ATLA BIBLIOGRAPHY SERIES
edited by Dr. Kenneth E. Rowe

An Index to
English Periodical Literature
on the Old Testament
and
Ancient Near Eastern Studies

Volume V

Compiled and Edited by

William G. Hupper

ATLA Bibliography Series, No. 21

Writing is the mother of orators, the father of scholars.
... *Sumerian Proverb*

The American Theological Library Association, and
The Scarecrow Press, Inc.
Metuchen, N.J., & London 1992

Illustration is an example of an "Hittite" Stag. Used by permission of ATATÜRK KÜLTÜR, DİL VE TARİH YÜKSEK KURUMU, TÜRK TARİH KURUMU BAŞKANLIĞI, Ankara, Turkey

Acknowledgment

The editor wishes to thank the Griffith Institute for permission to use the schema of the sign list from Alan Gardiner's *Egyptian Grammar, Third Edition,* which greatly facilitated the development of the various sections on Egyptian Lexicography.

British Library Cataloguing-in-Publication data available

Library of Congress Cataloging-in-Publication Data
(Revised for volume 5)

Hupper, William G.
    An index to English periodical literature on the Old
Testament and ancient Near Eastern studies.

    (ATLA bibliography series no. 21)
    1. Bible. O.T.—Periodicals—Indexes. 2. Middle
East—Periodicals—Indexes. I. American Theological
Library Association. II. Title. III. Series.
Z 7772.A1H86 1987 [BS1171.2]   016.221   86-31448
ISBN 0-8108-1984-8 (v. 1)
ISBN 0-8108-2126-5 (v. 2)
ISBN 0-8108-2319-5 (v. 3)
ISBN 0-8108-2393-4 (v. 4)
ISBN 0-8108-2618-6 (v. 5)

Table of Contents

Table of Contents

Table of Contents

Table of Contents

Table of Contents

vii

Table of Contents

Table of Contents

Table of Contents

---

1. Listed here as a matter of convenience due to geographical distribution. Actual linguistic family has not been determined.

Table of Contents

Table of Contents

Preface

With this volume the limits of word processing have been pushed to the extreme. It has been by far the most difficult volume to produce, requiring the use of over 22 different fonts including a large number of non-Roman fonts, Greek and Hebrew[1] notwithstanding. In some cases it was necessary to literally produce the needed fonts, e.g., Coptic, Egyptian Hieroglyphics, Cuneiform, Persian, and specific characters not available in Arabic and Syriac. The editor has also rescinded the self imposed mandate not to include additional journals. One more reference has been incorporated into this volume, namely: *Proceedings of the International Conference on Semitic Studies.*

Certainly great strides have been made in the past few decades in the decipherment of Cuneiform. Since we are all products of our own generation, many of the articles listed show obvious deficiencies compared with our present understanding. They have been included as being valuable for historical inquiry if nothing else.

While many hours have been spent by the editor, it has been only though the assistance of a number of people who cannot go unnamed that this volume has come to completion. The editor wishes to sincerely thank Dr. Frederick E. Greenspahn, University of Denver, for proofreading the sections of Semitic Grammar, Hebrew Grammar and Lexicography, and for making valuable comments on improving these and related sections; to Dr. James Hoffmeier, Wheaton College, for reading the sections on Egyptian Hieroglyphics and Grammar; to Dr. James Moyer, Southwestern Missouri State University for checking the sections on Cuneiform; to Randall S. Dugger Th.M., Harvard University, for proofreading the sections on Greek Grammar and Lexicography; and to Jay Ellison, Ph.D. candidate, Harvard University for a number of suggestions to improve the schema on the breakdown of the various languages and their family relations. As always, to Mrs. Florence Hall for her undiminished resolution in proofreading the entire manuscript, checking it against the original file cards. Numerous articles which might have discrepancies were additionally rechecked against the actual entries in attempting to insure as accurate a list of citations as possible. Hopefully there are no *desunt nonnulla,* and if perhaps an error has crept in, it is entirely the responsibility of the editor. Additionally, much benefit has been derived from the constructive criticism expressed by a number of reviewers. This has helped the editor improve the series and is greatly appreciated.

Melrose, MA
Mother's Day, 1992

---

1. A much improved Hebrew Postscript font, Hebraica, distributed by Linguist's Software, has been used for this volume.

Periodical Abbreviations*

A

A&A   *Art and Archaeology; the arts throughout the ages*
      (Washington, DC, Baltimore, MD, 1914-1934)

A/R   *Action/Reaction* (San Anselmo, CA, 1967ff.)

A&S   *Antiquity and Survival* (The Hague, 1955-1962)

A(A)   *Anadolu (Anatolia)* (Ankara, 1956ff.) [Subtitle varies;
      Volume 1-7 as: *Anatolia: Revue Annuelle*
      d'Archeologie]

AA   *Acta Archaeologica* (Copenhagen, 1930ff.)

AAA   *Annals of Archaeology and Anthropology* (Liverpool,
      1908-1948; Suspended, 1916-1920)

AAAS   *Annales archéologiques arabes Syriennes. Revue*
      d'Archéologie et d'Histoire (Damascus, 1951ff.)
      [Volumes 1-15 as: *Les Annales archéologiques de Syrie*
      - Title Varies]

AAASH   *Acta Antiqua Academiae Scientiarum Hungaricae*
      (Budapest, 1951ff.)

AAB   *Acta Archaeologica* (Budapest, 1951ff.)

AAI   *Anadolu Araştirmalari Istanbul Üniversitesi Edebiyat Fakültesi*
      eski Önasya Dilleri ve Kültürleri Kürsüsü Tarafindan
      Čikarilir (Istanbul, 1955ff.) [Supersedes: *Jahrbuch für*
      Kleinasiatische Forschungen]

AAOJ   *American Antiquarian and Oriental Journal* (Cleveland,
      Chicago 1878-1914)

AASCS   *Antichthon. The Australian Society for Classical Studies*
      (Sydney, 1967ff.)

ABBTS   *The Alumni Bulletin [of] Bangor Theological Seminary*
      (Bangor, ME; 1926ff.)

ABenR   *The American Benedictine Review* (St. Paul, 1950ff.)

ABR   *Australian Biblical Review* (Melbourne, 1951ff.)

Abr-N   *Abr-Nahrain, An Annual Published by the Department of*
      Middle Eastern Studies, University of Melbourne
      (Melbourne, 1959ff.)

ACM   *The American Church Monthly* (New York, 1917-1939)
      [Volumes 43-45 as: *The New American Church Monthly*]

*All the journals indexed are listed in the Periodical Abbreviations even though no specific citation may appear in the present volume. Although the titles of many foreign language journals have been listed, only English Language articles are included in this index (except as noted). Articles from Modern Hebrew Language Journals are referred to by their English summary page.

ACQ	*American Church Quarterly* (New York, 1961ff.) [Volume 7 on as: *Church Theological Review*]
ACQR	*The American Catholic Quarterly Review* (Philadelphia, 1876-1929)
ACR	*The Australasian Catholic Record* (Sydney, 1924ff.)
ACSR	*American Catholic Sociological Review* (Chicago, 1940ff.) [From Volume 25 on as: *Sociologial Analysis*]
ADAJ	*Annual of the Department of Antiquities of Jordan* (Amman, 1957ff.) [Volume 14 not published—destroyed by fire at the publishers]
AE	*Annales d'Ethiopie* (Paris, 1955ff.)
AEE	*Ancient Egypt and the East* (New York, London, Chicago, 1914-1935; Suspended, 1918-1919)
Aeg	*Aegyptus: Rivista Italiana di Egittologia e di Papirologia* (Milan,1920ff.)
AER	*American Ecclesiastical Review* (Philadelphia, New York, Cincinnati, Baltimore, 1889ff.) [Volumes 11-19 as: *Ecclesiastical Review*]
AfER	*African Ecclesiastical Review: A Quartlerly for Priests in Africa* (Masaka, Uganda, 1959ff.)
Aff	*Affirmation* (Richmond, VA, 1966ff.) [Volume 1 runs from 1966 to 1980 inclusive]
AfO	*Archiv für Orientforschung; Internationale Zeitschrift für Wissenschaft vom Vorderen Orient* (Berlin, 1923ff.)
AfRW	*Archiv für Religionswissenschaft* (Leipzig, 1898-1941)
AHDO	*Archives d'histoire du droit oriental et Revue internationale des droits de l'antiquité* (Brussels, 1937-38, 1947-1951, N.S., 1952-53)
AIPHOS	*Annuaire de l'institut de philologie et d'histoire orientales et slaves* (Brussels, 1932ff.)
AJ	*The Antiquaries Journal. Being the Journal of the Society of Antiquaries of London* (London, 1921ff.)
AJA	*The American Journal of Archaeology* (Baltimore, 1885ff.) [Original Series, 1885-1896 shown with *O. S;* Second Series shown without notation]
AJBA	*The Australian Journal of Biblical Archaeology* (Sydney, 1968ff.) [Volume 1 runs from 1968 to 1971 inclusive]
AJP	*The American Journal of Philology* (Baltimore, 1880ff.)
AJRPE	*The American Journal of Religious Psychology and Education* (Worcester, MA, 1904-1911)
AJSL	*The American Journal of Semitic Languages and Literatures* (Chicago, 1884-1941) [Volumes 1-11 as: *Hebraica*]
AJT	*American Journal of Theology* (Chicago, 1897-1920)
AL	*Archivum Linguisticum: A Review of Comparative Philology and General Linguistics* (Glasgow, 1949-1962)

ALUOS	*The Annual of the Leeds University Oriental Society* (Leiden,1958ff.)
Amb	*The Ambassador* (Wartburg Theological Seminary, Dubuque, IA, 1952ff.)
AmHR	*American Historical Review* (New York, Lancaster, PA, 1895ff.)
AmSR	*American Sociological Review* (Washington, DC, 1936ff.)
Anat	*Anatolica: Annuaire International pour les Civilisations de l'Asie Anterieure* (Leiden, 1967ff.)
ANQ	*Newton Theological Institute Bulletin* (Newton, MA, 1906ff.) [Title varies as: *Andover-Newton Theological Bulletin; Andover-Newton Quarterly, New Series,* beginning 1960ff.]
Anthro	*Anthropos; ephemeris internationalis ethnologica et linguistica* (Salzburg, Vienna, 1906ff.)
Antiq	*Antiquity: A Quarterly Review of Archaeology* (Gloucester, England, 1927ff.)
Anton	*Antonianum. Periodicum Philosophico-Theologicum Trimestre* (Rome, 1926ff.)
AO	*Acta Orientalia ediderunt Societates Orientales Bœtava Donica, Norvegica* (Lugundi Batavorum, Havniæ, 1922ff.)
AOASH	*Acta Orientalia Academiae Scientiarum Hungaricae* (Budapest, 1950ff.)
AOL	*Annals of Oriental Literature* (London, 1820-21)
APST	*Aberdeen Philosophical Society, Transactions* (Aberdeen, Scotland, 1840-1931)
AQ	*Augustana Quarterly* (Rock Island, IL, 1922-1948)
AQW	*Anthropological Quarterly* (Washington, DC, 1928ff.) [Volumes1-25 as: *Primitive Man*]
AR	*The Andover Review* (Boston, 1884-1893)
Arch	*Archaeology* (Cambridge, MA, 1948ff.)
Archm	*Archaeometry. Bulletin of the Research Laboratory for Archaeology and the History of Art, Oxford University* (Oxford,1958ff.)
ARL	*The Archæological Review* (London, 1888-1890)
ArOr	*Archiv Orientální. Journal of the Czechoslovak Oriental Institute, Prague* (Vlašska, Czechoslovakia, 1929ff.)
AS	*Anatolian Studies: Journal of the British Institute of Archaeology at Ankara* (London, 1951ff.)
ASAE	*Annales du service des antiquités de l'Égypte* (Cairo, 1899ff.)
ASBFE	*Austin Seminary Bulletin. Faculty Edition* (Austin, TX; begins with volume 71[sic], 1955ff.)

ASR	*Augustana Seminary Review* (Rock Island, IL, 1949-1967) [From volume 12 on as: *The Seminary Review*]
ASRB	*Advent Shield and Review* (Boston, 1844-45)
ASRec	*Auburn Seminary Record* (Auburn, NY, 1905-1932)
ASSF	*Acta Societatis Scientiarum Fennicae* (Helsinki, 1842-1926) [Suomen tideseura]
ASTI	*Annual of the Swedish Theological Institute (in Jerusalem)* (Jerusalem, 1962ff.)
ASW	*The Asbury Seminarian* (Wilmore, KY, 1946ff.)
AT	*Ancient Times: A Quarterly Review of Biblical Archaeology* (Melbourne, 1956-1961)
ATB	*Ashland Theological Bulletin* (Ashland, OH, 1968ff.)
ATG	*Advocate for the Testimony of God* (Richmond, VA, 1834-1839)
AThR	*The American Theological Review* (New York, 1859-1868) [*New Series* as: *American Presbyterian and Theological Review,* 1863-1868]
'Atiqot	*'Atiqot: Journal of the Israel Department of Antiquities* (Jerusalem, 1955ff.)
ATJ	*Africa Theological Journal* (Usa River, Tanzania, 1968ff.)
ATR	*Anglican Theological Review* (New York, Lancaster, PA; 1918ff.)
AubSRev	*Auburn Seminary Review* (Auburn, NY, 1897-1904)
Aug	*Augustinianum* (Rome, 1961ff.)
AULLUÅ	*Acta Universitatis Lundensis. Lunds Universitets Årsskrift. Första Avdelningen. Teologi, Juridik och Humanistika Ämnen* (Lund, 1864-1904; *N. S.,* 1905-1964)
AUSS	*Andrews University Seminary Studies* (Berrien Springs, MI, 1963ff.)
AusTR	*The Australasian Theological Review* (Highgate, South Australia, 1930-1966)

B

B	*Biblica* (Rome, 1920ff.)
BA	*The Biblical Archaeologist* (New Haven; Cambridge, MA; 1938ff.)
Baby	*Babyloniaca Etudes de Philologie Assyro-Babylonienne* (Paris, 1906-1937)
BASOR	*Bulletin of the American Schools of Oriental Research* (So. Hadley, MA; Baltimore, New Haven, Philadelphia, Cambridge, MA;1919ff.)
BASP	*Bulletin of the American Society of Papyrologists* (New Haven, 1963ff.)

BAVSS	*Beiträge zur Assyriologie und vergleichenden semitischen Sprachwissenschaft* (Leipzig, 1889-1927)
BBC	*Bulletin of the Bezan Club* (Oxford, 1925-1936)
BC	*Bellamire Commentary* (Oxon., England; 1956-1968)
BCQTR	*British Critic, Quarterly Theological Review and Ecclesiastical Record* (London, 1793-1843) [Superseded by: *English Review*]
BCTS	*Bulletin of the Crozer Theological Seminary* (Upland, PA, 1908-1934)
Bery	*Berytus. Archaeological Studies* (Copenhagen, 1934ff.)
BETS	*Bulletin of the Evangelical Theological Society* (Wheaton, IL, 1958ff.)
BFER	*British and Foreign Evangelical Review, and Quarterly Record of Christian Literature* (Edinburgh, London, 1852-1888)
BH	*Buried History. Quarterly Journal of the Australian Institute of Archaeology* (Melbourne, 1964-65; 1967ff.)
BibR	*Biblical Repertory* (Princeton, NJ; New York, 1825-1828)
BibT	*The Bible Today* (Collegeville, MN, 1962ff.)
BIES	*Bulletin of the Israel Exploration Society* (Jerusalem, 1937-1967) [*Yediot-* ידיעות בחקידת ארץ־ ישראל ועתיקותיה - Begun as: *Bulletin of the Jewish Palestine Exploration Society* through volume 15. English summaries discontinued from volume 27 on as translations published in: *Israel Exploration Journal*]
BIFAO	*Bulletin de l'institut français d'archéologie orientale au Caire* (Cairo, 1901ff.)
BJ	*Biblical Journal* (Boston, 1842-1843)
BJRL	*Bulletin of the John Rylands Library* (Manchester, 1903ff.)
BM	*Bible Magazine* (New York, 1913-1915)
BMB	*Bulletin du Musée de Byrouth* (Paris, 1937ff.)
BN	*Bible Numerics: a Periodical Devoted to the Numerical Study of the Scriptures* (Grafton, MA; 1904)
BO	*Bibliotheca Orientalis* (Leiden, 1944ff.)
BofT	*Banner of Truth* (London, 1955ff.)
BOR	*The Babylonian and Oriental Record: A Monthly Magazine of the Antiquities of the East* (London, 1886-1901)
BQ	*Baptist Quarterly* (Philadelphia, 1867-1877)
BQL	*Baptist Quarterly* (London, 1922ff.)
BQR	*Baptist Quarterly Review* (Cincinnati, New York, Philadelphia, 1879-1892)
BQRL	*The British Quarterly Review* (London, 1845-1886)
BR	*Biblical Review* (New York, 1916-1932)
BRCM	*The Biblical Review and Congregational Magazine* (London, 1846-1850)

BRCR   *The Biblical Repository and Classical Review* (Andover, MA,
              1831-1850) [Title varies as: *Biblical Repository; The
              Biblical Repository and Quarterly Observer; The
              American Biblical Repository*]
BRec   *Bible Record* (New York, 1903-1912) [Volume 1, #1-4 as:
              Bible Teachers Training School, New York City,Bulletin]
BRes   *Biblical Research: Papers of the Chicago Society of Biblical
              Research* (Amsterdam, Chicago, 1956ff.)
BS   *Bibliotheca Sacra* (New York, Andover, Oberlin, OH;
              St. Louis, Dallas, 1843, 1844ff.)
BSAJB   *British School of Archaeology in Jerusalem, Bulletin*
              (Jerusalem, 1922-1925)
BSOAS   *Bulletin of the School of Oriental and African Studies.
              University of London* (London, 1917ff.)
BSQ   *Bethel Seminary Quarterly* (St. Paul, MN; 1952ff.) [From
              Volume 13 on as: *Bethel Seminary Journal*]
BT   *Biblical Theology* (Belfast, 1950ff.)
BTF   *Bangalore Theological Forum* (Bangalore, India, 1967ff.)
BTPT   *Bijdragen Tijdschrift voor philosophie en theologie*
              (Maastricht,1938ff.) [Title varies as: *Bijdragen.
              Tijdschrift voor filosofie en theologie*]
BTr   *Bible Translator* (London, 1950ff.)
BUS   *Bucknell University Studies* (Lewisburg, PA; 1941ff.)
              [From Volume 5 on as: *Bucknell Review*]
BVp   *Biblical Viewpoint* (Greenville, SC, 1967ff.)
BW   *Biblical World* (Chicago, 1893-1920)
BWR   *Bible Witness and Review* (London, 1877-1881)
BWTS   *The Bulletin of the Western Theological Seminary* (Pittsburgh,
              1908-1931)
BZ   *Biblische Zeitschrift* (Paderborn, 1903-1939; *New Series,*
              1957ff.) [*N.S.* shown without notation]

C

C&C   *Cross and Crown. A Thomistic Quarterly of Spiritual
              Theology* (St. Louis, 1949ff.)
CAAMA   *Cahiers archéologiques fin de l'antiquité et moyen age*
              (Paris, 1961ff.)
CAAST   *Connecticut Academy of Arts and Sciences, Transactions*
              (New Haven, 1866ff.)
Carm   *Carmelus. Commentarii ab instituto carmelitano editi*
              (Rome, 1954ff.)
CBQ   *Catholic Biblical Quarterly* (Washington, DC; 1939ff.)
CC   *Cross Currents* (West Nyack, NY; 1950ff.)

CCARJ	*Central Conference of American Rabbis Journal* (New York,1953ff.)
CCBQ	*Central Conservative Baptist Quarterly* (Minneapolis, 1958ff.) [From volume 9, #2 on as: *Central Bible Quarterly*]
CCQ	*Crisis Christology Quarterly* (Dubuque, IA; 1943-1949) [Volume 6 as: *Trinitarian Theology*]
CD	*Christian Disciple* (Boston, 1813-1823) [Superseded by: *Christian Examiner*]
CdÉ	*Chronique d'Égypte* (Brussels, 1925ff.)
CE	*Christian Examiner* (Boston, New York, 1824-1869)
Cent	*Centaurus. International Magazine of the History of Science and Medicine* (Copenhagen, 1950ff.)
Center	*The Center* (Atlanta, 1960-1965)
CFL	*Christian Faith and Life* (Columbia, SC, 1897-1939) [Title varies: Original Series as: *The Bible Student and Religious Outlook,* volumes 1 & 2 as: *The Religious Outlook;* New Series as: *The Bible Student;* Third Series as: *The Bible Student and Teacher;* several volumes as: *Bible Champion*]
ChgoS	*Chicago Studies* (Mundelein, IL; 1962ff.)
CJ	*Conservative Judaism* (New York, 1945ff.)
CJL	*Canadian Journal of Linguistics* (Montreal, 1954ff.)
CJRT	*The Canadian Journal of Religious Thought* (Toronto, 1924-1932)
CJT	*Canadian Journal of Theology* (Toronto, 1955ff.)
ClR	*Clergy Review* (London, 1931ff.)
CM	*The Clergyman's Magazine* (London, 1875-1897)
CMR	*Canadian Methodist Review* (Toronto, 1889-1895) [Volumes 1-5 as: *Canadian Methodist Quarterly*]
CNI	*Christian News from Israel* (Jerusalem, 1949ff.)
CO	*Christian Opinion* (New York, 1943-1948)
Coll	*Colloquium. The Australian and New Zealand Theological Review* (Auckland, 1964ff.) [Volume 1 through Volume 2, #1 as: *The New Zealand Theological Review*]
CollBQ	*The College of the Bible Quarterly* (Lexington, KY, 1909-1965) [Break in sequence between 1927 and 1937, resumes in 1938 with volume 15 duplicated in number]
ColTM	*Columbus Theological Magazine* (Columbus, OH; 1881-1910)
CongL	*The Congregationalist* (London, 1872-1886)
CongML	*The Congregational Magazine* (London, 1818-1845)
CongQB	*The Congregational Quarterly* (Boston, 1859-1878)
CongQL	*The Congregational Quarterly* (London, 1923-1958)
CongR	*The Congregational Review* (Boston, Chicago, 1861-1871) [Volumes 1-6 as: *The Boston Review*]

CongRL	*The Congregational Review* (London, 1887-1891)
ConstrQ	*The Constructive Quarterly. A Journal of the Faith, Work, and Thought of Christendom* (New York, London, 1913-1922)
Cont	*Continuum* (St. Paul, 1963-1970)
ContextC	*Context (Journal of the Lutheran School of Theology at Chicago)* (Chicago, 1967-1968)
ContR	*Contemporary Review* (London, New York, 1866ff.)
CovQ	*The Covenant Quarterly* (Chicago, 1941ff.) [Volume 1, #1 as: *Covenant Minister's Quarterly*]
CQ	*Crozer Quarterly* (Chester, PA; 1924-1952)
CQR	*Church Quarterly Review* (London, 1875-1968)
CR	*The Church Review* (New Haven, 1848-1891) [Title varies; Volume 62 not published]
CraneR	*The Crane Review* (Medford, MA; 1958-1968)
CRB	*The Christian Review* (Boston, Rochester; 1836-1863)
CRDSB	*Colgate-Rochester Divinity School Bulletin* (Rochester, NY; 1928-1967)
Crit	*Criterion* (Chicago, 1962ff.)
CRP	*The Christian Review: A Quarterly Magazine* (Philadelphia, 1932-1941)
CS	*The Cumberland Seminarian* (McKenzie, TN; Memphis; 1953-1970)
CSQ	*Chicago Seminary Quarterly* (Chicago, 1901-1907)
CSQC	*The Culver-Stockton Quarterly* (Canton, MO; 1925-1931)
CSSH	*Comparative Studies in Society and History: An International Quarterly* (The Hague, 1958ff.)
CT	*Christian Thought* (New York, 1883-1894)
CTJ	*Calvin Theological Journal* (Grand Rapids, 1966ff.)
CTM	*Concordia Theological Monthly* (St. Louis, 1930ff.)
CTPR	*The Christian Teacher [and Chronicle]* (London, 1835-1838; *N.S.*, 1838-1844 as: *A Theological and Literary Journal*) [Continues as: *The Prospective Review; A Quarterly Journal of Theology and Literature*)
CTSB	*Columbia Theological Seminary Bulletin* (Columbia, SC; Decatur, GA; 1907ff.) [Title varies]
CTSP	*Catholic Theological Society, Proceedings* (Washingon, DC; Yonkers, NY; 1948ff.)
CTSQ	*Central Theological Seminary Quarterly* (Dayton, OH; 1923-1931)
CUB	*Catholic University Bulletin* (Washington, DC; 1895-1914) [Volumes 1-20 only]

D

DDSR	*Duke Divinity School Review* (Durham, NC; 1936ff.) [Volumes 1-20 as: *The Duke School of Religion Bulletin;* Volumes 21-29 as: *Duke Divinity School Bulletin*]
DG	*The Drew Gateway* (Madison, NJ; 1930ff.)
DI	*Diné Israel. An Annual of Jewish Law and Israeli Family Law* דיני ישראל, שנתון למשפט עברי ולדיני משפחה בישראל (Jerusalem, 1969ff.)
DJT	*Dialogue: A Journal of Theology* (Minneapolis, 1962ff.)
DownsR	*Downside Review* (Bath, 1880ff.)
DQR	*Danville Quarterly Review* (Danville, KY; Cincinnati; 1861-1864)
DR	*Dublin Review* (London, 1836-1968) [Between 1961 and 1964 as: *Wiseman Review*]
DS	*Dominican Studies. A Quarterly Review of Theology and Philosophy* (Oxford, 1948-1954)
DSJ	*The Dubuque Seminary Journal* (Dubuque, IA; 1966-1967)
DSQ	*Dubuque Seminary Quarterly* (Dubuque, IA; 1947-1949) [Volume 3, #3 not published]
DTCW	*Dimension: Theology in Church and World* (Princeton, NJ; 1964-1969) [Volumes 1 & 2 as: *Dimension* ; New format beginning in 1966 with full title, beginning again with Volume 1]
DTQ	*Dickinson's Theological Quarterly* (London, 1875-1883) [Superseded by *John Lobb's Theological Quarterly*]
DUJ	*The Durham University Journal* (Durham, 1876ff.; *N.S.,* 1940ff.) [Volume 32 of *O.S.* = Volume 1 of *N.S.*]
DUM	*Dublin University Magazine* (Dublin, London, 1833-1880)
DunR	*The Dunwoodie Review* (Yonkers, NY; 1961ff.)

E

EgR	*Egyptian Religion* (New York, 1933-1936)
EI	*Eretz-Israel. Archaeological, Historical and Geographical Studies* (Jerusalem, 1951ff.), ארץ-ישראל מחקרים בידיעת הארץ ועתיקותיה [English Summaries from Volume 3 on]

EJS   *Archives européennes de Sociologie / European Journal of Sociology / Europäisches Archiv für Soziologie* (Paris, 1960ff.)

EN   *The Everlasting Nation* (London, 1889-1892)

EQ   *Evangelical Quarterly* (London, 1929ff.)

ER   *Evangelical Review* (Gettysburg, PA; 1849-1870) [From Volume 14 on as: *Evangelical Quarterly Review*]

ERCJ   *Edinburgh Review, or Critical Journal* (Edinburgh, London, 1802-1929)

ERG   *The Evangelical Repository: A Quarterly Magazine of Theological Literature* (Glasgow, 1854-1888)

ERL   *The English Review, or Quarterly Journal of Ecclesiastical and General Literature* (London, 1844-1853) [Continues *British Critic*]

ESS   *Ecumenical Study Series* (Indianapolis, 1955-1960)

ET   *The Expository Times* (Aberdeen, Edinburgh, 1889ff.)

ETL   *Ephemerides Theologicae Lovanienses* (Notre Dame, 1924ff.)

Eud   *Eudemus. An International Journal Devoted to the History of Mathematics and Astronomy* (Copenhagen, 1941)

Exp   *The Expositor* (London, 1875-1925)

Exped   *Expedition* (Philadelphia, 1958ff.) [Continues: *The University Museum Bulletin*]

F

F&T   *Faith and Thought* (London, 1958ff.) [Supersedes: *Journal of the Transactions of the Victoria Institute, or Philosophical Society of Great Britain*]

FBQ   *The Freewill Baptist Quarterly* (Providence, London, Dover, 1853-1869)

FDWL   *Friends of Dr.Williams's Library (Lectures)* (Cambridge, Oxford, 1948ff.)

FLB   *Fuller Library Bulletin* (Pasadena, CA; 1949ff.)

FO   *Folia Orientalia* (Kraków, 1960ff.)

Focus   *Focus. A Theological Journal* (Willowdale, Ontario, 1964-1968)

Folk   *Folk-Lore: A Quarterly Review of Myth, Tradition, Institution & Custom being The Transactions of the Folk-Lore Society And Incorporating the Archæological Review and the Folk-Lore Journal* (London, 1890ff.)

Found   *Foundations (A Baptist Journal of History and Theology)* (Rochester, NY; 1958ff.)

FUQ   *Free University Quarterly* (Amsterdam-Centrum, 1950-1965)

G

GBT	*Ghana Bulletin of Theology* (Legon, Ghana; 1957ff.)
GJ	*Grace Journal* (Winona Lake, IN; 1960ff.)
GOTR	*Greek Orthodox Theological Review* (Brookline, MA; 1954ff.)
GR	*Gordon Review* (Boston; Beverly Farms, MA; Wenham, MA; 1955ff.)
GRBS	*Greek, Roman and Byzantine Studies* (San Antonio; Cambridge, MA; University, MS; Durham, NC; 1958ff.) [Volume1 as: *Greek and Byzantine Studies*]
Greg	*Gregorianum; Commentarii de re theologica et philosophica* (Rome, 1920ff.) [Volume 1 as: *Gregorianum; rivista trimestrale di studi teologici e filosofici*]
GUOST	*Glasgow University Oriental Society, Transactions* (Glasgow, 1901ff.)

H

H&T	*History and Theory: Studies in the Philosophy of History* (The Hague, 1960ff.)
HA	*Hebrew Abstracts* (New York, 1954ff.)
HDSB	*Harvard Divinity School Bulletin* (Cambridge, MA; 1935-1969)
Herm	*Hermathena; a Series of Papers on Literature, Science and Philosophy by Members of Trinity College, Dublin* (Dublin, 1873ff.) [Volumes 1-20; changes to issue number from #46 on]
HeyJ	*The Heythrop Journal* (New York, 1960ff.)
HJ	*Hibbert Journal* (London, Boston, 1902-1968)
HJAH	*Historia. Zeitschrift für alte Geschichte / Revue d'Histoire Ancienne / Journal of Ancient History / Rivista di Storia Antica* (Baden, 1950ff.)
HJud	*Historia Judaica. A Journal of Studies in Jewish History Especially in the Legal and Economic History of the Jews* (New York, 1938-1961)
HQ	*The Hartford Quarterly* (Hartford, CT; 1960-1968)
HR	*Homiletic Review* (New York, 1876-1934)
HRel	*History of Religions* (Chicago, 1961ff.)
HS	*Ha Sifrut. Quarterly for the Study of Literature* הספרות, רבעון למדע הספרות (Tel-Aviv, 1968ff.)
HSR	*Hartford Seminary Record* (Hartford, CT; 1890-1913)
HT	*History Today* (London, 1951ff.)

HTR	*Harvard Theological Review* (Cambridge, MA; 1908ff.)
HTS	*Hervormde Teologiese Studien* (Pretoria, 1943ff.)
HUCA	*Hebrew Union College Annual* (Cincinnati, 1904, 1924ff.)

I

IA	*Iranica Antiqua* (Leiden, 1961ff.)
IALR	*International Anthropological and Linguistic Review* (Miami, 1953-1957)
IAQR	*Asiatic Quarterly Review* (London, 1886-1966) [1st Series as: *Asiatic Quarterly Review*, (1886-1890); 2nd Series as: *The Imperial and Asiatic Quarterly and Oriental and Colonial Record*, (1891-1895); 3rd Series, (1896-1912); New Series, Volumes 1 & 2 as: *The Asiatic Quarterly Review* (1913); Volumes 3-48 (1914-1952) as: *Asiatic Review, New Series;* Volumes 49-59 (1953-1964) as: *Asian Review, New Series;* continued as: *Asian Review, Incorporating Art and Letters [and] the Asiatic Review, New Series,* Volumes 1-3 (1964-1966)]
ICHR	*Indian Church History Review* (Serampore, West Bengal, 1967ff.)
ICMM	*The Interpreter. A Church Monthly Magazine* (London, 1905-1924)
IEJ	*Israel Exploration Journal* (Jerusalem, 1950ff.)
IER	*Irish Ecclesiastical Record (A Monthly Journal under Episcopal Sanction)* (Dublin, 1864-1968)
IES	*Indian Ecclesiastical Studies* (Bangalore, India, 1962ff.)
IJA	*International Journal of Apocrypha* (London, 1905-1917) [Issues #1-7 as: *Deutero-Canonica,* pages unnumbered]
IJT	*Indian Journal of Theology* (Serampore, West Bengal, 1952ff.)
ILR	*Israel Law Review* (Jerusalem, 1966ff.)
Inter	*Interchange: Papers on Biblical and Current Questions* (Sydney, 1967ff.)
Interp	*Interpretation; a Journal of Bible and Theology* (Richmond, 1947ff.)
IPQ	*International Philosophical Quarterly* (New York, 1961ff.)
IR	*The Iliff Review* (Denver, 1944ff.)
Iran	*Iran: Journal of the British Institute of Persian Studies* (London, 1963ff.)
Iraq	*Iraq. British School of Archaeology in Iraq* (London, 1934ff.)
IRB	*International Reformed Bulletin* (London, 1958ff.)

IRM *International Review of Missions* (Edinburgh, London,
   Geneva, 1912ff.)
Isis *Isis. An International Review devoted to the History of Science
   and Civilization* (Brussels; Cambridge, MA; 1913ff.)
ITQ *Irish Theological Quarterly* (Dublin, Maynooth, 1906ff.)

J

JAAR *Journal of the American Academy of Religion* (Wolcott, NY;
   Somerville, NJ; Baltimore; Brattleboro, VT) [Volumes
   1-4 as: *Journal of the National Association of Biblical
   Instructors;* Volumes 5-34 as: *Journal of Bible and
   Religion*]
JANES *Journal of the Ancient Near Eastern Society of Columbia
   University* (New York, 1968ff.)
Janus *Janus; Archives internationales pour l'Histoire de la
   Médecine et pour la Géographie Médicale* (Amsterdam;
   Haarlem; Leiden; 1896ff.)
JAOS *Journal of the American Oriental Society* (Baltimore,
   New Haven, 1843ff.)
JAOSS *Journal of the American Oriental Society, Supplements*
   (Baltimore, New Haven, 1935-1954)
JARCE *Journal of the American Research Center in Egypt*
   (Gluckstadt, Germany; Cambridge, MA; 1962ff.)
JASA *Journal of the American Scientific Affiliation* (Wheaton, IL,
   1949ff.)
JBL *Journal of Biblical Literature* (Middletown, CT; New Haven;
   Boston; Philadelphia; Missoula, MT; 1881ff.)
JC&S *The Journal of Church and State* (Fresno, CA; 1965ff.)
JCE *Journal of Christian Education* (Sydney, 1958ff.)
JCP *Christian Philosophy Quarterly* (New York, 1881-1884)
   [From Volume 2 on as: *The Journal of Christian
   Philosophy*]
JCS *Journal of Cuneiform Studies* (New Haven; Cambridge,
   MA;1947ff.)
JCSP *Journal of Classical and Sacred Philology* (Cambridge,
   England, 1854-1857)
JEA *Journal of Egyptian Archaeology* (London, 1914ff.)
JEBH *Journal of Economic and Business History* (Cambridge,
   MA;1928-1932)
JEOL *Jaarbericht van het Vooraziatisch-Egyptisch Gezelschap
   Ex Oriente Lux* (Leiden, 1933ff.)
JES *Journal of Ethiopian Studies* (Addis Ababa, 1963ff.)

JESHO	*Journal of the Economic and Social History of the Orient* (Leiden, 1958ff.)
JHI	*Journal of the History of Ideas. A Quarterly Devoted to Intellectual History* (Lancaster, PA; New York;1940ff.
JHS	*The Journal of Hebraic Studies* (New York; 1969ff.)
JIQ	*Jewish Institute Quarterly* (New York, 1924-1930)
JJLP	*Journal of Jewish Lore and Philosophy* (Cincinnati, 1919)
JJP	*Rocznik Papirologii Prawniczej-Journal of Juristic Papyrology* (New York, Warsaw, 1946ff.) [Suspended 1947 & 1959-60]
JJS	*Journal of Jewish Studies* (London, 1948ff.)
JKF	*Jahrbuch für Kleinasiatische Forschungen* (Heidelberg, 1950-1953) [Superseded by *Anadolu Araştirmalari Istanbul Üniversitesi Edebiyat Fakültesi eski Önasya Dilleri ve Kültürleri Kürsüsü Tarafindan Čikarilir*]
JLTQ	*John Lobb's Theological Quarterly* (London, 1884)
JMUEOS	*Journal of the Manchester Egyptian and Oriental Society* (Manchester, 1911-1953) [Issue #1 as: *Journal of the Manchester Oriental Society*]
JMTSO	*Journal of the Methodist Theological School in Ohio* (Delaware, OH; 1962ff.)
JNES	*Journal of Near Eastern Studies* (Chicago, 1942ff.)
JP	*The Journal of Philology* (Cambridge, England; 1868-1920)
JPOS	*Journal of the Palestine Oriental Society* (Jerusalem, 1920-1948) [Volume 20 consists of only one fascicle]
JQR	*Jewish Quarterly Review* (London, 1888-1908; *N.S.,* Philadelphia, 1908ff.) [Includes 75th Anniversary Volume as: *JQR, 75th*]
JR	*Journal of Religion* (Chicago, 1921ff.)
JRAI	*Journal of the Royal Anthropological Institute of Great Britain and Ireland* (London, 1872-1965) [Volumes 1-69 as: *Journal of the Anthropological Institute* Continued as: *Man, N.S.*]
JRAS	*Journal of the Royal Asiatic Society of Great Britain and Ireland* (London, 1827ff.) [*Transactions,* 1827-1835 as *TRAS; Journal* from 1834 on: (Shown without volume numbers)]
JRelH	*Journal of Religious History* (Sydney, 1960ff.)
JRH	*Journal of Religion and Health* (Richmond, 1961ff.)
JRT	*Journal of Religious Thought* (Washington, DC; 1943ff.)
JSL	*Journal of Sacred Literature and Biblical Record* (London,1848-1868)
JSOR	*Journal of the Society of Oriental Research* (Chicago, 1917-1932)
JSP	*The Journal of Speculative Philosophy* (St. Louis, 1868-1893)

JSS   *Journal of Semitic Studies* (Manchester, 1956ff.)

JTALC   *Journal of Theology of the American Lutheran Conference* (Minneapolis, 1936-1943) [Volumes 1-5 as: *American Lutheran Conference Journal;* continued from volume 8, #3 as: *Lutheran Outlook* (not included)]

JTC   *Journal for Theology and the Church* (New York, 1965ff.)

JTLC   *Journal of Theology: Church of the Lutheran Confession* (Eau Claire, WI; 1961ff.)

JTS   *Journal of Theological Studies* (Oxford, 1899-1949; *N.S.,* 1950ff.)

JTVI   *Journal of the Transactions of the Victoria Institute, or Philosophical Society of Great Britain* (London, 1866-1957) [Superseded by *Faith & Thought*]

Jud   *Judaism. A Quarterly Journal of Jewish Life and Thought* (New York, 1952ff.)

JWCI   *Journal of the Warburg and Courtauld Institutes* (London,1937ff.)

JWH   *Journal of World History-Cahiers d'Histoire Mondiale -Cuadernos de Historia Mundial* (Paris, 1953ff.)

K

Kêmi   *Kêmi. Revue de philologie et d'archéologie égyptiennes et coptes* (Paris, 1928ff.)

Klio   *Klio. Beiträge zur alten Geschichte* (Leipzig, 1901ff.)

Kobez   *Kobez (Qobeṣ);* קובץ החברה העברית לחקירת ארץ־ישראל ועתיקתיה (Jerusalem, 1921-1945)

KSJA   *Kedem; Studies in Jewish Archaeology* (Jerusalem, 1942, 1945)

Kuml   *Kuml. Årbog for Jysk Arkæologisk Selskab* (Århus, 1951ff.)

Kush   *Kush. Journal of the Sudan Antiquities Service* (Khartoum, Sudan, 1953-1968)

KZ   *Kirchliche Zeitschrift* (St. Louis; Waverly, IA; Chicago; Columbus; 1876-1943)

KZFE   *Kadmos. Zeitschrift für vor-und frühgriechische Epigraphik* (Berlin, 1962ff.)

L

L	*Levant (Journal of the British School of Archaeology in Jerusalem)* (London, 1969ff.)
Lang	*Language. Journal of the Linguistic Society of America* (Baltimore, 1925ff.)
LCQ	*Lutheran Church Quarterly* (Gettysburg, PA; 1928-1949)
LCR	*Lutheran Church Review* (Philadelphia, 1882-1927)
Lěš	*Lěšonénu. Quarterly for the Study of the Hebrew Language and Cognate Subjects* לשוננו (Jerusalem, 1925ff.) [English Summaries from volume 30 onward]
LIST	*Lown Institute. Studies and Texts* (Brandeis University. Lown School of Near Eastern and Judaic Studies. Cambridge, MA; 1963ff.)
Listen	*Listening* (Dubuque, IA; 1965ff.) [Volume numbers start with "zero"]
LofS	*Life of the Spirit* (London, 1946-1964)
LQ	*The Quarterly Review of the Evangelical Lutheran Church* (Gettysburg, PA; 1871-1927; revived in1949ff.) [From 1878 on as: *The Lutheran Quarterly*]
LQHR	*London Quarterly and Holborn Review* (London, 1853-1968)
LS	*Louvain Studies* (Louvain, 1966ff.)
LSQ	*Lutheran Synod Quarterly* (Mankato, MN, 1960ff.) [Formerly *Clergy Bulletin* (Volume 1 of *LSQ* as *Clergy Bulletin,* Volume 20, #1 & #2)]
LTJ	*Lutheran Theological Journal* (North Adelaide, South Australia, 1967ff.)
LTP	*Laval Theologique et Philosophique* (Quebec, 1945ff.)
LTQ	*Lexington Theological Quarterly* (Lexington, KY; 1966ff.)
LTR	*Literary and Theological Review* (New York; Boston, 1834-1839)
LTSB	*Lutheran Theological Seminary Bulletin* (Gettysburg, PA; 1921ff.)
LTSR	*Luther Theological Seminary Review* (St. Paul, MN; 1962ff.)
LWR	*The Lutheran World Review* (Philadelphia, 1948-1950)

M

Man	*Man. A Monthly Record of Anthropological Science* (London,1901-1965; *N. S.,* 1966ff.) [Articles in original series referred to by *article* number not by *page* number - New Series subtitled: *The Journal of the Royal Anthropological Institute*]
ManSL	*Manuscripta* (St. Louis, 1957ff.)
MB	*Medelhavsmuseet Bulletin* (Stockholm, 1961ff.)
MC	*The Modern Churchman* (Ludlow, England; 1911ff.)
McQ	*McCormick Quarterly* (Chicago, 1947ff.) [Volumes 1-13 as: *McCormick Speaking*]
MCS	*Manchester Cuneiform Studies* (Manchester, 1951-1964)
MDIÄA	*Mitteilungen des deutsches Instituts für ägyptische Altertumskunde in Kairo* (Cairo, 1930ff.)
Mesop	*Mesopotamia* (Torino, Italy, 1966ff.)
MH	*The Modern Humanist* (Weston, MA; 1944-1962)
MHSB	*The Mission House Seminary Bulletin* (Plymouth, WI; 1954-1962)
MI	*Monthly Interpreter* (Edinburgh, 1884-1886)
MidS	*Midstream (Council on Christian Unity)* (Indianapolis, 1961ff.)
Min	*Ministry. A Quarterly Theological Review for South Africa* (Morija, Lesotho, 1960ff.)
Minos	*Minos. Investigaciones y Materiales Para el Estudio de los Textos Paleocretenses Publicados Bajo la Dirección de Antonio Tovar y Emilio Peruzzi* (Salamanca, 1951ff.) [From Volume 4 on as: *Minos Revista de Filología Egea*]
MIO	*Mitteilungen des Instituts für Orientforschung [Deutsche Akademie der Wissenschaften zu Berlin Institut für Orientforschung]* (Berlin, 1953ff.)
Miz	*Mizraim. Journal of Papyrology, Egyptology, History of Ancient Laws, and their Relations to the Civilizations of Bible Lands* (New York, 1933-1938)
MJ	*The Museum Journal. Pennsylvania University* (Philadelphia,1910-1935)
MMBR	*The Monthly Magazine and British Register* (London, 1796-1843) [*1st Ser.,* 1796-1826, Volumes 1-60; *N.S.,* 1826-1838, Volumes 1-26; *3rd Ser.,* 1839-1843, Volumes 1-9, however, Volumes 7-9 are marked 95-97*[sic]*]

ModR	*The Modern Review* (London, 1880-1884)
Monist	*The Monist. An International Quarterly Journal of General Philosophical Inquiry* (Chicago; La Salle, IL; 1891ff.)
Mosaic	*Mosaic* (Cambridge, MA; 1960ff.)
MQ	*The Minister's Quarterly* (New York, 1945-1966)
MQR	*Methodist Quarterly Review (South)* (Louisville, Nashville, 1847-1861; 1879-1886; 1886-1930) [*3rd Ser.* as: *Southern Methodist Review;* Volume 52 (1926) misnumbered as 53; Volume 53 (1927) misnumbered as 54; and the volume for 1928 is also marked as 54]
MR	*Methodist Review* (New York, 1818-1931) [Volume 100 not published]
MTSB	*Moravian Theological Seminary Bulletin* (Bethlehem, PA; 1959-1970) [Volume for 1969 apparently not published]
MTSQB	*Meadville Theological School Quarterly Bulletin* (Meadville, PA;1906-1933) [From Volume 25 on as: *Meadville Journal*]
Muséon	*Le Muséon. Revue d'Études Orientales* (Louvain, 1882-1915;1930/32ff.)
MUSJ	*Mélanges de l'Université Saint-Joseph. Faculté orientale* (Beirut, 1906ff.) [Title varies]
Mwa-M	*Milla wa-Milla. The Australian Bulletin of Comparative Religion* (Parkville, Victoria, 1961ff.)

N

NB	*Blackfriars. A Monthly Magazine* (Oxford, 1920ff.) [From Volume 46 on as: *New Blackfriars*]
NBR	*North British Review* (Edinburgh, 1844-1871)
NCB	*New College Bulletin* (Edinburgh, 1964ff.)
NEAJT	*Northeast Asia Journal of Theology* (Kyoto, Japan, 1968ff.)
NEST	*The Near East School of Theology Quarterly* (Beirut, 1952ff.)
Nexus	*Nexus* (Boston, 1957ff.)
NGTT	*Nederduitse gereformeerde teologiese tydskrif* (Kaapstad, N.G., Kerk-Uitgewers, 1959ff.)
NOGG	*Nihon Orient Gakkai geppo* (Tokyo, 1955-1959) [Being the *Bulletin of the Society for Near Eastern Studies in Japan*-Continued as: *Oriento*]
NOP	*New Orient* (Prague, 1960-1968)

NPR	*The New Princeton Review* (New York, 1886-1888)
NQR	*Nashotah Quarterly Review* (Nashotah, WI; 1960ff.)
NT	*Novum Testamentum* (Leiden, 1955ff.)
NTS	*New Testament Studies* (Cambridge, England; 1954ff.)
NTT	*Nederlandsch Theologisch Tijdschrift* (Wageningen, 1946ff.)
NTTO	*Norsk Teologisk Tidsskrift* (Oslo, 1900ff.)
Numen	*Numen; International Review for the History of Religions* (Leiden, 1954ff.)
NW	*The New World. A Quarterly Review of Religion, Ethics and Theology* (Boston, 1892-1900)
NYR	*The New York Review. A Journal of The Ancient Faith and Modern Thought (St. John's Seminary)* (New York, 1905-1908)
NZJT	*New Zealand Journal of Theology* (Christchurch, 1931-1935)

O

OA	*Oriens Antiquus* (Rome, 1962ff.)
OBJ	*The Oriental and Biblical Journal* (Chicago, 1880-1881)
OC	*Open Court* (Chicago, 1887-1936)
ONTS	*The Hebrew Student* (Morgan Park, IL; New Haven; Hartford; 1881-1892) [Volumes 3-8 as: *The Old Testament Student;* Volume 9 onwards as: *The Old and New Testament Student*]
OOR	*Oriens: The Oriental Review* (Paris, 1926)
OQR	*The Oberlin Quarterly Review* (Oberlin, OH; 1845-1849)
Or	*Orientalia commentarii de rebus Assyri-Babylonicis, Arabicis, and Aegyptiacis, etc.* (Rome 1920-1930)
Or, N.S.	*Orientalia: commentarii, periodici de rebus orientis antiqui* (Rome, 1932ff.)
Oriens	*Oriens. Journal of the International Society of Oriental Research* (Leiden, 1948ff.)
Orient	*Orient. The Reports of the Society for Near Eastern Studies in Japan* (Tokyo, 1960ff.)
Orita	*Orita. Ibadan Journal of Religious Studies* (Ibadan, Nigeria, 1967ff.)
OrS	*Orientalia Suecana* (Uppsala, 1952ff.)
OSHTP	*Oxford Society of Historical Theology, Abstract of Proceedings* (Oxford, 1891-1968) [Through 1919 as: *Society of Historical Theology, Proceedings*]
Osiris	*Osiris* (Bruges, Belgium; 1936-1968) *[Subtitle varies]*
OTS	*Oudtestamentische Studiën* (Leiden, 1942ff.)

OTW   *Ou-Testamentiese Werkgemeenskap in Suid-Afrika, Proceedings of die* (Pretoria, 1958ff.) [Volume 1 in Volume 14 of: *Hervormde Teologiese Studies*]

P

P   *Preaching: A Journal of Homiletics* (Dubuque, IA; 1965ff.)
P&P   *Past and Present* (London, 1952ff.) *[Subtitle varies]*
PA   *Practical Anthropology* (Wheaton, IL; Eugene, OR; Tarrytown, NY; 1954ff.)
PAAJR   *Proceedings of the American Academy for Jewish Research* (Philadelphia, 1928ff.)
PAOS   *Proceedings of the American Oriental Society* (Baltimore, New Haven; 1842, 1846-50, 1852-1860) [After 1860 all proceedings are bound with *Journal*]
PAPA   *American Philological Association, Proceedings* (Hartford, Boston, 1896ff.) *[Transactions* as: *TAPA. Transactions* and *Proceedings* combine page numbers from volume 77 on]
PAPS   *Proceedings of the American Philosophical Society* (Philadelphia, 1838ff.)
PBA   *Proceedings of the British Academy* (London, 1903ff.)
PEFQS   *Palestine Exploration Fund Quarterly Statement* (London, 1869ff.) [From Volume 69 (1937) on as: *Palestine Exploration Quarterly*]
PEQ   *Palestine Exploration Quarterly* [See: *PEFQS*]
PER   *The Protestant Episcopal Review* (Fairfax, Co., VA; 1886-1900) [Volumes 1-5 as: *The Virginian Seminary Magazine*]
Person   *Personalist. An International Review of Philosophy, Religion and Literature* (Los Angeles, 1920ff.)
PF   *Philosophical Forum* (Boston, 1943-1957; *N.S.,* 1968ff.)
PHDS   *Perspectives. Harvard Divinity School* (Cambridge, MA; 1965-1967)
PIASH   *Proceedings of the Israel Academy of Sciences and Humanities* (Jerusalem, 1967ff.)
PICSS   *Proceedings of the International Conference on Semitic Studies held in Jerusalem, 19-23 July 1965* (Jerusalem, 1969)
PIJSL   *Papers of the Institute of Jewish Studies, London* (Jerusalem,1964)
PJT   *Pacific Journal of Theology* (Western Samoa, 1961ff.)

PJTSA	*Jewish Theological Seminary Association, Proceedings* (New York, 1888-1902)
PP	*Perspective* (Pittsburgh, 1960ff.) [Volumes 1-8 as: *Pittsburgh Perspective*]
PQ	*The Presbyterian Quarterly* (New York, 1887-1904)
PQL	*The Preacher's Quarterly* (London, 1954-1969)
PQPR	*The Presbyterian Quarterly and Princeton Review* (New York, 1872-1877)
PQR	*Presbyterian Quarterly Review* (Philadelphia, 1852-1862)
PR	*Presbyterian Review* (New York, 1880-1889)
PRev	*The Biblical Repertory and Princeton Review* (Princeton, Philadelphia, New York, 1829-1884) [Volume 1 as: *The Biblical Repertory, New Series;* Volumes 2-8 as: *The Biblical Repertory and Theological Review*]
PRR	*Presbyterian and Reformed Review* (New York, Philadelphia, 1890-1902)
PSB	*The Princeton Seminary Bulletin* (Princeton, 1907ff.)
PSTJ	*Perkins School of Theology Journal* (Dallas, 1947ff.)
PTR	*Princeton Theological Review* (Princeton, 1903-1929)
PUNTPS	*Proceedings of the University of Newcastle upon Tyne Philosophical Society* (Newcastle upon Tyne, 1964-70)

Q

QCS	*Quarterly Christian Spectator* (New Haven, 1819-1838) *[1st Series* and *New Series* as: *Christian Spectator]*
QDAP	*The Quarterly of the Department of Antiquities in Palestine* (Jerusalem, 1931-1950)
QRL	*Quarterly Review* (London, 1809-1967)
QTMRP	*The Quarterly Theological Magazine, and Religious Repository* (Philadelphia, 1813-1814)

R

R&E	*[Baptist] Review and Expositor* (Louisville, 1904ff.)
R&S	*Religion and Society* (Bangalore, India, 1953ff.)
RAAO	*Revue d'Assyriologie et d'Archéologie Orientale* (Paris, 1886ff.)

Periodical Abbreviations

RChR   *The Reformed Church Review* (Mercersburg, PA; Chambersburg, PA; Philadelphia; 1849-1926) [Volumes 1-25 as: *Mercersburg Review;* Volumes 26-40 as: *Reformed Quarterly Review;* 4th Series on as: *Reformed Church Review*]

RCM   *Reformed Church Magazine* (Reading, PA; 1893-1896) [Volume 3 as: *Reformed Church Historical Magazine*]

RdQ   *Revue de Qumran* (Paris, 1958ff.)

RDSO   *Rivista degli Studi Orientali* (Rome, 1907ff.)

RÉ   *Revue Égyptologique* (Paris, 1880-1896; *N.S.,* 1919-1924)

RefmR   *The Reformation Review* (Amsterdam, 1953ff.)

RefR   *The Reformed Review. A Quarterly Journal of the Seminaries of the Reformed Church in America* (Holland, MI; New Brunswick, NJ; 1947ff.) [Volumes 1-9 as: *Western Seminary Bulletin*]

RÉg   *Revue d'Égyptologie* (Paris, 1933ff.)

RelM   *Religion in the Making* (Lakeland, FL; 1940-1943)

Resp   *Response—in worship—Music—The arts* (St. Paul, 1959ff.)

RestQ   *Restoration Quarterly* (Austin, TX; Abilene, TX; 1957ff.)

RFEASB   *The Hebrew University / Jerusalem: Department of Archaeology. Louis M. Rabinowitz Fund for the Exploration of Ancient Synagogues, Bulletin* (Jerusalem, 1949-1960)

RHA   *Revue Hittite et Asianique* (Paris, 1930ff.)

RIDA   *Revue internationale des droits de l'antiquité* (Brussels, 1948ff.)

RJ   *Res Judicatae. The Journal of the Law Students' Society of Victoria* (Melbourne, 1935-1957)

RL   *Religion in Life* (New York, 1932ff.)

RO   *Rocznik Orjentalistyczny. (Wydaje Polskie towarzystwo orjentalisyczne)* (Kraków, Warsaw, 1914ff.)

RP   *Records of the Past* (Washington, DC; 1902-1914)

RR   *Review of Religion* (New York, 1936-1958)

RS   *Religious Studies* (London, 1965ff.)

RTP   *Review of Theology and Philosophy* (Edinburgh, 1905-1915)

RTR   *Recueil de travaux relatifs à la philologie et à l'archéologie egyptiennes et assyriennes* (Paris, 1870-1923)

RTRM   *The Reformed Theological Review* (Melbourne, 1941ff.)

S

SAENJ	*Seminar. An Annual Extraordinary Number of the Jurist* (Washington, DC; 1943-1956)
SBAP	*Society of Biblical Archæology, Proceedings* (London, 1878-1918)
SBAT	*Society of Biblical Archæology, Transactions* (London, 1872-1893)
SBE	*Studia Biblica et Ecclesiastica* (Oxford, 1885-1903) Volume 1 as: *Studia Biblica*]
SBFLA	*Studii (Studium) Biblici Franciscani. Liber Annuus* (Jerusalem, 1950ff.)
SBLP	*Society of Biblical Literature & Exegesis, Proceedings* (Baltimore, 1880)
SBO	*Studia Biblica et Orientalia* (Rome 1959) [Being Volumes 10-12 respectively of *Analecta Biblica. Investigationes Scientificae in Res Biblicas*]
SBSB	*Society for Biblical Studies Bulletin* (Madras, India, 1964ff.)
SCO	*Studi Classici e Orientali* (Pisa, 1951ff.)
Scotist	*The Scotist* (Teutopolis, IL; 1939-1967)
SCR	*Studies in Comparative Religion* (Bedfont, Middlesex, England, 1967ff.)
Scrip	*Scripture. The Quarterly of the Catholic Biblical Association* (London, 1944-1968)
SE	*Study Encounter* (Geneva, 1965ff.)
SEÅ	*Svensk Exegetisk Årsbok* (Uppsala-Lund, 1936ff.)
SEAJT	*South East Journal of Theology* (Singapore, 1959ff.)
Sefunim	*Sefunim (Bulletin)* [היפה] ספונים (Haifa, 1966-1968)
SGEI	*Studies in the Geography of Eretz-Israel* מחקרים בניאוגרפיה של ארץ-ישראל (Jerusalem, 1959ff.) [English summaries in Volumes 1-3 only; continuing the *Bulletin of the Israel Exploration Society (Yediot)*]
SH	*Scripta Hierosolymitana* (Jerusalem, 1954ff.)
Shekel	*The Shekel* (New York, 1968ff.)
SIR	*Smithsonian Institute Annual Report of the Board of Regents* (Washington, DC; 1846-1964; becomes: *Smithsonian Year* from 1965 on]
SJH	*Seminary Journal* (Hamilton, NY; 1892)
SJT	*Scottish Journal of Theology* (Edinburgh, 1947ff.)
SL	*Studia Liturgica. An International Ecumenical Quarterly for Liturgical Research and Renewal* (Rotterdam, 1962ff.)

SLBR	*Sierra Leone Bulletin of Religion* (Freetown, Sierra Leone; 1959-1966)
SMR	*Studia Montes Regii* (Montreal, 1958-1967)
SMSDR	*Studi e Materiali di Storia Delle Religioni* (Rome, Bologna, 1925ff.)
SO	*Studia Orientalia* (Helsinki, 1925ff.)
SOOG	*Studi Orientalistici in Onore di Giorgio Levi Della Vida* (Rome, 1956)
Sophia	*Sophia. A Journal for Discussion in Philosophical Theology* (Parkville, Victoria, Australia, 1962ff.)
SP	*Spirit of the Pilgrims* (Boston, 1828-1833)
SPR	*Southern Presbyterian Review* (Columbia, SC; 1847-1885)
SQ/E	*The Shane Quarterly* (Indianapolis, 1940ff.) [From Volume 17 on as: *Encounter*]
SR	*The Seminary Review* (Cincinnati, 1954ff.)
SRL	*The Scottish Review* (London, Edinburgh, 1882-1900; 1914-1920)
SS	*Seminary Studies of the Athenaeum of Ohio* (Cincinnati, 1926-1968) [Volumes 1-15 as: *Seminary Studies*]
SSO	*Studia Semitica et Orientalia* (Glasgow, 1920, 1945)
SSR	*Studi Semitici* (Rome, 1958ff.)
ST	*Studia Theologica* (Lund, 1947ff.)
StEv	*Studia Evangelica* (Berlin, 1959ff.) [Being miscellaneous volumes of: *Text und Untersuchungen zur Geschichte der altchristlichen Literatur,* beginning with Volume 73]
StLJ	*The Saint Luke's Journal* (Sewanee, TN; 1957ff.) [Volume 1, #1 as: *St. Luke's Journal of Theology*]
StMR	*St. Marks Review: An Anglican Quarterly* (Canberra, A.C.T., Australia, 1955ff.)
StP	*Studia Patristica* (Berlin, 1957ff.) [Being miscellaneous volumes of: *Text und Untersuchungen zur Geschichte der altchristlichen Literatur,* beginning with Volume 63]
StVTQ	*St. Vladimir's Theological Quarterly* (Crestwood, NY; 1952ff. [Volumes 1-4 as: *St. Vladimir's Seminary Quarterly*]
Sumer	*Sumer. A Journal of Archaeology in Iraq* (Baghdad, 1945ff.)
SWJT	*Southwestern Journal of Theology* (Fort Worth, 1917-1924; *N.S.,* 1950ff.)
Syria	*Syria, revue d'art oriental et d'archéologie* (Paris, 1920ff.)

T

T&C	*Theology and the Church / SÎN-HÁK kap kàu-Hōe* *(Tainan Theological College)* (Tainan, Formosa, 1957ff.)
T&L	*Theology and Life* (Lancaster, PA; 1958-1966)
TAD	*Türk tarih, arkeologya ve etnoğrafya dergisi* (Istanbul, 1933-1949; continued as: *Türk arkeoloji Dergisi,* (Ankara, 1956ff.)
TAPA	*American Philological Society, Transactions* (See: *PAPA*)
TAPS	*Transactions of the American Philosophical Society* (Philadelphia, 1789-1804; *N.S.,* 1818ff.)
Tarbiz	*Tarbiz. A quarterly review of the humanities;* תרביץ‎ רבעון למדעי היהדות‎ (Jerusalem, 1929ff.) [English Summaries from Volume 24 on only]
TB	*Tyndale Bulletin* (London, 1956ff.) [Numbers 1-16 as: *Tyndale House Bulletin*]
TBMDC	*Theological Bulletin: McMaster Divinity College* (Hamilton, Ontario, 1967ff.)
TE	*Theological Education* (Dayton, 1964ff.)
Tem	*Temenos. Studies in Comparative Religion* (Helsinki, 1965ff.)
TEP	*Theologica Evangelica. Journal of the Faculty of Theology, University of South Africa* (Pretoria, 1968ff.)
Text	*Textus. Annual of the Hebrew University Bible Project* (Jerusalem, 1960ff.)
TF	*Theological Forum* (Minneapolis, 1929-1935)
TFUQ	*Thought. A Quarterly of the Sciences and Letters* (New York, 1926ff.) [From Volume 15 on as: *Thought. Fordham University Quarterly*]
ThE	*Theological Eclectic* (Cincinnati; New York, 1864-1871)
Them	*Themelios, International Fellowship of Evangelical Students* (Fresno, CA; 1962ff.)
Theo	*Theology; A Journal of Historic Christianity* (London, 1920ff.)
ThSt	*Theological Studies* (New York; Woodstock, MD; 1940ff.)
TLJ	*Theological and Literary Journal* (New York, 1848-1861)
TM	*Theological Monthly* (St. Louis, 1921-1929)
TML	*The Theological Monthly* (London, 1889-1891)
TPS	*Transactions of the Philological Society* (London, 1842ff.) [Volumes 1-6 as: *Proceedings*]
TQ	*Theological Quarterly* (St. Louis, 1897-1920)

Tr	*Traditio. Studies in Ancient and Medieval History, Thought and Religion* (New York, 1943ff.)
Trad	*Tradition, A Journal of Orthodox Jewish Thought* (New York, 1958ff.)
TRep	*Theological Repository* (London, 1769-1788)
TRFCCQ	*Theological Review and Free Church College Quarterly* (Edinburgh, 1886-1890)
TRGR	*The Theological Review and General Repository of Religious and Moral Information, Published Quarterly* (Baltimore, 1822)
TRL	*Theological Review: A Quarterly Journal of Religious Thought and Life* (London, 1864-1879)
TT	*Theology Today* (Lansdowne, PA; 1944ff.)
TTCA	*Trinity Theological College Annual* (Singapore, 1964-1969) [Volume 5 apparently never published]
TTD	*Teologisk Tidsskrift* (Decorah, IA; 1899-1907)
TTKB	*Türk Tarih Kurumu Belleten* (Ankara, 1937ff.)
TTKF	*Tidskrift för teologi och kyrkiga frågor (The Augustana Theological Quarterly)* (Rock Island, IL; 1899-1917)
TTL	*Theologisch Tijdschrift* (Leiden, 1867-1919) [English articles from Volume 45 on only]
TTM	*Teologisk Tidsskrift* (Minneapolis, 1917-1928)
TUSR	*Trinity University Studies in Religion* (San Antonio, 1950ff.)
TZ	*Theologische Zeitschrift* (Basel, 1945ff.)
TZDES	*Theologische Zeitschrift (Deutsche Evangelische Synode des Westens, North America)* (St. Louis, 1873-1934) [Continued from Volumes 22 through 26 as: *Magazin für Evangel. Theologie und Kirche;* and from Volume 27 on as: *Theological Magazine*]
TZTM	*Theologische Zeitblätter, Theological Magazine* (Columbus,1911-1919)

U

UC	*The Unitarian Christian* (Boston, 1947ff.) [Volumes 1-4 as: *Our Faith*]
UCPSP	*University of California Publications in Semitic Philology* (Berkeley, 1907ff.)
UF	*Ugarit-Forschungen. Internationales Jahrbuch für die Altertumskunde Syrien-Palästinas* (Neukirchen, West Germany; 1969ff.)
ULBIA	*University of London. Bulletin of the Institute of Archaeology* (London, 1958ff.)

UMB   *The University Museum Bulletin, University of Pennsylvania* (Philadelphia, 1930-1958)

UMMAAP   *University of Michigan. Museum of Anthropology. Anthropological Papers* (Ann Arbor, 1949ff.)

UnionR   *The Union Review* (New York, 1939-1945)

UPQR   *The United Presbyterian Quarterly Review* (Pittsburgh, 1860-1861)

UQGR   *Universalist Quarterly and General Review* (Boston, 1844-1891)

URRM   *The Unitarian Review and Religious Magazine* (Boston, 1873-1891)

USQR   *Union Seminary Quarterly Review* (New York, 1945ff.)

USR   *Union Seminary Review* (Hampden-Sydney, VA; Richmond; 1890-1946) [Volumes 1-23 as: *Union Seminary Magazine*]

UTSB   *United Theological Seminary Bulletin* (Dayton, 1905ff.) [Including: *The Bulletin of the Evangelical School of Theology; Bulletin of the Union Biblical Seminary,* later, *Bonebrake Theological Bulletin*]

UUÅ   *Uppsala Universitets Årsskrift* (Uppsala, 1861-1960)

V

VC   *Virgiliae Christianae: A Review of Early Christian Life and Language* (Amsterdam, 1947ff.)

VDETF   *Deutsche Vierteljahrsschrift für englisch-theologische Forschung und Kritik / herausgegeben von M. Heidenheim* (Leipzig, Zurich, 1861-1865) [Continued as: *Vierteljahrsschrift für deutsch – englisch- theologische Forschung und Kritik...* 1866-1873]

VDI   *Vestnik Drevnei Istoriĭ. Journal of Ancient History* (Moscow, 1946ff.) [English summaries from 1967 on only]

VDR   *Koinonia* (Nashville, 1957-1968) [Continued as: *Vanderbilt Divinity Review,* 1969-1971]

VE   *Vox Evangelica. Biblical and Historical Essays by the Members of the Faculty of the London Bible College* (London, 1962ff.)

Voice   *The Voice* (St. Paul, 1958-1960) [Subtitle varies]

VR   *Vox Reformata* (Geelong, Victoria, Australia, 1962ff.)

VT   *Vetus Testamentum* (Leiden, 1951ff.)

VTS   *Vetus Testamentum, Supplements* (Leiden, 1953ff.)

W

Way	*The Way. A Quarterly Review of Christian Spirituality* (London, 1961ff.)
WBHDN	*The Wittenberg Bulletin (Hamma Digest Number)* (Springfield, OH; 1903ff.) [Volumes 40-60 (1943-1963) only contain *Hamma Digest Numbers*]
WesTJ	*Wesleyan Theological Journal. Bulletin of the Wesleyan Theological Society* (Lakeville, IN; 1966ff.)
WLQ	*Wisconsin Lutheran Quarterly* (Wauwatosa, WI; Milwaukee;1904ff.) [Also entitled: *Theologische Quartalschrift*]
WO	*Die Welt des Orients . Wissenschaftliche Beiträge zur Kunde des Morgenlandes* (Göttingen, 1947ff.)
Word	*Word: Journal of the Linguistic Circle of New York* (New York, 1945ff.)
WR	*The Westminster Review* (London, New York, 1824-1914)
WSQ	*Wartburg Seminary Quarterly* (Dubuque, IA; 1937-1960) [Volumes 1-9, #1 as: *Quarterly of the Wartburg Seminary Association*]
WSR	*Wesleyan Studies in Religion* (Buckhannon,WV; 1960-1970) [Volumes 53-62 only*[sic]*]
WTJ	*Westminster Theological Journal* (Philadelphia, 1938ff.)
WW	*Western Watch* (Pittsburgh, 1950-1959) [Superseded by: *Pittsburgh Perspective*]
WZKM	*Wiener Zeitschrift für die Kunde des Morgenlandes* (Vienna, 1886ff.)

Y

YCCAR	*Yearbook of the Central Conference of American Rabbis* (Cincinnati, 1890ff.)
YCS	*Yale Classical Studies* (New Haven, 1928ff.)
YDQ	*Yale Divinity Quarterly* (New Haven, 1904ff.) [Volumes 30-62 as: *Yale Divinity News,* continued as: *Reflections*]
YR	*The Yavneh Review. A Religious Jewish Collegiate Magazine* (New York, 1961ff.) [Volume 2 never published]

Z

Z	*Zygon. Journal of Religion and Science* (Chicago, 1966ff.)
ZA	*Zeitschrift für Assyriologie und verwandte Gebiete* [Volumes 45 on as: *Zeitschrift für Assyriologie und vorderasiatische Archäologie]* (Leipzig, Strassburg, Berlin, 1886ff.)
ZÄS	*Zeitschrift für ägyptische Sprache und Altertumskunde* (Leipzig, Berlin, 1863ff.)
ZAW	*Zeitschrift für die alttestamentliche Wissenschaft* (Giessen, Berlin, 1881ff.)
ZDMG	*Zeitschrift der Deutschen Morgenländischen Gesellschaft* (Leipzig, Wiesbaden, 1847ff.)
ZDPV	*Zeitschrift des Deutschen Palästina-Vereins* (Leipzig, Wiesbaden, 1878ff.) [English articles from Volume 82 on only]
Zion	*Zion. A Quarterly for Research in Jewish History, New Series* ציון, רבעין לחורתולדוה ישראל (Jerusalem, 1935ff.) [English summaries from Volume 3 on only]
ZK	*Zeitschrift für Keilschriftforschung* (Leipzig, 1884-1885)
ZNW	*Zeitschrift für die neutestamentliche Wissenschaft und die Kunde des Urchristentums (...Kunde der älteren Kirche, 1921—)* (Giessen, Berlin, 1900ff.)
ZS	*Zeitschrift für Semitistik und verwandte Gebiete* (Leipzig, 1922-1935)

Sigla[1]

*   Indicates article is additionally listed in other sections of the index.

†   Indicates that title is from the table of contents; from the header; or a composite if title is completely lacking as in early journals.

‡   Indicates a bibliographical article on a specific subject.

---

1.   Compete information may be found in Volume I, page xxiii.

§417 **3.2.12 Religionsgeschichte - General Studies**

*†Anonymous, "Religious History of Mankind," *LQHR* 5 (1855-56) 289-334. *(Review)*

*W. I. Distant, "On the term 'Religion' as used in Anthropology," *JRAI* 6 (1876-77) 60-68. (Discussion, pp. 68-70)

*Alfred Cave, "Evolution and the Hebrews: A Review of Herbert Spencer's 'Hebrews and Phœnicians'," *BFER* 30 (1881) 17-39. *(Review)*

Anonymous, "The Origin of Religion," *WR* 115 (1881) 402-411.

Anonymous, "The Development of Religion," *WR* 116 (1881) 138-154.

S. H. Kellogg, "Professor Max Müller on the Origin and Growth of Religion," *BFER* 33 (1884) 320-343.

S. H. Kellogg, "Prof. Max Müller on the Origin and Growth of Religion," *BS* 41 (1884) 132-157.

*Anonymous, "The Origins of Religion and Language," *CQR* 18 (1884) 396-412. *(Review)*

S. H. Kellogg, "The Ghost Theory of the Origin of Religion," *BS* 44 (1887) 273-293.

Walter Lloyd, "The Secret History of Religions," *WR* 132 (1889) 566-580.

Edward Tylor, "On the Limits of Savage Religion," *JRAI* 21 (1891-92) 283-299. [Discussion, pp. 299-301]

†Anonymous, "Origins and Interpretations of Primitive Religions," *ERCJ* 186 (1897) 213-244. *(Review)*

†Anonymous, "The Making of Religion," *ERCJ* 188 (1898) 311-330. *(Review)*

I. W. Howerth, "Brinton's Theory of the Origin of Religion," *Monist* 10 (1899-1900) 293-298.

J. M'Caffrey, "The Development of Religion: A Criticism," *IER, 4th Ser.,* 10 (1901) 1-36.

P. Forde, "The Origin of Religion," *IER, 4th Ser.,* 10 (1901) 132-140.

*R. M. Wenley, "Philosophy of Religion and the Endowment of Natural Theology," *Monist* 12 (1901-02) 21-48.

*A[ndrew] C. Zenos, "The Philosophy of History in the Philosophy of Religion," *CFL, N.S.,* 7 (1903) 67-74.

*Lewis R. Farnell, "Sociological hypothesis concerning the position of women in ancient religion," *AfRW* 7 (1904) 70-94.

Edmund Buckley, "A Sketch of the Science of Religion," *BW* 23 (1904) 256-262, 349-357.

S[amuel] I[ves] Curtiss, "Survivals of Ancient Semitic Religion in Syrian Centres," *Exp, 6th Ser.,* 11 (1905) 415-431.

James Bissett Pratt, "Concerning the Origin of Religion," *AJRPE* 2 (1906-07) 257-271.

R. Fullerton, "The Origin of Religion," *IER, 4th Ser.,* 22 (1907) 113-126.

R. Fullerton, "Evolution of Religion," *IER, 4th Ser.,* 22 (1907) 225-243.

Grant Showerman, "The Ancient Religions in Universal History," *AJP* 29 (1908) 156-171.

Alfred E. Garvie, "The Development of the Religious Consciousness," *ET* 20 (1908-09) 256-261.

R. R. Marett, "The tabu-mana formula as a minimum definition of Religion," *AfRW* 12 (1909) 186-194.

*Charles Gelderd, "Prehistoric Man: His Civilization and Religion," *IER, 4th Ser.,* 27 (1910) 337-357.

George W. Gilmore, "Primitive Religious Phenomena. 1. Fundamentals and Sources," *HR* 63 (1912) 442-446.

George W. Gilmore, "Primitive Religious Phenomena. II. The Objects and Rationale of Worship," *HR* 64 (1912) 14-19.

George W. Gilmore, "Primitive Religious Phenomena. III. Social Religion-Totemism and Taboo," *HR* 64 (1912) 185-190.

George W. Gilmore, "Primitive Religious Phenomena. IV. Intellectual Religion—Magic and Mythology," *HR* 64 (1912) 273-279.

George W. Gilmore, "Primitive Religious Phenomena. V. Spiritual Religion," *HR* 64 (1912) 351-357.

George W. Gilmore, "Primitive Religious Phenomena. VI. The Religion of Ritual," *HR* 65 (1913) 13-19.

W. T. Shepherd, "Concerning the Origin of the Ideas of Gods," *AJRPE* 7 (1914-15) 237-244.

T. W. Rhys Davids, "The Beginnings of Religion," *JMUEOS* #4 (1914-15) 49-54.

A. L. Frothingham, "Ancient Orientation Unveiled," *AJA* 21 (1917) 55-76.

A. L. Frothingham, "Ancient Orientation Unveiled II," *AJA* 21 (1917) 187-201.

A. L. Frothingham, "Ancient Orientation Unveiled III," *AJA* 21 (1917) 313-336. *(Correction, p 448)*

A. L. Frothingham, "Ancient Orientation Unveiled IV," *AJA* 21 (1917) 420-448.

*Louis Matthews Sweet, "The Decay of Religion," *BR* 3 (1918) 69-88, 228-247.

H. W. Congdon, "The Primitive Religion," *CFL, 3rd Ser.,* 28 (1922) 130-132.

Bruce Byran, "Do the Old Gods Exist Today: Gods of Man - Past and Present: Tracing Religion in its Different Forms by God and Fetish Through the Ages," *A&A* 17 (1924) 169-176.

James H. Leuba, "Mysticism and Religion," *ATR* 7 (1924-25) 152-159.

Herbert H. Gowen, "The Theriomorphic in Theology," *ATR* 9 (1926-27) 365-377.

Hermann Gunkel, "The 'Historical Movement' in the Study of Religion," *ET* 38 (1926-27) 532-536.

T. W. E. Higgens, "Man and His God: The Origin of Religion Among Primitive Peoples," *JTVI* 59 (1927) 41-57, 63-64. [(Discussion, pp. 58-62) (Communication by A. T. Schofield, p. 63)]

D. A. McGregor, "Contemporary Theories of Primitive Religion," *ATR* 10 (1927-28) 343-357.

*I. F. Wood, "The Contribution of the Bible to the History of Religion," *JBL* 47 (1928) 1-19.

J[ohn] M. C[ooper], "The Origin and Early History of Religion," *AQW* 2 (1929) #3/4, 33-50.

Samuel M. Zwemer, "The Origin of Religion—By Evolution or by Revelation," *CRP* 3 (1934) 91-104.

Samuel M. Zwemer, "The Origin of Religion—By Evolution or by Revelation," *JTVI* 67 (1935) 184-197, 204. (Discussion and Communications, pp. 197-204)

John Murphy, "High gods among low races," *SMSDR* 11 (1935) 1-11.

Christopher R. North, "Religion and History," *ET* 47 (1935-36) 354-358.

J. Battersby Harford, "The Origin and Growth of Religion," *ET* 48 (1936-37) 68-74.

Rafael Karsten, "The Origins of Religion," *Man* 37 (1937) #26.

H. J. Rose, "The Origins of Religion," *Man* 37 (1937) #27.

Morton Smith, "The Common Theology of the Ancient Near East," *JBL* 70 (1951) x.

Morton Smith, "The Common Theology of the Ancient Near East," *JBL* 71 (1952) 135-147.

M[argaret] A. Murray, "Ancient and Modern Ritual Dances in the Near East," *Folk* 66 (1955) 401-409.

J. Stafford Wright, "An Examination of Evidence for Religious Beliefs of Palaeolithic Man," *F&T* 90 (1958) 4-15. (Communication by T. C. Mitchell, p. 144)

*E. O. James, "The Threshold of Religion. *The Marett Lecture,* 1958," *Folk* 69 (1958) 160-174.

S. G. F. Brandon, "The Origin of Religion," *HJ* 57 (1958-59) 349-355.

*Robin Horton, "A Definition of Religion, and its Uses," *HRAI* 90 (1960) 201-226.

*S. G. F. Brandon, "The Book of Job: Its Significance for the History of Religions," *HT* 11 (1961) 547-554.

L. E. Browne, "Religion in History," *HJ* 60 (1961-62) 16-23.

W. F. Jackson Knight, "Origins of Belief," *Folk* 74 (1963) 289-304.

C. J. Bleeker, "The significance of the religions of antiquity," *JEOL* #17 (1963) 249-252.

Robert N. Bellah, "Religious Evolution," *AmSR* 29 (1964) 358-374. [Primitive Religion, pp. 361-364; Archaic Religion, pp. 364-366; Historic Religion, pp. 366-368]

S. G. Brandon, "The origin of Religion: In Theory and Archæology," *HT* 17 (1967) 219-228.

*Th. C. Vriezen, "The study of the Old Testament and the History of Religion," *VTS* 17 (1969) 1-24.

§418 *3.2.12.1 Religionsgeschichte of Israel*

*Alfred Cave, "Evolution and the Hebrews: A Review of Herbert Spencer's 'Hebrews and Phœnicians'," *BFER* 30 (1811) 17-39. *(Review)*

Anonymous, "On the Study of Divinity. Chapter III. On the Jewish People and Their Religion," *MR* 2 (1819) 204-207.

†Anonymous, "A Believing Jew's Creed," *SP* 3 (1830) 377-378.

Anonymous, "Religion of the Bible," *CRB* 4 (1839) 1-20. *(Review)*

A. M. B., "On Religion considered with respect to its Source, its Forms, and its Developments," *CTPR, N.S.,* 2 (1840) 390-405. *(Review)*

*[Albert] Barnes, "The Patriarchal Religion, as developed in the Book of Job," *BRCR, N.S.,* 11 (1844) 163-179.

Tayler Lewis, "The Spirit of the Old Testament," *BRCR, 3rd Ser.,* 6 (1850) 1-39.

*†Anonymous, "Mackay on the Progress of Intellect," *BQRL* 12 (1850) 443-476. *(Review)*

I. E. Dwinell, "Advance in the Type of Revealed Religion," *BS* 14 (1857) 323-343.

†Anonymous, "The Mosaic Dispensation and Christianity," *BQRL* 25 (1857) 111-142. *(Review)*

S. T., "The Bible and Judaism," *JSL, 3rd Ser.,* 7 (1858) 106-120. *(Review)*

W. H. R., "The Jewish Church," *UQGR* 15 (1858) 301-323.

Henry Crossley, "Jewish Orthodoxy," *JSL, 3rd Ser.,* 12 (1860-61) 157-162; 13 (1861) 186-188; 14 (1861-62) 180-186.

Henry Constable*[sic]*, "Jewish Orthodoxy," *JSL, 3rd Ser.,* 14 (1861-62) 436-437.

†Anonymous, "Judaism after the Captivity," *LQHR* 30 (1868) 178-224. *(Review)*

*Charles Warren, "The Comparative Holiness of Mounts Zion and Moriah," *PEFQS* 1 (1869) 76-88.

*August Eisenlohr, "On the Political Condition of Egypt before the Reign of Ramses III; *probably in connection with the establishment of the Jewish Religion.* From the Great Harris Papyrus," *SBAT* 1 (1872) 355-384.

Anonymous, "The Religious Ideas of the Old Testament," *CongL* 2 (1873) 257-264.

*Anonymous, "The Old Testament and the New," *CongL* 2 (1873) 321-324.

Anonymous, "Genius of Judaism," *CR* 25 (1873) 435-452.

F. A. Gast, "Origin of Old Testament Religion," *RChR* 23 (1876) 598-616.

Anonymous, "History of the Jewish Church," *CQR* 3 (1876-77) 273-300. *(Review)*

John Wright, "Canon Mozley on the Old Testament," *TRL* 14 (1877) 252-260. *(Review)*

Charles H. Brigham, "Judaism in Rome," *URRM* 7 (1877) 261-285. *(Review)*

R. P. Stebbins, "The Religion of Israel to the Fall of the Jewish State," *URRM* 10 (1878) 297-315, 353-377. *(Review)*

*Alfred Cave, "The Critical Estimate of Mosaism," *DTQ* 5 (1879) 449-470.

*Alfred Cave, "The Critical Estimate of Mosaism," *PQPR* 55 (1879) 579-614. *(Review)*

*S. S. Hebberd, "The Religion of Abraham," *UQGR, N.S.,* 16 (1879) 341-359.

*Anonymous, "Was the Jewish Religion Ethical?" *OBJ* 1 (1880) 3-5.

Talbot W. Chambers, "The Theory of Professor Kuenen," *PR* 1 (1880) 304-320.

Claude Montefiore, "Is Judaism a Tribal Religion?" *ContR* 42 (1882) 361-382.

George H. Schodde, "The Evangelist of the Old Testament," *LQ* 12 (1882) 442-453.

Henry M. Harman, "Weber's System of Theology of the Old Synagogue of Palestine," *MR* 64 (1882) 5-28, 252-283. *(Review)*

Willis J. Beecher, "The Logical Methods of Professor Kuenen," *PR* 6 (1882) 701-731.

William C. Wilkinson, "The Levitical Law as a Tuition to Theism," *ONTS* 2 (1882-83) 161-162.

[Charles] A[ugustus] Briggs, "The Argument e Silentio, *with Special Reference to the Religion of Israel,*" *JBL* 3 (1883) 3-21.

James Scott, "Analysis of Rabbinical Judaism," *ONTS* 4 (1884-85) 345-352, 396-401.

J. Estlin Carpenter, "Through the Prophets to the Law," *ModR* 5 (1884) 1-28.

James Scott, "Analysis of Rabbinical Judaism," *BFER* 34 (1885) 72-87.

F. A. Gast, "Origin of the Old Testament Religion," *ONTS* 5 (1885-86) 52-61, 107-111. *(Review)*

*Archibald Duff, "Jeremiah, the Prophet of Personal Godliness: A Study in Hebrew Religion," *BS* 43 (1886) 652-662.

Thomas Barker, "Spencer's Origin of the Religious Idea," *CM* 23 (1886) 1-12.

S. R. Calthrop, "'The Word of God is not Bound'," *URRM* 25 (1886) 435-442.

*[S. R. Calthrop], "Traditional Records of Early Israel," *URRM* 25 (1886) 530-539.

*S. R. Calthrop, "'Jehovah of Hosts.'," *URRM* 25 (1886) 540-551.

*S. R. Calthrop, "The Prophets," *URRM* 26 (1886) 67-77, 128-140.

*S. R. Calthrop, "The Prophets and the Exile," *URRM* 26 (1886) 206-219.

*S. R. Calthrop, "'Israel's Last Word.'," *URRM* 26 (1886) 289-299.

Geo[rge] H. Schodde, "New Testament Judaism and Its Genesis," *ONTS* 6 (1886-87) 44-47.

S. Ives Curtiss, "The History of Israel from the Standpoint of Modern Criticism," *Exp, 3rd Ser.,* 6 (1887) 321-339.

*Archibald Duff, "Isaiah and Zion; or, the Development of Thought in Isaiah. A Study in the History of Hebrew Religion," *AR* 9 (1888) 426-431, 528-547.

George H. Schodde, "The Errors of Judaism in Christ's Day," *ColTM* 8 (1888) 381-392.

*Ismar J. Peritz, "Woman in Ancient Hebrew Cult," *JBL* 17 (1888) 111-148.

G. W. F. Hegel, "The Religion of the Old Testament," *JSP* 22 (1888-93) 253-280. *(Trans. by J. MacBride Sterrett)*

Walter Lloyd, "The Religion of the Semites," *WR* 133 (1890) 375-383. *(Review)*

*D. G. Lyon, "Judaism and Christianity," *ONTS* 12 (1891) 367-373. *(Review)*

*Edward L. Curtis, "Cheyne's Bampton Lectures on the Psalter," *ONTS* 14 (1892) 198-205. *(Review)*

*George H. Schodde, "Post-Exilic Legalism and Post-Exilic Literature," *ONTS* 15 (1892) 201-206.

O[swald] J[ohn] Simon, "Authority and Dogma in Judaism," *JQR* 5 (1892-93) 231-243.

M. Hyamson, "Authority and Dogma in Judaism, A Reply," *JQR* 5 (1892-93) 469-482. [Reply by Oswald John Simon, p. 715]

C. R. Blauvelt, "The Spencerian Theory of the Religion of Israel," *CT* 10 (1892-93) 261-282.

*Henry Hayman, "The Evidence of the Psalter to a Levitical System," *BS* 50 (1893) 238-260.

Oliver J. Thacher, "The Expansion of Judaism," *BW* 1 (1893) 99-108.

Owen C. Whitehouse, "The Principle of Centralisation in Early Israel," *OSHTP* (1893-94) 27-36.

P. H. Steenstra, "Theology of Moses," *JBL* 14 (1895) 72-88.

*C[arl] H[einrich] Cornill, "The Religion of Moses," *OC* 9 (1895) 4455-4458.

*F. Meinhold, "The Origins of the Religion and History of Israel," *NW* 4 (1895) 98-121.

*R. W. Dale, "The Place of Abraham in Religious History," *Exp, 5th Ser.,* 4 (1896) 338-350.

C[rawford] H. Toy, "The Preprophetic Religion of Israel," *NW* 5 (1896) 123-142.

Francis B. Denio, "Dillmann on the Nature and Character of the Old Testament Religion," *BW* 9 (1897) 349-353.

T. Witton Davies, "Milestones in Religious History: or Tent, Temple, Tabernacle, Synagogue, and Church," *BW* 10 (1897) 1-23.

Edward T. Harper, "Religious Life in Israel from the Division of the Kingdom to the Reform of Josiah," *BW* 10 (1897) 33-47.

Edwin Post, "Latin Pagan Side-Lights on Judaism," *MR* 79 (1897) 71-94.

Arthur E. Whatham, "The Early Religion of the Hebrews," *BS* 55 (1898) 629-655.

A. J. F. Behrends, "The Early Religion of the Hebrews," *BS* 55 (1898) 742-743.

Lewis B[ayles] Paton, "The Religion of Judah from Josiah to Ezra," *BW* 11 (1898) 410-421.

G. Margoliouth, "The Earliest Religion of the Ancient Hebrews. A New Theory," *ContR* 74 (1898) 581-592.

*G[rey] H[ubert] Skipwith, "Hebrew Tribal Names and the Primitive Traditions of Israel," *JQR* 11 (1898-99) 239-265

Arthur E. Whatham, "Rejoinder to Dr. Behrends' Criticisms," *BS* 56 (1899) 168-170.

Arthur E. Whatham, "Were the Israelites Ever Polytheists?" *BW* 13 (1899) 293-307.

Theo. G. Soares, "The Religious Idea of Judaism from Ezra to Maccabees," *BW* 13 (1899) 380-388.

*W. M. McPheeters, "Woman in the Ancient Hebrew Cult," *CFL, O.S.,* 3 (1899) 72-74.

*S. Baring-Gould, "Priest and Prophet," *ContR* 76 (1899) 832-841.

*Joseph Offord, "Dancing Worship," *SBAP* 21 (1899) 253.

Grey Hubert Skipwith, "The Origins of the Religion of Israel," *JQR* 12 (1899-1900) 381-414.

J. S. Riggs, "Some Types of Judaism in the Times of Jesus," *BW* 15 (1900) 105-111.

G. W. Stibitz, "The Centralization of Jehovah Worship in Israel," *RChR* 4 (1900) 81-89.

John P. Peters, "The Religion of Moses," *JBL* 20 (1901) 101-128.

*W. Ewing, "Palestine and Revelation," *GUOST* 2 (1901-07) 18-20.

D. H. MacVicar, "Is the Religion of the Old Testament a Religion of Fear?" *CFL, N.S.,* 6 (1902) 139-145.

W. Scott Watson, "The Rewards of the Old Testament Religion," *CFL, N.S.,* 6 (1902) 145-151.

*Jas. A. Quarles, "The Sociology of Joseph's Day. Religious," *CFL, N.S.,* 6 (1902) 164-175.

Lewis B[ayles] Paton, "The Religion of the Post-Exilic Prophets," *BW* 22 (1903) 258-267.

James Moffatt, "Post-Exilic Judaism," *Exp, 6th Ser.,* 8 (1903) 317-320.

Samuel Ives Curtiss, "The Transformation of the Local Divinities into Gods," *BW* 21 (1903) 7-16.

Eduoard König, "Budde's Hypothesis of the Kenite Origin of the Mosaic Religion of Israel," *HR* 47 (1904) 15-22.

Emil G. Hirsch, "In What Does the Originality of Judaism Consist?" *HUCA* (1904) 158-164.

*Grey Hubert Skipwith, "The Origins of the Religion of Israel," *JQR* 17 (1904-05) 57-64. [Preliminary; The Cretan Zeus; Babel and Bible]

Grey Hubert Skipwith, "The God of Sinai and Jerusalem," *JQR* 17 (1904-05) 489-513.

Anonymous, "Notes and Comments. Traces of Pre-Mosaic Religion Among the Israelites," *ICMM* 1 (1905) 286-288.

Crawford H. Toy, "The Triumph of Yahwism," *JBL* 24 (1905) 91-106.

*Edward E. Nourse, "The Book of Genesis and the Religious Development of Israel," *HSR* 16 (1905-06) 91-113.

Pierre Batiffol, "Was Judaism a Church?" *NYR* 1 (1905-06) 687-700.

*J. E. Odgers, "Notes on θεὸς Ὕψιστος," *OSHTP* (1905-06) 65-75.

W. H. Jones, "The Religion of Israel," *AAOJ* 28 (1906) 270-274.

Lewis Bayles Paton, "The Origin of Yahweh-Worship in Israel," *BW* 28 (1906) 6-22, 113-127.

L. W. Batten, "The Religion of Israel to Samuel," *BW* 28 (1906) 400-411.

Anonymous, "Editorial Notes. Hebrew Religion," *ICMM* 3 (1906-07) 8-10.

‡T. K. Cheyne, "Survey of Recent Literature on the History and Religion of Israel," *RTP* 2 (1906-07) 413-424, 477-487. *(Review)*

*S[tanley] A. Cook, "The Jewish Temple of Yahu, God of the Heavens, at Syene," *Exp, 7th Ser.,* 4 (1907) 497-505.

Grey Hubert Skipwith, "The Origins of the Religion of Israel," *JQR* 20 (1907-08) 738-776. [The Mountain of the World; The World of the Dead, and the Worship of Death; The Sons of the Gods]

C. F. Burney, "A Theory of the Development of Israelite Religion in Early Times," *JTS* 9 (1907-08) 321-352.

C. F. Burney, "A Theory of the Development of Israelite Religion in Early Times," *OSHTP* (1907-08) 61-64.

‡T. K. Cheyne, "Survey of Recent Progress of History of Israel and Israel's Religion," *RTP* 3 (1907-08) 393-410. *(Review)*

Willis J. Beecher, "The Idea of a Central Sanctuary New in the Time of Josiah?" *CFL, 3rd Ser.,* 9 (1908) 334-336.

Walter V. Couch, "Where Israel Got Its Religion," *CFL, 3rd Ser.,* 9 (1908) 363-364. *(Editorial Note)*

*R[obert] H[enry] Charles, "Man's Forgiveness of his Neighbour: a Study in Religious Development," *Exp, 7th Ser.,* 6 (1908) 492-505.

William Hayes Ward, "The Origin of the Worship of Yahwe," *AJSL* 25 (1908-09) 175-187.

H[arold] M. Wiener, "Some Reflexions on Dr. Burney's View of the Religion of Israel," *JTS* 10 (1908-09) 100-106.

*E. G. King, "Enoch and the Feast of Dedication. (A Study in Natural Religion)," *ICMM* 5 (1908-09) 287-295.

‡T. K. Cheyne, "Survey of Recent Literature on the History of Israel and Its Religion," *RTP* 4 (1908-09) 545-557. *(Review)*

*G. Buchanan Gray, "The Excavations at Gezer and Religion in Ancient Palestine," *Exp, 7th Ser.,* 7 (1909) 423-442

Paul Haupt, "The Burning Bush and the Origin of Judaism," *PAPS* 48 (1909) 354-369.

John E. M'Fadyen, "The Centralization of Israel's Worship," *ET* 21 (1909-10) 264-266.

*J. H. A. Hart, "Philo and the Catholic Judaism of the First Century," *JTS* 11 (1909-10) 25-42.

*E. F. Morison, "The Relation of Priest and Prophet in the History of Israel Before the Exile," *JTS* 11 (1909-10) 211-245.

*Caroline Breyfogle, "The Religious Status of Woman in the Old Testament," *BW* 35 (1910) 405-419.

*Ed[uard] König, "The Significance of the Patriarchs in the History of Religion," *Exp, 7th Ser.,* 10 (1910) 193-207.

R. W. Moss, "The Religious History of Israel," *LQHR* 113 (1910) 307-309.

*Joseph Strauss, "Woman's Position in Ancient and Modern Jewry," *WR* 174 (1910) 620-628.

*‡G. H. Box, "Survey of Recent Literature Concerned with Judaism in Its Relations to Christian Origins and Early Development," *RTP* 6 (1910-11) 65-87. *(Review)*

*I. G. Matthews, "Sennacherib's Invasion and Its Religious Significance," *BW* 37 (1911) 115-119.

George A. Barton, "Influence of the Babylonian Exile on the Religion of Israel," *BW* 37 (1911) 369-378.

*Lewis Bayles Paton, "Modern Palestine and the Bible. *X. The Religion of the Jews*," *HR* 62 (1911) 268-273.

W. H. Bennett, "Religious Antagonism in Israel," *OSHTP* (1911-12) 5-19.

Frank C. Porter, "Things Greater and Less in the Bible," *YDQ* 7 (1911-12) 111-122.

Eduard Friedrich König, "The History of the Religion of Israel and Its Newer Representation," *BS* 69 (1912) 513-521.

George Aaron Barton, "The Evolution of the Religion of Israel. I. Moses and the Covenant with Yahweh," *BW* 39 (1912) 17-26.

George Aaron Barton, "The Evolution of the Religion of Israel. II. The Pre-Prophetic Period in Canaan," *BW* 39 (1912) 88-98.

George Aaron Barton, "The Evolution of the Religion of Israel. III. The Prophets of the Eighth Century," *BW* 39 (1912) 157-166.

*George Aaron Barton, "The Evolution of the Religion of Israel. IV. Deuteronomy and Jeremiah," *BW* 39 (1912) 268-281.

George Aaron Barton, "The Evolution of the Religion of Israel. V. From Ezekiel to Nehemiah," *BW* 39 (1912) 307-314.

George Aaron Barton, "The Evolution of the Religion of Israel. VI. From Nehemiah to Christ," *BW* 39 (1912) 396-402.

W. H. Bennett, "Religious Controversy in the Old Testament," *Exp, 8th Ser.,* 4 (1912) 289-305, 508-525. [I. General; II. The Period of the Pre-Exilic Prophets, A. Foreign Policy, B. Differences on Personal Questions, C. Social Ethics, Religion and Morality, D. Theology, E. Ritual; Summary and Conclusion]

Eduard König, "The Beginnings of the True Religion of Israel," *HR* 64 (1912) 96-99.

F. J. Foakes-Jackson, "Religion of Northern Israel under the Monarchy," *ICMM* 9 (1912-13) 36-47.

‡G. H. Box, "Survey of Recent Literature on Late Pre-Christian and Early Post-Christian Judaism," *RTP* 8 (1912-13) 513-539. *(Review)*

*J. M. Powis Smith, "A Professional Reading Course on the Religion of the Hebrews and Modern Scholarship," *BW* 42 (1913) 234-239, 305-308, 373-377.

*A. Noordtzij, "The Old Testament Revelation of God and the Ancient-Oriental Life," *BS* 70 (1913) 622-652. *(Trans. by John H. de Vries)*

B. D. Eerdmans, "Primitive Religious Thought in the Old Testament," *Exp, 8th Ser.,* 6 (1913) 385-405.

*Lewis Bayles Paton, "Canaanite Influence on the Religion of Israel," *AJT* 18 (1914) 205-224.

*John H. deVries, "Does the Old Testament Contain Traces of Animism?" *BS* 71 (1914) 484-489.

*J. M. Powis Smith, "A Professional Reading Course on the Religion of the Hebrews and Modern Scholarship," *BW* 43 (1914) 44-48.

Bernard J. Snell, "Religious Development between the Old and New Testaments," *IJA* #39 (1914) 72-73. *(Review)*

Frank H. Ridgley, "Hebrew Spiritualism," *BWTS* 7 (1914-15) 15-24.

Leroy Waterman, "Our Religious Problem and Its Old Testament Analogies," *MTSQB* 9 (1914-15) #1, 3-18.

*J. M. Powis Smith, "Religion and War in Israel," *AJT* 19 (1915) 17-31.

*Stanley A. Cook, "The Significance of the Elephantine Papyri for the History of Hebrew Religion," *AJT* 19 (1915) 346-382.

*Herbert L. Willett, "The Religious and Social Ideals of Israel," *BW* 46 (1915) 193-200, 258-263, 326-333, 398-404. [Suggestions to Leaders, by Georgia L. Chamberlin, pp. 263-266, 333-336, 404-406]

*George W. Gilmore, "The Influence of Zoroastrianism on Jewish Doctrines in the Inter-Testamental Period," *IJA* #40 (1915) 12-13.

George H. Schodde, "The Judaism of the New Testament Era," *TZTM* 5 (1915) 469-472.

J. M. Powis Smith, "Some Problems in the Early History of Hebrew Religion," *AJSL* 32 (1915-16) 81-97.

*J. M. Powis Smith, "The Effect of the Disruption on the Hebrew Thought of God," *AJSL* 32 (1915-16) 261-269.

*Herbert L. Willett, "The Religious and Social Ideals of Israel," *BW* 47 (1916) 63-72, 133-144, 207-216, 279-288, 351-360, 421-430. [Suggestions to Leaders, by Georgia L. Chamberlin, pp. 142-144, 215-216, 286-288, 358-360, 428-430]

*W. F. Lofthouse, "The Mosaic Codes and Popular Hebrew Religion," *Exp, 8th Ser.,* 11 (1916) 66-80.

James Hope Moulton, "The Hebrew Genius for Religion," *HR* 72 (1916) 399-400.

Leander S. Keyser, "The Old Testament Religion. Was it a Revelation or an Evolution?" *LQ* 46 (1916) 548-564.

J. M. Powis Smith, "Jewish Religion in the Fifth Century B.C.," *AJSL* 33 (1916-17) 322-333.

Robert H. Kennett, "The Conflict Between Priestly and Prophetic Ideas in the Church of Israel," *ICMM* 14 (1917-18) 104-115.

Samuel Holmes, "Jewish Apostacy[sic]* according to the Apocrypha," *IJA* #48 (1917) 3-4.

*Louis Matthews Sweet, "The Decay of Religion," *BR* 3 (1918) 69-88, 228-247. [Hebrew Religion, pp. 72-81]

G. A. Cooke, "The Law and the Prophets," *OSHTP* (1918-19) 5-17.

*Harold M. Wiener, "The Religion of Moses," *BS* 76 (1919) 323-358.

*Gilbert Binns, "The Religion of the Pentateuch," *IER, 5th Ser.,* 14 (1919) 101-114.

*Joseph Rauch, "Apocalypse in the Bible," *JJLP* 1 (1919) 163-195. [IX. Contribution of Apocalypse to the Religion of Israel. The Book of Daniel, pp. 188-195]

David Neumark, "The Principles of Judaism in Historical Outline," *JJLP* 1 (1919) *paged separately at the end of part #4, as* 1-46.

A. J. Wensinck, "The significance of ritual in the religion of Israel," *TTL* 53 (1919) 95-105.

*Harold M. Wiener, "Professor Barton on 'The Religion of Moses'," *BS* 77 (1920) 334-344.

*George W. Gilmore, "The Samaritans: Their Testimony to the Religion of Israel," *HR* 80 (1920) 472-474. *(Review)*

*W. R. Aytoun, "The Rise and Fall of the 'Messianic' Hope in the Sixth Century," *JBL* 39 (1920) 24-43.

Robert George Raymer, "Hebrew Theology and Its Determinants in the Eighth Century B.C.," *MQR, 3rd Ser.,* 46 (1920) 555-563.

*Phillip Wendell Carnnell, "The Prophets and the Cultus," *R&E* 17 (1920) 137-157.

G. A. Cooke, "The Law and the Prophets," *Theo* 1 (1920) 75-82.

Theophile James Meek, "Some Religious Origins of the Hebrews," *AJSL* 37 (1920-21) 101-131.

John E. McFadyen, "The Spirit of Early Judaism. Contrast of the Post-Exilic with the Pre-Exilic Age," *ET* 32 (1920-21) 228-231.

John E. McFadyen, "The Spirit of Early Judaism. Contrasts within the Post-Exilic Age," *ET* 32 (1920-21) 277-280.

John E. McFadyen, "The Spirit of Early Judaism. Dominant Motive of the Post-Exilic Activity," *ET* 32 (1920-21) 312-316.

Ed[uard] König, "The Burning Problem of the Hour in Old Testament Religious History," *Exp, 8th Ser.,* 21 (1921) 81-106.

Julian Morgenstern, "The Historical Reconstruction of Hebrew Religion and Archaeology," *JR* 1 (1921) 233-254.

George Foot Moore, "Christian Writers on Judaism," *HTR* 14 (1921) 197-254.

*J. E. Walker, "The Supreme Object of Worship in Ancient China, Was it Jehovah?" *BS* 79 (1922) 23-42.

Samuel A. B. Mercer, "Did Judaism Fail?" *ConstrQ* 10 (1922) 135-143.

Ed[uard] König, "The So-Called 'Popular Religion of Israel'," *Exp, 8th Ser.,* 23 (1922) 383-400, 401-419.

*R. Travers Herford, "The Fundamentals of Religion, as Interpreted by Christianity and Rabbinical Judaism," *HJ* 21 (1922-23) 314-326.

S. P. T. Prideaux, "'Rabbinical Judaism'," *HJ* 21 (1922-23) 590.

W. K. Lowther Clarke, "In the Study. The Religion of Israel," *Theo* 7 (1923) 176-177.

*James H. Grier, "Israel's Vision of God," *BS* 81 (1924) 116-125.

George Foot Moore, "The Rise of Normative Judaism. I. To the Reorganization at Jamnia," *HTR* 17 (1924) 307-374.

Edward[sic] König, "The So-Called 'Popular Religion' of Israel," *MR* 107 (1924) 580-586.

Theophile J. Meek, "Light from the Old Testament on Primitive Religion," *CJRT* 2 (1925) 32-36.

George Foot Moore, "The Rise of Normative Judaism. II. To the Close of the Mishnah," *HTR* 18 (1925) 1-38.

*Adam C. Welch, "When Was the Worship of Israel Centralized at the Temple?" *ZAW* 43 (1925) 250-255.

*Campbell N. Moody, "Spiritual Power in Pagan Religions and in the Old Testament," *ET* 38 (1926-27) 180-184.

*Adam C. Welch, "Psalm LXXXI.: A Sidelight into the Religion of North Israel," *ET* 38 (1926-27) 455-458.

*Chester C. McCown, "Climate and Religion in Palestine," *JR* 7 (1927) 520-539.

‡John A. Maynard, "A Critical Bibliography of Studies on Hebrew Religion from 1918 to 1924," *JSOR* 11 (1927) 47-70.

*Anonymous, "Public Worship in the Bible," *MR* 110 (1927) 476-478.

A. Kampmeier, "The Actual History of the Origin of Judaism and Christianity in a Nutshell," *OC* 41 (1927) 526-536, 601-613. [I. Origin of Judaism, pp. 526-536]

R. W. Stewart, "The Newer Estimate of Judaism," *ET* 39 (1927-28) 374-378.

*I. F. Wood, "The Contribution of the Bible to the History of Religion," *JBL* 47 (1928) 1-19.

E. G. [H.] Kraeling, "The Real Religion of Ancient Israel," *JBL* 47 (1928) 133-159.

*Theophilus G. Pinches, "The Influence of the Heathenism of the Canaanites upon the Hebrews," *JTVI* 60 (1928) 122-142, 145-147. (Discussion, pp. 143-145)

J. R. Darbyshire, "The Structure of Religion in the Old Testament," *Theo* 18 (1929) 197-204.

*Robert S. Mathes, "'The Prophet Isaiah and the Growth of the Hebrew Religion'," *CTSQ* 7 (1929-30) #3, 6-10.

Eduard König, "The Present Dispute About the Truth of the Old Testament Religion," *MR* 113 (1930) 920-922. *(Trans. by E. W. Hammer)*

O. S. Rankin, "From the Institutum Judaicum," *ET* 42 (1930-31) 421-425.

S[tanley] A. Cook, "Semitic Theism," *JTS* 32 (1930-31) 228-250.

*S. H. Hooke, "The Mixture of Cults in Canaan in Relation to the History of the Hebrew Religion," *JMUEOS* #16 (1931) 23-30.

William Craighton Graham, "The Religion of the Hebrews," *JR* 11 (1931) 242-259.

*Abraham Cronbach, "The Psychoanalytic Study of Judaism," *HUCA* 8&9 (1931-32) 605-740.

Eduard König, "The Modern Attack on the Historicity of the Religion of the Patriarchs," *JQR, N.S.,* 22 (1931-32) 119-142.

A. H. Baldinger, "The Religion of Israel—Evolution or Revelation?" *BS* 89 (1932) 19-27.

J[ames] A. Montgomery, "Ascetic Strains in Early Judaism," *JBL* 51 (1932) 183-213.

*C. R. North, "The Religious Aspect of Hebrew Kingship," *ZAW* 50 (1932) 8-38.

E. P. Aderman, "Distinctive Features in the Religion of Israel," *NZJT* 2 (1932-33) 235-239.

*F. M. T. Böhl, "Some Notes on Israel in the Light of Babylonian Discoveries," *JBL* 52 (1933) 140-146. *[marked as "to be continued" but was not]*

Eduard König, "The Truth of Old Testament Religion," *JQR, N.S.,* 24 (1933-34) 103-111.

W. Harvey-Jellie, "Bridging the Gulf Between the Testaments. *II. The Faith,"* *HR* 107 (1934) 185-187.

Mordecai M. Kaplan, "The Effects of Intercultural Contacts upon Judaism," *JR* 14 (1934) 53-61.

*M. Kiddle, "Saul and David. A Study of the Conflict Between Northern Prophecy and Southern Priesthood," *Theo* 28 (1934) 95-101.

W. F. Lofthouse, "The Evolution of Religion in the Old Testament," *MC* 24 (1934-35) 259-274.

*T. H. W. Maxfield, "The Evolution of Judaism in the Post-Exilic Period with special reference to its literature," *MC* 24 (1934-35) 275-294.

Stanley A. Cook, "The 'Evolution' of Biblical Religion," *MC* 24 (1934-35) 471-484.

Richard Bernheimer, "Vitae prophetarum," *JAOS* 55 (1935) 200-203.

W. Emery Barnes, "The Mosaic Religion," *Theo* 31 (1935) 6-17.

*Solomon Zeitlin, "The Jews: Race, Nation or Religion—Which?" *JQR, N.S.,* 26 (1935-36) 313-347.

S[tanley] A. Cook, "The development of the religion of Israel," *AIPHOS* 4 (1936) 539-550.

Sheldon H. Blank, "Studies in Post-Exilic Universalism," *HUCA* 11 (1936) 159-191.

Samuel S. Cohon, "Authority in Judaism," *HUCA* 11 (1936) 593-646.

Leroy Waterman, "The Revolt of Israel's Prophets Against Nationalism in Religion," *RL* 5 (1936) 380-387.

*W. J. Ferrar, "The Jewish Kingship and the Sacred Combat," *Theo* 32 (1936) 37-43.

Erwin R. Goodenough, "New Light on Hellenistic Judaism," *JAAR* 5 (1937) 18-28.

J[ames] A. Montgomery, "(1) Aesthetic in Hebrew Religion," *JBL* 56 (1937) iv.

James A. Montgomery, "Aesthetic in Hebrew Religion," *JBL* 56 (1937) 35-41.

*Edward J. Young, "The God of Horeb," *EQ* 10 (1938) 10-29.

J. N. Schofield, "Religion in Palestine During the Monarchy," *JMUEOS* #22 (1938) 37-52.

Werner Jaeger, "Greeks and Jews. The First Greek Records of Jewish Religion and Civilization," *JR* 18 (1938) 127-143.

John J. Dougherty, "The Supernatural Origin of Israel's Religion," *CBQ* 1 (1939) 232-238.

Samuel Koch, "An Inventory of the Jew and Judaism at the Beginning of the Christian Era," *CQ* 16 (1939) 260-266.

*William F. Stinespring, "Old Testament Criticism. Archaeology, and Religion," *DDSR* 4 (1939) 61-69.

*H. P. Hamann, "The Evolutionistic Error with Regard to the God of Israel," *AusTR* 11 (1940) 42-48, 65-70.

William F[oxwell] Albright, "The Ancient Near East and the Religion of Israel," *JBL* 59 (1940) 85-112.

*Henry F. L. Lutz, "The Eighth Century B.C. and Its Religious Significance," *KZ* 64 (1940) 463-474.

Corwin C. Roach, "Prophet versus Priest: A False Antithesis," *RelM* 1 (1940-41) 327-338.

*James A. Montgomery, "Law and Religion in the Ancient World as Illustrated in the Bible," *ATR* 23 (1941) 293-306.

Herbert Gordon May, "The God of My Father—A Study of Patriarchal Religion," *JAAR* 9 (1941) 155-158, 199-200.

G. Ernest Wright, "The Terminology of Old Testament Religion and Its Significance," *JNES* 1 (1942) 404-414.

Corwin C. Roach, "The Secret of Conflict in the Old Testament," *RelM* 3 (1942-43) 176-184.

*G. Ernest Wright, "How Did Early Israel Differ from Her Neighbors?" *BA* 6 (1943) 1-10, 13-20. [What Civilization Owes to the Canaanites; Israel's Debt to Canaan; I. Official Religion of Early Israel not Polytheistic; II. No Mythology about God in the Old Testament; III. The Significance of Anthropomorphism; IV. The God of Israel Stood Alone; V. The Prohibition Against Images; V*[sic]* The Union of Religion and Morality; VII. Israel a Covenanted Group; VIII. The Ruler-Servant Motif in Early Israelite Religion; IX. Early Israelite Traditions of the Beginning of the World]

Cosslette Quin, "A Biblical Humanism," *Theo* 46 (1943) 1-3. *[O.T. Refs. pp. 1-2]*

Solomon Zeitlin, "Judaism as a Religion," *JQR, N.S.,* 34 (1943-44) 1-40, 207-241, 321-364; 35 (1944-45) 85-116, 179-225, 303-349.

Herbert Gordon May, "A Sociological Approach to Hebrew Religion," *JAAR* 12 (1944) 98-106.

L. Wallach, "From Hellenism to Christianity and Rabbinic Judaism—the Problem of Continuity," *JBL* 63 (1944) iii.

John L. McKenzie, "The Divine Sonship of Men in the Old Testament," *CBQ* 7 (1945) 326-339.

Paul E. Davies, "Early Christian Attitudes Toward Judaism and the Jews," *JAAR* 13 (1945) 72-82.

George Ricker Berry, "The Unrealistic Attitude of Postexilic Judaism," *JBL* 64 (1945) 309-317.

*U[mberto] Cassuto, "The Gods of the Jews of Elephantine," *KSJA* 2 (1945) VI.

Sheldon H. Blank, "The Dissident Laity in Early Judaism," *HUCA* 19 (1945-46) 1-42.

Abraham Cronbach, "New Studies in the Psychology of Judaism," *HUCA* 19 (1945-46) 205-273.

*James B. Pritchard, "The Hebrew Theologian and His Foreign Colleagues," *CQ* 23 (1946) 21-33.

R[obert] H. Pfeiffer, "The Growth of Old Testament Religion," *SQ/E* 8 (1947) 7-31.

Herbert Gordon May, "Theological Universalism in the Old Testament," *JAAR* 16 (1948) 100-107.

Nathan Rotenstreich, "On the Notion of Tradition in Judaism," *JR* 28 (1948) 28-36.

*Alan Robinson, "God, the Refiner of Silver," *CBQ* 11 (1949) 188-190.

*Norman W. Porteous, "Ritual and Righteousness. *The Relation of Ethics to Religion in the Prophetic Literature,*" *Interp* 3 (1949) 400-414.

*C. R. North, "Old Testament Theology and the History of Hebrew Religion," *SJT* 2 (1949) 113-126.

*H. H. Rowley, "Living Issues in Biblical Scholarship. The Antiquity of Israelite Monotheism," *ET* 61 (1949-50) 333-338.

*W[illiam] L. Reed, "Some Implications of *ḥēn* for Old Testament Religion," *JBL* 69 (1950) ix-x.

*A. S. Kapelrud, "Cult and Prophetic Words," *ST* 4 (1950) 5-12.

*Geo Widengren, "The Ascension of the Apostle and the Heavenly Book. (King and Saviour. III)," *UUÅ* (1950) #7, 1-117. [Israelitic-Jewish Religion in the Light of Comparative Research, pp. 22-39]

*A. R. Johnson, "Living Issues in Biblical Scholarship. Divine Kingship in the Old Testament," *ET* 62 (1950-51) 36-42.

*Alexander Guttmann, "Foundations of Rabbinic Judaism," *HUCA* 23 (1950-51) Part 1, 453-473.

*John Paterson, "The Psalms and the Cult," *GUOST* 14 (1950-52) 42-47.

*G. W. Anderson, "Some Aspects of the Uppsala School of Old Testament Study," *HTR* 43 (1950) 239-256. [II. The History of Old Testament Religion, pp. 249-253]

Bernard J. Bamberger, "Jewish Universalism," *RL* 20 (1951) 362-373.

*John Wick Bowman, "Response and Fellowship. *Devotional Life in the Bible,*" *Interp* 6 (1952) 279-289.

Solomon Zeitlin, "The Bet Ha-Shoebah and the Sacred Fire. A Historical Study of Religious Institutions During the Second Commonwealth," *JQR, N.S.,* 43 (1952-53) 217-224.

P[eter] R. Ackroyd, "Crisis and Evolution in the Old Testament," *EQ* 25 (1953) 69-82.

George E. Mendenhall, "Biblical Faith and Cultic Evolution," *LQ, N.S.,* 5 (1953) 235-258.

*Antonine DeGulielmo, "The Religious Life of the Jews in the Light of Their Coins," *CBQ* 16 (1954) 171-188.

*William L. Reed, "Some Implications of ḥēn for Old Testament Religion," *JBL* 73 (1954) 36-41.

*Chr. H. W. Brekelmans, "Exodus XVIII and the Origins of Yahwism in Israel," *OTS* 10 (1954) 214-224.

S. G. F. Brandon, "Divine Kings and Dying Gods," *HJ* 53 (1945-55) 327-333.

*George Weston Briggs, "Eastern Sage to Western Man," *RR* 19 (1954-55) 115-130. *[Influence of Zoroastrianism on the Hebrew Religion, esp. pp. 118-121]*

Steven Szikszai, "The Unbroken Line of Development of Israel's Faith," *BTSAB* 30 (1955) #4, 1-8.

John J. Dougherty, "The Origins of the Hebrew Religion: A Study in Method," *CBQ* 17 (1955) 258-276.

Ephraim Frisch, "Judaism, Distortion and Reality," *JAAR* 23 (1955) 38-41.

Harry L. Poppers, "Hasidism and Rabbinic Judaism," *Jud* 4 (1955) 70-77.

*D. W. Watts, "The People of God. A Study in the Doctrine in the Pentateuch," *ET* 67 (1955-56) 232-237.

Ronald J. Williams, "Theodicy in the Ancient Near East," *CJT* 2 (1956) 14-26.

*H. H. Rowley, "Ritual and the Hebrew Prophets," *JSS* 1 (1956) 338-360.

*W. Stewart McCullough, "Israel's Kings, Sacral and Otherwise," *ET* 68 (1956-57) 144-148.

*Aubrey R. Johnson, "Old Testament Exegesis, Imaginative and Unimaginative. A Reply to Professor McCullough's article 'Israel's Kings, Sacral and Otherwise'," *ET* 68 (1956-57) 178-179.

Maurice L. Zigmond, "Organized Religion in Israel," *CCARJ* #16 (1957) 8-9.

*James Barr, "The Problem of Old Testament Theology and the History of Religion," *CJT* 3 (1957) 141-149.

*Geo Widengren, "King and Covenant," *JSS* 2 (1957) 1-32.

Nahum Levison, "The Proselyte in Biblical and Early Post-Biblical Times," *SJT* 10 (1957) 45-56.

W[illiam] A. Irwin, "The Study of Israel's Religion," *VT* 7 (1957) 113-126.

Morton Smith, "The Image of God: Notes on the Hellenization of Judaism, with especial Reference to Goodenough's work on Jewish Symbols," *BJRL* 40 (1957-58) 473-512.

Robert B. Campbell, "An Analysis of the 'Recital' in the Religious Spirit of the Hebrews," *MH* 13 (1957-58) #2, 23-32.

*E[phraim] A. Speiser, "Census and Ritual Expiation in Mari and Israel," *BASOR* #149 (1958) 17-25.

B. Uffenheimer, "On the Question of Centralisation of Worship in Ancient Israel," *Tarbiz* 28 (1958-59) #2, I-II.

*M. Haran, "The Ark and the Cherubim: Their Symbolic Significance in Biblical Ritual," *IEJ* 9 (1959) 30-38, 89-94.

*Jacob Neusner, "Qumran and Jerusalem: Two Jewish Roads to Utopia," *JAAR* 27 (1959) 284-290.

Eliezer Berkovits, "From the Temple to Synagogue and Back," *Jud* 8 (1959) 303-311.

*Cyril S. Rodd, "Kingship and Cult," *LQHR* 184 (1959) 21-26.

*A. G. Hebert, "The Idea of Kingship in the Old Testament," *RTR* 18 (1959) 34-45.

Prescott H. Williams Jr., "The Covenant form in Old Testament worship," *ASBFE* 75 (June, 1960) #8, 6-19.

*David N. Freedman, "History and Eschatology. *The Nature of Biblical Religion and Prophetic Faith,*" *Interp* 14 (1960) 143-154.

*Allan R. McAllaster, "Hebrew Language and Israelite Faith. *Insights Provided by Language Structure,*" *Interp* 14 (1960) 421-432.

*Nicole Milne, "Prophet, Priest and King and their Effect on Religion in Israel," *Abr-N* 2 (1960-61) 55-67.

M. H. Segal, "The Religion of Israel Before Sinai," *Tarbiz* 30 (1960-61) #3, I-IV.

James M. Ward, "The Origin of Israel's Faith," *PSTJ* 14 (1960-61) #2, 24-30.

*William O. Walker Jr., "Critical Study and 'Historical' Traditions in the Old Testament," *TUSR* 7 (1960-63) 100-117.

E. R. Goodenough, "Judaism at Dura-Europos," *IEJ* 11 (1961) 161-170.

J. Philip Hyatt, "Yehezkel Kaufmann's View of the Religion of Israel," *JAAR* 29 (1961) 52-57. *(Review)*

*Gerald Cooke, "The Israelite King as Son of God," *ZAW* 73 (1961) 202-225.

*R. E. Clements, "Temple and Land: A Significant Aspect of Israel's Worship," *GUOST* 19 (1961-62) 16-28.

M. H. Segal, "The Religion of Israel Before Sinai," *JQR, N.S.,* 52 (1961-62) 41-68; 53 (1962-63) 226-256.

*Moshe Weinfeld, "The Change in the Conception of Religion in Deuteronomy," *Tarbiz* 31 (1961-62) #1, I-III.

Richard N. Longnecker, "Christian Piety of Pre-Destruction Hebraic Judaism," *BETS* 5 (1962) 51-63.

G. Ernest Wright, "Cult and History. *A Study of a Current Problem in Old Testament Interpretation,*" *Interp* 16 (1962) 3-20.

Andrew C. Tunyogi, "The Rebellions of Israel," *JBL* 81 (1962) 385-390.

Julius Guttmann, "On the Fundamentals of Judaism," *Mosaic* 3 (1962) #3, 23-30.

*Raphael Hallevy, "The Place of the Monarchy in the Israelite Religion," *Tarbiz* 32 (1962-63) #3, I-II.

*Roderick A. F. MacKenzie, "The City and Israelite Religion," *CBQ* 25 (1963) 60-70.

Jacob Neusner, "A Zoroastrian Critique of Judaism. (Škand Gumanik Vičar, Chapters Thirteen and Fourteen: A New Translation and Exposition)," *JAOS* 83 (1963) 283-294.

Moshe Weinfeld, "Universalism and Particularism in the Period of Exile and Restoration," *Tarbiz* 33 (1963-64) #3, I-II.

G. W. Anderson, "Israel's Creed: Sung, not Signed," *SJT* 16 (1963) 277-285.

Ludwig R. Dewitz, "The Concept of Balance in the Old Testament," *CTSB* 57 (1964) 1-18.

Wilfred Harrington, "The Law, The Prophets and the Gospel," *ITQ* 31 (1964) 283-302.

*M. Weinfeld, "Cult Centralization in Israel in the Light of a Neo-Babylonian Analogy," *JNES* 23 (1964) 202-212.

Elie Benamozegh, "Judaism and Christianity in the Light of Noachism. *2. The Universality of Judaism,*" *Jud* 13 (1964) 346-350.

*R. Davidson, "Orthodoxy and the Prophetic Word. A Study in the Relationship between Jeremiah and Deuteronomy," *VT* 14 (1964) 407-416.

Jacob Neusner, "Judaism at Dura-Europos," *HRel* 4 (1964-65) 81-102.

Judah Goldin, "Of Change and Adaptation in Judaism," *HRel* 4 (1964-65) 269-294.

J. A. Thompson, "The Near Eastern Suzerain-Vassal Concept in the Religion of Israel," *JRelH* 3 (1964-65) 1-19.

*M. Haran, "The Religion of the Patriarchs—An Attempt at a Synthesis," *ASTI* 4 (1965) 30-55.

*R. Vande Walle, "An Administrative Body of Priests and a Consecrated People," *IJT* 14 (1965) 57-72.

*Frank E. Eakin Jr., "Yahwism and Baalism Before the Exile," *JBL* 84 (1965) 407-414.

William A. Irwin, "Sources of Israel's Faith," *SQ/E* 26 (1965) 171-182.

Julian Morgenstern, "The Fire Upon the Altar Once Again," *SQ/E* 26 (1965) 215-224.

Anton T. Pearson, "The Church in the Old Testament," *BSQ* 14 (1965-66) #1, 3-15.

Kermit Schoonover, "Worship and Reality in the Old Testament," *PSTJ* 19 (1965-66) #1/2, 12-17.

*David Stacey, "Clues from the Old Testament," *PQL* 11 (1965) 18-24. [II. Worship (in OT)]

Blanche Thompson Richardson, "Judaism—Mother of Christianity," *ContR* 209 (1966) 296-298.

*Marten H. Woundstra, "The Religious Problem-Complex of Prophet and Priest in Contemporary Thought," *CTJ* 1 (1966) 39-66. *[O.T. Refs. pp. 42-47]*

David W. Wills, "Tradition and History in Ancient Israel and America," *DTCW* 1 (1966) #1, 90-113.

Ronald M. Hals, "The Old Testament Roots of Secularization," *LQ, N.S.,* 18 (1966) 36-42.

Jimmy J. Roberts, "The Decline of the Wellhausen Reconstruction of Israelite Religion," *RestQ* 9 (1966) 229-240.

*L. W. Barnard, "Hermas and Judaism," *StP* 8 (1966) 3-9.

D. A. Hubbard, "The Wisdom Movement and Israel's Covenant Faith," *TB* #17 (1966) 3-34.

*Bruce Vawter, "Church and State in Ancient Israel," *Focus* 3 (1966-67) #2, 5-17.

H. D. Beeby, "Incarnating the Gospel—An Old Testament Approach," *T&C* 6 (1966-67) #1/2, 4-12.

Maurice Friedman, "Martin Buber's Biblical Judaism," *BibT* #30 (1967) 2114-2120.

*W. R. Hanford, "Deutero-Isaiah and Luke-Acts: Straightforward Universalism?" *CQR* 168 (1967) 141-152.

Donald M. Gaymon, "The History of Israel and the Lay Revolution," *SE* 3 (1967) 128-135. (Comments by R. Martin-Achard and Roland de Corneille, pp. 136-138)

*Ulrich S. Leupold, "Worship Music in Ancient Israel: Its Meaning and Purpose," *Resp* 9 (1967-68) 116-124.

*James A. Wharton, "The Occasion of the Word of God: An unguarded essay on the character of the Old Testament as the memory of God's story with Israel," *ASBFE* 84 (1968) #1, 5-54.

*Samuel Amirtham, "To be near to and far away from Yahweh: The Witness of the individual psalms of lament to the concept of the presence of God," *BTF* 2 (1968) #2, 31-55.

*Delbert R. Hillers, "Ritual Procession of the Ark and Ps 132," *CBQ* 30 (1968) 48-55.

*Eugene B. Borowitz, "Judaism and the Secular State," *JR* 48 (1968) 22-34.

Jay A. Wilcoxen, "Some Anthropocentric Aspects of Israel's Sacred History," *JR* 48 (1968) 333-350.

*Walter Harrelson, "Guilt and Rites of Purification related to the Fall of Jerusalem in 587 B.C.," *Numen* 15 (1968) 218-221.

Erfaim Shmueli, "The 'Pariah-People' and its 'Charismatic Leadership': A Reevaluation of Max Weber's 'Ancient Judaism'," *PAAJR* 36 (1968) 167-247.

Jared Judd Jackson, "Once Again, 'The Religion of Israel'," *PP* 9 (1968) 267-285.

*Islwyn Blythim, "The Patriarchs and the Promise," *SJT* 21 (1968) 56-73.

*Menahem Haran, "Biblical Studies: The Idea of the Divine Presence in Israelite Cult," *Tarbiz* 38 (1968-69) #2, I-II. *(Review)*

*Ulrich S. Leupold, "Worship Music in Ancient Israel: Its Meaning and Purpose," *CJT* 15 (1969) 176-186.

*Bezalel Porten, "The Religion of the Jews of Elephantine in Light of the Hermopolis Papyri," *JNES* 28 (1969) 116-121. [Sabbath; Cult, I. Bethel, II. Nabu, III. Malkat Sh^emayin "Queen of Heaven"]

Jonathan Z. Smith, "Earth and Gods," *JR* 49 (1969) 103-127.

James A. Wharton, "Obedience and sacrifice: Some reflections on worship from the Old Testament side," *ASBFE* 85 (Nov, 1969) #3, 5-25.

*Emmanuel Lévinas, "Judaism and the Feminine Element," *Jud* 18 (1969) 30-38. *(Trans. by Edith Wyschogrod)*

*J. N. M. Wijngaards, "The Dramatization of Salvific History in the Deuteronomic Schools," *OTS* 16 (1969) 1-127.

*R. P. Carroll, "The Elijah-Elisha Sagas: Some Remarks on Prophetic Succession in Ancient Israel," *VT* 19 (1969) 400-415.

*Arthur E. Cundall, "Sacral Kingship—The Old Testament Background," *VE* 6 (1969) 31-41.

Dennis J. McCarthy, "The Religion of the Old Testament," *Way* 9 (1969) 175-183.

Dennis J. McCarthy, "What was Israel's Historical Creed?" *LTQ* 4 (1969) 46-53.

Th. C. Vriezen, "The study of the Old Testament and the History of Religion," *VTS* 17 (1969) 1-24.

§419 **3.2.12.2 Related Studies in Modern Judaism**

Anonymous, "Modern Judaism," *BFER* 18 (1869) 245-272.

Frances Power Cobbe, "Progressive Judaism," *ContR* 42 (1882) 745-763.

David Philipson, "Tendencies of Thought in Modern Judaism," *NW* 4 (1895) 601-625.

Anonymous, "Reformed Judaism," *CQR* 44 (1897) 164-182.

G. Deutsch and M. Mietziner, "Report of Committee on the Draft of Principles of Judaism," *YCCAR* 10 (1900) 148-164.

E. W. G. Masterman, "The Religious Life of the Orthodox Jews in Palestine," *BW* 21 (1903) 274-280.

Louis Grossmann, "Religious Education in Modern Judaism," *HUCA* (1904) 110-123.

Samuel Ives Curtiss, "Sacrifice Before Shrines in Modern Judaism," *CSQ* 7 (1907) #3, 37-38.

*Julian Morgenstern, "The Significance of the Bible for Reform Judaism in the Light of Modern Scientific Research," *YCCAR* 18 (1908) 217-238. [Responses by N. Krass, pp. 239-242; W. H. Ettelson, pp. 243-248]

*Joseph Strauss, "Woman's Position in Ancient and Modern Jewry," *WR* 174 (1910) 620-628.

H. G. Enelow, "What Do Jews Believe?" *MQR, 3rd Ser.,* 40 (1914) 565-572.

Alban G. Widgery, "Aspects of Liberal Judaism," *MC* 8 (1918-19) 490-502.

W. H. Bennett, "Liberal Judaism," *IAQR* 15 (1919) 101-105.

*Felix A. Levy, "God and Reform Judaism," *YCCAR* 45 (1935) 229-245.

Luitpold Wallach, "The Scientific and Philosophical Background of Zunz's 'Science of Judaism'," *HJud* 4 (1942) 51-70.

‡Joshua Loth Liebman, "Theological Bibliographies. IV. Judaism and Jewish Theology," *ANQ* 38 (1946) #2, 20.

Luitpold Wallach, "The Beginnings of the Science of Judaism in the Nineteenth Century. A Contribution to the Intellectual History of the Age," *HJud* 8 (1946) 33-60.

Benard Heller, "Authority in Judaism—Its Source, Scope and Limits," *YCCAR* 61 (1951) 319-364. [Preliminary Definitions, I. God; II. Torah; III. Israel]

Felix Eckstein, "Judaism—The Traditional, Existentialist, and Humanist Approach," *Jud* 2 (1953) 148-159.

Ephraim Fischoff, "Judaism and Modern Theology: *Discussion*," *YCCAR* 66 (1956) 216-230.

Richard L. Rubenstein, "Atonement and Sacrifice in Contemporary Jewish Liturgy," *Jud* 11 (1962) 131-143.

Steven S. Schwarzschild, "The Role and Limits of Reason in Contemporary Jewish Theology," *YCCAR* 73 (1963) 199-214.

Eugene B. Borowitz, "Faith and Method in Modern Jewish Theology," *YCCAR* 73 (1963) 215-228.

§420 *3.2.12.3 Studies on Monolatry and Monotheism*

*[Edward] Zeller, "The Development of Monotheism Among the Greeks," *ContR* 4 (1867) 359-379.

J. H. Titcomb, "On Prehistoric Monotheism, *considered in relation to Man as an Aboriginal Savage*," *JTVI* 6 (1872-73) 141-155. (Discussion, pp. 155-165)

†Anonymous, "The Monotheism of Paganism," *BQRL* 57 (1873) 342-381. *(Review)*

*O. Cone, "The Development of Monotheism among the Greeks," *UQGR*, *N.S.*, 10 (1873) 171-197.

A. Kuenen, "Yahveh and the 'other gods'," *TRL* 13 (1876) 329-366.

William Sanday, "On the Nature and Development of Monotheism in Israel," *TRL* 13 (1876) 486-499.

W. H. Rule, "Monotheism, a Truth of Revelation, not a Myth," *JTVI* 12 (1878-79) 343-361. (Discussion, pp. 361-369)

*A. G. Laurie, "Persian Influence on Jewish Monotheism," *UQGR, N.S.,* 16 (1879) 21-32.

*R. Brown, "'The System of Zoroaster considered in connexion with Archaic Monotheism'," *JTVI* 13 (1879-80) 246-305. [Discussion, pp. 306-314]

*Edward Zeller, "Development of Monotheism Among the Greeks," *MQR, 2nd Ser.,* 2 (1880) 217-230. *(Trans. by Dwight M. Lowrey)*

*Edward Zeller, "The Development of Monotheism Among the Greeks," *BS* 39 (1882) 619-647. *(Trans. by Edward D. Mead)*

E. A. Allen, "Is Monotheism a 'Primitive' Faith?" *AAOJ* 10 (1886) 246-249.

*C. Loring Brace, "Egyptian Monotheism," *NPR* 1 (1886) 346-361.

A. A. Berle, "Early Israelitish Monotheism," *BS* 52 (1895) 168-170.

W. O. E. Oesterley, "The Development of Monotheism in Israel," *Exp, 6th Ser.,* 6 (1902) 93-105.

*W. F. Warren, "Beginnings of Hebrew Monotheism—The Ineffable Name," *MR* 84 (1902) 24-35.

P. A. Peter, "The Prevalence of Monotheism Before Polytheism in the History of Mankind," *ColTM* 23 (1903) 188-192.

Friedrich Delitzsch, "Monotheism," *OC* 17 (1903) 409-417. *(Trans. by W. H. Carruth)*

Anonymous, "Monotheism in Semitic Religions," *CQR* 57 (1903-04) 300-318.

*C. H. W. Johns, "Babylonian Monotheism. A Personal Explanation," *ET* 15 (1903-04) 44-45.

Robert W. Rogers, "Fresh Light Upon Bible Problems: The Return to an Early Monotheism," *BRec* 3 (1906) 247-253.

W. F. Lofthouse, "Mythology and Monotheism," *LQHR* 105 (1906) 301-319. *(Review)*

*Harold M. Wiener, "Hebrew Monotheism," *BS* 64 (1907) 609-637.

Henry Preserved Smith, "Moses and Monotheism," *AJT* 12 (1908) 444-454.

James A. Kelso, "'Hebrew and the Older Semitic Monotheism'," *HR* 55 (1908) 426-433. *(or Vol. 56 (1909) pp. 266-272)*[1]

*W. F. Badè, "Not Monotheism, but Mono-Jahwism Asserted in Deuteronomy," *PAPA* 40 (1908) lii.

G. A. Grierson, "The Monotheistic Religion of Ancient India and its Descendant, the Modern Hindu Doctrine of Faith," *IAQR, 3rd Ser.,* 28 (1909) 115-126.

J. Edwin Odgers, "Notes on Pagan Monotheism," *OSHTP* (1912-13) 5-20.

Anonymous, "Was Israel's Monotheism Influenced by Babylon," *HR* 68 (1914) 203.

*Samuel A. B. Mercer, "Was Ikhnaton a Monotheist?" *JSOR* 3 (1919) 70-80.

A. M. Hocart, "The Origin of Monotheism," *Folk* 33 (1922) 282-293.

G. Buchanan Gray, "Hebrew Monotheism," *OSHTP* (1922-23) 5-28.

George Preston Mains, "The Monotheistic Quest," *Person* 4 (1923) 237-243.

W. L. Wardle, "The Origins of Hebrew Monotheism," *ZAW* 43 (1925) 193-209.

*H. M. DuBose, "Shechem and the Primeval Monotheism," *BR* 12 (1927) 171-188.

*Robert H. Pfeiffer, "The Dual Origin of Hebrew Monotheism," *JBL* 46 (1927) 193-206.

Anonymous, "Primeval Monotheism," *CFL, 3rd Ser.,* 34 (1928) 214-215.

*John Robert Towers, "Was Akhenaten a Monotheist Before His Accession?" *AEE* 16 (1931) 97-100.

*James Fleming, "Was There Monotheism in Israel Before Amos?" *ATR* 14 (1932) 130-142.

1 Page numbers in this journal vary as more than one edition was apparently issued!

S[tanley] A. Cook, "Primitive Monotheism," *JTS* 33 (1931-32) 1-17.

*Samuel A. B. Mercer, "The Wisdom of Amenemope and Monotheism," *EgR* 2 (1934) 18-20.

*S[tephen H.] Langdon, "Monotheism as the Predecessor of Polytheism in Sumerian Religion," *EQ* 9 (1937) 137-146.

Theophile J. Meek, "Primitive Monotheism and the Religion of Moses," *RR* 4 (1939-40) 286-303.

*J. Philip Hyatt, "Freud on Moses and the Genesis of Monotheism," *JAAR* 8 (1940) 85-88. *(Review)*

Theophile J. Meek, "Monotheism and the Religion of Isarel," *JBL* 61 (1942) 21-43.

*B. D. Eerdmans, "On the Road to Monotheism," *OTS* 1 (1942) 105-125.

R. T. O'Callaghan, "Monotheism and the Historical Process—A Recent Study," *Or, N.S.,* 20 (1951) 216-236.

*Joseph Klausner, "Monotheism and Ethics in Judaism," *Jud* 1 (1952) 325-333.

James Barr, "The Problem of Israelite Monotheism," *GUOST* 17 (1957-58) 52-62.

M. David Weiss, "Repression and Monotheism," *Jud* 10 (1961) 217-226.

Hamilton A. R. Gibb, "Pre-Islamic Monotheism in Arabia," *HTR* 55 (1962) 269-280.

N. H. Snaith, "The Advent of Monotheism in Israel," *ALUOS* 5 (1963-65) 100-113.

*Nathaniel S. Lehrman, "Moses, Monotheism, and Marital Fidelity," *JRH* 3 (1963-64) 70-89.

W. W. Meissner, "Notes on Monotheism: The Argument," *JRH* 6 (1967) 269-279.

W. W. Meissner, "Notes on Monotheism: Origins," *JRH* 7 (1968) 43-60.

W. W. Meissner, "Notes on Monotheism: Psychodynamic Aspects," *JRH* 7 (1968) 151-163.

*Yitzhak Baer, "The Persecution of Monotheistic Religion by Antiochus Epiphanes," *Zion* 33 (1968) #3/4, I-II.

§421 **3.2.12.4 Syncretism and the Old Testament (Influences on the Religion of Israel) [See also: §463 Studies in Comparative Religion→]**

*A. G. Laurie, "Persian Influence on Jewish Monotheism," *UQGR, N.S.,* 16 (1879) 21-32.

*T. K. Cheyne, "Possible Zoroastrian Influences on the Religion of Israel," *ET* 2 (1890-91) 202-208, 224-228, 248-253.

*George A. Barton, "Ashtoreth and her influence in the Old Testament," *JBL* 10 (1891) 73-91.

*T. K. Cheyne, "Old Testament Notes. Jewish Influences on Persian Beliefs," *Exp, 4th Ser.,* 5 (1892) 79-80.

*J. H. Moulton, "Zoroastrian Influences on Judaism," *ET* 9 (1897-98) 352-359.

*M[elvin] G[rove] Kyle, "The Religion of Israel in Its Relation to the Religions of Contiguous Peoples. I. Calf-Worship," *CFL, N.S.,* 6 (1902) 71-78.

*Anonymous, "'Zarathushtra, Philo: The Achæmenids and Israel'," *IAQR, 3rd Ser.,* 21 (1906) 314-317. *(Review)*

Leonard W. King, "Israel, Greece, and Babylon," *CQR* 75 (1912-13) 369-395. *(Review)*

C. T. Harley Walker, "Persian Influence on the Development of Biblical Religion," *ICMM* 10 (1913-14) 313-320.

Louis Wallis, "Amorite Influence in the Religion of the Bible," *BW* 45 (1915) 216-223.

*George W. Gilmore, "The Influence of Zoroastrianism on Jewish Doctrine in the Inter-Testamental Period," *IJA* #40 (1915) 12-13.

Max Loehr, "The Religion of Israel in the Light of the Religions of the Ancient East," *BS* 78 (1921) 295-318.

G. H. Box, "Judaism and Hellenism," *CQR* 95 (1922-23) 104-140.

J. A. Huffman, "Israel's Indebtedness to Other Nations," *CFL, 3rd Ser.,* 32 (1926) 516-517.

I. F. Wood, "Borrowing Between Religions," *JBL* 46 (1927) 98-110.

L. Elliott Binns, "Midianite Elements in Hebrew Religion," *JTS* 31 (1929-30) 337-354.

*S. H. Hooke, "The Mixture of Cults in Canaan in Relation to the History of the Hebrew Religion," *JMUEOS* #16 (1931) 23-30.

*S[tephen] Langdon, "Babylonian and Hebrew Demonology with reference to the supposed borrowing of Persian Dualism in Judaism and Christianity," *JRAS* (1934) 45-56.

*Walter G. Williams, "The Ras Shamra Inscriptions and Their Significance from the History of Hebrew Religion," *AJSL* 51 (1934-35) 233-246.

*George A. Barton, "The Origin of the Thought-Pattern which Survives in Baptism," *JAOS* 56 (1936) 155-165.

*J. Philip Hyatt, "Canaanite Religion and Its Influence on the Hebrews," *BA* 2 (1939) 6-7.

Beatrice L. Goff, "Syncretism in the Religion of Israel," *JBL* 58 (1939) 151-162.

Millar Burrows, "Syncretism and the Old Testament," *JAAR* 9 (1941) 10-16.

Carl H. Kraeling, "Method in the Study of Religious Syncretism," *JAAR* 9 (1941) 28-34, 66.

William Stevenson Smith, "The Relationship Between Egyptian Ideas and Old Testament Thought," *JAAR* 19 (1951) 12-15.

Maurice L. Zigmond, "Judaism and Its Cultural Setting—An Anthropological View," *YCCAR* 62 (1952) 340-359.

*George Weston Briggs, "Eastern Sage to Western Man," *RR* 19 (1954-55) 115-130. [Influence of Zoroastrianism on the Hebrew Religion, esp. pp. 118-121]

*J. N. Schofield, "Modern Issues in Biblical Studies. The Religion of the Near East and the Old Testament," *ET* 71 (1959-60) 195-198.

*L. Johnston, "Jeremiah and Morality," *ClR* 47 (1962) 142-147.

*Jacob Neusner, "Jewish Use of Pagan Symbols after 70 C.E.," *JR* 53 (1963) 303-314.

*David Winston, "The Iranian Component in the Bible, Apocrypha, and Qumran: A Review of the Evidence," *HRel* 5 (1965-66) 183-216.

*Raphael Hallevy, "The Canaanite Period: A Culture Clash," *Tarbiz* 35 (1965-66) #2, I-II.

*R. E. Clements, "Baal-Berith of Shechem," *JSS* 13 (1968) 21-32.

Henry O. Thompson, "A Suggested Influence on the Thought of Ancient Israel," *JRT* 25 (1968-69) 69-78.

§422 *3.2.12.5 Studies in Hebrew Worship*

*Anonymous, "Spirit of the Hebrew Scriptures.—No. III. Public Worship: Social Crime, and its Retribution," *CE* 17 (1834) 78-92.

*David B. Ford, "Significance of the Mosaic Tabernacle and Worship," *CRB* 28 (1863) 406-416.

*Cedron, "The Temple Ritual," *CongL* 2 (1873) 654-665; 3 (1874) 100-106, 142-148, 217-223, 291-298, 335-341, 482-488, 547-553, 726-732; 4 (1875) 41-47, 101-107, 161-167, 239-244, 358-365, 487-494, 540-546, 624-629, 673-679.

*[Alfred Edersheim], "The Hymnody of the Jewish Temple," *DTQ* 1 (1875) 475-478.

W[illiam] W. Evarts Jr., "The Place of Incense in the Mosaic Ritual," *ONTS* 4 (1884-85) 29-30.

S. J. Andrews, "The Worship of the tabernacle compared with that of the second temple," *JBL* 6 (1886) Part 1, 56-68.

David J. Burrell, "The Ceremonial Law. A Normal Lesson: with Mnemonic Helps," *ONTS* 7 (1887-88) 284-287.

Edward T. Horn, "The Worship of God in the Old Testament," *LCR* 14 (1895) 10-34.

*Herbert C. Alleman, "The Temple in Worship," *LQ* 28 (1898) 89-97.

*Joseph Offord, "Dancing Worship," *SBAP* 21 (1899) 253.

*William R. Harper, "Constructive Studies in the Priestly Element in the Old Testament II: The History of Worship in the Earlier Old Testament Period," *BW* 17 (1901) 121-134.

*William R. Harper, "Constructive Studies in the Priestly Element in the Old Testament III: The History of Worship in the Middle Old Testament Period," *BW* 17 (1901) 206-220.

*William R. Harper, "Constructive Studies in the Priestly Element in the Old Testament IV: The History of Worship in the Later Old Testament Period," *BW* 17 (1901) 366-381.

*William R. Harper, "Constructive Studies in the Priestly Element in the Old Testament VI: The Laws and Usages Concerning the Place of Worship, Considered Comparatively," *BW* 18 (1901) 56-63.

Maximilian J. Rudwin, "The Origin of Judeo-Christian Worship," *OC* 33 (1919) 287-295.

Alexander Nairne, "Semitic Sacramental Rites," *MC* 16 (1926-27) 296-309.

*Anonymous, "Public Worship in the Bible," *MR* 110 (1927) 476-478.

*C. R. North, "The Religious Aspect of Hebrew Worship," *ZAW* 50 (1932) 8-38.

*John Wick Bowman, "Response and Worship. *Devotional Life in the Bible,"* *Interp* 6 (1952) 279-289.

Walter Harrelson, "Worship in Early Israel," *BRes* 3 (1958) 1-14.

C. E. B. Cranfield, "Divine and Human Action. *The Biblical Concept of Worship,"* *Interp* 12 (1958) 387-398.

John D. W. Watts, "Elements of Old Testament Worship," *JAAR* 26 (1958) 217-221.

K. W. Clark, "Worship in the Jerusalem Temple after A.D. 70," *NTS* 6 (1959-60) 269-280.

*Richard L. Scheef Jr., "Worship and Ethics in the Bible," *T&L* 3 (1960) 198-207.

M[enahem] Haran, "The Uses of Incense in the Ancient Israelite Ritual," *VT* 10 (1960) 113-129.

*Solomon Zeitlin, "The Temple and Worship," *JQR, N.S.,* 51 (1960-61) 209-241.

Walter Harrelson, "Worship in Early Israel," *CRDSB* 36 (1964) #6, 11-21.

*David Stacey, "Clues from the Old Testament," *PQL* 11 (1965) 18-24. [II. Worship (in OT)]

*Ulrich S. Leupold, "Worship Music in Ancient Israel: Its Meaning and Purpose," *Resp* 9 (1967-68) 116-124.

*Ulrich S. Leupold, "Worship Music in Ancient Israel: Its Meaning and Purpose," *CJT* 15 (1969) 176-186.

§423 **3.2.12.6 The Priesthood - General Studies [See: §48 for Priests (including High Priests) ←]**

W. Milligan, "The Idea of Priesthood," *Exp, 3rd Ser.,* 8 (1888) 1-21.

W. Milligan, "Idea of Old Testament Priesthood Fulfilled in the New Testament," *Exp, 3rd Ser.,* 8 (1888) 161-180.

William J. Adams, "The Office of the Ancient Jewish Priest," *ET* 2 (1890-91) 244-246.

William J. Adams, "The Christian Ministry Viewed in the Light of the Ancient Jewish Priesthood," *ET* 2 (1890-91) 276-277.

*James Henry Breasted, "The Development of the Priesthood in Israel and Egypt—A Comparison," *BW* 2 (1893) 19-28.

*S. Baring-Gould, "Priest and Prophet," *ContR* 76 (1899) 832-841.

*F. Rendall, "The Scriptural Idea of Priesthood Embodied in Successive Types," *Exp, 3rd Ser.,* 9 (1889) 24-55.

T. K. Cheyne, "The Priesthood of David's Sons," *Exp, 5th Ser.,* 9 (1899) 453-457.

*William R. Harper, "Constructive Studies in the Priestly Element in the Old Testament V: The Laws and Usages Concerning the Priest, Considered Comparatively," *BW* 17 (1901) 450-462.

*William R. Harper, "Prophet and Priest," *BW* 20 (1902) 83-88. *[Editorial]*

*Charles Callaway, "The Prophet and the Priest in Hebrew Ethics," *WR* 161 (1904) 533-539.

R. H. Kennett, "The Origin of the Aaronite Priesthood," *JTS* 6 (1904-05) 161-186.

A.H.McNeile, "The Origin of the Aaronite Priesthood," *JTS* 7 (1905-06) 1-9.

Owen H. Gates, "The Relation of Priests to Sacrifice before the Exile," *JBL* 27 (1908) 67-92.

*Charles Lynn Pyatt, "The Prophet and the Priest in Judaism," *CollBQ* 14 (1923-24) #2, 15-29.

*Herbert Loewe, "The Sacramental Controversy Before A.D. 1," *ET* 39 (1927-28) 198-200. *[The Lighting of the Incense on the Day of Atonement]*

*A. E. J. Rawlinson, "Priesthood and Sacrifice in Judaism and Christianity," *ET* 60 (1948-49) 116-121.

S. M. Zwemer, "Melchizedek and Aaron," *EQ* 23 (1951) 164-170.

John W. Bailey, "The Usage in the Post Restoration Period of Terms Descriptive of the Priest and High Priest," *JBL* 70 (1951) 217-225. (Corr. p. 344)

*Walter G. Williams, "Studies in Prophecy. Part II. Priest and Prophet," *IR* 10 (1953) 110-115.

*J. L. Teicher, "Priests and Sacrifices in the Dead Sea Scrolls," *JJS* 5 (1954) 93-99.

*John Bowman, "Ezekiel and the Zadokite Priesthood," *GUOST* 16 (1955-56) 1-14.

Paul Winter, "Twenty-Six Priestly Courses," *VT* 6 (1956) 215-217.

*Clive A. Thomson, "Samuel, the Ark, and the Priesthood," *BS* 118 (1961) 259-263.

*R. B. Y. Scott, "Priesthood, Prophecy, Wisdom, and the Knowledge of God," *JBL* 80 (1961) 1-15.

*Eric Freidus, "The Priesthood of Christ and the Old Testament Priesthood: An Interpretation of Hebrews," *ACQ* 2 (1962) 162-165.

H. J. Katzenstein, "Some Remarks on the Lists of Chief Priests of the Temple of Solomon," *JBL* 81 (1962) 377-384.

H. D. Mantel, "Ordination and Appointment in the Days of the Temple," *Tarbiz* 32 (1962-63) #2, II-III.

*Saul Christensen, "Priests and Prophets—Old Testament Controversy," *Scotist* 20 (1964) 19-31.

*Martin A. Cohen, "The Role of the Shilonite Priesthood in the United Monarchy of Ancient Israel," *HUCA* 36 (1965) 59-98.

*R. Vande Walle, "An Administrative Body of Priests and Consecrated People," *IJT* 14 (1965) 57-72.

John Mauchline, "Aaronite and Zadokite Priests: Some Reflections on an Old Problem," *GUOST* 21 (1965-66) 1-11.

Lloyd Geering, "The Role of the Priest in the Bible," *Coll* 2 (1966-68) 97-104.

*J. Liver, "The 'Sons of Zadok the Priests' in the Dead Sea Sect," *RdQ* 6 (1967-69) 3-30.

§424 *3.2.12.6.1 The Levitical Priesthood*

Paul Haupt, "Babylonian elements in the Levitic ritual," *JBL* 19 (1890) 55-81.

*M. Berlin, "Notes on Genealogies of the Tribe of Levi in 1 Chron. XXIII-XXVI," *JQR* 12 (1899-1900) 291-298.

James Oscar Boyd, "Origin of 'The Levites'," *CFL, N.S.,* 2 (1900) 174-175.

Dean A. Walker, "The Levitical Priesthood, a Study in Social Development," *JBL* 19 (1900) 124-131.

*Ed[uard] König, "The Priests and the Levites in Ezekiel XLIV. 7-15," *ET* 12 (1900-01) 300-303.

*A. van Hoonacker, "Ezekiel's Priests and Levites—A Disclaimer," *ET* 12 (1900-01) 383.

*A. van Hoonacker, "Ezekiel's Priests and Levites," *ET* 12 (1900-01) 494-498.

G. R. Berry, "Priests and Levites," *JBL* 42 (1923) 227-238.

*Theodor H. Gaster, "The Name לֵוִי," *JTS* 38 (1937) 250-251. *[Levite]*

*Theophile J. Meek, "Moses and the Levites," *AJSL* 56 (1939) 113-120.

*H. H. Rowley, "Early Levite History and the Question of Exodus," *JNES* 3 (1944) 73-78.

Ralph Marcus, "Dositheus, Priest and Levite," *JBL* 64 (1945) 269-271.

Cuthbert Lattey, "The Tribe of Levi," *CBQ* 12 (1950) 277-291.

Moshe Greenberg, "A New Approach to the History of the Israelite Priesthood," *JAOS* 70 (1950) 41-47.

*M. Gertner, "The Masorah and the Levites. An Essay in the History of a Concept," *VT* 10 (1960) 241-272.

J. A. Emerton, "Priest and Levites in Deuteronomy," *VT* 12 (1962) 129-138.

*E[phraim] A. Speiser, "Unrecognized Dedication," *IEJ* 13 (1963) 69-73. *[Levites]*

E. Nielsen, "The Levites in Ancient Israel," *ASTI* 3 (1964) 16-27.

§425 *3.2.12.6.2 The High Priest*

S. F. Hancock, "The Urim and the Thummim," *ONTS* 3 (1883-84) 252-266.

Henry E. Dosker, "Urim and Thummim," *PRR* 3 (1892) 717-730.

B. Pick, "Jewish High Priests Subsequent to the Return from Babylon," *LCR* 17 (1898) 127-142, 370-374, 550-556, 655-664.

R. C. Ford, "The High Priest's Diadem," *ET* 8 (1896-97) 526-527.

W. Muss-Arnolt, "The Urim and Thummim. A Suggestion as to their Original Nature and Significance," *AJSL* 16 (1899-1900) 193-224.

J. Cleveland Hall, "Urim and Thummim," *PER* 13 (1899-1900) 227-233.

T.   C.   Foote,   "The   Ephod,"   *JBL*   21   (1902)   1-47.

L. Belleli, "The High Priest's Procession on the Date of Atonement," *JQR* 17 (1904-05) 163-167, 584-586.

Samuel Poznanski, "The High Priest's Procession," *JQR* 17 (1904-05) 388.

I[srael] Abrahams, "The High Priest's Procession and the Liturgy," *JQR* 17 (1904-05) 586.

*Geo. St. Clair, "Israel in Camp: A Study," *JTS* 8 (1906-07) 185-217. *[The Breast Plate of the High Priest]*

[Paul Carus], "The Oracle of Yahveh," *Monist* 17 (1907) 365-388. *[The Urim and Thummim, The Ephod, and the Breastplate of Judgment]*

*David Heumark, "Crescas and Spinoza. A Memorial Paper in Honor of the Five Hundredth Anniversary of the 'Or Adonoi'," *YCCAR* 18 (1908) 277-318. [III. Excursus on Urim ve-Thummim, Choshen, and Goral, pp. 319-348]

*John E. McFadyen, "The Mosaic Origin of the Decalogue," *Exp, 8th Ser.,* 11 (1915) 385-392. *[The Ephod]*

*A. H. Sayce, "Assyriological Notes," *SBAP* 39 (1917) 207-212. [The Ephod, p. 210]

*Anonymous, "Ephod and Ark," *HR* 75 (1918) 55-56. *(Review)*

J. E. Hogg, "A Note on two points in Aaron's Head-dress," *JTS* 26 (1924-25) 72-75.

F. C. Burkitt, "A Further note on Aaron's Head-dress," *JTS* 26 (1924-25) 180.

A. D. Hogg, "The inscription on Aaron's head-dress," *JTS* 28 (1926-27) 287-288.

*Jacob Z. Lauterbach, "A Significant Controversy Between the Sadducees and the Pharisees," *HUCA* 4 (1927) 173-205. *[How the High Priest should enter the Holy of Holies]*

*Herbert Loewe, "The Sacramental Controversy Before A.D. 1," *ET* 39 (1927-28) 198-200. *[The Lighting of the Incense on the Day of Atonement]*

*Charles W. Cooper, "Some of the Precious Stones of the Bible, with Special Reference to the High Priest's Breastplate and the Jasper of Rev. IV. 3," *JTVI* 61 (1929) 60-74, 83-85. (Discussion, pp. 75-83)

J. Ostersetzer, "An Inquiry into a Tannaitic Massorah Regarding the High Priesthood," *Zion* 4 (1938-39) #4, III.

E. A. Mangan, "The Urim and Thummim," *CBQ* 1 (1939) 133-138.

George Dahl, "The Problem of the Ephod," *ATR* 34 (1952) 206-210.

*J. S. Kennard, "The Jewish High Priest as Agent of the Imperial Cult," *JBL* 71 (1952) V.

Menahem Haran, "The Ephod According to Biblical Sources," *Tarbiz* 24 (1954-55) #4, II-III.

*H. G. Judge, "Aaron, Zadok, and Abiathar," *JTS, N.S.,* 7 (1956) 70-74.

*Solomon Zeitlin, "The Titles High Priest and the Nasi of the Sanhedrin," *JQR, N.S.,* 48 (1957-58) 1-5.

*Solomon Zeitlin, "The Temple and Worship," *JQR, N.S.,* 51 (1960-61) 209-241.

Carl Armerding, "The Breastplate of Judgment," *BS* 118 (1961) 54-58.

*R. E. Clements, "Temple and Land: A Significant Aspect of Israel's Worship," *GUOST* 19 (1961-62) 16-28.

*E. Mary Smallwood, "High Priests and Politics in Roman Palestine," *JTS, N.S.,* 13 (1962) 14-34.

Solomon Zeitlin, "Bouleuterion and Parhedrion," *JQR, N.S.,* 53 (1962-63) 169-170. *[Duties of the High Priest]*

J. S. Harris, "The Stones of the High Priest's Breastplate," *ALUOS* 5 (1963-65) 40-62.

Edward Robertson, "The Urīm and Thummīm; what were they?" *VT* 14 (1964) 67-74.

J. R. Bartlett, "Zadok and His Successors at Jerusalem," *JTS, N.S.,* 19 (1968) 1-18.

R. A. Stewart, "The Sinless High-Priest," *NTS* 14 (1967-68) 126-135.

Joseph Gutmann, "Torah Ornaments, Priestly Vestments, and the King James Bible," *CCARJ* 16 (1969) #1, 78-79.

§426 *3.2.12.7 Altars, High Places, Pillars and Sanctuaries*

*Charles W. Wilson, "On the Site of Ai and the Position of the Altar which Abram Built between Bethel and Ai," *PEFQS* 1 (1869) 123-126.

Claude R. Conder, "Identification of the Altar 'Ed'," *PEFQS* 6 (1874) 241-247.

*Claude R. Conder, "The Site of Nob and the High Places," *PEFQS* 7 (1875) 34-41.

R. F. Hutchinson, "The Identification of the Altar of Ed," *PEFQS* 8 (1876) 28-32. (Note by C[laude] R. Conder, pp. 31-32)

*Claude R. Conder, "The Moslem Mukams," *PEFQS* 9 (1877) 89-103. *[Holy Places]*

C[laude] R. Conder, "Rude Stone Monuments of the Bible," *PEFQS* 14 (1882) 139-142. *[Pillars]*

W. F. Birch, "The High Place at Gibeon," *PEFQS* 14 (1882) 264.

W. E. S., "The Cubical Stones of Moab," *PEFQS* 14 (1882) 271-272. *[Asheroth(?)]*

C[laude] R. Conder, "Notes. *Asheroth,*" *PEFQS* 15 (1883) 101. *[Pillars]*

C[laude] R. Conder, "Note. *Rude Stone Monuments,*" *PEFQS* 15 (1883) 102.

*†Ch. Clermont-Ganneau, "Description of an Altar found on Mount Gerizim," *SBAP* 6 (1883-84) 133, 182-184.

C[laude] R. C[onder], "Notes. *The Nâblus Altar,*" *PEFQS* 18 (1886) 18.

James Edward Hanauer, "The 'Rock Altar' of Zorah," *PEFQS* 19 (1887) 57-58.

C[onrad] Schick, "A Supposed Druidical Stone," *PEFQS* 22 (1890) 22-23. *[Pillars, etc.]*

Claude R. Conder, "Notes on the *Quarterly Statement,* July, 1890. *Pillar at Tell el Hesy,*" *PEFQS* 22 (1890) 329.

H. B. Greene, "Hebrew Rock Altars," *BW* 9 (1897) 329-340.

C. Clermont-Ganneau, "Notes on the October 'Quarterly Statement' P. 297. *Rude Stone Monuments in Palestine,*" *PEFQS* 32 (1900) 78.

*Samuel Ives Curtiss, "High Place and Altar at Petra," *PEFQS* 32 (1900) 350-355.

*George L. Robinson, "The Newly Discovered 'High Place' at Petra in Edom," *BW* 17 (1901) 6-16.

*George L. Robinson, "The 'High Place' at Petra in Edom," *AAOJ* 23 (1901) 229-241.

Anonymous, "High Place at Petra," *MR* 83 (1901) 138-140.

*W. Clarkson Wallis, "Note on the High Place at Petra," *PEFQS* 33 (1901) 65.

Willis J. Beecher, "'Pillars' in the Old Testament," *HR* 43 (1902) 397-403.

William Hayes Ward, "The Asherah," *AJSL* 19 (1902-03) 33-44.

William Hayes Ward, "The Asherah," *AAOJ* 25 (1903) 189-190.

*F. E. Hoskins, "The Second High Place at Petra," *BW* 21 (1903) 167-174.

*Paul Carus, "Stone Worship," *OC* 18 (1904) 661-686.

*Luther Link, "What is Asherah?" *USR* 16 (1904-05) 352-357.

W. Clarkson Wallis, "Notes and Queries. 2. *The 'Neolithic Altar' at Gezer,*" *PEFQS* 37 (1905) 164-165.

R. A. S[tewart] Macalister, "Notes and Queries. 1. *The Neolithic Altar,*" *PEFQS* 37 (1905) 364.

*F. E. Hoskins, "A Third 'High-Place' at Petra," *BW* 27 (1906) 385-390.

James C. Egbert, "Augustus' Altar of Peace," *RP* 5 (1906) 104-111.

*Arthur E. P. Weigall, "Report on Some Objects recently found in Sebakh and other Diggings," *ASAE* 8 (1907) 40-50. [Altar for Human Sacrifice, from Edfu, pp. 44-46]

*George L. Robinson, "The Vaulted Chambers of Petra's High Places," *AAOJ* 30 (1908) 67-72.

*George L. Robinson, "The High Places of Petra," *BW* 31 (1908) 8-21.

J.   P.   MacLean,   "Asherah,"   *AAOJ*   31   (1909)   1-6.

*Dow Covington, "Altar of Ptolemy Neos Dionysos XIII," *ASAE* 10 (1909) 34-35.

A. Forder, "A Causeway Across the Dead Sea, and a Moabite Monolith," *PEFQS* 42 (1910) 112-116. *[Pillar]*

*Laurence E. Browne, "A Jewish Sanctuary in Babylonia," *JTS* 17 (1915-16) 400-401.

Anonymous, "Sacred Stones," *MR* 102 (1919) 454-460. *[Pillars, etc.]*

*Douglas P. Blair, "Stone Altars and Cup-Marks in South Palestine," *PEFQS* 51 (1919) 167-174.

*W[illiam] F[oxwell] Albright, "The Babylonian Temple-Tower and the Altar of Burnt-Offering," *JBL* 39 (1920) 137-142.

*Stanley A. Cook, "The 'Holy Place' of 'Ain Duk," *PEFQS* 52 (1920) 82-87.

*Gerald M. FitzGerald, "Notes on Recent Discoveries. IV. *The Jewish Sanctuary of 'Ain Duk," PEFQS* 53 (1921) 185-186.

J. Battersby Harford, "Altars and Sanctuaries in the Old Testament," *ET* 40 (1928-29) 11-14, 60-64, 135-139, 168-172, 214-218, 281-285.

*D. Winton Thomas, "En-Dor: A Sacred Spring?" *PEFQS* 65 (1933) 205-206.

Millar Burrows, "From Pillar to Post," *JPOS* 14 (1934) 42-51.

*W[illiam] F[oxwell] Albright, "The Excavation of the Conway High Place at Petra," *BASOR* #57 (1935) 18-26.

D. Winton Thomas, "Naphath-Dor: A Hill Sanctuary?" *PEFQS* 67 (1935) 89-90.

*G. Ernest Wright, "'Sun-Image' or 'Altar of Incense?'" *BA* 1 (1938) 9-10.

Edmund H. Hunt, "High Places of Sacrifice in Palestine and Petra," *Man* 42 (1942) #23.

*Constantine G. Yavis, "The Earliest Hellenic Altars and Their Antecedents," *AJA* 52 (1948) 381.

*Oliver H. Myers, "The *Neter* Pole and the *Ashera*," *JEA* 36 (1950) 113-114.

*P. J. Riis, "An Augustan Altar from Tarentum," *AA* 23 (1952) 147-152.

*Herbert Hoffmann, "Foreign Influence and Native Invention in Archaic Greek Altars," *AJA* 57 (1953) 189-195.

*E. Douglas Van Buren, "Akkadian stepped altars," *Numen* 1 (1954) 228-234.

W[illiam] F[oxwell] Albright, "The high place in Ancient Palestine," *VTS* 4 (1957) 242-258.

*Ray L. Cleveland, "The Sacred Stone Circle of Khor Rori (Dhofar)," *BASOR* #155 (1959) 29-31.

*J. P. U. Lilley, "The Altar in Joshua and Judges," *TB* #5&6 (1960) 32-33.

*Sylvester [J.] Saller, "The archaeological Setting of the Shrine of Bethpage," *SBFLA* 11 (1960-61) 172-250.

A. S. Hiram, "A Votive Altar from Upper Galilee," *BASOR* #167 (1962) 18-22.

Sylvester J. Saller, "Sacred Places and Objects of Ancient Palestine," *SBFLA* 14 (1963-64) 161-228.

*B[enjamin] Mazar, "The Sanctuary of Arad and the Family of Hobab the Kenite," *JNES* 24 (1965) 297-303.

*Javier Teixidor, "The Altars Found at Hatra," *Sumer* 21 (1965) 85-92.

*Arthur E. Cundall, "Sanctuaries (Central and Local) in Pre-exilic Israel, with particular reference to the Book of Deuteronomy," *VE* 4 (1965) 4-27.

*Dawson Kiang, "The Mazarita Altar, A Hellenistic Relief from Egypt," *AJA* 70 (1966) 191.

*David Stronach, "The Kūh-i-Shahrak Fire Altar," *JNES* 25 (1966) 217-227. *[Sasanian]*

Eugene Stockton, "Stones at Worship," *AJBA* 1 (1968-71) #3, 58-81. *[Mazzeboth]*

*Edward F. Campbell Jr. and G. Ernest Wright, "Tribal League Shrines in Amman and Shechem," *BA* 32 (1969) 104-116.

§427 *3.2.12.7.1 The Tabernacle and Its Contents*

Anonymous, "The True Idea of the Sanctuary,"*AThR* 1 (1859) 528-542.

*David B. Ford, "Significance of the Mosaic Tabernacle and Worship," *CRB* 28 (1863) 406-416.

*T. O. Paine, "On the Holy Houses, or the Hebrew Tabernacle, the Temple of Solomon, and the Later Temple," *JAOS* 10 (1880) cxxv-cxxvi.

George D. Armstrong, "The Tabernacle," *USR* 1 (1889-90) 284-289.

John H. Hopkins, "The Molten Sea before Solomon's Temple," *CR* 63 (1891) 140-144.

[Theodore F. Wright], "The 'Horn of the Altar'," *AAOJ* 14 (1892) 229.

James Strong, "The Tabernacle," *BW* 1 (1893) 270-277.

*W.W. Davies, "House, Tabernacle and Temple," *HR* 26 (1893) 80-82.

William Henry Green, "Critical Views Respecting the Mosaic Tabernacle," *PRR* 5 (1894) 69-88.

*W. Brryman Ridges, "On the Structure of the Tabernacle," *PEFQS* 28 (1896) 189.

W. H. B. Proby, "Construction of the Tabernacle," *PEFQS* 28 (1896) 223-224.

*Dunlop Moore, "Have We in I. Sam. II. 22 a Valid Witness to the Existence of the Mosaic Tabernacle in the Days of Eli?" *ET* 8 (1896-97) 139-141.

Theodore F. Wright, "The Tabernacle Roof," *PEFQS* 29 (1897) 225-226.

Adolph Büchler, "Biblical Research and Discovery. The Fore-Court of Women," *CFL, O.S.,* 2 (1898) 239-240.

William Brown, "Construction of the Tabernacle," *PEFQS* 29 (1897) 154-155. [Correction, *PEFQS* 30 (1898) p. 70]

C[onrad] Schick, "Some Remarks on the Tabernacle Controversy," *PEFQS* 30 (1898) 241-244.

Theodore F. Wright, "Was the Tabernacle Oriental?" *JBL* 18 (1899) 195-198.

Theo[dore] F. Wright, "The Boards of the Tabernacle," *PEFQS* 31 (1899) 70.

A. R. S. Kennedy, "A New Theory of the Construction of the Tabernacle of the Priests' Code," *GUOST* 2 (1901-07) 16-17.

R. B. Pattie, "Another Theory of the Tabernacle," *GUOST* 2 (1901-07) 20-21.

Dunlop Moore, "Did the Tabernacle Described in Exodus Really Exist?" *CFL, N.S.,* 7 (1903) 171-177.

Henry T. Hooper, "The Tabernacle: Ideal or Actual?" *LQHR* 103 (1905) 340-346. *(Review)*

*Claude R. Conder, "Notes on New Discoveries," *PEFQS* 41 (1909) 266-275. [Incense, p. 270]

Harold M. Wiener, "The Position of the Tent of Meeting," *Exp, 8th Ser.,* 3 (1912) 476-480.

James Orr, "The Historicity of the Mosaic Tabernacle," *JTVI* 44 (1912) 103-115, 127-128. [(Discussion, pp. 115-124) (Communications by R. B. Girdlestone, pp. 124-125; J. J. Lias, pp. 125-127)]

Julian Morgenstern, "The Tent of Meeting," *JAOS* 38 (1918) 125-139.

*A. H. Finn, "The Tabernacle Chapters," *JTS* 16 (1914-15) 449-482.

*A. H. Sayce, "Assyriological Notes," *SBAP* 39 (1917) 207-212. [The Shew-bread, p. 211]

J[ames] L. Kelso, "The Hebrew Tabernacle as a Work of Architecture," *BS* 79 (1922) 62-71.

*Adam C. Welch, "The Sanctuary in Deuteronomy," *ET* 36 (1924-25) 568.

*Adam C. Welch, "The Two Descriptions of the Sanctuary in Deuteronomy," *ET* 37 (1925-26) 215-219, 442-444.

*R. B. Pattie, "Is the Tabernacle a Copy of the Temple, or the Temple a Copy of the Tabernacle?" *GUOST* 6 (1929-33) 4-7.

*Carl L. Steinbicker, "The Tabernacle and Mosaic Art," *SS* 5 (1931) 21-35.

*M. Narkiss, "The Snuff-Shovel as a Jewish Symbol. (A Contribution to the problem of Jewish decorative motifs)," *JPOS* 15 (1935) 14-28.

*Julian Morgenstern, "The *'otfe,* the *maḥmal,* the Ark, the 'Tent of Meeting,' and the *'efod,*" *JBL* 55 (1936) vi.

*John Vernon McGee, "Theology of the Tabernacle," *BS* 94 (1937) 153-175, 295-320, 409-429.

H. Th. Obbink, "The Horns of the Altar in the Semitic World, Especially in Jahwism," *JBL* 56 (1937) 43-49.

*John Vernon McGee, "The Theology of the Tabernacle," *BS* 95 (1938) 22-39.

*Herbert Gordon May, "*Ephod* and *Ariel,*" *AJSL* 56 (1939) 44-69.

*Julian Morgenstern, "The Ark, the Ephod, and the Tent of Meeting," *HUCA* 17 (1942-43) 153-265.

*Julian Morgenstern, "The Ark, the Ephod, and the Tent of Meeting, Part II," *HUCA* 18 (1944) 1-52.

Frank M. Cross Jr., "The Tabernacle," *BA* 10 (1947) 45-68. [The New Outlook on Israelite History; The Historical Status of the Priestly Tradition; The History of the Tabernacle Institution; The Promulgation of the Tent Ideal; The Archaeology of the Tabernacle; Reconstruction of the Priestly Tabernacle; The Tabernacle and the Davidic Tent; Light on Tabernacle Terminology; Conclusion]

Maximilian Kon, "The Menorah of the Arch of Titus," *PEQ* 82 (1950) 25-30.

*Cecil Roth, "The Priestly Laver as a Symbol on Ancient Jewish Coins," *PEQ* 84 (1952) 91-93.

Menahem Haran, "The Tent of Meeting," *Tarbiz* 25 (1956-57) #1, III-IV.

Menahem Haran, "The Censer Incense and *Tamid* Incense," *Tarbiz* 26 (1956-57) #2, I-II.

M. H. Segal, "The Tent of Meeting," *Tarbiz* 25 (1956-57) #2, VIII-IX.

M. L. G. Guillebaud, "The Tent Over the Tabernacle," *EQ* 31 (1959) 90-96.

H. Strauss, "The Fate and Form of the Menorah of the Maccabees," *EI* 6 (1960) 35*.

Menahem Haran, "The Nature of the ''Ohel Mo'edh' in Pentateuchal Sources," *JSS* 5 (1960) 50-65.

*W. Wirgin, "Two Notes," *IEJ* 11 (1961) 151-154. [I. On the Shape of the Foot of the *Menorah,* pp. 151-153]

Menahem Haran, "The Complex of Ritual Acts Performed Inside the Tabernacle," *SH* 8 (1961) 272-302.

*W. Wirgin, "The Menorah as a Symbol of Judaism," *IEJ* 12 (1962) 140-142.

*W. Wirgin, "The *Menorah* as a Symbol of After-Life," *IEJ* 14 (1964) 102-104.

Menahem Haran, "The Priestly Image of the Tabernacle," *HUCA* 36 (1965) 191-226.

*Baruch A. Levine, "The Descriptive Tabernacle Texts of the Pentateuch," *JAOS* 85 (1965) 307-318. [Exodus 35-39; Leviticus 8-9 & Numbers 7]

*Jan Dus, "The Dreros Bilingual and the Tabernacle of Ancient Israel," *JSS* 10 (1965) 54-57. (With Comment by Professor C. H. Gordon, pp. 57-58)

D. Sperber, "The History of the Menorah," *JJS* 16 (1965) 135-160.

Virgil W. Rabe, "The Identity of the Priestly Tabernacle," *JNES* 25 (1966) 132-134.

A. Negev, "The Chronology of the Seven-Branched Menorah," *EI* 8 (1967) 74*.

*Samuel Belkin, "Some Obscure Tradition Mutually Clarified in Philo and Rabbinic Literature," *JQR, 75th* (1967) 80-103. [1. The Horns of the Altar, pp. 80-83]

Joseph Gutmann, "A Note on the Temple Menorah," *ZNW* 60 (1969) 289-291.

§428 *3.2.12.7.2 The Ark of the Covenant*

Enoch Pond, "The Ark of the Testimony, and its Appendages," *BRCR, N.S.,* 10 (1843) 290-328.

Alvah Hovey, "The Ark of the Covenant," *CRB* 17 (1852) 572-593.

M. C. Read, "The Ark of the Hebrews," *AAOJ* 3 (1880-81) 320-321.

Carlos A. Butler, "The Ark of the Covenant. Study of a Model," *CR* 42 (1883) 423-438.

*A. L. Frothingham Jr., "Early Bronzes Discovered in the Cave of Zeus on Mount Ida in Krete," *AJA, O.S.,* 5 (1889) 48. [*Ref. Ark of the Covenant* תֵּבָה]

Daniel Kirkwood, "The Ark of the Covenant," *GUOST* 2 (1901-07) 48.

*John D. Davis, "The Ark and the Cloud During the March," *CFL, N.S.,* 6 (1902) 78-83.

T. C. Foote, "The Cherubim and the Ark," *JAOS* 25 (1904) 279-286.

Fritz Hommel, "The Ark of Jahweh," *ET* 18 (1906-07) 155-158.

*Wm. B. Stevenson, "Was the Ark Jehovah's Throne?" *ET* 18 (1906-07) 379-380.

B. D. Eerdmans, "The Ark of the Covenant," *Exp, 8th Ser.,* 3 (1912) 408-420.

Cuthbert Lattey, "The Ark of the Covenant," *IER, 5th Ser.,* 11 (1918) 150-160.

*Anonymous, "Ephod and Ark," *HR* 75 (1918) 55-56. *(Review)*

Herbert G[ordon] May, "The Ark—A Miniature Temple," *AJSL* 52 (1935-36) 215-234.

*Julian Morgenstern, "The *'otfe,* the *maḥmal,* the Ark, the 'Tent of Meeting,' and the *'efod,*" *JBL* 55 (1936) vi.

James Oscar Boyd, "What Was in the Ark?" *EQ* 11 (1939) 165-168.

*Julian Morgenstern, "The Ark, the Ephod, and the Tent of Meeting," *HUCA* 17 (1942-43) 153-265.

*Julian Morgenstern, "The Ark, the Ephod, and the Tent of Meeting, Part II," *HUCA* 18 (1944) 1-52.

J. H. Crehan, "The Ark of the Covenant," *ClR* 35 (1951) 301-311.

*N. H. Tur-Sinai, "The Ark of God at Beit Shemesh (1 Sam. VI) and Peres 'Uzza (2 Sam. VI; 1 Chron. XIII)," *VT* 1 (1951) 275-286.

T. Worden, "The Ark of the Covenant," *Scrip* 5 (1952-53) 82-90.

*Joseph Bourke, "Samuel and the Ark, a Study in Contrasts," *DS* 7 (1954) 73-103.

M[enahem] Haran, "The Ark of the Covenant and the Cherubs," *EI* 5 (1958) 88*.

*M[enahem] Haran, "The Ark and the Cherubim: Their Symbolic Significance in Biblical Ritual," *IEJ* 9 (1959) 30-38, 89-94.

Eduard Nielsen, "Some reflections on the history of the ark," *VTS* 7 (1960) 61-74.

*Clive A. Thomson, "Samuel, the Ark, and the Priesthood," *BS* 118 (1961) 259-263.

M[enahem] Haran, "The Disappearance of the Ark," *IEJ* 13 (1963) 46-58.

William McKane, "The Earlier History of the Ark," *GUOST* 21 (1965-66) 68-76.

G. H. Davies, "The Ark of the Covenant," *ASTI* 5 (1966-67) 30-47.

*Terence E. Fretheim, "The Ark in Deuteronomy," *CBQ* 30 (1968) 1-14.

§429 *3.2.12.7.3 The Sanctuary at Shiloh*

*L. W. Batten, "The Sanctuary at Shiloh and Samuel's sleeping therein," *JBL* 19 (1900) 29-33.

John D. Davis, "The Sanctuary of Israel at Shiloh," *PSB* 11 (1917) #3, 1-5.

John D. Davis, "The Sanctuary of Israel at Shiloh," *PTR* 16 (1918) 204-229.

*Menaḥem Haran, "Shiloh and Jerusalem," *Tarbiz* 31 (1961-62) #4, I.

*Menaḥem Haran, "Shiloh and Jerusalem: The Origin of the Priestly Tradition in the Pentateuch," *JBL* 81 (1962) 14-24.

*Anonymous, "Shiloh—A Lesson Ignored," *BH* 2 (1965) #4, 20-24.

§430 *3.2.12.8 Sacrifices and Offerings*

*Hermas, "Of the Perpetuity of the Jewish Ritual," *TRep* 5 (1786) 403-444.

Hermas, "Of the Perpetuity of the Jewish Ritual (continued from Vol. V. p. 444," *TRep* 6 (1788) 1-21.

†Anonymous, "Davidson on Primitive Sacrifices," *BCQTR, N.S.,* 23 (1825) 570-582. *(Review)*

†Anonymous, "Davidson and Molesworth on Sacrifice," *BCQTR, 3rd Ser.,* 3 (1826) 78-95. *(Review)*

†Anonymous, "Farber's Origin of Expiatory Sacrifice," *BCQTR, 4th Ser.,* 3 (1828) 72-86. *(Review)*

J. H. Kurtz, "The Sin-Offering," *BS* 9 (1852) 27-51. *(Trans. by David B. Ford)*

R. Abbey, "The Jewish Sacrifices," *MQR* 6 (1852) 79-106.

G. R. N., "The Scripture Doctrine of Sacrifice," *CE* 59 (1855) 234-280. *(Review)*

[William Outram], "Jewish Sacrifices, with Particular Reference to the Sacrifice of Christ," *BS* 16 (1859) 1-56. *[Derived from the work of William Outram]*

[William Outram], "Jewish Sacrifices, with particular reference to the Sacrifice of Christ," *JSL, 3rd Ser.,* 9 (1859) 25-67.

[Karl Christian Wilhelm Felix Bähr], "The Significance of the Jewish Sacrifices," *BS* 27 (1870) 593-613. *[Derived from the work of Bähr]*

R. G. Balfour, "On the Origin of Primitive Sacrifice," *BFER* 20 (1871) 489-505.

[John Spencer], "Origin and Significance of Jewish Sacrifices," *BS* 28 (1871) 145-183. *[Derived in part from John Spencer's* De Legibus Hebreaeorum]

*Calvin E. Park, "The Connection Between the Mosaic and Pagan Sacrifices," *BS* 31 (1874) 693-730.

Calvin E. Park, "On Certain Erroneous Theories of the Significance of Sacrifice," *BS* 32 (1875) 98-136.

*Cedron, "The Temple Ritual. The Sacrifice of the Red Heifer," *CongL* 4 (1875) 673-679.

Calvin E. Park, "On the Question of the Divine Institution of Sacrifice," *BS* 33 (1876) 102-132.

[Joseph] Barclay, "Biblical Notes. The Offering of the First Fruits," *Exp, 1st Ser.,* 7 (1878) 317-318.

Howard Crosby, "The Sacrifices," *ONTS* 5 (1884-85) 249-250.

Alvah Hovey, "Shekhar and Leaven in Mosaic Offerings," *ONTS* 6 (1886-87) 11-16.

S. W. Culver, "The Symbolism of Sacrifice," *BQR* 10 (1888) 447-465.

Frederic Gardiner, "Various Topics. II. On the reason for the selection of certain animals for sacrifice among the ancient Israelites," *JBL* 8 (1888) 146-150.

*P. A. Nordell, "Old Testament Word Studies: 7. Sacrifice and Worship," *ONTS* 8 (1888-89) 257-261. [Mĭnhāh *present, offering;* Qŏrbān *offering;* Zĕbhăḥ *sacrifice;* 'ōlāh *burnt offering;* Ḥăṭṭā'th *sin offering;* 'āshām *guilt offering;* Kĭppĕr *to make atonement*]

D. B. Lady, "The Origin and Development of the Idea of Sacrifices," *RChR* 39 (1892) 487-503.

*Andrew Harper, "The Prophets and Sacrifice," *Exp, 4th Ser.,* 9 (1894) 241-253.

*[H. Gollancz], "A.—Jewish Authorities on the Ram of Abraham," *IAQR, 2nd Ser.,* 8 (1894) 198-199.

[H. Gollancz], "B.—Nature of Jewish Sacrificial Animals," *IAQR, 2nd Ser.,* 8 (1894) 199-201.

*George A. Barton, "On the Sacrifices כלל and כלל שלם in the Marselles Inscription," *JAOS* 16 (1894-96) lxvi-lxix.

A. A. Berle, "The Real Meaning of Semitic Sacrifice," *BS* 52 (1895) 342-346.

Bernard Pick, "The Unscriptural Expiatory Sacrifice," *HR* 32 (1896) 409-410.

*G. A. Simcox, "II.—Tophet," *SBAP* 20 (1898) 302-303. *[Sacrifices]*

E. P. Boys-Smith, "Sacrifice in Ancient Religion and in Christian Sacrament," *ET* 11 (1899-1900) 104-107, 184-188.

Hermann Schultz, "The Significance of Sacrifice in the Old Testament," *AJT* 4 (1900) 257-313.

F. A. Gast, "The Idea of Sacrifice as Developed in the Old Testament," *RChR, 4th Ser.,* 4 (1900) 1-34.

John D. Davis, "The Sin Offering," *CFL, N.S.,* 1 (1900) 72-76.

*William R. Harper, "Constructive Studies in the Priestly Element of the Old Testament. VII: The Laws and Usages Concerning Sacrifice, Considered Comparatively," *BW* 18 (1901) 120-130.

Samuel Ives Curtiss, "Ancient Sacrifice among Modern Semites," *AJA* 6 (1902) 38.

*Motier A. Bullock, "Jehovah's Protest Against the Altar Service," *BS* 59 (1902) 529-536. [The Import of the Altar Service; The Use and Meaning of *Blood* in Sacrificial Offering; The New Testament Use of these Old Testament Symbols]

Samuel Ives Curtiss, "Discoveries of a Vicarious Element in Primitive Semitic Sacrifice," *Exp, 6th Ser.,* 6 (1902) 128-134.

Samuel Ives Curtiss, "The Semitic Sacrifice of Reconciliation," *Exp, 6th Ser.,* 6 (1902) 454-462.

*W. O. E. Oesterley, "The Sacrifice of Isaac," *SBAP* 24 (1902) 253-260.

*Samuel Ives Curtiss, "The Place of Sacrifice among the Primitive Semites," *AJA* 7 (1903) 83.

Samuel Ives Curtiss, "The Place of Sacrifice among the Primitive Semites," *BW* 21 (1903) 248-259.

M[elvin] G[rove] Kyle, "The Religion of Israel in Its Relation to the Religions of Contiguous Peoples. III. Sacrifices," *CFL, N.S.,* 8 (1903) 36-40, 85-92.

*James Oscar Boyd, "Samuel and the Law of Sacrifice," *CFL, N.S.,* 8 (1903) 69-74.

S[amuel] I[ves] Curtiss, "Firstlings and Other Sacrifices," *JBL* 22 (1903) 45-49.

Samuel Ives Curtiss, "The Origin of Sacrifice among the Semites as Deduced from Facts Gathered among Syrians and Arabs," *Exp, 6th Ser.,* 10 (1904) 461-472.

*Melvin Grove Kyle, "New Light from Egypt on the Sacrifices," *BS* 62 (1905) 323-336.

*Melvin Grove Kyle, "New Light from Egypt on the Sacrifices," *CFL, 3rd Ser.,* 3 (1905) 356-364.

*James A. Montgomery, "Notes from the Samaritan," *JBL* 25 (1906) 49-54. [V. Angels Attendant at the Sacrifices, p. 54]

Henry Nelson Bullard, "The Peace Offerings," *CFL, 3rd Ser.,* 6 (1907) 211-215.

*Franklin N. Jewett, "Questions from the Pew. The Place for Sacrificing. (Lev. xvii: 1-9; Deut. xii: 8-15.)," *OC* 21 (1907) 564-567.

Anonymous, "'Origin and Significance of Sacrifice'," *CFL, 3rd Ser.,* 10 (1909) 4-6. *(Editorial Comment)*

John Slattery, "The Sacrificial Idea," *ITQ* 5 (1910) 198-211.

A[dolph] Büchler, "Private Sacrifices before the Jewish Day of Atonement," *Exp, 8th Ser.,* 2 (1911) 239-243.

*T. Witton Davies, "Some Notes on Hebrew Matters, Literary and Otherwise. Anent Some Technical Terms for Old Testament Sacrifice," *R&E* 9 (1912) 553-555.

Michael M. McDivitt, "Sacrifice Among Primitive Peoples," *BWTS* 5 (1912-13) 34-48.

A. H. McNeil, "Law, Sin, and Sacrifice, in the Old Testament," *ICMM* 9 (1912-13) 376-383.

*[Parke] P. Flournoy, "Elephantine, and the Priest Code Theory," *USR* 24 (1912-13) 285-295. *[Laws of Sacrifice]*

*John P. Peters, "The Cock," *JAOS* 33 (1913) 363-396. *[Sacrifices]*

G. Buchanan Gray, "Interpretations of Jewish Sacrifice," *Exp, 8th Ser.,* 9 (1915) 385-404.

G. Buchanan Gray, "The Antiquity and Perpetuity of Sacrifice," *Exp, 8th Ser.,* 9 (1915) 528-552.

*G. Buchanan Gray, "The Sacrifice of Cain and Abel," *Exp, 8th Ser.,* 10 (1915) 1-23.

A. Berriedale Keith, "M. Reinarch's Theory of Sacrifice," *JRAS* (1916) 542-555.

Benedict Steuart, "Sacrifice and Oblation," *IER, 5th Ser.,* 10 (1917) 1-26.

G. Buchanan Gray, "The 'Gift' Element in Jewish Sacrifice," *OSHTP* (1918-19) 21.

Robert H. Kennett, "The Place of Sacrifice in the Church of Israel," *ICMM* 16 (1919-20) 251-263.

C. Reeves Palmer, "The Significance of Hebrew Sacrifice," *ICMM* 17 (1920-21) 68-73.

*William L. Baxter, "'Smooth Stone Out of the Brook'," *PTR* 19 (1921) 177-224. [Ezekiel the Sacrificial Pioneer, pp. 216-223]

*H. C. Ackerman, "The Decalogue and Sacrifice," *ATR* 4 (1921-22) 241-244.

J. A. Kelso, "The Water Libation of the Old Testament," *Exp, 8th Ser.,* 24 (1922) 226-240.

*Paul Haupt, "Philological Studies. 2. Wine and Blood," *AJP* 45 (1924) 48-50. *[Sacrifices]*

*Innes Logan, "Prophecy and Sacrifice: A Note," *Exp, 9th Ser.,* 3 (1925) 62-65.

S. S. Klyve, "The Bible Idea of Atoning Sacrifice: Over Against the Conception of Sacrifice Held in Ethnic Religions, Especially those of China," *TTM* 9 (1925-26) 241-263; 10 (1926-27) 65-80.

H. H. Gowen, "The Hair-Offering," *JSOR* 11 (1927) 1-20.

Harry M. Hubbell, "Horse Sacrifice in Antiquity," *YCS* 1 (1928) 181-192.

Arthur Stevens Phelps, "Incense or Perfumery," *R&E* 29 (1932) 166-171.

J. Russell Howden, "The Levitical Offerings," *BR* 17 (1932) 185-198.

*W[illiam] F[oxwell] Albright and P. E. Dumont, "A Parallel between Indic and Babylonian Sacrificial Ritual," *JAOS* 54 (1934) 107-128.

Christopher R. North, "Some Outstanding Old Testament Problems. V. Sacrifice in the Old Testament," *ET* 47 (1935-36) 250-254.

E. O. James, "After Fifty Years. III. Aspects of Sacrifice in the Old Testament," *ET* 50 (1938-39) 151-155.

James E. Coleran, "Origins of Old Testament Sacrifice," *CBQ* 2 (1940) 130-144.

*C. Lattey, "The Prophets and Sacrifice: A Study in Biblical Relativity," *JTS* 42 (1941) 155-165.

*H. Wheeler Robinson, "Hebrew Sacrifice and Prophetic Symbolism," *OSHTP* (1941-42) 26-27.

*H. Wheeler Robinson, "Hebrew Sacrifice and Prophetic Symbolism," *JTS* 43 (1942) 129-139.

*Arthur Darby Nock, "The Cult of Heroes," *HTR* 37 (1944) 141-173. [Appendix 4 (see p. 162): Theophrastus on the Contrast Between Jewish and Greek Sacrifice, p. 173]

*G. D. Hornblower, "Cain and Abel: The Choice of Kind of Sacrifice," *Man* 44 (1944) #31.

*James D. Coleran, "The Prophets and Sacrifice," *ThSt* 5 (1944) 411-438.

G. A. Hadjiantoniou, "Sacrifice: Its Origin and Purpose," *EQ* 17 (1945) 42-53.

P. P. Saydon, "Sin-offering and Trespass-offering," *CBQ* 8 (1946) 393-398.

E. Reim, "The Blood Sacrifices of the Old Testament," *WLQ* 43 (1946) 272-281; 44 (1947) 35-42, 179-191.

C. J. Cadoux, "The Religious Value of Sacrifice," *ET* 58 (1946-47) 43-46.

*Norman H. Snaith, "The Prophets and Sacrifice and Salvation," *ET* 58 (1946-47) 152-153.

*H. H. Rowley, "The Prophets and Sacrifice," *ET* 58 (1946-47) 305-307.

H. H. Rowley, "The Religious Value of Sacrifice," *ET* 58 (1946-47) 69-71.

*A. E. J. Rawlinson, "Priesthood and Sacrifice in Judaism and Christianity," *ET* 60 (1948-49) 116-121.

D. M. L. Urie, "Sacrifice among the West-Semites," *PEQ* 81 (1949) 67-82.

Harold H. Rowley, "The Meaning of Sacrifice in the Old Testament," *BJRL* 33 (1950-51) 74-110.

G. Constantine Yavis, "The Central Devotional Act in the Ritual of Sacrifice," *AJA* 55 (1951) 152-153.

*Cuthbert Lattey, "Vicarious Solidarity in the Old Testament," *VT* 1 (1951) 1267-274. *[Sacrifice]*

A. M. Ramsey, "Christian Theology and the Concept of Sacrifice," *OSHTP* (1951-52) 5-16.

*R. J. Zwi Werblowsky, "The Rebuilding of the Temple and the Re-introduction of Sacrifice in Light of Rabbinical Judaism," *Theo* 56 (1953) 82-88.

*J. L. Teicher, "Priests and Sacrifices in the Dead Sea Scrolls," *JJS* 5 (1954) 93-99.

*P. V. Glob, "Snake Sacrifices in Bahrain's Ancient Capital. The Danish Archaeological Bahrain Expedition's Fourth Campaign of Excavation," *Kuml* (1957) 125-127.

N[orman] H. Snaith, "Sacrifices in the Old Testament," *VT* 7 (1957) 308-317.

Carl Armerding, "The Atonement Money," *BS* 115 (1958) 334-340.

*Robert Dobbie, "Sacrifice and Morality in the Old Testament," *ET* 70 (1958-59) 297-300.

*H. H. Rowley, "Sacrifice and Morality: A Rejoinder," *ET* 70 (1958-59) 341-342.

J. E. Steinmueller, "Sacrificial Blood in the Bible," *B* 40 (1959) 556-567.

J. E. Steinmueller, "Sacrificial Blood in the Bible," *SBO* 1 (1959) 422-433.

*Robert Dobbie, "Deuteronomy and the Prophetic Attitude to Sacrifice," *SJT* 12 (1959) 68-82.

H. McKeating, "The Sacrifices of God," *PQL* 6 (1960) 369-373.

K. A. Dickson, "The Meaning of Sacrifice," *GBT* 2 (1961-66) #3, 12-19.

*K. A. Dickson, "A Note on the Laying on of Hands as a Sacrificial Rite," *GBT* 2 (1961-66) #7, 26-28.

*J. Liver, "The Half-Shekel in the Scrolls of the Judean Desert Sect," *Tarbiz* 31 (1961-62) #1, III-IV.

Hobart E. Freeman, "The Problem of the Efficacy of Old Testament Sacrifices," *BETS* 5 (1962) 73-90.

N[orman] H. Snaith, "The Wave Offering," *ET* 74 (1962-63) 127.

Hobart E. Freeman, "The Problem of the Efficacy of Old Testament Sacrifices," *GJ* 4 (1963) #1, 21-28.

J. Liver, "The Half-Shekel Offering in Biblical and Post-Biblical Literature," *HTR* 56 (1963) 173-198.

Raymond Firth, "Offering and Sacrifice: Problems of Organization," *JRAI* 93 (1963) 12-24.

Douglas Jones, "The Cessation and Sacrifice After the Destruction of the Temple in 586 B.C.," *JTS, N.S.,* 14 (1963) 12-31.

Th. P. van Baaren, "Theoretical speculations on sacrifice," *Numen* 11 (1964) 1-12.

N[orman] H. Snaith, "The sin-offering and the guilt-offering," *VT* 15 (1965) 73-80.

*Frederick [L.] Moriarty, "Abel, Melchizedek, Abraham," *Way* 5 (1965) 95-104.

*David Gill, "*Thysia* and *šelāmīm:* Questions to R. Schmid's *Das Bundesopfer in Israel,*" *B* 47 (1966) 255-262.

Alexander Guttmann, "The End of the Jewish Sacrificial Cult," *HUCA* 38 (1967) 137-148.

James Swetnam, "Temple Sacrifices: profile of a theological problem," *BibT* #34 (1968) 2377-2380.

Kevin G. O'Connell, "Sacrifice in the Old Testament," *BibT* #41 (1969) 2862-2867.

Dennis J. McCarthy, "The Symbolism of Blood and Sacrifice," *JBL* 88 (1969) 166-176.

M[enahem] Haran, "Zebaḥ Hayyamîm," *VT* 19 (1969) 11-22. *[The Yearly Sacrifice]*

*M[enahem] Haran, "*ZBḤ YMM* in the Karatepe inscriptions," *VT* 19 (1969) 372-373. *[The Yearly Sacrifice]*

*Leo Landman, "The Guilt-Offering of the Defiled Nazarite," *JQR, N.S.,* 60 (1969-70) 345-352.

§431 *3.2.12.8.1 Tithing and Stewardship*

†T. T., "Origin of Tithes," *MMBR* 43 (1817) 398-399.

*Albert A. Isaacs, "Charity in Talmudical Times," *EN* 1 (1889) 97-103.

Thos. E. Peck, "Moral Obligation of the Tithe," *USR* 1 (1889-90) 270-279.

C. R. Vaughan, "The Tithe Law," *USR* 7 (1895-96) 36-46, 115-123, 182-190.

*G. M. Mackie, "Giving: A Study in Oriental Manners," *ET* 9 (1897-98) 367-370.

*Henry Lansdell, "Tithe-giving Amongst Ancient Pagan Nations," *JTVI* 31 (1897-98) 123-137. [(Discussion, pp. 137-138) (Note by F. W. H.*[sic]* Petrie, pp. 138-139)]

Joseph Morris, "The Place of Charity or Almsgiving in the Old Testament," *ET* 21 (1909-10) 427-428.

*Robert Roberts, "Almsgiving in the Apocrypha, Talmud, and Qoran," *IJA* #21 (1910) 28-30.

J. M. Powis Smith, "The Deuteronomic Tithe," *AJT* 18 (1914) 119-126.

A. H. Godbey, "The Hebrew Tithe," *Monist* 26 (1916) 63-85.

A. H. Godbey, "The Decade of the Dead," *MQR, 3rd Ser.,* 51 (1925) 309-337. *[Tithing]*

Thos. E. Peck, "Moral Obligation of the Tithe," *USR* 1 (1889-90) 270-279.

C. R. Vaughan, "The Tithe Law," *USR* 7 (1895-96) 36-46, 115-123, 182-190.

H. W. Provence, "Tithing in the Bible," *R&E* 39 (1942) 432-438.

§432 *3.2.12.8.2 Human Sacrifice - General Studies*

*A. [H.] Sayce, "On Human Sacrifice among the Babylonians," *SBAT* 4 (1875) 25-31.

Manuel Orozco Y Berra, "Human Sacrifices in Ancient Times," *OBJ* 1 (1880) 67-70. *(Trans. by L. P. Gratacap)*

Charles H. H. Wright, "The Old Testament and Human Sacrifices," *BFER* 33 (1884) 401-402; 34 (1885) 56-72.

*William Hayes Ward, "Notes on Oriental Antiquities. VIII. 'Human Sacrifices' on Babylonian Cylinders," *AJA, O.S.,* 5 (1889) 34-43.

*W[illiam] H[ayes] Ward, "On some Babylonian cylinders supposed to represent human sacrifices," *JAOS* 13 (1889) cccii-ccciv.

*C. J. Ball, "Glimpses of Babylonian Religion," *SBAP* 14 (1891-92) 149-162. [I. Human Sacrifices, pp. 149-153]

W. H. Gardner, "Human Sacrifice," *OC* 8 (1894) 3991-3996, 4000-4004.

*Arthur E. Whatham, "The Origin of Human Sacrifice—including an Explanation of the Hebrew Asherah," *AJRPE* 2 (1906-07) 24-61.

[Paul Carus], "Foundations Laid in Human Sacrifice," *OC* 23 (1909) 494-501.

*W. H. Wood, "Jar-Burial Customs and the Question of Infant Sacrifice in Palestine," *BW* 36 (1910) 166-175, 227-234.

Anonymous, "Possible Evidence of Human Sacrifices in Babylon," *RP* 9 (1910) 120.

Myron W. Jacobs, "Human Sacrifice in the Old Testament," *JIQ* 1 (1924-25) 78-82.

O. G. S. Crawford, "Human Sacrifice in Antiquity," *Antiq* 8 (1934) 332-335.

J. Gwyn Griffiths, "Human Sacrifices in Egypt: The classical evidence," *ASAE* 48 (1948) 409-423.

R. H. Sales, "Human Sacrifice in Biblical Thought," *JAAR* 25 (1957) 112-117.

C. J. Gadd, "The Spirit of Living Sacrifices in Tombs," *Iraq* 22 (1960) 51-58.

§433 *3.2.12.9 Studies concerning the "Temples" - General Studies*

*E. Robinson, "Remains of the Ancient Bridge between the Jewish Temple and Mount Zion," *BS* 1 (1844) 794-800.

*G. J. C. D., "The Temple and the Synagogue," *BFER* 17 (1868) 275-288.

*[Alfred] Edersheim, "The Hymnody of the Jewish Temple," *DTQ* 1 (1875) 475-478.

Charles Warren, "Note on the Souterrains in the Noble Sanctuary, Jerusalem," *PEFQS* 7 (1875) 96-97.

T[homas] C[haplin] and C[harles] W[arren], "Aven Hash-Sheteyah," *PEFQS* 7 (1875) 182-183.

Jas. Fergusson, "The 'Speaker's Commentary' on the Temple at Jerusalem," *ContR* 27 (1875-76) 979-994.

Thomas Chaplin, "The Stone of Foundation and the Site of the Temple," *PEFQS* 8 (1876) 23-28.

Charles Warren, "The Stone of Foundation," *PEFQS* 8 (1876) 62.

C. Clermont-Ganneau, "The Veil of the Temple of Jerusalem at Olympia," *PEFQS* 10 (1878) 79-81.

Charles Warren, "The Site of the Temple of the Jews," *SBAP* 2 (1879-80) 70-71.

*T. O. Paine, "On the Holy Houses, or the Hebrew Tabernacle, the Temple of Solomon, and the Later Temple," *JAOS* 10 (1880) cxxv-cxxvi.

Charles W. Warren, "The Site of the Temple of the Jews," *SBAT* 7 (1880-82) 309-330.

*Thomas Chaplin, "Translations of the Middoth, &c.," *PEFQS* 19 (1887) 132-133.

T. O. Paine, "On the Holy Houses from the Hebrew Scriptures; also from the original texts of the Chronicles, Ezra, Maccabees, Septuagint, Coptic, Itala, Chaldee, Syriac, Samaritan, Talmud, and leading Rabbis," *JAOS* 13 (1889) xiii.

*H. Graetz, "Biblical Studies II—The Central Sanctuary of Deuteronomy," *JQR* 3 (1890-91) 219-230.

T. Wrightson, "On the Relation of Certain Arch Springings Found within the Area of the Temple of Jerusalem," *PEFQS* 23 (1891) 219-224.

Michael Adler, "The Emperor Julian and the Jews," *JQR* 5 (1892-93) 591-651. [II. Proposed Rebuilding of the Temple, pp. 615-651]

*W.W. Davies, "House, Tabernacle and Temple," *HR* 26 (1893) 80-82.

J. M. Tenz, "Paving Stones of the Temple," *PEFQS* 25 (1893) 330. [Note by C. R. Conder, *PEFQS* 26 (1894), p. 82]

J. A. Selbie, "A Central Sanctuary," *ET* 7 (1895-96) 472.

C. M. Watson, "The Site of the Temple," *PEFQS* 28 (1896) 47-60, 226-228. (Note by C. R. Conder, pp. 170, 340-341)

Edward Hull, "Where are the Sacred Vessels of the Temple?" *PEFQS* 28 (1896) 344.

Jas. Simpson, "Where are the Sacred Vessels of the Temple?" *PEFQS* 29 (1897) 77-80.

*William Simpson, "The Temple and the Mount of Olives," *PEFQS* 29 (1897) 307-308.

W. Bacher, "Statements of a Contemporary of the Emperor Julian on the Rebuilding of the Temple," *JQR* 10 (1897-98) 168-172.

Joseph Bruneau, "Biblical Research. I. Biblical Archaeology and Discoveries. *The Temple of Jerusalem*," *AER* 19 (1898) 48-49.

*Herbert C. Alleman, "The Temple in Worship," *LQ* 28 (1898) 89-97.

Vicomte Francois de Salignac Fenelon, "Note on the Site of the Temple," *PEFQS* 31 (1899) 272.

Anonymous, "Model of Jerusalem Temple," *ColTM* 22 (1902) 177-179.

Arthur Bumstead, "The Hebrew Sanctuary—Was it One or Manifold?" *MR* 84 (1902) 108-111.

C. Clermont-Ganneau, "Archaeological and Epigraphical Notes on Palestine. 22. *The 'Gate of Nicanor' in the Temple of Jerusalem,*" *PEFQS* 35 (1903) 125-131.

W. Shaw Caldecott, "The Temple Spoils Represented on the Arch of Titus," *PEFQS* 38 (1906) 306-315. (Note by J. D. Crace, p. 315)

*Lewis Bayles Paton, "Jerusalem in Biblical Times: I. The Location of the Temple," *BW* 29 (1907) 7-22.

*R. B. Pattie, "Ezekiel's Temple," *GUOST* 3 (1907-12) 17-21.

*Hugh Pope, "The Temple of Onias at Leontopolis," *ITQ* 3 (1908) 415-424.

James A. Kelso, "The Unity of the Sanctuary in the Light of the Elephantine Papyri," *JBL* 28 (1909) 71-82.

C. M. Watson, "The Position of the Altar of Burnt Sacrifice in the Temple of Jerusalem," *PEFQS* 42 (1910) 15-22.

J. M. Tenz, "The Position of the Altar of Burnt Sacrifice in the Temple of Jerusalem," *PEFQS* 42 (1910) 137-139.

*D. S. Margoliouth, "The Opening Sentences in Wellhausen's 'Prolegomena'," *Exp, 8th Ser.,* 1 (1911) 40-50.

Gustaf Dalman, "The Search for the Temple Treasure at Jerusalem," *PEFQS* 44 (1912) 35-39.

*William Fulton, "The Temple in the Psalter," *GUOST* 4 (1913-22) 24-25.

*R. B. Pattie, "Light from the Mishnah on the Earlier Temple," *GUOST* 4 (1913-22) 76-78.

*Theron H. Rice, "The House of God in the History of Redemption," *USR* 35 (1913-14) 305-312.

*Adam C. Welch, "When Was the Worship of Israel Centralized at the Temple?" *ZAW* 43 (1925) 250-255.

*R. B. Pattie, "Is the Tabernacle a Copy of the Temple, or the Temple a Copy of the Tabernacle?" *GUOST* 6 (1929-33) 4-7.

*Helen Rosenau, "Some Aspects of the Pictorial Influence of the Jewish Temple," *PEFQS* 68 (1936) 157-162.

*P. Romanoff, "Influence of the Temple on Ceremonial Objects and Art," *JBL* 59 (1940) xv.

G. Ernest Wright, "The Significance of the Temple in the Ancient Near East, Part III, The Temple in Palestine-Syria," *BA* 7 (1944) 65-77. [The Temple in Canaan; Temple-Form and Ritual in Canaan; The Temple in Israel; The Tabernacle; The Temple of Solomon; "The House of the Lord"; The Temple in Community Life]

Thomas Hannay, "The Temple," *SJT* 3 (1950) 278-287.

*M.D.Goldman, "Lexicographical Notes on the Hebrew Text of the Bible (2) From Whom Did David Buy the Temple Area?"*ABR* 1 (1951) 138-139.

Abram Spiro, "When Was the Samaritan Temple Built?" *JBL* 70 (1951) xi.

*R. J. Zwi Werblowsky, "The Rebuilding of the Temple and the Re-introduction of Sacrifice in the Light of Rabbinical Judaism," *Theo* 56 (1953) 82-88.

Yigael Yadin, "A Note on Dating the Shechem Temple," *BASOR* #150 (1958) 34.

G. Ernest Wright, "Comment on Yadin's Dating of the Shechem Temple," *BASOR* #150 (1958) 34-35.

Hugh Nibley, "Christian Envy of the Temple," *JQR, N.S.,* 50 (1959-60) 97-123, 229-240.

Robert J. Bull, "A Re-examination of the Shechem Temple," *BA* 23 (1960) 110-119.

*Bernice Strack, "The Temple-Model as a Visual Aid in the Study of Scripture," *Scotist* 16 (1960) 60-73.

*Solomon Zeitlin, "The Temple and Worship," *JQR, N.S.,* 51 (1960-61) 209-241.

*R. E. Clements, "Temple and Land: A Significant Aspect of Israel's Worship," *GUOST* 19 (1961-62) 16-28.

R. L. Fisher, "The Temple Quarter," *JSS* 8 (1963) 34-41.

William F. Stinespring, "Temple Research in Jerusalem," *DDSR* 29 (1964) 85-101.

H. C. Thomson, "The Right of Entry to the Temple in the O.T.," *GUOST* 21 (1965-66) 25-34.

*H. C. Kee, "Tell-er-Ras and the Samaritan Temple," *NTS* 13 (1966-67) 401-402.

Virgil W. Rabe, "Israelite Opposition to the Temple," *CBQ* 29 (1967) 228-233.

D. W. Gooding, "Temple specifications: a dispute in logical arrangement between the MT and the LXX," *VT* 17 (1967) 143-172.

*E. D. Stockton, "The Fortress Temple of Shechem and Joshua's Covenant," *AJBA* 1 (1968-71) #1, 24-28.

*G. R. H. Wright, "Temples at Shechem," *ZAW* 80 (1968) 1-35.

*Menahem Haran, "Biblical Studies: The Idea of the Divine Presence in the Israelite Cult," *Tarbiz* 38 (1968-69) #2, I-II. *(Review)*

*Edward F. Campbell Jr. and G. Ernest Wright, "Tribal League Shrines in Amman and Shechem," *BA* 32 (1969) 104-116.

§434 *3.2.12.9.1 Solomon's Temple*

J. E., "Solomon's Temple," *JSL, 2nd Ser.,* 2 (1852) 359-393. *(Review)*

*T. O. Paine, "On the Holy Houses, or the Hebrew Tabernacle, the Temple of Solomon, and the Later Temple," *JAOS* 10 (1880) cxxv-cxxvi.

(Mrs.) E. A. Finn, "The Rock (Sakhrah) Foundation of Solomon's Temple," *PEFQS* 21 (1889) 156-157.

Emanuel Schmidt, "Solomon's Temple," *BW* 14 (1899) 164-171.

Geo. St. Clair, "Jachin and Boaz," *WR* 154 (1900) 421-426.

W. E[mery] Barnes, "Jachin and Boaz," *JTS* 5 (1903-04) 447-451.

*Paul Carus, "Stone Worship," *OC* 18 (1904) 661-686. [Jachin and Boaz, pp. 662-666]

Reginald Walsh, "'Solomon's Temple: Its History and Structure'," *IER, 4th Ser.,* 23 (1908) 165-171. *(Review)*

*Phillips Endecott Osgood, "The Temple of Solomon. A Deductive Study of Semitic Culture," *OC* 23 (1909) 449-468, 526-549, 588-609.

*Clive A. Thomson, "Certain Bible Difficulties," *BS* 96 (1939) 459-478. [III. The Date of the Founding of the Temple, pp. 463-464, 475]

R. B. Y. Scott, "The Pillars *Jachin* and *Boaz,*" *JBL* 58 (1939) v.

R. B. Y. Scott, "The Pillars Jachin and Boaz," *JBL* 58 (1939) 143-150.

*W[illiam] F[oxwell] Albright, "Two Unpublished Phoenician 'Thymiateria' and the Temple of Solomon," *AJA* 45 (1941) 87.

G. Ernest Wright, "Solomon's Temple Resurrected," *BA* 4 (1941) 17-31. [Significances; The Temple Equipment]

*W[illiam] F[oxwell] Albright, "Two Cressets from Marisa and the Pillars of Jachin and Boaz," *BASOR* #85 (1942) 18-27.

Herbert Gordon May, "The Two Pillars Before the Temple of Solomon," *BASOR* #88 (1942) 19-27.

*Leroy Waterman, "The Damaged 'Blueprints' of the Temple of Solomon," *JNES* 2 (1943) 284-294.

Leroy Waterman, "The Treasuries of Solomon's Private Chapel," *JNES* 6 (1947) 161-163.

G. Ernest Wright, "Dr. Waterman's View Concerning the Solomonic Temple," *JNES* 7 (1948) 53.

Leroy Waterman, "A Rebuttal," *JNES* 7 (1948) 54-55.

*J. L. Myres, "King Solomon's Temple and Other Buildings and Works of Art," *PEQ* 80 (1948) 14-41. [The Temple and Sanctuary; Jachin and Boaz. 1 Kgs. 7:15ff; Which Member of the Composite Capitals was uppermost? Where did the Two Pillars Stand? Solomon's Temple and the Temple of Paphos in Cyprus; The House of the Forest of Lebanon (1 Kgs. 7:2-6); The Porch of Pillars. 1 Kgs. 7:6; The Palaces of Solomon and Pharaoh's Daughter; The "Sea of Brass." 1 Kgs. 7:23-26; The Ten Smaller Lavers: 1 Kgs. 7:27-38]

C. C. Wylie, "On King Solomon's Molten Sea," *BA* 12 (1949) 86-90.

M. B. Rowton, "The Date of the Founding of Solomon's Temple," *BASOR* #119 (1950) 20-22.

Paul Leslie Garber, "Reconstruction of Solomon's Temple," *BA* 14 (1951) 2-24. [The Temple Court; The Temple Exterior; Floor Plan; The Platform-Basement; The Steps; The Pillars Jachin and Boaz; The Porch; The Temple Doors; The Holy Place; The Side Chambers; The Holy of Holies; The Temple Designed with the Ark as Center; Significance]

P[aul] L[eslie] Garber, "Some Problems in Reconstructing Solomon's Temple," *JBL* 70 (1951) iv.

Paul Leslie Garber, "A Reconstruction of Solomon's Temple," *Arch* 5 (1952) 165-172.

G. Ernest Wright, "The Stevens' Reconstruction of the Solomonic Temple," *BA* 18 (1955) 41-44.

*Yigael Yadin, "The Third Season of Excavation at Hazor, 1957," *BA* 21 (1958) 30-47. [Area H, The Holy of Holies and Cult Furniture of the Temple, Alalakh and the Temple of Solomon]

S. Yeivin, "Jachin and Boaz," *EI* 5 (1958) 89*.

Paul Leslie Garber, "Reconsidering the Reconstruction of Solomon's Temple," *JBL* 77 (1958) 123-128.

William F[oxwell] Albright and G. Ernest Wright, "Comments on Professor Garber's Article," *JBL* 77 (1958) 129-131.

P[aul] L[eslie] Garber, "Additional Remarks," *JBL* 77 (1958) 132-133.

William F. Stinespring, "The Howland-Garber Model of Solomon's Temple," *DDSR* 24 (1959) 12-13.

S. Yeivin, "Jachin and Boaz," *PEQ* 91 (1959) 6-22.

S. Yeivin, "Was There a High Portal in the First Temple?" *VT* 14 (1964) 331-343.

Joshua Brand, "Remarks on the Temple of Solomon," *Tarbiz* 34 (1964-65) #4, III-V.

*D[avid] Ussishkin, "Building IV in Hamath and the Temples of Solomon and Tell Tayanat," *IEJ* 16 (1966) 104-110.

*Sh. Yeivin, "Philological Notes 10," *Lĕš* 32 (1967-68) #1/2, I-II. [3. Technical Terms describing Solomon's Temple]

§435 *3.2.12.9.2 The Temple of Zerubbabel (The Second Temple)*

Thomas Chaplin, "Middoth, or the Measurements of the Temple. With the Commentary of Rabbi Obadiah of Bartenora," *PEFQS* 18 (1886) 224-228.

Thomas Chaplin, "Middoth, or the Measurements of the Temple. With the Commentary of Rabbi Obadiah of Bartenora. *(Continued)*," *PEFQS* 19 (1887) 60-63.

Thomas Chaplin, "Middoth, or the Measurements of the Temple. With the Commentary of Rabbi Obadiah of Bartenora. *(Concluded)*," *PEFQS* 19 (1887) 116-128.

*John Skinner, "Requests and Replies," *ET* 3 (1891-92) 68. [The Second Temple and The Visions of Ezekiel (43:10, 11)]

W. R. Betterridge, "The Builders of the Second Temple," *BS* 53 (1896) 231-249.

G[eorge] A[dam] Smith, "The Second Temple, from Zechariah to Ezra," *Exp, 7th Ser.,* 1 (1906) 510-523.

Paul Haupt, "The Inauguration of the Second Temple," *JBL* 33 (1914) 161-169.

N. H. Baynes, "Zerubbabel's Rebuilding of the Temple," *JTS* 25 (1923-24) 154-160.

W. E. Hogg, "The Founding of the Second Temple," *PTR* 25 (1927) 457-461.

*Charles C. Torrey, "The Foundry of the Second Temple at Jerusalem," *JBL* 55 (1936) 247-260.

H. Lewy, "A Note on the Fate of the Sacred Vessels of the Second Temple," *KSJA* 1 (1942) XI.

Solomon Zeitlin, "A Note on the Chronology of the Destruction of the Second Temple," *JQR, N.S.,* 37 (1946-47) 165-167.

F. I. Andersen, "Who Built the Second Temple?" *ABR* 6 (1958) 1-35.

Joshua Brand, "Concerning an Article on the Second Temple," *Tarbiz* 29 (1959-60) #3, II-III.

A. Gelston, "The Foundation of the Second Temple," *VT* 16 (1966) 232-235.

Sidney B. Hoenig, "B'sar Ta'avah—'Flesh of Desire.'   A Study of Regulations Pertaining to the Economy of the Second Temple," *JQR, N.S.*, 59 (1968-69) 290-310.

§436 *3.2.12.9.3 "Herod's" Temple*

[Edward] Robinson, "Ancient Temple of the Jews," *BJ* 2 (1843) 281-286.

Charles Warren, "Lieut. Warren on 'The Temple of Herod'," *PEFQS* 1 (1869) 23-26.

*C. Clermont-Ganneau, "Discovery of a Tablet from Herod's Temple," *PEFQS* 3 (1871) 132-133.

Tyrwhitt Drake, "Limestone Column Discovered in the Russian Buildings at Jerusalem to the West of the New Church," *PEFQS* 3 (1871) 135.

George St. Clair, "Note on M. Ganneau's Discovery of an Inscribed Stone of the Temple of Jerusalem," *PEFQS* 3 (1871) 172-173.

Charles Warren, "The Temple of Herod," *PEFQS* 7 (1875) 97-101.

Thomas Chaplin, "The Herodian Temple, According to the Treatis Middoth and Flavius Josephus," *PEFQS* 18 (1886) 92-113.

Aldolf Buchler, "The Fore-court of the Women and the Brass Gate in the Temple of Jerusalem," *JQR* 10 (1897-98) 678-718.

J. L. Leeper, "Remains of the Temple at Jerusalem," *BW* 22 (1903) 329-341.

Clyde W. Votaw, "The Temple at Jerusalem in Jesus' Day," *BW* 23 (1904) 169-179.

Charles Kassel, "The Fall of the Temple," *OC* 19 (1905) 35-40.

A. R. S. Kennedy, "The Site and Arrangements of Herod's Temple," *GUOST* 3 (1907-12) 12.

A. R. S. Kennedy, "Some Problems of Herod's Temple," *ET* 20 (1908-09) 24-27, 66-69, 181-183, 270-273. [I. The Cubit used by Herod's Masons; II. The Area of Herod's Temple; III. The Gates of the Great Court; IV. Robinson's Arch; V. The Royal Porch; VI. The Position of the Temple Courts; VII. The Beautiful Gate of the Temple; VIII. The Position of the Temple on the Platform]

*M. H. Ben-Shammai, "The Legends of the Destruction of the Temple among the Paintings of the Dura Synagogue," *BIES* 9 (1941-42) #4, I.

*Floyd V. Filson, "Part IV—Temple, Synagogue, and Church," *BA* 7 (1944) 77-88. [Origin and Growth of the Synagogue; Herod Rebuilds the Temple; The Role of the Synagogue; The Church and the Temple; The Church and the Synagogue; The Church in the Home; Later Trends]

*Elias Bickerman, "The Warning Inscription of Herod's Temple," *JQR, N.S.,* 37 (1946-47) 387-405.

S[olomon] Zeitlin, "The Warning Inscription of the Temple," *JQR, N.S.,* 38 (1947-48) 111-116.

Spencer Corbett, "Some Observations on the Gateways to the Herodian Temple in Jerusalem," *PEQ* 84 (1952) 7-14.

Richard D. Barnett, "Reminiscences of Herod's Temple," *CNI* 12 (1961) #3, 13-18.

*Solomon Zeitlin, "There was no Synagogue in the Temple," *JQR, N.S.,* 53 (1962-63) 168-169.

*Norman Walker, "The Riddle of the Ass's Head and the Question of a Trigram," *ZAW* 75 (1963) 225-227.

Solomon Zeitlin, "There was no Court of Gentiles in the Temple area," *JQR, N.S.,* 56 (1965-66) 88-89.

§437 *3.2.12.9.4 The Temple at Elephantine*

Anonymous, "The Temple of Onias," *MR* 88 (1906) 990-991.

Melvin Grove Kyle, "Archaeological Department: A Jewish Temple in Egypt," *CFL, 3rd Ser.,* 7 (1907) 89-90. *(Editorial Note)*

Anonymous, "A Jewish Temple in Egypt, B.C. 525-411," *BS* 65 (1908) 170-173. *(Condensed from an article by S. R. Driver)*

*J. M. Powis Smith, "The Jewish Temple at Elephantine," *BW* 31 (1908) 448-459.

A. Kampmeier, "The Yahu-Temple in Elephantine," *OC* 22 (1908) 321-323.

G. Frederick Wright, "Significance of the Jewish Temple at Elephantine," *RP* 8 (1909) 245-246.

*Hermann Gunkel, "The Jâhû Temple in Elephantine," *Exp, 8th Ser.,* 1 (1911) 20-39.

*A. H. Sayce, "The Jewish Garrison and the Temple at Elephantine," *Exp, 8th Ser.,* 2 (1911) 97-116.

*A. H. Sayce, "The Jews and their Temple at Elephantine," *Exp, 8th Ser.,* 2 (1911) 417-434.

*Hugh Pope, "The Temple of Jahu in Syene and Pentateuchal Criticism," *AER* 47 (1912) 291-303.

Barnard C. Taylor, "A Jewish Temple in Elephantine," *BCTS* 4 (1912) 71-83.

*George W. Gilmore, "Aramaic Papyri and the Jewish Temple at Elephantine," *HR* 75 (1918) 56-57.

*Bezalel Porten, "The Structure and Orientation of the Jewish Temple at Elephantine—A Revised Plan of the Jewish District," *JAOS* 81 (1961) 38-42.

§438 *3.2.12.9.5 Studies of Persons or Groups associated with the Temple, other than Priests, or Levites*

*Joseph Jacobs, "The Nethinim," *BOR* 2 (1887-88) 66-71, 100-104.

*P. A. Nordell, "Old Testament Word Studies: 6. Theocratic Functionaries," *ONTS* 8 (1888-89) 220-224. [Rŏ'ĕh *seer;* Ḥŏzĕh *seer, gazer;* Nābhî' *prophet;*Kōhēn *priest;* Lēvî *Levite;* Mĕlĕk *king*]

Anonymous, "The Nethinim," *EN* 3 (1891) 518-521.

J. A. Selbie, "Koberle on 'The Temple Musicians'," *ET* 10 (1898-99) 497-498. *(Review)*

Hermann Vogelstein, "The Development of the Apostolate in Judaism and Its Transformation in Christianity," *HUCA* 2 (1925) 99-123.

*Beatrice A Brooks, "Fertility Cult Functionaries in the Old Testament," *JBL* 60 (1941) 227-253. *[Definitions of: Nethinim; Qedesh; Zonah;* צבאות;עלמה; יושבת; *Eunuch]*

*B. D. Eerdmans, "Thoda-Songs and Temple-Singers in the Pre-Exilic Period," *OTS* 1 (1942) 162-175.

*Alfred Guillaume, "Is Episcopacy a Jewish Institution?" *BSOAS* 13 (1949-51) 23-26.

*W[illiam] F[oxwell] Albright, "The Seal Impression from Jericho and the Treasurers of the Second Temple," *BASOR* #148 (1957) 28-30.

*J. L. McKenzie, "The Edlers in the Old Testament," *B* 40 (1959) 522-540.

*Everett Ferguson, "Ordination in the Ancient Church (I)," *RestQ* 4 (1960) 117-138. [The Jewish Background: Priests; Kings; Prophets; Elders, Judges, and Rabbis—Old Testament Precedents; Elders and Rabbis—the Rabbinic Literature; Elders and the Sanhedrin; Community and Synagogue Officers in the Diaspora; Functionaries in the Qumran Community]

*M[enahem] Haran, "The Gibeonites, the Nethinim, and the sons of Solomon's Servants," *VT* 11 (1961) 159-169.

Baruch A. Levine, "The Netînîm," *JBL* 82 (1963) 207-212.

§439 **3.2.12.10 The Sabbath [See also: Studies on Individual Commandments →]**

†Anonymous, "Thoughts on the Sabbath," *QTMRP* 1 (1813) 371-374.

H. J., "Was the Sabbath instituted before the time of Moses?" *QCS* 4 (1822) 297-298. [Reply by T. H. D., pp. 363-365]

Anonymous, "The Sabbath," *TRGR* 1 (1822) 47-63, 187-200, 366-368.

†Anonymous, "Septenary Institutions," *WR* 54 (1850-51) 153-178. *[Sabbaths]*

Anonymous, "Of Sabbaths, as observed by the Jews; and of the authority of the Jewish Scriptures," *WR* 54 (1850-51) 179-206.

W. N., "The Sabbath Day. On the Divine Authority, Early Origin, Universality, and Perpetuity of the Sabbath," *JSL, 2nd Ser.,* 1 (1851-52) 70-97.

R. W. Dickinson, "The Origin of the Sabbath," *TLJ 4* (1851-52) 395-415.

R. W. Dickinson, "The Sabbath and its Modern Assailants," *TLJ* 4 (1851-52) 614-648.

Anonymous, "The Claims of the Sabbath," *ERG, 1st Ser.,* 1 (1854-55) 288-303.

W. M. O'Hanlon, "The Scriptural Authority and Obligation of the Sabbath Examined," *BS* 13 (1856) 520-551, 698-725.

Anonymous, "History of the Sabbath under the Old Testament Dispensation; its Divine Origin and Universal Obligation," *JSL, 3rd Ser.,* 6 (1857-58) 83-116.

N. G. E., "Physiology and the Sabbath," *JSL, 3rd Ser.,* 7 (1858) 88-96.

*J. C. Murphy, "The Weekly Sabbath," *BS* 29 (1872) 78-113.

Richard A. Proctor, "Saturn and the Sabbath of the Jews," *ContR* 25 (1874-75) 610-622.

*Cedron, "The Temple Ritual. The Sabbath," *CongL* 4 (1875) 540-546.

Anonymous, "Perpetuity of the Sabbath," *PQPR* 5 (1876) 118-146.

*Anonymous, "The Feasts of Jehovah," *BWR* 1 (1877) 1-48. [I. Lecture I. The Sabbath, pp. 2-8]

Anonymous, "The Sabbath," *SPR* 28 (1877) 193-224.

William DeLoss Love, "The Sabbath Under the Old Dispensation," *BS* 36 (1879) 729-759.

William DeLoss Love, "The Sabbath Under the Old Dispensation," *DTQ* 6 (1880) 119-135.

Julius H. Seelye, "The Sabbath Question," *PRev* 56 (1880) Part 2, 335-352.

E. O. Frierson, "The Sabbath," *MQR, 2nd Ser.,* 3 (1881) 422-434.

Francis Brown, "The Sabbath in the Cuneiform Records," *PR* 3 (1882) 688-700.

J. H. McIlvaine, "The Holy Sabbath," *PR* 4 (1883) 253-274.

Arnold Guyot, "The Seventh Day," *ONTS* 3 (1883-84) 353-354.

K. M. McIntyre, "The Sabbath," *SPR* 35 (1884) 215-230.

*John P. Peters, "Miscellaneous Notes," *AJSL* 1 (1884-85) 115-119. [The Sabbath, pp. 117-118]

Joseph Agar Beet, "The Jewish Sabbath and the Lord's Day," *Exp, 2nd Ser.,* 8 (1884) 338-350.

*William C. Wilkinson, "Sabbath for Man; or, the Fourth Commandment Fundamental, not Ceremonial," *BQR* 8 (1886) 221-230.

*John Q. Bittinger, "Septenary Time and the Origin of the Sabbath," *BS* 46 (1889) 321-342.

*B. Pick, "The Rites, Ceremonies and Customs of the Jews," *HR* 17 (1889) 199-206. [VIII. The Jewish Sabbath, pp. 203-204]

R. N. Sledd, "The Law of the Sabbath," *MQR, 3rd Ser.,* 7 (1889-90) 36-50.

Clark S. Beardslee, "The Sabbath. A Proposed Course for Inductive Bible Study," *HSR* 1 (1890-91) 54-60.

*Howard Crosby, "The Sabbath," *HR* 19 (1890) 261-262.

J. T. Nichols, "The Origin of the Hebrew Sabbath," *ONTS* 12 (1891) 36-42.

J. T. Nichols, "The Development of the Sabbath Among the Hebrews," *ONTS* 12 (1891) 207-215.

Moncure D. Conway, "Civilising the Sabbath," *OC* 6 (1892) 3495-3500.

Jesse W. Brooks, "Extra-Biblical Evidence of the Primitive Sabbath," *HR* 25 (1893) 500-506.

*P. A. Peter, "The Sabbath in Genesis and Exodus," *ColTM* 16 (1896) 153-169.

William De Loss Love, "The Sabbath Under the Old Dispensation," *BS* 35 (1897) 729-759.

Morris Jastrow Jr., "The Original Character of the Hebrew Sabbath," *AJT* 2 (1898) 312-352.

James D. O'Neill, "The Pre-Mosaic Sabbath—I," *CUB* 5 (1899) 22-39.

James D. O'Neill, "The Pre-Mosaic Sabbath—II," *CUB* 5 (1899) 184-204.

Crawford H. Toy, "The Earliest form of the Sabbath," *JBL* 18 (1899) 190-194.

T. R. English, "The Sabbath," *USR* 11 (1899-1900) 262-273.

*William R. Harper, "Constructive Studies in the Priestly Element of the Old Testament: IX: Laws and Usages Concerning the Sabbath and Kindred Institutions, Considered Comparatively," *BW* 18 (1901) 297-307.

Jacob Voorsanger, "The Sabbath Question," *YCCAR* 12 (1902) 103-122. [Discussion of the Sabbath Question: Jacob S. Raisin, pp. 123-128; I. Lewinthal, pp. 128-130; H. G. Enelow, pp. 130-133; Louis Wolsey, pp. 133-135; M. Heller, pp. 135-136; Henry Cohen, p. 136; Joseph Krauskoff, pp. 137-139; T. Schanfarber, pp. 139-140; Adolph Guttmacher, pp. 140-141; Joseph Herz, pp. 141-142; G. Deutsch, pp. 142-143; I. L. Leucht, pp. 143-145; Joseph Silverman, pp. 145-146; W. Willner, pp. 146-147; S. H. Sonneschein, pp. 147-148; Closing Remarks on the Sabbath Question by Jacob Voorsanger, pp. 148-152]

Edward G. King, "The Sabbath in the Light of the Higher Criticism," *ET* 17 (1905-06) 438-443.

*C. H. W. Johns, "Statistics of Sabbath Keeping in Babylonia," *Exp, 7th Ser.,* 2 (1906) 433-440.

*G. Margoliouth, "The Calendar, the Sabbath, and the Marriage Law in the Geniza-Zadokite Document," *ET* 24 (1912-13) 553-558. [II. The Sabbath]

B.W. Bacon, "The Sabbath, Jewish and Christian,"*YDQ* 9 (1912-13) 117-124.

Theophile J. Meek, "The Sabbath in the Old Testament," *JBL* 33 (1914) 201-212.

Anonymous, "The Sabbath in the Old Testament," *HR* 70 (1915) 395-396.

William F. Badé, "The Jewish Sabbath in the Light of Babylonian Archaeology," *AJA* 20 (1916) 90.

*K. Kohler, "The Sabbath and Festivals in Pre-Exilic and Exilic Times," *JAOS* 37 (1917) 209-223.

*Theophilus G. Pinches, "The Creation-legend and the Sabbath in Babylonia and Amurru," *JRAS* (1920) 583-589.

J. Hugh Michael, "The Jewish Sabbath in the Light of Classical Writers," *AJSL* 40 (1923-24) 117-124.

*(   ) M., "Gen. 2, 1-3," *WLQ* 23 (1926) 118-135, 186-200, 267-279. *[The Sabbath]*

*W. E[mery] Barnes, "Prophecy and the Sabbath (A Note on the Teaching of Jeremiah)," *JTS* 29 (1927-28) 386-390.

*K. Budde, "The Sabbath and the Week," *JTS* 30 (1928-29) 1-15.

W. W. Cannon, "The weekly Sabbath," *ZAW* 49 (1931) 325-327.

E. G. [H.] Kraeling, "The Present Status of the Sabbath Question," *AJSL* 49 (1932-33) 218-228.

Israel Harburg, "Observance of Sabbath," *YCCAR* 47 (1937) 324-350.

*Sol Finesinger, "The Custom of Looking at the Fingernails at the Outgoing of the Sabbath," *HUCA* 12&13 (1937-38) 347-365.

*Jacob Z. Lauterbach, "The Origin and Development of Two Sabbath Ceremonies," *HUCA* 15 (1940) 367-424.

R. E. Wolfe, "New Moon and Sabbath," *JBL* 59 (1940) xiv.

Harold L. Creager, "An Evaluation of the Sabbath," *LCQ* 15 (1942) 34-47.

*S. K. Mirsky, "Allusions to Sabbath in the Ugaritic Texts in the Light of Midrashic Literature," *JBL* 69 (1950) viii.

R. North, "The Derivation of Sabbath," *B* 36 (1955) 182-201.

Franz Landsberger, "The Origin of the Ritual Implements for the Sabbath," *HUCA* 27 (1956) 387-415.

Olan Hicks, "The Hebrew Sabbath," *RestQ* 3 (1959) 23-35.

Bernard P. Robinson, "Jewish Sabbath and Christian Sunday," *LofS* 18 (1963-64) 412-419.

*S. T. Kimbrough Jr., "The Concept of Sabbath at Qumran," *RdQ* 5 (1964-66) 483-502.

Gary G. Cohen, "The Doctrine of the Sabbath in the Old and New Testaments," *GJ* 6 (1965) #2, 7-15.

*William H. Shea, "The Sabbath in the Epistle of Barnabas," *AUSS* 4 (1966) 149-175.

Merrill F. Unger, "The Significance of the Sabbath," *BS* 123 (1966) 53-59.

*J. M. Baumgarten, "The Counting of the Sabbath in Ancient Sources," *VT* 16 (1966) 277-286.

H. W. Huppenbauer, "The Sabbath," *GBT* 3 (1966-71) #5, 1-12.

*Theodore Friedman, "The Sabbath: Anticipation of Redemption," *Jud* 16 (1967) 445-452.

J. Heinemann, "The Triennial Lectionary Cycle," *JJS* 19 (1968) 41-48.

Mayer Gruber, "The Source of the Biblical Sabbath," *JANES* 1 (1968-69) 14-20.

*Bezalel Porten, "The Religion of the Jews of Elephantine in the Light of the Hermopolis Papyri," *JNES* 28 (1969) 116-121. [Sabbath, pp. 116-118]

§440 *3.2.12.11 The Feasts, Fasts, and Festivals - General Studies*

*Lyman Coleman, "The Festivals of the Christian Church compared with those of other Ancient Forms of Religion," *BS* 4 (1847) 650-671. [Relation of the Festivals of the Christian church to those of the Jews, pp. 658-662]

*Cedron, "The Temple Ritual," *CongL* 2 (1873) 654-665; 3 (1874) 100-106, 142-148, 217-223, 291-298, 335-341, 482-488, 547-553, 726-732; 4 (1875) 41-47, 101-107, 161-167, 239-244, 358-365, 487-494, 540-546, 624-629, 673-679.

*Anonymous, "The Feasts of Jehovah," *BWR* 1 (1877) 1-48. [I. Lecture I. The Sabbath; II. The Passover; III. The Feast of Unleavened Bread; Lecture II. The Wave-Sheaf and the Wave-Loaves, Lev. XXIII 9-22; Lecture III. The Feasts of the Future, Lev. XXIII 23-end: The Feast of Trumpets; The Day of Atonement; The Feast of Tabernacles]

*B. Pick, "The Rites, Ceremonies and Customs of the Jews," *HR* 17 (1889) 199-206. [IX. New Year's Day, p. 204; XI. Other Festivals, p. 205]

*W. St. C[had] Boscawen, "The Babylonian and Jewish Festivals," *BOR* 4 (1889-90) 34-38.

M. H. Harris, "Can We Revive the Succoth Celebration?" *YCCAR* 9 (1898-99) 76-80.

*William R. Harper, "Constructive Studies in the Priestly Element in the Old Testament. VIII: The Laws and Usages Concerning Feasts, Considered Comparatively," *BW* 18 (1901) 204-217.

K. Kohler, "History and Functions of Ceremonies in Judaism," *YCAAR* 17 (1907) 205-229. [The Origin and Development of Jewish Ceremonies; 1. The Mosaic Ceremonial; 2. The Ceremonies of Pharisaic and Rabbinical Judaism; 3. The Ceremonies of Modern Judaism]

*E. G. King, "Enoch and the Feast of Dedication. (A Study in Natural Religion)," *ICMM* 5 (1908-09) 287-295.

James A. Montgomery, "The Dedication Feast in the Old Testament," *JBL* 29 (1910) 29-40.

*B. D. Eerdmans, "The Hebrew Feasts in Leviticus xxiii," *Exp, 8th Ser.*, 4 (1912) 43-56.

*H. St. J. Thackeray, "The Song of Hannah and Other Lessons and Psalms for the Jewish New Year's Day," *JTS* 16 (1914-15) 177-203.

*K. Kohler, "The Sabbath and Festivals in Pre-Exilic and Exilic Times," *JAOS* 37 (1917) 209-223.

Edward König, "The Feast of Enthronement in Jerusalem Recently Discovered," *CFL, 3rd Ser.,* 32 (1926) 523-525. *(Trans. by E. W. Hammer)*

*H[erbert] G[ordon] May, "The Relation of the Passover to the Festival of Unleavened Cakes," *JBL* 55 (1936) 68-82.

*Zemach Green, "Restriction of Travel on New Moon Holidays in Biblical Judaism," *JBL* 63 (1944) v.

Reginald Ginns, "Rosh Hash-Shanah: Its Date and Significance," *DS* 2 (1949) 385-394. *(Review)*

Solomon Zeitlin, "The Second Day of *Rosh Ha-shanah* in Israel," *JQR, N.S.,* 44 (1953-54) 326-329.

Salomon Speier, "A Contribution to the Understanding of the Piyyutim," *EI* 3 (1954) XIII.

*Abraham Goldberg, "On the First Two Mishna Paragraphs of the Treatise *Rosh Hashshana*," *Tarbiz* 29 (1959-60) #4, II.

*Joseph H. Golner, "God, Satan and Atonement," *Jud* 9 (1960) 299-306. *[Holidays]*

*J. B. Segal, "The Hebrew Festivals and the Calendar," *JSS* 6 (1961) 74-94.

*Leon J. Leibreich, "Aspects of the New Year Liturgy," *HUCA* 34 (1963) 125-176.

H. McKeating, "The Bread of God: *A study of Harvest Festivals in Old Testament Times*," *PQL* 9 (1963) 184-193.

Judah Rosenthal, "The Four Commemorative Fast Days," *JQR, N.S., 75th* (1967) 446-459. [1. Asarah b'Tebet; 2. Shivah Asar b'Tammaz; 3. Tishah b'Ab; 4. Zom Gedaliah]

Ezra Fleischer, "'The Great New-Moon Day'," *Tarbiz* 37 (1967-68) #3, II-III. *[Rosh Ḥodesh]*

Francisco O. Garcia-Treto, "The Three-Day Festival Pattern in Ancient Israel," *TUSR* 9 (1967-69) 19-30.

§441 *3.2.12.11.1 The Passover*

F. Corbaux, "On the Historical Origin of the Passover," *JSL, 2nd Ser.,* 7 (1854-55) 25-39, 281-297.

H. F. W., "Hebrew Festivals:—The Passover," *JSL, 4th Ser.,* 1 (1862) 55-63.

*Cedron, "The Temple Ritual. The Passover or Pasque," *CongL* 4 (1875) 239-244.

*Anonymous, "The Feasts of Jehovah," *BWR* 1 (1877) 1-48. [I. Lecture I: II. The Passover, pp. 8-11; III. The Feast of Unleavened Bread, pp. 11-14]

Anonymous, "The Seder-Table," *EN* 3 (1891) 474-476.

Theodore E. Schmauk, "The Paschal Lamb," *LCR* 10 (1891) 127-163.

*Charles Warren, "Dates on Which Paschal Full Moons Occur," *PEFQS* 32 (1900) 157-164.

Robert Dick Wilson, "The Passover," *CFL, N.S.,* 4 (1901) 323-329.

George M. Mackie, "The Jewish Passover in the Christian Church," *ET* 13 (1901-02) 391-397.

S. Fyne, "The Exodus Festival and the Unleavened Bread," *ET* 16 (1904-05) 346-347.

B. D. Eerdmans, "The Passover and the Days of Unleavened Bread," *Exp, 7th Ser.,* 8 (1909) 448-462.

Eb. Nestle, "The Aramaic Name of the Passover," *ET* 21 (1909-10) 521-522.

*Samuel Daiches, "The Aramaic Ostracon from Elephantine and the Festival of Passover," *SBAP* 34 (1912) 17-23.

*A. H. Sayce, "The Passover Ostrakon from Elephantine," *SBAP* 34 (1912) 212.

*W. W. Cannon, "Passover and Priests Code," *Exp, 8th Ser.*, 19 (1920) 226-235.

*G. Róheim, "The Passage of the Red Sea," *Man* 23 (1923) #96. *[Passover]*

*G. Róheim, "Passover and Initiation: A Postscript to the Passage of the Red Sea. Man, 1923. 96," *Man* 23 (1923) #111. *[Passover]*

W. T. McCree, "The Covenant Meal in the Old Testament," *JBL* 45 (1926) 120-128.

Adam C. Welch, "On the Method of Celebrating Passover," *ZAW* 45 (1927) 24-29.

C. E. Walkowiak, "The Origin of the Passover," *SS* 5 (1931) 4-20.

Elias Newman, "The Jewish Passover and the Christian Lord's Supper," *TF* 6 (1934) 2-17.

*H[erbert] G[ordon] May, "The Relation of the Passover to the Festival of Unleavened Cakes," *JBL* 55 (1936) 68-82.

*G. B[uchanan] Gray, "Passover and Unleavened Bread: The Laws of J, E, and D," *JTS* 37 (1936) 241-253.

Jacob Z. Lauterbach, "The Date of the Slaughter of the Paschal Lamb," *PAAJR* 12 (1942) 49-50.

*Grace Amadon, "Important Passover Texts in Josephus and Philo," *ATR* 27 (1945) 109-115.

Solomon Zeitlin, "The Liturgy of the First Night of Passover," *JQR, N.S.*, 38 (1947-48) 431-460.

Harold M. Kamsler, "'This is the Sacrifice of the Passover'," *CJ* 6 (1949-50) #4, 5-7.

Louis Finkelstein, "The Origin of the Hallel," *HUCA* 23 (1950-51) Part 2, 319-337.

Solomon Zeitlin, "The Time of the Passover Meal," *JQR, N.S.*, 42 (1951) 45-50.

J. Rosenthal, "Passover and the Festival of Unleavened Bread," *JJS* 3 (1952) 178-180.

*L. Morris, "The Passover in Rabbinic Literature," *ABR* 4 (1954-55) 57-76.

Sidney B. Hoenig, "The Duration of the Festival of Matzot," *JQR, N.S.,* 49 (1958-59) 271-277.

Clifford W. Atkinson, "The Ordinances of Passover –Unleavened Bread," *ATR* 44 (1962) 70-85.

John H. O'Rourke, "The Passover in the Old Testament," *BibT* #5 (1963) 302-303, 306-309.

Jay A. Wilcoxen, "The Israelite Passover: Some Problems," *BRes* 8 (1963) 13-27.

Yehuda Leib Alter, "Reflections on Passover," *Jud* 12 (1963) 206-209. *[Sefath Emeth]*

Christopher Kiesling, "The Jewish Paschal Mystery," *C&C* 20 (1968) 175-183.

*Aaron Samuel Tameret, "Passover and Non-Violence," *Jud* 17 (1968) 203-210. *(Trans. by Everett E. Geudler)*

§442 *3.2.12.11.2 The Day of Atonement*

*Cedron, "The Temple Ritual. The Day of Expiation," *CongL* 4 (1875) 487-494.

*Anonymous, "The Feasts of Jehovah," *BWR* 1 (1877) 1-48. [Lecture III. The Day of Atonement, pp. 37-42]

[Thomas Chaplin], "Yoma, or the Day of Atonement. With the Commentary of Rabbi Obadiah of Barttenora*[sic]*," *PEFQS* 17 (1885) 197-207.

Thomas Chaplin, "Yoma, or the Day of Atonement—*Continued,*" *PEFQS* 18 (1886) 58-65, 115-118.

Thomas Chaplin, "Tamid, or the Continual Service. With the Commentary of Rabbi Obadiah of Bartenora," *PEFQS* 18 (1886) 119-130, 213-223.

*B. Pick, "The Rites, Ceremonies and Customs of the Jews," *HR* 17 (1889) 199-206. [X. The Day of Atonement, pp. 204-205]

Anonymous, "The Great Day of Atonement," *ET* 5 (1893-94) 76-78.

*G. S. Hitchcock, "Philo and the Day of Atonement," *NYR* 3 (1907-08) 52-55.

B. D. Eerdmans, "The Day of Atonement," *Exp, 8th Ser.,* 1 (1911) 493-504.

Hebert Loewe, "The Sacramental Controversy Before A.D. 1," *ET* 39 (1927-28) 198-200. *[The Day of Atonement]*

Jacob Gartenhaus, "The Jewish Day of Atonement," *R&E* 35 (1938) 45-53.

*Th. C. Vriezen, "The Term *Hizza:* Lustration and Consecration," *OTS* 7 (1950) 201-235. [The day of Atonement. Lev. xvi, pp. 219-233]

*Julian Morgenstern, "Two Prophecies of the Fourth Century B.C. and the Evolution of Yom Kippur," *HUCA* 24 (1952-53) 1-74.

Hermann Cohen, "The Day of Atonement," *CJ* 10 (1955-56) #4, 37-39.

Herman Cohen, "The Day of Atonement I," *Jud* 17 (1968) 352-357.

Herman Cohen, "The Day of Atonement II," *Jud* 18 (1969) 84-90.

Herman Cohen, "The Day of Atonement III," *Jud* 18 (1969) 216-222.

§443 *3.2.12.11.3 The Day of Pentecost*

Josiah Pratt, "Wave Sheaf and the Pentecost," *JSL, 4th Ser,* 10 (1866-67) 177-180.

*Anonymous, "The Feasts of Jehovah," *BWR* 1 (1877) 1-48. [Lecture II. The Wave-Sheaf and the Wave-Loaves, Lev. 23:9-22, pp. 14-29]

*B. Noack, "The Day of Pentecost in Jubilees, Qumran, and Acts," *ASTI* 1 (1962) 73-95.

§444 *3.2.12.11.4 The Feast of Tabernacles*

*Anonymous, "The Feast of Jehovah," *BWR* 1 (1877) 1-48. [Lecture III. The Feast of Tabernacles, pp. 42-48]

Anonymous, "The Feast of Tabernacles," *EN* 4 (1892) 185-187.

*E. C. Selwyn, "The Feast of Tabernacles, Epiphany and Baptism," *JTS* 13 (1911-12) 225-249.

*H. St. J. Thackeray, "Psalm LXXVI and Other Psalms for the Feast of Tabernacles," *JTS* 15 (1913-14) 425-431.

*W. E[mery] Barnes, "Psalm LXXVI and Other Psalms for the Feast of Tabernacles," *JTS* 15 (1913-14) 431-432.

F. J. Badcock, "The Feast of Tabernacles," *JTS* 24 (1922-23) 169-174.

*Hugo Gressmann, "The Mysteries of Adonis and the Feast of Tabernacles," *Exp, 9th Ser.,* 3 (1925) 416-432.

George W. MacRae, "The Meaning and Evolution of the Feast of Tabernacles," *CBQ* 22 (1960) 251-276.

§445 *3.2.12.11.5 Hanukkah*

I. Livingstone, "Chunnucah: the festival of the Maccabees," *IJA* #29 (1912) 27-29.

J. Abelson, "Maccabean Memories," *IJA* #45 (1916) 27-30. *[Hanukkah]*

S[olomon] Zeitlin, "The Festival of Hanukkah," *JBL* 53 (1934) xiii.

Solomon Zeitlin, "Hanukkah," *JQR, N.S.,* 29 (1938-39) 1-36.

*S. Atlas and M. Perlmann, "Saadia on the Scroll of the Hasmonaeans," *PAAJR* 14 (1944) 1-23. *[Hanukkah]*

*Julian Morgenstern, "The Chanukkah Festival and the Calendar of Ancient Israel," *HUCA* 20 (1947) 1-136; 21 (1948) 365-496.

H. F. Wickings, "The Feast of Lights," *ET* 73 (1961-62) 190.

§446 *3.2.12.11.6 The Feast of Purim*

C. H. W. Johns, "The Derivation of Purim," *Exp, 5th Ser.,* 4 (1896) 151-154.

*G. A. Simcox, "I.—Purim," *SBAP* 20 (1898) 300-302.

Paul Haupt, "Purim. Address delivered at the Annual Meeting of the Society of Biblical Literature and Exegesis, New York, December 27, 1905," *BAVSS* 6 (1906-09) Heft 2, 1-53.

*Israel Friedlaender, "Bonfires on Purim," *JQR, N.S.,* 1 (1910-11) 257-258.

*Maurice A. Canney, "Notes on Philology, Etc. Purim," *JMUEOS* #5 (1915-16) 103.

*B. Schneider, "Esther Revised According to the Maccabees," *SBFLA* 13 (1962-63) 190-218. *[Feast of Purim]*

§447 *3.2.12.12 Synagogue Worship [See: §194 for Synagogue Buildings←]*

*G. J. C. D., "The Temple and the Synagogue," *BFER* 17 (1868) 275-288.

Anonymous, "The Jewish Synagogue," *BFER* 19 (1870) 1-18.

*H. Friendlænder, "Rabbinical Preaching," *EN* 1 (1889) 130-133.

A. Buchler, "The Reading of the Law and the Prophets in a Triennial Cycle," *JQR* 5 (1892-93) 420-468.

A. Buchler, "The Reading of the Law and the Prophets in a Triennial Cycle, II," *JQR* 6 (1893-94) 1-73.

Ernest D[eWitt] Burton, "The Ancient Synagogue Service," *BW* 8 (1896) 143-148.

*D Kaufmann, "Art in the Synagogue," *JQR* 9 (1896-97) 254-269.

D. S. Margoliouth, "Lines of Defence of the Biblical Revelation. 6. The Calendar of the Synagogue," *Exp, 6th Ser.,* 2 (1900) 336-355.

G. H. Box, "The Jewish Prayer-Book. A Study in the Worship of the Synagogue," *ET* 15 (1903-04) 313-316, 362-366.

*I. Elbogen, "Studies in the Jewish Liturgy," *JQR* 18 (1905-06) 587-599. [I, A. פרם על שמע]

A. Lukyn Williams, "The Religion and Worship of the Synagogue," *Exp, 7th Ser.*, 7 (1909) 286-288. *(Review)*

Isidore Lewnithal, "The Origin and Growth of the Synagogue," *MQR, 3rd Ser.*, 42 (1916) 131-138.

Louis Finkelstein, "The Origin of the Synagogue," *PAAJR* 1 (1928-30) 49-59.

Solomon Zeitlin, "The Origin of the Synagogue. A Study in the Development of Jewish Institutions," *PAAJR* 2 (1930-31) 69-81.

Israel Bettan, "Israel and the Synagog," *YCCAR* 43 (1933) 294-312. {Discussion by: [David] Philipson, p. 312; [Samuel] Goldenson, pp. 312-313; [Abraham J.] Feldman, p. 313; [Julius] Rappaport, p. 313; Bernard Heller, pp. 313-314; Morris Clark, p. 314; [Max C.] Currick, p. 314; [Marius] Ranson, pp. 314-315; [Harry L.] Comins, p. 315; Reply by Israel Bettan, pp. 315-316}

N[orman] H. Snaith, "The Triennial Cycle on the Psalter," *ZAW* 51 (1933) 302-307.

Helen Rosenau, "A Note on Synagogue Orientation," *JPOS* 16 (1936) 33-36.

Helen Rosenau, "The Synagogue and the Diaspora," *PEQ* 69 (1937) 196-202.

Bernard J. Bamberger, "Factors in the History of the Synagog," *YCCAR* 47 (1937) 218-237. {Discussion by: Solomon B. Freehof, pp. 237-238; Samuel S. Cohon, p. 238; [Barnett R.] Brickner, pp. 239-240; [Samuel] Goldenson, p. 240; James G. Heller, pp. 240-241; [Solomon] Foster, p. 241; Charles E. Shulman, pp. 241-242; [Jacob] Singer, p. 242; Reply by Bernard J. Bamberger, pp. 242-243}

*R. G. Finch, "A Synagogue Sermon," *Theo* 45 (1942) 164-168. *[Pesiqta]*

David Daube, "A Modern Synagogue Sermon," *Theo* 46 (1943) 106-108. *[Sidrah/Mikketz]*

*Herbert Gordon May, "Synagogues in Palestine," *BA* 7 (1944) 1-20.
   [Synagogue Origins; The Earliest Synagogues Unearthed; Roman
   Period Synagogues in Palestine; The Synagogue at Dura-Europos;
   Byzantine Period Synagogues; The Synagogue Facade; Porch and
   Courts; Separation of Women in Worship; Locations of Synagogues;
   The Ark, or Shrine for the Law; Candlesticks, Seating Arrangements;
   The Priest; Synagogue Inscriptions; Pictures and Figures in the
   Synagogue]

*Floyd V. Filson, "Part IV—Temple, Synagogue, and Church," *BA* 7 (1944)
   77-88. [Origin and Growth of the Synagogue; Herod Rebuilds the
   Temple; The Role of the Synagogue; The Church and the Temple; The
   Church and the Synagogue; The Church in the Home; Later Trends]

Eric Werner, "The Oldest Sources of the Synagogal Chant," *PAAJR* 14
   (1946-47) 225-231. [Note by D. A. Jessurun Cardozo, pp. 231-232]

O. S. Rankin, "The Extent of the Influence of the Synagogue Service upon
   Christian Worship," *JSS* 1 (1948-49) 27-32.

Franz Landsberger, "The House of the People," *HUCA* 22 (1949) 149-155.
   [Synagogue]

Cecil Roth, "The 'Chair of Moses' and Its Survivals," *PEQ* 81 (1949) 100-
   111.

Israel Renov, "The Seat of Moses," *JBL* 70 (1951) vi.

*Cecil Roth, "Ecclesiasticus in the Synagogue Service," *JBL* 71 (1952) 171-
   178.

I. Renov, "The Seat of Moses," *IEJ* 5 (1955) 262-267.

A. Ehrhardt, "The Birth of the Synagogue and R. Akiba," *ST* 9 (1955) 86-
   111.

J[ulian] Morgenstern, "The Origin of the Synagogue," *SOOG* 2 (1956) 192-
   201.

Irenaeus Dalmais, "The Liturgy of the Synagogue and the Christian
   Liturgy," *LofS* 11 (1956-57) 173-181.

Franz Landsberger, "The Sacred Direction in Synagogue and Church,"
   HUCA 28 (1957) 181-203.

J. Guillet, "From Synagogue to Early Christian Assembly: I," *LofS* 12 (1957-58) 22-29.

J. Guillet, "From Synagogue to Early Christian Assembly: II," *LofS* 12 (1957-58) 64-73.

Isaiah Sonne, "Secondary Names for Synagogue," *Tarbiz* 27 (1957-58) #4, X-XI.

S. D. Goitein, "Ambōl —The Raised Platform in the Synagogue," *EI* 6 (1960) 37*-38*.

Jack P. Lewis, "The Synagogue," *RestQ* 4 (1960) 199-204.

Hayim Donin, "Havdalah—*The Ritual and the Concept,*" *Trad* 3 (1960-61) 60-72.

*Solomon Zeitlin, "There was no Synagogue in the Temple," *JQR, N.S.,* 53 (1962-63) 168-169.

S. Safrai, "Was there a Women's Gallery in the Synagogue of Antiquity?" *Tarbiz* 32 (1962-63) #4, II.

Sidney B. Hoenig, "The Supposititious Temple-Synagogue," *JQR, N.S.,* 54 (1963-64) 115-131.

Joseph Heinemann, "The 'Triennial' Cycle and the Calendar," *Tarbiz* 33 (1963-64) #4, III-IV.

J. Weingreen, "The origin of the synagogue," *Herm* #98 (1964) 68-84.

*Erick Werner, "The Role of Tradition in Music of the Synagogue," *Jud* 13 (1964) 156-163.

*Stanley S. Harakas, "The Relationship of the Church and Synagogue in the Apostolic Fathers," *StVTQ, N.S.,* 11 (1967) 123-138.

*A. Thomas Kraabel, "Ὕψιστος and the Synagogue at Sardis," *GRBS* 10 (1969) 81-93.

§448 *3.2.12.13 The Sects of Judaism - General Studies*

O. D. Miller, "Origin, History and Doctrines of the Ancient Jewish Sects,"
UQGR, N.S., 18 (1881) 261-281.

A.   Bernstein,   "Chasidaism,"   *EN*   1   (1889)   219-223,   269-274.

S. N. Deinard, "Nazarenes and Shramanas," *OC* 23 (1909) 702-703.
[Comments by A. Kampmeier, pp. 766-767] *[Nazarenes and Ebionites]*

A. Kampmeier, "The Pre-Christian Nasareans," *OC* 27 (1913) 85-90.

*Felix Perles, "The Hebrew Names of the Essenes and the Therapeutae,"
JQR, N.S., 17 (1926-27) 405-406.

J. P. Arendzen, "Jewish Monks in the Days of Christ," *IER, 5th Ser.,* 32
(1928) 236-249.

Leon Nemoy, "Al-Qirqisānī's Account of the Jewish Sects and
Christianity," *HUCA* 7 (1930) 317-397.

David M. Shohet, "The Sicarii," *CJ* 3 (1946-47) #3, 9-15.

*Y. Baer, "The Ancient Hassidim in Philo's Writings and in Hebrew
Tradition," *Zion* 18 (1953) #3/4, I.

*Joshua Finkel, "A Link Between Ḥasidism and Hellenic and Patristic
Literature," *PAAJR* 26 (1957) 1-24; 27 (1958) 19-41. *[Sects]*

Nahum Levison, "Theocracy, Hierocracy, and Early Jewish Sects," *GUOST*
17 (1957-58) 48-51.

*G. Vermes, "Essenes—Therapeutai—Qumran," *DUJ, N.S.,* 21 (1959-60)
97-115.

Jacob Neusner, "The Fellowship (חקורה) in the Second Jewish
Commonwealth," *HTR* 53 (1960) 125-142.

*H. A. Wolfson, "The Pre-Existent Angel of the Magharians and Al-
Nahāwandī," *JQR, N.S.,* 51 (1960-61) 89-106.

*S[olomon] Zeitlin, "Zealots and Sicarii," *JBL* 81 (1962) 395-398.

*Solomon Zeitlin, "I. Masada and the Sicarii. The Occupants of Masada," *JQR, N.S.,* 55 (1964-65) 299-317.

*P. Wernberg-Møller, "The Nature of the *YAḤAD* according to the *Manual of Discipline* and Related Documents," *ALUOS* 6 (1966-68) 56-81.

*Solomon Zeitlin, "The Sicarii and Masada," *JQR, N.S.,* 57 (1966-67) 251-270.

Julian Morgenstern, "The *Ḥªsîdîm*—Who Were They?" *HUCA* 38 (1967) 59-73.

*Isaiah Tishby, "The Messianic Idea and Messianic Trends in the Growth of Hasidism," *Zion* 32 (1967) #1/2, I-III.

*Jacob Neusner, "The Phenomenon of the Rabbi in Late Antiquity," *Numen* 16 (1969) 1-20.

*Leo Landman, "The Guilt-Offering of the Defiled Nazarite," *JQR, N.S.,* 60 (1969-70) 345-352.

§449 *3.2.12.13.1 The Essenes and Zadokites [For Qumran
"Essenes" see: Qumran
- The Community→]*

Wm. Hall, "The Essenes, Morally and Historically Considered," *BRCR, 3rd Ser.,* 3 (1847) 162-173.

P. S., "The Essenes," *JSL, 2nd Ser.,* 3 (1852-53) 176-186; 8 (1858-59) 186-187.

James Almes, "The Essenes," *JSL, 2nd Ser.,* 4 (1853) 170-178.

Edmond Stapfer, "The Sect of the Essenes," *DTQ* 3 (1877) 179-185.

Keningdale Cook, "The Tradition of the Essenes," *DUM* 96 (1880) 146-199.

George Foot Moore, "The Covenantors of Damascus; a Hitherto Unknown Jewish Sect," *HTR* 4 (1911) 330-377.

James A. Montgomery, "A Lost Jewish Sect," *BW* 38 (1911) 373-383. *[Zadokites]*

Anonymous, "A New Jewish Sect," *MR* 93 (1911) 308-311. *[Zadokites]*

Joseph Barnes, "The Jewish Sect of the New Covenant at Damascus," *CUB* 19 (1913) 533-546.

D. S. Margoliouth, "The Zadokites," *Exp, 8th Ser.,* 6 (1913) 157-164.

J. W. Lightley, "'The Essenes' their manner of life," *IJA* #48 (1917) 9-11.

*K. Kohler, "The Essenes and the Apocalyptic Literature," *JQR, N.S.,* 11 (1920-21) 145-168.

*Felix Perles, "The Hebrew Names of the Essenes and the Therapeutae," *JQR, N.S.,* 17 (1926-27) 405-406.

*Ralph Marcus, "Pharisees, Essenes, and Gnostics," *JBL* 73 (1954) 157-161.

*Solomon Zeitlin, "The Essenes and Messianic Expectations. A Historical Study of the Sects and Ideas During the Second Jewish Common-wealth," *JQR, N.S.,* 45 (1954-55) 83-119.

‡*Raymond F. Surburg, "Intertestamental Studies 1946—1955," *CTM* 27 (1956) 95-114. [III. The Dead Sea Scrolls and the Essenes, pp. 101-105]

*A. Dupont-Sommer, "On a Passage of Josephus Relating to the Essenes (Antiq. XVIII, §22)," *JSS* 1 (1956) 361-366.

J. L. Teicher, "The Essenes," *StP* 1 (1957) 540-545.

*Morton Smith, "The Description of the Essenes in Josephus and the Philosophumena," *HUCA* 29 (1958) 273-313.

*John Strugnell, "Flavius Josephus and the Essenes: *Antiquities* XVIII, 18-22," *JBL* 77 (1958) 106-115.

*Solomon Zeitlin, "The Account of the Essenes in Josephus and in the Philosophumena," *JQR, N.S.,* 49 (1958-59) 292-300.

L. Rabinowitz, "The First Essenes," *JSS* 4 (1959) 358-361.

*G. Vermes, "Essenes—Therapeutai—Qumran," *DUJ, N.S.,* 21 (1959-60) 97-115.

Matthew Black, "The Essene Problem," *FDWL* #14 (1960) 1-27.

*Bent Noack, "Are the Essenes Referred to in the Sibylinne Oracles?" *ST* 17 (1963) 90-102.

§450 *3.2.12.13.2 The Pharisees*

Henry Constable, "The Pharisees were the Orthodox Party among the Jews," *JSL, 3rd Ser.,* 11 (1860) 463-464.

*F. W. Farrar, "The Results of the Exile and the Origin of Pharisaism," *Exp, 1st Ser.,* 5 (1877) 87-98.

*Ernest D[eWitt] Burton, "The Ethical Teachings of Jesus in Relation to the Ethics of the Pharisees and of the Old Testament," *BW* 10 (1897) 198-208.

*James Moffatt, "The Righteousness of the Scribes and Pharisees," *ET* 13 (1901-02) 201-206.

Eb. Nestle, "Did the Pharisees Wear White Garments?" *ET* 20 (1908-09) 188-189.

*G. H. Box, "Survey of Recent Literature on the Pharisees and Sadducees," *RTP* 4 (1908-09) 129-151.

Israel Friedlaender, "The Rupture Between Alexander Jannai and the Pharisees," *JQR, N.S.,* 4 (1913-14) 443-448.

*B. D. Eerdmans, "Pharisees and Sadducees," *Exp, 8th Ser.,* 8 (1914) 299-315.

*M. H. Segal, "Pharisees and Sadducees," *Exp, 8th Ser.,* 13 (1917) 81-108.

M. D. Hussey, "Origin and Name of Pharisee," *JBL* 39 (1920) 66-69.

Burton S. Easton, "Mr. Herford on the Pharisees," *ATR* 7 (1924-25) 423-437.

J. P. Arendzen, "The Pharisees," *IER, 5th Ser.,* 25 (1925) 225-236.

Solomon Zeitlin, "The Pharisees," *JQR, N.S.,* 16 (1925-26) 383-392. *(Review)*

*Jacob Z. Lauterbach, "A Significant Controversy Between the Sadducees and the Pharisees," *HUCA* 4 (1927) 173-205. *[How the High Priest should enter the Holy of Holies]*

Louis Finkelstein, "The Pharisees: Their Origin and Their Philosophy," *HTR* 22 (1929) 185-261.

Jacob Z. Lauterbach, "The Pharisees and Their Teachings," *HUCA* 6 (1929) 69-139.

*H. St. John Thackeray, "On Josephus's Statement of the Pharisees' Doctrine of Fate (Antiq. xviii, 1, 3)," *HTR* 25 (1932) 93.

G. Allon, "The Attitude of the Pharisees toward Roman Rule and the Herodian Dynasty," *Zion* 3 (1937-38) #4, IV-VI.

*T. W. Manson, "Sadducee and Pharisee: The Origin and Significance of the Names," *BJRL* 22 (1938) 144-159.

*Solomon Gandz, "The dawn of literature. Prolegomena to a history of unwritten literature," *Osiris* 7 (1939) 261-522. [Chapter XVII., §10. The Pharisees, pp. 468-470]

B. J. Bamberger, "The Legalism of the Pharisees," *JBL* 66 (1947) iv.

John Bowman, "The Pharisees," *EQ* 20 (1948) 125-146.

Ralph Marcus, "The Pharisees in the Light of Modern Scholarship," *JR* 32 (1952) 153-164.

*Ralph Marcus, "Pharisees, Essenes, and Gnostics," *JBL* 73 (1954) 157-161.

*C. Rabin, "Alexander Jannaeus and the Pharisees," *JJS* 7 (1956) 3-12.

Louis Finkelstein, "The Ethics of Anonymity Among the Pharisees," *CJ* 12 (1957-58) #4, 1-12.

*Louis H. Feldman, "The Identity of Pollio, the Pharisee, in Josephus," *JQR*, N.S., 49 (1958-59) 53-62.

G. Allon, "The attitude of the Pharisees to the Roman government and the House of Herod," *SH* 7 (1961) 53-78.

Solomon Zeitlin, "The Pharisees," *JQR*, N.S., 52 (1961-62) 97-129.

*Cecil Roth, "The Pharisees in the Jewish Revolution of 66-73," *JSS* 7 (1962) 63-80.

Sidney B. Hoenig, "Pharisaism Reconsidered," *JQR*, N.S., 56 (1965-66) 337-353. *(Review)*

*Paul J. Camp, "The Attitudes of the Pharisees Toward the Law at the Time of Christ," *SS* 17 (1965) #2, 68-88. [Introduction; The Law; History of the Pharisees; The Social Milieu of the Pharisees; Theoretical Attitudes Towards the Law; A Dichotomy in the Face of the Law; Unmooring the Law; Practical Attitudes; The Pharisees and Politics; St. Paul, the Ideal Pharisee]

Louis Finkelstein, "The Origin of the Pharisees," *CJ* 23 (1968-69) #2, 25-36.

Solomon Zeitlin, "The Origin of the Pharisees Reaffirmed," *JQR, N.S.,* 59 (1968-69) 255-267.

Ellis Rivkin, "Defining the Pharisees: The Tannaitic Sources," *HUCA* 40 (1969) 205-249.

§451 *3.2.12.13.3 The Sadducees*

*G. H. Box, "Survey of Recent Literature on the Pharisees and Sadducees," *RTP* 4 (1908-09) 129-151.

*B. D. Eerdmans, "Pharisees and Sadducees," *Exp, 8th Ser.,* 8 (1914) 299-315.

*M. H. Segal, "Pharisees and Sadducees," *Exp, 8th Ser.,* 13 (1917) 81-108.

G. H. Box, "Who were the Sadducees?" *Exp, 8th Ser.,* 15 (1918) 19-38.

Anonymous, "Who were the Sadducees," *HR* 75 (1918) 280-281.

J. P. Arendzen, "The Sadducees," *IER, 5th Ser.,* 25 (1925) 486-500.

*Jacob Z. Lauterbach, "A Significant Controversy Between the Sadducees and the Pharisees," *HUCA* 4 (1927) 173-205. *[How the High Priest should enter the Holy of Holies]*

*T. W. Manson, "Sadducee and Pharisee: The Origin and Significance of the Names," *BJRL* 22 (1938) 144-159.

*Robert J. North, "The Qumran 'Sadducees'," *CBQ* 17 (1955) 164-188.

*Bernard J. Bamberger, "The Sadducees and the Belief in Angels," *JBL* 82 (1963) 433-435.

*E. E. Ellis, "Jesus, the Sadducees and Qumran," *NTS* 10 (1963-64) 274-279.

*Solomon Zeitlin, "The Sadducees and the Belief in Angels," *JBL* 83 (1964) 67-71.

Victor Eppstein, "When and How the Sadducees were Excommunicated," *JBL* 85 (1966) 213-224.

§452 *3.2.12.13.4 The Sanhedrin*

(　) Witsius, "On the Councils of the Hebrews," *PRev* 1 (1829) 252-266. *[The Sanhedrin]*

A. Kampmeier, "Did the Sanhedrin Exist at the Time of Jesus?" *OC* 25 (1911) 249-251.

E. Bickerman, "The Sanhedrin," *Zion* 3 (1937-38) #4, VII.

Hanoch Albeck, "The Sanhedrin and Its President," *Zion* 8 (1942-43) #4, I.

*Solomon Zeitlin, "The Political Synedrion and the Religious Sanhedrin," *JQR, N.S.,* 36 (1945-46) 109-140.

*Solomon Zeitlin, "Synedrion in the Judeo-Hellenistic Literature and Sanhedrin in Tannaitic Literature," *JQR, N.S.,* 36 (1945-46) 307-315.

*Solomon Zeitlin, "Synedrion in Greek Literature, the Gospels and the Institution of the Sanhedrin," *JQR, N.S.,* 37 (1946-47) 189-198.

*Solomon Zeitlin, "Is a Revival of a Sanhedrin in Israel Necessary for Modification of the Halaka?" *JQR, N.S.,* 47 (1951-52) 339-376.

Jacob B. Agus, "Ancient Sanhedrin or Sanhedrin-Academy?" *Jud* 1 (1952) 52-63.

T. A. Burkill, "The Competence of the Sanhedrin," *VC* 10 (1956) 80-96.

*Solomon Zeitlin, "The Titles High Priest and the Nasi of the Sanhedrin," *JQR, N.S.,* 48 (1957-58) 1-5.

Sidney B. Hoenig, "The Sanhedrin," *JQR, N.S.,* 52 (1961-62) 335-345. *(Review)*

J. Spencer Kennard Jr., "The Jewish Provincial Assembly," *ZNW* 53 (1962) 25-51. *[Sanhedrin]*

§453　*3.2.12.13.5　The Scribes as a Religious Group [See also: §92 for Scribe as a Profession ←]*

B. Pick, "The Scribes, Before and in the Time of Christ," *LQ* 8 (1878) 249-278.

H. L. Strack, "The Scribe," *AJSL* 1 (1884-85) 209-211.

*James Moffatt, "The Righteousness of the Scribes and Pharisees," *ET* 13 (1901-02) 201-206.

H. R. Mackintosh, "The Scribes of Palestine," *ET* 13 (1901-02) 403-404.

§454　*3.2.12.13.6　The Zealots*

Vernon Stauffer, "The Program of the Zealots and the Program of Jesus," *CollBQ* 14 (1924-25) #1, 3-14.

*Sidney B. Hoenig, "Maccabees, Zealots and Josephus," *JQR, N.S.,* 49 (1958-59) 75-80.

*Cecil Roth, "The Zealots in the War of 66-73," *JSS* 4 (1959) 332-355.

Cecil Roth, "The Zealots—A Jewish Religious Sect," *Jud* 8 (1959) 33-40.

*Solomon Zeitlin, "Josephus and the Zealots: A Rejoinder," *JSS* 5 (1960) 388.

*Solomon Zeitlin, "Zealots and Sicarii," *JBL* 81 (1962) 395-398.

*S. G. F. Brandon, "The Zealots: The Jewish resistance against Rome A.D. 6-73," *HT* 15 (1965) 632-641.

*B. Salomonsen, "Some Remarks on the Zealots with Special Regard to the Term 'Qannaim' in Rabbinic Literature," *NTS* 12 (1965-66) 164-176.

Gunther Baumbach, "The significance of the Zealots," *TD* 17 (1969) 241-246.

§455 *3.2.12.14 The Hebrew Cultus, includes Dreams, Divination, Idolatry, Magic, Necromancy, and Superstition [See also: §418 Religionsgeschichte of Israel ←]*

Anonymous, "The Science and Traditions of the Supernatural. Magic, Sorcery, and Witchcraft," *DUM* 61 (1863) 687-703.

Anonymous, "Ancient Magic and Astrology," *DUM* 73 (1869) 603-621.

Anonymous, "Ancient Magic, Legal and Illegal," *DUM* 76 (1870) 121-139.

*Anonymous, "Prophets and Prophecy," *SPR* 26 (1875) 138-159. [Dreams, pp. 149-151]

Claude R. Conder, "The Calves of Bethel and Dan," *PEFQS* 10 (1878) 27-29.

W. F. Birch, "The Golden Calf at Bethel," *PEFQS* 12 (1880) 103-104.

*Claude R. Conder, "Notes on Disputed Points," *PEFQS* 12 (1880) 172-174. [The calves of Bethel, pp. 172-173]

H. P. Smith, "The High Places," *ONTS* 2 (1882-83) 225-234. (Editorial note, pp. 246-247)

*Joseph Jacobs, "Are there Totem-Clans in the Old Testament?" *SBAP* 8 (1885-86) 39-41.

S. Louis, "Ancient Traditions of Supernatural Voices (Bath-Kol)," *SBAT* 9 (1886-93) 182-194.

*P. A. Nordell, "Old Testament Word Studies: 8. Idols and Images," *ONTS* 8 (1888-89) 296-301. [Mĭnhāh *present, offering;* Qŏrbān *offering;* Zēbhăh *sacrifice;* 'ōlāh *burnt offering;* Hăṭṭā'th *sin offering*]

Joseph Jacobs, "Are There Totem-Clans in the Old Testament?" *ARL* 3 (1889) 145-164.

A. H. Sayce, "Polytheism in Primitive Israel," *JQR* 2 (1889-90) 25-36.

R. C. H. Lenski, "Witchcraft and the Bible," *ColTM* 11 (1891) 229-240.

Barnard C. Taylor, "Israel's Greatest Sin: Idolatry," *ONTS* 12 (1891) 198-202.

*F. W. Farrar, "Was There a Golden Calf at Dan? A Note on 1 Kings XII, 29, 30 and Other Passages," *Exp, 4th Ser.,* 8 (1893) 254-265.

*William Hayes Ward, "Light on Scriptural Texts from Recent Discoveries. XI. The Shades of the Dead: Rephaim and Teraphim," *HR* 26 (1893) 508-510.

R. C. H. Lenski, "A Study of Witchcraft," *ColTM* 14 (1894) 17-34, 85-103, 149-163, 230-244, 290-301.

R. Winterbotham, "The Cultus of Father Abraham," *Exp, 5th Ser.,* 4 (1896) 177-186.

A. van Hoonacker, "Divination by the 'ôb Amongst the Ancient Hebrews," *ET* 9 (1897-98) 157-160.

*J. A. Selbie, "Demonology, Magic, etc.," *ET* 10 (1898-99) 326-328.

B[enjamin] B. Warfield, "Israel and Ancestor-Worship," *CFL, N.S.,* 2 (1900) 268-269.

Ross G. Murison, "Totemism in the Old Testament," *BW* 18 (1901) 176-184.

Stanley A. Cook, "Israel and Totemism," *JQR* 14 (1901-02) 413-448.

Charles Edward Smith, "Witchcraft and the Old Testament," *BS* 59 (1902) 26-35.

*M[elvin] G[rove] Kyle, "The Religion of Israel in Its Relation to the Religions of Contiguous Peoples. I. Calf-Worship," *CFL, N.S.,* 6 (1902) 71-78

R. Bruce Taylor, "Traces of Tree-Worship in the Old Testament," *ET* 14 (1902-03) 407-415.

*Ross G. Murison, "The Serpent in the Old Testament," *AJSL* 21 (1904-05) 115-130.

*Arthur E. Whatham, "The Origin of Human Sacrifice — including an Explanation of the Hebrew Asherah," *AJRPE* 2 (1906-07) 24-61.

Charles Edward Smith, "Witchcraft and the Old Testament," *CFL, 3rd Ser.,* 7 (1907) 37-42.

*Ed[uard] König, "Astrology Among the Babylonians and Israelites," *HR* 53 (1907) 407-410.

Sidney Zandstra, "The Theory of Ancestor Worship Among the Hebrews," *PTR* 5 (1907) 281-287.

*W. H. Wood, "Jar-Burial Customs and the Question of Infant Sacrifice in Palestine," *BW* 36 (1910) 166-175, 227-234.

*W[illiam] F[rederic] Badè, "Hebrew Funerary Rites as Survivals of Ancestor Worship," *PAPA* 42 (1910) lxxvii.

*William Frederic Badè, "The Iron-Taboo of the Hebrew," *PAPA* 43 (1911) lx.

*W. Sherwood Fox, "Old Testament Parallels to *Tabellae Defixionum*," *PAPA* 43 (1912) xxv-xxvi.

*C. Ryder Smith, "Some Indian Parallels to Hebrew Cult," *JTS* 14 (1912-13) 424-432.

*W. Sherwood Fox, "Old Testament Parallels to Tabellae Defixionum," *AJA* 17 (1913) 84.

*W. Sherwood Fox, "Old Testament Parallels to 'Tabellae Defixionum'," *AJSL* 30 (1913-14) 111-124.

W. M. Christie, "Jewish Superstition," *GUOST* 4 (1913-22) 41.

*John H. deVries, "Does the Old Testament Contain Traces of Animism?" *BS* 71 (1914) 484-489.

Ed[uard] König, "Image-Worship and Idol-Worship in the Old Testament," *Exp, 8th Ser.,* 7 (1914) 289-298.

Leroy Waterman, "Bull-Worship in Israel," *AJSL* 31 (1914-15) 229-255.

*J[ohn] E. McFadyen, "The Mosaic Origin of the Decalogue," *Exp, 8th Ser.,* 11 (1915) 152-160, 222-231, 311-320, 384-400. [The Teraphim, pp. 392-394; Calf Worship, pp. 394-400]

*Moïse Schwab, "Amulets and Bowls with Magic Inscriptions," *JQR, N.S.,* 7 (1916-17) 619-628. *(Review)*

Paul Haupt, "Crystal-Gazing in the Old Testament," *JBL* 36 (1917) 84-92.

*G[eorge] W. Gilmore, "Interpretation of Dreams, Hebrew and Babylonian," *HR* 75 (1918) 398-399.

*Joseph Offord, "Archaeological Notes on Jewish Antiquities. XLIV. *The Queen of Heaven*," *PEFQS* 50 (1918) 90-92.

H. J. D. Astley, "Survivals of Primitive Cults in the Old Testament," *ICMM* 15 (1918-19) 90-97, 206-215.

*Joseph Offord, "On—Anu, Heliopolis in a Semitic Inscription; and the Gilgals and Massebahs of Palestine," *PEFQS* 51 (1919) 123-133.

*Wilfred H. Schoff, "Cinnamon, Cassia and Somaliland," *JAOS* 40 (1920) 260-270. *[Totism]*

R[obert] H. Pfeiffer, "The Polemic Against Idolatry in the Old Testament," *JBL* 43 (1924) 229-240.

*R. A. S[tewart] Macalister, "On a Remarkable Group of Cult-Objects from the Ophel Excavation," *PEFQS* 56 (1924) 137-142.

*E. G. H. Kraeling, "The Early Cult of Hebron and Judges 16:1-3," *AJSL* 41 (1924-25) 174-178.

Allan H. Godbey, "Ariel, or David-Cultus," *AJSL* 41 (1924-25) 253-266.

*M. D. R. Willink, "Is Genesis I. a Manifesto Against Nature Worship?" *Theo* 11 (1925) 11-15.

*R[obert] H. Pfeiffer, "Images of Yahweh," *JBL* 45 (1926) 211-222.

*Eric Burrows, "The Dew Cult of Mount Hermon," *JSOR* 11 (1927) 76-77.

*Robert H. Pfeiffer, "Three Assyriological Footnotes to the Old Testament," *JBL* 47 (1928) 184-187. [3. The earliest reference to kiblah, pp. 186-187]

W. E[mery] Barnes, "Teraphim," *JTS* 30 (1928-29) 177-179.

*Charles Roads, "The Witch of Endor," *MR* 112 (1929) 454-456. [Necromancy, pp. 455-456]

*Allen H. Godbey, "Incense and Poison Ordeals in the Ancient Orient," *AJSL* 46 (1929-30) 217-238.

Sidney Smith, "What Were the Teraphim," *JTS* 33 (1931-32) 33-36.

*H[erbert] G[ordon] May, "The Fertility Cult in Hosea," *JTS* 48 (1931-32) 73-98.

George Ricker Berry, "Taboo in the Old Testament," *CRDSB* 4 (1931-32) 5-18.

*W. J. Ferrar, "The Jewish Kingship and the Sacred Combat," *Theo* 32 (1936) 37-43.

*W[illiam] F[oxwell] Albright, "The Golden Calf and the Cherubim," *JBL* 57 (1938) xviii.

*Martin Rist, "The God of Abraham, Isaac, and Jacob: A Liturgical and Magical Formula," *JBL* 57 (1938) 289-304.

H. Hamann, "Teraphim," *AustTR* 10 (1939) 84-87.

*John Pedersen, "Canaanite and Israelite Cultus," *AO* 18 (1939-40) 1-14.

*William A. Irwin, "Images of Yahweh," *CQ* 19 (1942) 292-301.

*E. L. Sukenik, "Installations in Connection with the Cult of the Dead in Canaanite Ugarit and in Israelite Samaria," *KSJA* 1 (1942) VIII-IX.

Rufus M. Jones, "Jewish Mysticism," *HTR* 36 (1943) 155-163.

*G. R. Driver, "Witchcraft in the Old Testament," *JRAS* (1943) 6-16.

J. Spencer Kennard Jr., "Judaism and Images," *CQ* 23 (1946) 259-265.

*H. Torczyner, "A Hebrew Incantation Against Night-Demons from Biblical Times," *JNES* 6 (1947) 18-29.

*Sidney Jellicoe, "The Prophets and the Cultus," *ET* 60 (1948-49) 256-258.

C[hester] C. McCown, "Hebrew High Places and Cult Remains," *JBL* 69 (1950) x.

C[hester] C. McCown, "Hebrew High Places and Cult Remains," *JBL* 69 (1950) 205-219.

*A. S. Kapelrud, "Cult and Prophetic Words," *ST* 4 (1950) 5-12.

Peter R. Ackroyd, "The Teraphim," *ET* 62 (1950-51) 378-380.

*Yehezkel Kaufmann, "The Bible and Mythological Polytheism," *JBL* 70 (1951) 179-197.

*J. S. Kennard, "The Jewish High Priest as Agent of the Imperial Cult," *JBL* 71 (1952) v.

*S. B. Gurewicz, "When Did the Cult Associated with the 'Golden Calves' Fully Develop in the Northern Kingdom?" *ABR* 3 (1953) 41-44.

Henry J. Cadbury, "The Single Eye," *HTR* 47 (1954) 69-74.

*Eduard Nielsen, "The Burial of Foreign Gods," *ST* 8 (1954) 103-122.

J. A. Thompson, "The 'Golden Calves' of Jeroboam (An Additional Note)," *ABR* 4 (1954-55) 79-84.

Cecil Roth, "An Ordinance Against Images in Jerusalem, A. D. 66," *HTR* 49 (1956) 169-177.

*A. Leo Oppenheim, "The Interpretation of Dreams in the Ancient Near East. With a Translation of an Assyrian Dream-Book," *TAPS, N.S.,* 46 (1956) 179-373.

*E. E. Urbach, "The Rabbinical Laws of Idolatry in the Second and Third Centuries in the Light of Archaeological and Historical Facts," *IEJ* 9 (1959) 149-165, 229-245.

*Roy Lee Honeycutt, "Jeremiah and the Cult," *R&E* 58 (1961) 464-473.

Karl Heinrich Rengstorf, "Old and New Testament Traces of a Formula of the Judean Royal Ritual," *NT* 5 (1962) 229-244.

Judah Goldin, "On Honi the Circle-Maker: A Demanding Prayer," *HTR* 56 (1963) 233-237.

R. Neher-Bernheim, "The Libel of Jewish Ass-Worship," *Zion* 28 (1963) #1/2, IV.

Martin J. Buss, "The Meaning of 'Cult' in the Interpretation of the Old Testament," *JAAR* 32 (1964) 317-325.

*M. Weinfeld, "Cult Centralization in Israel in the Light of a Neo-Babylonian Analogy," *JNES* 23 (1964) 202-212.

*Roy A. Rosenberg, "The God Ṣedeq," *HUCA* 36 (1965) 161-177.

Andrew F. Key, "Traces of the Worship of the Moon God Sîn Among the Early Israelites," *JBL* 84 (1965) 20-26.

*R. E. Clements, "Deuteronomy and the Jerusalem Cult-Tradition," *VT* 15 (1965) 300-312.

Baruch Abraham Levine, "Comments on Some Technical Terms of the Biblical Cult," *Lĕš* 30 (1965-66) #1, n.p.n.

Frank M. Cross Jr., "The Divine Warrior in Israel's Early Cult," *LIST* 3 (1966) 11-30.

*S. E. Loewenstamm, "The Making and Destruction of the Golden Calf," *B* 48 (1967) 481-490.

*Harry A. Hoffner, "The Linguistic Origins of Teraphim," *BS* 124 (1967) 230-238.

*Moses Aberbach and Leivy Smolar, "Aaron, Jeroboam, and the Golden Calves," *JBL* 86 (1967) 129-140.

[Clifford A. Wilson], "Snakes Alive! Would the serpent in the wilderness have any religious significance for the Israelites?" *BH* 4 (1968) 119-121.

*Richard L. Ruble, "The Doctrine of Dreams," *BS* 125 (1968) 360-364.

*Roy A. Rosenberg, "Who is the Moreh haṣṢedeq?" *JAAR* 36 (1968) 118-122.

Karen Randolph Joines, "The Bronze Serpent in the Israelite Cult," *JBL* 87 (1968) 245-256.

*J. N. M. Wijngaards, "'You shall not bow down to them or serve them'," *IJT* 18 (1969) 180-190.

§456 *3.2.12.15 Studies in Hebrew "Philosophy"*

Cantabrigiensis, "A History of the Ancient Philosophy," *MMBR, N.S.,* 22 (1836) 347-354, 471-478, 563-574; 23 (1837) 63-68, 301-306.

*Anonymous, "Philosophy of Philo," *PRev* 23 (1851) 624-635.

Richard J. H. Gottheil, "A Synopsis of Greek Philosophy by Bar 'Ebhrâyâ," *AJSL* 3 (1886-87) 249-254.

Richard J. H. Gottheil, "Two Corrections," *AJSL* 4 (1887-88) 186.

S. Schechter, "The Dogmas of Judaism," *JQR* 1 (1888-89) 48-61, 115-127.

John Owen, "Optimism and Pessimism in Jewish Philosophy," *JQR* 3 (1890-91) 182-207.

Anonymous, "Jewish Philosophy," *ONTS* 11 (1890) 381.

Karl Budde, "The Nomadic Ideal in the Old Testament," *NW* 4 (1895) 726-745.

R. M. Wenley, "Judaism and the Philosophy of Religion," *JQR* 10 (1897-98) 18-40.

D. R. Alexander, "Summary of Paper on 'Aspects of the Old Testament Outlook on Life'," *GUOST* 2 (1901-07) 40-41.

*Edouard König, "Physical Beauty as Valued in the Bible," *HR* 49 (1905) 117-120.

F. A. Gast, "The Hebrew Conception of Life," *RChR, 4th Ser.,* 9 (1905) 456-462.

*Edward Chauncey Baldwin, "The Hebrew and the Greek Ideas of Life," *BW* 36 (1910) 334-344.

Beresford Potter, "The Influence of Babylonian Conceptions on Jewish Thought," *JTVI* 44 (1912) 299-318, 333-338. [(Discussion, pp. 318-327) (Communications by J. J. Lias, pp. 327-329; S. R. Driver, p. 329; R. M. Curwen, p. 329; A. Irving, pp. 329-331; R. B. Girdlestone, pp. 331-332; M. L. Rouse, pp. 332-333)]

*S. Angus, "Hebrew, Greek, and Roman," *R&E* 10 (1913) 163-177.

*S. Angus, "Hebrew, Greek, and Roman. Part II.," *R&E* 10 (1913) 403-422.

*Norman Bentwich, "From Philo to Plotinus," *JQR, N.S.,* 4 (1913-14) 1-21.

W[illia]m J. Hinke, "The Old Testament View of Life," *ASRec* 10 (1914-15) 359-375.

*Francis B. Denio, "Israel's Philosophy of History," *BS* 72 (1915) 357-373.

Israel Isaac Efros, "The Problem of Space in Jewish Mediaeval Philosophy," *JQR, N.S.,* 6 (1915-16) 495-554; 7 (1916-17) 61-87, 223-251.

*Harry Austryn Wolfson, "Crescas on the Problem of Divine Attributes," *JQR, N.S.,* 7 (1916-17) 1-44, 175-221.

Meyer Waxman, "The Philosophy of Don Hasdai Crescas," *JQR, N.S.,* 8 (1917-18) 305-337, 455-475.

Meyer Waxman, "The Philosophy of Don Hasdai Crescas, Part II, Chapters III and IV," *JQR, N.S.,* 9 (1918-19) 181-213.

Harry Austryn Wolfson, "Note on Crescas's Definition of Time," *JQR, N.S.,* 10 (1919-20) 1-17.

Meyer Waxman, "The Philosophy of Don Hasdai Crescas, Chapters V to VII," *JQR, N.S.,* 10 (1919-20) 25-47, 291-308.

John W. Flight, "The Nomadic Idea and Ideal in the Old Testament," *JBL* 42 (1923) 158-266.

*Samuel Nirenstein, "The Problem of the Existence of God in Maimonides, Alanus and Averroes: A Study in the Religious Philosophy of the Twelfth Century," *JQR, N.S.,* 14 (1923-24) 395-454.

David Neumark, "Saadya's Philosophy—Sources, Characteristics, Principles," *HUCA* 1 (1924) 503-573

*Harry A[ustryn] Wolfson, "Notes on Proofs of the Existence of God in Jewish Philosophy," *HUCA* 1 (1924) 575-596.

Harry Austryn Wolfson, "The Classification of Sciences in Mediaeval Jewish Philosophy," *HUCA, Jubilee Volume* (1925) 263-315.

David Neumark, "The Philosophy of Judaism and How It Should Be Taught," *HUCA, Jubilee Volume* (1925) 513-521.

Alex. R. Gordon, "Agnostic Tendencies in the Old Testament," *CJRT* 3 (1926) 26-31.

Israel [Isaac] Efros, "Studies in Pre-Tibbonian Philosophical Terminology," *JQR, N.S.,* 17 (1926-27) 129-164, 323-368.

*George Foot Moore, "Fate and Free Will in the Jewish Philosophies According to Josephus," *HTR* 22 (1929) 371-389.

Israel [Isaac] Efros, "More About Abraham B. Hayya's Philosophical Terminology," *JQR, N.S.,* 20 (1929-30) 113-138.

Charles H. Patterson, "The Philosophy of the Old Testament," *JAAR* 2 (1934) #2, 60-66.

*John Paterson, "Prophecy and Asceticism," *RL* 3 (1934) 209-211.

*Harry Austryn Wolfson, "The Internal Senses in Latin, Arabic, and Hebrew Philosophic Texts," *HTR* 28 (1935) 69-133.

Gerhard Gershom Scholem, "Philosophy and Jewish Mysticism," *RR* 2 (1937-38) 385-402.

Margaret B. Crook, "Religious Philosophers in the Old Testament," *RL* 7 (1938) 553-564.

Henry Schaeffer, "Biblical Thinking versus Aristotelianism in Theology," *LCQ* 15 (1942) 23-33.

Abraham [J.] Heschel, "The Quest for Certainty in Saadia's Philosophy," *JQR, N.S.,* 33 (1942-43) 265-313.

Abraham [J.] Heschel, "Reason and Revelation in Saadia's Philosophy," *JQR, N.S.,* 34 (1943-44) 391-408.

Agathe H. F. Thornton, "The Hebrew Conception of Speech as a Creative Energy," *HJ* 44 (1945-46) 132-134.

*Harry [Austryn] Wolfson, "The Kalam Problem of Nonexistence and Saadia's Second Theory of Creation," *JQR, N.S.,* 36 (1945-46) 371-391.

Harry A[ustryn] Wolfson, "Atomism in Saadia," *JQR, N.S.,* 37 (1946-47) 107-124.

*Harry [Austryn] Wolfson, "Arabic and Hebrew Terms for Matter and Element with Especial Reference to Saadia," *JQR, N.S.,* 38 (1947-48) 47-61.

M. A. Skill, "Critical Notes," *JQR, N.S.,* 38 (1947-48) 214. *[Ref:* Wolfson, 'Atomism in Saadia'," *JQR, N.S.,* 37 (1946-47) *above]*

*E. L. Allen, "The Hebrew View of Nature," *JJS* 2 (1950-51) 100-104.

*William Cosser, "The Meaning of 'Life' *(Ḥayyim)* in Proverbs, Job, and Ecclesiastes," *GUOST* 15 (1953-54) 48-53.

E[dmund] F. Sutcliffe, "Effect as Purpose: a Study in Hebrew Thought Patterns," *B* 35 (1954) 320-327.

*Charles Lee Feinberg, "The Old Testament in Jewish Thought and Life," *BS* 111 (1954) 27-38, 125-136.

Bernard J. LeFrois, "Semitic Totality Thinking," *CBQ* 17 (1955) 315-323.

George Farr, "Is there Philosophy in the Old Testament?" *BQL* 16 (1955-56) 52-57.

*Henry Slonimsky, "The Philosophy Implicit in the Midrash," *HUCA* 27 (1956) 235-290.

Salomon Suskowicz, "Is There a Jewish Philosophy?" *Jud* 7 (1958) 195-207.

Quentin Lauder, "The Hebrew Point of View," *TD* 6 (1958) 101-106.

Louis H. Feldman, "Philo-semitism among Ancient Intellectuals," *Trad* 1 (1958-59) 27-39.

Robert T. Anderson, "The Role of the Desert in Israelite Thought," *JAAR* 27 (1959) 41-44.

*James Wood, "The Idea of Life in the Book of Job," *GUOST* 18 (1959-60) 29-37.

James Robinson, "The Biblical View of the World. *A Theological Evaluation*," *SQ/E* 20 (1959) 470-483.

Thomas Wieser, The Biblical View of the World. *A Theological Evaluation*," *SQ/E* 20 (1959) 484-493.

Eliezer Berkovits, "What is Jewish Philosophy?" *Trad* 3 (1960-61) 117-130.

Meir Ben-Horin, "The Ultimate and the Mystery, A Critique of Some Neo-Mystical Tenets," *JQR, N.S.,* 51 (1960-61) 55-71, 141-155.

Wallace I. Wolverton, "The Distinctive Character of Hebrew Thought. A Review Article," *CJT* 7 (1961) 201-204.

Steven S. Schwarzschild, "Do Noachites Have to Believe in Revelation? A Passage in Dispute between Maimonides, Spinoza, Mendelssohn and M. Cohen. A Contribution to a Jewish View of Natural Law," *JQR, N.S.,* 52 (1961-62) 297-308.

Michael Wyschogrod, "Directions for Contemporary Jewish Philosophy I. *Agenda for Jewish Philosophy,*" *Jud* 11 (1962) 195-199.

Arthur Hyman, "Directions for Contemporary Jewish Philosophy II. *The Task of Jewish Philosophy,*" *Jud* 11 (1962) 199-205.

Steven S. Schwazschild, "Directions for Contemporary Jewish Philosophy III. *To Re-Cast Rationalism,*" *Jud* 11 (1962) 205-209.

Arthur A. Cohen, "The Philosopher and the Jew," *Jud* 11 (1962) 309-319.

Steven S. Schwazschild, "Do Noachites Have to Believe in Revelation?" *JQR, N.S.,* 53 (1962-63) 30-66.

Israel [Isaac] Efros, "Maimonides' Treatise on Logic: The New Arabic Text and Its Light on the Hebrew Versions," *JQR, N.S.,* 53 (1962-63) 269-273.

Richard L. Rubenstein, "The Meaning of Torah in Contemporary Jewish Theology. An Existentialist Philosophy of Judaism," *JAAR* 32 (1964) 115-124.

*John E. Rexine, "Hebrew and Greek Thought and Culture Compared," *StVSQ, N.S.,* 9 (1965) 138-144.

Harry A[ustryn] Wolfson, "Two Comments Regarding the Plurality of Worlds in Jewish Sources," *JQR, N.S.,* 56 (1965-66) 245-247.

*G. Gerald Harrop, "'But Now Mine Eye Seeth Thee'," *CJT* 12 (1966) 80-84.

*Hugh R. Harcourt, "Hebrew, Greek and Roman Thought," *NEST* 13 (1966) #1, 10-25.

John F. Priest, "Humanism, Skepticism and Pessimism in Israel," *HQ* 8 (1968) #3, 19-37.

John F. Priest, "Humanism, Skepticism and Pessimism in Israel," *JAAR* 36 (1968) 311-326.

§457 *3.2.12.16 Studies in the Genre of Ḥokmah (Wisdom) Literature [including Job, Proverbs, Ecclesiastes, and Ecclesiasticus]*

A. B. Davidson, "The Wisdom of the Hebrews," *Exp, 1st Ser.,* 11 (1880) 321-340; 12 (1880) 381-400, 436-459.

Franz Delitzsch, "Characteristics of the Chokma," *ONTS* 3 (1883-84) 157-158.

R. V. Foster, "The Hebrew 'Wisdom'," *ONTS* 5 (1885-86) 104-107.

S. R. Driver, "Job and Solomon," *Exp, 3rd Ser.,* 6 (1887) 71-80. *(Review)*

S. G. Green, "The 'Wisdom' of the Old Testament.   Proverbs and Ecclesiastes," *CongRL* 1 (1887-88) 408-420.

Edward T. Root, "What is Meant by the Biblical 'Hokma' or Wisdom?" *ONTS* 9 (1889) 24-27.

T. K. Cheyne, "Old Testament Notes, The Hebrew Idea of Wisdom," *Exp, 4th Ser.,* 5 (1892) 78-79.

D. M. Welton, "The Old Testament Wisdom (Chokma)," *BW* 10 (1897) 183-189.

William R. Harper, "The Methods of the Sages in Teaching," *BW* 15 (1900) 326-330. *(Editorial)*

*D. S. Margoliouth, "Lines of Defence of the Biblical Revelation. II. The Wisdom of Ben-Sira and the Wisdom of Solomon," *Exp, 6th Ser.,* 1 (1900) 141-160, 186-193.

John Skinner, "The Cosmopolitan Aspect of the Hebrew Wisdom," *JQR* 17 (1904-05) 240-262.

Anonymous, "The Theology of the Wisdom Literature," *CQR* 64 (1907) 342-369.

*Norman R. Mitchell, "The Wisdom of the Hebrews in Relation to Greek Thought," *GUOST* 3 (1907-12) 16-17.

*C. F. Burney, "The Rise of a Belief in a Future Life in Israel," *ICMM* 4 (1907-08) 41-57. *[Wisdom Literature]*

H. E. Ryle, "The Wisdom Literature of the Bible. Outlines of an Opening Lecture," *ICMM* 4 (1907-08) 129-137. *[Also shows author as: Herbert E. Winton(sic)]*

[Herbert Pentin], "The Wisdom-Books of the Apocrypha. Some Hints to Students," *IJA* #27 (1911) 74-76.

John Franklin Genung, "The Development of Hebrew Wisdom," *BW* 42 (1913) 16-25.

*Robert F. Chisholm, "The Pre-Abrahamic Stories of Genesis as Wisdom Literature," *GUOST* 4 (1913-22) 80-82.

*E. G. King, "Job and the Alphabetical Psalms," *ICMM* 14 (1917-18) 31-39.

*Duncan Black Macdonald, "The Pre-Abrahamic Stories of Genesis, as a part of the Wisdom Literature," *SSO* 1 (1920) 115-125.

*Samuel A. B. Mercer, "Old Testament and Other Oriental Wisdom," *ATR* 6 (1923-24) 118-123.

W. R. Taylor, "Hellenism and Wisdom Literature," *CJRT* 1 (1924) 491-498.

*Emil Johnson, "The Ancient Hebrew Education. *A Study in Proverbs, Ecclesiastes, and Talmud*," *AQ* 4 (1925) 215-227, 338-349; 5 (1926) 8-24.

Robert H. Pfeiffer, "Edomitic Wisdom," *ZAW* 44 (1926) 13-26.

Herbert H. Gowen, "The Divine Wisdom," *ATR* 13 (1931) 377-387.

F. James, "Some Aspects of the Religion of Proverbs," *JBL* 51 (1932) 31-39.

*Samuel A. B. Mercer, "The Wisdom of Amenemope and his Religious Ideas," *EgR* 2 (1934) 27-69. [V. Amenemope and Other Wisdom Literature, p. 65]

R[obert] H. Pfeiffer, "Wisdom and Vision in the Old Testament," *ZAW* 52 (1934) 93-101.

*W. B. Stevenson, "A Mnemonic Use of Numbers in Proverbs and Ben Sira," *GUOST* 9 (1938-39) 26-38.

Robert Gordis, "Quotations in Wisdom Literature," *JQR, N.S.*, 30 (1939-40) 123-147.

Robert Gordis, "Social Background of Wisdom Literature," *JBL* 60 (1941) vi.

Robert Gordis, "The Social Background of Wisdom Literature," *HUCA* 18 (1944) 77-118.

*F. W. Dillistone, "Wisdom, Word, and Spirit. *Revelation in the Wisdom Literature*," *Interp* 2 (1948) 275-287.

T[erence] Y. Mullins, "The Origin and Development of Jewish Wisdom Literature through New Testament Times," *JBL* 67 (1948) xii.

*Terence Y. Mullins, "Jewish Wisdom Literature in the New Testament," *JBL* 68 (1949) 335-339.

*Neil G. Smith, "Family Ethics in the Wisdom Literature," *Interp* 4 (1950) 453-457.

*E. C. Burleigh, "The Influence of Hebrew Wisdom Literature upon Early Christian Doctrine," *ABR* 1 (1951) 75-87.

T[erence] Y. Mullins, "The Opposition of Reason and Anger in Wisdom Literature," *JBL* 72 (1953) vii.

*William Cosser, "The Meaning of 'Life' *(Ḥayyim)* in Proverbs, Job, and Ecclesiastes," *GUOST* 15 (1953-54) 48-53.

G. R. Webber, "Wisdom Doctrines in Old Testament Literature," *LQ, N.S.,* 6 (1954) 69-75.

*Lawrence E. Toombs, "O.T. Theology and the Wisdom Literature," *JAAR* 23 (1955) 193-196.

W[illiam] F[oxwell] Albright, "Some Canaanite-Phoenician sources of Hebrew wisdom," *VTS* 3 (1955) 1-15.

*P. A. H. de Boer, "The counsellor," *VTS* 3 (1955) 42-71.

*Johannes Lindblom, "Wisdom in the Old Testament prophets," *VTS* 3 (1955) 192-204.

*S[igmund] Mowinckel, "Psalms and wisdom," *VTS* 3 (1955) 205-224.

*J. Pedersen, "Wisdom and immortality," *VTS* 3 (1955) 238-246.

Norman W. Porteous, "Royal wisdom," *VTS* 3 (1955) 247-262.

*R. B. Y. Scott, "Solomon and the beginnings of wisdom in Israel," *VTS* 3 (1955) 262-279.

W. H. Gispen, "The wise men in Israel," *FUQ* 5 (1957-58) 1-18.

*Robert T. Siebeneck, "May Their Bones Return to Life!—Sirach's Praise of the Fathers," *CBQ* 21 (1959) 411-428.

H. L. Ellison, "The Wisdom Literature of the Old Testament," *F&T* 91 (1959-60) 198-207.

*Edmund I. Gordon, "A new look at the Wisdom of Sumer and Akkad," *BO* 17 (1960) 121-152.

*B. Gemser, "The instructions of 'Onchsheshoquy and Biblical wisdom literature," *VTS* 7 (1960) 102-128.

Charles C. Forman, "The Context of Biblical Wisdom," *HJ* 60 (1961-62) 125-132.

*Edwin [M.] Yamauchi, "The Sapiential Septuagint," *BETS* 5 (1962) 109-115.

*John Warwick Montgomery, "Wisdom as Gift. *The Wisdom Concept in Relation to Biblical Messianism,*" *Interp* 16 (1962) 43-57. [The Religious Meanings of Wisdom; The Wisdom Concept in the Canonical Old Testament; The Wisdom Concept in the Old Testament Apocrypha; Wisdom and the Christ in the New Testament; Contrast and Conclusion]

*E. W. Heaton, "Prophecy and wisdom," *OSHTP* (1962-63) 4-5.

Wilfrid Harrington, "The Wisdom of Israel," *ITQ* 30 (1963) 311-325.

John F. Priest, "Where is Wisdom to be Placed?" *JAAR* 31 (1963) 275-282.

*Roland E. Murphy, "A consideration of the classification 'Wisdom Psalms'," *VTS* 9 (1963) 156-167.

*T. Donald, "The Semantic Field of Rich and Poor in the Wisdom Literature of Hebrew and Accadian," *OA* 3 (1964) 27-41.

*Roland E. Murphy, "The Old Testament Wisdom Literature and the Problem of Retribution," *Scotist* 20 (1964) 5-18.

*Walther Zimmerli, "The Place and Limit of the Wisdom in the Framework of the Old Testament Theology," *SJT* 17 (1964) 146-158.

Alexander A. Di Lella, "Conservative and Progressive Theology: Sirach and Wisdom," *CBQ* 28 (1966) 139-154.

*D. A. Hubbard, "The Wisdom Movement and Israel's Covenant Faith," *TB* #17 (1966) 3-34.

*Robert Gordis, "Biblical Wisdom and Modern Existentialism," *CJ* 21 (1966-67) #4, 1-10.

Roland E. Murphy, "Assumptions and Problems in Old Testament Wisdom Research," *CBQ* 29 (1967) 407-418.

John L. McKenzie, "Reflections on Wisdom," *JBL* 86 (1967) 1-9.

*C. M. Carmichael, "Deuteronomic Laws, Wisdom, and Historical Traditions," *JSS* 12 (1967) 198-206.

Roger N. Carstensen, "The Persistence of the 'Elihu' Tradition in Later Jewish Writings," *LTQ* 2 (1967) 37-46.

*Carroll Mizicko, "Wisdom Literature in Israel and the Ancient Near East," *Scotist* 23 (1967) 47-73.

*Robert C. Hill, "The Dimensions of Salvation History in the Wisdom Books," *Scrip* 19 (1967) 97-106.

*James R. Boston, "The Wisdom Influence upon the Song of Moses," *JBL* 87 (1968) 198-202.

*Donald E. Gowan, "Habakkuk and Wisdom," *PP* 9 (1968) 157-166.

*Roland E. Murphy, "Form Criticism and Wisdom Literature," *CBQ* 31 (1969) 475-483.

Roland E. Murphy, "The Interpretation of Old Testament Wisdom Literature," *Interp* 23 (1969) 289-301.

*J. L. Crenshaw, "Method in Determining Wisdom Influence upon 'Historical' Literature," *JBL* 88 (1969) 129-142.

§458 *3.2.12.17 Studies in the Genre of Apocalyptic Literature [See also: §407 Daniel as an Apocalyptic Writing ←]*

*George H. Schodde, "The Messianic Idea in Pre-Christian Apocalyptic Literature," *LQ* 9 (1879) 346-370.

G[eorge] H. S[chodde], "Pre-Christian Apocalyptic Literature," *ColTM* 3 (1883) 14-32.

George H. Schodde, "The Jewish Apocalypses," *BW* 6 (1895) 97-104.

*Frank C. Porter, "Prophecy and Apocalypse," *BW* 14 (1899) 36-41.

G. S. Rollins, "The Importance of the Study of Apocalyptic Literature," *CSQ* 2 (1902-03) #1, 8-16.

John W. Bailey, "Jewish Apocalyptic Literature," *BW* 25 (1905) 30-42.

*C. F. Burney, "The Rise of a Belief in a Future Life in Israel," *ICMM* 4 (1907-08) 156-174. *[Apocalyptic Literature]*

Clyde W. Votaw, "The Apocalypse of John: I. Jewish Apocalyptic Literature," *BW* 31 (1908) 32-40.

Cyril W. Emmet, "The Apocalyptic Hope and the Teaching of Jesus," *IJA* #12 (1908) 34-36.

G. H. Box, "Some Characteristics of Apocalyptic Literature and its Writers," *IJA* #13 (1908) 7-9.

Lic. Carl Clemen, "The Jewish Apocalypses," *BW* 34 (1909) 33-44.

*Robert H. Kennet, "The Development of the Apocalyptic Style in the Old Testament," *ICMM* 8 (1911-12) 386-401.

David Frew, "The Jewish Apocalyptic," *GUOST* 4 (1913-22) 13-15.

*William Caldwell, "The Doctrine of Satan. II. Satan in Extra-Biblical Apocalyptic Literature," *BW* 41 (1913) 98-102.

George S. Hitchcock, "Apocalyptic," *ITQ* 8 (1913) 160-177.

B. K. Rattey, "The Apocalyptic Hope in the Maccabæan Age," *ICMM* 10 (1913-14) 191-201.

*Andrew C. Zenos, "Apocryphal Literature and Bible Study. I. Eschatology," *HR* 68 (1914) 451-453.

David Frew, "The Jewish Apocalyptic," *IJA* #38 (1914) 62-69.

*W. A. L. Elmslie, "The Doctrine of God in the Jewish Apocryphal and Apocalyptic Literature," *JTS* 16 (1914-15) 431-432. *(Review)*

*G. H. Box, "The Doctrine of God in the Jewish Apocryphal and Apocalyptic Literature," *IJA* #41 (1915) 37-39. *(Review)*

W. E. Orchard, "The Significance of Jewish Apocalypse," *IJA* #42 (1915) 45-50.

*Hewlett Johnson, "The Editor's Note," *ICMM* 12 (1915-16) 1-20, 111. *[Apocalyptic Literature]*

*H. J. Wicks, "The Doctrine of the Messiah in Jewish Apocrypha and Apocalyptic," *IJA* #46 (1916) 34-36.

H. D. A. Major, "The Apocalyptic Hope," *IJA* #47 (1916) 62-64.

*H. T. Andrews, "The Message of the Apocalyptic for Modern Times," *Exp, 8th Ser.,* 14 (1917) 58-71.

*Joseph Rauch, "Apocalypse in the Bible," *JJLP* 1 (1919) 163-195. [I. The Element of Hope; II. "Day of Judgment"; III. יום יהוה—National Aspect; IV. יום יהוה—Individual as Combined with National Aspects; V. אחרית הימים; VI. Transition: Ezekiel; VII. Growth of Apocalypse; VIII. Pseudonymity of Apocalypse; IX. Contribution of Apocalypse to the Religion of Israel. The Book of Daniel]

*E. J. Prince, "Jewish Apocalyptic and Mysteries," *HJ* 18 (1919-20) 95-112.

*T. Herbert Bindley, "Some Misunderstood Symbolism,"*ICMM* 16 (1919-20) 57-62.

Conrad Henry Moehlman, "The Apocalyptic Mind," *BW* 54 (1920) 58-69.

Edward William Winstanley, "The Outlook of Early Christian Apocalypse," *Exp, 8th Ser.,* 19 (1920) 161-184.

J. H. Lechie, "Beauties of Apocalyptic Literature," *Exp, 8th Ser.,* 19 (1920) 381-400.

S. P. T. Prideaux, "The Permanent Value of Apocalypse," *ICMM* 17 (1920-21) 189-194.

Anonymous, "Apocalyptic Literature," *MR* 103 (1920) 973-977.

*K. Kohler, "The Essenes and the Apocalyptic Literature," *JQR, N.S.,* 11 (1920-21) 145-168.

*R[obert] D[ick] Wilson, "Apocalypses and the Date of Daniel," *PTR* 19 (1921) 529-545.

G. H. Box, "Jewish Apocalyptic in the Apostolic Age," *Exp, 8th Ser.,* 24 (1922) 321-345, 437-459.

*L. Ginzberg, "Some Observations on the Attitude of the Synagogue Towards the Apocalyptic-Eschatological Writings," *JBL* 41 (1922) 115-136.

Donald W. Riddle, "The Physical Basis of Apocalypticism," *JR* 4 (1924) 174-191.

*Albion R. King, "Prophecy and Apocalypticism," *MR* 107 (1924) 852-866.

*G. H. Dix, "The Heavenly Wisdom and the Divine Logos in Jewish Apocalyptic," *JTS* 26 (1924-25) 1-12.

*C[hester] C. McCown, "Hebrew and Egyptian Apocalyptic Literature," *HTR* 18 (1925) 357-411. [I. The Relationships Between Egypt and Israel; II. Hebrew and Egyptian Literature; III. Egyptian Apocalyptic Literature in the Middle Kingdom; IV. Egyptian Apocalyptic Literature of Greek and Roman Times; V. The Influence of Egyptian Apocalyptic]

*C. Ryder Smith, "The Social Teaching of the Apocryphal and Apocalyptic Books," *ET* 37 (1925-26) 505-508.

D. W. Riddle, "From Apocalypse to Martyrology," *ATR* 9 (1927) 260-280.

*A. R. Gordon, "The Ethics of Jewish Apocalypse," *CJRT* 4 (1927) 19-27.

*Conrad Henry Moehlman, "The Apocalyptic Mind," *CRDSB* 3 (1930-31) 114-128.

*D. M. McIntyre, "Jewish Apocalyptic in Relation to the New Testament," *JTVI* 63 (1931) 172-191, 197-198. [Discussion and Communications, pp. 191-197]

W. Harvey-Jellie, "Bridging the Gulf Between the Testaments. *II. In Literature,*" *HR* 107 (1934) 103-105.

*J. W. Bailey, "The Temporary Messianic Reign in the Literature of Early Judaism," *JBL* 53 (1934) 170-187.

*E. E. Flack, "Motives for Pseudonymity in the Apocalypses: A Study in the Continuity of Revelation," *LCQ* 9 (1936) 1-17.

*Ismar J. Perita, "The New Biblical Approach to Social Problems," *JAAR* 5 (1937) 107-116. [III. The Principle of Differentiation in Biblical Opinion, *IV. The Social Ideals of the Apocalyptist,* p. 114]

N. H. Parker, "Jewish Apocalypse in the Time of Christ," *CQ* 17 (1940) 33-46.

George R. Berry, "The Apocalyptic Literature of the Old Testament," *JBL* 62 (1943) 9-16.

H. H. Rowley, "The Voice of God in Apocalyptic. *Eternal Values in the Apocalypses,*" *Interp* 2 (1948) 403-418.

*D. S. Russell, "The Apocalyptic Conception of the Unity of History," *BQL* 13 (1949-50) 68-75.

Lester J. Kuyper, "The Message of Apocalyptic," *RefR* 5 (1951-52) #3, 1-4.

T. Francis Glasson, "Apocalyptic—Some Current Delusions," *LQHR* 177 (1952) 104-110.

*B. J. Roberts, "The Dead Sea Scrolls and Apocalyptic Literature," *OSHTP* (1952-53) 29-35.

Charles T. Fritsch, "The Message of Apocalyptic for Today," *TT* 10 (1953-54) 357-366.

*E. W. Heaton, "The Affiliation of the Book of Daniel," *OSHTP* (1954-55) 23-24.

‡Raymond F. Surburg, "Intertestamental Studies 1946-1955," *CTM* 27 (1956) 95-114. [I. Apocrypha, Pseudepigrapha, Apocalypses, pp. 95-99]

*George E. Ladd, "The Revelation and Jewish Apocalyptic," *EQ* 29 (1957) 94-128.

William S. Sparks, "The Neo-Hebraic Apocalyptic Literature," *IR* 14 (1957) #3, 3-12. [The Book of Zerubbabel; The Book of Elijah, (Apocalypse of Elijah); The Secrets of Simeon Ben Yohai; Prayer of Rabbi Ben Yohai, (Ashkenazim), (Story of Daniel), (Midrash of the Ten Kings); Conclusion]

George E. Ladd, "The Origin of Apocalyptic in Biblical Religion," *EQ* 30 (1958) 140-146.

P. M. Hadfield, "Iranian Influences on Jewish and Christian Apocalyptic," *LQHR* 183 (1958) 216-220.

*Bo Reicke, "Official and Pietistic Elements of Jewish Apocalypticism," *JBL* 79 (1960) 137-150.

T. F[rancis] Glasson, "Apocalyptic Ideas of Judaism Contemporary with Our Lord," *LQHR* 185 (1960) 166-170.

J. A. Baker, "Some problems in the origins of Jewish apocalyptic," *OSHTP* (1961-62) 25-26.

George Howard, "Jewish Apocalyptic Literature," *RestQ* 6 (1962) 77-84.

Michael J. Cantley, "Introduction to Apocalyptic," *BibT* #8 (1963) 500-504.

*J. Licht, "Time and Eschatology in Apocalyptic Literature and in Qumran," *JJS* 16 (1965) 177-182.

*David J. Ellis, "Biblical Apocalyptic and Prophecy," *F&T* 96 (1967) #3, 27-40.

*William R. Murdock, "History and Revelation in Jewish Apocalypticism," *Interp* 21 (1967) 167-187.

*F. H. Drinkwater, "Jewish Apocalyptic and the Resurrection," *Cont* 6 (1968) 433-436.

Hans Dieter Betz, "On the Problem of the Religio-Historical Understanding of Apocalypticism," *JTC* 6 (1969) 134-156.

Frank M. Cross, "New Directions in the Study of Apocalyptic," *JTC* 6 (1969) 157-165.

*David Noel Freedman, "The Flowering of Apocalyptic," *JTC* 6 (1969) 166-174. [I. The Apocalyptic Era (ca. 165 BCE—135 CE); II. The Book of Daniel; III. Qumran, an Apocalyptic Community]

§459 **3.2.12.18 Messianic Expectation in Israel [See also:
Messianic Prophecy; and, Messiah→]**

W. H. J., "The Ancient Expectation of a Redeemer," *JSL, 3rd Ser.,* 3 (1856)
141-121.

David Green, "The Knowledge and Faith of the Old Testament Saints
Respecting the Promised Messiah," *BS* 14 (1857) 166-199.

Anonymous, "The Messianic Idea of the Old Testament," *MQR* 13 (1859)
194-213.

Anonymous, "The Messiah of the Jews," *CE* 68 (1860) 96-113. *(Review)*

Anonymous, "Jewish Conceptions of the Messiah," *TRL* 2 (1865) 241-254.

T[homas] B. Thayer, "The Ancient Promise of Redemption," *UQGR, N.S.,* 2
(1865) 308-323.

Anonymous, "Origin and Character of Messianic Hopes," *CE* 87 (1869) 71-
93.

P[aton] J. Gloag, "Messianic Views of the Modern Jews," *BFER* 25 (1876)
235-251. *(Review)*

*J. H. Allen, "The Messiah and the Christ of History," *URRM* 8 (1877) 608-
625.

J. Rawson Lumby, "The Coming of the Messiah. A Jewish Exposition,"
Exp, 1st Ser., 9 (1879) 393-397.

*George H. Schodde, "The Messianic Idea in Pre-Christian Apocalyptic
Literature," *LQ* 9 (1879) 346-370.

*A. G. Laurie, "The Jewish and Persian Messiahs," *UQGR, N.S.,* 16 (1879)
359-371.

Chars. W. Wendte, "The Messianic Hope," *URRM* 14 (1880) 268-281.

Anonymous, "The Doctrine of Two Messiahs among the Jews," *BQR* 3
(1881) 64-73. *(Trans. from the German by J. F. Morton)*

Anonymous, "The Study of the Messianic Element in the Old Testament,"
ONTS 3 (1883-84) 212-213.

Anonymous, "Jewish Theories of Messianic Interpretation," *ONTS* 3 (1883-84) 213.

*B. Pick, "Talmudic Notices Concerning the Messiah," *PR* 5 (1884) 505-510.

John P. Peters, "Suggestions on the Rise and Development of the Messianic Hope," *AR* 4 (1885) 75-96.

James Scott, "Historical Development of the Messianic Idea," *ONTS* 7 (1887-88) 176-180.

*J. G. Lansing, "The Messianic Element in the Book of Job," *CT* 6 (1888-89) 401-430.

G[eorge] H. Schodde, "The Messianic Views of Christ's Contemporaries," *ColTM* 11 (1891) 193-212.

Joseph M. Gleason, "History and Development of the Messianic Idea," *AER* 7 (1892) 30-47.

*R[obert] H[enry] Charles, "Messianic Doctrine in the Book of Enoch, and Its Influence on the New Testament," *ET* 4 (1892-93) 301-303.

*W. A. Shedd, "The Relation of the Messianic Teaching of Isaiah to Contemporary Events," *PPR* 5 (1894) 575-591.

*G. Buchanan Gray, "The References to the 'King' in the Psalter, in Their Bearing on the Question of Date and Messianic Belief," *JQR* 7 (1894-95) 658-686.

*Talbot W. Chambers, "The Messianic Idea in the Prophets," *PRR* 6 (1895) 224-238.

George S. Goodspeed, "Israel's Messianic Hopes," *BW* 12 (1898) 400-436.

Shailer Mathews, "The Jewish Messianic Expectations in the Time of Jesus," *BW* 12 (1898) 437-443.

*Henry T. Sell, "Christ in the Old Testament: or, the Development of the Messianic Idea," *BS* 60 (1903) 737-749.

*A. Smythe Palmer, "Michael the Messiah," *ET* 16 (1904-05) 287.

Thomas P. F. Gallagher, "The Messianic Idea," *IER, 4th Ser.,* 18 (1905) 1-19, 129-147, 226-244.

Jacob ben Aaron, "The Messianic Hope of the Samaritans," *OC* 21 (1907) 272-296. [Edited with introduction by William E. Barton, pp. 272-282] *(Trans. by Abdullah Ben Kori)*

*W. O. E. Oesterley, "Messianic Teaching in the Apocrypha," *IJA* #9 (1907) 7-9.

*W. O. E. Oesterley, "The Messianic Teaching of IV Esdras," *IJA* #11 (1907) 8-10; #12 (1908) 11-13; #17 (1909) 29-31.

Henry Preserved Smith, "The Origin of the Messianic Hope in Israel," *AJT* 14 (1910) 337-360.

Louis Matthews Sweet, "The Messiahship of Jesus," *BRec* 8 (1911) 109-111. [II. The Messianic Hope in the Old Testament]

*W[illia]m J. Hinke, "The Messianic Idea in Ancient Religions," *ASRec* 8 (1912-13) 159-184.

*C. G. Montefiore, "Modern Judaism and the Messianic Hope. A Reply to a Recent Indictment of Judaism," *HJ* 11 (1912-13) 366-377.

*G. H. Box, J. Albert Goldsmid, J. T. Turner, "Modern Judaism and the Messianic Hope," *HJ* 11 (1912-13) 885-889.

*A. Nairne, "The Transformation of the Messianic Hope by Our Lord and His Apostles," *ICMM* 9 (1912-13) 17-35.

Hugo Gressmann, "The Sources of Israel's Messianic Hope," *AJT* 17 (1913) 173-194.

*Hewlett Johnson, "The Editor's Notes," *ICMM* 12 (1915-16) 1-20, 111. *[Messianic Expectation]*

*Moses Gaster, "Jewish Coins and Messianic Traditions," *Exp, 8th Ser.,* 12 (1916) 241-259.

*H. J. Wicks, "The Doctrine of the Messiah in Jewish Apocrypha and Apocalyptic," *IJA* #46 (1916) 34-36.

*Edgar Rogers, "Jewish Coins and Messianic Traditions. A Reply to Dr. Gaster," *Exp, 8th Ser.,* 13 (1917) 29-43.

William Watson, "The Human and the Superhuman Messiahs," *Exp, 8th Ser.,* 13 (1917) 63-80.

*L. P. Smith, "The Messianic Ideal of Isaiah," *JBL* 36 (1917) 158-212.

A. F. Kirkpatrick, "The Hope of Israel," *ICMM* 14 (1917-18) 294-304.

*W. R. Aytoun, "The Rise and Fall of the 'Messianic' Hope in the Sixth Century," *JBL* 39 (1920) 24-43.

B. H. Streeter, "The Messianic Hope," *MC* 11 (1921-22) 587-596.

*John H. Raven, "Job's Messianic Hope," *BR* 7 (1922) 537-554.

*John H. Raven, "Job's Messianic Hope. II," *BR* 8 (1923) 35-60.

Frederick C. Grant, "The Economic Significance of Messianism," *ATR* 6 (1923-24) 196-213; 7 (1924-25) 281-289.

H. J. Wicks, "The Christ of Jewish Expectation—and the Christ who came," *BQL* 2 (1924-25) 207-212.

G. H. Dix, "The Messiah ben Joseph," *JTS* 28 (1925-26) 130-143.

G. H. Dix, "The Influence of Babylonian Ideas on Jewish Messianism," *JTS* 26 (1924-25) 241-256.

J. E. Hogg, "Note on 'The Messiah ben Joseph'," *JTS* 27 (1925-26) 411.

*R. B. Y. Scott, "The Expectation of Elijah," *CJRT* 3 (1926) 490-502.

H. Smith, "Ναζωραῖος κληθήσεται," *JTS* 28 (1926-27) 60.

*G. H. Dix, "The Seven Archangels and the Seven Spirits: A Study in the Origin, Development, and Messianic Associations of the Two Themes," *JTS* 28 (1926-27) 233-250.

H. Oscherowitz, "The Growth of the Messianic Idea," *OC* 43 (1929) 244-256.

A. Guillaume, "The Messiah in Judaism and Christianity," *ET* 43 (1931-32) 406-411.

I. G. Matthews, "An Episode in the Messianic Hope," *CQ* 12 (1935) 39-46.

*George Dahl, "The Messianic Expectation in the Psalter," *JBL* 57 (1938) 1-12.

J. Ridderbos, "The Messiah-King," *EQ* 11 (1939) 289-299.

*Michael J. Gruenthaner, "Messianic Concepts of Ezechiel," *ThSt* 2 (1941) 1-18.

*Cuthbert Lattey, "The Messianic Expectation in 'The Assumption of Moses'," *CBQ* 4 (1942) 9-21.

George E. Ganss, "The Messianic Ideas of Jesus' Contemporaries," *CBQ* 6 (1944) 37-52.

A. G. Hebert, "The Pattern of the Messianic Hope," *CQR* 142 (1946) 1-12.

Eugene Taeubler, "Jerusalem 201 to 199 B.C.E. on the History of a Messianic Movement," *JQR, N.S.,* 37 (1946-47) 1-30, 125-137, 249-263.

Cullen I. K. Story, "What Kind of Messiah Did the Jews Expect?" *BS* 104 (1947) 483-494; 105 (1948) 102-114, 233-247.

*G. R. Beasley-Murray, "The Two Messiahs in the Testament of the Twelve Patriarchs," *JTS* 48 (1947) 1-12.

Walter G. Williams, "The Long Expected Messiah," *IR* 6 (1949) 21-28.

*Abram Spiro, "Pseudo-Philo's Saul and the Rabbis' Messiah ben Ephraim," *PAAJR* 21 (1952) 119-137.

*Charles Lee Feinberg, "The Old Testament in Jewish Thought and Life," *BS* 111 (1954) 27-38, 125-136. [Messianic Expectation, pp. 33-38]

*Solomon Zeitlin, "The Essenes and Messianic Expectations. A Historical Study of the Sects and Ideas During the Second Jewish Commonwealth," *JQR, N.S.,* 45 (1954-55) 83-119.

*Cecil Roth, "Messianic Symbols in Palestine Archaeology," *PEQ* 87 (1955) 151-164.

Frank R. Neff Jr., "A Study in Jewish and Christian Messianism," *TUSR* 5 (1956-58) 69-85.

Eamonn O'Doherty, "The Organic Development of Messianic Revelation," *CBQ* 19 (1957) 16-24.

John L. McKenzie, "Royal Messiahs," *CBQ* 19 (1957) 25-52.

*Raymond E. Brown, "The Messianism of Qumran," *CBQ* 19 (1957) 53-82.

James Barr, "Tradition and Expectation in Ancient Israel," *SJT* 10 (1957) 24-34.

*George H. Cramer, "The Messianic Hope of Jeremiah," *BS* 115 (1958) 237-246.

R. J. Zwi Werblowsky, "Crises of Messianism," *Jud* 7 (1958) 106-120.

*S. L. Edgar, "New Testament and Rabbinic Messianic Interpretation," *NTS* 5 (1958-59) 47-54.

A. I. Polack, "The Messianic Idea in Contemporary Jewish Thought," *LofS* 15 (1960-61) 250-257.

R. H. Altus, "The Messianic Concept in Israel," *AusTR* 32 (1961) 131-133.

R. H. Beatty, "The Messianic Hope," *ACQ* 2 (1962) 15-25.

Joseph J. DeVault, "'The End of Days'—Messianic Expectation in Judaism," *BibT* #3 (1962) 181-186.

Vittorio Lanternari, "Messianism: Its Historical Origin and Morphology," *HRel* 2 (1962-63) 52-72.

*L. M. Muntingh, "Some aspects of West-Semitic kinship in the period of the Hebrew patriarchs," *OTW* 9 (1966) 106-115.

*A. J. B. Higgins, "Jewish Messianic Belief in Justin Martyr's *Dialogue with Trypho*," *NT* 9 (1967) 298-305.

*Isaiah Tishby, "The Messianic Idea and Messianic Trends in the Growth of Hasidism," *Zion* 32 (1967) #1/2, I-III.

*Roy A. Rosenberg, "Who is the Moreh haṣṢedeq?" *JAAR* 36 (1968) 118-122.

*J. Coert Rylaarsdam, "Jewish Hope and Christian Eschatology," *LTSB* 48 (1968) #2, 24-34.

*Jacob B. Agus, "Context and Challenge—A Response to Rylaarsdam," *LTSB* 48 (1968) #2, 35-44.

Anonymous, "The Search for the Messiah," *BH* 4 (1968) 77-80.

R. J. Zwi Werblowsky, "Messianism in Jewish History," *JWH* 11 (1968-69) 30-45.

R. M. Longenecker, "The Messianic Secret in the Light of Recent Discoveries," *EQ* 41 (1969) 207-215.

G. Scholem, "The Neutralisation of the Messianic Element in Early Hasidism," *JJS* 20 (1969) 25-56.

*N. Wieder, "The 'Land of Damascus' and Messianic Redemption," *JJS* 20 (1969) 86-88.

§460 **3.2.13 *Mythology in General - includes Folklore, Legends, and Superstitions in General***

†Anonymous, "Pantika: or, Traditions of the most Ancient Times," *BCQTR*, 4th Ser., 17 (1835) 332-344. *(Review)*

†Anonymous, "Introduction to a Scientific System of Mythology," *CTPR*, 3rd Ser., 1 (1845) 335-355. *(Review)*

A. S. Wilkins, "The Mythology of the Aryan Nations," *TRL* 7 (1870) 504-525. [Note, *TRL* 8 (1871) p. 130] *(Review)*

*(Miss) A. W. Buckland, "Mythological Birds Ethnologically Considered," *JRAI* 4 (1874-75) 227-292.

George W. Cox, "Goldziher's Hebrew Mythology," *TRL* 14 (1877) 358-374. *(Review)*

John W. Chadwick, "Goldziher's Hebrew Mythology," *URRM* 8 (1877) 278-288. *(Review)*

Rayner Winterbotham, "Divine Myths," *Exp, 1st Ser.,* 7 (1878) 137-155.

F. A. Paley, "On the Origin of the 'Solar Myth,' and Its Bearing on the History of Ancient Thought," *DR, 3rd Ser.,* 2 (1879) 90-111.

*(Miss) A. W. Buckland, "Surgery and Superstition in Neolithic Times," *JRAI* 11 (1881-82) 7-20 (Discussion, pp. 20-21)

*C[laude] R. Conder, "Jewish Superstitions," *PEFQS* 14 (1882) 145-146.

S. Louis, "Ancient Traditions of Supernatural Voices *(Bath-Kol),*" *SBAP* 8 (1885-86) 117-118.

†J. Marshall, "The Belief in Supernatural Voices," *SBAP* 8 (1885-86) 140-142.

J. P. MacLean, "Notes on Giants," *UQGR, N.S.,* 23 (1886) 464-474.

J. G. Frazer, "Some Popular Superstitions of the Ancients," *Folk* 1 (1890) 145-171.

H. Walter Featherstun, "The Origin of the Myths," *MQR* 8 (1890) 149-158.

*William Hayes Ward, "Light on Scriptural Texts from Recent Discoveries. XI. The Shades of the Dead: Rephaim and Teraphim," *HR* 26 (1893) 508-510. *[Ghosts]*

*W. St. Chad Boscawen, "The Hebrew Legend of Civilisation in the Light of Recent Discoveries," *ET* 5 (1893-94) 351-356.

Ernest Riess, "On Ancient Superstition," *TAPA* 26 (1895) 40-55.

*Fritz Hommel, "Belial and Other Mythological Terms," *ET* 8 (1896-97) 472-473. [Belial; Sheol; Zion; Earth]

*G. H. Skipwith, "The Burning Bush and the Garden of Eden: A Study in Comparative Mythology," *JQR* 10 (1897-98) 489-502.

*H. Colley March, "The Mythology of Wise Birds," *JRAI* 27 (1897-98) 209-232.

*Ed[uard] König, "The Latest Mythological Theory of the Patriarchs," *ET* 14 (1902-03) 217-219.

*Hans H. Spoer, "Notes on Jewish Amulets," *JBL* 23 (1904) 97-105.

Geo. W. Shaw, "Mythopœ Erudition," *OC* 18 (1904) 687-689.

Ghosn El-Howie, "The Evil Eye," *PEFQS* 36 (1904) 148-150.

George St. Clair, "Notes and Queries. *Earthquake Superstition,*" *PEFQS* 39 (1907) 243-244.

*O. Neufchotz de Jassy, "The Mythological Hebrew Terms Explained by the Sanskrit. *An Essay in Comparative Philology and Mythology,*" *Monist* 18 (1908) 126-138. [Editorial introduction, p. 126; Editorial Postscript, pp. 138-140; Rejoinder, pp. 140-142]

W. D. Moffat, "'The Myth and the Word'," *CFL, 3rd Ser.,* 13 (1910) 155-159.

*William Frederic Badè, "The Iron-Taboo of the Hebrews," *PAPA* 43 (1911) lx.

*Wilfred H. Schoff, "Tammuz, Pan and Christ. Notes on a Typical Case of Myth-Transference and Development," *OC* 26 (1912) 513-532.

Joseph Jacobs, "Legends of the Jew,"*JQR, N.S.,* 4 (1913-14) 499-504.

*Wilfred Schoff, "Tammuz, Pan and Christ. Further Notes on a Typical Case of Myth-Transference," *OC* 27 (1913) 449-460.

Karl Johan Karlson, "Psychoanalysis and Mythology," *AJRPE* 7 (1914-15) 137-213.

*[Julian] Morgenstern, "On Gilgames-Epic XI, 274-320. A Contribution to the Study of the Role of the Serpent in Semitic Mythology," *ZA* 29 (1914-15) 284-300.

Solomon T. Hurwitz, "Pygmy-Legends in Jewish Literature," *JQR, N.S.,* 6 (1915-16) 339-358.

L. R. Farnell, "The Value and the Methods of Mythological Study," *PBA* 9 (1919-20) 37-51.

*Armand Kaminka, "The Origin of the Ashmedai Legend in the Babylonian Talmud," *JQR, N.S.,* 13 (1922-23) 221-224.

Jacob Singer, "Taboo in the Hebrew Scriptures," *OC* 40 (1926) 443-448.

Alexander H. Krappe, "Acca Larentia," *AJA* 46 (1942) 490-499.

*Solomon Gandz, "The Zodiacal Light in Semitic Mythology," *PAAJR* 13 (1943) 1-39.

Samuel Krauss, "Jewish Giants in the Gentile Folklore," *JQR, N.S.,* 38 (1947-48) 135-149.

*Yehezkel Kaufmann, "The Bible and Mythological Polytheism," *JBL* 70 (1951) 179-197.

*John L. McKenzie, "The Hebrew Attitude towards Mythological Polytheism," *CBQ* 14 (1952) 323-335.

*S. B. Frost, "Eschatology and Myth," *VT* 2 (1952) 70-80.

*Luisa Banti, "Myth in Pre-Classical Art," *AJA* 58 (1954) 307-310.

*W[illiam] F[oxwell] Albright, "Dwarf-Craftsmen in the Keret Epic and Elsewhere in North-West Semitic Mythology," *IEJ* 4 (1954) 1-4.

Margaret A. Murray, "Folklore in History," *Folk* 66 (1955) 257-266.

S. H. Hooke, "Omens—Ancient and Modern," *Folk* 66 (1955) 330-339.

E. O. James, "The Nature and Function of Myth," *Folk* 68 (1957) 474-482.

*J. L. Benson, "The Griffin in the Minoan-Mycenaean World," *AJA* 63 (1959) 186.

*Tariq Madhloum, "More Notes on the Near Eastern Griffin," *Sumer* 20 (1964) 57-62.

*Patrick D. Miller Jr., "Fire in the Mythology of Canaan and Israel," *CBQ* 27 (1965) 256-261.

§461 *3.2.13.1 Studies in Folklore, Mythology, Demythology and the Old Testament*

*Anonymous, "Mythology and Revelation," *CRB* 21 (1856) 603-611.

*C. H., "Ancient Atheism and Superstition," *JSL, 4th Ser.,* 1 (1862) 24-55.

C. M. Cady, "The Use of Mythic Elements in the Old Testament," *BW* 6 (1895) 115-120, 194-202.

William Hayes Ward, "Light on Scriptural Texts from Recent Discoveries. Ancient Myths in the Hebrew Scriptures," *HR* 30 (1895) 315-317.

P. Gardner, "The Origins of Myth," *OSHTP* (1895-96) 5-17.

*T. K. Cheyne, "Hebrew Mythological Terms," *ET* 8 (1896-97) 525-526.

[Paul Carus], "The Fairy-Tale Element in the Bible," *Monist* 11 (1900-01) 405-447, 500-535.

A[ndrew] C. Zenos, Charles F. Kent, William G. Ballantine, George A. Barton, Benjamin W. Bacon, William H. Ryder, Sylvester Burnham, Henry S. Nash, and John E. McFadyen, "Myth and Fiction as Employed in the Bible. A Symposium," *BW* 22 (1903) 342-357.

*W. O. E. Oesterley, "Dioscurism in the Old Testament," *ET* 17 (1905-06) 477.

Margaret D. Gibson, "Folk-lore in the Old Testament," *ET* 19 (1907-08) 140-141. *(Review)*

D. S. Margoliouth, "Folklore in the Old Testament," *Exp, 7th Ser.*, 5 (1908) 304-314.

*E. Walter Maunder, "Jeremias and Astral-Mythology in the Old Testament," *LQHR* 118 (1912) 220-237. *(Review)*

Arthur C. Headlam, "Folk-lore in the Old Testament," *CQR* 88 (1919) 139-144. *(Review)*

M. Gaster, "Folk-lore in the Old Testament," *Folk* 30 (1919) 71-76. *(Review)*

W. O. E. Oesterley, "Old Testament Folk-Lore," *ERCJ* 229 (1919) 173-187. *(Review)*

*Herbert H. Gowen, "The Folk Lore of the Old Testament," *ATR* 3 (1920-21) 310-327.

Th. Graebner, "Little Journeys in the Higher Anticriticism. I. The Myth Hypothesis," *TM* 1 (1921) 297-303, 321-329, 359-365.

W. J. Perry, "An Interpretation of Old Testament Traditions," *JMUEOS* #10 (1923) 35-51.

H. F. B. Compston, "Old Testament Folk-lore and Fact," *CQR* 97 (1923-24) 255-273.

H. Hamann, "'Folk-lore in the Old Testament'," *AusTR* 9 (1938) 27-28.

*J. W. Jack, "Recent Biblical Archaeology," *ET* 52 (1940-41) 454-458. [Old Testament Mythology, pp. 457-458]

Herbert Gordon May, "Pattern and Myth in the Old Testament," *JR* 21 (1941) 285-299.

Evelyn W. Hippisley, "Some Examples of Folklore in the Old Testament," *Folk* 55&56 (1944-45) 16-21.

*Julian Morgenstern, "The Divine Triad in Biblical Mythology," *JBL* 64 (1945) 15-37.

*Philip E. Hughes, "Miracle and Myth," *EQ* 20 (1948) 184-195.

Cuthbert Lattey, "Old Testament Mysticism," *CQR* 154 (1953) 315-321.

E. L. Allen, "On Demythologizing the Old Testament," *JAAR* 22 (1954) 236-241.

Theodor H. Gaster, "Myth and Story," *Numen* 1 (1954) 184-212.

James Stewart, "Scripture and the Functions of Myth," *HJ* 54 (1955-56) 131-138.

*J. Stafford Wright, "The Place of Myth in the Interpretation of the Bible," *JTVI* 88 (1956) 17-30, 151-152. [(Discussion, pp. 145-149.) (Communications by H. L. Ellison, p. 149; B. B. Knopp, pp. 149-151)]

G. Henton Davies, "An Approach to the Problem of Old Testament Mythology," *PEQ* 88 (1956) 83-91.

G. R. Driver, "Mythical monsters in the Old Testament," *SOOG* 1 (1956) 234-249.

John L. McKenzie, "Myth and the Old Testament," *CBQ* 21 (1959) 265-282.

J. James Barr, "The Meaning of 'Mythology' in Relation to the Old Testament," *VT* 9 (1959) 1-10.

Lawrence E. Toombs, "The Formation of Myth Patterns in the Old Testament," *JAAR* 29 (1961) 108-112.

Iris V. Cully, "Biblical Mythology and Christian Education," *JAAR* 31 (1963) 40-46. [Myth in the Old Testament, pp. 41-43]

Edmund Hill, "Remythologising: The Key to Scripture," *Scrip* 16 (1964) 65-75.

*Patrick D. Miller Jr., "Fire in the Mythology of Canaan and Israel," *CBQ* 27 (1965) 256-261.

Klaus Rosenthal, "Myth and Symbol," *SJT* 18 (1965) 411-434.

Albert Strobel, "Myth in the Old Testament," *TD* 14 (1966) 218-222.

Avery Dulles, "Symbol, Myth, and Biblical Revelation," *ThSt* 27 (1966) 1-26. [Myth and the Old Testament, p. 15-17]

*Mircea Eliade, "Cosmic Myth and 'Sacred History'," *RS* 2 (1966-67) 171-184.

Donald Broadribb, "An Analytical Approach to Biblical Mythology," *Mwa-M* #7 (1967) 31-40.

*John Van Seters, "History and Myth in Biblical Interpretation," *ANQ, N.S.*, 8 (1967-68) 154-162.

*Warren Kliewer, "The Daughters of Lot: Legend and Fabliau," *IR* 25 (1968) #1, 13-28.

Trude Weiss-Rosmarin, "Demythologizing the Hebrew Bible," *CJ* 23 (1968-69) #4, 51-59.

D. Broadribb, "Myth and Development," *Abr-N* 8 (1969) 69-84.

*[Samuel] E. Loewenstamm, "The Ugaritic Myth of the Sea and its Biblical Counterparts," *EI* 9 (1969) 136. *[English Summary]*

*Mary K. Wakeman, "The Biblical Earth Monster in the Cosmogonic Combat Myth," *JBL* 88 (1969) 313-320.

*Jefim Schirmann, "The Battle Between Behemoth and Leviathan According to an Ancient Hebrew *Piyyuṭ*," *PIASH* 4 (1969-70) 327-369.

§462 *3.2.13.1.1 The Lilith Legend*

*(   ) Y., "Traditions of the East-From Herder," *CTPR, N.S.*, 2 (1840) 208-210. [Lilis*[sic]* pp. 208-209]

*P. A. Nordell, "Old Testament Word Studies: 9. Angels, Demons, etc.," *ONTS* 8 (1888-89) 341-345. [lîlîth *night monster*, p.345]

James A. Montgomery, "The Lilith Legend," *MJ* 4 (1913) 62-65.

Maximilian Rudwin, "The Legend of Lilith," *OC* 44 (1930) 513-521.

*Theodor H. Gaster, "A Canaanite Magical Text," *Or, N.S.*, 11 (1942) 41-79. [Lilith, p. 50]

*G. R. Driver, "Lilith: *Heb.* לילית *'goat-sucker, night jar'* (Is. xxxiv. 14).," *PEQ* 91 (1959) 55-57.

*Susan Lee Sherman and John Briggs Curtis, "Divine-Human Conflicts in the Old Testament," *JNES* 28 (1969) 231-242. [Lilith, pp. 234-235]

§463 *3.2.14 Studies in Comparative Religion*

*Lyman Coleman, "The Festivals of the Christian Church compared with those of other Ancient Forms of Religion," *BS* 4 (1847) 650-671. [Relation of the Festivals of the Christian church to those of the Jews, pp. 658-662; Analogy between the festivals of the Christian church and of Pagan nations, pp. 662-667]

*John Kitto, "On Sacred Trees," *JSL, 1st Ser.,* 1 (1848) 290-295. *[Ref.: Tree of Life and Tree of Good and Evil]*

*Edward Wilton, "A Parallel Between David and Titus Manilus Torquatus," *JSL, 1st Ser.,* 4 (1849) 374-378.

Asahel Abbot, "Vestiges of a Redeemer in the Religions of the Ancient World," *BRCR, 3rd Ser.,* 6 (1850) 362-375.

P. B. Spear, "The Genius of Hebrew and of Roman Learning," *BS* 11 (1854) 527-568. [I. Hebrew and Roman Learning treated Comparatively with the Greek; II. Hebrew and Roman Learning treated Comparatively with each other]

J. F. C., "Comparative Theology of Heathen Religions," *CE* 62 (1857) 183-199. *(Review)*

*T. S. K[ing], "India in Greece," *UQGR* 9 (1857) 221-241. *(Review)*

E. Burgess, "Sacred Traditions in the East," *BS* 15 (1858) 845-876.

H. C. Barlow, "Sacred Trees," *JSL, 4th Ser.,* 1 (1862) 273-292.

E. Burgess, "Oriental Sacred Traditions," *JSL, 4th Ser.,* 4 (1863-64) 302-327.

†Anonymous, "Islam," *QRL* 127 (1869) 293-353. *(Review)*

Max Müller, "A Chapter of Accidents in Comparative Theology," *ContR* 14 (1870) 1-19.

J. B. Hague, "Homer and the Old Testament," *BQ* 6 (1872) 443-468.

A. M. Fairbairn, "The Belief in Immortality. An Essay in Comparative History of Religious Thought," *ContR* 20 (1872) 27-55. *[Part I]*

A. M. Fairbairn, "The Belief in Immortality. An Essay in Comparative History of Religious Thought, Part II. The Belief in Greece," *ContR* 20 (1872) 370-402.

F. R. Conder, "The Central Ideas of Semitic and Aryan Faith," *TRL* 13 (1876) 104-119.

*B. W. Savile, "Heathen Cosmogonies Compared with Hebrew," *JTVI* 10 (1876-77) 251-301. (Discussion, pp. 301-315)

William Simpson, "The Tenno-Sama, or Mikoshi; Ark-Shrines of Japan," *SBAT* 5 (1876-77) 550-554.

Keningale Cook, "An Aryan Ancestor," *DUM* 92 (1878) 1-13, 177-191.

M. Eells, "Traditions of the 'Deluge' Among the Tribes of the North-west," *AAOJ* 1 (1878-79) 70-72.

Stephen D. Peet, "The Bible Narrative and Heathen Traditions. *The Traces of the Facts mentioned in the Traditions of all Nations,*" *AAOJ* 1 (1878-79) 150-160.

G. D. B. Pepper, "God and the Bibles," *BQR* 1 (1879) 323-331.

*A. G. Laurie, "The Persian, Jewish and Christian Resurrections," *UQGR, N.S.,* 16 (1879) 257-271.

*A. G. Laurie, "The Jewish and Persian Messiahs," *UQGR, N.S.,* 16 (1879) 359-371.

*François Lenormant, "Ararat and 'Eden. A Biblical Study," *ContR* 40 (1881) 453-478. *[Marked as "continued" but was not]*

William D. Whitney, "On the So-Called Science of Religion," *PRev* 57 (1881) Part 1, 429-452.

*F. G. Fleay, "On the Interpretation of the Early Mythologies of Greece and India," *AAOJ* 5 (1883) 1-17.

*Justin A. Smith, "Studies in Archaeology and Comparative Religion," *ONTS* 3 (1883-84) 295-304, 340, 346, 381-387.

*Anonymous, "The Samson-Saga and the Myth of Herakles," *WR* 121 (1884) 305-328. *(Review)*

*Talbot W. Chambers, "Sun Images and the Sun of Righteousness," *ONTS* 5 (1884-85) 193-203.

Justin A. Smith, "Incantations in Historical Religions," *ONTS* 5 (1884-85) 300-303.

Justin A. Smith, "The Future Life in Historical Religions," *ONTS* 5 (1884-85) 338-341.

Justin A. Smith, "Pagan Wisdom; Christian Inspiration," *ONTS* 5 (1884-85) 402-407.

*Justin A. Smith, "Studies in Archaeology and Comparative Religion: IX. The Literature of Paganism," *ONTS* 5 (1885-86) 16-24.

*Justin A. Smith, "Studies in Archaeology and Comparative Religion: X. Pagan Literature in Relation to Pagan Faith," *ONTS* 5 (1885-86) 75-82.

*Justin A. Smith, "Studies in Archaeology and Comparative Religion: XI. The Idea of Evil, as to Origin," *ONTS* 5 (1885-86) 128-135.

*Justin A. Smith, "Studies in Archaeology and Comparative Religion: XII. The Idea of Evil, as to Nature," *ONTS* 5 (1885-86) 171-177.

*Justin A. Smith, "Studies in Archaeology and Comparative Religion: XIII. The Idea of Redemption," *ONTS* 5 (1885-86) 228-233, 267-273.

Alexander Wilder, "Side-Lights," *HR* 12 (1886) 400-405, 482-486.

T. Powell, "A Samoan Tradition of Creation and the Deluge," *JTVI* 20 (1886-87) 147-163, 172-175. (Discussion, pp. 163-171)

Stephen D. Peet, "Animal worship and sun worship in the East and the West compared," *JAOS* 13 (1889) cclxx-cclxxiv.

Terrien de Lacouperie, "The Deluge-Tradition and its Remains in Ancient China," *BOR* 4 (1889-90) 15-24, 49-56, 79-88, 102-111.

Joseph Jacobs, "Recent Research in Comparative Religions," *Folk* 1 (1890) 384-397. *(Review)*

K. Kohler, "Comparative studies in Semitic mythology and religion," *JAOS* 14 (1890) clxvi-clxvii.

Anonymous, "The Unknown God," *CQR* 31 (1890-91) 180-194. *(Review)*

*C. J. Ball, "The First Three of the Five Autocrats. *(Wu-Ti),*" SBAP 13 (1890-91) 77-78. *[Akkadian Mythology]*

*J. F. Hogan, "The Sacrifice of Iphigenia," *IER, 3rd Ser.,* 12 (1891) 1070-1086.

*D. G. Loyon, "Judaism and Christianity," *ONTS* 12 (1891) 367-373. *(Review)*

†Anonymous, "The Golden Bough. A Study in Comparative Religion," *QRL* 172 (1891) 191-208. *(Review)*

*A. H. Huizinga, "Babylonian *versus* Hebrew Account of Creation," *PQ* 6 (1892) 385-398.

*W. St. Chad Boscawen, "Some Elements in the Babylonian Religion and Their Comparative Relationship to Judaism," *ET* 4 (1892-93) 203-209.

M. Adler, "Notes and Discussion. Was Homer Acquainted with the Bible?" *JQR* 5 (1892-93) 170-174.

*C. Taylor, "The Two Ways in Hermes and Xenophon," *JP* 21 (1892-93) 243-258.

*Moncure D. Conway, "Mothers and Sons of Gods," *OC* 7 (1893) 3671-3672, 3687-3688, 3703-3705.

*C. J. Ball, "Israel and Babylon," *SBAP* 16 (1893-94) 188-200. [3. Purification of Date Palms, pp. 193-195]

James Deans, "The Hidery Story of Creation," *AAOJ* 17 (1895) 61-67.

Stephen D. Peet, "The Story of the Creation Among the American Aborigines as Proof of Prehistoric Contact," *AAOJ* 17 (1895) 127-150.

*W. St. C[had] Boscawen, "The Creative Power of the Divine Word and Name," *BOR* 8 (1895-1900) 271-276.

*A. Cowley, "Samaritan Literature and Religion," *JQR* 8 (1895-96) 562-575.

C. G. Montefiore, "Unitarianism and Judaism in Their Relation to Each Other," *JQR* 9 (1896-97) 240-253.

Charles F. Aiken, "The Avesta and the Bible," *CUB* 3 (1897) 243-291.

*J. F. Hewitt, "The History of the Week as a Guide to Historic Chronology," *WR* 148 (1897) 8-22, 126-149, 237-250. [Part I.—The Week of the Pole-star Worshippers; Part II—The Week of the Moon Worshippers; Part III—The Week of the Sun-Worshippers]

P. De Roo, "The Bible Among the Indians Before the Discovery of America," *AER* 19 (1898) 232-259.

*Moncure D. Conway, "Solomonic Literature," *OC* 12 (1898) 385-410. [Wisdom in the Book of Proverbs, and the Avesta, pp. 390-410]

*Paul Carus, "Yahveh and Manitou," *Monist* 9 (1898-99) 382-415.

*Lawrence [H.] Mills, "The Bible, the Avesta, and the Inscriptions," *IAQR, 3rd Ser.,* 11 (1901) 315-321.

Crawford H. Toy, "Creator gods," *JAOS* 23 (1902) 29-37.

Alberta Field, "The Legend of Adam's Bridge," *AAOJ* 25 (1903) 39-40.

*W. Deans, "Tree-Worship and Similar Practices in China," *ET* 15 (1903-04) 384.

Anonymous, "Peruvian Story of the Deluge," *AAOJ* 26 (1904) 342-344.

Frederick Bliss*[sic]*, "Sophistry on the Subject of Comparative Religions," *AAOJ* 26 (1904) 370-373.

Samuel Ives Curtiss, "Survivals of Ancient Semitic Religion in Syrian Centres of Moslem and Christian Influence," *AJA* 8 (1904) 77-78.

*T[heophilus] G. P[inches], "Talmudische und Midraschische Parallelen zum Bablonischen Weltschöpfungsepos," *JRAS* (1904) 369-370. *[English Text]*

*Stephen D. Peet, "Ancient Alphabets and Sacred Books," *AAOJ* 27 (1905) 265-280.

*Melvin Grove Kyle, "New Light from Egypt on the Sacrifices," *BS* 62 (1905) 323-336.

*Melvin Grove Kyle, "New Light from Egypt on the Sacrifices," *CFL, 3rd Ser.,* 3 (1905) 356-364.

H. D. Griswold, "The Messiah of Qādiān," *JTVI* 37 (1905) 241-253. (Discussion, pp. 253-258)

*Anonymous, "The Massai and Higher Criticism," *MR* 87 (1905) 810-815.

*†[I. Schwab], "'The Kaddish'," *YCCAR* 15 (1905) 205-222. [II. The Kaddish and the Lord's Prayer, pp. 213-220]

George C. Cameron, "The Masi and Their Primitive Traditions," *ET* 17 (1905-06) 219-224, 254-258, 315-319. [I. The Creation; II. The Fall; III. The Permission to Eat Flesh; IV. The Flood; V. Abraham, Isaac, and Jacob; VI. Moses; VII. The Ten Commandments]

Albert R. Steggall, "The Masai and Their Traditions," *ET* 17 (1905-06) 429.

Leon Arpee, "The Reed," *ET* 18 (1906-07) 46-47. *[Armenian Creation Myth/Zulu Myth]*

*T. H. Weir, "Higher Criticism and the Korán," *ContR* 91 (1907) 388-398.

James Moffatt, "Some Parallels from Plautus," *ET* 19 (1907-08) 42-43.

*Wilfrid J. Moulton, "The Religion of the Old Testament in the Framework of the Other Ancient Oriental Religions," *ET* 19 (1907-08) 252-254. *(Review)*

*Stephen D. Peet, "The Cosmogony of the Bible Compared with that of the Ancient Pagans," *AAOJ* 30 (1908) 145-160.

*Joseph Offord, "Book of the Dead compared with the Bible," *AAOJ* 30 (1908) 276-278.

G. F. Hill, "Adonis, Baal, and Astarte," *CQR* 66 (1908) 118-141. *(Review)*

T. Holbein Hendley, "Resemblances between Indian and Jewish Ideas and Customs," *JTVI* 40 (1908) 77-101. (Discussion, pp. 101-103)

*O. Neufchotz de Jassy, "The Mythological Hebrew Terms Explained by the Sanskrit. *An Essay in Comparative Philology and Mythology,*" *Monist* 18 (1908) 126-138. [Editorial introduction, p. 126; Editorial Postscript, pp. 138-140; Rejoinder, pp. 140-142]

Berthold Laufer, "The Jonah Legend in India," *Monist* 18 (1908) 576-578.

S. S. Doran, "The Reed," *ET* 20 (1908-09) 45. *[African Creation Stories]*

*G. A. Grierson, "The Monotheistic Religion of Ancient India and its Descendant, the Modern Hindu Doctrine of Faith," *IAQR, 3rd Ser.,* 28 (1909) 115-126.

†Louis H. Jordan, "Survey of Recent Literature on Comparative Religion," *RTP* 5 (1909-10) 269-286, 333-353.

J. Torrend, "Likenesses of Moses' Story in the Central African Folk-Lore," *Anthro* 5 (1910) 54-70.

C. C. Martindale, "A Note on Comparative Religion," *DR* 147 (1910) 270-284. *(Review)*

Leon Arpee, "The Reed," *ET* 22 (1910-11) 282. *[Babylonian Creation Compared with African]*

Israel Friedlaender, "Jewish-Arabic Studies," *JQR, N.S.,* 1 (1910-11) 183-215. [I. Shiitic Elements in Jewish Sectarianism]

H. Hirschfeld, "Some notes on 'Jewish Arabic Studies'," *JQR, N.S.,* 1 (1910-11) 447-448.

Israel Friedlaender, "A Reply," *JQR, N.S.,* 1 (1910-11) 449-450.

*W. F. Lofthouse, "Kernel and Husk in the Old Testament Stories," *Exp, 8th Ser.,* 1 (1911) 97-117.

Thomas Patrick Hughes, "The Bibles of the World," *HR* 62 (1911) 138-139.

Edward W. Clark, "The Belief of the Ancient Egyptians, Etruscans, and Greeks in the Future World as Shown by their Stelae, Burial Jars and Grave Reliefs," *RP* 10 (1911) 123-132, 133-143, 203-212.

Israel Friedlaender, "Jewish-Arabic Studies," *JQR, N.S.,* 2 (1911-12) 481-516. [I. Shiitic Elements in Jewish Sectarianism, 1. The Raja Doctrine, 2. Docetism]

Wakeman Ryno, "Comparative Mythology," *AAOJ* 34 (1912) 41-46.

*Wilfred Schoff, "Tammuz, Pan and Christ. Notes on a Typical Case of Myth-Transference and Development," *OC* 26 (1912) 513-532.

*W. Sherwood Fox, "Old Testament Parallels to *Tabellae Defixionum*," *PAPA* 43 (1912) xxv-xxvi.

*W[illia]m J. Hinke, "The Messianic Idea in Ancient Religions," *ASRec* 8 (1912-13) 159-184.

*H. Townsend, "Job and Buddha," *ET* 24 (1912-13) 499-501.

Israel Friedlaender, "Jewish-Arabic Studies," *JQR, N.S.,* 3 (1912-13) 235-300. [I. Shiitic Elements in Jewish Sectarianism, 3. The One True Prophet, 4. Successive Incarnation, 5. Tafwīḍ, 6. Prophet and Messiah, 7. The Dāʿī, 8. Succession, 9. Anointment, 10. Inspiration, 11. Social Position, 12 Jihād, 13. Tabdīl, 14 Prohibition of Meat, 15. Number of Prayers]

*C. Ryder Smith, "Some Indian Parallels to Hebrew Cult," *JTS* 14 (1912-13) 424-432.

*W. Sherwood Fox, "Old Testament Parallels to Tabellae Defixionum," *AJA* 17 (1913) 84.

*Wilfred H. Schoff, "Tammuz, Pan and Christ. Further Notes on a Typical Case of Myth-Transference," *OC* 27 (1913) 449-460.

Morris Jastrow Jr., "Babylonian, Etruscan and Chinese Divination," *RP* 12 (1913) 13-16.

*W. Sherwood Fox, "Old Testament Parallels to 'Tabellae Defixionum'," *AJSL* 30 (1913-14) 111-124.

W. Arthur Cornaby, "Chinese Sidelights Upon Scripture Passages, I.," *ET* 25 (1913-14) 177-179.

S. B. Slack, "Had any Roman and Semitic Legends a Common Origin?" *AJA* 18 (1914) 75.

W. Arthur Cornaby, "Chinese Sidelights Upon Scripture Passages, II.," *ET* 26 (1914-15) 18-20. [The Portal of Scriptures; The Number Seven; Metaphor and Myth; Literary Parallelism]

W. Arthur Cornaby, "Chinese Sidelights Upon Scripture Passages, III.," *ET* 26 (1914-15) 60-63. [Vestiges of Paradise; The Fall of Man; Origin of Religion]

W. Arthur Cornaby, "Chinese Sidelights Upon Scripture Passages, IV.," *ET* 26 (1914-15) 369-372. [Patriarchal Childhood; Worship]

Dyson Hague, "The Ethnic Scriptures—A Friendly Critique," *HR* 68 (1914) 168-169. [Response by George W. Gilmore, p. 169]

*John S. Banks, "The Idea of God in Israel and Babylon," *LQHR* 122 (1914) 129-131.

Herbert H. Gowen, "A Qoheleth of the Far East," *OC* 28 (1914) 257-272.

Clifford Herschel Moore, "The Ethical Value of Oriental Religions Under the Roman Empire," *HTR* 8 (1915) 166-181.

*George A. Barton, "Tammuz and Osiris," *JAOS* 35 (1915) 213-223.

Lewis R. Farnell, "The Golden Bough," *QRL* 223 (1915) 464-484. *(Review)*

W. Arthur Cornaby, "Chinese Sidelights Upon Scripture Passages V," *ET* 27 (1915-16) 493-494. [Blood-Covenant; Betrothal Covenant]

Albert J. Carnoy, "Iranian Views of Origins in connection with Similar Babylonian Beliefs," *JAOS* 36 (1916) 300-320.

*James George Frazer, "Ancient Stories of a Great Flood. *The Huxley Memorial Lecture for* 1916," *JRAI* 46 (1916) 231-283.

Samuel Daiches, "Babylonian Dog-Omens and some Talmudic and Later Jewish Parallels," *SBAP* 39 (1917) 168-171.

*(Miss) C. Garlick, "Note on the Sacred Tree in Mesopotamia," *SBAP* 40 (1918) 111-112.

F. B. Jevons, "The Primitive Theory of Sacrifice," *ICMM* 15 (1918-19) 190-200.

George W. Gilmore, "Hebrew Tradition and Egyptian and Babylonian Myths," *HR* 78 (1919) 277-279. *(Review)*

R. R. Marett, "The Interpretation of Survivals," *QRL* 231 (1919) 445-461. *(Review)*

Herbert H. Gowen, "The Old Testament and Comparative Religion," *ACM* 6 (1919-20) 277-286.

Cornelia Steketee Hulst, "Homer and the Prophets or Homer and Now," *OC* 35 (1921) 1-9, 65-82, 744-766; 36 (1922) 217-229, 282-299.

*Sidney Smith, "The Relation of Marduk, Ashur, and Osiris," *JEA* 8 (1922) 41-44.

A. S. Geden, "Value and Purpose of the Study of Comparative Religion," *JTVI* 55 (1923) 98-112, 118 [(Discussion, pp. 112-117) (Communications by Sidney Collet, p. 117; J. J. B. Coles, p. 117)]

A[llen] H[oward] Godbey, "Blood: The Cult of the Dead," *MQR, 3rd Ser.,* 49 (1923) 704-728.

*Henry S. Gehman, "A Jonah-Parallel in Buddhism," *RChR, 5th Ser.,* 2 (1923) 369-371.

*Samuel A. B. Mercer, "Old Testament and Other Oriental Wisdom," *ATR* 6 (1923-24) 118-123.

*Maurice A. Canney, "The Goat-song," *ZAW* 42 (1924) 145-148.

John A. Maynard, "Method in the Study of Religious Ethnology," *ATR* 7 (1924-25) 469-476.

*Hugo Gressmann, "The Mysteries of Adonis and the Feast of Tabernacles," *Exp, 9th Ser.,* 3 (1925) 416-432.

J[ohn] A. Maynard, "Judaism and Mazdayasna: A Study in Dissimilarities," *JBL* 44 (1925) 163-170.

Paul Haupt, "Circe and Istar," *BAVSS* 10 (1927) Heft 2, 107-113.

George A. Barton, "A Comparison of Some Features of Hebrew and Babylonian Ritual," *JBL* 46 (1927) 79-89.

Dudley Joseph Whitney, "The Polynesian Creation Story," *CFL, 3rd Ser.,* 35 (1929) 130-134.

William R. Arnold, "The Relation of Primitive Christianity to Jewish Thought and Teaching," *HTR* 23 (1930) 161-179.

*G. A. Wainwright, "The Relationship of Amūn to Zeus, and his Connexion with Meteorites," *JEA* 16 (1930) 35-38.

Andrew Burgess, "The African and Arabian Influences Upon the Primitive Religious Beliefs of the Malagasy People," *TF* 4 (1932) 125-158, 221-222.

Alexander Haggerty Krappe, "Trophonios and Agamedes," *AfRW* 30 (1933) 228-241.

N. Schmidt, "Problems Concerning the Origin of Some of the Great Oriental Religions," *JAOS* 53 (1933) 191-214.

*A. H. Sayce, "The Astarte Papyrus and the Legend of the Sea," *JEA* 19 (1933) 56-59.

*W[illiam] F[oxwell] Albright and P. E. Dumont, "A Parallel between Indic and Babylonian Sacrificial Ritual," *JAOS* 54 (1934) 107-128.

James Moffatt, "The Sacred Book in Religion," *JBL* 53 (1934) 1-12.

W. N. Delevingne, "The Bible and the Bhagavadgitā," *JTVI* 66 (1934) 139-155, 158-159. (Discussion, pp. 155-158)

H. Wheeler Robinson, "History and Revelation," *BQL* 7 (1934-35) 1-13.

*Samuel A. B. Mercer, "Osiris and Marduk," *EgR* 3 (1935) 158-159.

*Harry Austryn Wolfson, "The Internal Senses in Latin, Arabic, and Hebrew Philosophic Texts," *HTR* 28 (1935) 69-133.

*Elizabeth G. K. Hewat, "Hebrew and Chinese Wisdom: A Comparative Study of the Book of Proverbs and the Analects of Confucius," *IRM* 24 (1935) 506-514.

Culbert G. Rutenber, "Creation Stories of Polynesia," *CRP* 6 (1937) 107-118.

*James A. Montgomery, "The Highest, Heaven, Aeon, Time, etc., in Semitic Religion," *HTR* 31 (1938) 143-150.

*H[enry] S. Gehman, "A Jonah and a David-Uriah Parallel in Buddhist Literature," *JBL* 57 (1938) ix.

*Raphael Patai, "The 'Control of Rain' in Ancient Palestine. A Study in Comparative Religion," *HUCA* 14 (1939) 251-286.

*J. Philip Hyatt, "The Deity Bethel and the Old Testament," *JAOS* 59 (1939) 81-98.

Fred V. Winnett, "Primitive Arabian and Semitic Religion," *RR* 4 (1939-40) 282-285.

Moses Hadas, "Livy as Scripture," *AJP* 61 (1940) 445-456.

W[illiam] F[oxwell] Albright, "The Near East and Israel," *JBL* 59 (1940) 85-110.

Herman Hailperin, "Saadia's Relation to Islamic and Christian Thought," *HJud* 4 (1942) 1-15.

Lev Gillet, "'Dialogue with Trypho'," *IRM* 31 (1942) 172-179.

Alfred E. Garvie, "Judaism and Christianity," *IRM* 32 (1943) 388-395.

J. Minto Robertson, "Aeschylus and the Messianic Idea. A Re-reading of 'Prometheus Bound'," *LQHR* 168 (1943) 33-41.

T[heodor] H. Gaster, "The Canaanite Story of Aqhart and the Myth of Orion," *JBL* 63 (1944) v.

*Thomas Dann Heald, "The Earlier Form of the Genesis Stories of the Beginning," *Folk* 55&56 (1944-45) 87-103.

M. E. L. Mallowan, "The Intellectual Adventure of Ancient Man," *Antiq* 21 (1947) 116-121. *(Review)*

Martin P. Nilsson, "Letter to Professor Arthur D. Nock on Some Fundamental Concepts in the Science of Religion," *HTR* 47 (1949) 71-107.

John Gray, "Cultic Affinities Between Israel and Ras Shamra," *ZAW* 62 (1949-50) 207-220.

*Rudolph Arbesmann, "Fasting and Prophecy in Pagan and Christian Antiquity," *Tr* 7 (1949-51) 1-71.

Hildegard Lewy, "Origin and Significance of the Mâgên Dâwîd: A Comparative Study in the Ancient Religions of Jerusalem and Mecca," *ArOr* 18 (1950) Part 3, 330-365.

Chester J. Droog, "Hebrew Religion and Canaanite Neighbors," *RefR* 4 (1950-51) #4, 7-10.

Carlton C. Allen, "Religions and Their Sources," *TUSR* 2 (1951-52) 17-27.

A. K. Reischauer, "Freedom and Authority in Eastern Faiths," *USQR* 7 (1951-52) #3, 23-31.

Monford Harris, "Two Ways: Halakah and Charisma," *Jud* 1 (1952) 69-79.

*E. R. Lacheman, "The Use of Comparative Religion, Literature and Archaeology in O.T. Studies," *JBL* 72 (1953) xvii.

*A. Marmorstein, "Greek Poet and Hebrew Prophet," *LQHR* 178 (1953) 42-44.

Paul Weiss, "Greek, Hebrew and Christian," *Jud* 4 (1955) 116-123.

S. Davis, "Divining Bowls: Their Uses and Origins—Some African Examples, and Parallels from the Ancient World," *Man* 55 (1955) #143.

R. Pettazzoni, "On the attributes of God," *Numen* 2 (1955) 1-27.

Howard M. Teeple, "Early Jewish-Christian Writing," *JAAR* 25 (1957) 301-305.

E. Dora Earthy, "A probable creation- and flood-myth in Portuguese East Africa," *Numen* 4 (1957) 232-234.

John Drewett, "The Bible and Other Religions," *MC, N.S.,* 1 (1957-58) 32-39.

*T. Worden, "Questions and Answers. Similarities with Pagan Religions. What attitude ought we to adopt to the parallels so frequently adduced from extra-biblical sources, in support of a denial that the Bible is the revealed word of God?" *Scrip* 10 (1958) 58-60.

Justus M. van der Kroef, "Javanese Messianic Expectations: their Origin and Cultural Context," *CSSH* 1 (1958-59) 299-323.

W. H. Hudspeth, "A Creation Story of the A-Hsi," *Folk* 70 (1959) 398-403.

Werner Vycichl, "Ancient Egyptian *Ka* and *Ba* in Africa," *Kush* 8 (1959) 282-284.

*William F[oxwell] Albright, "Archaeology and Religion," *OC* 9 (1959) 107-124. [I. The Scientific Study of Archaeology; II. The Scientific Study of Religion; III. Judaeo-Christianity in the Light of Archaeology; IV. Archaeology, History, and Religion; V. Theism and Religious Humanism in the Light of History]

E. A. Worms, "The Aboriginal Concept of the Soul," *ACR* 37 (1960) 100-115.

W. H. Hudspeth, "The A-Hsi Story of the Deluge," *Folk* 71 (1960) 109-118.

*C. S. Mann, "Sacral Kingship—An Ashanti Footnote," *JSS* 5 (1960) 378-387.

*William G. Braude, "The Church Fathers and the Synagogue," *Jud* 9 (1960) 112-119.

John Layard, "Œdipus and Job in West African Religion," *Man* 60 (1960) #76.

Toyozo W. Nakarai, "Shintoism and Hebraism," *SQ/E* 21 (1960) 469-473.

*Ruth Amiran, "Myths of the Creation of Man and the Jericho Statues," *BASOR* #167 (1962) 23-25.

*Robley Edward Whitson, "The Concept of Origins," *TFUQ* 37 (1962) 245-268.

Isma'il Ragi al Faruqi, "A Comparison of the Islamic and Christian Approaches to Hebrew Scripture," *JAAR* 31 (1963) 283-293.

*U. Milo Kaufmann, "Expostulation with the Divine. *Contrasting Attitudes in Greek and Hebrew Piety,*" *Interp* 18 (1964) 171-182.

*Edwin M. Yamauchi, "Tammuz and the Bible," *JBL* 84 (1965) 283-290.

*Song Nai Rhee, "'Fear God' and 'Honor Your Father and Mother'. Two Injunctions in the Book of Proverbs and the Confucian Classics," *SQ/E* 26 (1965) 207-214.

Elmer G. Suhr, "Krishna and Mithra as Messiahs," *Folk* 77 (1966) 205-221.

*W. Den Boer, "Graeco-Roman Historiography and its Relation to Biblical and Modern Thinking," *H&T* 7 (1968) 60-75.

M. E. Andrews, "Israelite and Canaanite Religion—Christianity and other Religions," *Orita* 2 (1968) 19-28.

Andrew Alföldi, "An Ugrian Creation Myth on Early Hungarian Phalerae," *AJA* 73 (1969) 359-361.

*Melford E. Spiro, "Religious Symbolism and Social Behavior," *PAPS* 113 (1969) 341-349. [Some Similarities Between Judaism and Buddhism, pp. 344-349]

§464 *3.2.15 Ancient Religions and Philosophy - General Studies
[See also: §417 Religionsgeschichte
- General Studies ←]*

†T[homas] Taylor, "Opinions of Ancient Theologists," *MMBR* 3 (1797) 259-260.

†Anonymous, "Religious System of the Ancients—Fate," *DR* 4 (1838) 32-67. *(Review)*

Anonymous, "Idolatry—Its Rise—Not Man's Primitive Religion—Hume's Argument Disposed of," *SPR* 10 (1857-58) 115-125.

Anonymous, "The Origin of Idolatry," *AThR* 4 (1862) 328-352.

E. L., "The Origin of Idolatry; a Criticism of Rawlinson and others," *AThR* 4 (1862) 429-471.

*C. H., "Ancient Atheism and Superstition," *JSL, 4th Ser.,* 1 (1862) 24-55.

*T. B. Thayer, "Ancient and Modern Unbelief," *UQGR, N.S.,* 1 (1864) 149-162.

*Philip Mules, "Was the Idolatry of Terah Sabaïsm?" *JSL, 4th Ser.,* 10 (1866-67) 182-183.

Anonymous, "The Gods of the Nations when Christ Appeared," *DR, N.S.,* 9 (1867) 80-109. *(Review) [Original numbering as Vol 61]*

†Anonymous, "Cox's *Aryan Mythology,*" *ERCJ* 132 (1870) 330-363. *(Review)*

C. Staniland Wake, "The Origin of Serpent-Worship," *JRAI* 2 (1872-73) 373-386. (Discussion, pp. 386-390)

*Calvin E. Park, "The Connection Between the Mosaic and Pagan Sacrifices," *BS* 31 (1874) 693-730.

*(Miss) A. W. Buckland, "Mythological Birds Ethnologically Considered," *JRAI* 4 (1874-75) 277-292.

J. S. Phené, "On Prehistoric Traditions and Customs in Connection with Sun and Serpent Worship *(with Subsequent Notes),*" *JTVI* 8 (1874-75) 321-356. (Discussion, pp. 356-361)

E. L. Brandreth, "On Some of the Sources of Aryan Mythology," *TPS* (1875-76) 142-163.

*W. Robertson Smith, "Animal worship and animal tribes among the Arabs and the Old Testament," *JP* 9 (1880) 75-100.

*O. D. Miller, "Solar Symbolism in the Ancient Religions," *AAOJ* 3 (1880-81) 218-227.

*William Hayes Ward, "The Serpent Tempter in Oriental Mythology," *BS* 38 (1881) 209-230.

*(Miss) A. W. Buckland, "Surgery and Superstition in Neolithic Times," *JRAI* 11 (1881-82) 7-20 (Discussion, pp. 20-21)

F. G. Fleay, "Lectures on Polytheism," *AAOJ* 6 (1884) 73-82.

W. G. Moorehead, "Universality of Serpent-Worship," *ONTS* 4 (1884-85) 205-210.

R. Collins, "Some Characteristics of Primitive Religion," *JTVI* 19 (1885-86) 216-241. [(Discussion, pp. 241-245) (Remarks by Saumarez Smith, pp. 246-248; Reply by R. Collins, pp. 248-252)]

Anonymous, "What is Astrology?" *SRL* 7 (1886) 72-92.

Justin A. Smith, "Ethical Value of Pagan Religions," *ONTS* 6 (1886-87) 17-21.

*J[ustin] A. Smith, "Religion as an Element in Civilization," *ONTS* 6 (1886-87) 106-109.

(Miss) E. M. Clerke, "Dragon Myths of the East," *IAQR, 1st Ser.,* 4 (1887) 98-117. *[O.T. Refs., p. 103]*

William Tucker, "Nature Worship in Ancient and Prehistoric Religions," *AAOJ* 10 (1888) 154-157.

W. St. C[had] Boscawen, "Oriental Eschatology," *BOR* 8 (1895-1900) 38-42.

F. Legge, "Serapis—A Study in Religions," *SRL* 28 (1896) 33-55.

William Crooke, "The Binding of a God: A Study of the Basis of Idolatry," *Folk* 8 (1897) 325-355.

K. Budde, "Imageless Worship in Antiquity," *ET* 9 (1897-98) 396-399.

*H. Colley March, "The Mythology of Wise Birds," *JRAI* 27 (1897-98) 209-232.

*Henry Lansdell, "Tithe-giving Amongst Ancient Pagan Nations," *JTVI* 31 (1897-98) 123-137. [(Discussion, pp. 137-138) (Note by F. W. H.*[sic]* Petrie, pp 138-139.)]

*William Hayes Ward, "Two Idols from Syria," *AJA* 4 (1900) 289-292.

*F. J. Coffin, "Third commandment," *JBL* 19 (1900) 166-188. [III. Concepts of the Divine Name among Primitive Peoples, pp. 171-177]

*Joseph Offord, "Herodotus and Palmyrene Inscriptions," *AAOJ* 25 (1903) 178. [Arabian God: Orotalt/Obotalt /Obdat and Alilat]

George F. Moore, "Baetylia and Other Holy Stones," *AJA* 7 (1903) 82.

Grey Hubert Skipwith, "Ashtoreth, the Goddess of the Zidonians," *JQR* 18 (1905-06) 715-738.

Geo. St. Clair, "The Subtle Serpent," *JTS* 7 (1905-06) 40-50. *[The Serpent in Ancient Religions and Serpent Worship]*

Samuel Ives Curtiss, "Survivals of Personality Surrendered to Deity Among Syrians and Arabs," *CSQ* 7 (1907) #3, 26-37.

G. E. White, "Survivals of Primitive Religion Among the People of Asia Minor," *JTVI* 39 (1907) 146-163. (Discussion, pp. 164-166)

Anonymous, "Twins in the Mythology of All Nations," *AAOJ* 30 (1908) 56-57.

Willis Brewer, "Names of Deity," *OC* 23 (1909) 119-123.

Sigmund Frey, "Deities and Their Names," *OC* 23 (1909) 314-316.

A. E. Whatham, "The Origin and Significance of the Worship of the Diana of the Ephesians," *AAOJ* 32 (1910) 35-40.

Lewis Bayles Paton, "The Cult of the Mother-Goddess in Ancient Palestine," *BW* 36 (1910) 26-38. *['Ashtart]*

Franz Cumont, "Why the Oriental Religions Spread," *OC* 24 (1910) 357-374. *(Trans. by A. M. Thielen)*

A. E. Whatham, "The Sign of the Mother-Goddess," *AJRPE* 4 (1910-11) 252-309.

*Lewis Bayles Paton, "Survivals of Primitive Religion in Syria," *AJA* 15 (1911) 63-64.

*Lewis Bayles Paton, "Modern Palestine and the Bible. *IX. Survivals of Primitive Religion,*" *HR* 62 (1911) 194-199.

Anonymous, "Adonis und Esmun," *ET* 23 (1911-12) 90. *(Review)*

L. C. Casartelli, "Religion of the Achæmenid Kings," *JMUEOS* #2 (1912-13) 65-67.

George Comack, "Heathen Messiahs," *ContR* 103 (1913) 856-864.

P[aul] C[arus], "An Ass-Headed Deity," *OC* 27 (1913) 574-575.

[Paul Carus], "The Mother Goddess," *OC* 27 (1913) 641-655.

Lina Eckenstein, "Moon-Cult in Sinai on the Egyptian Monuments," *AEE* 1 (1914) 9-13.

*L. A. Waddell, "The Indian Myth of 'Churning the Ocean' Interpreted: An Important New Chapter in Aryan Pre-History," *IAQR* 5 (1914) 377-380, 490-507. [Agreement with the Babylonian Creation-Myth, pp. 379-380, *repeated on pp.* 492-493 *[sic]*]

J. S. Banks, "Eastern Religions in the West," *ET* 27 (1915-16) 443-447.

W. Scott, "The Notion of Re-Birth in Some Pagan Religions," *OSHTP* (1917-18) 51-60.

G. Elliot Smith, "Dragons and Rain Gods," *BJRL* 5 (1918-20) 317-380.

Cuthbert Lattey, "Ruler-Worship in the Bible," *ITQ* 14 (1919) 238-257.

Lawrence Parmly Brown, "The Cosmic Eyes," *OC* 32 (1918) 685-701.

Lawrence Parmly Brown, "The Cosmic Hands," *OC* 33 (1919) 8-26.

Lawrence Parmly Brown, "The Cosmic Feet," *OC* 33 (1919) 345-363.

Lawrence Parmly Brown, "The Cosmic Mouth, Ears, and Nose," *OC* 33 (1919) 482-505.

Lawrence Parmly Brown, "The Cosmic Hemorrhage," *OC* 33 (1919) 753-762.

*Lawrence Parmly Brown, "The Cosmic Leprosy and Dropsy," *OC* 34 (1920) 15-33.

Lawrence Parmly Brown, "The Cosmic Multiplications," *OC* 34 (1920) 98-118.

Lawrence Parmly Brown, "The Cosmic Transmutations," *OC* 34 (1920) 279-301.

Lawrence Parmly Brown, "The Cosmic Resurrections," *OC* 34 (1920) 423-439, 494-505.

Lawrence Parmly Brown, "The Cosmic Parthenogenesis," *OC* 34 (1920) 600-618, 739-752.

Lawrence Parmly Brown, "The Cosmic Man and Homo Signorum," *OC* 35 (1921) 10-37. *[Marked as continued, but was not]*

Margaret C. Waites, "The Deities of the Sacred Axe," *AJA* 27 (1923) 25-56.

*C. Winckworth, "On Heathen Deities in the *Doctrine of Addai*," *JTS* 25 (1923-24) 402-403. [Appendix to Mr. Winckworth's Note, by F. C. Burkitt, p. 403]

[J.] Rendel Harris, "Valentine and Orson: A Study in Twin-Cult," *ContR* 126 (1924) 323-331.

*Maurice A. Canney, "The Goat-song," *ZAW* 42 (1924) 145-148.

Arthur Darby Nock, "Eunuchs in ancient religion," *AfRW* 23 (1925) 25-33.

*A. M. Tallgren, "The Copper Idols from Galich and Their Relatives," *SO* 1 (1925) 312-341.

*Campbell N. Moody, "Spiritual Power in Pagan Religions and in the Old Testament," *ET* 38 (1926-27) 180-184.

Alan Rowe, "Notes and Queries. Serpent-cult in *Palestine*," *PEFQS* 60 (1928) 110.

Maurice A. Canney, "The Ceremonial Use of Sand," *JMUEOS* #14 (1929) 35-52.

Lawrence Parmly Brown, "The Cosmic Teeth," *OC* 44 (1930) 1-20, 73-83, 162-172, 232-243.

G. D. Hornblower, "Temples and Kings in Ancient Egypt," *JMUEOS* #17 (1932) 21-39. *[Fertility rites]*

*Edward Ulback, "The Serpent in Myth and Scripture," *BS* 90 (1933) 449-455.

*Samuel A. B. Mercer, "Astarté in Egypt," *EgR* 3 (1935) 192-203.

C. N. Deedes, "The Double-Headed God," *Folk* 46 (1935) 194-243.

J. P. Hyatt, "New Light on the Deity Bethel," *JBL* 56 (1937) iii.

*E. Bikerman, "Anonymous Gods," *JWCI* 1 (1937-38) 187-196. [1. Foreign Gods Retaining their Original Names; 2. Foreign Gods Changing Their Original Names; 3. The Worship and Adoption of Anonymous Gods; 4. The Anonymous God of the Jews]

H. J. Fleure, "Ritual and Ethic: A Study of a Change in Ancient Religions about 800-500 B.C.," *BJRL* 22 (1938) 435-454.

J. P. Hyatt, "Iconic Representation of the Deified Sanctuary," *JBL* 58 (1939) v.

S. Vernon McCasland, "The Asklepios Cult in Palestine," *JBL* 58 (1939) 221-228.

*Alan S. Hoey, "Official Policy towards Oriental Cults in the Roman Army," *TAPA* 70 (1939) 456-481.

W[illiam] F[oxwell] Albright, "The Egypto-Canaanite Deity Ḥaurôn," *BASOR* #84 (1941) 7-12.

*Campbell Bonner, "Aeolus Figured on Colic Amulets," *HTR* 35 (1942) 87-93.

E. Douglas Van Buren, "Mountain Gods," *Or, N.S.*, 12 (1943) 76-84.

J. A. Thomson, "The God Molech," *JBL* 63 (1944) v-vi.

Frederick Poulsen, "Talking, Weeping and Bleeding Sculptures. A Chapter in the History of Religious Fraud," *AA* 16 (1945) 178-195.

Lillian B. Lawler, "Snake Dances," *Arch* 1 (1948) 110-113.

Leo A. Oppenheim, "The Golden Garments of the Gods," *JNES* 8 (1949) 172-193.

Henri Frankfort, "Ishtar at Troy," *JNES* 8 (1949) 194-200.

E. Douglas Van Buren, "Ancient Beliefs and Some Modern Interpretations," *Or, N.S.,* 18 (1949) 494-501.

*Geo Widengren, "The Ascension of the Apostle and the Heavenly Book. (King and Saviour. III)," *UUÅ* (1950) #7, 1-117. [Mesopotamian Religion, pp. 7-21 (Additional notes, pp. 86-100); Israelitic-Jewish Religion in the Light of Comparative Research, pp. 22-39; Samaritan, Jewish —and Samaritan-Gnostic, and Jewish Rabbinic Evidence, pp. 40-58]

E. Douglas Van Buren, "An Enlargement on a Given Theme," *Or, N.S.,* 20 (1951) 15-69. *[Use of Goat in Cultic Religion]*

*Geo Widengren, "The King and the Tree of Life in Ancient Near Eastern Religion. (King and Saviour IV)," *UUÅ* (1951) #4, 1-79.

*John L. McKenzie, "The Hebrew Attitude towards Mythological Polytheism," *CBQ* 14 (1952) 323-335.

E. Douglas Van Buren, "Foundation Rites for a New Temple," *Or, N.S.,* 21 (1952) 293-306.

Robert Redfield, "The Primitive World View," *PAPS* 96 (1952) 30-36.

Morton Smith, "The Religious History of Classical Antiquity," *JRT* 12 (1954-55) 90-99.

*Phyllis Ackerman, "The Gemini are born," *Arch* 8 (1955) 26-30.

*E. Douglas Van Buren, "How Representations of Battles of the Gods Developed," *Or, N.S.,* 24 (1955) 24-41.

G. Castellino, "Rituals and Prayers against 'Appearing Ghosts'," *Or, N.S.,* 24 (1955) 240-274.

M. Dothan, "Some Aspects of Religious Life in Palestine during the Hyksos Rule," *A&S* 2 (1957) #2/3, 121-130.

M. Avi-Yonah, "Places of Worship in the Roman and Byzantine Periods," *A&S* 2 (1957) #2/3, 262-286.

L. V. Grinsell, "The Ferryman and his Fee: a study in Ethnology, Archaeology, and Tradition," *Folk* 68 (1957) 257-269. *[Life after Death]*

*P. V. Glob, "Snake Sacrifices in Bahrain's Ancient Capital. The Danish Archaeological Bahrain Expedition's Fourth Campaign of Excavation," *Kuml* (1957) 125-127.

*Elias J. Bickerman, "The Altars of the Gentiles: A Note on the Jewish 'ius sacrum'," *RIDA, 3rd Ser.,* 5 (1958) 137-164.

M. Avi-Yonah, "Syrian Gods at Ptolemais-Accho," *IEJ* 9 (1959) 1-12.

*K. V. Mathew, "Ancient Religions of the Fertile Crescent—and the Sanathana Dharma," *IJT* 8 (1959) 83-90.

Paul Thieme, "The 'Aryan' Gods of the Mitanni Treaties," *JAOS* 80 (1960) 301-317.

E. O. James, "The Religions of Antiquity," *Numen* 7 (1960) 137-147.

S. G. F. Brandon, "The Personification of Death in Some Ancient Religions," *BJRL* 43 (1960-61) 317-335.

*Bernard Goldman, "A Snake Goddess, Asiatic Demonology and the Gorgon," *AJA* 65 (1961) 189.

G. A. Wainwright, "The Earliest Use of the Mano Cornuta," *Folk* 72 (1961) 492-495. *[Magical apotropaic gesture]*

E. O. James, "Primitive Religion: Past and Present," *Folk* 72 (1961) 496-508.

*M. A. Murray, "Egypt and Africa," *Man* 61 (1961) #12.

*W. Culican, "The Hasanlu Bowl," *Mwa-M* #1 (1961) 63-73.

Ernst H. Kantorowicz, "Gods in Uniform," *PAPS* 105 (1961) 368-393.

G. J. D. Aalders, "The Tolerance of Polytheism in Classical Antiquity and its Limits," *FUQ* 9 (1963-65) 223-242.

*Javier Teixidor, "The Altars Found at Hatra," *Sumer* 21 (1965) 85-92.

*B. Uffenheimer, "The 'Awakeners'—A Cultic Term From the Ancient Near East," *Lĕš* 30 (1965-66) #3 n.p.n. [עדרן]

S. G. F. Brandon, "The Origin of Death in Some Ancient Near Eastern Religions," *RS* 1 (1965-66) 217-228.

Harry A. Hoffner Jr., "Symbols for Masculinity and Femininity; Their Use in Ancient Near Eastern Sympathetic Magic Rituals," *JBL* 85 (1966) 326-334.

*Karl Oberhuber, "Polytheism and High Culture," *NOP* 6 (1967) 11-15.

*Edwin M. Yamauchi, "Anthropomorphism in Ancient Religions," *BS* 125 (1968) 29-44.

*Lloyd R. Bailey, "Israelite "*Ēl Šadday* and Amorite *Bêl Šadê*," *JBL* 87 (1968) 434-438.

*Robert A. Hadley, "Hieronymus of Cardia and Early Seleucid Mythology," *HJAH* 18 (1969) 142-152.

*Jean Ouellette, "More on 'Êl Šadday and Bêl Šadê," *JBL* 88 (1969) 470-471.

§465 *3.2.15.1 Semitic Religion - General Studies*

*A. H. Sayce, "Balaam's Prophecy (Numbers XXIV. 17-24) and the God Seth," *AJSL* 4 (1887-88) 1-6.

Morris Jastrow Jr., "General Features of Semitic Religions," *ONTS* 13 (1891) 175-176.

†Anonymous, "Semitic Religions," *ERCJ* 175 (1892) 325-341. *(Review)*

*George A. Barton, "Notes," *JAOS* 16 (1894-96) cxciii. [1. On the Semitic Ishtar Cult]

*George A. Barton, "West semitic deities with compound names," *JBL* 20 (1901) 22-27.

*Samuel Ives Curtiss, "The Place of Sacrifice among the Primitive Semites," *AJA* 7 (1903) 83.

W. M. Flinders Petrie, "Note on Semitic Worship in Sinai," *Man* 5 (1905) #104.

*G. Buchanan Gray, "The Excavations at Gezer and Religion in Ancient Palestine," *Exp, 7th Ser.,* 7 (1909) 423-442

*W. Max Müller, "The Semitic God of Tahpanhes. Probably an Ancient Relief of Yahveh," *OC* 23 (1909) 1-5.

C. J. Ball, "The Ass in Semitic Mythology," *SBAP* 32 (1909) 64-72.

*A. H. Sayce, "Assyriological Notes," *SBAP* 39 (1917) 207-212. [The Pig-god, p. 209] *[Amorite God]*

W[illiam] F[oxwell] Albright, "The Evolution of the West-Semitic Divinity 'An-'Anat-'Attâ," *AJSL* 41 (1924-25) 73-101.

W[illiam] F[oxwell] Albright, "Further Observations on the Name *'Anat-'Attah*," *AJSL* 41 (1924-25) 283-285.

W[illiam] F[oxwell] Albright, "Note on the Goddess 'Anat," *AJSL* 43 (1926-27) 233-236.

S[tephen] Langdon, "The Semitic Goddess of Fate, Fortuna-Tyche," *JRAS* (1930) 21-29.

*S[tephen H.] Langdon, "Minîtu, 'Fate.' A Correction," *JRAS* (1930) 402-403. [*lum-ni*]

*Edward A. Arbez, "The Relations Between Religion and Morality Among the Early Semites," *AQW* 4 (1931) #1/2, 1-11.

(Miss) M. A. Murray, "Female Fertility Figures," *JRAI* 64 (1934) 93-100.

*J. Philip Hyatt, "The Deity Bethel and the Old Testament," *JAOS* 59 (1939) 81-98. *[Western Semitic Religion]*

Julius Lewy, "The Šulmān Temple in Jerusalem," *JBL* 59 (1940) 519-522.

Julius Lewy, "The Old West Semitic Sun-God Ḥammu," *HUCA* 18 (1944) 429-488.

*Oliver H. Myers, "The *Neter* Pole and the *Ashera*," *JEA* 36 (1950) 113-114.

*Alfred Haldar, "The Notion of the Desert in Sumero-Accadian and West-Semitic Religions," *UUÅ* (1950) #3, 1-70.

Mitchell J. Dahood, "Ancient Semitic Deities in Syria and Palestine," *SSR* 1 (1958) 65-94.

*J[ulian] Morgenstern, "The King-God among the Western Semites and the Meaning of Epiphanies," *VT* 10 (1960) 138-197.

Peter J. Ucko, "The Interpretation of Prehistoric Anthropomorphic Figurines," *JRAI* 92 (1962) 38-54.

Michael C. Astour, "Semitic Elements in the Kumarbi Myth: An Onomastic Inquiry," *JNES* 27 (1968) 172-177.

*Lloyd R. Bailey, "Israelite "*Ēl Šadday* and Amorite *Bêl Šadê*," *JBL* 87 (1968) 434-438.

*Eugene Stockton, "Petra Revisited: A Review of a Semitic Cult Complex," *AJBA* 1 (1968-71) #4, 51-73.

*Jean Ouellette, "More on 'Êl Šadday and Bêl Šadê," *JBL* 88 (1969) 470-471.

*M. E. L. Mallowan, "Alabaster eye-idols from Tell Brak, North Syria," *MUSJ* 45 (1969) 391-396.

§466 *3.2.15.2 Religions of Assyria, Babylonia, Canaan, and Egypt - General Studies*

O. D. Miller, "The Chaldæo-Assyrian Doctrine of the Future Life; according to the Cuneiform Inscriptions," *UQGR, N.S.,* 17 (1860) 318-327.

T. B. Thayer, "Demonology of the Hindoos, Buddhists, and Chaldeans," *UQGR, N.S.,* 3 (1866) 308-320.

*Hyde Clarke, "Researches in Prehistoric and Protohistoric Comparative Philology, Mythology, and Archæology in Connection with the Origin of Culture in America, and its Propagation by the Sumerian or Akkad Families," *JRAI* 4 (1874-75) 148-212. (Discussion, pp. 212-231)

O. D. Miller, "The Antiquity of Sacred Writings in the Valley of the Euphrates," *AAOJ* 2 (1879-80) 290-295.

O. D. Miller, "The Assyro-Babylonian Doctrine of the Future Life:—Following the Cuneiform Inscriptions," *OBJ* 1 (1880) 58-62.

James T. Bixby, "Ancient Akkad and its Religion," *URRM* 13 (1880) 409-432.

J. N. Fradenbergh, "The Religion of Babylonia and Assyria," *MR* 65 (1883) 97-120, 279-301.

[Charles François] Lenormant, "Chaldean Imprecations," *ONTS* 4 (1884-85) 82-83.

Eberhard Schrader, "The Serpent in the Cuneiform Inscriptions," *ONTS* 5 (1885-86) 178.

E. de Presseense, "The Chaldæo-Assyrian Religion," *BFER* 36 (1887) 57-67.

D. G. Lyon, "Assyrian and Babylonian Royal Prayers," *JAOS* 14 (1890) xciii-xciv.

C. J. Ball, "The First Three of the Five Autocrats. *(Wu-Ti),*" *SBAP* 13 (1890-91) 77-78. *[Akkadian Mythology]*

*B. T. A. Evetts, "The Canephoros in Early Chaldean Art," *SBAP* 13 (1890-91) 153-159.

*Theo. G. Pinches, "Was 𒀭𒀪𒇥𒉌 The Most High God of Salem?" *SBAP* 16 (1893-94) 225-229.

William Hayes Ward, "Light on Scriptural Texts from Recent Discoveries. The Primitive Gods of Palestine," *HR* 29 (1895) 506-507.

W. St. C[had] Boscawen, "The Chaldean City God," *BOR* 8 (1895-1900) 176-183.

*J[oseph] Offord Jr., "The Nude Goddess in Assyrio-Babylonian Art," *SBAP* 18 (1896) 156-157.

*A. H. Sayce, "Recent Biblical and Oriental Archaeology. The Sumerian Original of the First Account of the Creation in Genesis," *ET* 14 (1902-03) 124-125.

Joseph Offord, "The Biblical Nisroch and the Assyrian and Babylonian Nusku," *AAOJ* 27 (1905) 127-128.

*Kerr Duncan MacMillan, "Some Cuneiform Tablets bearing on the Religion of Babylonia and Assyria," *BAVSS* 5 (1906) 531-712.

*Morris Jastrow Jr., "Hepatoscopy and Astrology in Babylonia and Assyria," *PAPS* 47 (1908) 646-676.

*Theophilus G. Pinches, "The Goddess Istar in Assyro-Babylonian Literature," *SBAP* 31 (1909) 20-37, 57-69.

*Morris Jastrow Jr., "Months and Days in Babylonian-Assyrian Astrology," *AJSL* 24 (1909-10) 151-155.

T. G. Pinches, "Notes upon the Beliefs of the Babylonians and Assyrians," *ET* 22 (1910-11) 163-167.

Lewis Bayles Paton, "Survivals of Primitive Religion in Syria," *AJA* 15 (1911) 63-64.

L. W. King, "The Origin of Animal Symbolism in Babylonia, Assyria, and Persia," *SBAP* 34 (1912) 276-278.

*Morris Jastrow Jr., "Sumerian and Akkadian Views of Beginnings," *JAOS* 36 (1916) 274-299.

*A. H. Sayce, "Assyriological Notes," *SBAP* 39 (1917) 207-212. [The Hamathite God אלור, p. 208]

George W. Gilmore, "Gesture in Sumerian and Babylonian Prayer," *HR* 79 (1920) 394.

J. T. Parfit, "Religion in Mesopotamia," *JTVI* 53 (1921) 177-184, 186-187. [(Discussion, pp. 184-186) (Communication by Langhorne Orchard, p. 186)]

*Samuel A. B. Mercer, "Liturgical Elements in Babylonian and Assyrian Seal Cylinders," *JSOR* 6 (1922) 106-116.

F. Harold Smith, "The Trinities of Non-Christian Religions," *CQR* 95 (1922-23) 75-103.

Theophilus G. Pinches, "The Completed Legend of Bel-Merodach and the Dragon," *JTVI* 59 (1927) 137-162, 164. (Discussion, pp. 161-164)

*John Robert Towers, "A Syrian God and Amen-Ra?" *AEE* 16 (1931) 75-76.

*Harold L. Creager, "Cultural and Religious Influence of Babylonia and Assyria on Western Asia," *LCQ* 4 (1931) 345-367.

W[illiam] F[oxwell] Albright, "The Syro-Mesopotamian God Šulmân-Ešmûn and Related Figures," *AfO* 7 (1931-32) 164-169.

Julius Lewy, "Some West Semitic Heroes and Deities in the Old Babylonian and Assyrian Texts," *JBL* 55 (1936) xvii-xviii.

E. Douglas Van Buren, "Sheep and Corn," *Or, N.S.,* 5 (1936) 127-137. *[Cultic Practices]*

*E. Douglas Van Buren, "The Scorpion in Mesopotamian Art and Religion," *AfO* 12 (1937-39) 1-28.

E. Douglas Van Buren, "Religious Rites and Ritual in the Time of Uruk IV—III," *AfO* 13 (1939-41) 32-45.

*T. Fish, "War and Religion in Ancient Mesopotamia," *BJRL* 23 (1939) 387-402.

*Julian Oberman, "Two Magic Bowls: New Incantation Texts from Mesopotamia," *AJSL* 57 (1940) 1-31.

*E. Douglas Van Buren, "The ṣalme in Mesopotamian Art and Religion," *Or, N.S.,* 10 (1941) 65-92.

E. Douglas Van Buren, "Concerning the Horned Cap of the Mesopotamian Gods," *Or, N.S.,* 12 (1943) 318-327.

*A. Leo Oppenheim, "II. The Mesopotamian Temple," *BA* 7 (1944) 54-63. [The Typical Mesopotamian Temple; Temple and Community in Mesopotamia]

E. Douglas Van Buren, "The giš-ti and the giš-ka-an-na," *Or, N.S.,* 13 (1944) 281-287.

*E. Douglas Van Buren, "Amulets in Mesopotamia," *Or, N.S.,* 14 (1945) 18-23.

Julius Lewy, "The Late Assyro-Babylonian Cult of the Moon and Its Culmination in the Time of Nabonidus," *HUCA* 19 (1945-46) 405-489.

E. Douglas Van Buren, "The Dragon in Ancient Mesopotamia," *Or., N.S.,* 15 (1946) 1-45.

A. L. Oppenheim, "Mesopotamian Mythology. I," *Or., N.S.,* 16 (1947) 207-238.

E. Douglas Van Buren, "A Further Note on the Dragon in Mesopotamia," *Or, N.S.,* 16 (1947) 251-254.

E. Douglas Van Buren, "The Guardians of the Gate in the Akkadian Period," *Or, N.S.,* 16 (1947) 312-332.

E. Douglas Van Buren, "Additional Note Concerning the Guardians of the Gate," *Or, N.S.,* 16 (1947) 477-480.

A. L. Oppenheim, "Mesopotamian Mythology. II," *Or, N.S.,* 17 (1948) 17-58.

*M. E. L. Mallowan, "Kingship and the Gods: a review," *Antiq* 23 (1949) 93-99. *(Review)*

A. L. Oppenheim, "Mesopotamian Mythology. III," *Or, N.S.,* 19 (1950) 129-158.

*H[enri] Frankfort, "State Festivals in Egypt and Mesopotamia," *JWCI* 15 (1952) 1-12.

*E. Douglas Van Buren, "Places of Sacrifice ('Opferstätten')," *Iraq* 14 (1952) 76-92. *[Assyrian and Babylonian]*

*H. G. Quaritch Wales, "The Sacred Mountain of the Old Asiatic Religion," *JRAS* (1953) 23-30.

E. Douglas Van Buren, "An Investigation of a New Theory concerning the Bird-Man," *Or, N.S.,* 22 (1953) 47-58.

J. Leibovitch, "The Cult of the Ass in Antiquity," *BIES* 18 (1953-54) #3/4, III.

*Maud W. Makemson, "Astronomy in Primitive Religion," *JAAR* 22 (1954) 163-171.

*Phyllis Ackerman, "The Gemini are Born," *Arch* 8 (1955) 26-30.

*E. Douglas Van Buren, "Representations of Fertility Divinities in Glyptic Art," *Or, N.S.,* 24 (1955) 345-376.

John Gray, "Royal Substitution in the Ancient Near East," *PEQ* 87 (1955) 180-182.

J. B. McMinn, "Fusion of the Gods: A Religio-Astrological Study of the Interpenetration of the East and West in Asia Minor," *JNES* 15 (1956) 201-213.

*E. Douglas Van Buren, "A Ritual Sequence," *Or, N.S.,* 25 (1956) 39-41. *[Assyrian and Babylonian]*

E. Douglas Van Buren, "The Rain-goddess as represented in Early Mesopotamia," *SBO* 3 (1959) 343-355.

G. W. Lambert, "The Great Battle of the Mesopotamian Religious Year. The Conflict in the Akītu House. (*A Summary*)," *Iraq* 25 (1963) 189-190.

Thorkild Jacobsen, "Ancient Mesopotamian Religion: The Central Concerns," *PAPS* 107 (1963) 473-484.

Raphael Patai, "Matronit: The Goddess of the Kabbala," *HRel* 4 (1964-65) 53-68. [Ancient Near Eastern mythologies, pp. 53-56]

*Samuel E. Loewenstamm, "Prostration from Afar in Ugaritic, Accadian and Hebrew," *BASOR* #188 (1967) 41-43.

§467 *3.2.15.2.1 Assyrian Religion - Specifically*

John Hogg, "On the Goddess Nanaea," *JSL, 4th Ser.,* 3 (1863) 181-182.

H. Fox Talbot, "Note on the Religious Belief of the Assyrians," *SBAT* 1 (1872) 106-115.

*H. F[ox] Talbot, "A Fragment of Ancient Assyrian Mythology," *SBAT* 1 (1872) 271-280.

H. Fox Talbot, "On the Religious Belief of the Assyrians. No. II, No. III," *SBAT* 2 (1873) 29-79.

H. Fox Talbot, "The Legend of Ishtar descending to Hades," *SBAT* 2 (1873) 179-212.

H. Fox Talbot, "On the Religious Beliefs of the Assyrians. No. IV," *SBAT* 2 (1873) 346-352.

H. Fox Talbot, "Revised Translation of the Descent of Ishtar, with a further Commentary," *SBAT* 3 (1874) 118-135.

H. Fox Talbot, "Addenda to Paper on the 'Descent of Ishtar'," *SBAT* 3 (1874) 357-360.

W. St. Chad Boscawen, "Notes on the Religion and Mythology of the Assyrians," *SBAT* 4 (1875) 267-301.

*H. F. Talbot, "The Fight between Bel and the Dragon, and the Flaming Sword which turned Every Way (Gen. iii. 24) *Translated from a Chaldean Tablet,*" *SBAT* 5 (1876-77) 1-21.

Ernest A. Budge, "Assyrian Incantations to Fire and Water," *SBAT* 6 (1878-79) 420-435.

William St. Chad Boscawen, "Notes on Assyrian Religion and Mythology," *SBAT* 6 (1878-79) 535-542.

*Theo[philus] G. Pinches, "Note upon the Divine Name ," *SBAP* 8 (1885-86) 27-28.

*A. H. Sayce, "Miscellaneous Notes," *ZA* 2 (1887) 331-340. [1. The god Ramman, pp. 331-333.]

*E. Bonavia, "Sacred Trees of the Assyrian Monuments," *BOR* 3 (1888-89) 7-12, 35-40, 56-61.

*A. H. Sayce, "Miscellaneous Notes," *ZA* 4 (1889) 382-393. [27. *Asipu* and Joseph, pp. 387-388 *(Assyrian word for "prophet")*]

*W. St. C[had] Boscawen, "Notes on the Assyrian Sacred Trees," *BOR* 4 (1889-90) 95-96.

D. G. Lyon, "The Pantheon of Assurbanipal," *JAOS* 14 (1890) xciv-xcv.

*Herbert E. Ryle, "The Early Narratives of Genesis, II. The Assyrian Cosmogony and the Days of Creation," *ET* 2 (1890-91) 197-201. [1. Assyrian Cosmogony, pp. 197-199]

George A. Barton, "The Semitic Ištar Cult," *AJSL* 9 (1892-93) 131-165; 10 (1893-94) 1-74.

*George A. Barton, "Tiamat," *JAOS* 15 (1893) 1-27. (corrigendia, p. v)

George A. Barton, "Notes. I. On the Semitic Ishtar Cult," *AJSL* 10 (1893-94) 202-205.

*William Hayes Ward, "Bel and the Dragon," *AJSL* 14 (1897-98) 94-105.

C. H. W. Johns, "The God Mani," *ET* 10 (1898-99) 526-527.

Fritz Hommel, "The God Mani," *ET* 10 (1898-99) 566-567.

*C. H. W. Johns, "Assyriological Notes," *SBAP* 21 (1899) 254-255. *[The god Allai or Alai]*

C. H. W. Johns, "Notes on Assyriology," *SBAP* 21 (1899) 284-285. *[Assyrian Gods]*

(Miss) E. M. Plunket, "Notes.—Ahura Mazda, etc.," *SBAP* 22 (1900) 80-85.

*Clifton Daggett Gray, "A Hymn to Šamaš," *AJSL* 17 (1900-01) 129-145.

Morris Jastrow Jr., "The God Ašur," *JAOS* 24 (1903) 282-311.

J. Dyneley Prince, "Nisroch and Nusku," *JBL* 23 (1904) 68-75.

*C. H. W. Johns, "The Divine Name Auršt in Assyrian," *ET* 16 (1904-05) 144.

Fritz Hommel, "The Assyro-Chaldaean Sabbath," *ET* 16 (1904-05) 184-185.

Paul Carus, "Assyrian Poems on the Immortality of the Soul," *OC* 19 (1905) 107-110.

A. H. Sayce, "The Assyrian god Au," *SBAP* 27 (1905) 111-112.

A. T. Clay, "Ellil, the God of Nippur," *AJSL* 23 (1906-07) 269-279.

*R. Campbell Thompson, "An Assyrian Incantation against Ghosts," *SBAP* 28 (1906) 219-227. [K. 2175]

*D. D. Luckenbill, "The Temple Women of the Code of Hammurabi," *AJSL* 34 (1917-18) 1-12.

*(Miss) C. Garlick, "Note on the Sacred Tree in Mesopotamia," *SBAP* 40 (1918) 111-112.

*D. D. Luckenbill. "The Egyptian Earth-God in Cuneiform," *AJSL* 40 (1923-24) 288-292.

Arthur Jeffery, "A Reference to the Ishtar-Cult in the Qur'an," *AJSL* 41 (1924-25) 280-282.

*Theophilus G. Pinches, "The Worship of Idols in Assyrian History in Relation to Bible References," *JTVI* 57 (1925) 10-29, 31-32. [Discussion, pp. 29-31]

*Sidney Smith, "Notes on 'The Assyrian Tree'," *BSOAS* 4 (1926-28) 69-76.

*John A. Maynard, "Short Notes on Assyrian Religious Texts," *JSOR* 12 (1928) 109. [1. Images of Lambs; 2. Sagullatu, סגלה; 3. Some Names of Demons]

*Cecil J. Mullo-Weir, "Restorations of Assyrian Rituals," *JRAS* (1931) 259-264.

*H[enri] Frankfort, "Gods and Myths on Sargonid Seals," *Iraq* 1 (1934) 2-29.

Cyrus H. Gordon, "Assyriac Incantation," *BASOR* #110 (1948) 26-27.

Hildegard Lewy and Julius Lewy, "The God Nusku," *Or, N.S.,* 17 (1948) 146-159.

*Hillel A. Fine, "Studies in Middle-Assyrian Chronology and Religion," *HUCA* 24 (1952-53) 187-273.

*Hillel A. Fine, "Studies in Middle-Assyrian Chronology and Religion, Part II," *HUCA* 25 (1954) 107-168.

I. J. Gelb, "The Name of the Goddess Innin," *JNES* 19 (1960) 72-79.

*W. Culican, "The Hasanlu Bowl," *Mwa-M* #1 (1961) 63-73.

*A. Leo Oppenheim, "Analysis of an Assyrian Ritual (KAR 139)," *HRel* 5 (1965-66) 250-265.

*A. Leo Oppenheim, "Divination and Celestial Observation in the Last Assyrian Empire," *Cent* 14 (1969) 97-135.

§468 *3.2.15.2.2 Babylonian and Sumerian Religion - Specifically*

A. [H.] Sayce, "Tammuz," *JSL, 4th Ser.,* 7 (1865) 441-445.

*A. [H.] Sayce, "On Human Sacrifice among the Babylonians," *SBAT* 4 (1875) 25-31.

A. H. Sayce, "Babylonian Augury by means of Geometrical Figures," *SBAT* 4 (1875) 302-314.

†Anonymous, "The Magic and Sorcery of the Chaldeans," *LQHR* 45 (1875-76) 1-24. *(Review)*

*O. D. Miller, "The Pyramidal Temple," *OBJ* 1 (1880) 169-178. *[Ziggurat]*

*Francis Brown, "The Cherubim in Babylonian Mythology," *PR* 3 (1882) 168-169.

W[illiam] Hayes Ward, "On the Contest between Bel-Merodach and the Dragon," *JAOS* 11 (1885) x.

W[illiam] Hayes Ward, "The Dragon and the Serpent in Chaldean Mythology," *JAOS* 11 (1885) xvii.

D. G. Lyon, "Was there at the head of the Babylonian Pantheon a deity bearing the name *El?*" *JAOS* 11 (1885) clxiv-clxviii.

*†Fritz Hommel, "The Babylonian Gish-du-bara to be identified with Biblical Nimrod," *SBAP* 8 (1885-86) 119-120.

W[illia]m Hayes Ward, "A god of Agriculture," *AJA, O.S.,* 2 (1886) 261-266. *[Raman (Bin) and Bel of Nippur]*

Henry George Tomkins, "Tammuz, Lakhmu, Ashera, Sutekh," *PEFQS* 18 (1886) 204-205.

W. St. C[had] Boscawen, "Babylonian Teraphim," *BOR* 1 (1886-87) 39-40.

Theo[philus] G. Pinches, "Babylonian Notes. III. The Deities Ilan and Ḫar," *BOR* 1 (1886-87) 55.

Thomas Tyler, "The Babylonian Idea of a Disembodied Soul," *BOR* 1 (1886-87) 55-57.

Cyrus Adler, "The Views of the Babylonians concerning Life After Death," *AR* 10 (1888) 92-101.

Anonymous, "Professor Sayce on the Babylonian Religion," *LQHR* 70 (1888) 327-337. *(Review)*

W. St. Chad Boscawen, "Lectures on the Religions of Babylonia," *BOR* 3 (1888-89) 118-120. *[Abstract by H. M. M.]*

James A. Craig, "The Babylonian Istar-Epic," *ONTS* 8 (1888-89) 249-256.

*[William Hayes] Ward, "On the meaning of the design on the stone tablet of Abu-Habba," *JAOS* 13 (1889) ccxxxiii-ccxxxiv.

Cyrus Adler, "On the views of the Babylonians concerning life after death," *JAOS* 13 (1889) ccxxxviii-ccxliii.

*Charles B. Warring, "The Babylonian Legend of Creation. Is it the Original of the Story in the First Chapter of Genesis?" *MR* 71 (1889) 809-820.

*A. H. Sayce, "Miscellaneous Notes," *ZA* 4 (1889) 382-393. [28. Xisuthros, pp. 388-389]

*William R. Warren, "The Gates of Sunrise in Ancient Babylonian Art," *BOR* 3 (1889-90) 241-244.

*W. St. C[had] Boscawen, "The Babylonian and Jewish Festivals," *BOR* 4 (1889-90) 34-38.

*W[illia]m Hayes Ward, "The Babylonian Caduceus," *JAOS* 14 (1890) lxxxv-lxxxviii.

*C. J. Ball, "Glimpses of Babylonian Religion," *SBAP* 14 (1891-92) 149-162. [I. Human Sacrifices; II. The Gods and their Images]

*W. St. Chad Boscawen, "Some Elements in the Babylonian Religion and Their Comparative Relationship to Judaism," *ET* 4 (1892-93) 203-209.

W. St. Chad Boscawen, "The Babylonian Story of the Fall," *ET* 4 (1892-93) 439-441.

*Fritz Hommel, "Gish-dubarra, Gibil-gamish, Nimrod," *SBAP* 15 (1892-93) 291-300.

*W[illiam] Hayes Ward, "The Babylonian Gods in Babylonian Art," *JAOS* 15 (1893) xv-xviii.

George Reisner, "The different classes of Babylonian spirits," *JAOS* 15 (1893) cxcv-cxcvi.

George A. Barton, "Notes. III. Was Ilu ever a Distinct Deity in Babylonia?" *AJSL* 10 (1893-94) 206-207.

*Fritz Hommel, "A Supplementary Note to Gibil-Gamish," *SBAP* 16 (1893-94) 13-15. *[Nimrod]*

*C. J. Ball, "Israel and Babylon," *SBAP* 16 (1893-94) 188-200. [4. Tammuz, the Swine God, pp. 195-200]

William Hayes Ward, "Light on Scriptural Texts from Recent Discoveries. The Serpent in Babylonian Mythology," *HR* 27 (1894) 318-319.

*Felix Robiou, "A Study of Egyptian and Babylonian Triads," *IAQR, 2nd Ser.,* 7 (1894) 119-136.

*George A. Barton, "Notes," *JAOS* 16 (1894-96) cxciii. [3.Was Ilu ever a Distinct Deity in Babylonia?]

Theo[philus] G. Pinches, "The Religious Ideas of the Babylonians," *JTVI* 28 (1894-95) 1-27, 37-38. [(Discussion, pp. 28-33) (Remarks by Fritz Hommel, pp. 34-36)]

*John Henry Wright, "'Homoroka' a corruption of Marduk ('*O MOPΔOKα*)," *ZA* 10 (1895-96) 71-74.

W. St. C[had] Boscawen, "Babylonian Witchcraft," *BOR* 8 (1895-1900) 205-210.

*W. W. Moore, "Oannes and Dagon," *USR* 7 (1895-96) 191-197.

J. A. Selbie, "A Babylonian Trinity," *ET* 8 (1896-97) 272.

*Fritz Hommel, "Assyriological Notes," *SBAP* 19 (1897) 78-90, 312-315. [§31. Babylonian gods, ⊢ ⟨ 𒂟 ⊢ and ⊢ 𒀭 ⟨; §32. The name of the god ⊢ ⟨ 𒂟 ⊢]

*Alexander Kohut, "The Talmudic Records of Persian and Babylonian Festivals Critically Illustrated," *AJSL* 14 (1897-98) 183-194.

W. St. Chad Boscawen, "Babylonian Witchcraft," *ET* 9 (1897-98) 228-230.

C. H. W. Johns, "Adar," *ET* 9 (1897-98) 425.

*C[rawford] H. Toy, "Esther as a Babylonian Goddess," *NW* 7 (1898) 130-144.

*Morris Jastrow Jr., "Nebopolassar and the Temple to the Sun-God at Sippar," *AJSL* 15 (1898-99) 65-86.

*Fritz Hommel, "Yahveh in Early Babylonia," *ET* 10 (1898-99) 42.

Anonymous, "The Religion of Babylonia," *MR* 81 (1899) 135-138.

*Fritz Hommel, "Yahweh in Early Babylonia: A Supplementary Note," *ET* 11 (1899-1900) 270.

*William Hayes Ward, "The Goddesses in Primitive Babylonian Art," *AJA* 4 (1900) 169-170.

George A. Barton, "An Androgynous Babylonian Divinity," *JAOS* 21 (1900) 185-187. *[Ishtar]*

George A. Barton, "The Genesis of the God Eshmun," *JAOS* 21 (1900) 188-190.

Ira Maurice Price, "Notes on the Pantheon of the Gudean Cylinders," *AJSL* 17 (1900-01) 47-53.

William F. Warren, "Babylonian and Pre-Babylonian Cosmology," *JAOS* 22 (1901) 138-144.

*Paul Carus, "The Babylonian and Hebrew Views of Man's Fate after Death," *OC* 15 (1901) 346-366.

*Hugo Radau, "The Creation-Story of Genesis I.," *Monist* 12 (1901-02) 568-625. *[A Sumerian Theogony and Cosmology]*

William Hayes Ward, "Symbols of Babylonian Gods," *AJA* 6 (1902) 39.

S[tephen] H. Langdon, "The Name of the Ferryman in the Deluge Tablets," *JAOS* 23 (1902) 48-50.

*Fritz Hommel, "The Logos in the Chaldean Story of Creation," *ET* 14 (1902-03) 103-109.

H[ugo] Radau, "The Cosmology of the Sumerians," *Monist* 13 (1902-03) 103-113.

*Joseph Offord, "The Myths and Laws of Babylonia, and the Bible," *AAOJ* 25 (1903) 258-261.

Theophilus G. Pinches, "The Babylonian Story of the Creation, including Bel's Fight with the Dragon," *JTVI* 35 (1903) 17-48, *note p. 56* (Discussion, pp. 48-56)

Anonymous, "Gilgames, The Hero of the Flood," *RP* 2 (1903) 124-125.

A. H. Sayce, "Gilgames," *SBAP* 25 (1903) 266.

J. Dyneley Prince, "The Assyro-Babylonian Scape goat Controversy," *AJSL* 20 (1903-04) 173-181.

*C. H. W. Johns, "Babylonian Monotheism. A Personal Explanation," *ET* 15 (1903-04) 44-45.

A. H. Sayce, "Merodach," *ET* 15 (1903-04) 514.

Hugo Radau, "Bel, the Christ of Ancient Times," *Monist* 14 (1903-04) 67-119.

Joseph Offord, "Hymns to Tammuz: A New Recovery of Babylonian Literature," *AAOJ* 26 (1904) 337-341. *(Review)*

Anonymous, "The Devil and Evil Spirits of Babylonia," *RP* 3 (1904) 286-287.

Theophilus G. Pinches, "Sapattu, the Babylonian Sabbath," *SBAP* 26 (1904) 51-56.

Theophilus G. Pinches, "Sapattu, the Babylonian Sabbath. Additional Note," *SBAP* 26 (1904) 162-163.

H[enry] H. Howorth, "The god Asshur and the Epic of 'Marduk and Tiamat'," *SBAP* 26 (1904) 275-282; 27 (1905) 7-12.

W. O. E. Oesterley, "Asteroth Karnaim," *ET* 16 (1904-05) 132-134.

A. H. Sayce, "The Babylonian Sabbath," *ET* 16 (1904-05) 140.

A. H. Sayce, "The Name of the Babylonian God Usually Transcribed Ninip," *ET* 16 (1904-05) 140-141.

*A. H. Sayce, "The Babylonian and Biblical Accounts of Creation," *AJT* 9 (1905) 1-9.

J. Dyneley Prince, "The God-Name Ninib," *JBL* 24 (1905) 54-57.

*Anonymous, "Nina and Nineveh," *RP* 4 (1905) 61.

*Theophilus G. Pinches, "Nina and Nineveh," *SBAP* 27 (1905) 69-79, 155.

*C. H. W. Johns, "Statistics of Sabbath Keeping in Babylonia," *Exp, 7th Ser.*, 2 (1906) 433-440.

C. H. W. Johns, "The Babylonian Sabbath," *ET* 17 (1905-06) 566-567; 18 (1906-07) 140-142.

Anonymous, "The Doctrine of Sin in the Babylonian Religion," *AAOJ* 28 (1906) 40-43.

Morris Jastrow Jr., "A Babylonian Job," *ContR* 90 (1906) 801-808.

*C. H. W. Johns, "Statistics of Sabbath Keeping in Babylonia," *Exp, 7th Ser.,* 2 (1906) 433-440.

*Theophilus G. Pinches, "The Babylonian Gods of War and their Legends," *SBAP* 28 (1906) 203-218, 270-283.

C. H. W. Johns, "The Babylonian God Ninib," *ET* 18 (1906-07) 428-429.

*Ed[uard] König, "Has the Name 'Jahweh' Been Discovered in the Babylonian Monuments?" *ET* 18 (1906-07) 429-430.

*Ed[uard] König, "Astrology Among the Babylonians and Israelites," *HR* 53 (1907) 407-410.

Paul Haupt, "The name Istar," *JAOS* 28 (1907) 112-119.

Albert T. Clay, "The Origin and real Name of NIN-IB," *JAOS* 28 (1907) 135-144.

*Geo. W. Shaw, "Samson and Shemesh Once More," *Monist* 17 (1907) 620-626.

*Anonymous, "Job of the Cuneiform Inscriptions," *MR* 89 (1907) 307-310.

Albert T. Clay, "The Liver in Babylonian Divination," *RP* 6 (1907) 307-316.

*Morris Jastrow Jr., "The Signs and Names for the Liver in Babylonian," *ZA* 20 (1907) 105-129.

J. Dyneley Prince, "A Hymn to the Goddess Bau," *AJSL* 24 (1907-08) 62-75.

Stephen [H.] Langdon, "Lamentation to the Goddess of Širpurla," *AJSL* 24 (1907-08) 282-285.

Stephen [H.] Langdon, "A lament to Enlil and its later redactions," *Baby* 2 (1907-08) 275-281.

*G. Buchanan Gray, "The Heavenly Temple and the Heavenly Altar: Some Babylonian and Jewish Conceptions," *OSHTP* (1907-08) 65-67.

Theophilus G. Pinches, "The Legend of Merodach," *SBAP* 30 (1908) 53-62, 77-85.

A. H. Sayce, "The Babylonian Christ," *ET* 19 (1908-09) 43-44.

*Eduard König, "The Relations of Babylonian and Old Testament Culture. V. *Comparison Between Babylonian and Old-Testament Prophecy*," *HR* 58 (1909) 283-286.

Anonymous, "Babylonian Divination and Kindred Arts," *MR* 91 (1909) 474-478.

Alan S. Hawkesworth, "In How Far was Bel the Christ of Ancient Times?" *Monist* 19 (1909) 309-310.

*C. A. Browne, "Mars Dux and Mar(u)duk," *OC* 23 (1909) 444-445.

Stephen [H.] Langdon, "A chapter from the Babylonian books of private devotion," *Baby* 3 (1909-10) 1-32.

*Stephen [H.] Langdon, "A fragment of Nippurian liturgy," *Baby* 3 (1909-10) 241-249.

Stephen D. Peet, "The Babylonian Gods and Goddesses," *AAOJ* 32 (1910) 155-159.

*William Hayes Ward, "The Representation of Babylonian Gods in Art," *AJA* 14 (1910) 83-85.

Regina Miriam Bloch, "'Istar in the Underworld'," *ContR* 97 (1910) 333-345.

Crawford H. Toy, "Panbabylonianism," *HTR* 3 (1910) 47-84. *[Correction on insert slip at end of book]*

[Paul Carus], "The Babylonian Good Friday," *OC* 24 (1910) 138-142.

*[Paul Carus], "Tabi-utul-Bel, The Pious Sufferer," *OC* 24 (1910) 505-509.

*Clara Bewick Colby, "The Story of Tabi-utul-Bel and Nebuchadnezzar," *OC* 24 (1910) 766-767. [Editorial comment, pp. 767-768]

*J. Dyneley Prince, "A Hymn to Tammuz," *AJSL* 27 (1910-11) 84-89.

Frederick A. Vanderburgh, "Babylonian Tammuz Lamentations," *AJSL* 27 (1910-11) 312-321.

Stephen [H.] Langdon, "A liturgy of the cult of Tammuz," *Baby* 4 (1910-11) 229-245.

*George A. Barton, "On the Etymology of Ishtar," *JAOS* 31 (1910-11) 355-358.

*Leonard W. King, "'Heart and Reins' in Relation to Babylonian Liver Divination," *JMUEOS* #1 (1911) 95-98.

T[heophilus] G. Pinches, "Enlil and Ninlil, the Older Bel and Beltis," *SBAP* 33 (1911) 77-95.

*Samuel Daiches, "Job XXVI 12-13 and the Babylonian Story of Creation," *ZA* 25 (1911) 1-8.

Stephen [H.] Langdon, "Babylonian Eschatology," *Baby* 6 (1912) 193-215.

*Wilfred Schoff, "Tammuz, Pan and Christ. Notes on a Typical Case of Myth-Transference and Development," *OC* 26 (1912) 513-532.

J. Dyneley Prince, "The God Name ✳ ▤◁ ," *AJSL* 29 (1912-13) 284-287. *[Zaq-qar]*

Stephen H. Langdon, "The Scape-goat in Babylonian Religion," *ET* 24 (1912-13) 9-13.

W. F. Lofthouse, "Babylonian and Astral Mythology," *LQHR* 119 (1913) 331-334.

*Wilfred H. Schoff, "Tammuz, Pan and Christ. Further Notes on a Typical Case of Myth-Transference," *OC* 27 (1913) 449-460.

*A. H. Sayce, "The Solution of the Hittite Problem," *SBAP* 35 (1913) 6-12. [V. The Name of Istar, pp. 8-12]

Theophilus G. Pinches, "Ancestor-Worship and the Deification of Babylonian Kings," *ET* 25 (1913-14) 126-128.

*Stephen [H.] Langdon, "Methods of Theological Redactors in Babylonia," *ET* 25 (1913-14) 369-371.

Stephen [H.] Langdon, "The Sister of Tammuz," *Baby* 7 (1913-23) 20-28.

*Eduard König, "The Idea of God in Babylonia and in Israel," *HR* 68 (1914) 3-7.

*L. A. Waddell, "The Indian Myth of 'Churning the Ocean' Interpreted: An Important New Chapter in Aryan Pre-History," *IAQR* 5 (1914) 377-380, 490-507. [Agreement with the Babylonian Creation-Myth, pp. 379-380, *repeated on pp.* 492-493 *[sic]*]

*George A. Barton, "Religious Conceptions Underlying Sumerian Proper Names," *JAOS* 34 (1914) 315-320.

*John S. Banks, "The Idea of God in Israel and Babylon," *LQHR* 122 (1914) 129-131.

*Theophilus G. Pinches, "The Niffer Story of the Creation and the Flood," *ET* 26 (1914-15) 490-494.

Stephen [H.] Langdon, "The Origin and Evolution of Liturgic Forms in Babylonia," *OSHTP* (1914-15) 41-44.

*Francis A. Cunningham, "Daonos and the Babylonian God Ea," *AJA* 19 (1915) 81.

*George A. Barton, "Tammuz and Osiris," *JAOS* 35 (1915) 213-223.

Joseph Offord, "The Deity of the Crescent Venus in Ancient Western Asia," *JRAS* (1915) 197-203.

Theo. G. Pinches, "Notes on the Deification of Kings, and Ancestor-Worship, in Babylonia," *SBAP* 37 (1915) 87-95, 126-134.

Stephen H. Langdon, "The Sumerian Epic of the Fall of Man," *ET* 27 (1915-16) 165-168.

*A. L. Frothingham, "Babylonian Origin of Hermes the Snake-God and of the Caduceus," *AJA* 20 (1916) 175-211.

*Samuel A. B. Mercer, "'Emperor'-Worship in Babylonia," *JAOS* 36 (1916) 360-380.

*S[tephen H.] Langdon, "Lexigraphical Notes," *SBAP* 38 (1916) 37-40. [IV. The Sumerian Original of the Descent of Ishtar, pp. 55-57]

*Morris Jastrow Jr., "Sumerian Myths of Beginnings," *AJSL* 33 (1916-17) 91-144.

J. Dyneley Prince, "A Hymn to Ninkasi," *AJSL* 33 (1916-17) 40-44.

*Stephen [H.] Langdon, "The Necessary Revision of the Sumerian Epic of Paradise," *AJSL* 33 (1916-17) 245-249.

*George A. Barton, "A Word with reference to 'Emperor'-Worship in Babylonia," *JAOS* 37 (1917) 162-163.

George A. Barton, "Takku," *JAOS* 37 (1917) 163-164.

George A. Barton, "Ancient Babylonian Expressions of the Religious Spirit," *JAOS* 37 (1917) 23-42.

*A[lbert] T. Clay, "Name of the so-called deity Za-mal-mal," *JAOS* 37 (1917) 328-329. *[Baal Zebûb]*

*Samuel A. B. Mercer, "'Emperor'-worship in Babylonia—A Reply," *JAOS* 37 (1917) 331.

J[ohn] P. Peters, "The Worship of Tammuz," *JBL* 36 (1917) 100-111.

*A. H. Sayce, "Assyriological Notes," *SBAP* 39 (1917) 207-212. [The Name of the God Ea, pp. 211-212]

*Otto H. Boström, "The Babylonian Temple and its Place in the Ancient Community," *TTKF* 19 (1917) 28-36.

S[tephen H.] Langdon, "The Gardener in the Epic of Paradise," *ET* 29 (1917-18) 218-221. *[Sumerian Theology]*

Theophilus G. Pinches, "The Babylonian Paradise and Its Rivers," *ET* 29 (1917-18) 181-184, 288.

Paul Haupt, "Omoroka and Thalatth," *AJP* 39 (1918) 306-311.

*G[eorge] W. Gilmore, "Interpretation of Dreams, Hebrew and Babylonian," *HR* 75 (1918) 398-399.

S[tephen H.] Langdon, "The Babylonian Conception of the Logos," *JRAS* (1918) 433-449.

*S[tephen H.] Langdon, "A Hymn to the Moon-god, adapted for the use of Shamash-shum-ukîn, Viceroy of Babylon," *SBAP* 40 (1918) 104-110.

D. D. Luckenbill, "On the Reading of the Names of Some Babylonian Gods," *AJSL* 35 (1918-19) 55-61.

W[illiam] F[oxwell] Albright, "The Mouth of the Rivers," *AJSL* 35 (1918-19) 161-195.

*Hildegard Lewy, "The Babylonian Background of the Kay Kâûs Legend," *ArOr* 17 (1919) Part 2, 28-109. [Introduction, 1. The Astronomers among the Kings of Babylonia; 2. A Rebellion against the Religion of God in al-'Irâq; 3. A Royal Throne in the Vault of Heaven, 4. The Development of the Kay Kâûs Legend]

Theophilus G. Pinches, "The Legend of the Divine Lovers: Enlil and Ninlil," *JRAS* (1919) 185-205, 575-580.

S[tephen H.] Langdon, "Gesture in Sumerian and Babylonian Prayer. *A Study in Babylonian and Assyrian Archaeology*," *JRAS* (1919) 531-556.

*S[tephen H.] Langdon, "The religious interpretation of babylonian seals and a new prayer of Shamash-sum-ukîn (BM. 78219)," *RAAO* 16 (1919) 49-68.

W[illiam] F[oxwell] Albright, "The Goddess of Life and Wisdom," *AJSL* 36 (1919-20) 258-294. [I. Siduri Sâbîtu; II. The Vine and the Serpent; III. The Vineyard Paradise; IV. The Goddess of Life and Wisdom]

W[illiam] F[oxwell] Albright, "Uttu, the Sumerian god of commerce," *JAOS* 40 (1920) 73-74.

*W[illiam] F[oxwell] Albright, "The Babylonian Temple-Tower and the Altar of Burnt-Offering," *JBL* 39 (1920) 137-142.

Theophilus G. Pinches, "Babylonian Ritual Sacrifices and Offerings," *JRAS* (1920) 25-29.

*Theophilus G. Pinches, "The Creation-legend and the Sabbath in Babylonia and Amurru," *JRAS* (1920) 583-589.

Samuel A. B. Mercer, "The Sumerian Paradise of the Gods," *JSOR* 4 (1920) 51-81.

John P. Peters, "Notes and Suggestions on the Early Sumerian Religion and its Expression," *JAOS* 41 (1921) 131-149.

George A. Barton, "Note on Dr. Peters' Notes and Suggestions on the Early Sumerian Religion and its Expression," *JAOS* 41 (1921) 150-151.

Stephen [H.] Langdon, "The Incantation Title E-NU-SUB," *JSOR* 5 (1921) 81-83.

D. D. Luckenbill, *"Shût-Abni,* 'Those of Stone'," *AJSL* 38 (1921-22) 97-102.

*L. A. Waddell, "The Chaldee Father-God and the Pillar of Cloud," *ET* 33 (1921-22) 501-503.

Samuel A. B. Mercer, "Divine Service in Early Lagash," *JAOS* 42 (1922) 91-104. *[Sumerian Religion]*

W[illiam] F[oxwell] Albright, "The Name and Nature of the Sumerian God Uttu," *JAOS* 42 (1922) 197-200.

*H. F. Lutz, "Nin-Uraš and Nippur," *JAOS* 42 (1922) 210-211.

*Sidney Smith, "The Relation of Marduk, Ashur, and Osiris," *JEA* 8 (1922) 41-44.

*Step[hen H.] Langdon, "Hymn concerning the Cohabitation of the Earth God and the Earth Goddess, the begetting of the Moon God," *RAAO* 19 (1922) 67-77.

*Edward Chiera, "A Sumerian Tablet Relating to the Fall of Man," *AJSL* 39 (1922-23) 40-51.

*S[tephen H.] Langdon, "Two Sumerian Hymns from Eridu and Nippur," *AJSL* 39 (1922-23) 161-186.

S[tephen H.] Langdon, "Tagtug a Male Deity," *AJSL* 39 (1922-23) 197.

G. W Broomfield, "The Babylonian Moon God," *ICMM* 19 (1922-23) 271-281.

*Theophile J. Meek, "Babyloniaca," *JAOS* 43 (1923) 353-357. [The god ᵈE-ul, pp. 353-354]

*W[illiam] F[oxwell] Albright, "The Sumerian Conception of *Giš-Xar*—A Correction," *JSOR* 7 (1923) 79.

*C. Winckworth, "On Heathen Deities in the *Doctrine of Addai*," *JTS* 25 (1923-24) 402-403. [Appendix to Mr. C. Winckworth's Note, by F. C. Burkitt, p. 403]

*Sidney Smith, "The Face of Hambaba," *AAA* 11 (1924) 107-114.

Edward Chiera, "TAK-KU a Female Deity," *JAOS* 44 (1924) 54-60. *[Sumerian]*

*Aylward M. Blackman, "The Rite of Opening the Mouth in Ancient Egypt and Babylonia," *JEA* 10 (1924) 47-59.

*Stephen [H.] Langdon, "The Babylonian and Persian Sacaea," *JRAS* (1924) 65-72.

*G. R. Driver, "Some Recent Discoveries in Babylonian Literature. IV.—The Death and Resurrection of Bel," *Theo* 8 (1924) 190-197.

*Paul Haupt, "Philological and Linguistic Studies," *AJP* 46 (1925) 197-212. [7. The Waters of Death and the Plant of Life, pp. 211-212]

Sidney Smith, "The Babylonian Ritual for the Consecration and Induction of a Divine Statue," *JRAS* (1925) 37-60.

*S[tephen H.] Langdon, "Philological Note on *Nalbaš Šamê* = *Ishtar,*" *JRAS* (1925) 717.

W[illiam] F[oxwell] Albright, "The Babylonian Gazelle-god Arwîum-Sumuḳan," *AfO* 3 (1926) 181-183.

George A. Barton, "The Problem of the Origin and Early History of the Deity Nin-IB (Nin-urta, Nin-urash)," *JAOS* 46 (1926) 231-236.

*Sidney Smith, "Archaeological Notes," *JRAS* (1926) 433-446. [The Face of Hambaba, pp. 440-442]

*C. Leonard Woolley, "Babylonian Prophylactic Figures," *JRAS* (1926) 689-713.

*Theophilus G. Pinches, "Notes on the Discoveries at Ur and Tel al-Obeid, and the Worship of the Moon-God," *JTVI* 58 (1926) 32-54, 59-62. (Discussion, pp. 54-59)

Paul Haupt, "Istar's Azure Necklace," *BAVSS* 10 (1927) Heft 2, 96-106.

T. Fish, "The Cult of King Dungi During the Third Dynasty of Ur," *BJRL* 11 (1927) 322-328.

G. A. Barton, "When the Goddess Nin-shakh became a God," *JAOS* 47 (1927) 268-269.

Joseph Poplicha, "A Sun Myth in the Babylonian Deluge Story," *JAOS* 47 (1927) 289-301.

S. H. Hooke, "The Babylonian New Year Festival," *JMUEOS* #13 (1927) 29-38.

*Samuel A. B. Mercer, "Babylonian and Egyptian Triads," *JSOR* 11 (1927) 137-141.

T. Fish, "The Contemporary Cult of Kings of the Third Dynasty of Ur," *BJRL* 12 (1928) 75-82.

*T. Fish, "The City of Ur and Its God Nanna(r) in the Third Dynasty of Ur," *BJRL* 12 (1928) 336-346.

*S[tephen H.] Langdon, "The Legend of the kiškanu," *JRAS* (1928) 843-848.

*Sidney Smith, "Assyriological Notes," *JRAS* (1928) 849-875. [A Babylonian Fertility Cult, pp. 849-868]

E. Burrows, "Tilmun, Baḥrain, Paradise," *Or* #30 (1928) 3-34.

*O. E. Ravn, "The Rise of Marduk," *AO* 7 (1928-29) 81-90. *[Marked as "to be continued" but never was]*

*Cecil J. Mullo-Weir, "Four Hymns to Gula," *JRAS* (1929) 1-18.

Thorkild Jacobsen, "How did Gilgames oppress Uruk?" *AO* 8 (1929-30) 62-74.

C. J. Mullo-Weir, "Babylonian Private Rituals," *GUOST* 6 (1929-33) 61-62.

*Ira M. Price, "Light Out of Ur—The Devotion of the Elamite Kings to Sumerian Deities," *JAOS* 51 (1931) 164-169.

*J. G. Matthews, "Tammuz Worship in the Book of Malachi," *JPOS* 11 (1931) 42-50.

*S[tephen H.] Langdon, "New Fragments of the Commentaries on the Ritual of the Death and Resurrection of Bel," *JRAS* (1931) 111-116. [K. 6330 + 9138; K. 6359]

*S[tephen H.] Langdon, "The Sumero-Babylonian Origin of the Legend of Adam," *ET* 43 (1931-32) 45.

*Ira M. Price, "The Relation of Certain Gods to the Equity and Justice in Early Babylonia," *JAOS* 52 (1932) 174-178.

E. Douglas Van Buren, "The God Ningizzida," *Iraq* 1 (1934) 60-89.

*H[enri] Frankfort, "A Tammaz Ritual in Kurdistan (?)," *Iraq* 1 (1934) 137-145.

*W[illiam] F[oxwell] Albright and P. E. Dumont, "A Parallel between Indic and Babylonian Sacrificial Ritual," *JAOS* 54 (1934) 107-128.

*O. R. Gurney, "Babylonian Prophylactic Figures and their Rituals," *AAA* 22 (1935) 31-96. [K. 6068 + K. 7860 + K. 7823; K. 4625; K. 3241]

*Samuel A. B. Mercer, "Osiris and Marduk," *EgR* 3 (1935) 158-159.

*S[tephen H.] Langdon, "Monotheism as the Predecessor of Polytheism in Sumerian Religion," *EQ* 9 (1937) 137-146.

*M. Rostovtzeff, "The Squatting Gods in Babylonia and at Dura," *Iraq* 4 (1937) 19-20.

C. J. Gadd, "The Infancy of Man in a Sumerian Legend," *Iraq* 4 (1937) 33-34.

*W. F. J. Knight, "The Sumerian Provenience of Greek Defensive Sanctity," *PAPA* 68 (1937) xxxiv-xxxv.

S[amuel] N[oah] Kramer, "Inanna's Descent into the Nether World," *RAAO* 34 (1937) 93-134.

S[amuel] N[oah] Kramer, "Additional Material to 'Inanna's Descent into the Nether World'," *RAAO* 36 (1939) 68-80.

*Samuel N[oah] Kramer, "Ishtar in the Nether World According to a New Sumerian Text," *BASOR* #79 (1940) 18-27.

John Mauchline, "Ishtar—'Ashtart," *GUOST* 10 (1940-41) 11-20.

T. Fish, "The Piety of the Sumerian Kings," *JMUEOS* #23 (1942) 6-7. *[Summary]*

*T. Fish, "Religion and Community in Sumer," *JMUEOS* #23 (1942) 13-15.

T. Fish, "Food of the Gods in Ancient Sumer," *BJRL* 27 (1942-43) 308-322.

*A. Leo Oppenheim, "Assyriological Gleanings I," *BASOR* #91 (1943) 36-38. [II. Styled maledictions, pp. 37-38]

S[amuel] N[oah] Kramer, "The Death of Gilgamesh," *BASOR* #94 (1944) 2-12.

*Doro Levi, "Gleanings from Crete," *AJA* 49 (1945) 270-329. [1. The Dragon God of Babylon in Crete? pp. 271-280]

Thorkild Jacobsen, "Sumerian Mythology: A Review Article," *JNES* 5 (1946) 128-152. *(Review)*

Pablo Guzman-Rivas, "On a Sumerian 'Paradise' Myth," *MH* 3 (1946-47) #3, 15-18.

Samuel N[oah] Kramer, "Gilgamesh and the Land of the Living," *JCS* 1 (1947) 3-46.

E. Douglas Van Buren, "Fish-Offerings in Ancient Mesopotamia," *Iraq* 10 (1948) 101-121.

*E. Douglas Van Buren, "The Rod and Ring," *ArOr* 17 (1949) Part 2, 434-450.

S[amuel] N[oah] Kramer, "A Blood-Plague Motif in Sumerian Mythology," *JBL* 68 (1949) ix.

I[gnace] J. Gelb, "Šullat and Ḫaniš," *ArOr* 18 (1950) Part 1/2, 189-198. *[Sumerian gods]*

Ferris J. Stephens, "Lipit-Ishtar's Hall of Justice," *JAOS* 70 (1950) 179-181.

J. B. Pritchard, "Notes on Tammuz in the Light of Recent Discovery and Study," *JBL* 69 (1950) xiii-xiv.

Nels M. Bailkey, "A Babylonian Philosopher of History," *Osiris* 9 (1950) 106-130.

*T. Fish, "Miscellany," *MCS* 1 (1951) 56-57. [2. (d) Ha-ni. *(Night sky deity of Ur III)*, p. 57]

*Edith Porada and Faraj Basmachi, "Nergal in the Old Babylonian Period," *Sumer* 7 (1951) 66-68.

Henry L[udwig] F. Lutz, "Plaga Septentrionalis in Sumero-Akkadian Mythology," *UCPSP* 11 (1951) 297-309.

Ida Boboula, "The Great Stag: A Sumerian Divinity and its Affiliations," *AJA* 56 (1952) 171.

Henry Ludwig F. Lutz, "Concerning the Possible Egypto-Libyan Background of Nergal," *JAOS* 72 (1952) 30-33.

Ida Boboula, "The Sumerian Goddess BA-Ú," *AJA* 57 (1953) 104-105.

*H. H. Figulla, "Accounts concerning Allocation of Provisions for Offerings in the Ningal-Temple at Ur," *Iraq* 15 (1953) 88-122, 171-192.

Thorkild Jacobsen and Samuel N[oah] Kramer, "The Myth of Inanna and Bilulu," *JNES* 12 (1953) 160-188. *[Sumerian]*

Sidney Smith, "On a Study of the Babylonian Religion," *CQR* 155 (1954) 249-258.

T. Francis Glasson, "The Descent of Istar: From Ashtoreth to the Incarnation," *CongQL* 32 (1954) 313-321.

E. Douglas Van Buren, "New Evidence Concerning an Eye-divinity," *Iraq* 17 (1955) 164-175.

*Samuel Noah Kramer, "Sumerian Theology and Ethics," *HTR* 49 (1956) 45-62.

T. Fish, "d.GÌR," *MCS* 7 (1957) 13-14. *[Babylonian Deity]*

*G. G. Garner, "*Writing and the Bible:* Gods Stolen and Restored," *AT* 2 (1957-58) #4, 8-10.

Ida Boboula, "The Symbol of the Magna Mater," *AJA* 62 (1958) 221-222.

Samuel Noah Kramer, "Death and the Nether World according to the Sumerian Literary Texts," *Iraq* 22 (1960) 59-68.

*D. J. Wiseman, "The Goddess Lama at Ur," *Iraq* 22 (1960) 166-171.

Erica Reiner, "Fortune-Telling in Mesopotamia," *JNES* 19 (1960) 23-55.

*D. Cracknell, "*Abraham and Ur:* Mesopotamian Commerce and Religion," *AT* 5 (1960-61) #1, 6-8.

Thorkild Jacobsen, "Toward the Image of Tammuz," *HRel* 1 (1961-62) 189-213.

Joseph Fontenrose, "Concerning Kramer's Review of *Python*," *AJA* 66 (1962) 189-191. *[Tammuz]*

O. R. Gurney, "Tammuz Reconsidered: Some Recent Observations," *JSS* 7 (1962) 147-160.

Samuel Noah Kramer, "The Ieros Gamos in Sumer: The Data, New and Old," *AJA* 67 (1963) 213.

S[amuel] N[oah] Kramer, "Dilmun: Quest for Paradise," *Antiq* 37 (1963) 111-115.

Edwin C. Kingsbury, "A Seven Day Ritual in the Old Babylonian Cult at Larsa," *HUCA* 34 (1963) 1-34.

Samuel Noah Kramer, "The Indus Civilization and Dilmun, the Sumerian Paradise Land," *Exped* 6 (1963-64) #3, 44-52.

Ruth Stiehl, "The Origin of the Cult of Sarapis," *HRel* 3 (1963-64) 21-33.

*Edwin M. Yamauchi, "Tammuz and the Bible," *JBL* 84 (1965) 283-290.

*Roy A. Rosenberg, "The God Ṣedeq," *HUCA* 36 (1965) 161-177.

*Willy Hartner, "The Earliest History of the Constellations in the Near East and the Motif of the Lion-Bull Combat," *JNES* 24 (1965) 1-16.

S[amuel] N[oah] Kramer, "Dumuzi's Annual Resurrection: An Important Correction to 'Inanna's Descent'," *BASOR* #183 (1966) 31.

E[dwin] M. Yamauchi, "Additional Notes on Tammuz," *JSS* 11 (1966) 10-15.

Richard Caplice, "Participants in the Namburbi Rituals," *CBQ* 29 (1967) 346-352.

*A. R. Miller, "A New Babylonian 'Genesis' Story," *TB* #18 (1967) 3-28.

*Daniel Hammerly-Dupuy, "Some Observations on the Assyro-Babylonian and Sumerian Flood Stories," *AUSS* 6 (1968) 1-18.

*Miguel Civil, "Išme-Dagan and Enlil's Chariot," *JAOS* 88 (1968) 3-14. [CBS 6136] *[Sumerian]*

William W. Hallo, "Individual Prayer in Sumerian: The Continuity of a Tradition," *JAOS* 88 (1968) 71-89.

Thorkild Jacobsen, "The Battle between Marduk and Tiamat," *JAOS* 88 (1968) 104-108.

W. G. Lambert, "Myth and Ritual as Conceived by the Babylonians," *JSS* 13 (1968) 104-112.

*Ichiro Nakata, "Problems of the Babylonian *akītu* Festival," *JANES* 1 (1968-69) #1, 41-49.

David B. Weisberg, "An Old Babylonian Forerunner to *Šumma Ālu*," *HUCA* 40 (1969) 87-104. *[Divination]*

Hope Nash Wolff, "Gilgamesh, Enkidu, and the Heroic Life," *JAOS* 89 (1969) 392-398.

§469 *3.2.15.2.3 Canaanite and Phoenician Religion, including Ugaritic Mythology*

*†Anonymous, "Discourses on Elijah and John the Baptist," *BCQTR, 4th Ser.,* 17 (1835) 295-309. [Baal, pp. 306-308] *[Review]*

Anonymous, "Derceto, the Goddess of Ascalon," *JSL, 4th Ser.,* 7 (1865) 1-20.

[Joseph] Barclay, "Biblical Notes. The Worship of Molech," *Exp, 1st Ser.,* 7 (1878) 318.

*W. St. Chad Boscawen, "A Phœnician Funeral Tablet," *PEFQS* 14 (1882) 38-47.

[A. H.] Sayce, "The Phœnician Ritual," *ONTS* 4 (1884-85) 322-323.

*A. L. Frothingham Jr., "On the Meaning of Baalim and Ashtaroth in the Old Testament," *JAOS* 11 (1885) ccxxviii-ccxxix.

James S. Blackwell, "Ashtôreth, the Canaanitish Goddess," *PAPA* 18 (1886) viii-ix.

C[laude] R. C[onder], "Notes. *The Chimæra*," *PEFQS* 18 (1886) 18.

G. W. Collins, "'Ashtoreth and the 'Ashera," *SBAP* 11 (1888-89) 291-303.

J. Pollard, "On the Baal and Ashtoreth Altar discovered at Kanawat in Syria, now in the Fitzwilliam Museum at Cambridge," *SBAP* 13 (1890-91) 286-297.

†A. S. Murray, "Letter on the Altar from Kanawat," *SBAP* 13 (1890-91) 438.

*George A. Barton, "Ashtoreth and her influence in the Old Testament," *JBL* 10 (1891) 73-91.

†Joseph Pollard, "Letter from R. Hamilton Lang, with reference to the Altar from Kanawat," *SBAP* 14 (1891-92) 32.

*William Hayes Ward, "Light on Texts from Recent Discoveries. VII. The Immortality of the Soul in the Inscription of Panammu I," *HR* 26 (1893) 127-128.

*G. Schumacher, "Reports from Galilee," *PEFQS* 27 (1895) 110-114. [Idol, p. 113]

*W. W. Moore, "Oannes and Dagon," *USR* 7 (1895-96) 191-197.

*George F. Moore, "Biblical Notes," *JBL* 16 (1897) 155-165. [The Image of Moloch, pp. 161-165]

Karl Budde, "Ashera in the Old Testament," *NW* 8 (1899) 732-740.

Joseph Offord, "Ashteroth-Karnaim," *SBAP* 21 (1899) 173-174. *[Ashteroth = Venus = Karnaim]*

*Fritz Hommel, "Asherah Among the Ancient Minaeans," *ET* 11 (1899-1900) 190.

*Ghosn-el Howie, "Gezer Foundation Deposits and Modern Beliefs," *RP* 3 (1904) 212-216.

*E[duard] König, "Has the Name 'Jehweh' Been Found Among the Canaanites?" *ET* 17 (1905-06) 331-333.

Henry W. A. Hanson, "The Religion of Palestine at the Time of the Israelitic Conquest," *LQ* 37 (1907) 239-258.

*F. de P. Castells, "The Earliest Hebrew Script," *ET* 20 (1908-09) 429-431. *[Ashtoreth*, pp. 430-431]

Stanley A. Cook, "The Cult of Baal and Astarte in England," *PEFQS* 41 (1909) 280-284.

D. D. Luckenbill, "The Early Religion of Palestine," *BW* 35 (1910) 296-308, 365-379.

Stanley A. Cook, "Notes on the Old Canaanite Religion," *Exp, 7th Ser.,* 10 (1910) 111-127.

W. Carleton Wood, "The Religion of Canaan. From Earliest Times to the Hebrew Conquest," *JBL* 35 (1916) 1-133, 163-279.

G. W. Gilmore, "The Pre-Hebraic Religion of Canaan," *HR* 73 (1917) 231-232.

A[lbert] T. Clay, "Name of the so-called deity Za-mal-mal," *JAOS* 37 (1917) 328-329. *[Baal Zebûb]*

*Theophilus G. Pinches, "The Creation-legend and the Sabbath in Babylonia and Amurru," *JRAS* (1920) 583-589.

Samuel A. B. Mercer, "Divine Service in Ur," *JSOR* 5 (1921) 1-17.

*Theophilus G. Pinches, "The Influence of the Heathenism of the Canaanites upon the Hebrews," *JTVI* 60 (1928) 122-142, 145-147. (Discussion, pp. 143-145)

Ch. Virolleaud, "The Gods of Phoenicia," *Antiq* 5 (1931) 405-414.

Elmer A. Leslie, "Light from Archaeology on the Religion of Canaan," *MR* 114 (1931) 387-395.

*W[illiam] F[oxwell] Albright, "The North-Canaanite Epic of 'Al'êyân Ba'al and Môt," *JPOS* 12 (1932) 185-208.

*W[illiam] F[oxwell] Albright, "More Light on the Canaanite Epic of Aleyân Baal and Môt," *BASOR* #50 (1933) 13-20.

*W[illiam] F[oxwell] Albright, "The North-Canaanite Poems of Al'êyân Ba'al and the 'Gracious Gods'," *JPOS* 14 (1934) 101-140. [The Myth of the Gracious Gods, pp. 134-140]

H. L. Ginsberg, "The Victory of the Land-God over the Sea-God," *JPOS* 15 (1935) 327-333.

W[illiam] F[oxwell] Albright, "New Canaanite Historical and Mythological Data," *BASOR* #63 (1936) 23-32.

W[illiam] F[oxwell] Albright, "Zabûl Yam and Thâpiṭ Nahar in the Combat between Baal and the Sea," *JPOS* 16 (1936) 17-20.

H. L. Ginsberg, "Ba'lu and his Brethren," *JPOS* 16 (1936) 138-149.

W[illiam] F[oxwell] Albright, "The Canaanite God Ḥaurôn (Ḥôrôn)," *AJSL* 53 (1936-37) 1-12.

Cyrus H. Gordon, "A Marriage of the Gods in Canaanite Mythology," *BASOR* #65 (1937) 29-33.

Theodor H. Gaster, "Groupings of Deities in the Ritual Tariffs from Ras Shamra-Ugarit," *AfO* 12 (1937-39) 148-150.

*W[illiam] F[oxwell] Albright, "Was the Patriarch Terah a Canaanite Moon-God?" *BASOR* #71 (1938) 35-40.

*H. L. Ginsberg, "Women Singers and Wailers Among the Northern Canaanites," *BASOR* #72 (1938) 13-15.

J. Philip Hyatt, "The Deities of Ugarit," *BA* 2 (1939) 4-6.

J. Philip Hyatt, "An Early Daniel, and Other Parallels," *BA* 2 (1939) 8.

*J. Philip Hyatt, "Canaanite Religion and Its Influence on the Hebrews," *BA* 2 (1939) 6-7.

Theodor H. Gaster, "'Ba'al is Risen...': An Ancient Hebrew Passion Play from Ras Shamra-Ugarit," *Iraq* 6 (1939) 109-143.

*H. L. Ginsberg, "Two Religious Borrowings in Ugaritic Literature. I. A Hurrian Myth in Semitic Dress," *Or, N.S.*, 8 (1939) 317-327.

*John Pedersen, "Canaanite and Israelite Cultus," *AO* 18 (1939-40) 1-14.

*J. W. Jack, "Recent Biblical Archaeology. The Rephaim," *ET* 51 (1939-40) 421-422. *[Religious Attendants]*

*H. L. Ginsberg, "Two Religious Borrowings in Ugaritic Literature. II. The Egyptian God Ptaḥ in Ugaritic Mythology," *Or, N.S.*, 9 (1940) 39-44.

Albrecht Goetze, "The Ugaritic Deities *pdgl* and *ibnkl*," *Or, N.S.*, 9 (1940) 223-228.

H. L. Ginsberg, "The Ugaritic Deity *'Ibnkl*. A Rejoinder," *Or, N.S.*, 9 (1940) 228-229.

H. L. Ginsberg, "Did Anath Fight the Dragon?" *BASOR* #84 (1941) 12-14.

W[illiam] F[oxwell] Albright, 'Anath and the Dragon," *BASOR* #84 (1941) 14-16.

G. Levi Della Vida, "The Phoenician God Satrapes," *BASOR* #87 (1942) 29-32.

J. B. Pritchard, "Some Aspects of *Anat*," *JBL* 61 (1942) ix.

Umberto Cassuto, "The Palace of Baal," *JBL* 61 (1942) 51-56.

W[illiam] F[oxwell] Albright and George F. Mendenhall, "The Creation of the Composite Bow in Canaanite Mythology," *JNES* 1 (1942) 227-229.

*E. L. Sukenik, "Installations in Connection with the Cult of the Dead in Canaanite Ugarit and in Israelite Samaria," *KSJA* 1 (1942) VIII-IX.

*Theodor H. Gaster, "A Canaanite Magical Text," *Or, N.S.,* 11 (1942) 41-79.

W[illiam] F[oxwell] Albright, "The Furniture of El in Canaanite Mythology," *BASOR* #91 (1943) 39-44.

T[heodor] H. Gaster, "The Furniture of El in Canaanite Mythology," *BASOR* #93 (1944) 20-23.

W[illiam] F[oxwell] Albright, "In Reply to Dr. Gaster's Observations," *BASOR* #93 (1944) 23-25.

H. L. Ginsberg, "Baal's Two Messengers," *BASOR* #95 (1944) 25-30.

T[heodor] H. Gaster, "Folklore Myths in Canaanite Myth," *JRAS* (1944) 30-51.

H. L. Ginsberg, "The North-Canaanite Myth of Anath and Aqhat I," *BASOR* #97 (1945) 3-10.

H. L. Ginsberg, "The North-Canaanite Myth of Anath and Aqhat," *BASOR* #98 (1945) 15-23. [Part II]

Vivian Jacobs and Rosensohn Jacobs, "The Myth of Môt and 'Al'eyan Ba'al," *HTR* 38 (1945) 77-109.

H. L. Ginsberg, "Astarte and Anath," *JBL* 64 (1945) iv.

T[heodor] H. Gaster, "The Canaanite Myth of Baal and the Dragon," *JBL* 64 (1945) iv.

*J. H. Iliffe, "A Model Shrine of Phoenician Style," *QDAP* 11 (1945) 91-92.

*Theodor H. Gaster, "The King Without a Castle—Baal's Appeal to Asherat," *BASOR* #101 (1946) 21-30.

*Theodor H. Gaster, "A Canaanite Ritual Drama. The Spring Festival at Ugarit," *JAOS* 66 (1946) 49-76.

*Julian Obermann, "How Daniel was Blessed with a Son. An Incubation Scene in Ugaritic," *JAOSS* #6 (1946) 1-30.

T[heodor] H. Gaster, "The Canaanite Seasonal Myth: Observations on the Ugaritic Poem of Baal," *JBL* 65 (1946) iv-v.

Yigael Sukenik, "The Composite Bow of the Canaanite Goddess Anath," *BASOR* #107 (1947) 11-15.

*Julian Obermann, "How Baal Destroyed a Rival. *A Mythological Incantation Scene*," *JAOS* 67 (1947) 195-208.

J. B. Pritchard, "The Restatement of the Problem of Palestine Figurines," *JBL* 66 (1947) v.

*Sabatino Moscati, "The Wind in Biblical and Phoenician Cosmology," *JBL* 66 (1947) 305-310.

*J[ohn] Gray, "The Wrath of God in Canaanite and Hebrew Literature," *JMUEOS* #25 (1947-53) 9-19.

*David Neiman, "PGR: A Canaanite Cult-Object in the Old Testament," *JBL* 67 (1948) 55-60.

Theodor H. Gaster, "Ugaritic Mythology," *JNES* 7 (1948) 184-193.

D. M. L. Urie, "Officials of the Cult at Ugarit," *PEQ* 80 (1948) 42-47.

W[illiam] F[oxwell] Albright, "Baal-Zephon," *JBL* 68 (1949) xix.

John Gray, "The Canaanite God Horon," *JNES* 8 (1949) 27-34.

John Gray, "The Desert God 'Aṯtr in the Literature and Religion of Canaan," *JNES* 8 (1949) 72-83.

Merrill F. Unger, "Archaeology and the Religion of the Canaanites," *BS* 107 (1950) 168-174.

*John Gray, "Canaanite Mythology and Hebrew Traditions," *GUOST* 14 (1950-52) 47-57.

Frank J. Montalbano, "Canaanite Dagon: Origin, Nature," *CBQ* 13 (1951) 381-397.

John Gray, "The Hunting of Ba'al: Fratricide and Atonement in the Mythology of Ras Shamra," *JNES* 10 (1951) 146-155.

*Theodor H. Gaster, "The Egyptian 'Story of Astarte' and the Ugaritic Poem of Baal," *BO* 9 (1952) 82-85.

M. Avi-Yonah, "Mount Carmel and the God of Baalbek," *IEJ* 2 (1952) 118-124.

Cyrus H. Gordon, "Notes on the Legend of Keret," *JNES* 11 (1952) 212-213.

*R. T. O'Callaghan, "The Word *ktp* in Ugarit and Egypto-Canaanite Mythology," *Or, N.S.,* 21 (1952) 37-46.

*Cyrus H. Gordon, "Marginal Notes on the Ancient Middle East," *JKF* 2 (1952-53) 50-61. [III. Phoeniciana: b. The Phoenician worship of a heptad called the κάβειροι = כְּבִּירִים, p. 53]

Matitiahu Tsevat, "The Ugaritic Goddess Nikkal-Wïb," *JNES* 12 (1953) 61-62.

John Gray, "The God *YW* in the Religion of Canaan," *JNES* 12 (1953) 278-283.

*C[yrus] H. Gordon, "Sabbatical Cycle or Seasonal Pattern? Reflections on a New Book," *Or, N.S.,* 22 (1953) 79-81. *(Review) [Baal in Ras-Shamra Texts]*

Y. Leibovitz, "The Canaanite God Hôrûn," *EI* 3 (1954) III.

Matitiahu Tsevat, "The Canaanite God Šälaḥ," *VT* 4 (1954) 41-49.

Matitiahu Tsevat, "Additional Remarks to 'The Canaanite God Šälaḥ'," *VT* 4 (1954) 322.

Antonine A. DeGuglielmo, "Sacrifice in the Ugaritic Texts," *CBQ* 17 (1955) 196-216.

M. H. Pope, "El in the Ugaritic Texts," *VTS* 2 (1955) i-x, 1-116.

F[rede] Løkkegaard, "The House of Baal," *AO* 22 (1955-57) 10-27.

*H. St. J. Hart, "The face of Baal: the interest of ancient coin types and legends for biblical studies," *OSHTP* (1955-56) 35-36.

Frede Løkkegaard, "The Canaanite Divine Wetnurses," *ST* 10 (1956) 53-64. *[Anat]*

Joseph Fontenrose, "Dagon and El," *Oriens* 10 (1957) 277-279.

Mary Neely, "The Canaanites: The Depths of Religious Corruption," *AT* 3 (1958-59) #3, 13-15.

Mary Neely, "The Canaanites: The Bloodthirsty Anat," *AT* 3 (1958-59) #4, 8-10.

S. E. Loewenstamm, "The Muzzling of the Tannin in Ugaritic Myth," *IEJ* 9 (1959) 260-261.

*Svi Rin, "The מות of Grandeur," *VT* 9 (1959) 324-325. *[Mot]*

Mary Neely, "The Canaanites: Baal—Rider of the Clouds," *AT* 4 (1959-60) #1, 12-14.

*Mary Neely, "The Canaanites: The God that Answered by Fire," *AT* 4 (1959-60) #2, 6-8.

*Charles F. Pfeiffer, "Lotan and Leviathan," *EQ* 32 (1960) 208-211.

*G. Garbini, "The God 'Astar in the Inscription from Byblos," *Or, N.S.,* 29 (1960) 322.

*G. Garbini, "The Phoenician 'Goddess' in the Louvre," *Or, N.S.,* 29 (1960) 323-328.

*Julian Morgenstern, "The King-God Among the Western Semites and the Meaning of Epiphanies," *VT* 10 (1960) 138-197. [I. The Tyrian King-God, pp. 138-176]

Samuel Iwry, "New Evidence for Belomancy in Ancient Palestine and Phoenicia," *JAOS* 81 (1961) 27-34.

Samuel E. Loewenstamm, "The Climax of Seven Days in the Ugaritic Epos," *Tarbiz* 31 (1961-62) #3, I.

*U[mberto] Cassuto, "Baal and Mot in the Ugaritic Texts," *IEJ* 12 (1962) 77-86.

S[amuel] E. Loewenstamm, "The Ugaritic Fertility Myth—the Result of a Mistranslation," *IEJ* 12 (1962) 87-88.

*Norman Walker, "'Adam' and 'Eve' and 'Adon'," *ZAW* 74 (1962) 66-68. *[Phoenician god: '- d-n]*

R. N. Whybray, "Canaanite Creation Myth," *ET* 74 (1962-63) 309.

*E. C. B. MacLaurin, "The Development of the Idea of God in Ancient Canaan," *JRelH* 2 (1962-63) 277-294.

*A. S. Kapelrud, "Baal and Mot in the Ugaritic Texts," *IEJ* 13 (1963) 127-129.

S[amuel] E. Loewenstamm, "The Ugaritic Fertility Myth—a Reply," *IEJ* 13 (1963) 130-132.

*Harry A. Hoffner Jr., "An Anatolian Cult Term in Ugaritic," *JNES* 22 (1963) 66-68.[*dg̃t*]

A. S. Kapelrud, "Temple Building, a Task for Gods and Kings," *Or, N.S.,* 32 (1963) 56-62.

Hans Kosmala, "Mot and the Vine: The Time of the Ugaritic Fertility Rite," *ASTI* 3 (1964) 147-151.

*Anonymous, "Recent Acquisitions by the Institute. A Bronze Cast of the Goddess Asherah," *BH* 1 (1964) #1, 8-9.

*Anonymous, "Recent Acquisitions by the Institute. Baal, God of The Canaanites," *BH* 1 (1964) #1, 10-11.

Anson F. Rainey, "Organized Religion at Ugarit," *CNI* 15 (1964) #1, 16-24.

*B. Landsberger and H. Tadmor, "Fragments of Clay Liver Models from Hazor," *IEJ* 14 (1964) 201-218.

*Anonymous, "Jezebel and the Goddess of Love. Canaanite myths referring to the goddess Anat provide an interesting background to the story of Naboth's vineyard, 1 Kings 21," *BH* 2 (1965) #3, 4-9.

*Patrick D. Miller Jr., "Fire in the Mythology of Canaan and Israel," *CBQ* 27 (1965) 256-261.

*Frank E. Eakin Jr., "Yahwism and Baalism Before the Exile," *JBL* 84 (1965) 407-414.

Clark Hopkins, "Astrological Interpretations of Some Phoenician Bowls," *JNES* 24 (1965) 28-36.

Raphael Patai, "The Goddess Asherah," *JNES* 24 (1965) 37-52.

*John Pairman Brown, "Kothar, Kinyras, and Kythereia," *JSS* 10 (1965) 197-219.

Th. C. Vriezen, "The Edomitic Deity Qaus," *OTS* 14 (1965) 330-353.

*L. R. Fisher, "Creation at Ugarit and in the Old Testament," *VT* 15 (1965) 313-324.

John Gray, "Social Aspects of Canaanite Religion," *VTS* 15 (1965) 170-192.

Ora Negbi and S. Moskowitz, "The 'Foundation Deposits' or 'Offering Deposits' of Byblos," *BASOR* #184 (1966) 21-26.

Michael C. Astour, "Some New Divine Names from Ugarit," *JAOS* 86 (1966) 277-284.

F. C[harles] Fensham, "Winged Gods and Goddesses in the Ugaritic Tablets," *OA* 5 (1966) 157-164.

N[orman] H. Snaith, "The Cult of Molech," *VT* 16 (1966) 123-124.

*Samuel E. Loewenstamm, "Prostration from Afar in Ugaritic, Accadian and Hebrew," *BASOR* #188 (1967) 41-43.

Barch A. Levine, "Offerings to the Temple Gates at Ur," *HUCA* 38 (1967) 17-58.

*Frank E. Eakin Jr., "The Reed Sea and Baalism," *JBL* 86 (1967) 378-384.

F. Charles Fensham, "A possible explanation of the name Baal-Zebub of Ekron," *ZAW* 79 (1967) 361-364.

Frank L. Benz, "The Lady and the Lamp," *Amb* 16 (1967-68) #2, 8-9. *[Canaanite Religion]*

Anonymous, "A Greater than Baal is here," *BH* 4 (1968) 35-41.

*R. E. Clements, "Baal-Berith of Shechem," *JSS* 13 (1968) 21-32.

*Frank M. Cross, "The Song of the Sea and Canaanite Myth," *JTC* 5 (1968) 1-25.

J. C. de Moor, "Murices in Ugaritic Mythology," *Or, N.S.,* 37 (1968) 212-215.

Arthur L. Merrill, "The House of Keret: A Study of the Keret Legend," *SEÅ* 33 (1968) 5-17.

W[illiam] Culican, "Dea Tyria Gravida," *AJBA* 1 (1968-71) #2, 35-50. *[Astarte]*

William Culican, "Problems of Phoenicio-Punic Iconography—A Contribution," *AJBA* 1 (1968-71) #3, 28-57.

*R. D. Barnett, "'Anath, Ba'al and Pasargadae," *MUSJ* 45 (1969) 405-422.

§470　3.2.15.2.4 *Egyptian Religion and "Philosophy"*

†Anonymous, "Prichard's Analysis of Egyptian Mythology," *BCQTR, N.S.,* 14 (1820) 55-69. *(Review)*

*†Anonymous, "Lane's *Manners and Customs of the Modern Egyptians,*" *QRL* 59 (1837) 165-208. *(Review)* [Note on Egyptian Magic, pp. 203-208]

*G. Seyffarth, "Three Lectures on Egyptian Antiquities, &c., delivered at the Stuyvesant Institute, New York, May 1856," *ER* 8 (1856-57) 34-104. [IV. The Judicium Mortuorum, *(Judgment of the dead),* pp. 69-70; VI. The Phœnix, pp. 70-72]

W. R. A[lger(?)], "The Egyptian Doctrine of the Future Life," *UQGR* 13 (1856) 136-147.

Joseph P. Thompson, "The Egyptian Doctrine of a Future State," *BS* 25 (1868) 69-112.

Joseph P. Thompson, "On The Egyptian Doctrine of the Future Life," *JAOS* 9 (1871) xxxii-xxxiii.

C. W. Goodwin, "On the name Astennu," *ZÄS* 10 (1872) 108-109. *[A Name of the god Thoth]*

W. R. Cooper, "Observations on the Serpent Myths of Ancient Egypt," *JTVI* 6 (1872-73) 321-393. (Discussion, pp. 393-403)

*C. W. Goodwin, "Translation of an Egyptian Hymn to Amen," *SBAT* 2 (1873) 250-263.

*C. W. Goodwin, "Hymns to Amen," *SBAT* 2 (1873) 353-359.

*C. W. Goodwin, "Notes by C. W. Goodwin," *ZÄS* 11 (1873) 12-15. [6. The vessels of the brain, pp. 14-15]

(   ) Nichols, "Side-Lights. Egyptian Ritual of the Dead," *DTQ* 1 (1875) 143.

Keningale Cook "The Ancient Faith of Egypt," *DUM* 90 (1877) 27-51.

*W. R. Cooper, "On the Myth of Ra (the Supreme Sun-God of Egypt), with copious Citations from the Solar and Pantheistic Litanies," *JTVI* 11 (1877-78) 294-339, 343-345. (Discussion, pp. 339-343)

Robert Brown Jr., "The Archaic Solar-Cult of Egypt.—Part I. Ra," *TRL* 15 (1878) 513-533.

Hyde Clarke, "On the Relations between Pasht, the Moon, and the Cat, in Egypt," *SBAT* 6 (1878-79) 316-322.

Robert Brown Jr., "The Archaic Solar-Cult of Egypt. Part II. Uasar," *TRL* 16 (1879) 22-44.

T. O. Paine, "Osirids of Ancient Egypt," *OBJ* 1 (1880) 62-66.

P. le Page Renouf, "Egyptian Mythology, Mist and Cloud," *SBAP* 4 (1881-82) 75-76.

P. le Page Renouf, "The Bow in the Egyptian Sky," *SBAP* 6 (1883-84) 131-132.

P. le Page Renouf, "The Egyptian god ⟨hieroglyphs⟩," *SBAP* 6 (1883-84) 187-189.

P. le Page Renouf, "Egyptian Mythology, particularly with reference to Mist and Cloud," *SBAT* 8 (1883-84) 198-229.

Samuel Birch, "On the Shade or Shadow of the Dead," *SBAT* 8 (1883-84) 386-397.

F. G. Fleay, "Lectures on Polytheism. II. On the Egyptian Mythologies," *AAOJ* 6 (1884) 159-167.

Howard Osgood, "The Dogma of the Resurrection Among the Ancient Egyptians," *ONTS* 4 (1884-85) 267-275.

Samuel Birch, "On the Egyptian Belief concerning the Shade or Shadow of the Dead," *SBAP* 7 (1884-85) 45-49.

S[amuel] Birch, "On some Egyptian Rituals of the Roman Period," *SBAP* 7 (1884-85) 49-50.

*†J. Lieblein, "The 'Great Cackler'," *SBAP* 7 (1884-85) 99-100. *[Seb]*

*P. le Page Renouf, "Seb, the Great Cackler," *SBAP* 7 (1884-85) 152-154.

Lysander Dickermann, "The Deities of Ancient Egypt," *AR* 3 (1885) 374-390. [I. The Classification of the Gods; II. The Relation of the Gods to each Other; III. The Nature of the Egyptian Gods; IV. The Divine Attributes; V. The Egyptian Theory of Divine Government]

(   ) E., "Brugsch's Religion and Mythology of the Ancient Egyptians," *Exp, 3rd Ser.,* 1 (1885) 156-158. *(Review)*

T. O. Paine, "On the doctrine of God and the Soul among the most ancient Nile-dwellers," *JAOS* 11 (1885) xcii.

*A. Wiedemann, "Notes on the Cult of Set and on the Hyksos-Kings," *SBAP* 8 (1885-86) 92-95.

P. le Page Renouf, "The Myth of Osiris Unnefer," *SBAP* 8 (1885-86) 111-116.

*C. Loring Brace, "Egyptian Monotheism," *NPR* 1 (1886) 346-361.

P. le Page Renouf, "The Name of the Egyptian God Seb," *SBAP* 9 (1886-87) 83-97.

P. le Page Renouf, "The Myth of Osiris Unnefer," *SBAT* 9 (1886-93) 281-294.

F. Ll. Griffith, "Letter from Egypt," *BOR* 2 (1887-88) 146-147. *[Egyptian Religion]*

Georgia Louise Leonard, "The Occult Science in the Temples of Ancient Egypt," *OC* 1 (1887-88) 470-472, 496-498.

P. le Page Renouf, "Notes. 1. The Horus Standard and the Seat of Horus," *SBAP* 14 (1887-88) 17-21.

G. Maspero, "Egyptian Souls and Their Worlds," *NPR* 6 (1888) 23-36.

Lewis G. Janes, "Egyptian Doctrine of the Future Life," *URRM* 29 (1888) 33-48.

*P. le Page Renouf, "The Names of Isis and Osiris," *SBAP* 12 (1889-90) 343-346.

P. le Page Renouf, "Neith of Sais. *Nomina numina,*" *SBAP* 12 (1889-90) 347-352.

*P. le Page Renouf, "The Sunstroke in Egyptian," *SBAP* 12 (1889-90) 460-461.

F. C. H. Wendel, "Prolegomena to a Historical Account of the Egyptian Religion," *JAOS* 14 (1890) cxxix-cxxxi.

P. le Page Renouf, "Nile Mythology," *SBAP* 13 (1890-91) 4-11.

W. S. Kress, "Religion of the Ancient Egyptians," *ACQR* 16 (1891) 703-722.

*Anonymous, "The Future Life in Egypt and Israel," *ONTS* 13 (1891) 120-121.

Joseph Offord Jr., "The Myth of Osiris and Isis," *SBAP* 14 (1891-92) 371-373.

P. le Page Renouf, "The Gods Akar and Seb," *SBAP* 15 (1892-93) 385-386.

Camden M. Cobern, "A peculiarly Sacred Posture avoided in Ancestor Worship," *SBAP* 15 (1892-93) 521.

*James Henry Breasted, "The Development of the Priesthood in Israel and Egypt—A Comparison," *BW* 2 (1893) 19-28.

*J. Norman Lockyer, "The Early Temple and Pyramid Builders," *SIR* (1893) 95-105.

F. L. Griffith, "The God Set of Ramessu II and an Egypto-Syrian Deity," *SBAP* 16 (1893-94) 87-90.

George A. Barton, "Notes. II. On the God Mut," *AJSL* 10 (1893-94) 205-206.

J. Hunt Cooke, "Exploration and Discovery. The Banquet of Paheri," *BW* 4 (1894) 444-446.

*Felix Robiou, "A Study of Egyptian and Babylonian Triads," *IAQR, 2nd Ser.,* 7 (1894) 119-136.

W. St. Chad Boscawen, "Egyptian Eschatology," *ET* 6 (1894-95) 392-395.

W. St. Chad Boscawen, "Egyptian Psychology," *ET* 6 (1894-95) 458-459.

W. St. Chad Boscawen, "The Egyptian Heaven," *ET* 6 (1894-95) 535-538.

*George A. Barton, "Notes," *JAOS* 16 (1894-96) cxciii. [2. On the God Mut]

Paul Carus, "The Conceptions of Death and Immortality in Ancient Egypt," *OC* 9 (1895) #41, 4666-4670.

*W. St. C[had] Boscawen, "The Creative Power of the Divine Word and Name," *BOR* 8 (1895-1900) 271-276.

Ebenezer   Davis,   "Serapis,"   *PEFQS*   28   (1896)   337-339.

P. le Page Renouf, "The God [hieroglyphs]," *SBAP* 18 (1896) 111-112.

*Walter L. Nash, "A Bronze Uraeus of unusual form," *SBAP* 20 (1898) 145-146.

Josephine Williams, "Religious Ideas of the Ancient Egyptians," *WR* 150 (1898) 655-669.

F. G. Hilton Price, "Notes on Some Egyptian Deities," *SBAP* 21 (1899) 239-241. [Set, Ȧpuat, and Ȧnupt]

F. Ll. Griffith, "Notes on Mythology. Eileithyia in Egypt. The God of Busiris, Hermes Trismegistus," *SBAP* 21 (1899) 277-279.

*Percy E. Newberry, "Egyptian Historical Notes. (IV)," *SBAP* 23 (1901) 218-224. [23. A Priest of Astarte, pp. 219-220]

George St. Clair, "Pasht and the Sed Festival," *SBAP* 23 (1901) 225-229.

James Henry Breasted, "The Philosophy of a Memphite Priest," *ZÄS* 39 (1901) 39-54.

P. Henderson Aitken, "Divination in Ancient Egypt," *GUOST* 2 (1901-07) 30-31.

Isaac Myer, "An Egyptian Idea of Heaven," *RP* 1 (1902) 278-280.

*(Mrs.) Alice Grenfell, "The Iconography of Bes, and of Phoenician Bes-Hand Scarabs," *SBAP* 24 (1902) 21-40.

James Henry Breasted, "The Philosophy of a Memphite Priest," *OC* 17 (1903) 458-479.

W. L. Nash, "Ha-Mhyt. Goddess of the Mendesian Nome," *SBAP* 25 (1903) 112.

J. Herbert Walker, "The Egyptian Doctrine of the Transformation of Funeral Offerings," *SBAP* 26 (1904) 70-71.

*G. A. Wainwright, "The formula ⸗ in the light of mythology," *SBAP* 26 (1904) 101-104.

W. M. Flinders Petrie, "Animal Worship in Egypt," *SBAP* 26 (1904) 113-114.

*E. Naville, "The Mention of a Flood in the Book of the Dead," *SBAP* 26 (1904) 251-257, 287-294.

[Paul Carus], "The Conception of the Soul and the Belief in the Resurrection Among the Egyptians," *Monist* 15 (1905) 409-428.

Anonymous, "Offerings and Sacrifices in Egypt," *RP* 4 (1905) 159-160.

Anonymous, "Egyptian Serpent Gods," *RP* 4 (1905) 319.

M[elvin] G[rove] Kyle, "Egyptian Sacrifices, a Study of sacrificial scenes in painting and sculpture," *RTR* 27 (1905) 161-169.

(Mrs.) Alice Grenfell, "Egyptian Mythology and the Bible," *Monist* 16 (1906) 169-200.

*Edgar L. Larkin, "The Waning of the Light of Egypt," *OC* 20 (1906) 228-242.

*Margaret A. Murray, "The Astrological Character of the Egyptian Magical Wands," *SBAP* 28 (1906) 33-43.

Valdemar Schmidt, "Two Statuettes of the Goddess Buto," *SBAP* 28 (1906) 201-202.

*Alan H. Gardiner, "The goddess Ningal in an Egyptian text," *ZÄS* 43 (1906) 97.

Joseph Offord, "The Religion of the Ancient Egyptians," *AAOJ* 29 (1907) 95-100.

James H. Breasted, "The Message of the Religion of Egypt," *BW* 29 (1907) 427-434.

*W. M. Flinders Petrie, "The Soul-House in Egypt," *Man* 7 (1907) #71.

W. M. Flinders Petrie, "Soul-Houses in Egypt," *RP* 6 (1907) 195-201.

Percy E. Newberry, "Two Cults of the Old Kingdom," *AAA* 1 (1908) 24-29.

Anonymous, "Egyptian View of Death," *AAOJ* 30 (1908) 42-44.

*Anonymous, "The Pyramid Texts and the Future Life," *AAOJ* 30 (1908) 346-348.

Arthur E. Whatham, "The Origin and Significance of the Egyptian Ankh," *AJRPE* 3 (1908-09) 381-384.

Beresford Potter, "Some Christian Conceptions of Immortality and Resurrection in the Ancient Egyptian Religion," *ICMM* 5 (1908-09) 197-202.

Percy E. Newberry, "A Bird Cult of the Old Kingdom," *AAA* 2 (1909) 49-51.

*Arthur E. P. Weigall, "Religion and the Empire in Ancient Egypt," *QRL* 210 (1909) 44-66. *(Review)*

M[elvin] G[rove] Kyle, "Some further Observations concerning the Holocaust among the Ancient Egyptians," *RTR* 31 (1909) 49-54.

*Aylward M. Blackman, "The Nubian God Arsenuphis as Osiris," *SBAP* 32 (1909) 33-36.

G. Foucart, "An Entrance into the Lower World at Thebes," *SBAP* 32 (1909) 102-114.

F. Ll. Griffith, "Herodotus II 90. Apotheosis by drowning," *ZÄS* 46 (1909) 132-134.

Percy E. Newberry, "The Egyptian cult-Object ⊸⊶ and the 'Thunderbolt'," *AAA* 3 (1910) 50-52.

Franz Cumont, "The Religion of Egypt," *OC* 24 (1910) 553-573. *(Trans. by A. M. Thielen)*

Alan H. Gardiner, "The goddess Nekhbet at the Jubilee Festival of Ramses III," *ZÄS* 48 (1910) 47-51.

*Arthur E. P. Weigall, "Miscellaneous notes," *ASAE* 11 (1911) 170-176. [11. The *ka* receiving offerings , pp. 173-174]

F. Legge, "The Legend of Osiris," *SBAP* 33 (1911) 139-154.

Percy E. Newberry, "The Cult-animal of Set," *Klio* 12 (1912) 397-401.

*Aylward M. Blackman, "Remarks on an Incense-Brazier depicted in Thuthotep's Tomb at El-Berscheh," *ZÄS* 50 (1912) 66-68.

Aylward M. Blackman, "The Significance of Incense and Libations in Funerary and Temple Ritual," *ZÄS* 50 (1912) 69-75.

Percy E. Newberry, "Some Cults of Prehistoric Egypt," *AAA* 5 (1912-13) 123-136.

M[argaret] A. Murray, "The Cult of the Drowned in Egypt," *ZÄS* 51 (1913) 127-135.

Duncan H. Brodie, "Religion in Ancient Egypt," *GUOST* 4 (1913-22) 54-55.

W. M. Flinders Petrie, "Egyptian Beliefs in a Future Life. *(The Drew Lecture, November,* 1913)," *AEE* 1 (1914) 16-31.

M[argaret] A. Murray, "Evidence for the Custom of Killing the King in Ancient Egypt," *Man* 14 (1914) #12.

Anonymous, "Ancient Egypt and Immortality," *MR* 96 (1914) 478-483.

*F. Legge, "The Greek Worship of Serapis and Isis," *SBAP* 36 (1914) 79-99.

Ed. Mahler, "The Jackal-Gods on Ancient Egyptian Monuments," *SBAP* 36 (1914) 143-164.

*Percy E. Newberry, "Egyptian Historical Notes. III," *SBAP* 36 (1914) 168-174. [14. A Priest of the Goddess *Nebtu*, p. 169]

*George A. Barton, "Tammuz and Osiris," *JAOS* 35 (1915) 213-223.

*(Mrs.) Alice Grenfell, "The Ka on Scarabs," *RTR* 37 (1915) 77-93.

Alan H. Gardiner, "Some Personifications. I," *SBAP* 37 (1915) 253-262. [*Ḥike'*, The God of Magic; "To become Ḥike'"; Commentary]

*C. G. Seligman, "An Early Representation of Taurt," *AEE* 3 (1916) 53.

Battiscombe Gunn, "The Religion of the Poor in Egypt," *JEA* 3 (1916) 81-94.

Aylward M. Blackman, "Some Remarks on an Emblem upon the Head of an ancient Egyptian Birth-goddess," *JEA* 3 (1916) 199-206.

Aylward M. Blackman, "The Pharaoh's Placenta and the Moon-god Khons," *JEA* 3 (1916) 235-249.

F. Ll. Griffith, "An Omphalos from Napata," *JEA* 3 (1916) 255.

Joseph Offord, "Archaeological Notes. VIII. *Isis Worship*," *PEFQS* 48 (1916) 41-42.

*Alan H. Gardiner, "Some Personifications. II," *SBAP* 38 (1916) 43-54, 83-95. [*ḤU*, "Authoritative Utterance"; *SAI'* "Understanding"; "To become ḤU"; Commentary; Sequence of the Fourteen *KAS* of RĒ' and the King]

Lina Eckenstein, "The God Sopt," *AEE* 4 (1917) 103-108.

W. M. Flinders Petrie, "The Geography of the Gods," *AEE* 4 (1917) 109-119.

Anonymous, "A Little-Known Phase of Egyptian Religion," *HR* 73 (1917) 143-144.

*Battiscombe Gunn, "Interpreters of Dreams in Ancient Egypt," *JEA* 4 (1917) 252.

*Samuel A. B. Mercer, "'Emperor'-Worship in Egypt," *JSOR* 1 (1917) 10-18.

[Paul Carus], "The Egyptian Account of the Creation," *OC* 31 (1917) 437-439.

*Gustave Jéquier, "The Most Ancient Representation of the Sign ☥," *SBAP* 39 (1917) 87-88.

*Alan H. Gardiner, "Postscripta," *SBAP* 39 (1917) 133-140. [**2.** Some Personifications: i. *Ḥĭke, the god of Magic;* **3.** *Some Personifications:* ii. *Ḥu, "Authoritative Utterance"; Sia' "Understanding",* pp. 133-139]

W[illiam] F[oxwell] Albright, "The Solar Barks of Morning and Evening," *AJSL* 34 (1917-18) 142-143.

G. van der Leeuw, "The Moon-god Khons and the King's Placenta," *JEA* 5 (1918) 64.

Aylward M. Blackman, "'The House of the Morning'," *JEA* 5 (1918) 148-165.

Anonymous, "The Egyptian Mother Goddess," *OC* 32 (1918) 383-384. [*Nut*]

*W. L. Nash, "The Origin of the Mediaeval Representations of the Weighing of the Soul after Death," *SBAP* 40 (1918) 19-29.

Aylward M. Blackman, "The Sequence of the Episodes in the Egyptian Daily Temple Liturgy," *JMUEOS* #8 (1918-19) 27-53.

Aylward M. Blackman, "Sacramental Ideas and Usages in Ancient Egypt," *SBAP* 40 (1918) 57-66, 86-91.

H. F. Lutz, "The D̲D̲-Emblem of Osiris," *JAOS* 39 (1919) 196-205.

*Samuel A. B. Mercer, "Was Ikhnaton a Monotheist?" *JSOR* 3 (1919) 70-80.

M. A. Moret, "The Religious Revolution of Amenhotep IV," *OC* 33 (1919) 369-384.

N. W. Thomas, "What is the *Ka*?" *JEA* 6 (1920) 265-273.

A. C. Mace, "Communications II: Hathor Dances," *JEA* 6 (1920) 297.

A[ylward] M. Blackman, "Sacramental ideas and usages in Ancient Egypt," *RTR* 39 (1920-21) 44-78.

F. F. Bruijning, "The Tree of the Herakleopolite Nome," *AEE* 6 (1921) 104-109; 7 (1922) 1-8.

*T. Eric Peet, "The Problem of Akhenaton," *JMUEOS* #9 (1921) 39-48.

*Sidney Smith, "The Relation of Marduk, Ashur, and Osiris," *JEA* 8 (1922) 41-44.

Winifred S. Blackman, "Some Occurrences of the Corn-'arūseh in Ancient Egyptian Tomb Paintings," *JEA* 8 (1922) 235-240.

Samuel A. B. Mercer, "Divine Service in the Old Kingdom," *JSOR* 6 (1922) 41-59.

*Battiscombe Gunn, "'Finger-Numbering' in the Pyramid Texts," *ZÄS* 57 (1922) 71-72.

G. D. Hornblower, "Traces of a *Ka-* Belief in Modern Egypt and Old Arabia," *AEE* 8 (1923) 67-70.

*G. A. Wainwright, "The Red Crown in Early Prehistoric Times," *JEA* 9 (1923) 26-33.

Battiscombe Gunn, "Notes on the Aten and his Names," *JEA* 9 (1923) 168-176.

Samuel A. B. Mercer, "Sacrifice in Ancient Egypt," *JSOR* 7 (1923) 49-52.

*D. D. Luckenbill, "The Egyptian Earth-God in Cuneiform," *AJSL* 40 (1923-24) 288-292. *[Keb]*

Archibald Duff, "The Spiritual Legacy of Egypt to Us. An Essay on the Spiritual Result of the Life of Akhn-Aton, of the XVIIth Dynasty in Egypt, 1375-1358 B.C.," *HJ* 22 (1923-24) 335-349.

*Kete Denny McKnight, "The Persistence of Egyptian Traditions in Art and Religion After the Pharaohs," *A&A* 17 (1924) 43-53.

*Aylward M. Blackman, "The Rite of Opening the Mouth in Ancient Egypt and Babylonia," *JEA* 10 (1924) 47-59.

John Lewis, "The Mother Worship in Egypt," *JMUEOS* #11 (1924) 47-58.

R. O. Faulkner, "The God Setekh in the Pyramid Texts," *AEE* 10 (1925) 5-10.

*C[hester] C. McCown, "Hebrew and Egyptian Apocalyptic Literature," *HTR* 18 (1925) 357-411. [I. The Relationships Between Egypt and Israel; II. Hebrew and Egyptian Literature; III. Egyptian Apocalyptic Literature in the Middle Kingdom; IV. Egyptian Apocalyptic Literature of Greek and Roman Times; V. The Influence of Egyptian Apocalyptic]

Alan W. Shorter, "A Possible Late Representation of the God 'Ash," *JEA* 11 (1925) 78-79.

W. J. Perry, "The Cult of the Sun and the Cult of the Dead in Egypt," *JEA* 11 (1925) 191-200.

Aylward M. Blackman, "Osiris or the Sun-God? A Reply to Mr. Perry," *JEA* 11 (1925) 201-209.

*L. B. Ellis, "Isis at Cologne and Aix," *AEE* 11 (1926) 97-101. *[Roman Statue]*

*Battiscombe Gunn, "A shawabti-figure of Puyamrē' from Saqqara," *ASAE* 26 (1926) 157-159.

W. Spiegelberg, "The God Panepi," *JEA* 12 (1926) 34-37.

Samuel A. B. Mercer, "The Religion of Ikhnaton," *JSOR* 10 (1926) 14-33.

G. D. Hornblower, "Phallic Offerings to Hat-hor," *Man* 26 (1926) #52.

Henry [Ludwig] F. Lutz, "The Analysis of the Egyptian Mind," *OOR* 1 (1926) #1, 19-21.

*L. B. Ellis, "The Sistrum of Isis," *AEE* 12 (1927) 19-25.

*Samuel A. B. Mercer, "Babylonian and Egyptian Triads," *JSOR* 11 (1927) 137-141.

G. D. Hornblower, "Further Notes on Phallism in Ancient Egypt," *Man* 27 (1927) #97.

*M[argaret] A. Murray, "The Dying God," *AEE* 13 (1928) 8-11.

L. B. Ellis, "Refreshing in the Underworld," *AEE* 13 (1928) 17.

[W. M.] Flinders Petrie, "Osiris in the Tree and Pillar," *AEE* 13 (1928) 40-44.

William Wallace Martin, "THE HARPER'S LAMENT From the Tomb of Nefer-heteph, in the XVIII Dynasty of Egypt," *BR* 13 (1928) 349-352.

*P[ercy] E. Newberry, "The Pig and the Cult-animal of Set," *JEA* 14 (1928) 211-225.

Samuel A. B. Mercer, "A Study in Egyptian Religious Origins," *JSOR* 12 (1928) 83-96.

Harry W. Cartwright, "The Iconography of Certain Egyptian Divinities as Illustrated by the Collections in the Haskell Oriental Museum," *AJSL* 45 (1928-29) 179-196.

*J. G. Milne, "Alexander and Ammon," *AEE* 14 (1929) 74-78.

G. D. Hornblower, "A Further Note on the *Ka*," *AEE* 14 (1929) 104-107.

G. D. Hornblower, "Ancestor Cult in Ancient Egypt," *AEE* 15 (1930) 20-22.

G. D. Hornblower, "Altar and Bell in Later Egyptian Rites," *AEE* 15 (1930) 40-42.

G. D. Hornblower, "Postscript to 'Ancestor-Cult in Ancient Egypt'," *AEE* 15 (1930) 43-44.

*M[argaret] A. Murray, "The Bundle of Life," *AEE* 15 (1930) 65-73.

*G. A. Wainwright, "The Relationship of Amūn to Zeus, and his Connexion with Meteorites," *JEA* 16 (1930) 35-38.

T. J. C. Baly, "Notes on the Ritual of Opening the Mouth," *JEA* 16 (1930) 173-186.

G. D. Hornblower, "A Sacred Grove in Egypt," *Man* 30 (1930) #16.

*R. Engelbach, "An alleged winged Sun-disk of the first Dynasty," *ZÄS* 65 (1930) 115-116.

*John Robert Towers, "A Syrian God and Amen-Ra?" *AEE* 16 (1931) 75-76.

*John Robert Towers, "Was Akhenaten a Monotheist Before His Accession?" *AEE* 16 (1931) 97-100.

G. A. Wainwright, "The Emblem of Min," *JEA* 17 (1931) 185-195.[∞]

T. J. Colin Baly, "A Note on the Origin of Osiris," *JEA* 17 (1931) 221-222.

Henry L[udwig] F. Lutz, "The Ever-Blossoming Wreaths of Tindium as a Feature of Memphitic Legends," *UCPSP* 10 (1931-46) 281-286.

Henry L[udwig] F. Lutz, "Canopus the City of the 'Chest of Heaven'," *UCPSP* 10 (1931-46) 295-300.

M[argaret] A. Murray, "An Early Sed-Festival," *AEE* 17 (1932) 70-72.

Albert N. Corpening, "Studies in the Hermetica," *CQ* 9 (1932) 66-79.

E. G. Sihler, "The Religion of Ancient Egypt," *CTM* 3 (1932) 561-569.

*F. G. Gordon, "The Keftiu spell," *JEA* 18 (1932) 67-68.

*Alan W. Shorter, "Two statuettes of the goddess Sekhmet-Ubastet," *JEA* 18 (1932) 121-124.

G. A. Wainwright, "Letopolis," *JEA* 18 (1932) 159-172.

*Joshua Bloch, "Is the Egyptian Sun God *Re* Mentioned in the Bible? (A Note on Exodus X, 10)," *JSOR* 16 (1932) 57.

W. J. Perry, "Theology and Physiological Paternity," *Man* 32 (1932) #218. *[Fatherhood of the Sun God]*

John A. Wilson, "The Kindly God," *AJSL* 49 (1932-33) 150-153. *[Amon]*

*Battiscombe Gunn, "On the Supposed Mention of the Egyptian God *Re'* in Exodus," *EgR* 1 (1933) 33-34.

Samuel A. B. Mercer, "Some Religious Elements in the Civilization of Predynastic Egypt," *EgR* 1 (1933) 121-126.

*A. H. Sayce, "The Astarte Papyrus and the Legend of the Sea," *JEA* 19 (1933) 56-59.

E. S. Thomas, "Theology and Physical Paternity," *Man* 33 (1933) #26. *[Fatherhood of the Sun God]*

G. A. Wainwright, "A Ram-headed God at Hermopolis," *JEA* 19 (1933) 160-161.

M[argaret] A. Murray, "The God 'Ash," *AEE* 19 (1934) 115-117.

F. H. Hallock, "Christianity and the Old Egyptian Religion," *EgR* 2 (1934) 6-17.

Samuel A. B. Mercer, "The Nature of Sacrifice in Ancient Egypt," *EgR* 2 (1934) 20-22.

[Samuel A. B. Mercer], "Probabilities and Possibilities," *EgR* 2 (1934) 22-23. *[Bust-statuettes symbolizing the resurrection of the Osirinized dead]*

*Samuel A. B. Mercer, "The Wisdom of Amenemope and his Religious Ideas," *EgR* 2 (1934) 27-69. [I. Introduction; II. Contents; III. Translation; IV. The Wisdom of Amenemope and the Book of Proverbs; V. Amenemope and Other Wisdom Literature; VI. The Religious Ideas of Amenemope]

G. van der Leeuw, "The Contendings of Horus and Seth," *EgR* 2 (1934) 106-110.

Alexander Piankoff, "The Sky-Goddess Nut and the Night Journey of the Sun," *JEA* 20 (1934) 57-61.

G. A. Wainwright, "Some Aspects of Amūn," *JEA* 20 (1934) 139-153.

*A[lexander] Piankoff, "A Pantheistic Representation of Amon in the Petrie Collection," *AEE* 20 (1935) 49-51.

*Samuel A. B. Mercer, "Osiris and Marduk," *EgR* 3 (1935) 158-159.

*Samuel A. B. Mercer, "Astarté in Egypt," *EgR* 3 (1935) 192-203.

Samuel A. B. Mercer, "Abbreviations for the Use of Writers on Egyptian Religion," *EgR* 3 (1935) 204-227.

Alan W. Shorter, "The God Neḥebkau," *JEA* 21 (1935) 41-48.

G. A. Wainwright, "Some Celestial Associations of Min," *JEA* 21 (1935) 152-170.

*H. W. Fairman, "The Myth of Horus at Edfu—I," *JEA* 21 (1935) 26-36. [A. The Legend of the Winged Disk; B. *Not Published*]

*E. E. Boughey, "An Ancient Egyptian Flood-Legend?" *JMUEOS* #19 (1935) 27-31.

G. A. Wainwright, "Amun's Meteorite and Omphaloi," *ZÄS* 71 (1935) 41-44.

*Warren R. Dawson, "The Magicians of the Pharaoh: The Frazer Lecture, 1936" *Folk* 47 (1936) 234-262.

John A. Wilson, "Illuminating the Thrones at the Egyptian Jubilee," *JAOS* 56 (1936) 293-296.

Sterling Dow, "The Egyptian Cults in Athens," *HTR* 30 (1937) 183-232.

G. D. Hornblower, "Osiris and his rites: I," *Man* 37 (1937) #186.

G. D. Hornblower, "Osiris and his rites: II," *Man* 37 (1937) #200.

*O. H. E. Burmester, "Egyptian Mythology in the Coptic Apocrypha," *Or, N.S.,* 7 (1938) 355-367.

Selim Bey Hassan, "A representation of the solar disk with human hands and arms in the form of Horus of Beḥdet, as seen on the stela of Amenhetep IInd in the mud-brick temple at Giza," *ASAE* 38 (1938) 53-62.

*Moharram Kamal, "Some fragments from *Shawabti*-figures of Akhenaten in the Egyptian Museum," *ASAE* 39 (1939) 381-382.

*J. Gwyn Griffiths, "P. Oslo. 1, 105-9 and Metternich Stela, 85-6," *JEA* 25 (1939) 101.

*Battiscombe Gunn, "P. Chester Beatty I, 6, 6," *JEA* 25 (1939) 101-102.

*G. A. Wainwright, "Seshat's nš-shrine," *JEA* 25 (1939) 104.

*N. M. Davies and N. de G. Davies, "Harvest Rites in a Theban Tomb," *JEA* 25 (1939) 154-156.

*H[ermann] R[anke], "A Statue of the Goddess Hathor," *UMB* 8 (1939-40) #4, 10-12.

G. A. Wainwright, "Seshat and the Pharaoh," *JEA* 26 (1940) 30-40.

*H. L. Ginsberg, "Two Religious Borrowings in Ugaritic Literature. II. The Egyptian God Ptaḥ in Ugaritic Mythology," *Or, N.S.,* 9 (1940) 39-44.

George C. Ring, "The God of Egypt's Wise Men," *ThSt* 1 (1940) 251-268.

*A. Rowe, "Newly-identified monuments in the Egyptian Museum showing the deification of the dead together with brief details of similar objects elsewhere," *ASAE* 40 (1940-41) 1-50.

*G. A. Wainwright, "The Attempted Sacrifice of Sesostris," *JEA* 27 (1941) 138-143.

*S[amuel] Rosenblatt, "A Reference to the Egyptian God Re' in the Old Testament," *JBL* 60 (1941) xi.

*Samuel Rosenblatt, "A Reference to the Egyptian God Re' in the Rabbinic Commentaries," *JBL* 60 (1941) 183-185.

G. D. Hornblower, "Osiris and the Fertility-Rite," *Man* 41 (1941) #71.

*H. J. Rose, "The Name of Isis in Plutarch: Psychostasia," *Man* 41 (1941) #103.

*A[ylward] M. Blackman and H. W. Fairman, "The Myth of Horus at Edfu—II," *JEA* 28 (1942) 32-38. [C. The Triumph of Horus over his Enemies: A Sacred Drama]

*Mary S. Shaw, "Individuality according to the thought and practice of Ancient Egypt," *JMUEOS* #23 (1942) 11-12. *[Ka]*

*Harold H. Nelson, "The Identity of Amon-Re of United-With Eternity," *JNES* 1 (1942) 127-155.

Meta E. Williams, "Hecate in Egypt," *Folk* 53&54 (1942-43) 112-113.

†H. J. Rose, "Misunderstanding," *Folk* 53&54 (1942-43) 173-174. *[Hecate]*

Ambrose Lansing, "Pictorial Aspects of the Religion of Akh-en-Aten," *AJA* 47 (1943) 88.

G. A. Wainwright, "Amûn's sacred object at Thebes," *ASAE* 42 (1943) 183-185.

*A[ylward] M. Blackman and H. W. Fairman, "The Myth of Horus at Edfu—II," *JEA* 29 (1943) 2-36. [C. The Triumph of Horus over his Enemies: A Sacred Drama *(Continued)*]

Alan H. Gardiner, "The God Semseru," *JEA* 29 (1943) 75-76.

G. D. Hornblower, "The Egyptian Fertility-Rite: Postscript," *Man* 43 (1943) #16.

*G. D. Hornblower, "The Divine Cat and the Snake in Egypt," *Man* 43 (1943) #65.

*Harold H. Nelson, "I. The Egyptian Temple with particular reference to the Theban Temples of the Empire Period," *BA* 7 (1944) 44-53. [The Symbolism of the Egyptian Temple; Deity and the Temple in Egypt; Temple and Community in Egypt]

*A[ylward] M. Blackman and H. W. Fairman, "The Myth of Horus at Edfu—II," *JEA* 30 (1944) 5-22. [C. The Triumph of Horus over his Enemies: A Sacred Drama *(Concluded)*]

Alan H. Gardiner, "Horus the Beḥdetite," *JEA* 30 (1944) 23-60.

*Nina M. Davies, "A Scene of worshipping Sacred Cows," *JEA* 30 (1944) 64.

*A[ylward] M. Blackman and H. W. Fairman, "Additions and Corrections to A. M. Blackman and H. W. Fairman, "The Myth of Horus at Edfu—II," in *JEA* XXIX-XXX," *JEA* 30 (1944) 79-80.

A. S. Yahuda, "The Osiris Cult and the Designation of Osiris Idols in the Bible," *JNES* 3 (1944) 194-197.

Alan H. Gardiner, "Additions and Corrections to 'Horus the Beḥdetite' in *JEA* XXX, 23 ff.," *JEA* 31 (1945) 116.

G. D. Hornblower, "The Establishing of Osiris," *Man* 45 (1945) #38.

G. D. Hornblower, "Min and His Functions," *Man* 46 (1946) #103.

Elise J. Baumgartel, "Herodotus on Min *(A reinterpretation of Book* II, 4; 99; *and* 145/6)," *Antiq* 21 (1947) 145-150.

*Alexander Badawy, "A collection of Foundation-Deposits of Tuthmosis IIIrd," *ASAE* 47 (1947) 145-156. [I.-Description of the Collection; II.-Were Those Tools Intended for Practical or Votive Purposes? III.-To Which Monument were Those Tools Dedicated?]

Percy E. Newberry, "The Cult of the ⊣ - pole," *JEA* 33 (1947) 90-91.

Marie-Louise Buhl, "The Goddesses of the Egyptian Tree Cult," *JNES* 6 (1947) 80-97.

*Martin Rist, "The Metamorphosis of Apelius and the Zoolatry of the Egyptian Mysteries," *IR* 5 (1948) 134-141.

Harold Bell, "Popular Religion in Graeco-Roman Egypt: I. The Pagan Period," *JEA* 34 (1948) 82-97.

Jaroslav Černý "Thoth as Creator of Languages," *JEA* 34 (1948) 121-122.

*A[ylward] M. Blackman and H. W. Fairman, "The Significance of the Ceremony *Ḥwt Bḥsw* in the Temple of Horus at Edfu," *JEA* 35 (1949) 98-112; 36 (1950) 63-81.

*Bernard V. Bothmer, "Statuettes of W3ḏ't as Ichneumon Coffins," *JNES* 8 (1949) 121-123.

*Winifred Needler, "A Hathor from Eleventh-Dynasty Egypt," *Arch* 3 (1950) 194-195.

G. H. Lang, "An Ancient Egyptian Prayer," *EQ* 22 (1950) 188-204.

Alan [H.] Gardiner, "The Baptism of Pharaoh," *JEA* 36 (1950) 3-12.

*Oliver H. Myers, "The *Neter* Pole and the *Ashera*," *JEA* 36 (1950) 113-114.

Marian Goodlander, "Significant Trends in Ancient Egypt," *Person* 31 (1950) 20-28.

*Hermann Ranke, "The Egyptian Collections of the University Museum," *UMB* 15 (1950) #2/3, 5-109. [Egyptian Deities and Their Sacred Animals, pp. 17-20]

*S. G. F. Brandon, "The Problem of Change in the Ancient World," *Folk* 61&62 (1950-51) 88-97. *[Weltanschauurgen]*

*William Stevenson Smith, "The Relationship Between Egyptian Ideas and Old Testament Thought," *JAAR* 19 (1951) 12-15.

Labib Habachi, "Notes on the Altar of Sekhemrē'-sewadjtowě Sebkḥotpe from Sehēl," *JEA* 37 (1951) 17-19.

Mustafa el-Amir, "The Cult of *Ḥryw* at Thebes in the Ptolemaic Period," *JEA* 37 (1951) 81-85.

Alan [H.] Gardiner, "Addendum to 'The Baptism of Pharaoh', *JEA* 36, 3-12," *JEA* 37 (1951) 111.

Alan H. Gardiner, "The benefit conferred by reburial," *JEA* 37 (1951) 112.

*Theodor H. Gaster, "The Egyptian 'Story of Astarte' and the Ugaritic Poem of Baal," *BO* 9 (1952) 82-85.

*R. T. O'Callaghan, "The Word *ktp* in Ugarit and Egypto-Canaanite Mythology," *Or, N.S.*, 21 (1952) 37-46.

*Arthur Darby Nock, "Neotera, queen or goddess?" *Aeg* 33 (1953) 283-296.

*David Magie, "Egyptian Deities in Asia Minor in Inscriptions and on Coins," *AJA* 57 (1953) 163-187.

*H[enri] Frankfort, "Pyramid Temples and the Religion of the Old Kingdom," *BO* 10 (1953) 157-162.

William Kelly Simpson, "New Light on the God Reshef," *JAOS* 73 (1953) 86-89.

Joseph Leibovitch, "Gods of Agriculture and Welfare in Ancient Egypt," *JNES* 12 (1953) 73-113. *[28 pages of illustrations]*

S. R. K. Glanville and T. C. Skeat, "Eponymous Priesthoods of Alexandria from 211 B.C.," *JEA* 40 (1954) 45-58.

Louis V. Žabkar, "The Theocracy of Amarna and the Doctrine of Ba," *JNES* 13 (1954) 87-101.

*Rudolf Anthes, "Remarks on the Pyramid Texts and the Early Egyptian Dogma," *JAOS* 74 (1954) 35-39.

H. W. Fairman, "Worship and Festivals in an Egyptian Temple," *BJRL* 37 (1954-55) 165-203.

Abdel Moneim Abubakr, "Divine Boats of Ancient Egypt," *Arch* 8 (1955) 96-101.

*Hans Goedicke, "A Deification of a Private Person in the Old Kingdom," *JEA* 41 (1955) 31-33.

Jaroslav Černý "A Note on a Recently Discovered Boat of Cheops," *JEA* 41 (1955) 75-79.

A. J. Arkell, "An archaic representation of Ḥatḥōr," *JEA* 41 (1955) 125-126.

M. Herma van Voss, "The jackals of the sun-boat," *JEA* 41 (1955) 127.

*J. Gwyn Griffiths, "The costume and insignia of the king in the *sed*-festival," *JEA* 41 (1955) 127-128.

Hans Goedicke, "The Egyptian Idea of Passing from Life to Death (An Interpretation)," *Or, N.S.,* 24 (1955) 225-239.

Alexandre Piankoff, "The Theology of the New Kingdom in Ancient Egypt," *A&S* 1 (1955-56) 488-500.

Y. Leibovitz, "The Cult of Ptah with Non-Egyptians," *EI* 4 (1956) VI.

*Cyril Aldred, "The Carnarvon, Statuette of Amūn," *JEA* 42 (1956) 3-7

Elizabeth Thomas, "Solar Barks Prow to Prow," *JEA* 42 (1956) 65-79.

*M[argaret] A. Murray, "Burial Customs and Beliefs in the Hereafter in Predynastic Egypt," *JEA* 42 (1956) 89-96.

Elizabeth Thomas, "A further note on rock-cut boats," *JEA* 42 (1956) 117-118.

Alan [H.] Gardiner, "The daily income of Sesostris II's funerary temple," *JEA* 42 (1956) 119.

Labib Habachi, "Amenwahsu Attached to the Cult of Anabis, Lord of the Dawning Land," *MDIÄA* 14 (1956) 52-62.

*John A. Wilson, "The Royal Myth in Ancient Egypt," *PAPS* 100 (1956) 439-442.

W[illiam] K[elly] Simpson, "A Running of the Apis in the Region of the ʿAḥa and Passages in the Manethome Aelian," *Or, N.S.,* 26 (1957) 139-142.

Hans Goedicke, "A Lion-Cult of the Old Kingdom connected with the Royal Temple," *RÉg* 11 (1957) 57-60.

Siegfried Herrmann, "Isis in Byblos," *ZÄS* 82 (1957-58) 48-55.

J. Gwyn Griffiths, "The Horus-Seth Motif in the Daily Temple Liturgy," *Aeg* 38 (1958) 1-10.

J. Gwyn Griffiths, "The Interpretation of the Horus-Myth of Edru," *JEA* 44 (1958) 75-85.

J. Gwyn Griffiths, "Remarks on the Mythology of the Eyes of Horus," *CdÉ* 33 (1958) 182-193.

A. J. Arkell, "An Archaic Representation of Ḥatḥōr," *JEA* 44 (1958) 5.

C. J. Bleeker, "Isis and Nephthys as Wailing Women," *Numen* 5 (1958) 1-27.

S. G. F. Brandon, "A problem of the Osirian judgment of the dead," *Numen* 5 (1958) 110-127.

Hans Goedicke, "A note on the early cult of Horus in Upper Egypt," *ASAE* 56 (1959) 59-62.

Moh. Hasan Abd-ur-Rahmah, "The Four-feathered Crown of Akhenaten," *ASAE* 56 (1959) 247-249.

Elizabeth Thomas, "Terrestrial Marsh and Solar Mat," *JEA* 45 (1959) 38-51.

Rudolf Anthes, "Egyptian Theology in the Third Millennium B.C.," *JNES* 18 (1959) 169-212.

*J. Gwyn Griffiths, "Seth or Anubis?" *JWCI* 22 (1959) 367. [Rejoinder by A. A. Barb, pp. 367-371]

S. G. F. Brandon, "The Ritual Perpetuation of the Past," *Numen* 6 (1959) 112-129.

*J. Gwyn Griffiths, "Some Remarks on the Enneads of Gods," *Or., N.S.,* 28 (1959) 34-56.

Alexander Badawy, "Min, the cosmic fertility god of Egypt," *MIO* 7 (1959-60) 163-179.

S. G. F. Brandon, "Osiris: The Royal Mortuary God of Egypt," *HT* 10 (1960) 589-597.

*H. M. Stewart, "Some Pre-ʿAmārnah Sun Hymns," *JEA* 46 (1960) 83-90.

Alan [H.] Gardiner, "Was Osiris an ancient king subsequently deified?" *JEA* 46 (1960) 104.

*J. Vercoutter, "The Napatan Kings and Apis Worship (*Serepeum Burials of the Napatan Period*)," *Kush* 8 (1960) 62-76.

W. K. Simpson, "Reshep in Egypt," *Or., N.S.,* 29 (1960) 63-74.

*Samuel Tobias Lachs, "An Egyptian Festival in Canticles Rabba," *JQR, N.S.,* 51 (1960-61) 47-54.

Hans Goedicke, "Seth as a fool," *JEA* 47 (1961) 154.

E. P. Uphill, "A Joint Sed-Festival of Thutmose III and Queen Hatshepsut," *JNES* 20 (1961) 248-251.

*M[argaret] A. Murray, "Egypt and Africa," *Man* 61 (1961) #12.

J. A. S. Evans, "A Social and Economic History of an Egyptian Temple in the Greco-Roman Period," *YCS* 17 (1961) 149-283.

*C. Bradford Welles, "The Discovery of Sarapis and the Foundation of Alexandria," *HJAH* 11 (1962) 271-298.

R. Whiston, "Immortality and Transcendence in Egyptian Thought," *IPQ* 2 (1962) 515-537.

Henry George Fischer, "The Cult and Nome of the Goddess Bat," *JARCE* 1 (1962) 7-23.

*Alan [H.] Gardiner, "The Gods of Thebes as Guarantors of Personal Property," *JEA* 48 (1962) 57-69.

E. A. E. Reymond, "The Primeval Djeba," *JEA* 48 (1962) 81-88.

E. A. E. Jelinková, "The Shebtiw in temple at Edfu," *ZÄS* 87 (1962) 41-54.

L. Kákosy, "Problems of the Thoth-Cult in Roman Egypt," *AAB* 15 (1963) 123-128.

E. A. E. Reymond, "Worship of the Ancestor Gods at Edfu," *CdÉ* 38 (1963) 49-70.

*Alexander Badawy, "The Architectural Symbolism of the Massisi-Chapels in Egypt," *CdÉ* 38 (1963) 78-90.

*C. Bradford Welles, "Sarapis and Alexandria, an Addendum," *HJAH* 12 (1963) 512.

*William K. Simpson, "Studies in the Twelfth Egyptian Dynasty: I-II," *JARCE* 2 (1963) 53-63. [II. The Sed Festival in Dynasty XII, pp. 53-59]

G. A. Wainwright, "The Origin of the Storm-Gods in Egypt," *JEA* 49 (1963) 13-20.

G. A. Wainwright, "The Origin of Amūn," *JEA* 49 (1963) 21-23.

Louis V. Zabka, "Herodotus and the Egyptian Idea of Immortality," *JNES* 22 (1963) 57-63.

Eric Uphill, "The Sed-Festivals of Akhenaton," *JNES* 22 (1963) 123-127.

Alan R. Schulman, "The Cult of Ramesses III at Memphis," *JNES* 22 (1963) 177-184.

Hans Goedicke, "Early References to Fatalistic Concepts in Egypt," *JNES* 22 (1963) 187-190.

Herbert Hoffmann, "Helios," *JARCE* 2 (1963) 117-124.

*Rudolf Anthes, "Affinity and Difference Between Egyptian and Greek Sculpture and Thought in the Seventh and Sixth Centuries B.C.," *PAPS* 107 (1963) 60-81.

Erik Iversen, "Horapollon and the Egyptian Conceptions of Eternity," *RDSO* 38 (1963) 177-186.

Labib Habachi, "Edjo, Mistress of Nebt (Bilifya, near to Ihnâsya El-Medîneh)," *ZÄS* 90 (1963) 41-49.

L. Kákosy, "Ideas about the Fallen State of the World in Egyptian Religion: Decline of the Golden Age," *AOASH* 17 (1964) 205-216.

J. Gwyn Griffiths, "Isis in Oxford," *CdÉ* 39 (1964) 67-71.

Alan R. Schulman, "The God *Nḥj*," *JNES* 23 (1964) 275-279.

R. O. Faulkner, "Some notes on the God Shu," *JEOL* #18 (1964) 266-270.

*H. M. Stewart, "Egyptian Funerary Statuettes and the Solar Cult," *ULBIA* 4 (1964) 165-170.

S. G. F. Brandon, "Life After Death—IV. The After-Life in Ancient Egyptian Faith and Practice," *ET* 76 (1964-65) 217-220.

Anonymous, "The Egyptian After-Life," *BH* 2 (1965) #2, 10-15.

E. A. E. Reymond, "A late Edfu Theory of the Nature of God," *CdÉ* 40 (1965) 61-71.

E. A. E. Reymond, "The Cult of the Spear in the Temple of Edfu," *JEA* 51 (1965) 144-148.

Eric Uphill, "The Egyptian Sed-Festival Rites," *JNES* 24 (1965) 365-382.

Labib Habachi, "A Triple Shrine of the Theban Triad in Luxor Temple," *MDIÄA* 20 (1965) 93-97.

*Peter J. Ucko, "Anthropomorphic Ivory Figurines from Egypt," *JRAI* 95 (1965) 214-239.

Svein Bjerke, "Remarks on the Egyptian Ritual of 'Opening the Mouth' and its Interpretation," *Numen* 12 (1965) 201-216.

E. A. E. Reymond, "The Children of Tanen. (Part 1)," *ZÄS* 92 (1965-66) 116-128.

*L. Kákosy, "Prophecies of the Ram Gods," *AOASH* 19 (1966) 331-357.

R. O. Faulkner, "The King and the Star-Religion in the Pyramid Texts," *JNES* 25 (1966) 153-161.

C. J. Bleeker, "Guilt and Purification in ancient Egypt," *Numen* 13 (1966) 81-87.

*R. E. Witt, "The Importance of Isis for the Fathers," *StP* 8 (1966) 135-145.

Alan R. Schulman, "Ex-votos of the Poor," *JARCE* 6 (1967) 153-156.

*John Ruffle, "Four Egyptian Pieces in the Birmingham City Museum," *JEA* 53 (1967) 39-46. [4. Part of the relief depicting the Opening-of-the-mouth Ceremony (688' 66), pp. 45-46]

H. M. Stewart, "The mythical Sea of Knives," *JEA* 53 (1967) 164.

Eric Uphill, "The Date of Osorkon II's Sed-Festival," *JNES* 26 (1967) 61-62.

G. A. Gaballa, "New Evidence on the Birth of Pharaoh," *Or, N.S.,* 36 (1967) 299-304.

James M. Fennelly, "Roman Involvement in the Affairs of the Egyptian Shrine," *BJRL* 50 (1967-68) 317-335.

*J. Murtagh, "The 'Name' in Egypt and Israel," *BibT* #37 (1968) 2585-2589.

H. te Velde, "The Egyptian God Seth as a Trickster," *JARCE* 7 (1968) 37-40.

R. O. Faulkner, "The Pregnancy of Isis," *JEA* 54 (1968) 40-44.

*R. I. Rubinshtein, "On the Nature of the 'ushebtis'," *VDI* (1968) #2, 88-89.

*Abdel-Aziz Saleh, "Plural Sense and Cultural Aspects of the Ancient Egyptian *mdw-ntr*," *BIFAO* 68 (1969) 15-38. *['Word of God']*

Dia' Abou-Ghazi, "The First Appearance of Re' and his Continuous Being as Depicted in the Pyramid Texts," *BIFAO* 68 (1969) 47-51.

Cyril Aldred, "The 'New Year' Gifts to the Pharaoh," *JEA* 55 (1969) 73-81.

Labib Habachi, "Divinities Adored in the Area of Kalabsha, with Special Reference to the Goddess Miket," *MDIÄA* 24 (1969) 169-183.

Abdel-Aziz Saleh, "The So-called 'Primeval Hill' and other Related Elevations in Ancient Egyptian Mythology," *MDIÄA* 25 (1969) 110-120.

G. A. Gaballa and K. A. Kitchen, "The Festival of Sokar," *Or, N.S.,* 38 (1969) 1-76.

*O. D. Berlev, "'Falcon in Boat', a Hieroglyph and a God," *VDI* (1969) #1, 30.

H. te Velde, "The god Heka in Egyptian theology," *JEOL* #21 (1969-70) 175-186.

E. A. E. Reymond, "The Children of Tanen. Part II: The-God-of-the-Temple in the Edfu Tradition," *ZÄS* 96 (1969-70) 36-47.

*Miroslav Verner, "Statue of Twēret (Cairo Museum no. 39145) Dedicated by Pabēsi and Several Remarks on the Role of the Hippopotamus Goddess," *ZÄS* 96 (1969-70) 52-63.

§471 *3.2.15.2.5 Hittite and Hurrian Religion*

George St. Clair, "Sutekh, Chief God of the Hittites," *PEFQS* 22 (1890) 210-211.

Claude R. Conder, "Notes on the *Quarterly Statement,* July, 1890. *Sutekh,*" *PEFQS* 22 (1890) 330.

William Hayes Ward, "Oriental Antiquities. 2. Nehushtan," *AJA* 2 (1898) 162-165.

*William Hayes Ward, "The Hittite Gods in Hittite Art," *AJA* 3 (1899) 1-39.

C[laude] R. Conder, "Notes on Biblical Antiquities. 5. *Hittite Gods,*" *PEFQS* 37 (1905) 157-158.

William M. Ramsay, "Two Notes on Religious Antiquities in Asia Minor. II. The Armed Priestesses in the Hittite Religion," *ET* 21 (1909-10) 66.

A. H. Sayce, "The Hittite Communion Table at Mar'ash," *SBAP* 32 (1910) 253-254.

*Anonymous, "Ancient Bronze Statue Found at Cairo," *RP* 10 (1911) 116. [Hittite Deity]

*A. H. Sayce, "Notes on Hittite Inscriptions and Mythology: The Rock Sculptures of Boghaz Keui," *SBAP* 35 (1913) 55-62.

A. H. Sayce, "The Attys-Priest among the Hittites," *SBAP* 35 (1913) 251.

John Garstang, "The Sun God(dess) of Arenna," *AAA* 6 (1913-14) 109-115.

Anonymous, "Hittite Use of an Ox Head to Scare Away Powers of Evil," *RP* 12 (1913) 99-100.

*A. H. Sayce, "The Scapegoat Among the Hittites," *ET* 31 (1919-20) 283-284.

A. H. Sayce, "The Hittite Legend of the Great Serpent," *JRAS* (1922) 177-190.

*Samuel Raffaeli, "A Supposed Hittite Deity," *PEFQS* 54 (1922) 179. *[Heth(?)]*

*E. J. Pilcher, "The Supposed 'Hittite Deity'," *PEFQS* 55 (1923) 50.

W. M. Calder, "Notes on Anatolian Religion," *JMUEOS* #11 (1924) 19-35.

A. H. Sayce, "Hittite Legends," *JRAS* (1927) 87-93.

Eric Burrows, "Ḥurrian Sala(s)," *JRAS* (1927) 318-320.

W[illiam] F[oxwell] Albright, "The Anatolian Goddess Kubaba," *AfO* 5 (1928-29) 229-231.

*A. T. Olmstead, "Two Stone Idols from Asia Minor at the University of Illinois," *Syria* 10 (1929) 311-313.

Archibald H. Sayce, "Atamma-Attys and the Murrians," *RHA* 1 (1930-32) 213-217.

*A. H. Sayce, "The Astarte Papyrus and the Legend of the Sea," *JEA* 19 (1933) 56-59.

*E. H. Sturtevant, "A Hittite Text on the Duties of Priests and Temple Servants," *JAOS* 54 (1934) 363-406.

Giuseppe Furlani, "The Basic Aspect of Hittite Religion," *HTR* 31 (1938) 251-262.

E[phraim] A. Speiser, "An Intrusive Hurro-Hittite Myth," *JAOS* 62 (1942) 98-102.

Alexander H. Krappe, "The Anatolian Lion God," *JAOS* 65 (1945) 144-154.

Albrecht Goetze, "The Priestly Dress of the Hittite King," *JCS* 1 (1947) 176-185.

*E. Laroche, "Ḥattic Deities and Their Epithets," *JCS* 1 (1947) 187-216.

*G. Levi Della Vida, "A Hurrian Goddess at Carthage?" *JAOS* 68 (1948) 148-149.

Roger T. O'Callaghan, "An Approach to Some Religious Problems of Karatepe," *ArOr* 18 (1950) Parts 1/2, 354-365.

Theodor [H.] Gaster, "The Child-Stealing Witch among the Hittites," *SMSDR* 23 (1951-52) 134-137.

*L. J. Krušina-Černý, "Three New Circular Alabaster Idols from Kültepe," *ArOr* 20 (1952) 601-606.

Winifred Lamb, "Some Early Anatolian Shrines," *AS* 6 (1956) 87-94.

Seton Lloyd and James Mellaart, "An Early Bronze Age Shrine at Beycesultan," *AS* 7 (1957) 27-36.

*Nimet Özgüç, "Marble Idols and Statuettes from the Excavations at Kültepe," *TTKB* 21 (1957) 71-80.

*Hans G. Güterbock, "The Composition of Hittite Prayers to the Sun," *JAOS* 78 (1958) 237-245.

*J. G. Macqueen, "Hattian Mythology and Hittite Monarchy," *AS* 9 (1959) 171-188.

Arvid S. Kapelrud, "The interrelationship between religion and magic in Hittite religion," *Numen* 6 (1959) 32-50.

*Hans G. Güterbock, "An Outline of the Hittite *AN.TAḪ.ŠUM* Festival," *JNES* 19 (1960) 80-89.

H[ans] G. Güterbock, "The god Šuwaliyat reconsidered," *RHA* 19 (1961) 1-18.

H. A. Hoffner, "The Elkunirsa Myth Reconsidered," *RHA* 23 (1965) 5-16.

*Ph[ilo] H. J. Houwink ten Cate and F. Josephson, "Muwatallis' Prayer to the Storm-God of Kummanni (KBo XI 1)," *RHA* 25 (1967) 101-140.

*Robert L. Alexander, "The Mountain-God at Eflatun Pinar," *Anat* 2 (1968) 77-85.

Philo H. J. Houwink ten Cate, "Muwatallis' 'Prayer to be Spoken in an Emergency'," *JNES* 28 (1968) 204-208.

*George M. A. Hanfmann and Jane C. Waldbaum, "Kybebe and Artemis: Two Anatolian Goddesses at Sardis," *Arch* 22 (1969) 264-269.

*Ph[ilo] H. J. Houwink ten Cate, "Hittite Royal Prayers," *Numen* 16 (1969) 81-98.

*Harry A. Hoffner Jr., "Some Contributions of Hittitology to Old Testament Study," *TB* #20 (1969) 27-55. [C. Hittite Religion and the Old Testament, pp. 44-51; D. Hittite Mythology and the Old Testament, pp. 51-55]

§472 *3.2.15.2.6 Samaritan Religion*

*†Ch. Clermont-Ganneau, "Description of an Altar found on Mount Gerizim," *SBAP* 6 (1883-84) 133, 182-184.

A. Cowley, "The Samaritan Liturgy, and Reading of the Law," *JQR* 7 (1894-95) 121-140.

John E. H. Thomson, "The Samaritan Passover," *PEFQS* 34 (1902) 82-92.

W. J. Moulton, "The Samaritan Passover," *JBL* 22 (1903) 187-194.

Roland G. Stafford, "The Samaritan Passover," *PEFQS* 35 (1903) 90-92.

William E. Barton, "The Samaritan Passover," *OC* 22 (1908) 193-215.

Albert Edward Bailey, "The Samaritan Passover," *BW* 34 (1909) 8-14.

M. Gaster, "The Chain of Samaritan High Priests," *JRAS* (1909) 393-402.

Jeremiah Zimmerman, "The Samaritan Passover," *RP* 9 (1910) 131-153.

Jacob, the Son of Aaron, "The Book of Enlightenment," *BS* 70 (1913) 313-346, 457-485.

M. Gaster, "Samaritan Phylacteries and Amulets," *SBAP* 37 (1915) 96-107, 163-174; 38 (1916) 70-79, 96-104, 186-195, 202-222; 39 (1917) 16-26, 45-50.

Anonymous, "The Samaritan Passover," *MR* 102 (1919) 796-801.

*George W. Gilmore, "The Samaritans: Their Testimony to the Religion of Israel," *HR* 80 (1920) 472-474. *(Review)*

William Ewing, "The Samaritans and Their Sacred Law," *BS* 79 (1922) 418-451.

*P. P. McKenna, "The Samaritans and Their Paschal Sacrifice," *IER, 5th Ser.,* 32 (1928) 291-299.

J. N. Schofield, "The Samaritan Passover," *PEFQS* 68 (1936) 93-96.

*Harold H. Rowley, "Sanballat and the Samaritan Temple," *BJRL* 38 (1955-56) 166-198.

John Macdonald, "Comprehensive and Thematic Reading of the Law by the Samaritans," *JJS* 10 (1959) 67-74.

Donald J. Boys, "The Creed and Hymns of the Samaritan Liturgy," *LQHR* 186 (1961) 32-37.

A. D. Crown, "Dositheans, Resurrection and a Messianic Joshua," *AASCS* 1 (1967) 70-85.

*B. N. Grakov, "Survivals of Scythian Religion and Epos among the Samaritans," *VDI* (1969) #3, 72.

§473 *3.2.15.2.7 Persian Religions, especially Zoroastrianism*

†T. Taylor, "Collection of the Chaldæan Oracles," *MMBR* 3 (1797) 509-526. [The Oracles of Zoroaster, pp. 512-516]

Anonymous, "Zoroaster and His Religion," *CE* 1 (1824) 35-38.

†Anonymous, "Zoroaster, and the Persian Fire-Worshipers," *BQRL* 7 (1848) 49-73. *(Review)*

William D. Whitney, "On the Avesta, or the Sacred Scriptures of the Zoroastrian Religion," *JAOS* 5 (1855-56) 337-383.

W. R. Alger, "On the Persian Doctrine of the Future Life," *PAOS, May* (1858) 8.

S. R., "The Religion of Zoroaster," *UQGR* 17 (1860) 221-253, 358-377; 18 (1861) 5-29, 221-236, 329-347.

Henry J. Rose, "The Zend-Avesta," *ContR* 4 (1867) 50-72.

*R. Brown, "'The System of Zoroaster considered in connexion with Archaic Monotheism'," *JTVI* 13 (1879-80) 246-305. (Discussion, pp. 306-314)

J. N. Fradenburgh, "Zoroaster and Zoroastrianism," *BFER* 30 (1881) 692-708.

J. N. Fradenburgh, "Zoroaster and Zoroastrianism," *MR* 63 (1881) 61-77.

Anonymous, "The Oracles of Zoroaster," *JSP* 16 (1882) 285-296. *(Trans. by Thomas Stanley)*

†Anonymous, "The Faith of Iran," *ERCJ* 162 (1885) 386-410. *[Zoroastrianism] (Review)*

*M. Stein, "Zoroastrian Deities on Indo-Scythian Coins," *BOR* 1 (1886-87) 155-166.

*C. de Harlez, "The Deities of the Indo-Scythic Coins," *BOR* 1 (1886-87) 206-207.

Robert Young, "The Parsees, or Zoroastrian Fire-Worshipers," *ERG, 9th Ser.,* 2 (1887) 169-181.

David G. Hubbard, "The Religion of Zoroaster," *URRM* 29 (1888) 122-138.

*A[lexander] Kohut, "The Zendavesta and the First Eleven Chapters of Genesis," *JQR* 2 (1889-90) 223-229.

*T. K. Cheyne, "Possible Zoroastrian Influences on the Religion of Israel," *ET* 2 (1890-91) 202-208, 224-228, 248-253.

M. Monier Williams, "Remarks on the Monism, Pantheism, and Dualism of Brahmanical and Zoroastrian Philosophers," *JTVI* 25 (1891-92) 1-14, 27. [(Discussion, pp. 14-24) (Remarks by F. A. Orde-Ward, pp. 25-26; W. Martin Wood, pp. 26-27; Note by C. G. Chittenden, pp. 28-29)]

*T. K. Cheyne, "Old Testament Notes, Jewish Influences on Persian Beliefs," *Exp, 4th Ser.,* 5 (1892) 79-80.

A. V. W[illiams] Jackson, "Avesta, the Bible of Zoroaster," *BW* 1 (1893) 420-431.

F. Max Müller, "The Age of the 'Zend-Avesta'," *ContR* 64 (1893) 869-872.

A. V. Williams Jackson, "Where was Zoroaster's Native Place?" *JAOS* 15 (1893) 221-232.

A. V. Williams Jackson, "The doctrine of the resurrection among the Ancient Persians," *JAOS* 16 (1894-96) xxxviii-xxxix.

A. V. Williams Jackson, "Notes on Zoroaster and the Avesta," *JAOS* 16 (1894-96) cxxvi-cxxix. [I. Allusion to Zoroaster in the Snorra Edde Preface; II. Plutarch's *Artaxerxes,* Ch. iii. 1-10]

A. V. Williams Jackson, "On the question of the date of Zoroaster," *JAOS* 16 (1894-96) ccxxvii-ccxxviii.

Lawrence H[eyworth] Mills, "Three Hymns of Zoroaster," *IAQR, 2nd Ser.,* 9 (1895) 133-138.

L[awrence] H[eyworth] Mills, "The God of Zoroaster," *NW* 4 (1895) 47-56.

Paul Carus, "Persian Dualism," *OC* 9 (1895) #43, 4683-4685.

W. St. Chad Boscawen, "Persian Religions," *BOR* 8 (1895-1900) 49-50.

Kanga Navrijo Maneckji, "The Zoroastrian Theology of the present day," *BOR* 8 (1895-1900) 222-228. [Note by L. C. Casartelli, pp. 228-229]

L[awrence] H[eyworth] Mills, "Zoroastrian Lore; Yasna XLIII.," *IAQR, 3rd Ser.,* 1 (1896) 340-346.

Anonymous, "The Five Zoroastrian Gathas," *IAQR, 3rd Ser.,* 2 (1896) 370-373.

A. V. Williams Jackson, "The Ancient Persian Doctrine of a Future Life," *BW* 8 (1896) 149-163.

[Paul Carus], "Mazdaism," *OC* 11 (1897) 141-149. *[Zoroastrianism]*

Alexander Kohut, "The Talmudic Records of Persian and Babylonian Festivals Critically Illustrated," *AJSL* 14 (1897-98) 183-194.

*J. H. Moulton, "Zoroastrian Influences on Judaism," *ET* 9 (1897-98) 352-359.

A. V. Williams Jackson, "Notes on Ancient Persian Cosmology," *PAPA* 31 (1899) ix.

Louis H. Gray, "The Indo-Iranian Deity Apam Napāt," *AfRW* 3 (1900) 18-51.

John Beames, "Zoroaster, the Prophet of Ancient Iran," *IAQR, 3rd Ser.,* 9 (1900) 108-112.

A. V. Williams Jackson, "The Religion of the Achaemenian Kings. First Series. The Religion according to the Inscriptions," *JAOS* 21 (1900) 160-184.

J. Telleen, "The Sacred Books of the East," *TTKF* 2 (1900) 129-140. 129-140. [The Zend Avesta, pp. 134-140]

*Lawrence [H.] Mills, "The Bible, the Avesta, and the Inscriptions," *IAQR, 3rd Ser.,* 11 (1901) 315-321.

*Lawrence [Heyworth] Mills, "Philo's δυνάμεις and the Amesha Spenta," *JRAS* (1901) 553-568.

Mehrjibhai Noshirwanji Kuka, "The Era of Zoroaster in the Light of Recent Babylonian Researches," *IAQR, 3rd Ser.,* 16 (1903) 122-164.

A. V. Williams Jackson, "The Modern Zoroastrians of Persia," *HR* 48 (1904) 14-19.

Louis H. Gray, "The Double Nature of the Iranian Archangels," *AfRW* 7 (1904) 345-372.

Henry Goodwin Smith, "Persian Dualism," *AJT* 8 (1904) 487-501.

Rastamji Edalji Dastur Peshotun Sanjana, "Ahura-Mazda in the Avesta," *ET* 16 (1904-05) 183-184.

*Lawrence [H.] Mills, "The Dualism of Isaiah XLV. 7: Was it Zoroastrian?" *IAQR, 3rd Ser.,* 20 (1905) 286-294.

J. A. Cunningham, "The Parsees and Zoroaster," *IER, 4th Ser.,* 18 (1905) 305-315.

*Anonymous, "'Zarathushtra, Philo: The Achæmenids and Israel'," *IAQR, 3rd Ser.,* 21 (1906) 314-317. *(Review)*

Paul Carus, "The Zoroastrian Religion and the Bible," *OC* 20 (1906) 434-435.

James Hope Moulton, "A Zoroastrian Idyll," *ET* 18 (1906-07) 536-537.

Palmer A. Smythe, "The Zoroastrian Messiah," *HJ* 5 (1906-07) 156-165.

L. C. Casartelli, "'The Zoroastrian Messiah'," *HJ* 5 (1906-07) 435-436.

Palmer A. Smythe, "'The Zoroastrian Messiah'," *HJ* 5 (1906-07) 674.

E[velyn] Martinengo Cesaresco, "The Faith of Iran," *ContR* 92 (1907) 489-503.

*L[awrence Heyworth] Mills, "The 'Ahuna-Vairya' and the Logos," *IAQR, 3rd Ser.,* 24 (1907) 92-97.

*L[awrence Heyworth] Mills, "Exilic Jewish Eschatology: In How Far was it Zoroastrian," *IAQR, 3rd Ser.,* 23 (1907) 98-105.

L[awrence Heyworth] Mills, "The Avesta as the Document of Subjective Recompense," *IAQR, 3rd Ser.,* 24 (1907) 312-317.

Abraham Yohannan and A. V. Williams Jackson, "Some Persian References to Zoroaster and his Religion," *JAOS* 28 (1907) 183-188.

*Lawrence Heyworth Mills, "Avesta Eschatology Compared with the Books of Daniel and Revelation," *Monist* 17 (1907) 321-346, 583-609.

L[awrence Heyworth] Mills, "A Hymn of Zarathushtra," *IAQR, 3rd Ser.,* 25 (1908) 334-337.

L[awrence Heyworth] Mills, "A Hymn of Zarathushtra. Yasna XLVI. Vicissitudes, Revenge, and Victory," *IAQR, 3rd Ser.,* 26 (1908) 322-326.

Louis H. Gray, "Additional Classical Passages Mentioning Zoroaster's Name," *Muséon* 27 (1908) 311-318.

Lawrence Heyworth Mills, "Our Own Religion in Ancient Persia. Zoroaster (Zarathushtra) and the Bible," *OC* 23 (1909) 385-404, 675-689.

L[awrence Heyworth] Mills, "Two Hymns from the Gāthas," *IAQR, 3rd Ser.,* 27 (1909) 343-350.

L[awrence Heyworth] Mills, "The Avesta is Veda: a Plea for Joint Study," *IAQR, 3rd Ser.,* 29 (1910) 347-351.

L[awrence Heyworth] Mills, "Yasna XXVIII," *IAQR, 3rd Ser.,* 31 (1911) 87-97.

L[awrence Heyworth] Mills, "Yasna XLIV," *IAQR, 3rd Ser.,* 32 (1911) 122-131.

L[awrence Heyworth] Mills, "The Pre-Christian Religion in Ancient Persia," *IAQR, 3rd Ser.,* 32 (1911) 321-343.

G. F. Moore, "Zoroastrianism," *HTR* 5 (1912) 180-226.

A. V. Williams Jackson, "The Ancient Persian Conception of Salvation According to the Avesta, or Bible of Zoroaster," *AJT* 17 (1913) 195-205.

Louis H. Gray, "Zoroastrian and Other Ethnic Religious Material in the Acta Sanctorum," *JMUEOS* #3 (1913-14) 37-55.

L. C. Casartelli, "Early Zoroastrianism. A Review," *JMUEOS* #3 (1913-14) 79-81. *(Review)*

*George W. Gilmore, "The Influence of Zoroastrianism on Jewish Doctrine in the Inter-Testamental Period," *IJA* #40 (1915) 12-13.

James Hope Moulton, "The Zoroastrian Conception of a Future Life," *JTVI* 47 (1915) 233-247, 252. (Discussion, pp. 248-252)

L. A. Waddell, "A 'Zoroastrian' Period of Indian History," *IAQR* 8 (1916) 28-31. *[Patna, the "Palibothra" of the Greeks]*

[Lawrence Heyworth] Mills, "The Temptation of Zarathushtra—Vendīdād XIX," *IAQR* 8 (1916) 162-165.

Albert J. Carnoy, "The Moral Deities of Iran and India and Their Origins," *AJT* 21 (1917) 58-78.

Alban G. Widgery, "Some Liberal Aspects of Zoroastrianism," *MC* 7 (1917-18) 114-123.

A[lbert J.] Carnoy, "The Iranian Gods of Healing," *JAOS* 38 (1918) 294-307.

Abraham Yohannah, "Another Old Syriac Reference to Zoroaster," *JAOS* 43 (1923) 239-242.

Jarl Charpentier, "The Date of Zoroaster," *BSOAS* 3 (1923-25) 747-755.

*Stephen [H.] Langdon, "The Babylonian and Persian Sacaea," *JRAS* (1924) 65-72.

J. M. Unvala, "Some old Zoroastrian customs," *AO* 4 (1925) 311-319.

*Sidney Smith, "Notes on 'The Assyrian Tree'," *BSOAS* 4 (1926-28) 69-76.

V. Lesný, "The Representation of Zarathushtra Based on Misunderstanding," *ArOr* 1 (1929) 251-252.

*Ira M. Price, "Light Out of Ur—The Devotion of the Elamite Kings to Sumerian Deities," *JAOS* 51 (1931) 164-169.

S. H. Taqizadeh, "A New Contribution to the Materials concerning the Life of Zoroaster," *BSOAS* 8 (1935-37) 947-954.

R. C. Zaehner, "A Zervanite Apocalypse I," *BSOAS* 10 (1939-42) 377-398.

R. C. Zaehner, "A Zervanite Apocalypse II," *BSOAS* 10 (1939-42) 606-631.

A. T. Olmstead, "Zoroaster," *RR* 4 (1939-40) 3-16.

M. Sprengling, "Karīr, Founder of Zoroastrianism," *AJSL* 57 (1940) 197-228.

M. Sprengling, "From Karīr to Shahpuhr I," *AJSL* 57 (1940) 330-340.

M. Sprengling, "Shahpuhr I the Great on the Kaabah of Zoroaster," *AJSL* 57 (1940) 341-420.

C. N. Seddon, "Zoroastrianism and Its Influence," *MC* 31 (1941-42) 507-515.

*W. B. Henning, "The Murder of the Magi," *JRAS* (1944) 133-144.

*Judah Rosenthal, "Ḥiwi al-Balkhi: A Comparative Study," *JQR, N.S.,* 38 (1947-48) 317-342, 418-430; 39 (1948-49) 79-94. [The Zoroastrians, pp. 418-426]

S. H. Taqizadeh, "The 'Era of Zoroaster'," *JRAS* (1947) 33-40.

Arthur Darby Nock, "The Problem of Zoroaster," *AJA* 53 (1949) 272-285.

[Chester] C. McCown, "Religion in the Inscriptions of Darius I and Xerxes," *JBL* 68 (1949) vi.

Jehangir C. Tavadia, "From Aryan Mythology to Zoroastrian Theology. A Review of Dumézil's Researches," *ZDMG* 103 (1953) 344-353.

*George Weston Briggs, "Eastern Sage to Western Man," *RR* 19 (1954-55) 115-130. [Influence of Zoroastrianism on the Hebrew Religion, esp. pp. 118-121]

Otakar Klíma, "The Date of Zoroaster," *ArOr* 27 (1959) 556-564.

V. V. Strouvé, "The Religion of the Achaemenides and Zoroastrianism," *JWH* 5 (1959-60) 529-545.

Star M. Heimsath, "Zoroastrianism," *TUSR* 7 (1960-63) 34-40.

J. C. Hindley, "A Prophet Outside Israel? Thoughts on the Study of Zoroastrianism," *IJT* 11 (1962) 96-107.

P. W. Avery, "Zoroaster," *NB* 43 (1962) 175-180.

*S. G. F. Brandon, "Zarathustra and the Dualism of Iran," *HT* 13 (1963) 250-259.

E. S. Kennedy and B. L. van der Waerden, "The World-Year of the Persians," *JAOS* 83 (1963) 315-327.

D. N. Mackenzie, "Zoroastrian Astrology in the *Bundahišn*," *BSOAS* 27 (1964) 511-529.

Jacob Neusner, "Note on Barukh ben Neriah and Zoroaster," *JAAR* 32 (1964) 359-360.

Ilya Gershevitch, "Zoroaster's Own Contribution," *JNES* 23 (1964) 12-38.

Jacob Neusner, "Note on Barukh ben Neriah and Zoroaster," *Numen* 12 (1965) 66-69.

R. C. Zaehner, "Zoroastrian Survivals in Iranian Folklore," *Iran* 3 (1965) 87-96.

*David Stronach, "The Kūh-i-Shahrak Fire Altar," *JNES* 25 (1966) 217-227. *[Sasanian]*

Douglas A. Fox, "Darkness and Light: The Zoroastrian View," *JAAR* 35 (1967) 129-137.

Mary Boyce, "On the Sacred Fires of the Zoroastrian," *BSOAS* 31 (1968) 52-68.

Mary Boyce, "The Pious Foundations of the Zoroastrians," *BSOAS* 31 (1968) 270-289.

Marina U. Vesci, "Suffering in Zoroastrianism and its Way Out," *Numen* 15 (1968) 222-232.

Mary Boyce, "On Mithra's Part in Zoroastrianism," *BSOAS* 32 (1969) 10-34.

Shaul Shaked, "Esoteric Trends in Zoroastrianism," *PIASH* 3 (1969) 175-221.

§474 *3.2.15.3 Other Mediterranean Area Religions - General Studies*

*C[laude] R. C[onder], "Moabite Idols," *CongL* 2 (1873) 410-420.

C[laude] R. Conder, "Sun Worship in Syria," *PEFQS* 13 (1881) 80-84.

*Fritz Hommel, "Asherah Among the Ancient Minaeans," *ET* 11 (1899-1900) 190.

G. E. White, "A Primitive Cattle Shrine in Asia Minor," *RP* 6 (1907) 99-102.

*Aylward M. Blackman, "The Nubian God Arsenuphis as Osiris," *SBAP* 32 (1909) 33-36.

*Fritz Hommel, "The God Ashima of Hamath," *ET* 23 (1911-12) 93.

Arthur C. Headlam, "The Religion of Syria," *CQR* 81 (1915-16) 433-441. *[Atargatis] (Review)*

F. Legge, "The Most Ancient Goddess Cybele," *JRAS* (1917) 695-714.

A. L. Frothingham, "The Cosmopolitan Religion of Tarsus and the Origin of Mithra," *AJA* 22 (1918) 63-64.

*Hildegard Lewy, "The Babylonian Background of the Kay Kâûs Legend," *ArOr* 17 (1919) Part 2, 28-109. [Introduction, 1. The Astronomers among the Kings of Babylonia; 2. A Rebellion against the Religion of God in al-'Irâq; 3. A Royal Throne in the Vault of Heaven, 4. The Development of the Kay Kâûs Legend]

J. H. Dunbar, "The Holy Mountain," *Antiq* 3 (1928) 408-413. *[Gebel Barkal in Ethiopia]*

Theodor H. Gaster, "The Deity Yaz," *PEFQS* 64 (1932) 103-104. *[Syrian god]*

*Mary H. Swindler, "The Goddess with Upraised Arms," *AJA* 45 (1941) 87.

Harold Mattingly, "The Later Paganism." *HTR* 35 (1942) 171-179.

A. F. L. Beeston, "The Ritual Hunt: A Study in Old South Arabian Religious Practice," *Muséon* 61 (1948) 183-196.

Constantine G. Yavis, "Origins of Chthonic Worship," *AJA* 54 (1950) 263.

*Joseph Fontenrose, "White Goddess and Syrian Goddess," *UCPSP* 11 (1951) 125-148.

Michael Grant, "Mithras and the Roman World," *HT* 4 (1954) 771-777.

Irene Ringwood Arnold, "Agnostic Festivals in Italy and Sicily," *AJA* 62 (1958) 221; 64 (1960) 245-251.

John Strugnell, "The Nabataean Goddess Al-Kutba' and Her Sanctuaries," *BASOR* #156 (1959) 29-36. [Note by W. F. Albright, pp. 37-38]

*C. J. Classen, "The Libyan God Ammon in Greece before 331 B.C.," *HJAH* 8 (1959) 349-355.

Isaac Rabinowitz, "Another Aramaic Record of the North-Arabian Goddess Han-'Ilat," *JNES* 18 (1959) 154-155.

Machteld J. Mellink, "Early Cult-Images of Cybele in Asia Minor," *AJA* 64 (1960) 188.

Elmer G. Suhr, "The Phrygian Goddess of Bogazkoy," *AJA* 64 (1960) 188-189.

A. M. Honeyman, "Two Votaries of Han-'Ilat," *JNES* 19 (1960) 40-41.

J. T. Milik and J. Teixidor, "New Evidence on the North-Arabic Deity Aktab-Kutabâ," *BASOR* #163 (1961) 22-25.

C. H. Emilie Haspels, "Relics of a Dionysiac Cult in Asia Minor," *AJA* 66 (1962) 285-287.

*Rudolf Jonas, "A Diadem of the cult of Kybele from the Neapolis Region (Samaria)," *PEQ* 94 (1962) 118-128.

*Donald White, "Demeter's Sicilian Cult as a Political Instrument," *GRBS* 5 (1965) 261-279.

F. Sokolowski, "A New Testimony on the Cult of Artemis of Ephesus," *HTR* 58 (1965) 427-431.

Walther Hinz, "The Elamite God *d.GAL*," *JNES* 24 (1965) 351-354.

Nelson Glueck, "Nabataean Symbols of Immortality," *EI* 8 (1967) 37*-41*.

Diana Kirkbride, "Ancient Arabian Ancestor Idols. Part I: The Discovery of the Sanctuary at Risqeh," *Arch* 22 (1969) 116-121.

Diana Kirkbride, "Ancient Arabian Ancestor Idols. Part II: The Interpretation of the Sanctuary at Risqeh," *Arch* 22 (1969) 188-195.

*George M. A. Hanfmann and Jane C. Waldbaum, "Kybebe and Artemis: Two Anatolian Goddesses at Sardis," *Arch* 22 (1969) 264-269.

*B. N. Grakov, "Survivals of Scythian Religion and Epos among the Samaritans," *VDI* (1969) #3, 72.

Theresa Howard Carter, "The Stone Spirits," *Exped* 12 (1969-70) #2, 22-40. *[From Tell al-Rimah]*

§475 *3.2.15.3.1 Religions of Carthage*

Stephen [H.] Langdon, "The History and Significance of Carthaginian Sacrifice," *JBL* 23 (1904) 79-93.

W. Max Müller, "Remarks on the Carthaginian Deity," *JAOS* 32 (1912) 429-433. *[Tanit]*

*G. Levi Della Vida, "A Hurrian Goddess at Carthage?" *JAOS* 68 (1948) 148-149.

§476 *3.2.15.4 The Mystery Religions and Judaism*

*J. Abelson, "Mysticism and Rabbinical Literature." *HJ* 10 (1911-12) 426-443.

J. H. Hertz, "Jewish Mysticism. An Historical Survey." *HJ* 14 (1915-16) 784-798.

*E. J. Price, "Jewish Apocalyptic and the Mysteries," *HJ* 18 (1919-20) 95-112.

Doro Levi, "Mors Voluntaria, Mystery Cults on Mosaics from Antioch." *Bery* 7 (1942) 19-55. *[Antioch-on-Orontas]*

Leo Baeck, "Jewish Mysticism." *JSS* 2 (1950-51) 3-16.

Karl Lehmann, "The Mystery Cult of Samothrace." *Arch* 7 (1954) 91-95.

*Z. Werblowsky, "Philo and the Zohar: A Note on the Methods of the *Scienza Nova* in Jewish Studies," *JJS* 10 (1959) 25-44.

*Z. Werblowsky, "Philo and the Zohar (Part II)," *JJS* 10 (1959) 113-136.

§477 *3.2.15.4.1 Gnosticism - General Studies*

*Alexander Altmann, "The Gnostic Background of the Rabbinic Legends." *JQR, N.S.,* 35 (1944-45) 371-391.

*Raphael Patai, "Note to the Gnostic Background of the Rabbinic Adam Legends." *JQR, N.S.,* 36 (1945-46) 416-417.

Luitpold Wallach, "A Jewish Polemic Against Gnosticism." *JBL* 65 (1946) 393-396.

*Ralph Marcus, "Pharisees, Essenes, and Gnostics." *JBL* 73 (1954) 157-161.

*J. G. Weiss, "On the formula melekh ha-'olam as anti-Gnostic protest." *JJS* 10 (1959) 169-171.

*Søren Giversen, "The Apocryphon of John and Genesis." *ST* 17 (1963) 60-76.

Arthur Darby Nock, "Gnosticism." *HTR* 57 (1964) 255-279.

§478 *3.2.15.5 Cypriote, Minoan and Mycenaean Religions*

Louis Dyer, "New Aspects of Mycenaean Cultus," *AJA* 5 (1901) 20-21.

R. Bruce Taylor, "'Tree and Pillar Cult'," *ET* 13 (1901-02) 309-310. *(Review) [Mycenaean Cult]*

Anonymous, "A Cretan Prophet," *QRL* 231 (1919) 378-395. *(Review)*

*E. Power, "The ancient gods and language of Cyprus revealed by the Accadian inscriptions of Amathus," *B* 10 (1929) 126-169.

*M[argaret] A. Murray, "Sacred Stones in Ancient Malta," *AEE* 19 (1934) 29-31.

*Martin P. Nilsson, "Mycenaean and Homeric Religion," *AfRW* 33 (1936) 84-99.

*Lillian B. Lawler, "The Dancing Figures from Palaikastro—A New Interpretation," *AJA* 44 (1940) 106-107.

Spyrido N. Marinatos, "The Cult of the Cretan Caves," *RR* 5 (1940-41) 129-136.

*Doro Levi, "Gleanings from Crete," *AJA* 49 (1945) 270-329. [1. The Dragon God of Babylon in Crete?, pp. 271-280]

George E. Mylonas, "The Cult of the Dead in Mycenaean Times," *AJA* 55 (1951) 149-150.

*Luisa Banti, "Myth in Pre-Classical Art," *AJA* 58 (1954) 307-310.

Mortimer Hardin Chambers, "The Twelve Gods at Cos," *HTR* 48 (1955) 153-154.

John Chadwick, "Potnia," *Minos* 5 (1957) 117-129.

Michael Jameson, "Mycenaean Religion," *Arch* 13 (1960) 33-39.

Cyrus H. Gordon, "The Minoan Cult," *AJA* 67 (1963) 211.

C. F. A. Schaeffer, "An Ingot God from Cyprus." *Antiq* 39 (1965) 57-58.

Terry E. Small, "A Possible 'Shield-Goddess' from Crete," *KZFE* 5 (1966) 103-107.

B. C. Dietrich, "Some Light from the East on Cretan Cult Practice," *HJAH* 16 (1967) 386-413.

S. Spyridakis, "The Itanian Cult of Tyche Protogeneia," *HJAH* 18 (1969) 42-48. *[Cretan Cult]*

§479 *3.2.15.6 Greek and Roman Religions - General Studies*

F. A. Paley, "Pantheistic Theories of the Soul." *ACQR* 2 (1877) 30-51.

*N. Vaschide and H. Piéron, "Prophetic Dreams in Greek and Roman Antiquity." *Monist* 11 (1900-01) 161-194. *(Trans. by Thomas J. McCormick)*

M. H. Morgan, "Greek and Roman Rain-Gods and Rain-Charms." *TAPA* 32 (1901) 83-109.

Anonymous, "Recent Literature on the Religions of Greece and Rome." *ET* 15 (1903-04) 346-351. *(Review)*

G. F. Hill, "Some Palestinian Cults in the Graeco-Roman Age." *PBA* 5 (1911-12) 411-427.

Ernest E. Genner, "The Religions of Greece and Rome." *LQHR* 119 (1913) 274-288.

William Sherwood Fox, "An Infernal Postal Service." *A&A* 1 (1914-15) 205-207. *[Curses in Greek and Roman Religion]*

Shirley Jackson Case, "The Religion of Lucretius." *AJT* 19 (1915) 91-107.

*Shirley Jackson Case, "Religion and War in the Graeco-Roman World." *AJT* 19 (1915) 179-199.

*Elizabeth Hazelton Haight, "The Story of Cupid and Psyche. I.—In Ancient Art." *A&A* 3 (1916) 43-53.

Ernest Abell Dale, "Theories of the Primitive Life and Development of Man in Greek and Latin Literature." *CJRT* 1 (1924) 133-143, 248-257.

Edwyn Bevan, "Classical Ghosts." *QRL* 246 (1926) 60-74.

*Martin R. P. McGuire, "The Relations Between Religion and Morality Among the Early Greeks and Romans." *AQW* 4 (1931) #1/2, 11-22.

H. J. Rose, "Numen Inest: 'Animism' in Greek and Roman Religion." *HTR* 28 (1935) 237-257.

*George M. A. Hanfmann, "Gigantomacy." *AJA* 41 (1937) 113-114.

Arthur Darby Nock, "The Cult of Heroes." *HTR* 37 (1944) 141-173.

*Herbert C. Youtie, "The *Kline* of Sarapis." *HTR* 41 (1948) 9-30.

Herbert Jennings Rose, "Mana in Greece and Rome." *HTR* 42 (1949) 155-174.

Herbert Jennings Rose, "Nvmen*[sic]* and Mana," *HTR* 44 (1951) 109-120.

Abe Malherbe, "Notes on Religious Washings in the Graeco-Roman World." *RestQ* 1 (1957) 152-158.

W. F. Jackson Knight, "The After-Life in Greek and Roman Antiquity." *Folk* 69 (1958) 217-236.

C. B. Pascal, "Catullus and the di Parentes." *HTR* 52 (1959) 75-84.

§480 *3.2.15.6.1 Greek Mythology, Philosophy and Religion*

Pelagius, "Of the Doctrine of Plato concerning God, and the general System of Nature," *TRep* 4 (1784) 77-97.

H. G. Tschirner, "The Relation of Philosophy to Religion in Ancient Greece. Translated from the German, with an Introductory Note," *CRB* 2 (1837) 515-536.

[Johann] Schweighauer, "The Morals of Socrates," *BRCR, N.S.,* 1 (1839) 161-179. *(Trans. by F. M. Hubbard)*

†G[eorge] G[rote], "Grecian Legends and Early History," *WR* 39 (1843) 151-174. *(Review)*

William S. Tyler, "Sketches in Grecian Philosophy," *BRCR, N.S.,* 12 (1844) 425-454; *3rd Ser.,* 1 (1845) 421-456; 2 (1846) 1-34.

J. T. C[hamplin], "The Religion of Ancient Greece," *CRB* 10 (1845) 530-544. *(Review)*

(   ) Trithen, "On the Origin of Hemēs," *TPS* 3 (1846-48) 201-204.

T. S. K[ing], "Plato's View of Immortality," *UQGR* 4 (1847) 73-107.

*†Anonymous, "Mackay on the Progress of Intellect," *BQRL* 12 (1850) 443-476. *(Review) [Religious Development Among the Greeks and Hebrews]*

†Anonymous, "Mackay's Religious Development in Greece," *BQRL* 17 (1853) 154-202. *(Review)*

Anonymous, "Religion of the Ancient Greeks," *CRB* 21 (1856) 425-451.

Anonymous, "Greek Philosophy," *FBQ* 4 (1856) 175-186.

N. M. Williams, "The Phædon: or, Plato on the Immortality of the Soul," *CRB* 22 (1857) 507-532.

John Proudfit, "Homeric Ideas of the Soul and a Future Life," *BS* 15 (1858) 753-805.

N. M. Williams, "Plato on Atheism," *CRB* 23 (1858) 547-568.

William S. Tyler, "The Theology of Aeschylus," *BS* 16 (1859) 354-403.

William S. Tyler, "The Theology of Sophocles," *BS* 17 (1860) 575-619; 18 (1861) 53-94.

†Anonymous, "On the Origin and Influences of Greek Philosophy," *DR* 48 (1860) 1-36. *(Review)*

W[illia]m S. Tyler, "The Homeric Doctrine of the Gods," *AThR* 3 (1861) 599-631.

†Anonymous, "Rawlinson's Herodotus," *DR* 49 (1861) 348-367. *(Review)*

W[illiam] S. Tyler, "The Homeric Doctrine of Sin," *AThR* 4 (1862) 276-296.

J. C. Moffat, "On a Revolution in the Ancient Religion of Greece," *JAOS* 7 (1862) v-vi.

Friedrich Koster, "Origin of Homer's Purer Religious Ideas," *AThR, N.S.,* 3 (1865) 56-61.

Anonymous, "The Twilight of Faith; or, Foreshadowings of Christianity in the Writings of Plato," *DUM* 66 (1865) 243-257, 423-436.

Anonymous, "De Quincey and the Religion of the Greeks," *CE* 80 (1866) 154-174.

Brooke F. Wescott, "Æschylus as a Religious Teacher," *ContR* 3 (1866) 351-373.

*[Edward] Zeller, "The Development of Monotheism Among the Greeks," *ContR* 4 (1867) 359-379.

Anonymous, "Aristotle—His Works and Philosophy," *DUM* 72 (1868) 3-20.

*Anonymous, "Aristotle on Land-tenure, Commerce, Free-trade, Education, Domestic Life, the True and False Democracy, and the Model State," *DUM* 75 (1870) 361-376.

*Hyde Clarke, "On the Niobe of Magnesia ad Sipylum; and, On the Newly discovered Lydo-Assyrian Monument of Smyrna," *JAOS* 9 (1871) ix-x.

*H. J. Van Lennep, "On the Niobe of Mt. Sipylus,"*JAOS* 9 (1871) xvi.

H.   Sidgwick,   "The   Sophists,"   *JP*   4   (1872)   288-307.

T. D. Woolsey, "On the Greek Kronos," *PAOS, May and October* (1872) xv-xvi.

Tayler Lewis, "Primitive Greek Religion," *PQPR* 1 (1872) 429-467.

*Francis Wharton, "Unconscious Greek Prophecy," *BS* 30 (1873) 144-165.

*O. Cone, "The Development of Monotheism among the Greeks," *UQGR, N.S.,* 10 (1873) 171-197.

Stewart D. F. Salmond, "The Homeric Conception of Life and Immortality," *BFER* 24 (1875) 1-34.

Anonymous, "The Life and Teachings of Sophocles," *DTQ* 3 (1877) 267-281.

S. S. Hebberd, "The Orientalism of Plato," *JSP* 11 (1877) 122-128.

Percy Gardner, "The Greek Mind in Presence of Death, interpreted from Reliefs and Inscriptions on Athenian Tombs," *ContR* 31 (1877-78) 144-166.

*Keningale Cook, "Theism and Ethics in Ancient Greece," *DUM* 92 (1878) 584-592, 641-655.

François Lenormant, "The Eleusinian Mysteries. A Study of Religious History," *ContR* 37 (1880) 847-871; 38 (1880) 121-149, 412-433.

T. D. Woolsey, "On the Sacred Stones called by the Greeks *Bœtyli* or *Bœtylia,*" *JAOS* 10 (1880) xxxi-xxxii.

T. D. Woolsey, "On the Greek Kronos," *JAOS* 10 (1880) lvii-lviii.

*Edward Zeller, "Development of Monotheism Among the Greeks, *MQR,* 2nd Ser.,* 2 (1880) 217-230. *(Trans. by Dwight M. Lowrey)*

Anonymous, "Early Greek Thought," *WR* 113 (1880) 8-24. *(Review)*

*[J. P.] Lesley, "Ιακχος from [Hor-m] αχα, the Sphinx name of the Solar disc on the Horizon," PAPS 19 (1880-81) 110-111.

Lewis R. Packard, "The Morality and Religion of the Greeks," *PAPA* 13 (1881) 7-9. *[Bound with Transactions, but paged separately]*

Sumner Ellis, "Plato's Argument for Immortality," *UQGR, N.S.,* 18 (1881) 389-398.

*Edward Zeller, "The Development of Monotheism Among the Greeks," *BS* 39 (1882) 619-647. *(Trans. by Edward D. Mead)*

Anonymous, "The Stoics," *WR* 117 (1882) 33-64. *(Review)*

Anonymous, "Epicurus and Lucretius," *WR* 117 (1882) 299-346. *(Review)*

*F. G. Fleay, "On the Interpretation of the Early Mythologies of Greece and India," *AAOJ* 5 (1883) 1-17.

W. Scott, "The physical constitution of the Epicurean gods," *JP* 12 (1883) 212-247.

*C. K. Nelson, "The Force of Δίκη in Greek Theosophy," *PAPA* 15 (1883) ix.

Anonymous, "Classic Concepts of Heaven and Hell," *WR* 120 (1883) 95-110.

J. C. C. Newton, "Greek Mythology and Philosophy," *MQR, 2nd Ser.,* 6 (1884) 1-16, 415-424.

Frank B. Tarbell, "Greek Ideas as to the Effect of Burial on the Future of the Soul," *TAPA* 15 (1884) 36-45.

*Anonymous, "The Samoson-Saga and the Myth of Herakles," *WR* 121 305-328. *(Review)*

*W. S. Scarborough, "Fatalism in Homer and Virgil," *PAPA* 17 (1885) xxxvi-xxxvii.

Edward Maguire, "Greek Mythology—'Prometheus Vinctus'," *IER, 3rd Ser.,* 7 (1886) 339-350.

Edward Maguire, "Greek Philosophy.—Plato's 'Phaedo' and 'Timaeus'," *IER, 3rd Ser.,* 7 (1886) 577-589.

Richard M. Smith, "The Revelation to the Greeks," *MQR, 3rd Ser.,* 4 (1888) 291-298; 5 (1888-89) 323-332; 6 (1889) 235-248.

*J. Freudenthal, "Are There Any Traces of Greek Philosophy in the Septuagint?" *JQR* 2 (1889-90) 205-222. [1. Ψυχή; 2. Πνοή; 3. Νοῦς; 4. Φρόνησις, φρόνιμος, ἄφρων; 5, 6. - Δοξα and λογός; 7. Αἰσθάνομαι, αἴσθησις; 8. Ἀρετή; 9. Ἀνδρεία, ἀνδρεῖος; 10 Μεγαλοπρεπής, μεγαλοπρέπεια; 11 Πρόνοια; 12. Κόσμος]

*H. J. Clarke, "The Meaning and History of the Logos of Philosophy," *JTVI* 23 (1889-90) 249-267, 275-276. (Discussion, pp. 267-275)

Paul Wolters, "ΖΕΥΣ ῾ΗΛΙΟΠΛΙΤΗΣ," *AJA, O.S.,* 6 (1890) 65-68. *[Zeus of Heliopolis]*

F. B. Jevons, "Report on Greek Mythology," *Folk* 2 (1891) 220-241. *(Review)*

*J. F. Hogan, "The Sacrifice of Iphigenia," *IER, 3rd Ser.,* 12 (1891) 1070-1086.

Augustine F. Hewit, "The Theodicy of Aristotle," *AER* 7 (1892) 321-332.

J. D. Butler, "How Many Gods on Olympus?" *AAOJ* 14 (1892) 228-229.

*Julia Wedgwood, "Greek Mythology and the Bible," *ContR* 61 (1892) 368-381.

*C. Taylor, "The Two Ways in Hermes and Xenophon," *JP* 21 (1892-93) 243-258.

*J. E. Hanauer, "Notes on the Winged Figure at Jaffa, on Bether, &c.," *PEFQS* 26 (1894) 148-150. *[Greek Goddess - Psyche]*

J. B. Bury, "The Works and Days; A Study in Greek Realism," *SRL* 23 (1894) 31-42.

Arthur Fairbanks, "The Conception of the Future Life in Homer," *AJT* 1 (1897) 741-757.

Arthur Fairbanks, "Attitudes of Worship in Greece. (Illustrated)," *BW* 9 (1897) 98-111.

[Paul Carus], "The Greek Idea of Salvation," *OC* 12 (1898) 675-689.

George Santayana, "Greek Religion," *NW* 8 (1899) 401-417.

James Iverach, "Religion in Greek Literature," *LQHR* 93 (1900) 85-90. *(Review)*

[Paul Carus], "The Greek Mysteries, a Preparation for Christianity," *Monist* 11 (1900-01) 87-123.

Paul Carus, "On Greek Religion and Mythology," *OC* 14 (1900) 513-538, 577-606, 641-658, 705-727; 15 (1901) 1-22.

Anonymous, "The Early Greek Philosophers," *CQR* 52 (1901) 387-404.

Arthur Stoddard Cooley, "Zeus the Heaven," *PAPA* 32 (1901) cxl-cxlii.

Susan Braley Franklin, "Public Appropriations for Individual Offerings and Sacrifices in Greece," *TAPA* 32 (1901) 72-82.

W. A. Leonard, "The Myths of Greece," *WR* 155 (1901) 432-438. *(Review)*

Alfred H. Lloyd, "A Study in the Logic of the Early Greek Philosophy. Being, Not-Being, and Becoming," *Monist* 12 (1901-02) 404-415.

P. Gardner, "Pre-Hellenic Religion in Greece," *OSHTP* (1901-02) 32-33.

*Ernst Riess, "Some Names found on Coan Inscriptions," *AJA* 6 (1902) 32-33.

Arthur Stoddard Cooley, "Nature Aspects of Zeus," *PAPA* 34 (1902) lxv-lxvii.

Wm. Prentiss Drew, "The Faith of Socrates," *MR* 85 (1903) 443-446.

Bernard Bosanquet, "Plato's Conception of Death," *HJ* 2 (1903-04) 98-109.

Lewis R. Farnell, "Sacrificial Communion in Greek Religion," *HJ* 2 (1903-04) 306-322.

Evelyn Martinengo Cesaresco, "The Greek Conception of Animals," *ContR* 85 (1904) 430-439.

James Hope Moulton, "Recent Work on Greek Religion," *LQHR* 102 (1904) 94-110. *(Review)*

Thomas D. Seymour, "The Homeric Hades and the Dead," *PAPA* 36 (1904) xiii.

*N. P. Vlachos, "Religious Prophetism Among the Greeks," *RChR, 4th Ser.,* 8 (1904) 495-510; 9 (1905) 60-80, 500-516.

*Frederic Blass, "Science and Sophistry," *ET* 16 (1904-05) 8-15. *(Trans. by Mrs. Gibson)*

*James M. Paton,."The Death of Thersites on an Amphora in the Boston Museum of Fine Arts," *AJA* 9 (1905) 82-83.

W. T. Davison, "The Myths of Plato," *LQHR* 104 (1905) 60-81. *(Review)*

Herbert Weir Smyth, "Aspects of Greek Conservatism," *PAPA* 37 (1905) xx-xxiv.

Arthur Fairbanks, "Note on the Standpoint for the Study of Religion in Homer," *PAPA* 37 (1905) xlviii-xlix.

Gilbert Murray, "The Wanderings of Odysseus," *QRL* 202 (1905) 344-370. *(Review)*

John B. Kieffer, "The Greek Conception of Life," *RChR, 4th Ser.,* 9 (1905) 446-455.

L. R. Farnell, "Pre-Anthropomorphic Stage of Religion as Illustrated by Cult of Hestia," *OSHTP* (1906-07) 5-21.

George D[epue] Hadzsits, "Aphrodite and the Dione Myth," *AJA* 11 (1907) 64-65.

*James M. Paton, "Two Representations of the Birth of Dionysus," *AJA* 11 (1907) 65.

Anonymous, "Artemis Ephesia," *RP* 6 (1907) 64.

*Norman R. Mitchell, "The Wisdom of the Hebrews in Relation to Greek Thought," *GUOST* 3 (1907-12) 16-17.

[Paul Carus], "Olympian Brides," *OC* 22 (1908) 79-100.

Edwin A. Rumball, "Sin in the Greek Cults," *OC* 22 (1908) 398-406.

*Willis Brewer, "Ethnology of Greek Mythological Terms," *OC* 22 (1908) 480-484.

*C. A. Browne, "Etymology of Greek Mythological Terms According to Plato," *OC* 22 (1908) 680-685.

*R. C. Bosanquet, "Greek Temples and Early Religion," *QRL* 208 (1908) 252-279. *(Review)*

George Depue Hadzsits, "Significance of Worship and Prayer among the Epicureans," *TAPA* 39 (1908) 73-88.

Arthur E. Whatham, "The Magic Girdle of Aphrodite," *AJRPE* 3 (1908-09) 366-377.

*Dow Covington, "Altar of Ptolemy Neos Dionysos XIII," *ASAE* 10 (1909) 34-35.

J. Rendel Harris, "The Cult of the Heavenly Twins," *ContR* 95 (1909) 50-61. *[Dioscurism]*

E. E. Sikes, "Four-Footed Man: A Note on Greek Anthropology," *Folk* 20 (1909) 421-431.

Edward B. Clapp, "Greek Religion and Morality as set forth by Pindar," *HJ* 8 (1909-10) 283-300.

Thomas Spencer Jerome, "A Note on the Esoteric Doctrines of the Eleusinian Mysteries," *AJA* 14 (1910) 89-90.

*Edward Chauncey Baldwin, "The Hebrew and the Greek Ideas of Life," *BW* 36 (1910) 334-344.

W. M. Calder, "Zeus and Hermes at Lystra," *Exp, 7th Ser.*, 10 (1910) 1-6.

W. M. Calder, "The 'Priest' of Zeus at Lystra," *Exp, 7th Ser.*, 10 (1910) 148-155.

Maurice Hutton, "The Mind of Herodotus," *TAPA* 42 (1911) 35-43.

B. A. G. Fuller, "The Gods of Epicurus. A Plea for Their Serious Consideration," *HJ* 10 (1911-12) 892-910.

*Wilfred Schoff, "Tammuz, Pan and Christ. Notes on a Typical Case of Myth-Transference and Development," *OC* 26 (1912) 513-532.

[Paul Carus], "Pan the Rustic," *OC* 26 (1912) 533-545.

A. Kampmeier, "Pan, the Arcadian God," *OC* 26 (1912) 702.

Joseph William Hewitt, "On the Development of the Thank-offering among the Greeks," *TAPA* 43 (1912) 95-111.

*William Scott Ferguson, "Legalized Absolution en Route from Greece to Rome," *AmHR* 18 (1912-13) 29-47.

Paul Wendland, "Hellenistic Ideas of Salvation in the Light of Ancient Anthropology," *AJT* 17 (1913) 345-351.

John Bouton Lawrence, "The Theology of 'Prometheus Bound'," *BS* 70 (1913) 421-433.

*Cuthbert Lattey, "Alexander the God," *Exp, 8th Ser.,* 5 (1913) 97-113.

*Ernest E. Genner, "The Religions of Greece and Rome," *LQHR* 119 (1913) 274-288. *(Review)*

*Wilfred Schoff, "Tammuz, Pan and Christ. Further Notes on a Typical Case of Myth-Transference," *OC* 27 (1913) 449-460.

*S. Angus, "Hebrew, Greek, and Roman," *R&E* 10 (1913) 163-177.

*S. Angus, "Hebrew, Greek, and Roman. Part II.," *R&E* 10 (1913) 403-422.

Robert B. English, "Heraclitus and the Soul," *TAPA* 44 (1913) 163-184.

J. Rendel Harris, "The Origin of the Cult of Dionysos," *OSHTP* (1913-14) 42-44.

Lewis R. Farnell, "Magic and Religion in Early Hellenic Society," *AfRW* 17 (1914) 17-34.

F. Legge, "The Greek Worship of Serapis and Isis," *SBAP* 36 (1914) 79-99.

Joseph William Hewitt, "The Thank-offering and Greek Religious Thought," *TAPA* 45 (1914) 77-90.

John B. Kelso, "Greek Religion," *BWTS* 7 (1914-15) 25-43.

*W. Sherwood Fox, "A Problem of Cultus and Agriculture," *PAPA* 47 (1915) xvi-xvii.

Adela Marion Adam, "The Mysticism of Greece," *ET* 27 (1915-16) 343-346, 395-398, 460-463.

*A. L. Frothingham, "Babylonian Origin of Hermes the Snake-God and of the Caduceus," *AJA* 20 (1916) 175-211.

J. Rendel Harris, "The Origin of the Cult of Dionysos," *BJRL* 2 (1914-15) 114-128.

J. Rendel Harris, "The Origin of the Cult of Apollo," *BJRL* 3 (1916-17) 10-47.

J. Rendel Harris, "The Origin of the Cult of Artemis," *BJRL* 3 (1916-17) 147-184.

J. Rendel Harris, "The Origin of the Cult of Aphrodite," *BJRL* 3 (1916-17) 354-381.

William C. Lawton, "Hermes, the Friend of Man," *A&A* 6 (1917) 101-111.

Orlando O. Norris, "Greek Ideas of An Afterworld. A Study of the Relation between Practice and Belief," *Monist* 27 (1917) 57-82.

Anonymous, "Aphrodite as Mother Goddess," *OC* 31 (1917) 248-249.

*A. H. Sayce, "Assyriological Notes," *SBAP* 39 (1917) 207-211. [The God Kadmos, p. 209]

Hartley B. Alexander, "Plato's Conception of the Cosmos," *Monist* 28 (1918) 1-24.

Margaret C. Waites, "The Meaning of the 'Dokana'," *AJA* 23 (1919) 1-18.

Harry Ranston, "Xenophanes the Iconoclast," *LQHR* 132 (1919) 205-215.

*Lillian M. Wilson, "Contributions of Greek Art to the Medusa Myth," *AJA* 24 (1920) 232-240.

W. Sherwood Fox, "Aphrodite: Mother Earth," *AJP* 41 (1920) 283-286.

Dorothy Tarrant, "The Conception of the Soul in Greek Philosophy," *HJ* 20 (1921-22) 70-87.

E. W. Adams, "The Philosophy of Epicurus," *HJ* 20 (1921-22) 88-89.

A. L. Frothingham, "Medusa as Artemis in the Temple at Corfu," *AJA* 26 (1922) 84-85.

Claude C. H. Williamson, "The Delphic Oracle," *ACQR* 47 (1922) 196-216.

Michael Tierney, "The Origins of Orphism," *ITQ* 17 (1922) 112-127.

J. W. Hewitt, "The Gratitude of the Gods," *PAPA* 53 (1922) xix-xx.

*J. Rendel Harris, "Athena, Sophia, and the Logos," *BJRL* 7 (1922-23) 56-72.

B. A. G. Fuller, "The Eleusian and Orphic Mysteries," *HJ* 21 (1922-23) 141-157.

John Wright Buckham, "The Mysticism of Plato," *OC* 37 (1923) 463-467.

Jonathan Wright, "The Wisdom of Herodotus," *OC* 37 (1923) 610-621.

G. M. Sargeaunt, "A Stoic Vision of a Living Universe." *HJ* 22 (1923-24) 561-573.

Clyde Murley, "Pausanias and the Atlas Metope," *AJA* 28 (1924) 79-80.

*Stephen Bleecker Luce, "Studies on the Exploits of Hercules on Vases," *AJA* 28 (1924) 296-325.

G. M. Sargeaunt, "The Greek Fear of Life," *QRL* 242 (1924) 41-54.

*Kate McK. Elderkin, "Aphrodite Worship on a Minoan Gem," *AJA* 29 (1925) 53-58.

*Horace W. Wright, "The Janus Shrine at the Forum," *AJA* 29 (1925) 79-81.

J. R[endel] Harris, "Apollo's Birds," *BJRL* 9 (1925) 372-416.

H. Ranston, "The Orphic Mysteries," *Exp, 9th Ser.,* 4 (1925) 141-150.

A. H. Krappe, "The Story of Iason*[sic]* and Medeia," *Folk* 36 (1925) 308-321.

Alexander Kadison, "The Greek Idea of Sin," *OC* 39 (1925) 433-435.

J[ulius] A. Bewer, "The Hellenistic Mystery Religion and the Old Testament," *JBL* 45 (1926) 1-13.

(Mrs.) [Cornelia Steketee] Henry Hulst, "On Greek Religion," *OC* 40 (1926) 641-647.

L. W. Grensted, "Apollo in the Sky," *BJRL* 11 (1927) 51-56.

F. Melian Stawell, "Greek Religion," *QRL* 248 (1927) 64-81. *(Review)*

G. M. Sargeaunt, "The Greek View of Life," *QRL* 249 (1927) 350-362. *(Review)*

John Murray, "The Tradition of the Soul's Immortality in Greek Thought," *TFUQ* 2 (1927-28) 215-229.

Walter Miller, "The Eumenides Shrines at Athens," *AJA* 32 (1928) 61-62.

J. Rendel Harris, "The Origin of the Cult of Hermes," *BJRL* 13 (1929) 107-122.

J. Rendel Harris, "A Further Note on Hermes," *BJRL* 13 (1929) 305-308.

George M. A. Grube, "The God of Plato," *CJRT* 6 (1929) 165-172.

S. M. Adams, "The Religious Thought of Aeschylus," *CJRT* 6 (1929) 309-316.

*Arthur Darby Nock, "Σύνναος θεός," *PAPA* 60 (1929) xxvii.

Roy Kenneth Hack, "Homer and the Cult of Heroes," *TAPA* 60 (1929) 57-74.

*Stephen Bleecker Luce, "Studies on the Exploits of Hercules on Vases," *AJA* 34 (1930) 313-333. [II. The Theft of the Delphic Tripod]

Alexander Haggerty Krappe, "The Karneia," *AfRW* 28 (1930) 380-384.

*Philip H. Davis, "The Eleusinion in Athens and the Plutonion," *AJA* 34 (1930) 51.

*G. A. Wainwright, "The Relationship of Amūn to Zeus, and his Connexion with Meteorites," *JEA* 16 (1930) 35-38.

*H. N. Couch, "An Inscribed Votive Bronze Bull," *AJA* 35 (1931) 44-47.

Alfred C. Schlesinger, "Associated Divinities in Greek Temples," *AJA* 35 (1931) 161-169.

Edwyn Beavan, "Greek Oracles," *DR* 188 (1931) 57-67. *(Review) [Delphi Oracles]*

*Helena Carus, "Galatea Comes Alive," *OC* 45 (1931) 725-736.

T. Carlyle Hutton, "The Soul in Homer," *PAPA* 62 (1931) xxxviii-xxxix.

R. F. A. Hoernlé, "Plato's 'Forms' and Plato's 'God'. Part I," *Person* 12 (1931) 118-121.

R. F. A. Hoernlé, "Plato's 'Forms' and Plato's 'God'. Part II," *Person* 12 (1931) 175-182.

R. F. A. Hoernlé, "Plato's 'Forms' and Plato's 'God'. Part III," *Person* 12 (1931) 250-257.

Paul A. Clement, "The Cults of Pherae and the Artemis Pheraea Goddess," *AJA* 36 (1932) 40-41.

*Robert C. Horn, "Symbolic Acts of Greek Philosophers and Hebrew Prophets," *LCQ* 5 (1932) 190-201.

Norman W. DeWitt, "Notes on the History of Epicureanism," *TAPA* 63 (1932) 166-176.

Arthur E. Gordon, "On the Origin of Diana," *TAPA* 63 (1932) 177-192.

Joseph Eddy Fontenrose, "Zeus Didymaeus," *TAPA* 63 (1932) 245-255.

*M. Narkiss, "A Dioscuri Cult in Sebustiya," *PEFQS* 64 (1932) 201-212.

Irene Ringwood Arnold, "Local Festivals at Delos," *AJA* 37 (1933) 452-457.

*Charles F. Edson Jr., "Legitimus Honor. A Note on Hellenistic Ruler-Worship," *HTR* 26 (1933) 324-325.

*W. W. Tarn, "Alexander the Great and the Unity of Mankind," *PBA* 19 (1933) 123-166.

Clark Hopkins, "Assyrian Elements in the Perseus-Gorgon Story," *AJA* 38 (1934) 341-358.

*C[hester] C. McCown, "A New Deity in a Jerash Inscription," *JAOS* 54 (1934) 178-185. [πακειδᾶ]

Martin P. Nilsson, "Early Orphism and Kindred Religious Movements," *HTR* 28 (1935) 181-230.

George Miller Calhoun, "Zeus the Father in Homer," *TAPA* 66 (1935) 1-17.

Alexander Haggerty Krappe, "Apollon Σμινθεύς and the Teutonic Mysing," *ARW* 33 (1936) 40-56.

*Martin P. Nilsson, "Mycenaean and Homeric Religion," *ARW* 33 (1936) 84-99.

Harriet Boyd Hawes, "The Ancient Temple of the Goddess on the Acropolis," *AJA* 40 (1936) 120-121.

Friedrich Solmsen, "The Background of Plato's Theology," *TAPA* 67 (1936) 208-218.

Harold J. Stukey, "Purity in Fifth and Fourth Century Religion," *TAPA* 67 (1936) 286-295.

*George M. A. Hanfmann, "Gigantomachy," *AJA* 41 (1937) 113-114.

G. W. Elderkin, "The Marriage of Zeus and Hera and its Symbol," *AJA* 41 (1937) 424-435.

*M. H. Fisch, "Alexander and the Stoics, Part I," *AJP* 58 (1937) 59-82.

*M. H. Fisch, "Alexander and the Stoics (Cont.)," *AJP* 58 (1937) 129-151.

*W. F. J. Knight, "The Sumerian Provenience of Greek Defensive Sanctity," *PAPA* 68 (1937) xxxiv-xxxv.

George M[iller] Calhoun, "Homer's Gods: Prolegomena," *TAPA* 68 (1937) 11-25.

Ben Edward Perry, "The Early Greek Capacity for Viewing Things Separately," *TAPA* 68 (1937) 403-427.

Stuart Piggott, "The Hercules Myth—beginnings and ends," *Antiq* 12 (1938) 323-331.

Francis Redding Walton, "The Date of the Adonia at Athens," *HTR* 31 (1938) 65-72.

Hermann Fränkel, "Heraclitus on God and the Phenomenal World," *TAPA* 69 (1938) 230-244.

M. I. Rostovtzeff, "The Mentality of the Hellenistic World and the After-Life," *HDSB* 4 (1938-39) 5-25.

*Karl Lehmann-Hartleben, "Note on the Potnia Taurōn," *AJA* 43 (1939) 669-671.

*A. Cameron, "Sappho's Prayer to Aphrodite," *HTR* 32 (1939) 1-17.

*A. Cameron, "Inscriptions Relating to Sacral Manumission and Confession," *HTR* 32 (1939) 143-179.

*R[obert] H. Pfeiffer, "The Ages of Mankind in Genesis and Hesiod," *JBL* 58 (1939) iv.

S. V. McCasland, "The Asklepios Cult in Palestine," *JBL* 58 (1939) xvi.

Harold J. Stukey, "Pollution of the Soul by the Body," *PAPA* 70 (1939) xlv-xlvi.

John Wright Buckham, "The Humor of Plato," *Person* 20 (1939) 10-20.

Lillian B. Lawler, "The Dance of the Owl and Its Significance in the History of Greek Religion and the Drama," *TAPA* 70 (1939) 482-502.

Martin P. Nilsson, "The Origin of Belief Among the Greeks in the Divinity of the Heavenly Bodies," *HTR* 33 (1940) 1-8.

Kurt Latte, "The Coming of the Pythia," *HTR* 33 (1940) 9-18.

Arthur Darby Nock, "Orphism or Popular Philosophy?" *HTR* 33 (1940) 301-315.

John Brodie McDairmid, "Theophrastus on the Eternity of the World," *TAPA* 71 (1940) 239-247.

*Frank E. Brown, "The Temple of Zeus Olympios at Dura and the Religious Policy of the Seleucids," *AJA* 45 (1941) 94.

Irene Ringwood Arnold, "Festivals of the Aegean Islands, Chiefly from Inscriptional Evidence," *AJA* 45 (1941) 96.

Arthur Darby Nock, "A Cabiric Rite," *AJA* 45 (1941) 577-581.

Herbert Jennings Rose, "Greek Rites of Stealing," *HTR* 34 (1941) 1-5.

*H[erbert] J[ennings] Rose, "The Name of Isis in Plutarch: Psychostaisa," *Man* 41 (1941) #103.

Alexander H. Krappe, "The Birth of Adonis," *RR* 6 (1941-42) 3-17.

Ananda K. Coomaraswamy, "The 'E' at Delphi," *RR* 6 (1941-42) 18-19.

Hetty Goldman, "The Origin of the Greek Herm," *AJA* 46 (1942) 58-68.

*Sterling Dow, "Corinthiaca. I. The Month Phoinikaois," *AJA* 46 (1942) 69-72.

*Elisabeth Jastrow, "The Great Goddess of Nature in Funeral Art of Magna Graecia," *AJA* 46 (1942) 119.

Stanley Casson, "How Homer wrote the Odyssey," *Antiq* 16 (1942) 71-84.

Colin Hardie, "Homer and the Odyssey: Another Point of View," *Antiq* 16 (1942) 265-275. (Rejoinder by Stanley Casson, pp. 275-277)

Arthur Darby Nock, "Religious Attitudes of the Ancient Greeks," *PAPS* 85 (1942) 472-482.

H[erbert] J[ennings] Rose, "The Grief of Persephone," *HTR* 36 (1943) 247-250.

Martin P. Nilsson, "Problems of the History of Greek Religion in the Hellenistic and Roman Age," *HTR* 36 (1943) 251-275.

R. T. Norman, "Some Implications of Greek Views of Immortality," *DUJ, N.S.,* 5 (1943-44) 20-28.

Alexander H. Krappe, "Phaëthon," *RR* 8 (1943-44) 115-130.

William Scott Ferguson, "The Attic Orgeones," *HTR* 37 (1944) 61-140.

*Doro Levi, "Gleanings from Crete," *AJA* 49 (1945) 270-329. [2. The Siren from Parisos, pp. 280-293; 3. Zeus, Apollo, Athena, pp. 293-313]

L. A. Post, "The Divine in Homer," *CQ* 22 (1945) 20-27.

Farrand Sayre, "Greek Cynicism," *JHI* 6 (1945) 113-118.

Walter Woodburn Hyde, "Atheism Among the Greeks," *PAPA* 76 (1945) xxxiv-xxxv.

Kurt von Fritz, "Greek Prayers," *RR* 10 (1945-46) 5-39.

Howard J. B. Ziegler, "Psychology and Ethics in Epicetus," *USQR* 1 (1945-46) #3, 15-21.

George E. Mylonas, "The Eagle of Zeus," *AJA* 50 (1946) 286.

Herbert Jennings Rose, "Theology and Mythology in Aeschylus," *HTR* 39 (1946) 1-24.

*Truesdell S. Brown, "Euhemerus and the Historians," *HTR* 39 (1946) 259-274.

*W. L. Hildburgh, "Apotropaism in Greek Vase-Paintings," *Folk* 57&58 (1946-47) 154-178.

Martin P. Nilsson, "The Psychological Background of Late Greek Paganism," *RR* 11 (1946-47) 115-125.

Kurt von Fritz, "Pandora, Prometheus, and the Myth of the Ages," *RR* 11 (1946-47) 227-260.

Friedrich Solmsen, "Strata of Greek Religion in Aeschylus," *HTR* 40 (1947) 211-226.

Frederick J. Teggart, "The Argument of Hesiod's *Works and Days*," *JHI* 8 (1947) 45-77.

*Constantine G. Yavis, "The Earliest Hellenic Altars and Their Antecedents," *AJA* 52 (1948) 381.

*Herbert C. Youtie, "The *Kline* of Sarapis," *HTR* 41 (1948) 9-30.

*Martin Rist, "The Metamorphosis of Apelius and the Zoolatry of the Egyptian Mysteries," *IR* 5 (1948) 134-141.

*Julien L. Tondrian, "Comparisons and Identifications of Rulers with Deities in the Hellenistic Period," *RR* 13 (1948-49) 24-47.

*Gregory Vlastos, "Religion and Medicine in the Cult of Asclepius: A Review Article," *RR* 13 (1948-49) 269-290. *(Review)*

Richard C. Gilman, "The Soul in Early Greek Philosophy," *PF* 7 (1949) 19-24.

Gerald F. Else, "God and Gods in Early Greek Thought," *TAPA* 80 (1949) 24-36.

Archibald W. Allen, "Solon's Prayer to the Muses," *TAPA* 80 (1949) 50-65.

*Lloyd W. Daly, "The Cow in Greek Art and Cult," *AJA* 54 (1950) 261.

H[erbert] J[ennings] Rose, "Ghost Ritual in Aeschylus," *HTR* 43 (1950) 257-280.

Alice Sperduti, "The Divine Nature of Poetry in Antiquity," *TAPA* 81 (1950) 209-240.

Martin P. Nilsson, "Second Letter to Professor Noch on the Positive Gains in the Science of Greek Religion," *HTR* 44 (1951) 143-151.

Richard Hope, "Plato's Phaedo on Deathlessness," *Person* 32 (1951) 19-25.

*Joseph Fontenrose, "White Goddess and Syrian Goddess," *UCPSP* 11 (1951) 125-148.

Wilford O. Cross, "The Blessing of the Sower," *RR* 16 (1951-52) 27-39.

Richard Haywood, "The Delphic Oracle," *Arch* 5 (1952) 110-118.

Frederick C. Grant, "Greek Religion in the Hellenistic-Roman Period," *ATR* 34 (1952) 11-25. *(Review)*

Francis R. Walton, "Athens, Eleusis, and the Homeric Hymn to Demeter," *HTR* 45 (1952) 105-114.

H. Chadwick, "The Attis from a Domestic Shrine," *JTS, N.S.,* 3 (1952) 90-92.

*R[obert H.] Pfeiffer, "The Image of the Delian Apollo and Apolline Ethics," *JWCI* 15 (1952) 20-32.

Norman O. Brown, "The Birth of Athena," *TAPA* 83 (1952) 130-143.

*Ernest H. Kantorowicz, "ΣΥΝΘΡΟΝΟΣ ΔΙΚΗΙ," *AJA* 57 (1953) 65-70.

Charles H. Morgan, "Two Pheidian Legends and How They Grew," *AJA* 57 (1953) 109.

*Herbert Hoffmann, "Foreign Influence and Native Invention in Archaic Greek Altars," *AJA* 57 (1953) 189-195.

Elmer G. Suhr, "Herakles and Omphale," *AJA* 57 (1953) 251-263.

Thalia Phillies Howe, "The Origin and Function of the Gorgon-Head," *AJA* 58 (1954) 209-221.

*F. Sokolowski, "Fees and Taxes in the Greek Cults," *HTR* 47 (1954) 153-164.

*F. Sokolowski, "On *Prothysia* and *Promanteia* in Greek Cults," *HTR* 47 (1954) 165-171.

*F. Sokolowski, "The Real Meaning of Sacral Manumission," *HTR* 47 (1954) 173-181.

T. B. L. Webster, "Personification as a Mode of Greek Thought," *JWCI* 17 (1954) 10-21.

Donald Heiney, "Mythos and Ethos," *Person* 35 (1954) 152-159.

Ward Hooker, "Apuleius's 'Cupid and Psyche' as Platonic Myth," *BUS* 5 (1954-55) #3, 24-38.

Robert F. Healey, "In the Beginning: A study of Some Greek Ideas on Theogony, Cosmogony and Creation," *MH* 11 (1954-55) #1, 7-27.

*Oscar Broneer, "The Isthmian Sanctuary of Poseidon," *Arch* 8 (1955) 56-62.

H. T. Rose, "Divine Disguisings," *HTR* 49 (1956) 63-72.

F. Sokolowski, "Heracles Thasios." *HTR* 49 (1956) 153-158.

J. Gwyn Griffiths, "Archaeology and Hesiod's Five Ages," *JHI* 17 (1956) 109-119.

H. C. Baldry, "Hesiod's Five Ages," *JHI* 17 (1956) 553-554.

S. Sambursky, "On the Possible and the Probable in Ancient Greece," *Osiris* 12 (1956) 35-48.

Livio C. Stecchini, "The Delphian Column of the Dancers," *AJA* 61 (1957) 187.

Erland Ehnmark, "Transmigration in Plato," *HTR* 50 (1957) 1-20.

F. Sokolowski, "Partnership in the Lease of Cults in Greek Antiquity," *HTR* 50 (1957) 133-143.

Douglas D. Feaver, "Historical Development in the Priesthoods of Athens," *YCS* 15 (1957) 123-158.

*Christoph W. Clairmont, "Studies in Greek Mythology and Vase-Painting," *YCS* 15 (1957) 161-178.

Michael H. Jameson, "The Prehistory of Greek Sacrifice," *AJA* 62 (1958) 223.

Charlotte R. Long, "Greeks, Carians, and the Purification of Delos," *AJA* 62 (1958) 297-306.

*E. Badian, "Alexander the Great and the Unity of Mankind," *HJAH* 7 (1958) 425-444.

H[erbert] J[ennings] Rose, "Divine Names in Classical Greece," *HTR* 51 (1958) 3-32.

J. Gwyn Griffiths, "Did Hesiod Invent the 'Golden Age'?" *JHI* 19 (1958) 91-93.

*R. E. Wycherley, "Two Athenian Shrines," *AJA* 63 (1959) 67-72. [1. Herakleion in Melite; 2. Olympion]

F. Sokolowski, "On the Rules Regulating the Celebration of the Eleusinian Mysteries," *HTR* 52 (1959) 1-7.

Werner Jaeger, "The Greek Ideas of Immortality," *HTR* 52 (1959) 135-147.

F. Sokolowski, "From the History of the Worship of Apollo at Actium," *HTR* 52 (1959) 215-221.

Rudolph E. Siegel, "The Paradoxes of Zeno: Some Similarities Between Ancient Greek and Modern Thought," *Janus* 48 (1959) 24-47.

George Boas, "Some Assumptions of Aristotle," *TAPS, N.S.,* 49 (1959) Part 6, 3-98.

Chrysoula Kardara, "Problems of Hera's Cult-Images," *AJA* 64 (1960) 343-358.

*Rudolph E. Siegel, "On the relation between early Greek scientific thought and mysticism: is Hestia, the central fire, an abstract astronomical concept?" *Janus* 49 (1960) 1-20.

A. N. Marlow, "Myth and Ritual in Early Greece," *BJRL* 43 (1960-61) 373-402.

Clark Hopkins, "The Sunny Side of the Greek Gorgon," *AJA* 65 (1961) 190.

*Jerome Quinn, "Cape Phokas, Lesbos—Site of an Archaic Sanctuary for Zeus, Hera and Dionysus?" *AJA* 65 (1961) 391-393.

William Sale, "The Hyperborean Maidens on Delos," *HTR* 54 (1961) 75-89.

Bernard Goldman, "The Asiatic Ancestry of the Greek Gorgon," *Bery* 14 (1961-63) 1-22.

Clark Hopkins, "The Sunny Side of the Greek Gorgon," *Bery* 14 (1961-63) 25-35.

Momolina Marconi, "Can the Cosmogony of the Greeks Be Reconstructed?" *HRel* 1 (1961-62) 274-280.

Robert Fisher Healy, "A Deityless Sacrifice in the Athenian State Calendar," *AJA* 66 (1962) 197-198.

Ruth Ilsley Hicks, "Egyptian Elements in Greek Mythology," *TAPA* 93 (1962) 90-108.

Elmer G. Suhr, "Poseidon: Wind or Sea God?" *BUS* 11 (1962-63) #4, 1-11.

Marie Delcourt, "The Legend of Sarpedon and the Saga of the Archer," *HRel* 2 (1962-63) 33-51.

*Clark Hopkins, "The Canopy of Heaven and the Aegis of Zeus," *AJA* 67 (1963) 212.

Elmer G. Suhr, "Poseidon—God of the Wind or the Sea?" *AJA* 67 (1963) 217-218.

*Martin P. Nilsson, "The High God and the Mediator," *HTR* 56 (1963) 101-120.

Raghauveer, Singh, "Herakleitos and the Law of Nature," *JHI* 24 (1963) 457-472.

Friedrich Solmsen, "Nature as Craftsman in Greek Thought," *JHI* 24 (1963) 473-496.

*Rudolf Anthes, "Affinity and Difference Between Egyptian and Greek Sculpture and Thought in the Seventh and Sixth Centuries B.C.," *PAPS* 107 (1963) 60-81.

Donald P. Verene, "Plato's Conception of Philosophy and Poetry," *Person* 44 (1963) 528-538.

E. N. Lane, "A Re-Study of the God Men. Part I: The Epigraphic and Sculptural Evidence," *Bery* 15 (1964) 5-58.

*Clark Hopkins, "The Canopy of Heaven and the Aegis of Zeus," *BUS* 12 (1964) #3, 1-16.

*R. E. Wycherley, "The Olympieion at Athens," *GRBS* 5 (1964) 169-179. [Appendix: Synopsis of Zeus Cults at Athens, pp. 175-177]

F. Sokolowski, "Aphrodite as Guardian of Greek Magistrates," *HTR* 57 (1964) 1-8.

Robert F. Healey, "A Sacrifice Without a Deity in the Athenian State Calendar," *HTR* 57 (1964) 153-159.

*A. Cameron, "Sappho and the Aphrodite Again," *HTR* 57 (1964) 237-239.

*Olof Vessberg, "A New Variant of the Helena Myth," *MB* #4 (1964) 54-62.

Marie Delcourt, "The Last Giants," *HRel* 4 (1964-65) 209-242.

*Sterling Dow and David H. Gill, "The Greek Cult Table," *AJA* 69 (1965) 103-114.

*Robert F. Healey, "A Calendar of Sacrifices of Eleusis," *AJA* 69 (1965) 169.

Elmer J.*[sic]* Suhr, "Eros and the Marathon Boy," *AJA* 69 (1965) 176.

Elmer J.*[sic]* Suhr, "An Interpretation of the Medusa," *Folk* 76 (1965) 90-103.

C. R. Whittaker, "The Delphic Oracle: Belief and Behavior in Ancient Greece—and Africa," *HTR* 58 (1965) 21-47.

Henry G. Wolz, "Plato's Discourse on Love in the Phaedrus," *Person* 46 (1965) 157-170.

*George Devereux, "The abduction of Hippodameia as 'aition' of a Greek animal husbandry rite. A structural analysis," *SMSDR* 36 (1965) 3-25.

*John E. Rexine, "Hebrew and Greek Thought and Culture Compared," *StVSQ, N.S.,* 9 (1965) 138-144.

Robert Luyster, "Symbolic Elements in the Cult of Athena," *HRel* 5 (1965-66) 133-163.

Walter Burkert, "Greek Tragedy and Sacrificial Ritual," *GRBS* 7 (1966) 87-121.

*Hugh R. Harcourt, "Hebrew, Greek and Roman Thought," *NEST* 13 (1966) #1, 10-25.

Robert R. Dyer, "The Iconography of the *Oresteia* after Aeschylus," *AJA* 71 (1967) 175-176.

*John G. Griffith, "Aegisthus Citharista," *AJA* 71 (1967) 176-177.

Susan Downey, "A Local Form of Hercules at Hatra," *AJA* 71 (1967) 186.

*Robert F. Healey, "A Gennetic Sacrifice List in the Athenian State Calendar," *AJA* 71 (1967) 189.

*Donald White, "The Post-Classical Cult of Malophoros at Selinus," *AJA* 71 (1967) 335-352.

Michael Grant, "The myth of Orpheus and Eurydice," *HT* 17 (1967) 368-377.

*Harry Neumann, "Kierkegaard and Socrates on the Dignity of Man," *Person* 48 (1967) 453-460.

*Rosamond Kent Sprague, "Logic and Literary Form in Plato," *Person* 48 (1967) 560-572.

E. N. Lane, "A Re-Study of the God Men. Part II: The Numismatic and Allied Evidence," *Bery* 17 (1967-68) 13-47.

E. N. Lane, "A Re-Study of the God Men. Part III: Conclusions," *Bery* 17 (1967-68) 81-106.

J. B. Skemp, "Plato's Account of Divinity," *DUJ, N.S.,* 29 (1967-68) 26-33.

*Sp.   Marinatos,   "Αἰώρα,"   *AASCS*   2   (1968)   1-14.

Colin N. Edmonson, "Brauronian Artemis in Athens," *AJA* 72 (1968) 164-165.

*Friedrich Solmsen, "Greek Ideas of the Afterlife in Virgil's Roman Epic," *PAPS* 112 (1968) 8-14.

K. J. McKay, "Crime and Punishment in the Kallimachos' *Hymn to Delos,*" *AASCS* 3 (1969) 27-28.

Eva Keuls, "The Iconography of the Ass of Dionysus," *AJA* 73 (1969) 239.

E[lmer] G. Suhr, "The Daughter of the Dragon," *Folk* 80 (1969) 1-11. *[Athena]*

W. Harold Mare, "The Greek Altar in the New Testament and Inter-Testamental Periods," *GJ* 10 (1969) #1, 26-35.

*Nathaniel L. Gerber, "The Wise Man in Rabbinic Judaism and Stoic Philosophy,"*YR* 7 (1969) 40-62.

Edward L. Ochsenschlager, "The Cosmic Significance of the *Plamochoe*," *HRel* 9 (1969-70) 316-336.

§481 *3.2.15.6.2 Etruscan, Roman and Venetic Mythology and Religion*

J. N. B., "Cicero on the Immortality of the Soul [From the Tusculan Questions.]," *CE* 33 (1842-43) 129-150, 316-338.

C. G. Zumpt, "The Religion of the Romans," *BRCM* 2 (1846) 186-206.

C. G. Zumpt, "The Religion of the Ancient Romans," *JSL, 4th Ser.,* 1 (1862) 257-266.

Anonymous, "The Religion of the Romans," *MQR, 2nd Ser.,* 2 (1880) 443-459.

*W. S. Scarborough, "Fatalism in Homer and Virgil," *PAPA* 17 (1885) xxxvi-xxxvii.

Robert Brown Jr., "Etruscan Divinity-Names.—Part I," *BOR* 5 (1891) 153-160.

Karl P. Harrington, "Conceptions of Death and Immortality in Roman Sepulchral Inscriptions," *PAPA* 31 (1899) xxviii-xxxi.

Charles S. Sanders, "Jupiter Dolichenus," *JAOS* 23 (1902) 84-92.

F. G. Ballentine, "The Cult of the Nymphs as Water-Deities among the Romans," *PAPA* 35 (1903) vi-viii.

Jesse Benedict Carter, "Abstract Deities in Early Roman Religion," *PAPA* 37 (1905) xxxiv-xxxv.

R. S. Conway, "The Messianic Idea in Virgil," *HJ* 5 (1906-07) 309-328.

W. M. Ramsay, "The Divine Child in Virgil," *Exp, 7th Ser.,* 4 (1907) 97-111.

*C. A. Browne, "Mars Dux and Mar(u)duk," *OC* 23 (1909) 444-445.

Franz Cumont, "Asia Minor," *OC* 24 (1910) 277-294. *[Roman Religion]*

Franz Cumont, "The Transformation of Roman Paganism," *OC* 25 (1911) 129-139. *(Trans. by A. M. Thielen)*

*W. Sherwood Fox, "Old Testament Parallels to *Tabellae Defixionum,*" *PAPA* 43 (1912) xxv-xxvi.

F. Legge, "The Lion-Headed God of the Mithraic Mysteries," *SBAP* 34 (1912) 125-142; 37 (1915) 151-162.

G. Ancey, "The Spirits of the Departed among the Etruscans," *SBAP* 34 (1912) 191-196.

*W. Sherwood Fox, "The Old Testament Parallels to Tabellae Defixionum," *AJA* 17 (1913) 84.

*Ernest E. Genner, "The Religions of Greece and Rome," *LQHR* 119 (1913) 274-288. *(Review)*

*S. Angus, "Hebrew, Greek, and Roman," *R&E* 10 (1913) 163-177.

*S. Angus, "Hebrew, Greek, and Roman. Part II.," *R&E* 10 (1913) 403-422.

*W. Sherwood Fox, "The Old Testament Parallels to 'Tabellae Defixionum'," *AJSL* 30 (1913-14) 111-124.

Gordon J. Laing, "The Cults of the City of Rome as seen in the Inscriptions," *AJA* 18 (1914) 80-81.

Adela Marion Adam, "The Mysticism of Rome," *ET* 27 (1915-16) 491-492.

R. S. Conway, "Some Votive Offerings to the Venetic Goddess Rehtia," *JRAI* 46 (1916) 221-229.

A. L. Frothingham, "The Wheel of Life and the Story of Myrtilus," *AJA* 22 (1918) 68. *[Etruscan Religion]*

George Depue Hadzsits, "Lucretius as a Student of Roman Religion," *TAPA* 49 (1918) 145-160.

*John Gamble, "The Messiahs of Virgil and Isaiah," *MC* 8 (1918-19) 386-389. *(Review)*

*Margaret C. Waites, "The Nature of the Lares and Their Representation in Roman Art," *AJA* 24 (1920) 241-261.

Joshua Whatmough, "Rehtia, the Venetic Goddess of Healing," *JRAI* 52 (1922) 212-229.

W. A. Heidel, "Vergil's*[sic]* Messianic Expectations," *AJP* 45 (1924) 205-237.

Lily Ross Taylor, "The Mother of the Lares," *AJA* 29 (1925) 299-313.

E. A. Dale, "The Religious Purpose of the Aeneid: Aeneus and His Gods," *CJRT* 5 (1928) 111-121.

H[erbert] J[ennings] Rose, "On the Relations Between Etruscan and Roman Religion," *SMSDR* 4 (1928) 161-168.

*Eli Edward Burriss, "The Use and Worship of Water Among the Romans," *A&A* 30 (1930) 221-228, 233.

Eli Edward Burriss, "The Place of the Roman Child in Superstition and Religion," *PAPA* 61 (1930) xli-xlii.

R. S. Conway, "The Etruscan Influence on Roman Religion," *BJRL* 16 (1932) 376-395.

Inez Scott Ryberg, "The Significance of Mars in Early Roman Religion," *PAPA* 63 (1932) lxiii-lxiv.

*Harry Austryn Wolfson, "The Internal Senses in Latin, Arabic, and Hebrew Philosophic Texts," *HTR* 28 (1935) 69-133.

*George M. A. Hanfmann, "Gigantomachy," *AJA* 41 (1937) 113-114.

Harold Mattingly, "The Roman 'Virtues'," *HTR* 30 (1937) 103-117.

Aline Abaecherli Boyce, "The Expiatory Rites of 207 B.C.," *TAPA* 68 (1937) 157-171.

Kenneth Scott, "Notes on Augustus' Religious Policy," *AfRW* 35 (1938) 121-130.

Arthur Darby Nock, "A Feature of Roman Religion," *HTR* 32 (1939) 83-96. *[uer sacrum]*

Joseph E. Fontenrose, "Apollo and Sol in the Latin Poets of the First Century B.C.," *TAPA* 70 (1939) 439-455.

*Alan S. Hoey, "Official Policy towards Oriental Cults in the Roman Army," *TAPA* 70 (1939) 456-481.

*C[hester] C. McCown, "The Underworld in a Painted Tomb in Transjordan," *JBL* 59 (1940) vi.

Valentine*[sic]* Müller, "The Shrine of Janus Geminus in Rome, *AJA* 47 (1943) 437-440.

Arthur Darby Nock, "The Cult of Heroes," *HTR* 37 (1944) 141-173. [Appendix 2 *(see page 154):* Evidence Against Table Fellowship in Roman Sacrifice, pp. 169-170]

Walter Woodburn Hyde, "The Religion of the Romans," *CQ* 22 (1945) 109-129.

*Herbert Jennings Rose, "Keres and Lemures," *HTR* 41 (1948) 217-228.

*P. J. Riis, "An Augustan Altar from Tarentum," *AA* 23 (1952) 147-152.

*Arthur Darby Nock, "The Roman Army and the Roman Religious Year," *HTR* 45 (1952) 187-252. [I The Feriale Duranum; II Festivals and the army, (i) The keeping of holy days, (ii) Planning for the army; III Purpose of official policy (i) The meaning of Romanization, (ii) Hellenistic intervention in religious matters, Antiochus Epiphanes, (iii) Official Roman intervention in religious matters, (iv) Pagans and Christians in the Roman army (v) Conclusions on the Feriale Duranum; IV Popular awareness of holy days; V Emperors and gods; VI Conclusions; APPENDIX 'Themes son of Mocimus, priest']

H. H. Huxley, "Some Observations on the Gods in Roman Poetry," *HJ* 54 (1955-56) 384-391.

George M. A. Hanfmann, "An Etruscan Goddess," *Arch* 9 (1956) 230-232.

Stefan Weinstock, "Victor and Invictus," *HTR* 50 (1957) 211-247.

John A. Hanson, "Plautus as a Source Book for Roman Religion," *TAPA* 90 (1959) 48-101.

*Andrew Alföldi, "Diana Nemorensis," *AJA* 64 (1960) 137-144.

*Enrico Paribeni, "Note on 'Diana Nemorensis' (*AJA* 1960, 137-144)," *AJA* 65 (1961) 55-56.

I. A. Richmond, "The Roman Army and Roman Religion," *BJRL* 45 (1962-63) 185-197.

*D. R. Dudley, "Stoicism and Roman Politics: Introduction and Prospectus," *HT* 13 (1963) 767-773.

J. H. Waszink, "Agmina Furirum," *HTR* 56 (1963) 7-11.

David E. Hahm, "Roman Nobility and the Three Major Priesthoods, 218-167 B.C.," *TAPA* 94 (1963) 73-85.

*Robert E. A. Palmer, "The Censors of 312 B.C. and the State Religion," *HJAH* 14 (1965) 293-324.

P. J. Riis, "The Cult Image of Diana Nemorensis," *AA* 37 (1966) 67-75.

*Hugh R. Harcourt, "Hebrew, Greek and Roman Thought," *NEST* 13 (1966) #1, 10-25.

L. Castiglione, "Inverted Footprints Again," *AAASH* 16 (1968) 187-189.

*Friedrich Solmsen, "Greek Ideas of the Afterlife in Virgil's Roman Epic," *PAPS* 112 (1968) 8-14.

Colin Martin, The Gods of the Imperial Roman Army," *HT* 19 (1969) 255-263.

§482 *3.2.15.6.2.1 Emperor Worship*

Anonymous, "The Deification of Roman Emperors," *DR, N.S.,* 25 (1875) 375-404. *(Review) [Original numbering as Vol. 77]*

A. C. Merriam, "The Caesareum and the Worship of Augustus at Alexandria," *PAPA* 15 (1883) ix-xi.

Allan P. Ball, "The Theological Utility of the Caesar Cult," *PAPA* 41 (1909) xvii-xviii.

Frederick Stanley Dunn, "The First Steps in the Deification of Julius Caesar," *PAPA* 41 (1909) xxvii-xxviii.

Walter D. D. Hadzsits, "The Theory of the Worship of the Roman Emperors," *PAPA* 41 (1909) xxxix-xl.

[Paul Carus], "The Religion of Ancient Gaul and Cæsar Worship," *OC* 24 (1910) 724-743.

Henry Fairfield Burton, "The Worship of the Roman Emperors," *BW* 40 (1912) 80-91.

William Peterson, "The Deification of the Roman Emperors," *AJA* 18 (1914) 82-83.

*Samuel A. B. Mercer, "'Emperor'-Worship in Babylonia," *JAOS* 36 (1916) 360-380.

*George A. Barton, "A Word with reference to 'Emperor'-Worship in Babylonia," *JAOS* 37 (1917) 162-163.

*Samuel A. B. Mercer, "'Emperor'-worship in Babylonia—A Reply," *JAOS* 37 (1917) 331.

*Samuel A. B. Mercer, "'Emperor'-Worship in Egypt," *JSOR* 1 (1917) 10-18.

*Cuthbert Lattey, "Ruler-Worship in the Bible," *ITQ* 14 (1919) 238-257.

*Lily Ross Taylor, "The Worship of Augustus in Italy during His Lifetime," *TAPA* 51 (1920) 116-133.

J. M. Powis Smith, "Traces of Emperor-Worship in the Old Testament," *AJSL* 39 (1922-23) 32-39.

Kenneth Scott, "Emperor Worship in Ovid," *TAPA* 61 (1930) 43-69.

Kenneth Scott, "The Significance of Statues in Precious Metals in Emperor Worship," *TAPA* 62 (1931) 101-123.

Kenneth Scott, "The Elder and Younger Pliny on Emperor Worship," *TAPA* 63 (1932) 156-165.

*Charles F. Edson Jr., "Legitimus Honor. A Note on Hellenistic Ruler-Worship," *HTR* 26 (1933) 324-325.

Martin Percival Charlesworth, "Some Observations on Ruler-Cult, Especially in Rome," *HTR* 28 (1935) 5-44.

Aline L. Abaecherli, "The Institution of the Imperial Cult in the Western Provinces of the Roman Empire," *SMSDR* 11 (1935) 153-186.

Vagn Häger Poulsen, "Studies in Julio-Claudian Iconography," *AA* 17 (1946) 1-48.

Antony E. Raubitschek, "Octavia's Deification at Athens," *TAPA* 77 (1946) 146-150.

*Julien L. Tondrian, "Comparisons and Identifications of Rulers with Deities in the Hellenistic Period," *RR* 13 (1948-49) 24-47.

Charles Seltman, "The Ruler-Cult: From Alexander of Macedon to Elizabeth I of England," *HT* 3 (1953) 311-320.

H. W. Pleket, "An Aspect of the Emperor Cult: Imperial Mysteries," *HTR* 58 (1965) 331-347.

§483 *3.2.15.7 Non-Hebrew "Prophecy"*

Anonymous, "The Prophecies of Heathendom," *AThR* 1 (1859) 306-318.

*Francis Wharton, "Unconscious Greek Prophecy," *BS* 30 (1873) 114-165.

*N. Vaschide and H. Piéron, "Prophetic Dreams in Greek and Roman Antiquity," *Monist* 11 (1900-01) 161-194. *(Trans. by Thomas J. McCormack)*

*N. P. Valchos, "Religious Prophetism Among the Greeks," *RChR, 4th Ser.,* 8 (1904) 495-510; 9 (1905) 61-80, 500-516.

F. Cridland Evans, "Pagan Prophecy. Some Curious Facts in the History of Religious Development," *OC* 26 (1912) 641-653.

A. Kampmeier, "The Chasm at Delphi," *OC* 27 (1913) 61-62.

I. M. Casanowicz, "The Significance of Sibyls," *A&A* 20 (1925) 222-223.

*Robert C. Horn, "Symbolic Acts of Greek Philosophers and Hebrew Prophets," *LCQ* 5 (1932) 190-201.

*Rudolph Arbesmann, "Fasting and Prophecy in Pagan and Christian Antiquity," *Tr* 7 (1949-51) 1-71.

*A[braham] Malamat, "'Prophecy' in the Mari Documents," *EI* 4 (1956) VI-VII.

*A[braham] Malamat, "History and Prophetic Vision in a Mari Letter," *EI* 5 (1958) 86*-87*.

*Abraham Malamat, "Prophetic revelations in new documents from Mari and the Bible," *VTS* 15 (1965) 207-227.

L. Kákosy, "Prophecies of the Ram Gods," *AOASH* 19 (1966) 331-357. *[Egyptian]*

*Herbert B. Huffmon, "Prophecy in the Mari Letters," *BA* 31 (1968) 101-124. [Prophecy Outside Israel; The 'Answerer'; The Ecstatic; Private Persons; Hair and Hem; Mari and Israel; Appendix]

§484 *3.3 Philological and Epigraphical Studies*

†Meirion, "Comparison of Ancient and Modern Language," *MMBR* 42 (1816-17) 29-31.

F. Bopp, "Analytical Comparison of the Sanskrit, Greek, Latin, and Teutonic Languages, shewing the original identity of their grammatical structure," *AOL* 1 (1820-21) 1-65.

[F. Bopp], "Analytical Comparison of the Sanskrit, Greek, Latin and Teutonic Languages," *BibR* 2 (1826) 165-204, 349-385.

*( ) K., "Upon the Origin of Language," *MMBR, N.S.,* 4 (1827) 248-253. *(Review)*

T. Parker, "The Origin of Writing in Greece and Egypt," *BRCR, N.S.,* 2 (1839) 71-90.

F. A. Tholuck, "Theological Encyclopedia and Methodology, Part I, §9 Oriental Philology," *BS* 1 (1844) 196-199.

Richard Garrett, "On the Origin and Import of the Genitive Case," *TPS* (1844-46) 165-176.

Anonymous, "An Inquiry Concerning the Early History and Origin of Written Language," *CRB* 10 (1845) 519-529.

*Anonymous, "Comparative Grammar," *BRCM* 4 (1847-48) 1-22. *(Review)*

†Anonymous, "Comparative Philology," *ERCJ* 94 (1851) 297-339. *(Review)*

Anonymous, "One Primeval Language," *DUM* 39 (1852) 226-234. *(Review)*

[T. Hewitt] Key, "On the Imperfect Infinitive, Imperfect Participles, and those Substantives which fall under the definition *'nomen actionis',*" *TPS* (1852-53) 62-72.

*( ) M., "Theology, Philology, Geology," *JSL, 3rd Ser.,* 2 (1855-56) 66-81; 3 (1856) 184-188.

[W. D.] Whitney, "The Origin of Language," *PAOS, November* (1858) 8-9.

*[C.] Lottner, "Remarks on the nation by which the cuneiform mode of writing was invented.—On the most ancient ethnographical state of Western Asia historically known," *TPS* (1858) 124-136, 137-142.

*L. Tafel and R. L. Tafel, "Semitic Comparative Philology," *BS* 19 (1862) 516-550.

Anonymous, "The Science of Language," *CongR* 2 (1862) 539-548. *(Review)*

Anonymous, "The Origin and Course of Language," *DUM* 59 (1862) 749-755. *(Review)*

R. C. Ketchum, "The Relations of Language," *SPR* 15 (1862-63) 205-229.

Oscar Howes, "The Origin of Language," *CRB* 28 (1863) 383-406.

William D. Whitney, "On the Origin of Language," *JAOS* 8 (1866) lv.

†Anonymous, "The Science of Language," *QRL* 119 (1866) 394-435. *(Review)*

Anonymous, "The Origin of Language," *WR* 86 (1866) 88-122. *(Review)*

J. R. Young, "On the Language of Gesticulation; and on the Origin of Speech," *JTVI* 1 (1866-67) 231-246. (Discussion, pp. 246-255)

Frederic W. Farrar, "The growth and development of language," *JP* 1 (1868) #2, 1-23.

William A. Stevens, "Growth and History of Language," *BQ* 3 (1869) 419-435.

John O. Means, "Recent Theories of the Origin of Language," *BS* 27 (1870) 162-179.

*William Taylor, "The Variation of Languages and Species," *BFER* 20 (1871) 695-719.

W[illiam] D. Whitney, "On the Classification of Languages," *JAOS* 9 (1871) xi.

*G. W. Samson, "Reciprocal Influence of Languages developed amid Ancient Mediterranean Civilization," *PAPA* 4 (1872) 15-17. *[Bound with Transactions, but paged separately]*

*A. H. Sayce, "The Origin of Semitic Civilization, chiefly upon Philological Evidence," *SBAT* 1 (1872) 294-309.

F. A. March, "The Future of Philology," *PQPR* 3 (1874) 698-714.

*Hyde Clarke, "Researches in Prehistoric and Protohistoric Comparative Philology, Mythology, and Archæology in Connection with the Origin of Culture in America, and its Propagation by the Sumerian or Akkad Families," *JRAI* 4 (1874-75) 148-212. (Discussion, pp. 212-231)

*A. H. Sayce, "Language and Race," *JRAI* 5 (1875-76) 212-216. (Discussion, pp. 216-220)

*W. Chad Boscawen, "The Pre-Historic Civilisation of Babylonia," *JRAI* 8 (1878-79) 21-35. *[Philological Comparisons]*

R. Brown, "Language and the Theories of its Origin," *JTVI* 15 (1881-82) 309-355.

F. B., "Theological Education, No. X—The Study of Languages cognate with Hebrew," *BS* 39 (1882) 555-566.

*J. A. Smith, "The Language of Primitive Man," *ONTS* 2 (1882-83) 193-199.

Gustav Oppert, "On the Classification of Languages in conformity with Ethnology," *JRAI* 13 (1883-84) 32-50. [Discussion, pp. 50-52]

*Anonymous, "The Origins of Religion and Language," *CQR* 18 (1884) 394-412. *(Review)*

George H. Schodde, "On the Semitic Languages in General," *AJSL* 1 (1884-85) 247-248.

Edward Jacker, "Primitive Man and His Speech," *ACQR* 11 (1886) 226-241.

George H. Schodde, "The Study of the Cognates," *ONTS* 9 (1889) 335-340.

Ludwig Noire, "The Origin of Language," *OC* 4 (1890-91) 2221-2225, 2252-2255, 2266-2268.

F. Max Müller, "Critical Remarks on Noire's Theory of Language," *OC* 4 (1890-91) 2272-2274.

Anonymous, "Philology and Practical Linguistics: Sense, Counter-Sense, and Double Sense; or Words Like Dreams, go by 'Contraries'," *IAQR, 2nd Ser.,* 1 (1891) 260-261.

A. Neubauer, "On Non-Hebrew Languages Used by the Jews," *JQR* 4 (1891-92) 9-19.

*H. C. Alexander, "The Doctrine of Inspiration as Affected by the Essential Relation Between Thought and Language," *PQ* 7 (1893) 157-186.

R. C.*[sic]* Conder, "The Early Languages of Syria," *SRL* 21 (1893) 279-296.

*Edward Montet, "Mr. Le Pasteur Fesquet's New Theory of the Origin of Languages," *IAQR, 3rd Ser.,* 8 (1899) 386-388.

Ed[uard] König, "Did the Israelites down to the time of Joshua speak 'a pure Arabic dialect'?" *ET* 12 (1900-01) 143.

*C. J. Ball, "A Study in Biblical Philology," *SBAP* 33 (1911) 243-253.

*Allison Emery Drake, "Some Evidences of Aryo-Semitic Kinship," *BS* 70 (1913) 607-621.

*J. Iverach Munro, "The Witness of Philology to the Truth of the Old Testament," *JTVI* 49 (1917) 199-216. (Discussion, pp. 216-220)

E. Washburn Hopkins, "The Origin of the Ablative Case," *JAOS* 38 (1918) 47-59.

*Samuel Raffaeli, "The Epigraphy of Jewish Coinage," *PEFQS* 54 (1922) 154-156.

*W[illiam] F[oxwell] Albright, "Contributions of Biblical Archaeology and Philology," *JBL* 43 (1924) 363-393.

*Paul Haupt, "Philological and Linguistic Studies," *AJP* 46 (1925) 197-212. [4. Transposition, Assimilation, Conformation, pp. 205-206]

*John E. McFadyen, "The Place of Languages in Theological Education," *ET* 43 (1931-32) 294-300.

Roland G. Kent, "Linguistic Science and the Orientalist," *JAOS* 55 (1935) 115-137.

Robert Gordis, "Some Effects of Primitive Thought on Language," *JBL* 55 (1936) xviii.

Henry Fr. Lutz, "Speech consciousness among Egyptians and Babylonians," *Osiris* 2 (1936) 1-27.

W. B. Stevenson, "Illustrations of the Growth of Language, taken from the Semitic Languages," *GUOST* 8 (1936-37) 6-8.

Frank R. Blake, "The Origin and Development of Language and the Emergence of the Parts of Speech," *PAPA* 68 (1937) xxx.

Robert Gordis, "Some Effects of Primitive Thought on Language," *AJSL* 55 (1938) 270-284.

John Henry Bennetch, "The Advantage in Knowing the Biblical Languages," *BS* 100 (1943) 177-187.

F. A. Tholuck, "Oriental Philology," *BS* 102 (1945) 167-169. *[Reprint of an original article from* BS *(1844)]*

Alfons Nehring, "Plato and the Theory of Language," *Tr* 3 (1945) 13-48.

*William Young, "What the Bible Teaches About the Origin of Races and Languages," *CO* 3 (1945-46) 3-7.

W. S. Allen, "Ancient Ideas on the Origin and Development of Language," *TPS* (1948) 35-60.

Vladimír Skalička, "The Structure of Language of the Ancient Orient," *ArOr* 18 (1950) Parts 1/2, 485-488.

*N. W. Porteous, "Semantics and the Old Testament," *OTS* 8 (1950) 1-14.

Richard Paget, "The Origins of Language, with Special Reference to the Paleolithic Age," *JWH* 1 (1953-54) 399-414.

Alf Sommerfelt, "The Origin of Language: *Theories and Hypotheses,*" *JWH* 1 (1953-54) 885-902.

Malcom Guthrie, "The Bible and Current Theories about Language," *JTVI* 86 (1954) 50-60, 119-120. (Discussion, pp. 113-116) (Communications by F. F. Bruce, p. 116-117; J. B. Phillips, pp. 117-118; B. B. Knopp, 118-119)

Daniel J. Theron, "Some Thoughts on the Study of the Biblical Languages," *PSB* 49 (1956) #4, 22-25.

R. H. Pfeiffer, "Clues to the pronunciation of ancient languages," *SOOG* 2 (1956) 338-349.

M. H. Goshen-Gottstein, "Biblical Philology and the Concordance," *JJS* 8 (1957) 5-12.

Helen Homeyer, "Some Observations on Bilingualism and Language Shift in Italy from the Sixth to the Third Century B.C.," *Word* 13 (1957) 415-440.

C. F. Pfeiffer, "Figures of Speech in Human Language," *BETS* 2 (1959) #4, 17-21.

*W. D. McHardy, "Philology and Textual Criticism," *LQHR* 184 (1959) 4-9.

A. G. Spirkin, "The Origin of Language," *JWH* 5 (1959-60) 293-309.

V. V. Bunak, "Present State of the Problem of the Origin of Speech and the Early Stages of Its Evolution," *JWH* 5 (1959-60) 310-324.

*Howard McKaughan, "Bible Translation and Linguistics," *JCE* 4 (1961) 7-16.

Edward Ullendorff, "The Knowledge of Languages in the Old Testament," *BJRL* 44 (1961-62) 455-465.

*James Barr, "Hypostatization of Linguistic Phenomena in Modern Theological Interpretation," *JSS* 7 (1962) 85-94.

Henry A. Gleason Jr., "Some Contributions of Linguistics to Biblical Study," *HQ* 4 (1963-64) #1, 47-56.

Ramsay MacMullen, "Provincial Languages in the Roman Empire," *AJP* 87 (1966) 1-16.

Walter Harrelson, "Biblical Languages in the Theological Curriculum," *TE* 3 (1966-67) 441-447.

*E. Y. Kutscher, "Canaanite (=C)—Hebrew (=H)—Phoenician (=Ph)—Aramaic (=A)—Mishnaic Hebrew (=MH)—Punic (=P)," *Lěš* 33 (1968-69) #2/3, n.p.n.

M[itchell] Dahood, "Comparative Philology Yesterday and Today," *B* 50 (1969) 70-79.

S. Morag, "Oral Traditions and Dialects ÷ Towards a Methodology for Evaluating the Evidence of an Oral Tradition," *PICSS* (1969) 180-189.

§485 *3.3.1 The Alphabet - General Studies*

*†R. H., "Hieroglyphics and the Origin of Alphabetic Writing," *MMBR* 7 (1799) 185-186.

*†Anonymous, "Hammar on Ancient Alphabets," *BCQTR* 30 (1807) 15-23. *(Review)*

(   ) Magee, "On the Divine origin of Language and Alphabetical Letters," *QTMRP* 1 (1813) 310-318.

U. V., "On the original number of the letters in the Greek Alphabet," *QCS* 2 (1820) 347-349.

Adam Clarke, "Remarks Concerning the Origin of Language and Alphabetical Characters," *MR* 15 (1833) 212-223.

†Anonymous, "On the Origin of Alphabetic Writing," *DUM* 8 (1836) 623-644. *(Review)*

*†Anonymous, "Wall *on Egyptian Hieroglyphs, and on the Origin of Alphabetic Writing ,*" *ERCJ* 64 (1836-37) 82-93. *(Review)*

Anonymous, "Dr. Wall on Alphabetic Writing," *DUM* 16 (1840) 129-139. *(Review)*

Hensleigh Wedgewood, "On Traces of an Egyptian Origin of the Alphabets of Greece and Rome," *TPS* (1850-52) 1-6.

*[Joseph Fullonton], "Invention of Writing;—The Alphabet;—and Printing," *FBQ* 10 (1862) 431-441. [The Alphabet, pp. 436-438]

*†[Pliny E.] Chase, "Chinese characters and classical Alphabets," *PAPS* 9 (1862-64) 172-182.

(   ) Bruckner, "On the Invention of the Alphabet," *JSL, 5th Ser.,* 2 (1867-68) 178-191.

C. B. Cayley, "On the Modern Names of the Letters of the Alphabet," *TPS* (1870) 5-16.

*Hyde Clarke, "The Hamath Inscriptions.—Alphabets," *JRAI* 3 (1873-74) 135-136.

John C. C. Clarke, "History in Alphabets," *BS* 31 (1874) 333-355.

Isaac Taylor, "The History of the Alphabet," *JTVI* 12 (1878-79) 308-309. (Discussion, pp. 309-311)

[John] C. C. Clarke, "The Origin of the Semitic Alphabet," *ONTS* 2 (1882-83) 309-315.

*James Gow, "The Greek Numerical Alphabet," *JP* 12 (1883) 278-284.

John P. Peters, "The Babylonian Origin of the Phoenician Alphabet," *SBAP* 6 (1883-84) 73-76. (Remarks by Isaac Taylor, pp. 77-85, Geo. Bertin, 83-84)

†John P. Peters, "Reply to remarks by Dr. Isaac Taylor on his Paper, 'The Babylonian Origin of the Phoenician Alphabet'," *SBAP* 6 (1883-84) 225-228.

A. H. Sayce, "The origin of the Persian cuneiform alphabet," *ZK* 1 (1884) 19-27.

John C. C. Clarke, "The Varieties of the Semitic Alphabet," *AJSL* 1 (1884-85) 52-59.

A. H. Sayce, "The Origin of the Alphabet," *ContR* 48 (1885) 794-807.

John P. Peters, "On the Egyptian and Old Babylonian Theories of the Origin of the Phœnician Alphabet compared," *JAOS* 11 (1885) clxxv-clxxviii.

L. J. Hickey, "The Alphabet," *IER, 3rd Ser.,* 8 (1887) 147-156, 350-359.

C[laude] R. Conder, "The Alphabet," *PEFQS* 21 (1889) 17-20.

†Anonymous, "The Origin of Alphabets," *ERCJ* 172 (1890) 112-140. *(Review)*

Charles W. Super, "On the Early History of Our Alphabet," *BS* 49 (1892) 496-515.

C. J. Ball, "The Origin of the Phoenician Alphabet," *SBAP* 15 (1892-93) 392-408.

Anonymous, "The Alphabet Mycenæan, not Phœnician," *AAOJ* 18 (1896) 281.

John Henry Wright, "The Origin of the Sigma Lunatum," *TAPA* 27 (1896) 79-89. *[Greek Alphabet]*

Anonymous, "Alphabetic Writing," *MR* 79 (1897) 641-644.

C. V. Anthony, "'Alphabetic Writing'," *MR* 79 (1897) 973.

Anonymous, "Alphabetic Writing," *MR* 80 (1898) 480.

Mortimer Lamson Earle, "On the Supplementary Signs of the Greek Alphabet," *AJA* 4 (1900) 175-176.

John P. Peters, "Notes on Recent Theories of the Origin of the Alphabet," *JAOS* 22 (1901) 177-198.

William N. Bates, "The Early Greek Alphabets in the Light of Recent Discoveries in Egypt," *PAPA* 33 (1901) lxxvi-lxxvii.

M[elvin] G[rove] Kyle, "The Egyptian Origin of the Alphabet. An Historical Instance in Support of de Rougé's Alphabetic Prototypes," *RTR* 23 (1901) 151-156.

Arthur J. Evans, "The Origin of the Alphabet," *AAOJ* 24 (1902) 183-184.

Mortimer Lamson Earle, "Notes on the Greek Alphabet," *AJA* 6 (1902) 46-47. [I. Of the Evolution of the Supplementary Aspirate (Spirant) and Assibilate Signs; II. Of the Names of the Original Letters of the Greek Alphabet; III. Of the Beta Signs; IV. Of the Sixteen-letter Alphabet]

W. M. Patton, "The Origin of the Semitic Alphabet," *MR* 84 (1902) 400-411.

*Arthur J. Evans, "Pre-Phœnician Writing in Crete and its Bearing on the History of the Alphabet," *Man* 3 (1903) #28.

*Joseph Offord, "Notes and Queries. 4. *The Origin of the Cuneiform Syllabary,*" *PEFQS* 36 (1904) 181-182.

E. J. Pilcher, "The Origin of the Alphabet," *SBAP* 26 (1904) 168-173. [I. The Proto-Alphabet; II. The Baal-Lebanon Alphabet; III. The Earliest Greek Alphabet; IV. The Zenjerli Alphabet; V. The Formello Alphabet; VI. Alphabet from Assyrian Lion-Weights]

Henry Proctor, "Alphabetic Origins," *AAOJ* 27 (1905) 128-130.

*Stephen D. Peet, "Ancient Alphabets and Sacred Books," *AAOJ* 27 (1905) 265-280.

E. J. Pilcher, "The Order of the Letters of the Alphabet," *SBAP* 27 (1905) 65-68.

*C[laude] R. Conder, "Notes on Palestinian Archaeology. III. The Aramean Alphabet," *PEFQS* 38 (1906) 149-151.

Anonymous, "Origin of the Canaanaic Alphabet," *RP* 6 (1907) 118.

Franz Prætorius, "The Origin of the Canaanite Alphabet," *SIR* (1907) 595-604.

A. H. Sayce, "The Origin of the Phoenician Alphabet," *SBAP* 32 (1910) 215-222.

Hartwig Hirschfield, "Recent Theories on the Origin of the Alphabet," *JRAS* (1911) 963-977.

Anonymous, "Origin of the Phœnician Alphabet," *RP* 10 (1911) 55.

*Henry Proctor, "Egyptian Hieroglyphics and Alphabetic Origins," *AAOJ* 34 (1912) 293-294.

Anonymous, "Origin of the Alphabet," *RP* 11 (1912) 51.

E. Naville, "The Canaanite Alphabet," *SBAP* 34 (1912) 27-34.

M. Gaster, "Jewish Knowledge of the Samaritan Alphabet in the Middle Ages," *JRAS* (1913) 613-626.

W. B. Stevenson, "Recent Research Regarding the Early History of the Alphabet," *GUOST* 4 (1913-22) 73-76.

N. Kolkin, "The Origin of Our Alphabet," *AAOJ* 36 (1914) 28-30.

Anonymous, "The Formation of the Alphabet," *MR* 96 (1914) 303-307.

A. H. Sayce, "The Origin of the Meroitic Alphabet," *SBAP* 36 (1914) 177-180.

*James H. Breasted, "The Physical Processes of Writing in the Early Orient and Their Relation to the Origin of the Alphabet," *AJSL* 32 (1915-16) 230-249.

Alan H. Gardiner, "The Egyptian Origin of the Semitic Alphabet," *JEA* 3 (1916) 1-16.

A. E. Cowley, "The Origin of the Semitic Alphabet," *JEA* 3 (1916) 17-21.

D. D. Luckenbill, "Possible Babylonian Contributions to the So-Called Phoenician Alphabet," *AJSL* 36 (1919-20) 27-39.

William N. Bates, "Recent Theories on the Origin of the Alphabet," *AJA* 24 (1920) 80.

Warren R. Dawson, "The Egyptian Origin of the Alphabet," *IAQR* 16 (1920) 124-126.

A. H. Sayce, "The Origin of the Semitic Alphabet," *JRAS* (1920) 297-303.

W. M. Flinders Petrie, "The Alphabet of the XIIth Dynasty," *AEE* 6 (1921) 1-3.

Robert Eisler, "Introduction of the Cadmeian Alphabet into the Aegean World in the light of Ancient Traditions and Recent Discoveries," *JRAS* (1923) 34-73, 169-207. [I. Early Phenician*[sic]* Inscriptions on Copper Ingots from Crete and Sardinia; II. The Ancient Traditions about the introduction of the "Camean" Alphabet; III. The Graeco-Egyptian Traditions about the "Camean" Colonization of the Ægean during the Hyksos Period]

C[harles] C. Torrey, "The Early Alphabet," *AJA* 30 (1926) 86-87.

B[erthold] L[ouis] Ullman, "The Origin and Development of the Alphabet," *AJA* 31 (1927) 311-328.

*Anonymous, "The Primitive Alphabetic Inscriptions in Sinai," *BASOR* #27 (1927) 12-13.

E. E. W. Gs. Schröder, "A Phoenician Alphabet on Sumatra," *JAOS* 47 (1927) 25-35.

Ferris J. Stephens, "Did the Early Semites of Asia Minor Use the Alphabet?" *JAOS* 49 (1929) 122-127.

*Alan H. Gardiner, "The Sinai Script and the Origin of the Alphabet," *PEFQS* 61 (1929) 48-55.

*S. Yeivin, "The Sign and the True Nature of the Early Alphabets," *ArOr* 4 (1932) 71-78.

Rhys Carpenter, "The Antiquity of the Greek Alphabet," *AJA* 37 (1933) 8-29.

*R. Butin, "The Protosinaitic Inscriptions of Serabit and the Origin of the Alphabet," *AJA* 37 (1933) 115.

Berthold Louis Ullman, "How Old Is the Greek Alphabet?" *PAPA* 64 (1933) lvii.

*J. Penrose Harland, "Scripta Helladica and the Dates of Homer and the Hellenic Alphabet," *AJA* 38 (1934) 83-92.

B[erthold] L[ouis] Ullman, "How Old is the Greek Alphabet?" *AJA* 38 (1934) 359-381.

Trude Weiss Rosmarin, "The Origin of the Alphabet of Ras Shamra and its Bearing on the Origin of the Phoenician Alphabet," *JAOS* 55 (1935) 101-102.

T[heodor] H. Gaster, "The Chronology of Palestinian Epigraphy," *PEFQS* 67 (1935) 128-140.

*Eric Burrows, "Origins of the Ras Shamra Alphabet," *JRAS* (1936) 271-277.

*R. Butin, "Some Egyptian Hieroglyphs of Sinai and their Relationship to the Hieroglyphs of the Proto-Sinaitic Semitic Alphabet," *Miz* 2 (1936) 52-56.

Alan H. Gardiner, "Origin of Our Alphabet," *Antiq* 11 (1937) 359-360.

Rhys Carpenter, "The Greek Alphabet Again," *AJA* 42 (1938) 58-69.

Rodney [S.] Young, "Ceramic Evidence for the Introduction of the Greek Alphabet," *AJA* 42 (1938) 124-125.

Rhys Carpenter, "Origin and Diffusion of the Greek Alphabet," *AJA* 42 (1938) 125.

*John Day, "The Letters of Cadmus," *AJA* 42 (1938) 125.

B[erthold] L[ouis] Ullman, "The History of the Alphabet," *AJA* 42 (1938) 125-126.

*Julian Obermann, "The Archaic Inscriptions from Lachish. A Non-Phoenician System of the North Semitic Alphabet," *JAOSS* #2 (1938) 1-148.

*C[hester] C. McCown, "Two Years' Achievements in Palestinian Archaeology," *RL* 8 (1939) 97-108. [History of the Alphabet, pp. 100-101]

Frank R. Blake, "The Development of Symbols for the Vowels in Alphabets Derived from Phoenician," *JAOS* 60 (1940) 391-413.

Rodney S. Young, "The Early Alphabet in Attica," *AJA* 46 (1942) 124-125.

William Nickerson Bates, "Cadmus and the Greek Alphabet," *CQ* 19 (1942) 126-134.

David Diringer, "The Origin of the Alphabet," *Antiq* 17 (1943) 77-90.

R. O. Faulkner, "Had the Egyptians an Alphabet?" *Antiq* 17 (1943) 207-208. (Rejoinder by David Diringer, pp. 208-209)

*David Diringer, "The Palestinian Inscriptions and the Origin of the Alphabet," *JAOS* 63 (1943) 24-30.

F. J. Richards, "Semitic, Greek, and Indian Alphabets," *Man* 43 (1943) #30.

Rhys Carpenter, "The Alphabet in Italy," *AJA* 49 (1945) 452-464.

W[illiam] F[oxwell] Albright, "The Early Alphabetic Inscriptions from Sinai and Their Decipherment," *BASOR* #110 (1948) 6-22.

F. F. Bruce, "The Origin of the Alphabet," *JTVI* 80 (1948) 1-10, 11. (Communication by H. Biddulph, pp. 10-11)

*W[illiam] F[oxwell] Albright, "Some Important Recent Discoveries: Alphabetic Origins and the Idrimi Statue," *BASOR* #118 (1950) 11-20. [1. New Light on the Beginnings of the Alphabet, pp. 12-14.]

W[illiam] F[oxwell] Albright, "The Origin of the Alphabet and the Ugaritic ABC Again," *BASOR* #119 (1950) 23-24.

Manfred Cassirer, "Two Semitic Letters," *JEA* 36 (1950) 113.

C[yrus] H. Gordon, "The Ugaritic 'ABC'," *Or, N.S.,* 19 (1950) 374-376.

H. (Torczyner) Tur-Sinai, "The Origin of the Alphabet," *JQR, N.S.,* 41 (1950-51) 83-109, 159-179, 277-301.

E[phraim] A. Speiser, "A Note on Alphabetic Origins," *BASOR* #121 (1951) 17-21.

S[amuel] E. Loewenstamm, "New Light on the History of the Alphabet," *BIES* 16 (1951) #3/4, v.

Frederick L. Moriarty, "Early Evidence of Alphabetic Writing," *CBQ* 13 (1951) 135-145.

Julian Huxley, "Books and Alphabets," *HT* 1 (April, 1951) 19-28.

*Albrecht Goetze, "A Seal Cylinder with an Early Alphabetic Inscription," *BASOR* #129 (1953) 8-11.

Frank M. Cross Jr., "The Evolution of the Proto-Canaanite Alphabet," *BASOR* #134 (1954) 15-24.

W[illiam] F[oxwell] Albright, "Some Observations on the New Material for the History of the Alphabet," *BASOR* #134 (1954) 26.

Franklin P. Johnson, "Notes on the Early Greek Alphabet," *AJP* 77 (1956) 29-37.

David Diringer, "Problems of the Present Day on the Origin of the Phoenician Alphabet," *JWH* 4 (1957-58) 40-58.

R. M. Cook and A. G. Woodhead, "The Diffusion of the Greek Alphabet," *AJA* 63 (1959) 175-178.

Frank M. Cross Jr. and Thomas O. Lambdin, "A Ugaritic Abecedary and the Origins of the Proto-Canaanite Alphabet," *BASOR* #160 (1960) 21-26.

*Otto Eissfeldt, "The alphabetical cuneiform texts from Ras Shamra published in 'Le Palais Royal D'Ugarit', Vol. II, 1957," *JSS* 5 (1960) 1-49.

G. P. Goold, "Homer and the Alphabet," *TAPA* 91 (1960) 272-291.

S[tanislav] Segert, "The Alphabet Conquests*[sic]* the World," *NOP* 3 (1962) 136-139, 186-190.

David Diringer, "The Early Greek Alphabets," *Antiq* 37 (1963) 270-273.

Frank Moore Cross Jr., "The Origin and Early Evolution of the Alphabet," *EI* 8 (1967) 8*-24*.

B. N. Grakov, "Letters of the Archaic Megaro-Corinthian Alphabet," *VDI* (1969) #1, 101.

§486 *3.3.1.1 The Hebrew Alphabet*

*†[Pliny E.] Chase, "Chinese characters and classical Alphabets," *PAPS* 9 (1862-64) 172-182 [Hebrew Alphabet, pp. 177-181]

*C. Graham, "Note on the Hebrew Alphabet and Vowel Points," *JTVI* 6 (1872-73) 404.

C[laude] R. Conder, "The Seal of Haggai," *PEFQS* 22 (1890) 121-122. *[Alphabet]*

*E. J. Pilcher, "Herodian Pottery and the Siloam Inscription," *SBAP* 20 (1898) 213-222. [Plate II. Table of Alphabets, pp. 221-222]

R. A. Stewart Macalister, "Alphabet of Letters used on Old-Hebrew Jar Seals," *PEFQS* 32 (1900) 341.

Henry Proctor, "The Hebrew Alphabet," *AAOJ* 27 (1905) 97-98.

Henry Proctor, "The History of the Hebrew Alphabets," *AAOJ* 28 (1906) 329-334.

*Henry Proctor, "Symbolism of the Hebrew Alphabet," *AAOJ* 31 (1909) 16-18.

*Stanley A. Cook, "The Old Hebrew Alphabet and the Gezer Tablet," *PEFQS* 41 (1909) 284-309.

*Joseph Offord, "Archaeological Notes on Jewish Antiquities. LII. *The Alphabet of the Hebrew Bible*," *PEFQS* 50 (1918) 180-181.

*Solomon Gandz, "The knot in Hebrew literature, or from the knot to the alphabet," *Isis* 14 (1930) 189-214.

C. Levias, "The Order of the Hebrew Alphabet," *PAAJR* 4 (1932-33) 131-133.

W[illiam] F[oxwell] Albright, "The Early Evolution of the Hebrew Alphabet," *BASOR* #63 (1936) 8-12.

N. H. (Torczyner) Tur-Sinai, "On the Slavonic Parallels to the Origin of the Names in the Hebrew Alphabet," *JQR, N.S.,* 42 (1951-52) 233.

§487 **3.3.1.2 Studies in the Transliteration of
      Non-Roman Languages**

†Anonymous, "The Roman Alphabet applied to Eastern Languages," *LQHR*
11 (1858-59) 143-156. *(Review)*

J. B. A., "Universal Alphabet," *JSL, 3rd Ser.,* 10 (1859-60) 386-388.
[Transliteration of Hebrew]

M. P., "The Alphabet Question," *JSL, 3rd Ser.,* 11 (1860) 198-202.
[Transliteration of Hebrew]

Francis Barham, "Simplification of Oriental Languages," *JSL, 4th Ser.,* 4
(1863-64) 173-175.

†Anonymous, "The Transliteration of Hebrew," *AJSL* 1 (1884-85) 69-70.
(Untitled Editorial Note)

Edgar P. Allen, "On a new system of transliteration for the Semitic sounds,
based upon phonetic principles," *JAOS* 13 (1889) ccxliii-ccxliv.

M. Monier-Williams, "On the Transliteration of Oriental Languages," *IAQR,
2nd Ser.,* 2 (1891) 397-403. *[Sanskrit in particular]*

Stanley Leathes, "The Study and Transliteration of Hebrew," *IAQR, 2nd
Ser.,* 2 (1891) 404-406.

J. A. Selbie, "The Transliteration of Hebrew," *ET* 8 (1896-97) 451.

Eb. Nestle, "The Transliteration of Hebrew," *ET* 8 (1896-97) 525.

George B. Mitchell, "The Transliteration of Hebrew," *ET* 9 (1897-98) 48.

J. B. Ansted, "Hebrew and Arabic in Roman Type. Suggestions for a
uniform system of transliteration from Hebrew and Arabic into Roman
Print," *ET* 15 (1903-04) 564-565.

J. R. Madan, "Hebrew in Roman Type. Suggestions for a uniform system of
transliteration from Hebrew and Arabic into Roman Print," *ET* 16
(1904-05) 187-188.

Adolph A. Brux, "A Simplified System of Hebrew-English and Aramaic-
English Transliteration," *AJSL* 58 (1941) 57-69.

H. Merḥavya, "On the Transliteration of Hebrew Words in a 13th Century Latin Manuscript," *Lěš* 30 (1965-66) #1, n.p.n.

Werner Weinberg, "Transliteration and Transcription of Hebrew," *HUCA* 40 (1969-70) 1-32.

§488 *3.3.2 Onomatology and Teknonymy [See: §161 for Place Names and Town Lists ←]*

†Virgilus, "Observations on Prophetic Names," *TRep* 3 (1771) 309-316.

*†Q. P., "Etymology of Tigris," *MMBR* 13 (1802) 204.

H. Rood, "Origin of the national names applied to Abraham and his Posterity," *BJ* 1 (1842) 37-43.

Anonymous, "Philological Contributions. I. Scripture Proper Names of Persons, with their Signification," *TLJ* 4 (1851-52) 82-89.

*H. B. Hackett, "Scripture Facts and Illustrations, Collected During a Journey in Palestine," *CRB* 18 (1853) 405-424, 517-537. [Transmission of Scripture Names, pp. 534-536]

J. G., "On the Origin and Meaning of Roman Names," *JCSP* 2 (1855) 257-270.

H[enry] C. Rawlinson, "On the Orthography of some of the later Royal Names of Assyrian and Babylonian History," *JRAS* (1855) 398-402. (Reply by Ed[win Young] Hincks, pp. 402-403)

*S. F. D., "The Origin of Ancient Names of Countries, Cities, Individuals, and Gods," *CE* 61 (1856) 75-99.

[Gustav Friedrich] Oehler, "Origin and Significance of the Bible Names," *ThE* 6 (1867) 463-474. *(Trans. by W. F. Warren)*

C. W. Goodwin, "Coptic and Graeco-Egyptian names," *ZÄS* 6 (1868) 64-69.

*C. W. Goodwin, "On the name ⟨ Anepu," *ZÄS* 10 (1872) 58-59.

*J. P. Lesley, "Notes on an Egyptian element in the Names of the Hebrew kings, and its bearing on the History of the Exodus," *PAPS* 19 (1880-81) 409-435.

Anonymous, "Some Hebrew Names," *MQR, 2nd Ser.,* 4 (1882) 535-536.

†*A. H. Sayce, "On the names Shem and Japhet," *SBAP* 5 (1882-83) 154-155.

*Edgar C. S. Gibson, "Some Names in Genesis," *Exp, 2nd Ser.,* 6 (1883) 259-272, 350-362.

*A. H. Sayce, "The Names of the First Three Kings of Israel," *ModR* 5 (1884) 158-169.

*Maurice G. Hansen, "The Name Lucifer," *ONTS* 4 (1884-85) 71-73.

F. L. Griffith, "Notes on some Royal Names and Families. *Ameni; Menthu-hotep;* The Cartouche of the Ebers Calendar," *SBAP* 14 (1887-88) 39-44.

*J. G. Lansing, "Egyptian Notes," *AJSL* 4 (1887-88) 43-45. [II. The Egyptian Name of Joseph, pp. 44-45]

*Max Müller, "The supposed Name of Judah in the List of Shoshenq," *SBAP* 10 (1887-88) 81-83. (Note by P. le Page Renouf, pp. 83-86)

*Henry George Tomkins, "The Name Genubath," *SBAP* 10 (1887-88) 372. (Note by W. Harry Rylands, "The Ḳenbetu and the Semitic South," pp.

373-376 [جذرب]) [גנבת] // Γανηβάθ]

C. J. Ball, "Iranian names among the Hetta-hatte," *SBAP* 10 (1887-88) 424-436.

*Henry George Tomkins, "On the name ⌒ 𝄐 ᗯ ," *RTR* 10 (1888) 97-98.

W. St. Chad Boscawen, "Notes on Early Semitic Names," *BOR* 3 (1888-89) 228-231.

W. St. Chad Boscawen, "Notes on Early Semitic Names [Second Article]," *BOR* 3 (1888-89) 282-285.

*A. Lowy, "On the Origin of the Name Dameshek (Damascus)," *SBAP* 11 (1888-89) 237.

A. Lowy, "The Elohistic and Jehovistic Names of Men and Women in the Bible," *SBAP* 11 (1888-89) 238-247.

Thomas Laurie, "Divine Human Names," *BS* 46 (1889) 184-188.

*Morris Jastrow Jr., "Note on the proper name Bu-du-ilu," *JAOS* 13 (1889) cxlvi-cxlvii. *[Ammonite King]*

*P. le Page Renouf, "The Names of Isis and Osiris," *SBAP* 12 (1889-90) 343-346.

A. Löwy, "Elohistic and Jehovistic Proper Names," *EN* 2 (1890) 41-43.

Daniel G. Brinton, "On Etruscan and Libyan Names," *PAPS* 28 (1890) 39-52.

*B. H. T., "The Names of the Antediluvian Patriarchs Translated," *EN* 3 (1891) 141.

*Anonymous, "The Name Jerusalem," *ONTS* 13 (1891) 120.

W. St. C[had] Boscawen, "Syrian Names at Tel El-Amarna," *BOR* 6 (1892-93) 241-247.

*W. Taylor Smith, "Joshua and Jesus," *ET* 4 (1892-93) 47-48. [יְהוֹשׁוּעַ]

*Theo[philus] G. Pinches, "Yâ and Yâwa (Jah and Jahweh) in Assyro-Babylonian Inscriptions," *SBAP* 15 (1892-93) 13-15.

*James Henry Breasted, "Some Egyptian Names in Genesis—A New Inscription of the Oldest Period, etc.," *BW* 2 (1893) 285-288.

G. F. Moore, "The etymology of the name *Canaan*," *JAOS* 15 (1893) lxvii-lxx.

D. A. Lincke, "Continuance of the Name Assyria and Nineveh After 607-6 B.C.," *IAQR, 2nd Ser.,* 7 (1894) 371-378.

*Morris Jastrow Jr., "The element בשת in Hebrew proper names," *JBL* 13 (1894) 19-30.

Morris Jastrow Jr., "Hebrew proper names compounded with יה and יהו," *JBL* 13 (1894) 101-127.

Henry L. Gilbert, "A Study in Old Testament Names," *AJSL* 11 (1894-95) 209-234.

A[lbert] T. Clay, "Dr. Jastrow, Jr., and Assyrian Proper Names in 'Ia'," *LCR* 14 (1895) 196-201.

[J.] Chotzer, "Curiosities of Certain Hebrew Proper Names in the Old Testament," *IAQR, 3rd Ser.,* 2 (1896) 392-394.

Eberhard Nestle, "Some Contributions to Hebrew Onomatology," *AJSL* 13 (1896-97) 169-176.

G. Buchanan Gray, "Professor Hommel on the Evidential Value of Hebrew Proper Names," *ET* 8 (1896-97) 555-558.

T. K. Cheyne, "Hebrew Proper Names: An Explanation," *ET* 8 (1896-97) 329.

J. A. Selbie, "Hebrew Proper Names," *ET* 8 (1896-97) 561.

Anonymous, "Old Testament Proper Names," *CFL, O.S.,* 1 (1897) 120.

Theophilus G. Pinches, "Hebrew Names in Inscriptions from Babylonia," *PEFQS* 30 (1898) 137-138.

*A. H. Sayce, "Recent Biblical Archaeology, Note on the Name of Sisera," *ET* 10 (1898-99) 203.

G. Buchanan Gray, "Nebo as an Element in Hebrew Proper Names: Machnadebai and Barnabas," *ET* 10 (1898-99) 232-234.

*Samuel Krauss, "Notes on Sirach," *JQR* 11 (1898-99) 150-158. [1. The Name Sirach, pp. 150-153]

*G[rey] H[ubert] Skipwith, "Hebrew Tribal Names and the Primitive Traditions of Israel," *JQR* 11 (1898-99) 239-265

*Fritz Hommel, "Assyriological Notes *(Continuation),*" *SBAP* 21 (1899) 115-139.[§49. *Proper names;* pp. 136-137]

W. E. C[rum], "I.—The Name Pachomius," *SBAP* 21 (1899) 247-249.

*C. H. W. Johns, "Assyriological Notes," *SBAP* 21 (1899) 254-255. *[Assyrian Names]*

G. Buchanan Gray, "'The Encyclopedia Biblica' (Vols. I and II) and the Textual Tradition of Hebrew Proper Names," *JQR* 13 (1900-01) 375-391.

*Ernst Riess, "Some Names found on Coan Inscriptions," *AJA* 6 (1902) 32-33.

*E. J. Pilcher, "*Ana-pani-Ili,* illustrated from the Hebrew," *SBAP* 24 (1902) 185.

Joseph Offord, "Semitic Analogies for Old Testament Names," *SBAP* 24 (1902) 242-243.

*E[douard] Naville, "The Egyptian Name of Joseph," *SBAP* 25 (1903) 157-161. *[Chap. 41:45]*

Stephen [H.] Langdon, "List of Proper Names in the Annals of Ashurbanipal," *AJSL* 20 (1903-04) 245-252.

*Ed[uard] König, "The Name 'Ahab'," *ET* 16 (1904-05) 566-567. [אחב]

J. N. Fradenburgh, "The Religion of Biblical Proper Names," *HR* 48 (1904) 358-361.

*A. H. Sayce, "Recent Biblical and Oriental Archaeology. The Name of Adam," *ET* 17 (1905-06) 416-417.

*P. Scott-Moncrieff, "Note on the name Zaphnath Paaneaḥ," *SBAP* 29 (1907) 87-88. *[Egyptian Name of Joseph]*

Henry Preserved Smith, "Theophorous Proper Names in the Old Testament," *AJSL* 24 (1907-08) 34-61.

C. J. Ball, "Four Biblical Names," *ET* 19 (1907-08) 473. [אוה, אבה, אוי, אבי,]

John Urquhart, "'What May Lie in a Name'—the Name 'Samuel'," *CFL,* 3rd Ser., 9 (1908) 51-53.

*A. F. R. Platt, "The Origin of the Name of the Island Elephantine," *SBAP* 30 (1908) 206-207.

*James Wallace, "'History' Manufactured from 'Bogus' Etymology," *CFL,* 3rd Ser., 10 (1909) 295-296. *(Editorial)*

*A. H. Sayce, "The Name of the Ethiopian King, found at Basa," *SBAP* 31 (1909) 268. [⌐⌐ i(?)-b(?)]

*D. D. Luckenbill, "Some Hittite and Mitannian Personal Names," *AJSL* 26 (1909-10) 96-104.

G. L. Young, "Biblical Names and Titles as Illustrated from the Monuments,"*CFL, 3rd Ser.,* 12 (1910) 354-358.

*J. Dyneley Prince, "The name Hammurabi," *JBL* 29 (1910) 21-23.

*E. Naville, "The Egyptian Name of Joseph," *SBAP* 32 (1910) 203-210.

*Harold M. Wiener, "The Egyptian Name of Joseph," *BS* 68 (1911) 156-159.

*Sarah F. Hoyt, "The Name of the Red Sea," *JAOS* 32 (1912) 115-119.

*L. H. Gray, "Iranian Miscellanies. c) The Iranian Name בגדאנא," *JAOS* 33 (1913) 285.

*J. Dyneley Prince, "Ichabod," *JBL* 32 (1913) 151-154.

*A. H. Sayce, "The Solution of the Hittite Problem," *SBAP* 35 (1913) 6-12. [V. The Name of Istar, pp. 8-12]

*W. T. Pilter, "Eastern and Western Semitic Personal Names. The Equivalence of Hammurapi and Amraphel," *SBAP* 35 (1913) 171-186. (Supplementary Note, pp. 244-245)

*W. T. Pilter, "Some Amorite Personal Names in Genesis XIV: Bera', Birsha', Shinab, and Shemē'ber," *SBAP* 35 (1913) 205-226.

Knut L. Tallqvist, "Assyrian Personal Names," *ASSF* 43 (1914) #1, i-xxxii, 1-328.

*George A. Barton, "Religious Conceptions Underlying Sumerian Proper Names," *JAOS* 34 (1914) 315-320.

Oric Bates, "The Name *Osiris,*" *JEA* 2 (1915) 207-208.

*W. T. Pilter, "The Personal Names Abram and Abraham," *SBAP* 37 (1915) 175-191.

G. Buchanan Gray, "A Group of Hebrew Names of the Ninth Century B.C.," *ET* 27 (1915-16) 57-62.

Joseph Offord, "Babylonian and Hebrew Theophoric Names," *PEFQS* 48 (1916) 85-94.

Joseph Offord, "Archaeological Notes on Jewish Antiquities. XXI. *The Name* Zakarbaal," *PEFQS* 48 (1916) 192.

*W. T. Pilter, "Some Groups of Arabian Personal Names borne by the Israelites of the Mosaic Period," *SBAP* 38 (1916) 149-157, 171-180. [I. The Group in *'Amm, 'Ammi;* II. The Groups in *AB(I)* and *AḪ(I);* III. The Group in *TSUR;* IV. Was the name "Parnach" (Numb. XXXIV, 25) Persian?]

*D. D. Luckenbill, "The Name Hammurabi," *JAOS* 37 (1917) 250-253.

Joseph Offord, "Archaeological Notes on Jewish Antiquities. XXXI. *Some Hebrew Patriarch Names in Babylonia,*" *PEFQS* 49 (1917) 100-101.

Joseph Offord, "Archaeological Notes on Jewish Antiquities. XXXIII. *Semitic Names and Conceptions,*" *PEFQS* 49 (1917) 137-140.

W. T. Pilter, "Index of the Southern Arabian Proper Names contained in the *Corpus Inscriptionum Semiticarum (Pars Quarta, Fasciculi* 1-5)," *SBAP* 39 (1917) 99-112, 115-132.

*A. H. Sayce, "Assyriological Notes," *SBAP* 39 (1917) 207-212. [Baal and Yahveh, p. 208; The Nunnation in Arabic, p. 209; The Babylonian Name of NIN-IP, p. 212]

*Alan H. Gardiner, "The Supposed Egyptian Equivalent of the Name of Goshen," *JEA* 5 (1918) 218-223.

*Joseph Offord, "Archaeological Notes on Jewish Antiquities. LVIII. *The Semitic Name of Pithom,*" *PEFQS* 51 (1919) 182-184.

*J. Dyneley Prince, "A possible Sumerian original of the Name Nimrod," *JAOS* 40 (1920) 201-202.

W[illiam] F[oxwell] Albright, "The Name Rebecca," *JBL* 39 (1920) 165-166. (Addenda, p. 172)

Douglas Henry Corley, "Isidore in Jewry," *AJSL* 37 (1920-21) 240.

Maurice A. Canney, "The Significance of Names," *JMUEOS* #9 (1921) 21-37.

*L. H. Dudley Buxton, "Personal and Place Names in Malta," *Man* 21 (1921) #91.

*W[illiam] F[oxwell] Albright, "The Amonite Form of the Name Hammu-rabi," *AJSL* 38 (1921-22) 140-141.

*Max Radin, "Teknonymy in the Old Testament," *HTR* 15 (1922) 293-297.

*H. R. Hall, "The Egyptian Transliteration of Hittite Names," *JEA* 8 (1922) 219-222.

*D. D. Luckenbill, "Assyriological Notes," *AJSL* 39 (1922-23) 56-65. [VII. On some "Hittite" Proper Names, pp. 63-65]

James A. Montgomery, "The nominal prefix *n* in some Hebrew Names," *JAOS* 43 (1923) 50-51.

G. R. Driver, "The Name Kurd and its Philological Connexions," *JRAS* (1923) 393-403.

*M[argaret] A. Murray, "The Derivation of the Name Thebes," *AEE* 9 (1924) 55.

[W. M.] Flinders Petrie, "The Historical Value of Egyptian Names," *AEE* 9 (1924) 76-83.

*Paul Haupt, "Philological Studies," *AJP* 45 (1924) 47-63. [9. The Adventures of Odysseus, pp. 61-63.] *[Etymology of the name Odysseus]*

*R. Engelbach, "The Egyptian Name of Joseph," *JEA* 10 (1924) 204-206.

*Herbert Loewe, "The Name אוֹפִיר," *JQR, N.S.,* 15 (1924-25) 503-506.

G[eo.] P. G. Sobhy, "Studies in the Coptic Proper Names," *AEE* 10 (1925) 41-44.

*E. G. H. Kraeling, "Geographical Notes," *AJSL* 41 (1924-25) 193-194. [II. the Names "Rachel" and "Reu"]

*Edouard Naville, "The Egyptian Name of Joseph," *JEA* 12 (1926) 16-18.

*Battiscombe Gunn, "Notes on two Egyptian Kings," *JEA* 12 (1926) 250-253. [2. The Name Tutᶜankhamūn, pp. 252-253]

*Frederick A. Baepler, "A Study on the Hebrew Name for Eve," *TM* 6 (1926) 363-367. [חַוָּה]

*W[illiam] F[oxwell] Albright, "The Names 'Israel' and 'Judah' with an Excursus on the Etymology of Tôdâh and Tôrâh," *JBL* 46 (1927) 151-185.

*W. E. Staples, "The Hebrew of the Septuagint," *AJSL* 44 (1927-28) 6-30.

*W[illiam] F[oxwell] Albright, "The Name of Bildad the Shuhite," *AJSL* 44 (1927-28) 31-36.

Harry Joshua Leon, "The Names of the Jews of Ancient Rome," *TAPA* 59 (1928) 205-224.

*A. A. Bevan, "The Origin of the Name Maccabee," *JTS* 30 (1928-29) 191-193.

*M[argaret] A. Murray, "The Cerastes in Royal Names," *AEE* 14 (1929) 18-21.

Israel Eitan, "Two Onomatological Studies," *JAOS* 49 (1929) 30-33. [1. The Name Eve; 2. The Name Abraham]

*E[phraim] A. Speiser, "The Name Bildad," *AfO* 6 (1930-31) 23.

*Arno Poebel, "The Name of Elam in Sumerian, Akkadian, and Hebrew," *AJSL* 48 (1931-32) 20-26.

Jacob Z. Lauterbach, "The Naming of Children in Jewish Folklore, Ritual and Practice," *YCCAR* 42 (1932) 316-360.

L. A. Mayer and A. Reifenberg, "A jewish titulus from Egypt," *ASAE* 33 (1933) 81-82.

*Edgar J. Goodspeed, "The Shulammite," *AJSL* 50 (1933-34) 102-104.

*J. H. Hertz, "An Explanation of Bathsheba, Beersheba, Elisheba," *ET* 45 (1933-34) 142.

*R. Engelbach, "A New spelling of the name of king Kakai," *ASAE* 34 (1934) 157-158.

*James A. Montgomery, "Some Hebrew Etymologies," *JQR, N.S.,* 25 (1934-35) 261-269. [(1) Proper Names, pp. 261-265]

W[illiam] F[oxwell] Albright, "The Names *Shaddai* and *Abram,*" *JBL* 54 (1935) 173-204.

*Theophile James Meek, "The Iterative Names in the Old Akkadian Texts from Nuzi," *RAAO* 32 (1935) 51-55.

Alan H. Gardiner, "The Egyptian Origin of Some English Personal Names," *JAOS* 56 (1936) 189-197.

Pierre M. Purves, "Nuzi Names," *JAOS* 58 (1938) 462-471.

*H. H. Rowley, "The Meaning of 'The Shulammite'," *AJSL* 56 (1939) 84-91.

G. R. Driver, "New Aramaeo-Jewish Names in Egypt," *JEA* 25 (1939) 175-176.

*J. W. Jack, "Recent Biblical Archaeology," *ET* 51 (1939-40) 544-548. [The Name Jacob, p. 547]

E. G. [H.] Kraeling, "The Origin of the Name 'Hebrews'," *AJSL* 58 (1941) 237-253.

*Ralph Marcus, "The Hebrew Sibilant *śin* and the name *Yiśrāēl*," *JBL* 60 (1941) x.

*R. W. Hutchinson, "Sipylos and *S-P-L-L*," *ASAE* 41 (1942) 159-160.

Jaroslav Černý, "Greek Etymology of the name of Moses," *ASAE* 41 (1942) 349-354.

W[illiam] F[oxwell] Albright, "Abbreviated Canaanite and Hebrew Names ending in *an*," *JBL* 61 (1942) xii.

G. R. Driver, "Notes on Some Recently Recovered Proper Names," *BASOR* #90 (1943) 34.

*A. Leo Oppenheim, "Assyriological Gleanings I," *BASOR* #91 (1943) 36-38. [Neo-Babylonian Personal Name *Ša-pî-kalbi*, pp. 36-37]

*Alan H. Gardiner and H. I. Bell, "The Name of Lake Moeris," *JEA* 29 (1943) 37-50.

A. M. Honeyman, "A Note on the Names Shebaniah, Shebna, Etc.," *PEFQS* 76 (1944) 168-169.

*G. R. Driver, "(III) Two Gods (*ḤW* and *MWT*) in Proper Names," *PEQ* 77 (1945) 12-14.

*Roland G. Kent, "The Name Hystaspes," *Lang* 21 (1945) 55-58.

W[illiam] F[oxwell] Albright, "Cuneiform Material for Egyptian Prosopography, 1500-1200 B.C.," *JNES* 5 (1946) 7-25.

*A. S. Yahuda, "The Meaning of the name Esther," *JRAS* (1946) 174-178.

*G. R. Driver, "Theological and Philological Problems in the Old Testament," *JTS* 47 (1946) 156-166. [I. (i) *The god* Ym *in proper names,* pp. 156-157]

Henry M. Hoenigswald, "The Phonology of Etrusco-Roman Names," *TAPA* 77 (1946) 319.

*B. Maisler, "The Scribe of King David and the Problem of the High Officials in the Ancient Kingdom of Israel," *BIES* 13 (1946-47) #3/4, IV-V.

P.-E. Dumont, "Indo-Aryan Names from Mitanni, Nuzi and Syrian Documents," *JAOS* 67 (1947) 251-253.

*M. F. Laming Macadam, "On a Late Napatan or Early Meroitic King's Name," *JEA* 33 (1947) 93-94.

A. M. Honeyman, "The Evidence for Regnal Names Among the Hebrews," *JBL* 67 (1948) 13-25.

Guy Burton, "The title *Khnumt Nefer-Hezt,*" *ASAE* 49 (1949) 99-110.

E. R. Lacheman, "Nuzi Personal Names," *JNES* 8 (1949) 48-55.

*Julius Lewy, "Tabor, Tibar, Atabyros," *HUCA* 23 (1950-51) Part 1, 357-386. *[Etymological Study of the name Mount Tabor]*

J. Gwyn Griffiths, "Is Chalbes a greek name?" *ASAE* 51 (1951) 219-220.

Frank Zimmermann, "Abram and Abraham," *JBL* 70 (1951) vi.

Ralph Marcus, "The Name 'Makkabaios'," *JBL* 70 (1951) vii-viii.

*D. Winton Thomas, "Mount Tabor: The Meaning of the Name," *VT* 1 (1951) 229-230.

I[gnace] J. Gelb, "The Double Names of the Hittite Kings," *RO* 17 (1951-52) 146-154.

Albrecht Goetze, "The Theophorous Element of the Anatolian Proper Names from Cappadocia," *Lang* 29 (1953) 263-277.

Milka Cassuto-Salzmann, "Greek Names among the Jews," *EI* 3 (1954) XII.

*W[illiam] F[oxwell] Albright, "Northwest-Semitic Names in a List of Egyptian Slaves from the Eighteenth Century B.C.," *JAOS* 74 (1954) 222-233.

*Albrecht Goetze, "The Linguistic Continuity of Anatolia as Shown by its Proper Names," *JCS* 8 (1954) 74-81.

Albrecht Goetze, "Some Groups of Ancient Anatolian Names," *Lang* 30 (1954) 349-359.

*R. P. C. Hanson, "Interpretations of Hebrew Names in Origen," *VC* 10 (1956) 103-123.

*C. A. Wilson, "The Local Colour of the Bible Records: Part 3. The Israelites in Egypt: The Egyptian Titles Used," *AT* 1 (1956-57) #3, 6-8.

Y. F. Gumpertz, "On the Names of the Jews," *Tarbiz* 25 (1956-57) #3, IX-XI; #4, V-VI.

G. R. Driver, "Aramaic Names in Accadian Texts," *RDSO* 32 (1957) 41-57.

*Albrecht Goetze, "Remarks on Some Names Occurring in the Execration Texts," *BASOR* #151 (1958) 28-33.

*J. Gwyn Griffiths, "Remarks on the Horian elements in the Royal Titulary," *ASAE* 56 (1959) 63-86.

*A[lbrecht] Goetze, "Suffixes in 'Kanishite' Proper Names," *RHA* 18 (1960) 45-55.

Joseph A. Fitzmyer, "The Name Simon," *HTR* 56 (1963) 1-5. [שמעון]

*D. N. Freedman, "The Original Name of Jacob," *IEJ* 13 (1963) 124-125.

*Howard R. Bailey, "On Naming," *IR* 20 (1963) #1, 43-50.

*W. A. Ward, "Notes on Some Semitic Loan-Words and Personal Names in Late Egyptian," *Or, N.S.,* 32 (1963) 413-436.

Cecil Roth, "The Name Simon—A Further Discussion," *HTR* 57 (1964) 60. (Reply by Joseph A. Fitzmyer, pp. 60-61.)

*Andrew F. Key, "The Giving of Proper Names in the Old Testament," *JBL* 83 (1964) 55-59.

Michael C. Astour, "Greek Names in the Semitic World and Semitic Names in the Greek World," *JNES* 23 (1964) 193-201.

*John Bennett, "The meaning of the royal nomen and prenomen," *JEA* 51 (1965) 206-207.

K. A. Kitchen, "A Late Luvian Personal Name in Aramaic," *RHA* 23 (1965) 25-28.

Frank Zimmermann, "Folk etymology of Biblical names," *VTS* 15 (1965) 311-326.

*Edwin Yamauchi, "Slaves of God," *BETS* 9 (1966) 31-50.

*P. J. van Zijl, "'tb'l in the Phoenician and Biblical Literature," *OTW* 9 (1966) 159-162.

J. M. Sasson, "Remarks on two 'Anatolian' Personal Names from Mari," *RHA* 24 (1966) 155-159.

Fortunato A. Carfagna, "The Biblical Concept of Name," *SS* 18 (1966-67) #1, 3-15.

Naomi G. Cohen, "Historical conclusions gleaned from the names of the Jews of Elephantine," *Lĕš* 31 (1966-67) #2, n.p.n.; #3, n.p.n.

*N. B. Jankowska, "A System of Rotation of Eponyms of the Commercial Association at Kaniš (Asia Minor XIX B.C.)," *ArOr* 35 (1967) 524-548.

A. Jamme, "The So-called Thamudic Divine Name *wt* = *wtn*," *BO* 24 (1967) 279-288.

*Samuel Belkin, "Some Obscure Traditions Mutually Clarified in Philo and Rabbinic Literature," *JQR, 75th* (1967) 80-103. [2. Abraham's Name, pp., 83-86]

Robert D. Biggs, "Semitic Names in the Fara Period," *Or, N.S.,* 36 (1967) 55-66.

G. [M.] Bauer, "Some Problems of the Eponymate in Ancient South Arabia," *VDI* (1967) #2, 147.

A. M. Price, "The Aphal Name-Form in the Old Testament," *GUOST* 22 (1967-68) 56-63.

*Harry A. Hoffner Jr., "Birth and Name-giving in Hittite Texts," *JNES* 27 (1968) 198-203.

Eric P. Hamp, "The Name of Demeter," *Minos* 9 (1968) 198-204.

A. G. Lundin, "The Discussion over the Sabaean Eponymate (an answer to G. M. Bauer)," *VDI* (1968) #1, 126.

V. D. Blavatsky, "ΒΟΡΥΣΘΕΝΙϚ*[sic]*," *VDI* (1968) #4, 122.

Anonymous, "Naming the New-born Child," *BH* 5 (1969) 53-55.

*M. B. Rowton, "The Abu Amurrim," *Iraq* 31 (1969) 68-73.

*Michael H. Silverman, "Aramean Name-Types in the Elephantine Documents," *JAOS* 89 (1969) 691-709.

Eric P. Hamp, "Postscript to Demeter and Poseidon," *Minos* 10 (1969) 93-95.

*A. H. van Zyl, "The meaning of the name Samuel," *OTW* 12 (1969) 122-129.

*Ilya Gershevitch, "Iranian Nouns and Names in Elamite Garb," *TPS* (1969) 165-200.

A. Al-Ansary, "Lihyanite Personal Names *A Comparative Study*," *ALUOS* 7 (1969-73) 5-16.

§489 *3.3.3 Afroasiatic Languages*

*Israel Eitan, "Hebrew and Semitic Particles. Comparative Studies in Semitic Philology," *AJSL* 44 (1927-28) 177-205, 254-260.

*Israel Eitan, "Hebrew and Semitic Particles. Comparative Studies in Semitic Philology—*Continued*," *AJSL* 45 (1928-29) 48-63, 130-145, 197-211; 46 (1929-30) 22-51.

Joseph H. Greenberg, "The Afro-Asiatic (Hamito-Semitic) Present," *JAOS* 72 (1952) 1-9.

*Cyrus H. Gordon, "Marginal Notes on the Ancient Middle East," *JKF* 2 (1952-53) 50-61. [VII. Egypto-Semitica: Eg. *y* = Aram. הא; a. Eg. *ktt* = Ugar. *kdd* ; b. Two Egypto-Semitic uses of *-ny* ; c. Eg. 'man' *s* ; f. *s.t* 'woman' and the combination *s.t-ḥm.t* ; d. The vocalization of the Syriac enclitic *gêr*; pp. 57-58]

Cyrus H. Gordon, "Egypto-Semitica," *RDSO* 32 (1957) 269-277.

Joseph H. Greenberg, "An Afro-Asiatic Pattern of Gender and Number Agreement," *JAOS* 80 (1960) 317-321.

*Gérard Janssens, "Contributions to the Hamito-Semitic and the Egyptian Phonetic Laws," *CdÉ* 42 (1967) 86-122.

§490 *3.3.3.1 Hamitic - General Studies*

*E[phraim] A. Speiser, "Pitfalls of Polarity," *Lang* 14 (1938) 187-202.

*W. H. Worrell, "Noun Classes and Polarity in Hamitic and their bearing upon the Origin of the Semites," *JPOS* 1 (1920-21) 15-21.

§491 *3.3.3.1.1 Egyptian - General Studies*

*†R. H., "Hieroglyphics and the Origin of Alphabetic Writing," *MMBR* 7 (1799) 185-186.

*†Anonymous, "Hammar on Ancient Alphabets," *BCQTR* 30 (1807) 15-23. *(Review) [Hieroglyphics]*

Anonymous, "Summary of the Hieroglyphical System of the Ancient Egyptians, as established by the results of M. Champollion's recent Researches," *MMBR* 58 (1824-25) 304-306.

Anonymous, "Researches in Egypt," *MMBR* 59 (1825) 8-11, 297-300. *[Hieroglyphics compared with Chinese]*

†Anonymous, "Dr. Young's and M. Champollion's *System of Phonetic Hieroglyphics*," *WR* 4 (1825) 40-60.

†Anonymous, "Hieroglyphics," *ERCJ* 45 (1826-27) 96-147. *(Review)*

†Anonymous, "Hieroglyphics of Ancient Egypt," *BCQTR, 4th Ser.,* 1 (1827) 141-162. *(Review)*

*†Anonymous, "Egyptian Method of Notation," *WR* 13 (1830) 227-239.

*†Anonymous, "Wall *on Egyptian Hieroglyphs, and on the Origin of Alphabetic Writing*," *ERCJ* 64 (1836-37) 82-93. *(Review)*

Anonymous, "Egyptian Hieroglyphics," *QCS, 3rd Ser.,* 9 (1837) 29-42.

R. D. C. Robbins, "The Language of Ancient Egypt," *BRCR, N.S.,* 11 (1844) 137-162.

†Anonymous, "Discoveries in Picture Writing," *BQRL* 12 (1850) 79-110. *(Review)*

*G. Seyffarth, "Three Lectures on Egyptian Antiquities, &c., delivered at the Stuyvesant Institute, New York, May 1856," *ER* 8 (1856-57) 34-104. [II. The key to the Hieroglyphics, pp. 46-62]

†[Phiny E.] Chase, "Egyptian Hieroglyphics and Chinese Characters," *PAPS* 9 (1862-64) 231-232.

M. F. Chabas, "A Note on the Footmark in Hieroglyphic Script," *PAPS* 12 (1871-72) 193. [Rejoinder by J. P. Lesley, p. 194]

*Hyde Clarke, "On the Egyptian Colony and Language in the Caucasus, and its Anthropological Relation," *JRAI* 3 (1873-74) 178-198. (Discussion, pp. 198-200)

*A. H. Sayce, "On the Study of Assyrian and Egyptian: An Opening Address," *BFER* 24 (1875) 294-301.

*Claude R. Conder, "On Comparisons of Hieroglyphics," *PEFQS* 20 (1888) 252-259.

P. le Page Renouf, "Egyptian Phonology. I," *SBAP* 11 (1888-89) 107-115.

*C[laude] R. Conder, "The Three Hieroglyphic Systems," *ARL* 3 (1889) 99-117.

*[Wm.] Flinders Petrie, "Epigraphy in Egyptian Research," *IAQR, 2nd Ser.,* 2 (1891) 315-323.

*Anonymous, "Hieroglyphics and Pre-Phœnician Script," *AAOJ* 16 (1894) 310-311.

Anonymous, "A Dictionary of the Egyptian Language. An Appeal to Custodians and Owners of Inscriptions and Papyri," *SBAP* 20 (1898) 167-168.

F. Ll. Griffith, "The System of Writing in Ancient Egypt," *JRAI* 30 (1900) 153-159.

Kurt Sethe, M. G. Benedite, M. E. Montet, and J. H. Breasted, "The Transliteration of Egyptian. *The following letters on this subject have been received,"* *SBAP* 24 (1902) 355-361. *[Extracts of letters]*

†A. Wiedemann, "Letter from Prof. Dr. A. Wiedemann on the Transliteration of Egyptian," *SBAP* 25 (1903) 212-214.

*A. M. Skelly, "The Resurrection of Ancient Egypt and Assyria," *IER, 4th Ser.,* 23 (1908) 510-522.

Alan H. Gardiner, "The Nature and Development of the Egyptian Hieroglyphic Writing," *JEA* 2 (1915) 61-75.

W. M. F[linders] P[etrie], "Early Hieroglyphic Readings of Sir William Gell," *AEE* 4 (1917) 162-166.

W[illiam] F[oxwell] Albright, "Notes on Egypto-Semitic Etymology. I," *AJSL* 34 (1917-18) 81-98.

W[illiam] F[oxwell] Albright, "Notes on Egypto-Semitic Etymology. II," *AJSL* 34 (1917-18) 215-255.

Warren R. Dawson, "A Hieroglyphic Dictionary," *IAQR* 16 (1920) 644-651.

M[argaret] A. Murray, "Origins of Some Signs," *AEE* 6 (1921) 35-38.

Geo. P. G. Subḥy, "Survivals of Ancient Egyptian in Modern Dialect," *AEE* 6 (1921) 70-75.

Geo. P. G. Subḥy, "Egyptian Words Remaining in Modern Use. *(Continued from* p. 75, Part III, 1921)," *AEE* 7 (1922) 47-49. *[Marked as continued, but was not]*

*H. R. Hall, "The Egyptian Transliteration of Hittite Names," *JEA* 8 (1922) 219-222.

*Sidney Smith and C. J. Gadd, "A Cuneiform Vocabulary of Egyptian Words," *JEA* 11 (1925) 230-239. (Additional Note by T. Eric Peet, pp. 239-240)

*W[illiam] F[oxwell] Albright, "The New Cuneiform Vocabulary of Egyptian Words," *JEA* 12 (1926) 186-190.

*A[aron] Ember, "Several Egypto-Semitic Etymologies," *OOR* 1 (1926) #1, 5-8.[1. - Eg. mꜥbꜣ. *harpoon, spear* = Eth. mâʾbal, *sharp instrument, arrow;* 2. - Eg. mꜥbꜣ. *thirty* = Post-Biblical מְעֻבָּר *intercalated;* 3. Eg.

Fnḫ-ụ =(Φοῖνιξ, Phoenician) = Arab فَلَّح *fellah* < Aram. פלח *split, plough, cultivate the ground;* 4. Eg. ꜥr, *enter* = Aram. עלל *enter;* 5. Eg.

gm-ụ, *grief, mourning* = Arab. غَمّ ğamm, *grief, sadness;* 6. Eg. pzḫ,

be dishevelled, disarray, dismayed = Arab. فزع, *be frightened, terrified, dismayed;* 7. Eg. ḫꜣm, *catching of fish and birds* = חִים *net for catching fish;* 8. ḫꜣp, erroneously חפה لحف *cover;* 9. Eg. ḫnğ, *thigh,*

hip-bone (Pyr. Texts 124, 133, 1547) = Assyr. ḫinçu, Arab. خَضِر, Heb.

חֲלָצִים, *lion, hip;* 10. Eg. ꜥinꜥ, *chin (Pyr. Texts* 1308) = Heb. לַע *jaw-*

bone (probably = Arab. نيع *jaw, mandible*)]

W[illiam] F[oxwell] Albright, "Notes on Egypto-Semitic Etymology. III," *JAOS* 47 (1927) 198-237.

Alan H. Gardiner, "The Transcription of New Kingdom Hieratic," *JEA* 15 (1929) 48-55.

T. George Allen, "The Great Egyptian Dictionary is Finished," *AJSL* 49 (1932-33) 193-196.

Gilbert Bagnani, "The Transcription of Late Hieratic," *JEA* 19 (1933) 162-166.

Raymond O. Faulkner, "Some Further Remarks on the Transcription of Late Hieratic," *JEA* 21 (1935) 49-51.

*R. Butin, "Some Egyptian Hieroglyphs of Sinai and their Relationship to the Hieroglyphs of the Proto-Sinaitic Semitic Alphabet," *Miz* 2 (1936) 52-56.

Alan H. Gardiner, "Some Aspects of the Egyptian Language," *PBA* 23 (1937) 81-104.

T. G[eorge] Allen, "Egyptian Dictionary Notes," *AJSL* 56 (1939) 158.

T. George Allen, "Egyptian Dictionary Notes," *AJSL* 57 (1940) 97-98.

*Hermann Ranke, "The Egyptian Pronunciation of the Royal Name 'Khefren' and its Cognates," *JAOS* 70 (1950) 65-68.

F. Ll. Griffith, "The Decipherment of the Hieroglyphs," *JEA* 37 (1951) 38-46.

William F. Edgerton, "On the Theory of Writing," *JNES* 11 (1952) 287-290. *[Egyptian]*

*Thomas O. Lambdin, "Egyptian Loanwords in the Old Testament," *JAOS* 73 (1953) 145-155.

*Alexandre Badawy, "Philological evidence about methods of construction in ancient Egypt," *ASAE* 54 (1956-57) 51-74.

W[illiam] F[oxwell] Albright and T[homas] O. Lambdin, "New Material for the Egyptian Syllabic Orthography," *JSS* 2 (1957) 113-127.

John Bennett, "Motifs and phrases on funerary stelae of the later Middle Kingdom," *JEA* 44 (1958) 120-121.

Werner Vycichl, "Is Egyptian a Semitic Language?" *Kush* 7 (1959) 27-44.

Elizabeth Bowman, "A Note on the Development of Egyptian Writing," *JNES* 19 (1960) 46-48.

*William A. Ward, "Comparative Studies in Egyptian and Ugaritic," *JNES* 20 (1961) 31-40.

*Elizabeth Thomas, "*P₃ ḤR ḤN' I ḤNW/N HNW ḤN'I,* A Designation of the Valley of the Kings," *JEA* 49 (1963) 57-63.

R[aymond] O. Faulkner, "*Concise Dictionary of Middle Egyptian:* Corrigenda," *JEA* 49 (1963) 172.

John Bennett, "Pyramid names," *JEA* 52 (1966) 174-176.

R. A. Caminos, "The Talbotype Applied to Hieroglyphics," *JEA* 52 (1966) 65-70. *[Modern Printing of Hieroglyphics]*

§492 *3.3.3.1.2 Egyptian Hieroglyphics - Multiple Sign Articles*

J. F. Thrupp, "Explanation of certain hieroglyphic signs," *JCSP* 2 (1855) 232. [⌂, ◠, ▱(?)]

P. le P[age] Renouf, "Miscellanea," *ZÄS* 4 (1866) 58-60. [1. ⚬ = ⊻ or ⊔;

2. ⬠▱ must be read ⬠⌐; 3. ○ = ⟨⟩; *also* 1. ≈ is not *men* or *nen*, but ⲁⲛ or ⲛ̇ ; 2. No trace of *men* in old Egyptian; 3. No

trace in Coptic of ⬠; 4. ≈ has the sense of *deficere* not ⲡⲙⲟⲧ;

5. ⬠ and the verb ⬠ *jungere* are pronounced ChNeM; 6.

⬠, *to hear* should be read ⲥⲱⲧⲉⲙ; 7. "year" is ◠ not ◠; 8. ⬠ = ⬠; 9. ⟂⟂⟂; 10. ≈ = ⊙ = ▱]

S. Birch, "Adversaria Hieroglyphica," *ZÄS* 4 (1866) 85-88. [◠

Kebni, ▱ *neht*, ≈ *χp*; ▱ *sems*; ⬠ *ur, hur*; ▱ *ta* or

ma; ▱ *ka*; ▱ *tut*; ▱ ░ s-*χt*; ▱ *sat*

replaces ▱ *sat*; ▱ *sa n hemu*; ▱ *ptar*;

▱ *t'alt*; ▱ *stem*; ▱ *em beh*; ⌐; ◠ ;

▱ *han*; ▱ *apu* or *tpuru*; ▱; ▱ *peh.t*]

S. Birch, "Adversaria Hieroglyphica," *ZÄS* 4 (1866) 98-101. [⬛;

⬛ *sesunnu;* ⬛ *kahs;* ⬛; ⬛; ⬛ *tebn;*

⬛ *ntr;* ⬛ *baksu;* ⬛; ⬛ *tuau;*

⬛ *mahat;* ⬛ *beka;* ⬛ *tr;* ⬛

tertera; ⬛ *maut;* ⬛ *āb;* ⬛ *aχ;* ⬛

sessu; ⬛ *ba;* ⬛ determinative of *Tama;* ⬛ *nχχ*]

S. Birch, "Varia," *ZÄS* 5 (1867) 14-15. [⬛ *Mut* = ⬛ *mu-t;* ⬛ *hsbi;*

⬛ or ⬛ = ⬛ *χmu*]

P. le Page Renouf, "Miscellanea II," *ZÄS* 5 (1867) 32-33. [1. ⬛ =

⬛; 2. *water* written phonetically as ⬛;

3. Question on the transcription of ⬛; 4. ⬛ ≠ ⬛ therefore

⬛ is *mer;* 5. Confusion of ⬛ with ⬛; 6. Ithyphallic transcrip-

tion of Ammon or Horus is *Min;* 7. ⬛ has the value of *cha;* 8. ⬛ in

⬛; 9. ⬛]

P. le Page Renouf, "Miscellanea II," *ZÄS* 5 (1867) 41-43. [10. On the value

of [hieroglyph]; 11. [hieroglyphs]; 12. [hieroglyph] as *set;* 13. [hieroglyph] interchangeable

with [hieroglyph]; 14. ⲙⲟⲧⲧ *vincullum, junctura* = [hieroglyphs]; 15. [hieroglyph] identi-

fied with ⲟϯ; 16. [hieroglyphs] *extendere;* 17. [hieroglyph] = [hieroglyph] or [hieroglyph] and [hieroglyph] is

an ideograph = [hieroglyph] or [hieroglyphs]]

P. le Page Renouf, "Miscellanea II," *ZÄS* 5 (1867) 52-54. [18. [hieroglyph] as *mer*

χetem; 19. [hieroglyph] substitute for [hieroglyphs]; 20. [hieroglyph] as a complement to [hieroglyph];

21. [hieroglyph] [hieroglyph]; 22. No phonetic variant for [hieroglyphs]]

P. le Page Renouf, "Miscellanea III," *ZÄS* 5 (1867) 60-63, 65-66, 96. [1. An-

cient phonetic reading of [hieroglyph] not *Amenti;* 2. Three words using [hieroglyph] having

the value of *nem;* 3. *māfka* signifies *copper;* 4. [hieroglyphs] *χesteb;* 5.

[hieroglyphs] *em sχer auau;* 6. [hieroglyphs] as a disjunctive; 7. [hieroglyph];

8. Coptic ⲁⲉⲋⲱ and ⲛⲁⲉⲋⲱ signify [hieroglyph] and [hieroglyph]; 9. [hieroglyph] and [hieroglyph]; 10. [hieroglyph]]

S. Birch, "Varia," *ZÄS* 5 (1867) 63-64. [[hieroglyphs] *trau;* [hieroglyphs] =

[hieroglyphs] *ap;* [hieroglyph] *n-ka;* [hieroglyph] *s* = [hieroglyphs] *su;* [hieroglyph]; [hieroglyphs] *usf,* ⲟⲩⲱⲥϥ;

[hieroglyph]; [hieroglyph] *atn;* [hieroglyphs] *gar* = ⲍⲉⲗ; [hieroglyphs]; [hieroglyphs] *tb*]

P. le Page Renouf, "Miscellanea III," *ZÄS* 6 (1868) 7-9. [1. ⟨glyph⟩ pronounced
nāa; 2. Observations on ⟨glyph⟩ and ⟨glyph⟩; 3. Observations on ⟨glyph⟩ and ⟨glyph⟩; Additional note on number 10 ⟨glyph⟩ *(above)*]

S. Birch, "Varia," *ZÄS* 6 (1868) 9-12. [⟨glyphs⟩ *kaš;* ⟨glyphs⟩

makar; ⟨glyphs⟩; ⟨glyphs⟩ *mafkata* = ⟨glyph⟩; ⟨glyphs⟩ *tes;* ⟨glyphs⟩

hbai; ⟨glyphs⟩ *kabti;* ⟨glyphs⟩ *strt;* ⟨glyphs⟩ *hbi[sic];*

⟨glyphs⟩ *suh-ti;* ⟨glyphs⟩ *tesm;* ⟨glyphs⟩ *tui;* ⟨glyphs⟩; ⟨glyphs⟩

kiš = ϭⲱϣ; ⟨glyphs⟩ *mehi;* ⟨glyphs⟩ *nbt;* ⟨glyphs⟩ *χuu;*

⟨glyphs⟩ *at;* ⟨glyphs⟩ *uršu;* ⟨glyphs⟩ *nm* = ⲛⲙ or ⲛⲉⲙ]

P. le Page Renouf, "Miscellanea IV," *ZÄS* 6 (1868) 45-48. [1. ⟨glyphs⟩; 2. ⟨glyph⟩

and ⟨glyph⟩; 4. ⟨glyphs⟩ as a single group?; 5. ⟨glyphs⟩; 6. *Uas* as

one value of ⟨glyph⟩; 7. ⟨glyph⟩ read as *teb;* 8. Latin *ipse* = ⟨glyphs⟩ and ⟨glyphs⟩; 9.

⟨glyphs⟩; 10. ⟨glyphs⟩ with ⟨glyph⟩]

S. Birch, "Varia—Aethiopica," *ZÄS* 6 (1868) 61-64.

S. Birch, "Varia," *ZÄS* 6 (1868) 110-112. [*lubarita*, ⬚ or

⬚ *huatáhath;* ⬚ *Hakr;* ⬚ *trau;*

⬚ *aaχu;* ⬚ *mtn* (Coptic ⲙⲧⲟⲛ);
⬚]

S. Birch, "Varia," *ZÄS* 7 (1869) 25-27. [⬚ *tit; Wadhy Maghara tablet*
inscriptions: ⬚ , ⬚ *variant for sebt;* ⬚ *Hui;*
⬚ *χu bat*]

S. Birch, "Varia," *ZÄS* 7 (1869) 115-116. [1. ⬚ *reχ;* 2. ⬚

; 3. ⬚ = ⬚ *seš;* 4. ⬚ *variant of* ⬚ *mχnnu;* 5.

⬚ *kat;* 6. *Papyrus Amenneb c. 125 l. 6;* 7. ⬚

am but; 8. *Papyrus Amenneb c.3 l. 1* ⬚ =

⬚]

S. Birch, "Varia," *ZÄS* 7 (1869) 133-135. [9. ⟨hieroglyphs⟩ *ari-t, ali-t;* 10.

⟨hieroglyphs⟩ *au* variant of ⟨hieroglyph⟩; 11. ⟨hieroglyphs⟩ *Set;* 12. ⊗ = ⟨hieroglyphs⟩

sba; 13. ⟨hieroglyph⟩ *uta =* ⟨hieroglyph⟩ *uat;* 13.*[sic]* ⟨hieroglyphs⟩ *tna;* 14. ⟨hieroglyphs⟩

kamt; 15. ⟨hieroglyphs⟩ *btnnu;* 16. ⟨hieroglyphs⟩ *atri;* 17.

⟨hieroglyphs⟩ *amf;* 17.*[sic]* The Papyrus of Harsiesis-variant; 18.

⟨hieroglyphs⟩ *hmka;* 18.*[sic]* ⟨hieroglyphs⟩ *št*]

S. Birch, "Varia," *ZÄS* 8 (1870) 19-21. [1. ⟨hieroglyphs⟩ *neχn;* 2. ⟨hieroglyph⟩; 3. ⟨hieroglyph⟩ ;

4. ⟨hieroglyphs⟩ *mum-t;* 5. ⟨hieroglyphs⟩ *neb;* 6. ⟨hieroglyphs⟩ *haui;*

7. ⟨hieroglyphs⟩ variant of ⟨hieroglyphs⟩ ; 8. ⟨hieroglyphs⟩ *mautt;* 9. ⟨hieroglyphs⟩ *mut;* 10.

⟨hieroglyphs⟩ *tet en χm;* 11. ⟨hieroglyphs⟩ *ušau;* 12. ⟨hieroglyphs⟩ ;

13. ⟨hieroglyphs⟩ *pasu;* 14. ⟨hieroglyphs⟩ *χnt;* 15. ⟨hieroglyphs⟩ ; 16

⟨hieroglyphs⟩ *χu*]

S. Birch, "Varia," *ZÄS* 8 (1870) 66-68. [1. ⟨hieroglyphs⟩; 2. ⟨hieroglyphs⟩ *heba;* 3.

⟨hieroglyphs⟩; 4. "The chapter of exorcising the scorpion...at" *in the Hay*

Papyrus collection; 5. Ritual of *Sai* - variant of *nru* as *rχ;* 6. ⟨hieroglyphs⟩ *šu;*

7. ⟨hieroglyphs⟩ *ḵaruheb;* 8. ⟨hieroglyphs⟩ *ntr ba*

f ma netri]

S. Birch, "Varia," *ZÄS* 8 (1870) 130-132. [⟨hieroglyphs⟩ *sn-nχt;* ⟨hieroglyphs⟩

mateni-t; ⟨hieroglyphs⟩ *aḵhu;* ⟨hieroglyphs⟩ *maḵasu;* ⟨hieroglyphs⟩

pru; ⟨hieroglyphs⟩ *χn;* ⟨hieroglyphs⟩ *hatau;* ⟨hieroglyphs⟩ *kar*

nar at na; ⟨hieroglyphs⟩ *anχ;* ⟨hieroglyphs⟩ *kam*]

S. Birch, "Varia," *ZÄS* 9 (1871) 51-52. [1. ⟨hieroglyphs⟩ *âab-t;* 2.

⟨hieroglyphs⟩ *fnt;* 3. ⟨hieroglyphs⟩ replaces ⟨hieroglyphs⟩; 4. ⟨hieroglyphs⟩ *er enti;* 5.

⟨hieroglyphs⟩ *ḵar;* 6. ⟨hieroglyphs⟩ *tatfi nb;* 7. ⟨hieroglyphs⟩ *aχu;* 8.

⟨hieroglyphs⟩ *ruhiu* replaces "*ahu* the god"; 9. ⟨hieroglyphs⟩ *rema še pm;* 10. [hieroglyphs] *kapu-t na;* 11. [hieroglyphs] *spu;* 12. [hieroglyphs] *ar*]

S. Birch, "Varia," *ZÄS* 9 (1871) 64-66. [13. [hieroglyphs] *apr;* 14.

[hieroglyphs] *r atp ku em ar tn;* 15. [hieroglyphs] *ḳaft;* 16.

[hieroglyphs] *kat;* 17. [hieroglyphs] *al ki ťet māā;* 18.

[hieroglyphs] *šaš;* 19. [hieroglyphs] *hebs mnχ;* 20.

[hieroglyphs] *ubn m neb anχ maχru;* 21.

[hieroglyphs] *uat samta;* 22. [hieroglyphs] *hr χa sn;* 23.

[hieroglyphs] *(am) āmam ar er rem [s];* 24.

[hieroglyphs] *aiut;* 25. [hieroglyphs] *basaḳ;* 26. [hieroglyphs] *sšan* = Coptic

ⲱⲓⲥⲛⲉ; 27. [hieroglyphs] *aama* instead of *maau;* 28.

[hieroglyphs] *r matr-ut;* 29. [hieroglyphs]

š-sn nuhi apitut; 30. [hieroglyphs] *sn m (mtm) en ta*

(ru) ta; 31. [hieroglyphs] *pst*]

S. Birch, "Varia," *ZÄS* 9 (1871) 118-120. [[hieroglyphs] *kamtu;* miscellaneous papyrus fragments]

P. le Page Renouf, "On several hieroglyphic words," *ZÄS* 9 (1871) 129-137.

[1. Most feminine nouns end in ◁; 2. ⁓⁓⁓ ı ı ı ; 3. Demonstrative pronoun

▢⁓⁓ *pen;* 4. 🦶◠ ; 5. ⅃ ⅃ or ⅃ ; 6. *Passage from 2nd Berlin Papyrus;* 7. "1001 Nights" and "Two Brothers" - ◁ ⳩ ⳩ and ⳡ ⲏⲧ]

S. Birch, "Varia," *ZÄS* 10 (1872) 59. [Papyrus of Petharpaχrat c. 148;

⁓⁓ ⳩ *tnf;* 🅟 ⳩ 🅱 *sut;* 🅟 🅱 *sut an*]

*P. le Page Renouf, "Miscellanea V," *ZÄS* 10 (1872) 72-79. [1. ı ı ı merely ideographic; 2. Coptic feminine form with ⲥ; and ⳩⳩; 3. ⁓⁓⁓ ⳩ ◠ ; 4.

🅰 transcribed as *tep;* 5. Coptic ⲟⲩⲣⲟ, ⲉⲡⲡⲟ, ⲉⲡⲡⲁ]

S. Birch, "Varia," *ZÄS* 10 (1872) 96-98. [Various cartouches; Additional chapter to Book of the dead (Lepsius Todt. XXX, c. 80—XXXII, c. 87;

🅟 ⳩ 🅱 *sut;* ⁓⳩⳩◯🅱; unknown ideograph ⳩◯⳩ ı ı ı]

S. Birch, "Varia," *ZÄS* 10 (1872) 120-122. [🦶 ⳩ ⳩ ⁓⁓ ⳩ ⳩!

🦶 ⅃ ◠ ⁓⁓ 🅟 ⳩ ⳩ ⳩ ⁓⁓ ⳩ı ◯ ⁓ ⳩ ⳩ ⳩ı ⁓ı *maat en ka ntru em kat en sutut hna bau nu sahu au;* 🅟 ⳩ı *nfnu;* 🦶 ◠ı *uh =*

Coptic ⲟⳉ ⲉ or ⲟⲩⳉ ⲉ; ⳩ ⳩ *tun;* 🅟◠🅱 *sχet*]

S. Birch, "Varia," *ZÄS* 11 (1873) 151-152 [1. ⚏ *sen;* 2. 𓁷𓂝𓃭𓏤

baad; 3. 𓅮 *ba;* 4. 𓏭𓅓𓅓𓆟 *snemm;* 5. 𓏲 ; 6. 𓐪 𓊠 *sek;* 7.

𓏥𓊖𓈖 *mnχ;* 8. 𓏭��𓏲 *senb;* 9. 𓂝𓏲 *tfa;* 10. 𓏭 𓎟 *ant;* 11.

𓅭𓄿𓏏𓏭 ⤳ *sat;* 12. 𓆭𓏭𓎺 *neter aft;* 13. 𓎟𓂝𓏤 *rasr;*

14. 𓆓𓂝𓏤 *naus;* 15. 𓉻𓏭𓈖𓏥𓊹 *pessen kaf;* 16. 𓈖𓏲𓏏

m-tef; 17. 𓏏𓂝𓏭 *am-b ru;* 18. 𓈖𓏭� *m-ṭa-t;* 19. 𓃭𓂻 *hu*]

*C. W. Goodwin, "Miscellaneous Notes," *ZÄS* 12 (1874) 37-39.

[1. 𓏭𓂝𓄿 *nenau (or nau)* the Ostrich; 2. 𓏤; 3. Dual number ex-

pressed by ⑊ or ⑊ or 𓈖; 4. 𓏴𓅂𓏤 *set-em-ra*]

*D. H. Haigh, "𓏤𓅆𓏤 𓏭𓏭𓏭𓏪, 𓊖𓈖 𓏭𓏭, 𓏭𓅆𓏛𓏭 𓏭𓏭,"
ZÄS 13 (1875) 29-32, 60-64.

C. W. Goodwin, "Miscellanea," *ZÄS* 14 (1876) 101-106. [1. 𓏭𓂝𓊖;

2. 𓏭⑊ 𓏭; 3. 𓅨𓂝𓏭𓏏 *mārṭ;* 4. 𓉐�ª𓍯𓏫 *ás-t ári;* 5.

𓏭𓎺𓏤 *áss;* 6. 𓈖𓂝𓏭 *em-ar-tat* (or *em-rā*)]

S. Birch, "Varia," *ZÄS* 15 (1877) 31-34. [⟨hieroglyphs⟩ *kas-met;* ⟨hieroglyphs⟩

θášeps or *θáás;* ⟨hieroglyphs⟩ *qann;* ⟨hieroglyphs⟩ *uía;* ⟨hieroglyphs⟩ *bai árq;* ⟨hieroglyphs⟩

χeri; ⟨hieroglyphs⟩ *sšep;* ⟨hieroglyphs⟩ *seχam;* ⟨hieroglyphs⟩ = *per er χeru;* ⟨hieroglyphs⟩; ⟨hieroglyphs⟩;

⟨hieroglyphs⟩; ⟨hieroglyphs⟩; Three cartouches]

*P. le Page Renouf, "Miscellanea VI," *ZÄS* 15 (1877) 97-106. [Phonetic reading of: 1) ⟨hieroglyphs⟩, 2) ⟨hieroglyphs⟩ 3) of ⟨hieroglyphs⟩; 4) Egyptian names of wheat and corn-land; 5) supposed goddesss of Amenti; 6) phonetic reading of ⟨hieroglyphs⟩, 7) the forms ⟨hieroglyphs⟩, ⟨hieroglyphs⟩, ⟨hieroglyphs⟩ etc.; 8) phonetic values of the signs in ⟨hieroglyphs⟩ Osiris; 9) meaning of ⟨hieroglyphs⟩; 10) ⟨hieroglyphs⟩]

†P. le Page Renouf, "The Name (1) of the Ithyphallic Horus ⟨hieroglyph⟩, and (2) of the Heliopolitan Nome ⟨hieroglyphs⟩ ," *SBAP* 8 (1885-86) 246-253.

W. Max Muller, "On a Hieroglyphic Sign," *SBAP* 18 (1896) 187-191. [1. The value of ⟨hieroglyphs⟩ "AU" of ⟨hieroglyph⟩ . 2. The alleged old value of "FU"; 3. The common Ptolemaic use of ⟨hieroglyph⟩ "AU"; 4. The late pronunciation of "FAU," or "FU"]

Percy E. Newberry, "Extracts from my Notebooks (II)," *SBAP* 22 (1900) 59-66. [12. The Hieroglyphics ⟷ and ⣿, p. 65]

Percy E. Newberry, "Extracts from my Notebooks (III)," *SBAP* 22 (1900) 152-154. [20. Notes on Some Hieroglyphic Signs: (a) ⟡ *ááḥ;* (b) ⊜ <u>kh</u> and ⑪ *sep;* (c) ⚖]

†Fr. W. v. Bissing, "Notes," *SBAP* 22 (1900) 167-168. [⟚; ⟡; ⟡]

Arthur E. Weigall, "Egyptian Notes. The Sacerdotal Title Gemât," *SBAP* 23 (1901) 10-11. [Variations of ⚘]

James Henry Breasted, "Varia. II.—Three Obscure Phrases," *SBAP* 23 (1901) 237-243. [1. ⟿ ⟰ ⟐ ⟐ *arn[á] m kt ábá;* 2. ⟐ ; 3. ⟐ ⟛ *ua-r*]

*Henry Proctor, "Egyptian Hieroglyphics and Alphabetic Origins," *AAOJ* 34 (1912) 293-294.

Percy E. Newberry, "The ⟿ ⟡ of Methen = the ⟿ of the Nome Lists," *ZÄS* 50 (1912) 124.

W. M. F[linders] Petrie, "The Queenly Title, XXIInd Dynasty," *AEE* 3 (1916) 70.

*[W. M.] Flinders Petrie, "The Palace Titles," *AEE* 9 (1924) 109-122.

*[W. M.] Flinders Petrie, "The Cultivators and Their Land," *AEE* 10 (1925) 105-110.

*G. W. B. Huntingford, "On the Connection Between Egypt and the Masai-Nandi Group of East Africa," *AEE* 11 (1926) 10-11.

[W. M.] Flinders Petrie, "Supplies and Defence[sic]*," *AEE* 11 (1926) 15-23.

*Warren R. Dawson, "Three Anatomical Terms," *ZÄS* 62 (1927) 20-23. [I. 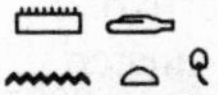 *mnd.t,* "Cheeks"; II.  *wdd,* "gall, gall-bladder"; III. 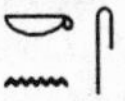 *kns,* "pubes, hypogastric region"]

Alan H. Gardiner, "Additions to the New Hieroglyphic Fount (1928)," *JEA* 15 (1929) 95. [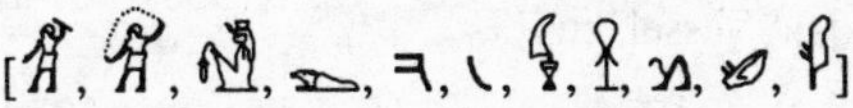]

Alan H. Gardiner, "Additions to the Hieroglyphic Fount (1931)," *JEA* 17 (1931) 245-247. [  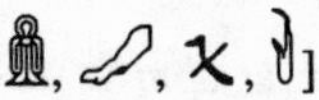]

*Battiscombe Gunn, "Notes on Egyptian Lexicography," *JEA* 27 (1941) 144-148. [I. The idiomatic expressions *ẖr tp, tp mꜣʿ*; 1. *Ḥr tp* > *ẖr ḏꜣḏꜣ* > ϩⲁⲧⲛ̄-, ϩⲁⲧⲱ⸗; 2. *Tp mꜣʿ*; II. *'Iṯ m* 'to take possession of' or the like]

Alan Rowe, "Some remarks on *A Collection of Hieroglyphs from the Monuments of Ḥor-Aḥa* forming Appendix IV of the Volume *Ḥor-Aḥa,* 1939, by W. B. Emery," *ASAE* 41 (1942) 342-345.

H. W. Fairman, "Notes on the alphabetic signs employed in the hieroglyphic inscriptions of the temple of Edfu," *ASAE* 43 (1943) 191-310.

H. W. Fairman, "Ptolemaic notes," *ASAE* 44 (1944) 263-278. [I. ; II. 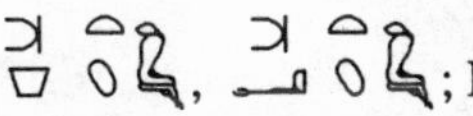; III. ]

H. W. Fairman, "An Introduction to the Study of Ptolemaic Signs and their Values," *BIFAO* 43 (1945) 51-138.

E. Jelínková-Reymond, "Some Notes on the Reading of the Group 𝕌𝕌 ,"
JEA 39 (1953) 80-83.

Th. O. Lambdin, "Egyptian Words in Tell El Amarna Letter No. 14," *Or,
N.S.*, 22 (1953) 362-369. [*imȝw*, tent; *imȝw*, red material; *ikn*,
amphora; *itḫ*, to draw; *'ȝ*, large; *'fḏ.t*, box, chest; *'nḫ*, vessel; *'š*, vessel;
wḏ, vessel; *wdḥw*, offering table; *pȝq.t*, fine linen; *mhn*, wooden chest;
mhn, vessel; *mḏq.t*, vessel; *nmš.t*, vessel; *rhd.t*, kettle; *hbn.t*, vessel;
hnw, vessel; *hn(n)w*, box; *ḫnm.t*, vessel; *š'ḥ'*, upright; *šwbt*, vessel;
šrd, carved wood; *qby*, vessel; *kȝ*, genius, double; *kȝ – ḫr – kȝ;* vessel;
kȝš, metal vessel; **kuba*, vessel; *ṭȝ.t*, vessel; *ṭ(ȝ)b – n – kȝ*, vessel; *dš*,
vessel; *ḏȝḏȝw*, vessel, cup]

C. de Wit, "Some values of Ptolemaic signs," *BIFAO* 55 (1955) 111-121.

Hans Goedicke, "Juridical Expressions of the Old Kingdom," *JNES* 15
(1956) 27-32. [I. *'Iri pḥw;* II. *š'*]

*A. M. Bakir, "The groups with ⸚ and ⌂⸗ in the light of the Cairo
Calendar," *ASAE* 56 (1959) 203-206.

Henry G. Fischer, "A supplement to Janssen's list of dogs' names," *JEA* 47
(1961) 152-153.

*W[illiam] A. Ward, "Some Egypto-Semitic Roots," *Or, N.S.*, 31 (1962)
397-412. [I. Egyptian *təḥ* = Semitic *dlḫ;* II. Egyptian *tr* = Semitic
d(w)r; III. Egyptian *qri(qəi)* = Semitic *qry;* IV. Egyptian *tm* = Semitic
dm(m); V. Egyptian *jř* = Semitic *šr;* VI. Egyptian *sči* = Semitic *nsk;*
VII. Egyptian *sti* = Semitic *št;* VIII. Egyptian *šd* = Semitic *šd;* IX.
Egyptian *wbə* = Semitic *wbl;* X. Egyptian *išf/nšf* = Semitic **fṭ;* XI.
Egyptian *ĵ'* = Semitic **z'*]

*Henry G. Fischer, "Varia Aegyptiaca," *JARCE* 2 (1963) 17-51. [9. Some

Occurrences of the Emblem of U.E. Nome 2, pp. 47-49.] [𝕌𝕌 ⸗ et al]

H. W. Fairman, "Some unrecorded Ptolemaic words," *ZÄS* 91 (1964) 4-11.

[I. ⊹⌐⌐ *imi-st-'* 'heart'; II. ⌐⌐ *itnt* (*idnt*) 'perch, resting

place'; III. ⌐⌐ *'t-ist* 'law- court'; IV. ⌐ o ı ı ı *wnf*

'beer'; V. ⌐ *bty* 'lips'; VI. ⌐ \\ ı ı ı *wnf* 'beer'; VII. ⌐

nfrt 'throat, gullet'; VIII. ⌐ o ı ı ı *nhfkw* 'pots for milk'; IX.

⌐ ı ⌐ o 'night, evening']

William A. Ward, "Notes on Some Egypto-Semitic Roots," *ZÄS* 95 (1968-
69) 65-72. [I. Egyptian *wjˁ* = Semitic *bṣˁ;* II. Egyptian *bn* = Semitic
bny; III. Egyptian *ˁwn* = Semitic *ˁwl;* IV. Egyptian *pts* = Semitic *pṭs;*
V. Egyptian *pds* = Semitic *pṭs;* VI. Egyptian *jˁ* = Semitic *ˁz(z);* VII. A
Term for Relatives by Marriage: Egyptian *sm* = Semitic *ḥm;* VIII.
Egyptian **df,* "to drip, overflow" = Semitic *ṭp,* "to drip, overflow"]

§493 *3.3.3.1.2.1 Sign List - (Gardiner's Schema)*

A - Man and his Occupations

William F. Edgerton, " as Dependent Pronoun," *AJSL* 50 (1933-34) 66.

F. Ll. Griffith, "On the Reading of ," *SBAP* 20 (1898) 299.

F. Ll. Griffith, "Notes on Hieroglyphics. The Head. The Papyrus Roll. The Soldier," *SBAP* 21 (1899) 269-272. [, 270-272]

*Alan H. Gardiner, "The Egyptian word for 'herdsman' &c.," *ZÄS* 42 (1905) 116-123. [ ]

B - Woman and her Occupations

[No Entries]

C - Anthropomorphic Deities

[No Entries]

D - Parts of the Human Body

P. le Page Renouf, "Note on the Values of the Sign ," *SBAP* 10 (1887-88) 571-578.

*F. Ll. Griffith, "Notes on Hieroglyphics. The Head. The Papyrus Roll. The Soldier," *SBAP* 21 (1899) 269-272. [ ]

P. le Page Renouf, "Note by Mr. Renouf on No. 24," *SBAP* 13 (1890-91) 120. [ ]

P. le Page Renouf, "Remarks," *SBAP* 13 (1890-91) 281-282. *[Remarks on 'Les textes Hieroglyphiques sont des Transcriptions des hieratiques']*

[𓏶]

Alan [H.] Gardiner, "The Reading of the Geographical Term 𓈖𓏤," *JEA* 43 (1957) 6-9.

†P. le Page Renouf, "The Meaning of the Word *Hotep*," *SBAP* 3 (1880-81)

117-121. [𓊵𓏤]

*James H. Breasted, "Varia. I.—Supplementary," *SBAP* 23 (1901) 236-237.

[𓊵𓈖]

Hans Goedicke, "*Ḥry-'* a word for infant," *JEA* 47 (1961) 154. [𓊵𓈖𓃒

and 𓊵𓈖𓃒]

*L[udwig] Keimer, " 𓊵𓏤𓃒𓈖 𓏥 'Falcon-face'," *AEE* 14 (1929) 47-48.

*C. W. Goodwin, "On the symbolic Eye, Uta," *ZÄS* 10 (1872) 124. [𓂀]

Henry G. Fischer, "An Old Kingdom Monogram 𓂀," *ZÄS* 93 (1966) 56-69.

†P. le Page Renouf, "On the true sense of an important Egyptian Word (𓂓, *Ka*)," *SBAP* 1 (1878-79) 26-27; 6 (1878-79) 494-508. [Remarks by A. Lowy and W. F Birch, *SBAP* 1 (1878-79) p. 27]

Samuel A. B. Mercer, "The *Ka* in the Pyramid Texts," *ArOr* 20 (1952) 194-196.

P. le Page Renouf, "The Egyptian word for Battle, 𓃀𓎡," *SBAP* 6 (1883-84) 229-231.

P. le Page Renouf, "The Egyptian Silurus Fish and its functions in Hiero-

glyphics. The true Phonetic Value of the Sign 𓃀𓎡, ideographic of Strife and War, and its homophones," *SBAP* 7 (1884-85) 100-108.

*A. M. Bakir, "The groups with 𓏙 and 𓊌 in the light of the Cairo Calendar," *ASAE* 56 (1959) 203-206.

*C. W. Goodwin, "On the word 𓃀𓎡𓅓𓏤," *ZÄS* 10 (1872) 30-31.

P. le Page Renouf, "Note on the Silurus Fish 𓃀𓎡𓅓𓄿 *āba*, and the Hieroglyphic Sign of Battle 𓃀𓎡," *SBAP* 9 (1886-87) 313-317.

*P. le Page Renouf, "The Negative Particle 𓂝," *SBAP* 6 (1883-84) 95-101.

Battiscombe Gunn, "A Negative Word in Old Egyptian," *JEA* 34 (1948) 27-30. [𓂝𓏭]

Aylward M. Blackman, "The Infinitive Form *sḏm.t-f* with Preceding 𓂝

and 𓈖 ," *ZÄS* 49 (1911) 103-105.

T. Eric Peet, "Can 𓈖 be used to negative *śḏmtf* ?" *ZÄS* 52 (1914) 109-111.

*Alan H. Gardiner, "(1) ⌒\\ and ⌒\\ . (2) The demonstrative ⌍⌍⌍ , and its derivatives," *SBAP* 22 (1900) 321-325.

Alan H. Gardiner, "The Egyptian Word for 'Dragoman'," *SBAP* 37 (1915) 117-125. [⌑]

T. Eric Peet, "A Further Note on the Egyptian Word for 'Dragoman'," *SBAP* 37 (1915) 224. [⌑]

*Alan H. Gardiner, "Postscripta," *SBAP* 39 (1917) 113-140. [1. The Egyptian word for 'dragoman', pp. 133-134. (⌑)]

*C. W. Goodwin, "Interrogative particle ⳬ ⋀ ," *ZÄS* 6 (1868) 6-7.

*T. W. Thacker, "On the Structure of the Expressions denoting Existence and Non-existence in Middle Egyptian," *JEA* 35 (1949) 31-37. [I. ⳾⳾ ⌒ ⌍⌍⌍ and ⌍⌍⌍ ⌍⌍⌍; II. ⌒ ⌍⌍⌍ and ⌍⌍⌍]

*G. H. Tomkins, "On the name ⌒⌒ ⳾ ⌂ ," *RTR* 10 (1888) 97-98.

R. E. Walker, "The determinative of *psḏ* 'back'," *JEA* 50 (1964) 177. [⌘]

E - Mammals

Alan H. Gardiner, "The word [hieroglyphs]," *ZÄS* 41 (1904) 130-135.

Alan [H.] Gardiner, "A word for 'representative', 'substitute', or the like," *JEA* 37 (1951) 111. [[hieroglyphs]]

John Ruffle, "A new meaning of the word [hieroglyphs]," *JEA* 50 (1964) 177-178.

F - Parts of Mammals

*Aylward M. Blackman, "On the Name of an Unguent used for Ceremonial Purposes," *JEA* 6 (1920) 58-60. [[hieroglyphs]]

*†P. le Page Renouf, "The Egyptian god [hieroglyphs] Apuat," *SBAP* 8 (1885-86) 157-158.

R. O. Faulkner, "*Wpwtyw* 'bystanders'," *JEA* 45 (1959) 102. [[hieroglyphs]]

Alan H. Gardiner, "A hitherto unnoticed negative in Middle Egyptian," *RTR* 40 (1923) 79-82. [[hieroglyphs]]

W. S. Blackman and A. M. Blackman, "An Ancient Egyptian Symbol as a Modern Egyptian Amulet," *AIPHOS* 3 (1935) 91-95. [[hieroglyphs]]

T. Eric Peet, "An unrecognised meaning of the verb [hieroglyphs]," *JEA* 1 (1914) 209-211.

Hans Goedicke, "The phonetic value of the sign ∠⅀ ," *JEA* 51 (1965) 200-202.

Warren R. Dawson, "The Writing of the Name *Ḥike'*," *JEA* 24 (1938) 128.

[ᛏ̄]

Warren R. Dawson, "The Writing of the Name *Ḥike'*. Second Note," *JEA*

31 (1945) 105. [ᛏ̄]

Alan [H.] Gardiner, "A Grim Metaphor," *JEA* 37 (1951) 29-31. [⛎]

W. Vycichl, "The hieroglyph ♎ ," *JEA* 39 (1953) 112-113.

*C. W. Goodwin, "On the ⏰ šet, and Egyptian weight," *ZÄS* 11 (1873) 16-17.

G - Birds

Ludwig Keimer, "A Note on Two Hieroglyphs 🦅 and 🦅 ," *AJSL* 43 (1926-27) 226-231.

Hans Goedicke, "The Title ⇌⌷ in the Old Kingdom," *JEA* 46 (1960) 60-64.

*O. D. Berlev, "'Falcon in Boat', a Hieroglyph and a God,"*VDI* (1969) #1,

30. [🦅]

Percy E. Newberry, "The Horus-title 🦅 of the Kings of Egypt," *SBAP* 26 (1904) 295-299.

P. le Page Renouf, "The Name of 🦅, the Blind Horus," *SBAP* 8 (1885-86) 155-157.

G. D. Hornblower, "The 'Golden Horus' Title," *JEA* 24 (1938) 129. [🦅]

*J. Gwyn Griffiths, "Remarks on the Horian elements in the Royal Titulary," *ASAE* 56 (1959) 63-86. [III. The 🦅 Title, pp. 64-86]

M[argaret] A. Murray, "Pharaoh's Third Title," *AEE* 18 (1933) 27-28. *[The Golden Hawk]* [🦅]

C. W. Goodwin, "Adversaria," *ZÄS* 6 (1868) 39. [1. The phonetic character 🦅 mak]

P. le Page Renouf, "The Royal Titles 🦅 ," *SBAP* 16 (1893-94) 53.

Nina M. Davies, "The Hieroglyph for the Fledgling," *JEA* 27 (1941) 133-134. [🦅]

C. W. Goodwin, "The vulture used for the word 'man'," *ZÄS* 6 (1868) 57-58. [🦅]

*Arthur E. P. Weigall, "Miscellaneous notes," *ASAE* 11 (1911) 170-176. [7. A composite hieroglyph 🦅, p. 172]

Battiscombe Gunn, "A note on the verb *wrš*," *RTR* 39 (1920-21) 108-109.

[🦅]

H - Parts of Birds

[No Entries]

I - Amphibious Animals, Reptiles, etc.

A. J. Arkell, "The Signs ⌐ and ☒," *JEA* 19 (1933) 175-176.

*M[argaret] A. Murray, "The Cerastes in Royal Names," *AEE* 14 (1929) 18-21. [☒]

M[agaret] A. Murray, "The Serpent Hieroglyph," *JEA* 34 (1948) 117-118. [☒]

K - Fishes and parts of Fishes

†P. le Page Renouf, "On the Value of the Hieroglyphic Sign ☒ &c., &c.," *SBAP* 5 (1882-83) 13-18.

R. Engelbach, "Notes on the Fish of Mendes," *ASAE* 24 (1924) 161-168. [☒]

L - Invertebrata and Lesser Animals

P. le Page Renouf, "Notes. 3. ☒ ⌒ not the king of Upper Egypt, and not to be read *bit* or *bat*," *SBAP* 14 (1887-88) 23-25.

P. le Page Renouf, "A Second Note on the Royal Title ☒ ," *SBAP* 14 (1891-92) 396-402.

Percy E. Newberry, "Note. the àåf 'flies'," *SBAP* 22 (1900) 166-167. [☒]

M - Trees and Plants

Percy E. Newberry, "The hieroglyphs 〔 and 〕 ," *JEA* 34 (1948) 119.

Percy E. Newberry, "The Word 〔〔〕 *Kh* a, a '*diwan*' or 'office',"
SBAP 22 (1900) 99-105.

P. le Page Renouf, "The Egyptian Prepositions 〔 and 〔〔〕," *SBAP* 6
(1883-84) 93-95.

A[lan] H. Gardiner, "On the Meaning of the Preposition 〔〕," *SBAP* 25
(1903) 334-336.

*Aylward M. Blackman, "On the reading of 〔 as *ny-św .t*," *RTR* 38
(1917) 69. [Additional note by Alan H. Gardiner, p. 70]

Alfred C. Bryant and F. W. Read, "On the Royal Titles 〔〕," *SBAP* 16
(1893-94) 225-257.

G. A. Wainwright, "The Formula 〔〔〕 in the light of mythology,"
SBAP 26 (1904) 101-104.

*Arthur E. P. Weigall, "Miscellaneous notes," *ASAE* 11 (1911) 170-176. [1.

The Title 〔〕 in the Middle Kingdom, p. 170]

N - Sky, Earth, Water

John Bennett, "Notes on the 'aten'," *JEA* 51 (1965) 207-209. [〔〕]

*Percy E. Newberry, "*Ta Ṭeḥenu*—'Olive Land'," *AEE* 2 (1915) 97-102.

[⚊ ⟩ ☖]

J[aroslav] Černý, "A Possible Egyptian word for 'astronomer'," *JEA* 49

(1963) 173. [✶ 𓏏𓏏 𓇼 𓇼𓈖𓈖]

P. J. de Horrack, "On the Phonetic Value of the sign ⚌ ," *SBAP* 16 (1893-94) 142-144.

O-Buildings, Parts of Buildings, etc.

Battiscombe Gunn, "An Egyptian expression for 'home'," *JEA* 36 (1950)

111-112. [▭ 𓏺 𓏭𓏭𓏭]

*James Henry Breasted, "A City of Inkhenaton in Nubia," *ZÄS* 40 (1902-03)

106-113. [𓉐 𓃀 𓅢 𓏭 𓊖 or 𓉐 𓃀 𓅢 𓏏]

*Alexander Badawy, "About Three Egyptian Hieroglyphs," *JNES* 15 (1956)

175-179. [The Sign 𓉐 𓉐 , pp. 175-176]

G. Willoughby Fraser, "Hat-Nub 𓊹 𓃀 𓈗 ," *SBAP* 16 (1893-94) 73-82.

Hans Goedicke, "The pronunciation of ▭ in the Middle Kingdom," *ZÄS* 81 (1956) 62.

*G. Legge, "Is the 𓊖 𓉐 𓇼 a heliacal rising," *RTR* 31 (1908) 106-112.

Alan H. Gardiner, "The term ⌐⌐ ~~Λ *pr-n-stȝ* in Pap. Mayer A.," *ZÄS* 59 (1924) 72.

Battiscombe Gunn, "An Egyptian expression for 'home'," *JEA* 36 (1950) 111-112. [⌐ꟼ ~~ ꟼꟼꟼ]

Alan H. Gardiner, "The Mansion of Life and the Master of the King's Largess," *JEA* 24 (1938) 33-91.[⌸ ⌐ , var. ⌸]

Alan H. Gardiner, "The House of Life," *JEA* 24 (1938) 157-179. [⌐ ♀ ⌐]

P - Ships and Parts of Ships

P. le Page Renouf, "On the sign ☙ and the words in which it occurs," *ZÄS* 10 (1872) 91-96. [Addenda et Corrigenda, *ZÄS* 12 (1874) 105]

*Jaroslav Černý, "Philological and etymological notes," *ASAE* 51 (1951) 441-446. [III. 7. The Cryptogram of Mentemḥēt (⍦), 442-443]

*Percy E. Newberry, "Extracts from my Notebooks (III)," *SBAP* 22 (1900) 142-154. [16. The ⍦⍦⍦ *Nefu*, 'Root of the *Cyperus esculentus*, L.', pp. 146-148]

Q - Domestic and Funerary Furniture

G. Lefebvre, "'A Pure Place'," *JEA* 25 (1939) 219. [⌐⌐⌐ *št wꜥbt*]

R - Temple Furniture and Sacred Emblems

E. A. Wallis Budge, "Neter. The Egyptian Word for God by E. A. Wallis Budge," *Monist* 13 (1902-03) 481-492. [⌐]

F. Legge, "The Sign ⌐ (Nutir or Neter)," *SBAP* 21 (1899) 310-311.

A. J. Arkell, "The Signs ⌐ and ⌐," *JEA* 19 (1933) 175-176.

[Samuel A. B. Mercer], "Queries," *EgR* 2 (1934) 23. [The Sign ⌐]

Alan H. Gardiner, "'The Reading of the Egyptian word for Necropolis'," *JEA* 24 (1938) 244-245. [⌐]

*Hans Goedicke, "A Deification of a Private Person in the Old Kingdom," *JEA* 41 (1955) 31-33. [⌐]

S - Crowns, Dress, Staves, etc.

Gustave Jéquier, "The Sign ⌐ ," *SBAP* 37 (1915) 246-252.

Gustave Jéquier, "The Most Ancient Representation of the Sign ⌐ ," *SBAP* 39 (1917) 87-88.

Alan H. Gardiner, "The Reading of ⌐ ...," *ZÄS* 41 (1904) 73-76.

R. Engelbach, "The Sign ⌐ *st*," *ASAE* 29 (1929) 33-39.

*P. le Page Renouf, "On the Metal ⌐ ," *ZÄS* 11 (1873) 119-123. [Addenda, *ZÄS* 12 (1874) p. 105]

R - Temple Furniture and Sacred Emblems

E. A. Wallis Budge, "Neter. The Egyptian Word for God by E. A. Wallis Budge," *Monist* 13 (1902-03) 481-492. [⌐]

F. Legge, "The Sign ⌐ (Nutir or Neter)," *SBAP* 21 (1899) 310-311.

A. J. Arkell, "The Signs ⌐ and ⌐," *JEA* 19 (1933) 175-176.

[Samuel A. B. Mercer], "Queries," *EgR* 2 (1934) 23. [The Sign ⌐]

Alan H. Gardiner, "'The Reading of the Egyptian word for Necropolis'," *JEA* 24 (1938) 244-245. [⌐]

*Hans Goedicke, "A Deification of a Private Person in the Old Kingdom," *JEA* 41 (1955) 31-33. [ ]

S - Crowns, Dress, Staves, etc.

Gustave Jéquier, "The Sign ⌒," *SBAP* 37 (1915) 246-252.

Gustave Jéquier, "The Most Ancient Representation of the Sign ♀," *SBAP* 39 (1917) 87-88.

Alan H. Gardiner, "The Reading of ⌐...," *ZÄS* 41 (1904) 73-76.

R. Engelbach, "The Sign ⌐ *st*," *ASAE* 29 (1929) 33-39.

*P. le Page Renouf, "On the Metal ⌐ °," *ZÄS* 11 (1873) 119-123. [Addenda, *ZÄS* 12 (1874) p. 105]

T - Warfare, Hunting, Butchery

Percy E. Newberry, "Note on the Hieroglyph ⌠," *ZÄS* 73 (1937) 139.

Percy E. Newberry, "Extracts from My Notebooks (II).," *SBAP* 22 (1900) 59-66. [13. The sign ⯑ , pp. 65-66]

W. M. Flinders Petrie, "The Title ⬦ ," *AAA* 1 (1908) 96.

U - Agriculture, Crafts, and Professions

R. O. Faulkner, "*Mȝst* 'knee'," *JEA* 45 (1959) 104. [⯑⯑⌐⌠]

*John Bennett, "A new interpretation of B.M. stela 1203," *JEA* 48 (1962) 158-159. [⌐ ⯑]

*Arthur E. P. Weigall, "Miscellaneous notes," *ASAE* 11 (1911) 170-176. [13. The Hieroglyph ⯑, p. 176]

C. W. Goodwin, "On the word [⯑ ı ı ı ı] *Ubrau*," *ZÄS* 6 (1868) 89-91.

Alan H. Gardiner, "Late writings of ⯑⯑⌐ 'magistrates'," *ZÄS* 73 (1937) 74.

Alan [H.] Gardiner, "The hieroglyph ⯑ with the value *šps*," *JEA* 37 (1951) 110.

*Alan H. Gardiner, "The Word *ḥm* in 'His Majesty' and the like," *JEA* 29 (1943) 79. [⯑]

V - Rope, Fibre, Baskets, Bags, etc.

Paul C. Smither, "The Transcription of the w3ḫ y-hall in P. Westcar," *JEA* 25

　　(1939) 104. [🐦 🦅 ⸜ 𓉐 ⬓ but 𓉐 should be 🐦]

C. G. Seligmann and Margaret A. Murray, "Note on the 'Sa' Sign," *Man* 11

　　(1911) #73. [𓊿]

Alan H. Gardiner, "Two Hieroglyphic Signs and the Egyptian Words for

　　'Alabaster' and 'Linen', etc.," *BIFAO* 30 (1931) 161-183. [δ]

*Percy E. Newberry, "Extracts from My Notebooks (II).," *SBAP* 22 (1900)

　　59-66. [The Hieroglyphs ⸺ and ⸻ , p. 65]

Battiscombe Gunn, "The Expresssion for the Recipient in Middle Kingdom

　　Letters," *JEA* 31 (1945) 107-108. [𓏌]

L. B. Ellis, "The Meaning of ⬭╤⬭," *AEE* 7 (1922) 77.

Alan H. Gardiner, "Two Hieroglyphic Signs and the Egyptian Words for

　　'Alabaster' and 'Linen', etc.," *BIFAO* 30 (1931) 161-183. [δ]

W - Vessels of Stone and Earthenware

[No Entries]

X - Loaves and Cakes

†P. le Page Renouf, "An Egyptian Preposition," *SBAP* 5 (1882-83) 135.

　　[⬭🐍🇮🇮, *tui*]

*Arthur E. P. Weigall, "Upper-Egyptian Notes," *ASAE* 9 (1908) 105-112.

[14. Note on a Hieroglyph at Karnak, p. 111 (Ⓠ)]

Y - Writings, Games, Music

*F. Ll. Griffith, "Notes on Hieroglyphics. The Head. The Papyrus Roll.

The Soldier," *SBAP* 21 (1899) 269-272. [◁ as ▭]

*Henry G. Fischer, "Varia Aegyptiaca," *JARCE* 2 (1963) 17-51. [11. *Bȝ.t* in

the New Kingdom (𓏞𓆇), pp. 50-51]

*Battiscombe Gunn, "Interpreters of Dreams in Ancient Egypt," *JEA* 4

(1916) 252. [𓀀𓏤 *sḫ pr- ꜥnḫ*]

*J[aroslav] Černý, "An alternative etymology of the Bohairic word for

'interpreter of dreams'," *JEA* 50 (1964) 184. [𓀀𓏤 *s pr- ꜥnḫ*]

Z - Strokes, Signs derived from Hieratic, Geometrical Figures

J[aroslav] Černý, "Philological and Etymological notes (II)," *ASAE* 42 (1943) 341-350. [3. The sign ✠ in the inscriptions of the naos of El-'Arîsh, pp. 341-345]

AA - Unclassified

Aylward M. Blackman, "The Porridge Stirrer as an Egyptian Hieroglyph," *Man* 9 (1909) #96 [𓏤]

*Paul Chalioungui, "Some body swellings illustrated in two tombs of the ancient Empire and their possible Relation to âaâ," *ZÄS* 87 (1962) 108-114.

C. W. Goodwin, "On the word ⊂⊃ ⚏ mekrer," *ZÄS* 10 (1872) 107-108.

*C. W. Goodwin, "Notes by C. W. Goodwin," *ZÄS* 11 (1873) 12-15. [5.

⊂⊃ 𓎣 ℗ , p. 15]

Hans Goedicke, "On the Origin of the Hieroglyph ⊿ ," *JEA* 45 (1959) 99-100.

E. Iversen, "The Hieroglyph 𓎺 ," *JEA* 42 (1956) 54-57.

*J. Gwyn Griffiths, "The Meaning of 𓉔 𓈖 *nd* and *nd-ḥr*," *JEA* 37 (1951) 32-37.

*Alexander Badawy, "About Three Egyptian Hieroglyphs," *JNES* 15 (1956) 175-179. [The Sign ⌐ , pp. 176-177; The Sign 𓏺, pp. 177-178]

*Arthur E. P. Weigall, "Miscellaneous notes," *ASAE* 11 (1911) 170-176. [9.

An unusual hieroglyph, pp. 172-173 (𓄿 𓏺 ⌒)]

*H. W. Fairman, "Two Ptolemaic numerals," *JEA* 49 (1963) 179-180. [⚏]

P. le Page Renouf, "The Name of the Winged Solar Disk on Egyptian Monuments. 𓅨 ," *SBAP* 8 (1885-86) 143-144.

P. le Page Renouf, "The Bow in the Egyptian Sky (2)," *SBAP* 17 (1895) 37-38, 94. [𓏏]

§494 ***3.3.3.1.2.2 "Alphabetical" Listing***

3 𓄿

*S. Yeivin, "The Sign 𓄿 and the True Nature of the Early Alphabets," *ArOr* 4 (1932) 71-78.

*Henry G. Fischer, "Varia Aegyptiaca," *JARCE* 2 (1963) 17-51. [2. A Realistic Example of the Hieroglyph for *'I3w* "Old", pp. 23-24]

Jaroslav Černý, " *'Inn* in Late Egyptian," *JEA* 27 (1941) 106-112. [Postscript by Alan H. Gardiner, p. 112]

Sarah Israelit-Groll, " *'IW-F [ḤR] TM SḌM* in Late Egyptian," *JEA* 55 (1969) 89-92.

*Erik Iversen, "Some Remarks on the Terms ⸗𓄿𓄿𓂋 and 𓄿𓏺𓂋 ," *JEA* 33 (1947) 47-51.

R. O. Faulkner, "*3pd* = 'duck'," *JEA* 38 (1952) 128. [𓄿 ▫ 𓅬]

A[ylward] M. Blackman, "A Note on *Lebensmüder, 86-88*," *Or., N.S.,* 7 (1938) 67-68. [𓄿𓏤𓂝 𓏥]

i 𓇋

R. O. Faulkner, "The Verb *'I* 'To Say' and its Developments," *JEA* 21 (1935) 177-190. [𓇋 or 𓇋𓄿]

J. Gwyn Griffiths, "The Inverted Use of *'Imy*," *JEA* 28 (1942) 66-67.

Sarah [Israelit-]Groll, "*iw·sḍm.f* in Late Egyptian," *JNES* 28 (1969) 184-191.

Edward F. Wente, *"iwiw·f sdm* in Late Egyptian," *JNES* 20 (1961) 120-123.

Charles F. Nims, "The Demotic Group from 'Small Cattle'," *JEA* 22 (1936) 51-54. [(M. Eg. *i wt;* Late Eg. *i ꜣwt*]

P. le Page Renouf, "Notes. 2. ⌇ 𓅱 ⌇ ⌇ Plague or Frog?" *SBAP* 14 (1887-88) 21-23.

Hans Goedicke, "A sportive writing of the interrogative *im + m,*" *JEA* 47 (1961) 155. [⌇ ⌇ ⌇ 𓅱 ⌇]

*C. W. Goodwin, "On the name ⌇ ⌇ ⌇ Anepu," *ZÄS* 10 (1872) 58-59.

*P. le Page Renouf, "Reply to M. Golenischeff. ⌇ ⟍, ⌇ ⲓⲓⲓ never conjunction but always preposition like ⌇ 𓅱 ⟍⟍ , ⌇ 𓅱 ," *ZÄS* 15 (1877) 106-111.

*M[argaret] A. Murray, "The Sign Oăbt ⌇," *AEE* 14 (1929) 43-45.

*T. W. Thacker, "On the Structure of the Expressions denoting Existence and Non-existence in Middle Egyptian," *JEA* 35 (1949) 31-37.

[I. ⌇ 𓅱 ⌇ and ⌇ ⌇ ; II. ⌇ ⌇ and ⌇]

Alan H. Gardiner, "The Idiom *it̲ i̲n,*" *JEA* 24 (1938) 124-125.

y⌇ ⟍

[No Entries]

Jaroslav Černý, "Note on *ˁзwy-pt* 'Shrine'," *JEA* 34 (1948) 120. [▭▭ ▯ ◠▭]

*F. Ll. Griffith, "Notes on Hieroglyphics. The Head. The Papyrus Roll. The Soldier," *SBAP* 21 (1899) 269-272. [▱ as ▭]

F. W. Read, "The sense of the word ▭ 𓄿𓀀𓀀𓀀," *BIFAO* 13 (1917) 141-144.

Hans Goedicke, "An additional note on *ˁз* 'foreigner'," *JEA* 52 (1966) 172-173.

*Charles F. Nims, "Notes on University of Michigan Demotic Papyri from Philadelphia," *JEA* 24 (1938) 73-82. [5. The Title *ˁrbṭ* and the "Letters of Agreement", pp. 78-82]

*H. W. Fairman, "Two Ptolemaic Alphabetic Values of ▱ ," *JEA* 36 (1950) 110-111. [2. ▱ = ▭]

*Erik Iversen, "Some Remarks on the Terms ▭𓄿𓄿◦ and 𓄿𓏤◦ ," *JEA* 33 (1947) 47-51.

*Girgis Mattha, "The *ἀπροκοπεῖον* in demotic texts," *BIFAO* 45 (1947) 59-60. [*ˁypsy*]

*Ludwig Keimer, "A Semitic Loan-Word in Egyptian," *AJSL* 42 (1925-26) 205-208. [*ˁgзynз*]

w 𓅱

Klaus Baer, "Temporal *WNN* in Late Egyptian," *JEA* 51 (1965) 137-143.

Alan H. Gardiner, "A late-Egyptian idiom," *ZÄS* 47 (1910) 134-136.

[𓃀𓈖𓅓 𓈖 𓂝]

b 𓃀

*N. Shiah, "Some remarks on the *Bekhen* -stone," *ASAE* 41 (1942) 180-205.

[II. The Word 𓃀𓈖𓏤 𓊌 , pp. 197-199]

*Henry G. Fischer, "Varia Aegyptiaca," *JARCE* 2 (1963) 17-51. [11. *Bꜣt* in the New Kingdom, pp. 50-51]

P. le Page Renouf, "A Difficult Passage in the Pyramid Text of King Teta,"

　　SBAP 14 (1891-92) 108-111. [𓃀 𓏺 𓂝 𓏭]

William F. Edgerton, "On the Late Egyptian Negative 𓃀𓈖 ," *AJSL* 48 (1931-32) 27-44.

p𓊪

*Henry G. Fischer, "The Butcher *Pḥ-r-ntr*," *Or, N.S.*, 29 (1960) 168-190.

*H. W. Fairman, "Two Ptolemaic numerals," *JEA* 49 (1963) 179-180. [𓊖]

*Abd-el-Mohsen Bakir, "a New approach to Middle Egyptian demonstra-

　　tives," *JEA* 39 (1953) 111-112. [𓊪𓊖]

f

*H. W. Fairman, "Two Ptolemaic Alphabetic Values of ⟨glyph⟩ ," *JEA* 36 (1950) 110-111. [1. ⟨glyph⟩ = ⟨glyph⟩ ; 2. ⟨glyph⟩ = ⟨glyph⟩]

Percy E. Newberry, "*Fy* 'cerastes'," *JEA* 34 (1948) 118. [⟨glyphs⟩]

*H. R. Hall, "Does *FENKHU* = Φοίνιξ?" *RTR* 34 (1912) 35-36. [⟨glyphs⟩]

m

P. le Page Renouf, "The negative particle ⟨glyph⟩ ," *ZÄS* 15 (1877) 89-97.

G. D. Hornblower, "The Ancient Egyptian Word *Maneros*," *Man* 47 (1947) #156.

*Alan H. Gardiner, "The word ⟨glyph⟩ in the Inscription of ⟨glyph⟩: and a Note on Millingen Papyrus I, 3, 4," *SBAP* 24 (1902) 349-354.

Rudolf Anthes, "The Original Meaning of *Mȝ'ḤRW*," *JNES* 13 (1954) 21-50.

Rudolf Anthes, "Note Concerning the Great Corporation of Heliopolis," *JNES* 13 (1954) 191-192. [mȝ 'ḥrw]

*Henry Fr. Lutz, "A Sumerian loanword in Egyptian," *AfO* 5 (1928-29) 185-186. [Sumerian *unu* written: *(áb-ku)* = Egyptian *mniw*]

Alan R. Schulman, "*Mhr* and *Mškb,* Two Egyptian Military Titles of Semitic Origin," *ZÄS* 93 (1966) 123-132.

Alan H. Gardiner, "The Group 𓄓 'Overseer'," *ZÄS* 40 (1902-03) 142-144.

*W[illiam] F[oxwell] Albright, "Mitannian maryannu, 'chariot-warrior', and the Canaanite and Egyptian Equivalents," *AfO* 6 (1930-31) 217-221. [m-ra-ya-na]

Alan H. Gardiner, "The Egyptian for 'in other words', 'in short'," *JEA* 24 (1938) [𓄓𓄓𓄓𓄓]

Alan H. Gardiner, "The word *m ꜥḏ₃* and its various uses," *JEA* 26 (1940) 157-158. [𓄓𓄓𓄓 𓏥]

Roger T. O'Callaghan, "New Light on the *Maryanna* as 'Chariot- Warrior'," *JFK* 1 (1950-51) 309-324.

*Charles F. Nims, "Notes on University of Michigan Demotic Papyri from Philadelphia," *JEA* 24 (1938) 73-82. [4. The Use of *m-s₃* with the Meaning "pertaining to", p. 78]

Battiscombe Gunn, "*Ms ₃* 'except' in Middle Egyptian?" *JEA* 25 (1939) 218. [𓄓𓄓𓄓]

Alec N. Dakin, "*M-s₃* 'pestering'," *JEA* 27 (1941) 159.

*Thomas O. Lambdin, "Another Cuneiform Transcription of Egyptian *msḥ*, 'Crocodile'," *JNES* 12 (1953) 284-285. [𓄓𓄓𓄓]

R. O. Faulkner, "A Misconstrued Particle in the Pyramid Texts," *JEA* 16 (1930) 171-172. [𓄓𓏭𓏭]

Alan H. Gardiner, "The proposed new reading of the word 'Overseer'," *JEA* 41 (1955) 121-122. [𓄓𓂺𓂺𓄓𓄓]

*Henry G. Fischer, "*Biȝ* and the Deified Vizier *Mḥw*," *JARCE* 4 (1965) 49-53.

*G. Lefebvre, "A Note on Brit. Mus. 828 (Stela of Simontu)," *JEA* 25 (1939) 218. (Note by Battiscombe Gunn, pp. 218-219) [mḏḥ]

*Charles F. Nims, "Notes on University of Michigan Demotic Papyri from Philadelphia," *JEA* 24 (1938) 73-82. [3. The Independent Use of the Conjunctive *mtw=*, pp. 77-78]

*Abdel-Aziz Saleh, "Plural Sense and Cultural Aspects of the Ancient Egyptian *mdw-nṯr*," *BIFAO* 68 (1969) 15-38.

⌇ n

*F. Ll. Griffith, "The Millingen Papyrus (teaching of Amenemhet). With note on the compounds formed with substantived *n*," *ZÄS* 34 (1896) 35-51.

*Alan H. Gardiner, "(1) ⌒\\ and ⌒\\ . (2) The demonstrative ⌇ , and its derivatives," *SBAP* 22 (1900) 321-325.

*Abd-el-Mohsen Bakir, "*Nḥḥ* and *ḏt* reconsidered," *JEA* 39 (1953) 110-111.

*Alan H. Gardiner, "The Original of Coptic ⲛⲁⲩ 'see'," *JEA* 31 (1945) 113.[⌇ 𓆑 𓂀 𓂻]

Alan H. Gardiner, "An Unrecognized Egyptian Adverb," *SBAP* 40 (1918) 5-7. [𓈖𓈖]

Battiscombe Gunn, "A Summary Writing of the Adverb *nii* in Old Egyptian?" *JEA* 24 (1938) 128-129. [𓈖𓈖]

*Aylward M. Blackman, "Philological Notes," *JEA* 11 (1925) 210-215. [2.

A Note on the Word ⬮ 𓇋𓃀𓅱𓆛 *nḫ3w* in *Papyrus Westcar*, 5, 15 foll., pp. 212-213]

C. W. Goodwin, "On the word ⬳𓃀𓎺 ," *ZÄS* 10 (1872) 31-33.

*G. A. Wainwright, "Seshat's nš-shrine," *JEA* 25 (1939) 104. [⬓ & 𓏏𓊽𓏏]

J. Gwyn Griffiths, "The Relative *NTY* with Generic Reference," *JEA* 54 (1968) 60-66.

Alan H. Gardiner, "The supposed particle 𓂋 ," *ZÄS* 69 (1933) 70-71.

Alan H. Gardiner, "The particle 𓊃 𓃀 𓏤 ," *ZÄS* 43 (1906) 160.

[Margaret A. Murray], "The Origin of 𓎛𓏏 𓏮 ," *AEE* 9 (1924) 55.

*J. Gwyn Griffiths, "The Meaning of 𓏏 𓎺 *nḏ* and *nḏ-ḥr*," *JEA* 37 (1951) 32-37.

Hans Goedicke, "The Egyptian word for 'comb'," *JEA* 49 (1963) 173. [⬳𓏭]

Jac. J. Janssen, "Once more the Egyptian word for 'comb'," *JEA* 50 (1964), 178-179. [𓎻]

Alan H. Gardiner, "The Relative Adjective ⬳\\ ," *SBAP* 22 (1900) 37-42.

Henry George Tomkins, "Note on the Name ▫ 〰 ＼＼𓆑𓆑 𓃥 ﹏ ١ 𓃥,

Nepiriuriu, in the Karnak List of Northern Syria," *SBAP* 11 (1888-89) 78-79.

Richard A. Parker, "Another variant of *nṯr ꜥꜣ wr (n) š ꜣ ꜥ ḫpr*," *JEA* 42 (1956) 122.

⊂⊃ r

H. F. Lutz, "A Remark on Egyptian *r* 'part'," *JAOS* 40 (1920) 359.

Max W. Müller, "The false *r* in archaic Egyptian orthography," *RTR* 31 (1909) 182-201.

Hans Goedicke, "'80' as a sportive writing," *CdÉ* 40 (1965) 28-33.

⊂⊃∩∩∩∩
[⇔∩∩∩∩]

Battiscombe Gunn, "The Word 𓂝 𓏤𓃀 𓈖 𓂧," *ZÄS* 62 (1927) 83-85.

*A Poebel, "Sumerian Mu-an-na 'year' and Egyptian *Rnpt* 'year'," *AJSL* 49

(1932-33) 1-8. [⊂⊃ 𓈖𓏭 ⊙]

▫ h

*William A. Ward, "The Semitic Root *HWY* in Ugaritic and Derived Stems in Egyptian," *JNES* 28 (1969) 265-267.

Paul C. Smither, "A New Reading of *Lebensmüde,* 131-2," *JEA* 25 (1939)

220. [▫𓏭𓃀𓃟 not ▫𓏭𓃀𓃟]

Ernest S. Thomas, "Oracular Responses," *AEE* 6 (1921) 76-78.

[Hen ⌐ ⌐]

Charles F. Nims, "The Term *HP,* 'Law, Right,' in Demotic," *JNES* 7 (1948) 243-260.

*[J. P.] Lesley, "Ιακχος from [Hor-m] aχu, the Sphinx name of the Solar disc on the Horizon," *PAPS* 19 (1880-81) 110-111.

A. M. Blackman, "The Use of the Egyptian Word *ht* 'house' in the Sense of 'stanza'," *Or, N.S.,* 7 (1938) 64-66.

Paul C. Smither, "The Writing of *HTP-D' I-NSW* in the Middle and New Kingdom," *JEA* 25 (1939) 34-37.

ḥ

*P. le Page Renouf, "The Sunstroke in Egyptian," *SBAP* 12 (1889-90) 460-461. [ ]

*Alan H. Gardiner, "The Egyptian name of the Nile," *ZÄS* 45 (1908) 140-141. [*ḥꜥpr [sic]*]

Alan H. Gardiner, "The hieratic writing of the verb *ḥw* 'to strike'," *ZÄS* 44 (1907) [ꓹ]126-129.

Battiscombe Gunn, "The Egyptian for 'short'," *RTR* 39 (1920-21) 101-104.

[ ]

*Alan H. Gardiner, "The Word *ḥm* in 'His Majesty' and the like," *JEA* 29 (1943) 79. [ ]

Hans Goedicke, "*Ḥry-ḏbꜥ*, 'suckled calf'," *RÉg* 11 (1957) 159-161.

Henry George Fischer, "An Early Occurence of ḥm 'servant' in Regulations Referring to a Mortuary Estate,"*MDIÄA* 16 (1958) 131-137.

W[illiam] F[oxwell] Albright, "The etymology of Egyptian ḥmt 'woman'," *RTR* 40 (1923) 71-72.

C. W. Goodwin, "On the numeral ⌇⌇⌇⌇," *ZÄS* 9 (1871) 126-128.

†P. Le Page Renouf, "The Meaning of the Word *Hotep[sic]*," *SBAP* 3 (1880-81) 117. [ḥotep]

F. Ll. Griffith, "A specialized hieratic group for ḥotep," *ZÄS* 29 (1891) 54-56.

Henry G. Fischer, "An Occurrence of Ḥnn-nśwt 'Ehnasya' on Two Statuettes of the Late Old Kingdom," *JAOS* 81 (1961) 423-425.

*S. Yeivin, "Topographic and Ethnic Notes," *'Atiqot* 2 (1959) 155-164. [ḤQ3/N/ÌŚNNWŚ TYḤRŚ, pp. 164]

*Henry G. Fischer, "A First Dynasty Bowl Inscribed with the Group Ḥt," *CdÉ* 36 (1961) 19-22.

C. J. C. Bennett, "The Writing of *Htp-di-Nsw*," *JEA* 27 (1941) 157.

*Alan H. Gardiner, "Some Personifications. II," *SBAP* 38 (1916) 43-54, 83-95. [ḤU, "Authoritative Utterance"; *SAI'* "Understanding"; "To become ḤU"; Commentary; Sequence of the Fourteen *KAS* of RĒ' and the King]

ḫ ⊜

*Theodor Herzl Gaster, "An Egyptian Loan-Word at Ras Shamra," *AEE* 18 (1934) 21. [ḫptš]

*Frithiof Rundgren, "The Root šft in the Modern Ethiopic Language (Tigrē, Tigrina, and Amharic) and Old Egyptian ḫfty, Coptic šft," *OrS* 2 (1953) 19-25.

Theodor Herzl Gaster, "An Egyptian Loan-Word in a Tell-Amarna Letter," *AEE* 18 (1934) 21. [ḫa-ab-ši]

Hermann Ranke, "The Egyptian Pronunciation of the Royal Name 'Khefren' and its Cognates," *JAOS* 70 (1950) 65-68.

C. H. Goodwin, "A rebus for the word χesteb," *ZÄS* 6 (1868) 7. [━ ◎ ┛ ⌐ °]

*W. Spiegelberg, "Note on the Word *khetemy*, 'a Seal-maker'," *SBAP* 27 (1905) 287. [◎ Ω ⳼⳼]

━ ḫ

W. Max Müller, "A Semitic Loan-word in Egyptian," *SBAP* 16 (1893-94) 118-120. ≈ *ḫnp*]

Alan H. Gardiner, " ▭ 𓄿 𓂝 ○ = 'umbilical cord'," *ZÄS* 66 (1931) 71.

━ ⸢ s

†E. Towry Whyte, "Note," *SBAP* 22 (1900) 402. [⸢]

Klaus Baer, "The oath *sḏfꜣ-tryt* in Papyrus Lee, 1, 1," *JEA* 50 (1964) 179-180.

*Battiscombe Gunn, "A Special Use of the *śḏm.f* and *śḏm.n.f* Forms," *JEA* 35 (1949) 21-24.

*R. A. Parker, "The Function of the Imperative *śḏm.f* in Middle Egyptian," *RÉg* 10 (1955) 49-59.

*H. Jacob Polotsky, "The 'Emphatic' *śḏm.n.f*. Form," *RÉg* 11 (1957) 109-117.

*Charles F. Nims, "Notes on University of Michigan Demotic Papyri from Philadelphia," *JEA* 24 (1938) 73-82. [2. The *sš n s'nḫ* of Marriage Settlements, pp. 74-77]

*†J. Lieblein, "The 'Great Cackler'," *SBAP* 7 (1884-85) 99-100. *[seb]*

*H. W. Fairman, "Two Ptolemaic Alphabetic Values of ⟿ ," *JEA* 36 (1950) 110-111. [⟿ = 𓏲]

Margaret [A.] Murray, "On the Title 𓊪𓏏 𓂋𓏏 ," *AAA* 1 (1908) 23.

⟿ š

David Lorton, "A Note on the Expression *Šms-ib*," *JARCE* 8 (1969-70) 55-57.

George R. Hughes, "Are there Two Demotic Writings of *šw*?" *MDIÄA* 14 (1956) 80-88.

△ ḳ

R. O. Faulkner, "*Ḳni* = 'bundle'," *JEA* 37 (1951) 114. [△𓎛𓏏]

John D. Cooney, "On the Meaning of ○ 𓏤 ⟿ ," *ZÄS* 93 (1966) 43-47.

H. F. Lutz, "*Ḳû*, 'thread, cord' in Egyptian," *JAOS* 42 (1922) 209-210.

⌴ k

C. W. Goodwin, "On the word ⌴🦅⌴ ⌴ Kamen," *ZÄS* 11 (1873) 17-18.

*Aylward M. Blackman, "Philological Notes," *JEA* 11 (1925) 210-215. [1.

A Further Note on the Word ⌴🦅⌴ ⌴ ⌴⌴⌴, *ḳȝ-rȝ-šw,* in *Papyrus Lansing,* verso, 1, 9, pp. 210-212.]

*Alan H. Gardiner, *"Kjj-bm* 'foreigners'," *ZÄS* 43 (1906) 160.

[⌴⌴⌴⌴] *[sic]*

A. J. Arkell, *"Kūr,* the title of the king of Cush," *BIFAO* 55 (1955) 123-124.

⌴ g

Hans Goedicke, "An Old Kingdom word for 'door-socket'," *JEA* 51 (1965) 200. [⌴⌴⌴⌴⌴]

⌴ t

Mustafa El Amir, "Note on 't ḫyr t ' in boundaries of Ptolemaic houses at Thebes," *ASAE* 53 (1955) 135-138.

A[ylward] M. Blackman, "The Hieroglyph ⌴ a Jar Sealing," *Man* 11 (1911) #10.

Herbert Thompson, "Note on t ḫyr (.t) in Boundaries of Ptolemaic Conveyances of Land," *JEA* 23 (1937) 258.

⇒ ṭ

Paul Haupt, "The Etymology of Egypt. ṭsm, greyhound," *JAOS* 45 (1925) 318-320.

*H. F. Lutz, "A Loanword in Egyptian," *JAOS* 40 (1920) 71. [ṭaḳapu - Assy. zaqapu]

⇒ d

R. O. Faulkner, "*Dw, wdi, rdi,*" *JEA* 45 (1959) 102-103. [⇔, 🖐⇔, and

⟿ or ⟿ (var. 𓂁 or 𓂀)]

Hans Goedicke, "*Dbt* 'Work-bench'," *JARCE* 7 (1968) 128.

*Warren R. Dawson, "The Substance called *Didi* by the Ancient Egyptians," *JRAS* (1927) 497-503. *[Nubian Hæmatite?]*

*Percy E. Newberry, Extracts from my Notebooks (III).," *SBAP* 22 (1900) 142-154. [17. The ⇔🖐⌐ᔆ *ṭab arḳ* (?) 'string of dried figs,' in ancient lists of offerings, p. 148]

ᔆ d

M[argaret] A. Murray, "The Serpent Hieroglyph," *JEA* 34 (1948) 117-118.

[ᔆ]

Richard H. Pierce, "*Ḏnf,* A Problem in Demotic Lexicography," *JARCE* 4 (1965) 73-78.

*Abd-el-Mohsen Bakir, "*Nḥḥ* and *ḏt* reconsidered," *JEA* 39 (1953) 110-111.

P[ercy] E. Newberry, "The Elephant's Trunk called its *drt (ḏrt)* 'Hand'," *JEA* 30 (1944) 75.

§495 *3.3.3.1.2.3 Word Studies Keyed to English*

William F. Edgerton, "A-lk=k 'Cease'!" *ZÄS* 70 (1934) 123-124.

P. le Page Renouf, "'Conscience' in Egyptian texts," *SBAP* 9 (1886-87) 207-210.

*George R. Hughes, "The Sixth Day of the Lunar Month and the Demotic Word for 'Cult Guild'," *MDIÄA* 16 (1958) 147-160.

*Labib Habachi, "God's fathers and the role they played in the history of the first intermediate period," *ASAE* 55 (1958) 167-190. *[God's father]*

*Battiscombe Gunn, "Miszellen. The writings of the word for 'grapes'," *ZÄS* 59 (1924) 71-72.

S[amuel] Birch, "On Formulas relating to the heart," *ZÄS* 4 (1866) 89-92; 5 (1867) 16-17, 54-56; 8 (1870) 30-34, 46-48, 73-81.

Alan H. Gardiner, "The Egyptian for 'in other words', 'in short'," *JEA* 24 (1938) 243-244.

Eric Uphill, "The Nine Bows," *JEOL* #19 (1965-66) 393-420.

Alan [H.] Gardiner, "The proposed new reading of the word for 'Overseer'," *JEA* 41 (1955) 121-122.

Walter Federn, "'...As does a potter's wheel'," *ZÄS* 93 (1966) 55-56.

Battiscombe Gunn, "'To have recourse to' in Egyptian," *RTR* 39 (1920-21)

105-107. [ ]

Alan [H.] Gardiner, "The Reading of the Word for Regnal Year," *JNES* 8 (1949) 165-171.

A. Leo Oppenheim, "Assyriological Gleanings IV[sic]*," *BASOR* #107 (1947) 7-11. [The Shadow of the King] *[Should be part V]*

Alan H. Gardiner, "'To wait for' in Egyptian," *ZÄS* 49 (1911) 100-102.

Alan H. Gardiner, "'To await' in Middle Egyptian," *JEA* 43 (1957) 112-113.

William F. Edgerton, "'Year' in Egyptian," *AJSL* 50 (1933-34) 66.

*W[illiam] F[oxwell] Albright, "The Words for 'Year' in Egyptian and Sumerian," *AJSL* 51 (1934-35) 126-127.

N. Shiah, "A Chinese Parallel to an Egyptian Idiom," *JEA* 24 (1938) 127-128. [*P. Chester Beatty* I, 3, 8] [*Youth*]

§496 3.3.3.1.2.4 Egyptian Grammar

R. S. Poole, "The Linguistic Affinities of the Ancient Egyptian Language," *JRAS* (1863) 313-322.

†[Pliny E.] Chase, "Short Egyptian—English Vocabulary," *PAPS* 10 (1865-68) 69-94.

C. W. Goodwin, "On the interchange of the letters ﹀﹀ and ⌒ in Egyptian," *ZÄS* 5 (1867) 85-88.

*C. W. Goodwin, "Notes on Egyptian Numerals," *ZÄS* 5 (1867) 94-95, 98-101; 6 (1868) 106-108.

*C. W. Goodwin, "Interrogative particle 𓊃𓏭 ," *ZÄS* 6 (1868) 6-7.

S[amuel] Birch, "Egyptian expressions of Value," *ZÄS* 6 (1868) 37-39.

P. le Page Renouf, "Assimilation of letter," *ZÄS* 10 (1872) 25-27.

*P. le Page Renouf, "Miscellanea V," *ZÄS* 10 (1872) 72-79. [1. ｜ ｜ ｜ merely ideographic; 2. Coptic feminine form with ｓ; and ＼＼; 3. 𓏴𓏤𓂀 ; 4. 𓃀 transcribed as *tep;* 5. Coptic ⲟⲩⲣⲟ, ⲉⲡⲡⲟ, ⲉⲡⲡⲁ]

P. le Page Renouf, "Note on Egyptian Prepositions," *SBAT* 2 (1873) 301-320.

*C. W. Goodwin, "Miscellaneous Notes," *ZÄS* 12 (1874) 37-39.

[1. ⎯☉🦅 *nenau (or nau)* the Ostrich; 2. 🕯; 3. Dual number expressed by ⦚ or ⦚ or ⌒; 4. ⌐🦅ᵢ *set-em-ra*]

*P. le Page Renouf, "Reply to M. Golenischeff. 🦆⦚, 🦆ᵢᵢᵢᵢ never conjunction but always preposition like 🦆⦚, 🦆," *ZÄS* 15 (1877) 106-111.

P. le Page Renouf, "Wrong Values commonly assigned to Hieroglyphic Groups," *SBAP* 4 (1881-82) 60-67.

Edwin Yorke McCauley, "A Manual for the Use of Students in Egyptology," *PAPS* 20 (1881-83) 1-89.

*P. le Page Renouf, "The Negative Particle ⌒," *SBAP* 6 (1883-84) 95-101.

*P. le Page Renouf, "Seb, the Great Cackler," *SBAP* 7 (1884-85) 152-154.

P. le Page Renouf, "Pronominal Forms in Egyptian," *SBAP* 10 (1887-88) 247-264.

*P. le Page Renouf, "Is אַבְרֵךְ (Gen. xli. 43) Egyptian? The Thematic Vowel in Egyptian," *SBAP* 11 (1888-89) 5-10.

P. le Page Renouf, "Pronominal Forms in Egyptian," *SBAP* 11 (1888-89) 18-21.

*A. H. Sayce, "Pronominal Forms in Egyptian," *SBAP* 11 (1888-89) 80-82. [Remarks by P. le Page Renouf, pp. 82-83]

†W. H. Rylands, A. H. Sayce, A. Neubauer, and P. le Page Renouf, "(Pronominal Forms in Egyptian.) Letter from Dr. Neubauer," *SBAP* 11 (1888-89) 283-285.

F. C. H. Wendel, "Notes on the history of Egyptian grammar," *JAOS* 14 (1890) cxcviii-ccii.

Edward Y[orke] McCauley, "A Dictionary of the Egyptian Language," *TAPS, N.S.,* 16 (1890) 1-241.

F. Ll. Griffith, "Note on Demotic Philology," *SBAP* 18 (1896) 103-105.

F. Ll. Griffith, "Transliteration of Demotic," *SBAP* 21 (1899) 273-276.

Edmund F. Schreiner, "The Vowel in the Writing of Ancient Egypt," *PAPA* 33 (1901) cxxxix.

F. Ll. Griffith, "Notes on Demotic Philology: The Khamuas Stories," *SBAP* 23 (1901) 16-18.

F. Legge, "The History of the Transliteration of Egyptian," *SBAP* 24 (1902) 273-282. [Note by Ernest Sibree, p. 340]

James Teackle Dennis, "The Transliteration of Egyptian," *JAOS* 24 (1903) 275-281.

Jacob Krall, "The Transliteration of Egyptian," *SBAP* 25 (1903) 209-212.

Christopher Johnston, "Erman's Egyptian Grammar," *JAOS* 25 (1904) 88.

Alan H. Gardiner, "An use of the later absolute pronoun," *ZÄS* 41 (1904) 135-136.

*Alan H. Gardiner, "Note on the 'ring' and its relation to the *dbn,*" *ZÄS* 43 (1906) 45-47.

F. Legge, "The Titles of the Thinite Kings," *SBAP* 30 (1908) 86-94, 121-128, 163-177.

Aaron Ember, "Semito-Egyptian sound-changes," *ZÄS* 49 (1911) 87-92.

Alan H. Gardiner, "A late-Egyptian use of the older absolute pronouns," *ZÄS* 50 (1912) 114-117.

Aaron Ember, "Mehri parallels to the Egyptian stems with prefixed *ḥ,*" *ZÄS* 51 (1913) 138-139.

Aaron Ember, "Several Semito-Egyptian Particles," *ZA* 28 (1913-14) 302-306.

*W. M. F[linders] P[etrie], "Boat Names in Egypt," *AEE* 2 (1915) 136-137.

H. R. Hall, "Letters of Champollion le Jeune and of Seyffarth to Sir William Gell," *JEA* 2 (1915) 76-87.

H. R. Hall, "Letters to Sir William Gell from Henry Salt, [Sir] J. G. Wilkinson, and Baron von Bunsen," *JEA* 2 (1915) 133-167.

Alan H. Gardiner, "On certain participial formations in Egyptian," *RÉg, N.S.,* 2 (1921-24) 42-55.

H. F. Lutz, "An Elucidation of the adverbial phrase *n mt n š.t*.," *JAOS* 43 (1923) 330-331.

W[illiam] F[oxwell] Albright, "The principles of Egyptian phonological development," *RTR* 40 (1923) 64-70.

*Nathaniel Reich, "A Grammatical Exercise of an Egyptian Schoolboy," *JEA* 10 (1924) 285-288.

Aylward M. Blackman, "Some Philological and other Notes," *JEA* 13 (1927) 187-192. [1. A Note on Prince Ḥardedef's salutation to the Sage Dedi, *Papyrus Westcar*, 7. 17ff.; 2. A Note on *Papyrus Westcar*, XI, 6ff.; 3. A Note on *Eloquent Peasant*, B 1, 168-171= Vogelsang, *Kommentar*, page 139; 4. *Pi'onkhi Stela*, Line 1]

*W[illiam] F[oxwell] Albright, "Another case of Egyptian *û* = Coptic *ê*," *ZÄS* 62 (1927) 64.

T. George Allen, "A New Landmark in the Field of Egyptian Grammar," *AJSL* 44 (1927-28) 116-133.

*Alan H. Gardiner, "An Egyptian Split Infinitive and the Origin of the Coptic Conjunctive Tense," *JEA* 14 (1928) 86-96.

John A. Maynard, "Note on R. O. Faulkner's Review of an Egyptian Grammar by S. A. B. Mercer," *JSOR* 12 (1928) 54-55.

R. Engelbach, "The direction of the Inscriptions on Obelisks," *ASAE* 29 (1929) 25-30.

Cyrus H. Gordon, "The Feminine Singulars of the Egyptian Demonstrative Pronouns," *JAOS* 49 (1929) 58-60.

T. George Allen, "'Independent' Uses of the Egyptian Qualitative," *JAOS* 49 (1929) 160-167.

William F. Edgerton, "A Clause in the Marriage Settlements," *ZÄS* 64 (1929) 59-62.

Aylward M. Blackman, "Notes on Certain Passages in Various Middle Egyptian Texts," *JEA* 16 (1930) 63-72.

*Alan H. Gardiner, "The Origin of Certain Coptic Grammatical Elements," *JEA* 16 (1930) 220-234. [I. The tense-formative ⲉⲡⲉ- in Late Egyptian, A. Examples showing ⊂⊃ before the infinitive, B. Examples without ⊂⊃ before the infinitive; C. Example with before the infinitive, D. Examples with ⊂⊃ for ⊂⊃ and without ⊂⊃ before the infinitive; II. The origin of ⲙⲡⲁⲧϥ, with some remarks on method; III. "Until he hears" in Coptic and Late Egyptian]

Henry Ludwig F. Lutz, "Verb Qualifiers in Egyptian," *UCPSP* 10 (1931-46) 265-274.

*John A. Wilson, "Ancient text corrections in Madient Habu," *ZÄS* 68 (1932) 48-56.

*William F. Edgerton, "Demotic writings of ⲙⲡⲁⲧⲉ-.," *ZÄS* 69 (1933) 123-125.

Alan H. Gardiner, "Two Employments of the Independent Pronouns," *JEA* 20 (1934) 13-17.

*R. O. Faulkner, "The Verb *Ỉ* 'To Say' and its Developments," *JEA* 21 (1935) 177-190. [𓇌 or 𓏤]

*S. Yeivin, "Studies in comparative Egypto-Semitics, IV," *Kêmi* 6 (1936) 63-80. [Parts I & II published in לְשׁוֹנֵנוּ]

*Jaroslav Černý, "The Gender of Tens and Hundreds in Late Egyptian," *JEA* 23 (1937) 57-59.

J. J. Clère, "A Note on the Grammatical Gender of the Names of Towns," *JEA* 23 (1937) 261.

*Charles F. Nims, "Notes on University of Michigan Demotic Papyri from Philadelphia," *JEA* 24 (1938) 73-82. [3. The Independent Use of the Conjunctive *mtw=*, pp. 77-78]

Paul C. Smither, "A New Use of the Preposition *m*," *JEA* 25 (1939) 166-169.

William F. Edgerton, "Egyptian Phonetic Writing, from its Invention to the Close of the Nineteenth Dynasty," *JAOS* 60 (1940) 473-506.

C. J. C. Bennett, "Growth of the *Htp-Di-Nsw* Formula in the Middle Kingdom," *JEA* 27 (1941) 77-82.

Battiscombe Gunn, "The Use of Red for Amounts of Cereals in Hieratic," *JEA* 27 (1941) 157.

*J[aroslav] Černý,, "Philological and Etymological Notes. I," *ASAE* 41 (1942) 335-338. [2. The opening words of the tales of the Doomed Prince and the Two Brothers, pp. 336-338]

Battiscombe Gunn, "The Split Determined Infinitive," *JEA* 32 (1946) 92-96.

Girgis Mattha, "The Egyptian conjunctive," *BIFAO* 45 (1947) 43-55.

William F. Edgerton, "Stress, Vowel Quality, and Syllable Division in Egyptian," *JNES* 6 (1947) 1-17.

Alan [H.] Gardiner, "The First Two Pages of the *Wöterbuch*," *JEA* 34 (1948) 12-18.

Alan [H.] Gardiner, "Adversaria Grammatica," *JEA* 34 (1948) 23-26. [I. The Negative Relative Adjective]

Ronald J. Williams, "On Certain Verbal Forms in Demotic," *JNES* 7 (1948) 223-235.

*Battiscombe Gunn, "A Special Use of the *śḏm.f* and *śḏm.n.f* Forms," *JEA* 35 (1949) 21-24.

Jaroslav Černý, "On the Origin of the Egyptian Conjunctive," *JEA* 35 (1949) 25-30.

Keith C. Seele, "A Rare Grammatical Construction in a Neglected Egyptian Text," *JNES* 8 (1949) 359-364.

William F. Edgerton, "Early Egyptian Dialect Interrelationships," *BASOR* #122 (1951) 9-12.

*Ronald J. Williams, "Grammatical Notes on the Demotic of Papyrus Insinger," *JEA* 38 (1952) 62-64.

*Abd-el-Mohsen Bakir, "A new approach to Middle Egyptian demonstratives," *JEA* 39 (1953) 111-112.

*J. Gwyn Griffiths, "Three notes on Herodotus, Book II," *ASAE* 53 (1955) 139-152. [1. Greek and Egyptian Writing, pp. 139-144]

*R. A. Parker, "The Function of the Imperative *śḏm.f* in Middle Egyptian," *RÉg* 10 (1955) 49-59.

Hans Goedicke, "Alternation of *ḫ* and *ḏ* in Egyptian," *ZÄS* 80 (1955) 32-34.

William A. Ward, "Notes on Egyptian Group-Writing," *JNES* 16 (1957) 198-203.

*H. Jacob Polotsky, "The 'Emphatic' *sḏm.n.f.* Form," *RÉg* 11 (1957) 109-117.

*Thomas O. Lambdin, "The Bivalence of Coptic *eta* and Related Problems in the Vocalization of Egyptian," *JNES* 17 (1958) 177-193.

Werner Vycichl, "A Late Egyptian Dialect of Elephantine," *Kush* 6 (1958) 176-178.

William A. Ward, "Some Effects of Varying Phonetic Conditions on Semitic Loan Words in Egyptian," *JAOS* 80 (1960) 322-327.

*Jacob J. Rabinowitz, "An Egyptian Parallel to the *Šalmukēnu* Clause of Accadian Documents," *JNES* 20 (1961) 50-51.

Richard A. Parker, "The Durative Tenses in P. Rylands IX," *JNES* 20 (1961) 180-187.

J. R. Harris, "A Hitherto Unrecognized Substantive," *Or, N.S.,* 30 (1961) 366-370.

Ebbe E. Knudsen, "Word Stress and Syllable Structure in Egyptian. A Review Article," *AO* 26 (1961-62) 193-203. *(Review)*

*Wolf Leslau, "Semitic and Egyptian Comparisons," *JNES* 21 (1962) 44-49.

Edward F. Wente, "The Late Egyptian Conjunctive as a Past Continuative," *JNES* 21 (1962) 304-311.

M. Korostovtsev, "Does the model *iw .f ḥr sḏm* of the Late Egyptian Praesens II refer to the future?" *JEA* 49 (1963) 173-175.

Donald B. Redford, "The Pronunciation of *pr* in Late Toponyms," *JNES* 22 (1963) 119-122.

Henry G. Fischer, "Graphic Transposition of the Indirect Genitive," *JARCE* 3 (1964) 123-124.

*John Bennett, "The meaning of the royal nomen and prenomen," *JEA* 51 (1965) 206-207.

Jac. J. Janssen, "Semitic Loan-words in Egyptian ostraca," *JEOL* #19 (1965-66) 443-448.

H. J. Polotsky, "Egyptian Tenses," *PIASH* 2 (1965-67) #5, 1-26.

A. M. Bakir, "Varia Grammatica," *JEA* 52 (1966) 34-38. [I. 1. 'Idiomatic phrases used as nouns; II. 1. *The indirect genitive,* 2. *The independent pronoun,* 3 *The function of* 'Iw, 4. *Some remarks on the* sḏm.n.f]

*Gérard Janssens, "Contributions to the Hamito-Semitic and the Egyptian Phonetic Laws," *CdÉ* 42 (1967) 86-122.

Charles F. Nims, "Second Tenses in Wenamūn," *JEA* 54 (1968) 161-164.

M[ordechai] Gilula, "An Adjectival Predicative Expression of Possession in Middle Egyptian," *RÉg* 20 (1968) 55-61.

M. A. Korostovtsev, "The Categories Transitive and Intransitive in Egyptian Verbs," *VDI* (1968) #4, 118.

M. [A.] Korostovtsev, "Notes on Late-Egyptian Punctuation," *AJBA* 1 (1968-71) #2, 13-18.

Gerard Janssens, "Word Accent and Vocalization in Old Egyptian," *CdÉ* 44 (1969) 241-262.

Mordechai Gilula, "Negative sentences in a Letter to the Dead," *JEA* 55 (1969) 216-217.

Edward F. Wente, "A Late Egyptian Emphatic Tense," *JNES* 28 (1969) 1-14.

Mordechai Gilula, "Two New Conjunctions in Middle Egyptian," *JNES* 28 (1969) 122-123. [1. m-znw, "after"; 2. n-msdwt, "in order that ... not"]

*J. Vergote, "The Plural Nouns in Egyptian and in Coptic," *Or, N.S.,* 38 (1969) 77-96.

*H. C. Jelgersma, "A grammatical peculiarity in the tomb inscriptions of the sons of Ramses III in the Valley of the Queens in Thebes," *JEOL* #21 (1969-70) 169-174.

Miroslav Verner, "Preparation of a Palaeographic Study on Old Kingdom Hieroglyphs," *ZÄS* 96 (1969-70) 49-52.

§497 *3.3.3.1.3 Coptic Grammar and Lexicography*

Anonymous, "The Coptic Language," *PRev* 27 (1855) 388-395.

Carl Abel, "On the Coptic Language," *TPS* (1855) 51-61.

C. W. Goodwin, "Gleanings in Coptic Lexicography," *ZÄS* 7 (1869) 129-131, 141-146; 8 (1870) 132-137; 9 (1871) 22-24, 45-48, 120-124; 14 (1876) 148 [Corrections].

*P. le Page Renouf, "Miscellanea V," *ZÄS* 10 (1872) 72-79. [5. Coptic oγpo,eππo,eππa, pp. 77-79]

*J. G. Lansing, "Egyptian Notes," *AJSL* 4 (1887-88) 43-45. [I. Bashmuric, p. 43]

W. E. C[rum], "II.—'Above' and 'Below' in Coptic," *SBAP* 21 (1899) 251-252.

Alan H. Gardiner, "The origin of the Coptic tense Futurum I," *ZÄS* 43 (1906) 97-98.

Alan H. Gardiner, "The origin of the Coptic negative ̇ππe," *ZÄS* 45 (1908) 73-79.

Aaron Ember, "A few Semitic Stems in Coptic," *ZÄS* 49 (1911) 94.

G. P. G. Sobhy, "The Pronunciation of Coptic in the Church of Egypt," *JEA* 2 (1915) 15-19.

*Battiscombe·Gunn, "Interpreters of Dreams in Ancient Egypt," *JEA* 4 (1916) 252 [ⲥⲫⲣⲁⲛϣ]

Alan H. Gardiner, "Some Coptic Etymologies," *SBAP* 38 (1916) 181-185. [I. S. A. ⲙⲥⲛⲉ: B. ⲙⲥⲛⲥ "kind," "sort"; II. S.B. ϣⲟⲗ: A. ⲥⲁⲗ "tooth," "tusk"; III. S. ⲥⲥⲟⲧ *ἀρούρα;* IV. S. ⲍⲱⲣⲡ "to stumble"]

Geo. P. G. Sobhy, "Studies in coptic lexicography," *BIFAO* 14 (1918) 57-64.

*Joseph Offord, "Archaeological Notes on Jewish Antiquities. *Coptic Terms and the Old Testament*," *PEFQS* 50 (1918) 137-138.

*H. I. Bell and W. E. Crum, "A Greek-Coptic Glossary," *Aeg* 6 (1925) 177-226.

*W[illiam] F[oxwell] Albright, "Another case of Egyptian *û* = Coptic *ê*," *ZÄS* 62 (1927) 64.

*Alan H. Gardiner, "An Egyptian Split Infinitive and the Origin of the Coptic Conjunctive Tense," *JEA* 14 (1928) 86-96.

Henry S. Gehman, "ⲈⲂⲞⲖ ⲞⲦⲦⲈ and ⲈⲂⲞⲖ ⲞⲦⲀⲈ to Express Comparison of Inequality in Bohairic," *JSOR* 12 (1928) 151-152.

W. H. Worrell, "The Evolution of Velar, Palatal and Dental Stops in Coptic," *JEA* 15 (1929) 191-193.

W. H. Worrell, "The Pronunciation of Coptic," *JAOS* 50 (1930) 144-149.

*Alan H. Gardiner, "The Origin of Certain Coptic Grammatical Elements," *JEA* 16 (1930) 220-234. [I. The tense-formative ⲉⲣⲉ– in Late Egyptian, A. Examples showing ⟳ before the infinitive, B. Examples without ⟳ before the infinitive; C. Example with before the infinitive, D. Examples with ⟳ for ⟴ and without ⟳ before the infinitive; II. The origin of ⲙ̄ⲡⲁ̄ⲧ̄ϥ, with some remarks on method; III. "Until he hears" in Coptic and Late Egyptian]

William F. Edgerton, "Etymologies of ⲦⲎⲚⲞⲞⲨ and ⲌⲞⲞⲨ," *AJSL* 48 (1931-32) 53-54.

*William F. Edgerton, "Demotic writings of ⲘⲠⲀⲦⲈ–," *ZÄS* 29 (1933) 123-125.

W. H. Worrell, "Syllabic Consonants in Sahidic Coptic," *ZÄS* 69 (1933) 130-131.

*De Lacy O'Leary, "Notes on the Coptic Language. II. How far can Coptic influence be traced in the Egyptian dialect of Arabic?" *Or, N.S.*, 3 (1934) 249-258.

William F. Edgerton, "On the Origin of Certain Coptic Verbal Forms," *JAOS* 55 (1935) 257-267.

W. H. Worrell, "Popular Traditions of the Coptic Language," *AJSL* 54 (1937) 1-11.

C. R. C. Allberry, "Three Points in Coptic Lexicography," *JEA* 25 (1939) 170-172. [I. 'ⲈⲔⲥⲀ' 'anent'; II. Ⲍⲥ ⲞⲨⲀⲒ̈ⲩ 'have access to'; III. ⲚⲞⲨⲞⲨⲅ 'to turn']

W. E. Crum, "A Bushmûric Word," *JEA* 26 (1940) 156-157. [ⲱⲡⲥⲩ and ⲦⲥⲐⲥ]

*Battiscombe Gunn, "Notes on Egyptian Lexicography," *JEA* 27 (1941) 144-148. [I. 1. *Ḥr tp > ḥr d̲ʒd̲ʒ* > ⲅⲀⲌⲚ–,ⲅⲀⲌⲰⲌ]

Alan H. Gardiner, "The expression ⲦⲘⲠⲤⲞⲠ," *JEA* 27 (1941) 158-159.

C. R. C. Allberry, "ⲦⲞⲨⲞ(Ⲉ)Ⲓ̈," *JEA* 27 (1941) 160.

*J[aroslav] Černý, "Philological and Etymological Notes. I," *ASAE* 41 (1942) 335-338. [1. On the etymology of coptic Ⲁⲅⲟ "treasure", pp. 335-336]

*Alan H. Gardiner, "The Original of Coptic ⲚⲀⲨ 'see'," *JEA* 31 (1945) 113.

Alan H. Gardiner, "Second Thoughts on the Origin of the Coptic ⲉⲣⲉ–,"
JEA 32 (1946) 101.

Girgis Mattha, "The origin of the explanatory particles ⲛ̄ and ⲛ̄ⲅ̄ⲥ:
ⲛ̄ⲭⲉ," *BIFAO* 45 (1947) 61-64.

*M[argaret] A. Murray, "The Serpent Hieroglyph," *JEA* 34 (1948) 117-118.
[ⲉⲍⲱ]

*Frithiof Rundgren, "The Root *šft* in the Modern Ethiopic Language (Tigrē,
Tigrina, and Amharic) and Old Egyptian *ḫfty,* Coptic *šft,*" *OrS* 2
(1953) 19-25.

Herbert Pierrepont Houghton, "The Coptic Infinitive," *Aeg* 35 (1955) 275-
291.

Herbert Pierrepont Houghton, "Coptic Substantive Relationship," *Aeg* 36
(1956) 153-177.

Herbert Pierrepont Houghton, "The Coptic Sentence," *Aeg* 37 (1957) 226-
242.

Jaroslav Černý, "Some Coptic etymologies III," *BIFAO* 57 (1958) 203-213.
[Parts I and II published in Coptic Studies in Honor of Walter Ewing
Crum, *pp. 35-47; and* Ägyptologische Studien Hermann Grapow zum
70. Geburstag gewidmet, *pp. 30-7 respectively]*

H. S. Smith, "Three Coptic etymologies," *JEA* 44 (1958) 122. [ⲙⲓ̈ⲕⲉ[SF]
ⲛ̄ⲱⲥⲧ[S], ⲱⲟ.ⲙ[SB], f. ⲱⲱⲙⲉ[S], pl. ⲱ.ⲙⲟⲩⲥ[S], ⲱ.ⲙⲱⲟⲩ[B]]

*Thomas O. Lambdin, "The Bivalence of Coptic *eta* and Related Problems
in the Vocalization of Egyptian," *JNES* 17 (1958) 177-193.

Herbert Pierrepont Houghton, "A study of the Coptic prefixed prepositional
particles," *Aeg* 39 (1959) 211-222.

*Wilson B. Bishai, "Notes on the Coptic Substratum in Egyptian Arabic,"
JAOS 80 (1960) 225-229.

H. J. Polotsky, "The Coptic Conjunction System," *Or, N.S.,* 29 (1960) 392-
422.

Theodore Petersen, "The Biblical Scholar's Concern with Coptic Studies," *CBQ* 23 (1961) 241-249.

*Wilson B. Bishai, "Nature and Extent of Coptic Phonological Influence on Egyptian Arabic," *JSS* 6 (1961) 175-182.

Ebbe E. Knudsen, "Saidic Coptic Vowel Phonemes," *AO* 26 (1961-62) 29-42.

Herbert Pierrepont Houghton, "The Akhmîmic Dialect of Coptic, with a brief Glossary," *Aeg* 42 (1962) 1-26.

*Wilson B. Bishai, "Coptic Grammatical Influence on Egyptian Arabic," *JAOS* 82 (1962) 285-289.

Jaroslav Černý, "Bohairic verbal prefix ⲁⲛⲛⲉϥ–," *ZÄS* 90 (1963) 13-16.

J[aroslav] Černý, "An alternative etymology of the Bohairic word for 'interpreter of dreams'," *JEA* 50 (1964) 184. [ⲥ ϥ ⲡ ⲁ ⲛ ⲯ]

H. W. Fairman, "The Origin of ⲣ ⲓ ⲱ ⲙ ⲉ," *JEA* 54 (1968) 236-238.

H. J. Polotsky, "The 'Weak' Plural Article in Bohairic," *JEA* 54 (1968) 243-245.

Dwight W. Young, "Unfulfilled Conditions in Shenoute's Dialect," *JAOS* 89 (1969) 399-407.

*James Drescher, "Graeco-Coptica," *Muséon* 82 (1969) 85-100.

*J. Vergote, "The Plural Nouns in Egyptian and in Coptic," *Or, N.S.,* 38 (1969) 77-96.

Georg Barth Magnus, "Autographemes and Vowel Phonemes in Saidic Coptic," *OrS* 18 (1969) 3-44.

*Heikki Palva, "Notes on the Alleged Coptic Morphological Influence on Egyptian Arabic," *OrS* 18 (1969) 128-136.

§498   **3.3.3.2 Semitic - General Studies**

*John Davies, "On the Semitic Languages, and their relations with Indo-European Class. Part I. On the Nature and Development of Semitic Roots," *TPS* (1854) 169-198.

*John Davies, "On the Semitic Languages, and their relations with Indo-European Class. Part II. On the Connexion of Semitic Roots with the corresponding forms in the Indo-European Class of Languages," *TPS* (1854) 238-281.

C. Lottner, "On Sister families of Languages, especially those connected with the Semitic Family," *TPS* (1860-61) 20-27.

C. Lottner, "On Sister families of Languages, especially those connected with the Semitic Family. Part II," *TPS* (1860-61) 112-132.

W[illiam] Henry Green, "On the Species or Derivative Forms of Semitic Verbs," *JAOS* 7 (1862) liii.

*Richard Cull, "A ח Conjugation, such as exists in Assyrian, shown to be a character of early Shemitic speech, by its vestiges found in the Hebrew, Phoenician, Aramaic, and Arabic Languages," *SBAT* 2 (1873) 83-109.

*W. D. Whitney, "The Question of Indo-European and Semitic Relationship," *PAPA* 8 (1875-76) 26-28. *[Bound with Transactions, but paged separately]*

*James F. McCurdy, "Relations of the Aryan and Semitic Languages. I.—History and Present State of Inquiry," *BS* 33 (1876) 78-101.

*James F. McCurdy, "Relations of the Aryan and Semitic Languages. II—Criteria of Relationship," *BS* 33 (1876) 352-381.

*Paul Haupt, "Studies on the Comparative Grammar of the Semitic Languages, with Special Reference to Assyrian. The Oldest Semitic Verb-Form," *JRAS* (1877-78) 244-252.

C[rawford] H. Toy, "On Shemitic Derived Stems," *PAPA* 11 (1878-79) 22. *[Bound with Transactions, but paged separately]*

C[rawford] H. Toy, "Expressions of Modal Ideas in Shemitic," *PAPA* 11 (1878-79) 27-28. *[Bound with Transactions, but paged separately]*

*J. F. McCurdy, "Relations of the Aryan and Semitic Languages, No. III.—Comparative Phonology," *BS* 36 (1879) 674-706.

Crawford H. Toy, "Modal Development of the Shemitic Verb," *TAPA* 10 (1879) 5-25.

C[rawford] H. Toy, "Problems of General Semitic Grammar," *AJP* 1 (1880) 416-426.

*J. F. McCurdy, "Relations of the Aryan and Semitic Languages IV.— Morphology of Roots," *BS* 37 (1880) 528-565.

*J. F. McCurdy, "Relations of the Aryan and Semitic Languages V.— Comparison of Roots," *BS* 37 (1880) 752-776.

C[rawford] H. Toy, "Remarks on J. G. Müller's Semitic Theory," *JAOS* 10 (1880) lxxii-lxxiii.

C[rawford] H. Toy, "The Semitic vowel *a*," *AJP* 2 (1881) 446-457.

*J. F. McCurdy, "Relations of the Aryan and Semitic Languages V.— Comparison of Roots (Continued)," *BS* 38 (1881) 116-146.

*G. Bertin, "Suggestions on the Formation of the Semitic Tenses. A Comparative and Critical Study," *JRAS* (1881) 105-118.

F. A. Gast, "The Claims of the Semitic Languages," *RChR* 28 (1881) 131-146.

C[rawford] H. Toy, "The Semitic Personal Pronouns," *PAPA* 14 (1882) x-xii.

C[rawford] H. Toy, "Remarks on Guyard's theory of Semitic Internal Plurals," *JAOS* 11 (1885) lix-lx.

L. C. Casartelli, "Pehlevi Notes—III. The Semitic Suffix -*man* and its origin," *BOR* 2 (1887-88) 129-132.

Cyrus Adler, "Semitic Languages in the Encyclopedia Britannica," *PAPA* 19 (1887) xiv-xvii.

William Hayes Ward, "Retrospect and Prospect," *AJSL* 5 (1888-89) 80-82.

*†‡Paul Haupt, "On a new periodical devoted to Assyriology and comparative Semitic grammar," *JAOS* 13 (1889) cclxvii-cclxx. *[Beiträge zur Assyriologie und vergleichenden semitischen Sprachwissenschaft]*

George F. Moore, "On a new theory of the nature of the so-called Emphatic Consonants in the Semitic languages," *JAOS* 13 (1889) ccciv-cccvii.

Abel H. Huizinga, "Analogy in the Semitic Languages. I," *AJP* 11 (1890) 471-481.

Edgar P. Allen, "On the Semitic Emphatic Consonants," *JAOS* 14 (1890) cviii-cxii.

Abel H. Huizinga, "Analogy in the Semitic Languages. II," *AJP* 12 (1891) 30-48.

Abel H. Huizinga, "Analogy in the Semitic Languages. III," *AJP* 12 (1891) 133-156.

*W. Muss-Arnolt, "On Semitic Words in Greek and Latin," *TAPA* 23 (1892) 35-156. *[Index of words, pp. 151-156]*

Max L. Margolis, "Notes on Semitic Grammar," *AJSL* 10 (1893-94) 188-192. [I. The First Vowel of the Imperfect Tense-Stem]

Paul Haupt, "Transitive and intransitive verbs in Semitic," *JAOS* 16 (1894-95) ci-cii.

*Max L. Margolis, "Notes on Semitic Grammar. II," *AJSL* 12 (1895-96) 197-229. [The Feminine Ending *T* in Hebrew; The Aramaic System of Nominal Inflection, Biliterals, Triliterals; The Feminine Ending in Aramaic; Our Problem Answered on Aramaic Ground; The Aramaic Method in Hebrew Nominal Inflection, Biliterals, Triliterals, Pluriliterals; Roots with a Semivowel as Third Radical; דְּמוּת Gen. 1:26]

*Dean A. Walker, "The Semitic Negative with special reference to the Negative in Hebrew," *AJSL* 12 (1895-96) 230-267.

William Rosenau, "Semitic Studies in American Colleges," *YCCAR* 7 (1896-97) 99-113.

Duncan B. Macdonald, "The Interchange of Sibilants and Dentals in Semitic," *AJSL* 15 (1898-99) 100-104.

*Edward Montet, "Mr. Le Pasteur Fesquet's New Theory of the Origin of Languages," *IAQR, 3rd Ser.,* 8 (1899) 386-388. *[Semitic]*

Max L. Margolis, "Pleonastic Formative Elements in the Semitic Languages," *PAPA* 32 (1900) lix.

Frank R. Blake, "The Internal Passive in Semitic," *JAOS* 22 (1901) 45-54.

*Max L. Margolis, "Notes on Semitic Grammar. III," *AJSL* 19 (1902-03) 45-48. [An Abnormal Hebrew Form]

*S[tephen] Langdon, "Lexicographical Notes," *SBAP* 31 (1909) 74-77. [III. Semitic Words for "sorrow," "distress;" Sumerian *sag-dib,* Br., 8072-7, pp. 74-75]

*Max L. Margolis, "Complete Induction for the Identification of the Vocabulary in the Greek Versions of the Old Testament with its Semitic Equivalents: Its Necessity and the Means of obtaining it," *JAOS* 30 (1909-10) 301-312.

*Alan S. Hawkesworth, "Semitic and Sumerian; A Study in Origins," *OC* 24 (1910) 574-575.

Frank R. Blake, "Vocalic r, l, m, n in Semitic," *JAOS* 31 (1910-11) 217-222.

Frank R. Blake, "Comparative Syntax of the Combinations formed by the Noun and its Modifiers in Semitic," *JAOS* 32 (1912) 135-200, 201-267.

*Allison Emery Drake, "Some Evidences of Aryo-Semitic Kinship," *BS* 70 (1913) 607-621.

‡*T. Witton Davies, "Survey of Recent Work on Semitic Philology and Hebrew Grammar," *RTP* 9 (1913-14) 685-713.

S[tephen] Langdon, "The Semitic *iau,*" *ET* 26 (1914-15) 474.

*Frank R. Blake, "Studies in Semitic Grammar," *JAOS* 35 (1917) 375-385. [I. Apparent Interchange between ה and א in Semitic; II. The Etymology of the Aramaic particle אִית, יתי‎; III. The Multiplicative Numerals in Aramaic and Hebrew; IV. Mixed Constructions in Hebrew and Aramaic]

Theodore H. Robinson, "Some Features of the Sibilants in the Semitic Languages," *JMUEOS* #8 (1918-19) 81-89.

*Hartwig Hirschfeld, "The Dot in Semitic Palaeography," *JQR, N.S.,* 10 (1919-20) 159-183. [I. The Dot Disjunctive; II. The Dot Diacritical; III. The Dot Vocalic; IV. The Dot Grammatical]

*Paul Haupt, "Philological and Linguistic Studies," *AJP* 46 (1925) 197-212. [5. The Origin of Semitic Case-endings, pp. 207-208]

Paul Haupt, "The Ending of the Semitic Genitive," *JAOS* 45 (1925) 311-315.

Ephraim Avigdor Speiser, "Secondary Developments in Semitic Phonology: An Application of the Principle of Sonority," *AJSL* 42 (1925-26) 145-169.

James A. Montgomery, "Alleged intensive noun-formations in the Semitic," *JAOS* 46 (1926) 56-58.

*A[aron] Ember, "Several Egypto-Semitic Etymologies," *OOR* 1 (1926) #1, 5-8.[1. - Eg. m'bȝ. *harpoon, spear* = Eth. mâ'bal, *sharp instrument, arrow;* 2. - Eg. m'bȝ. *thirty* = Post-Biblical מְעֻבָּר *intercalated;* 3. Eg. Fnḫ-u =(Φοῖνιξ, Phoenician) = Arab فَلَّاح *fellah* < Aram. פלח *split, plough, cultivate the ground;* 4. Eg. 'r, *enter* = Aram. עלל *enter;* 5. Eg. gm-u, *grief, mourning* = Arab. غُمّ *ğamm, grief, sadness;* 6. Eg. pzḫ, *be dishevelled, disarray, dismayed* = Arab. فزع, *be frightened, terrified, dismayed;* 7. Eg. ḫȝm, *catching of fish and birds* = חים *net for catching fish;* 8. ḫȝp, erroneously חפה لخَفّ *cover;* 9. Eg. ḫnğ, *thigh, hip-bone* (*Pyr. Texts* 124, 133, 1547) = Assyr. ḫinçu, Arab. خَضِر, Heb. חֲלָצַיִם, *lion, hip;* 10. Eg. ʾinʿ, *chin* (*Pyr. Texts* 1308) = Heb. לְעַ *jawbone* (probably = Arab. نيع *jaw, mandible*)]

Paul Haupt, "Misinsertion of Nasals," *BAVSS* 10 (1927) Heft 2, 193-197.

*J[ames] A. Montgomery, "The *Hemzah-h* in the Semitic," *JBL* 46 (1927) 144-146.

*Oswald T. Allis, "The Blessing of Abraham," *PTR* 25 (1927) 263-298. [I. The Passives and Reflexives in Semitics, pp. 271-278]

*Israel Eitan, "Hebrew and Semitic Particles. Comparative Studies in Semitic Philology," *AJSL* 44 (1927-28) 177-205, 254-260.

*Israel Eitan, "Hebrew and Semitic Particles—*Continued.* Comparative Studies in Semitic Philology," *AJSL* 45 (1928-29) 48-63, 130-145, 197-211; 46 (1929-30) 22-51.

*John C. Grandbery, "Languages of Bible Lands," *MQR, 3rd Ser.,* 55 (1929) 114-119. [Semitic Languages, pp. 117-119; Turkish, p. 119]

A. S. Tritton, "The Place of *n* in forming Semitic Roots," *BSOAS* 7 (1933-35) 595-597.

E[phraim] A. Speiser, "Studies in Semitic Formatives," *JAOS* 56 (1936) 22-46. [I. The "Causative" Conjugation; II. The So-called Feminine Ending -(a)t]

G. R. Driver, "Problems of Semitic Grammar," *ZDMG* 91 (1937) 373-351.

*E[phraim] A. Speiser, "Pitfalls of Polarity," *Lang* 14 (1938) 187-202.

J. J. Obermann, "The Semitic Third Person Singular," *JBL* 58 (1939) vi.

Meir M. Bravmann, "Some Aspects of the Development of Semitic Diphthongs," *Or, N.S.,* 8 (1939) 244-253; 9 (1940) 45-60.

Albrecht Goetze, "The So-Called Intensive of the Semitic Languages," *JAOS* 62 (1942) 1-8.

*Frank R. Blake, "Studies in Semitic Grammar II," *JAOS* 62 (1942) 109-118. [1. The Long Vowels in Stems *mediae infirmae;* 2. The Origin of the Semitic Causative Formations; 3. The Semitic Demonstrative Particle *ḥ;* 4. The Influence of Analogy in determining the Initial Syllables of the Forms of the Derived Conjugations in Semitic; 5. Distributive Expressions in Ethiopic; 6. Syriac Connecting Vowel *â* before Verbal Suffixes; 7. The Orthography of the Syriac Ittafal; 8. New Syriac *ke;* 9. Mandaic האנאתה; 10. Lihyanic and Thamudic *b* 'son'; 11. Some Lihyanic and Thamudic Prepositions; 12. The Lihyanic Article; 13. The Personal Pronoun 'I' at the beginning of Inscriptions; 14. Akkadian *qâtu* 'hand']

A. M. Honeyman, "Some Developments in the Semitic Root *'by*," *JAOS* 64 (1944) 81-82.

*Frank R. Blake, "Studies in Semitic Grammar III," *JAOS* 65 (1945) 111-116. [1. *E* for *a* Adjacent to Gutturals in Akkadian; 2. Supposed Influence of Preceding and Following *i* in Akkadian]

*Frank R. Blake, "Studies in Semitic Grammar IV," *JAOS* 66 (1946) 212-218. [1. The "Emphatic" Consonants in Semitic; 2. The Vocalization of the Pretonic Open Syllable in Hebrew; 3. Aramaic z for Semitic z_1 and d]

J. M. J. Paul Brauchet, "Notes on Semitic Philology," *CBQ* 10 (1948) 315-317. [I. Semitic Roots; II. Some Peculiarities of Semitic Roots]

J. H. Greenberg, "The Patterning of Root Morphemes in Semitic," *Word* 6 (1950) 162-181.

Edward J. Young, "Adverbial—*u* in Semitic," *WTJ* 13 (1950-51) 151-154.

*Frank R. Blake, "Studies in Semitic Grammar V," *JAOS* 73 (1953) 7-16. [1. The Semitic Accusative Suffix *-nî*; 2. Additional note on Etymology of Aramaic *'ît*; 3. The Hebrew Possessive Suffixes *-ām, -ān*; 4. The ending *ēh* in Hebrew verbs tertiae *h*; 5. The Construct Ending *-ē(h)* in Hebrew; 6. The Aramaic plural endings *-ôn* and *-ên*; 7. The mixing of forms of verbs tert.*j* and tert. ' in verbs tertiae infirmae in Aramaic; 8. The confusion in the forms of Aramaic nouns derived from monosyllabic and dissyllabic bases with short vowels; 9. Apparent exceptions in the treatment of the diphthong *aj* in Biblical Aramaic; 10. Peculiar Hephel forms in Biblical Aramaic; 11. Peculiar passive forms in Biblical Aramaic; 12. Addendum to Study 4.]

M[eir M.] Bravmann, "On a Case of Quantitative Ablaut in Semitic," *Or, N.S.,* 22 (1953) 1-24.

*Jaan Puhvel, "Semitic affinities of Hittite ḫar-aš-zi," *JAOS* 74 (1954) 86-88.

*E[phraim] A. Speiser, "The Durative Hipthpaʻel: A *tan-* Form," *JAOS* 75 (1955) 118-121.

*A. M. Honeyman, "Ugarit and Semitic Usage," *JAOS* 75 (1955) 121-122.

W. J. Martin, "Some notes on the imperative in the Semitic languages," *RDSO* 32 (1957) 315-319.

Sabatino Moscati, "On Semitic Case-Endings," *JNES* 17 (1958) 142-144.

E. Ullendorff, "What is Semitic Language? (A Problem of Linguistic Identification)," *Or, N.S.,* 27 (1958) 66-75.

*Moshe Held, "*mḫṣ/*mḫš* in Ugaritic and Other Semitic Languages (A Study in Comparative Lexicography)," *JAOS* 79 (1959) 169-176.

*W[olf] Leslau, "Traces of the Laryngeals in the Ethiopic Dialect of Ennemor. A Contribution to Semitic Laryngeals," *Or, N.S.,* 28 (1959) 257-270.

*F. C. Fensham, "The Judges and Ancient Israelite Jurisprudence," *OTW* 2 (1959) 15-22. [The meaning of špḥṭ in the Semitic languages except Hebrew, pp. 15-17]

*Stanislav Segert, "Considerations on Semitic Comparative Lexicography," *ArOr* 28 (1960) 470-487. [I. Past and Future of Semitic Comparative Lexicons; II. A Transliteration of Semitic Alphabets for the Purpose of Comparative Linguistics]

*Robert Gordis, "A West-Semitic Cognate to Akkadian 'Suhatu'," *JSS* 5 (1960) 151-152. [שֵׁחִי or שִׁחוֹ]

William C. Cowan, "Arabic evidence for Proto Semitic */awa/ and */ō/," *Lang* 36 (1960) 60-62.

*C. Rabin, "The Hebrew Development of the Proto-Semitic ā," *Tarbiẓ* 30 (1960-61) #2, I.

Meir M. Bravmann, "Genetic Aspects of the Genitive in the Semitic Languages," *JAOS* 81 (1961) 386-394.

Edward Ullendorff, "Comparative Semitics," *SSR* 4 (1961) 13-32.

John Wm. Wevers, "Semitic bound structures," *CJL* 7 (1961-62) #1, 9-14.

*Wolf Leslau, "Semitic and Egyptian Comparisons," *JNES* 21 (1962) 44-49.

*Bruno W. W. Dombrowski, "Some Remarks on the Hebrew Hithpaʻel and Inversative -t- in the Semitic Languages," *JNES* 21 (1962) 220-223.

*W[illiam] A. Ward, "Some Egypto-Semitic Roots," *Or, N.S.,* 31 (1962) 397-412. [I. Egyptian *təḥ* = Semitic *dlḫ;* II. Egyptian *tr* = Semitic *d(w)r;* III. Egyptian *qri(qəi)* = Semitic *qry;* IV. Egyptian *tm* = Semitic *dm(m);* V. Egyptian *jř* = Semitic *šr;* VI. Egyptian *sči* = Semitic *nsk;* VII. Egyptian *sti* = Semitic *št;* VIII. Egyptian *šd* = Semitic *šd;* IX. Egyptian *wbə* = Semitic *wbl;* X. Egyptian *išf/nšf* = Semitic **fṯ;* XI. Egyptian *ʃʻ* = Semitic **zʻ*]

J. B. Fischer, "The Origin of the Tripartite Division of Speech in Semitic Grammar," *JQR, N.S.,* 53 (1962-63) 1-21.

*W[illiam] A. Ward, "Notes on Some Semitic Loan-Words and Personal Names in Late Egyptian," *Or, N.S.,* 32 (1963) 413-436.

J. B. Fischer, "The Origin of Tripartite Division of Speech in Semitic Grammar," *JQR, N.S.*, 54 (1963-64) 132-160.

J. Macdonald, "New Thoughts on a Biliteral Origin for the Semitic Verb," *ALUOS* 5 (1963-65) 63-85.

*A. Haldar, "The Position of Ugaritic among the Semitic Languages," *BO* 21 (1964) 267-277.

*A. Shaffer, "Hurrian *kirezzi*, West-Semitic *krz*," *Or, N.S.*, 34 (1965) 32-34.

M. Dahood, K. Deller, R.Köbert, "Comparative Semitics. Some Remarks on a Recent Publication," *Or, N.S.*, 34 (1965) 35-44. *(Review)*

Stanislav Segert, "Aim and Terminology of Semitic Comparative Grammar," *RDSO* 40 (1965) 1-8.

*Harry A. Hoffner Jr., "A Native Akkadian Cognate to West Semitic *GBN* 'Cheese'?" *JAOS* 86 (1966) 27-31. [גְּבִינָה]

A. Murtonen, "The Semitic Sibilants," *JSS* 11 (1966) 135-150.

P. J. van Zijl, "The elements w-, p-, 'p-, and p'- in the Semitic Languages," *OTW* 11 (1968) 86-94.

James Barr, "The Ancient Semitic Languages—the conflict between Philology and Linguistics," *TPS* (1968) 37-55.

H. Shy, "Tanhum Hayĕrušalmi's *Almuršid Alkafi* (Some Examples from the Letter *Taw*)," *Lĕš* 33 (1968-69) #4, 2-3.

Maximilian Ellenbogen, "The Common Prehistoric Origin of Certain Non-Synonymous Semitic Roots," *JHS* 1 (1969) 61-66.

*William A. Ward, "The Semitic Root *HWY* in Ugaritic and Derived Stems in Egyptian," *JNES* 28 (1969) 265-267.

*R. Hetzron, "The Evidence for Perfect *y'aqtul* and Jussive *yaqt'ul* in Proto-Semitic," *JSS* 14 (1969) 1-21. [3. Hebrew, pp. 8-18]

Meïr M. Bravmann, "The Semitic Causative-Prefix *Š/SA*," *Muséon* 82 (1969) 517-522.

Robert Hetzron, "Third Person singular pronoun suffixes in Proto-Semitic," *OrS* 18 (1969) 101-127.

*H. Blanc, "The Fronting of Semitic *g* and the *qāl-gāl* Dialect Split in Arabic," *PICSS* (1969) 7-37.

J. Blau, "Some Problems of the Formation of the Old Semitic Languages in the Light of Arabic Dialects," *PICSS* (1969) 38-44.

G. R. Driver, "Some Uses of *qtl* in the Semitic Languages," *PICSS* (1969) 49-64.

M. H. Goshen-Gottstein, "The System of Verbal Stems in the Classical Semitic Languages," *PICSS* (1969) 70-91.

C. Rabin, "The Structure of the Semitic System of Case Endings," *PICSS* (1969) 190-204.

*Stanislav Segert, "Hebrew Bible and Semitic comparative lexicography," *VTS* 17 (1969) 204-211.

*Federico C. Corriente, "A Survey of Spirantization in Semitic and Arabic Phonetics," *JQR, N.S.,* 60 (1969-70) 147-171.

§499 *3.3.3.2.1 Levantine (Northwest Semitic)*

*E[phraim] A. Speiser, "A Figurative Equivalent for Totality in Akkadian and West-Semitic," *JAOS* 54 (1934) 200-203.

E[phraim] A. Speiser, "Addendum to the Phrase מן חם ועד חוט," *JAOS* 54 (1934) 299.

*E[phraim] A. Speiser, "The 'Elative' in West-Semitic and Akkadian," *JCS* 6 (1952) 81-92.

*George E. Mendenhall, "Puppy and Lettuce in Northwestern-Semitic Covenant Making," *BASOR* #133 (1954) 26-30.

*Horace D. Hummel, "Enclitic *Mem* in Early North-West Semitic, Especially Hebrew," *JBL* 76 (1957) 85-107.

I. J. Gelb, "New Evidence in Favor of the Syllabic Character of West Semitic Writing," *BO* 15 (1958) 1-7.

*M[itchell] Dahood, "Qoheleth and Northwest Semitic Philology," *B* 43 (1962) 349-365.

E. Y. Kutscher, "Contemporary Studies in North-western Semitic," *JSS* 10 (1965) 21-53.

W. Watson, "Shared Consonants in Northwest Semitic," *B* 50 (1969) 525-533.

*Pinḥas Artzi, "On the Cuneiform Background of the Northwest-Semitic Form of the Word *BRDL, B(A)RZ(E)L,* 'Iron'," *JNES* 28 (1969) 268-270.

§500 *3.3.3.2.1.1 Canaanite - General Studies*

*A. F. Simpson, "The Speech and Culture of Canaan," *DTQ* 6 (1880) 605-622.

*W[illiam] F[oxwell] Albright, "Canaanite Ḥofšî, 'Free', in the Amarna Tablets," *JPOS* 4 (1924) 169-170.

*W[illiam] F[oxwell] Albright, "Canaanite Ḥapši and Hebrew Ḥofsî Again," *JPOS* 6 (1926) 106-108.

*W[illiam] F[oxwell] Albright, "Mitannian maryannu, 'chariot-warrior', and the Canaanite and Egyptian Equivalents," *AfO* 6 (1930-31) 217-221. [na'arôn *written* na-'a-ru-na]

*W[illiam] F[oxwell] Albright, "New Light on Early Canaanite Language and Literature," *BASOR* #46 (1932) 15-20.

W[illiam] F[oxwell] Albright, "Recent Progress in North-Canaanite Research," *BASOR* #70 (1938) 18-24. [The North-Canaanite Tongue; The Geography of the North-Canaanite Epics]

E[phraim] A. Speiser, "Concatenated Sound-shift in Canaanite," *JBL* 58 (1939) vi-vii.

*I. Mendelsohn, "The Canaanite term for 'Free Proletarian'," *BASOR* #83 (1941) 36-39. *[ḥpṯ]*

A. M. Honeyman, "Canaanite Pronominal Suffixes at Byblos and elsewhere," *JRAS* (1941) 31-36.

J. H. Patton, "An Unrecognized Canaanite Particle in the Bible," *JBL* 62 (1943) v. *[hm]*

*W[illiam] F[oxwell] Albright, "b) Hebrew *bêth-ḥeber* in Proverbs and Canaanite *bêth-ḥubûri,* 'Granary'," *JBL* 62 (1943) vi.

*W[illiam] L. Moran, "The Use of the Canaanite Infinitive as a Finite Verb in the Amarna Letters from Byblos," *JCS* 4 (1950) 169-172.

*Julian Obermann, "Survival of an Old Canaanite Participle and its Impact on Biblical Exegesis," *JBL* 70 (1951) 199-209.

William L. Moran, "New Evidence on Canaanite *taqtulū(na)*," *JCS* 5 (1951) 33-35.

*Matitiahu Tsevat, "Alalakhiana," *HUCA* 29 (1958) 109-134. [II. The Alalakh Texts—The Language of Canaan—The Bible, pp. 124-133]

W[illiam] L. Moran, "Early Canaanite *yaqtula*," *Or, N.S.*, 29 (1960) 1-19.

M. Martin, "Revision and Reclassification of the Protobyblian Signs," *Or, N.S.*, 31 (1962) 250-271, 339-363.

*E. Y. Kutscher, "Canaanite (=*C*)—Hebrew (=*H*)—Phoenician (=*Ph*)—Aramaic (=*A*)—Mishnaic Hebrew (=*MH*)—Punic (=*P*)," *Lěš* 33 (1968-69) #2/3, n.p.n.

*Moshe Held, "Rhetorical Questions in Ugaritic and Biblical Hebrew," *EI* 9 (1969) 71-79. [Non-Hebrew Section]

*J. C. Greenfield, "Amurrite, Ugaritic and Canaanite," *PICSS* (1969) 92-101.

A. Demsky, "תהחפך כסא מלכה‎—The Cultural Continuum of a Canaanite Curse," *Lěš* 34 (1969-70) #3, n.p.n.

§501 *3.3.3.2.1.2 Amorite*

Matitiahu Tesvat, "On the 'Amorite' *ta/te* 'with'," *BASOR* #156 (1959) 40-41.

*Albrecht Goetze, "Amurrite Names in Ur III and Early Isin Texts," *JSS* 4 (1959) 193-203.

*Lloyd R. Bailey, "Israelite *ʾĒl Šadday* and Amorite *Bêl Šadê*," *JBL* 87 (1968) 434-438.

C. R. Krahmolkov, "The Amorite Enclitic Particle *TA/I*," *JSS* 14 (1969) 201-204.

*J. C. Greenfield, "Amurrite, Ugaritic and Canaanite," *PICSS* (1969) 92-101.

§502 *3.3.3.2.1.3 Edomite*

Eliezer ben Yehuda, "The Edomite Language," *JPOS* 1 (1920-21) 113-115.

§503 *3.3.3.2.1.4 Hebrew Philology - General Studies (includes History of the Hebrew Language)*

†Meirion, "Affinity of Welsh and Hebrew," *MMBR* 2 (1796) 609-611.

Charles Hodge, "On the Antiquity, History, &c. of the Hebrew Language," *BibR* 2 (1826) 293-316.

Anonymous, "Illustrations of the Elementary Principles of the Structure of Language," *BibR* 3 (1827) 519-535. *[Hebrew]*

Samuel H. Turner, "The Claims of the Hebrew Language and Literature," *BRCR* 1 (1831) 491-530.

*[Wilhelm] Gesenius, "Sources of Hebrew Philology and Lexicography," *BRCR* 3 (1833) 1-44. *(Trans. by Edward Robinson)*

*William M. Willett, "The History of the Hebrew Text, with Some Considerations for the Study of the Hebrew," *MR* 21 (1839) 164-176.

*C., "The Importance of a Knowledge of Hebrew to the Interpreter of the Scripture," *CongML* 25 (1842) 85-91.

Franz Delitzsch, "Outlines of the History of Hebrew Philology," *BRCR, N.S.,* 10 (1843) 190-219. *(Trans. by Wm. W. Turner)*

A. B., "History of the Early Study of Hebrew in England," *JSL, 1st Ser.,* 6 (1850) 1-25.

Anonymous, "On the Study of Hebrew," *JSL, 2nd Ser.,* 5 (1853-54) 138-144.

*W[illiam] Henry Green, "On the Relation of Hebrew to the Indo-European Tongues," *PAOS* (November, 1858) 7-8.

Russell Martineau, "On the Study of Hebrew: An Address at the Opening of the Session of Manchester New College, London, Oct. 10, 1864," *TRL* 1 (1864) 574-592.

George H. Whittemore, "Literature and Language of the Hebrews. A Translation," *BQ* 7 (1873) 237-244. [Translation of Renen's *Histoire Générale Des Langues Sémitiques*, Book II, Chap. 1, §4]

Wm. Henry Green, "The Study of the Hebrew Language," *PQPR* 5 (1876) 40-55.

R. B. Girdlestone, "The Preacher's Tools, and How to Use Them," *CM* 9 (1879) 310-319. [Part II.—Linguistic Helps to the Study of the Old Testament]

F. W. Lewis, "A Plea for the Study of Hebrew," *SPR* 30 (1879) 84-91.

Edward J. Young, "The Value of the Study of Hebrew for a Minister," *URRM* 11 (1879) 479-500.

John Currie, "The Study of Hebrew: Its Claims Upon Theological Students and Christian Ministers," *ONTS* 2 (1882-83) 1-13. *[Extra number following the December issue]*

B. Pick, "The Study of the Hebrew Language Among Jews and Christians," *BS* 41 (1884) 450-477.

‡Hermann L. Strack, "Books for the Study of the Neo-Hebraic Language," *AJSL* 1 (1884-85) 49-51.

R. F. Weidner, "The Hebrew Language," *ONTS* 4 (1884-85) 371-373.

John P. Peters, "Hebrew in College," *ONTS* 5 (1884-85) 397-399.

B. Pick, "The Study of the Hebrew Language Among Jews and Christians, Period II. The Study of Hebrew among Christians (A.D. 1500-1700)," *BS* 42 (1885) 470-495.

*Morris Jastrow Jr., "Assyrian, in its Relation to Hebrew and Arabic," *PAPA* 18 (1886) xviii-xix.

*W. O. Sproull, "The Native Language of Abraham," *AJSL* 4 (1887-88) 186.

Shailer Mathews, "The Rhetorical Value of the Study of Hebrew," *ONTS* 7 (1887-88) 276-280.

Morris Jastrow Jr., "The Present Status of Semitic Studies in this Country," *AJSL* 5 (1888-89) 77-79.

William R. Harper, "Semitic Study in the University," *AJSL* 5 (1888-89) 83-85.

Francis Brown, "Semitic Study in the Theological Seminary," *AJSL* 5 (1888-89) 86-88.

Crawford H. Toy, "Brief Addresses in Connection with the Same Topics," *AJSL* 5 (1888-89) 88.

William Henry Green, "Brief Addresses in Connection with the Same Topics," *AJSL* 5 (1888-89) 89-90.

Paul Haupt, "Brief Addresses in Connection with the Same Topics," *AJSL* 5 (1888-89) 89.

[David G.] Lyon, "Brief Addresses in Connection with the Same Topics," *AJSL* 5 (1888-89) 90-91.

Morris Jastrow Jr., "Postscript to Semitic Studies in America," *AJSL* 5 (1888-89) 198-199.

W. Bacher, "The view of Jehuda Halevi Concerning the Hebrew Language," *AJSL* 8 (1891-92) 136-149.

L. W. Batten, "Is It Necessary for a Clergyman to Know Hebrew?" *ONTS* 15 (1892) 124-128.

*H. C. Hatcher, "The language and literature of the Old Testament," *CMR* 7 (1895) 20-29. [I. The Old Testament language, pp. 21-25]

Ed. König, "'Arabisms' in the Old Testament?" *ET* 9 (1897-98) 430-432, 474-479.

Henry Hyvernat, "The Place of Hebrew in the Programs of Our Seminaries," *CUB* 4 (1898) 387-389.

*Edward Montet, "Mr. Le Pasteur Fesquet's New Theory of the Origin of Languages," *IAQR, 3rd Ser.,* 8 (1899) 386-388. *[Hebrew]*

David Prince, "The Homiletic Value of a Knowledge of Hebrew," *HR* 41 (1901) 162-166.

W. M. Christie, "Hebrew as a Spoken Tongue," *GUOST* 3 (1907-12) 61-62.

James C. Walker, "Can a Blind Man Learn Hebrew?" *USR* 19 (1907-08) 273-277.

W. N. Donovan, "The Homiletical Worth of the Study of Hebrew," *BW* 32 (1908) 51-62.

H. D. Catlin, "Is Our Present Seminary Hebrew Worth While," *BW* 32 (1908) 205-210.

Hilary G. Richardson, "The Use of Hebrew to a Minister," *HTR* 2 (1909) 73-84.

*O Neufchotz de Jassy, "The Mythological Hebrew Terms Explained by Sanskrit. *An Essay in Comparative Philology and Mythology*," *Monist* 18 (1908) 126-138. [Editorial introduction, p. 126; Editorial Postscript, pp. 138-140; Rejoinder, pp. 140-142]

M. H. Segal, "Hebrew in the Period of the Second Temple," *IJA* #23 (1910) 79-82.

Irwin Hoch De Long, "The Importance of the Study of Hebrew in a Theological Course," *RChR, 4th Ser.,* 14 (1910) 1-23.

Max L. Margolis, "The Scope and Methodology of Biblical Philology," *JQR, N.S.,* 1 (1910-11) 5-41.

W. St. Clair Tisdall, "The Āryan Words in the Old Testament I," *JQR, N.S.,* 1 (1910-11) 335-339.

W. St. Clair Tisdall, "The Āryan Words in the Old Testament," *JQR, N.S.,* 2 (1911-12) 213-219, 365-375. *[Parts II and III]*

*T. Witton Davies, "Some Notes on Hebrew Matters, Literary and Otherwise," *R&E* 9 (1912) 551-556.

*J. Oscar Boyd, "The Science of Semantics and the Words of the Old Testament," *BM* 1 (1913) 336-345.

W. St. Clair Tisdall, "The Āryan Words in the Old Testament," *JQR, N.S.,* 4 (1913-14) 97-105. *[Part IV]*

‡*T. Witton Davies, "Survey of Recent Work on Semitic Philology and Hebrew Grammar," *RTP* 9 (1913-14) 685-713.

*Anonymous, "The Value of Hebrew and Greek to the Minister," *MR* 96 (1914) 307-311.

*J. Iverach Munro, "The Witness of Philology to the Truth of the Old Testament," *JTVI* 49 (1917) 199-216 (Discussion, pp. 216-220)

Maurice A. Canney, "The Study of Hebrew," *ICMM* 15 (1918-19) 324-327.

W. K. Lowther Clarke, "In the Study. On Learning Hebrew," *Theo* 4 (1922) 283-284.

Robert F. Gribble, "The Minister and His Hebrew Old Testament," *USR* 36 (1924-25) 70-81.

*Samuel Poznanski, "New Material on the History of Hebrew and Hebrew-Arabic Philology during the X-XII Centuries," *JQR, N.S.,* 16 (1925-26) 237-266.

*W. E. Staples, "The Hebrew of the Septuagint," *AJSL* 44 (1927-28) 6-30.

R. B. Y. Scott, "The Case for Hebrew," *CJRT* 6 (1929) 105-116.

John A. Maynard, "The Renaissance in Hebrew," *CJRT* 8 (1931) 172-176.

W. M. Christie, "The Renaissance of Hebrew," *JTVI* 63 (1931) 67-80, 86-87. [(Discussion, pp. 80-85)(Communication by Harry Biddulph, p. 85)]

C. Hougstad, "Classical Training, Including Hebrew, as a Preparation of the Study of Theology," *TF* 4 (1932) 104-124, 220.

P. E. Kretzmann, "Why Hebrew?" *CTM* 4 (1933) 939.

*Charles C. Torrey, "Hebrew and Aramaic from Beth Shemesh," *JAOS* 55 (1935) 307-310.

Barnard C. Taylor, "The Hebrew Language—Some Characteristics," *CRP* 7 (1938) 39-47.

Alexander Sperber, "Hebrew Based Upon Biblical Passages in Parallel Transmission," *HUCA* 14 (1939) 153-249.

Zellig S. Harris, "Linguistic Structure in Hebrew," *JAOS* 61 (1941) 143-167.

Pinchos Wechter, "Ibn Barūn's Contribution to Comparative Hebrew Philology," *JAOS* 61 (1941) 172-187.

W. J. Martin, "The Genius of the Language of the Old Testament," *JTVI* 74 (1942) 195-205. [(Discussion, pp. 205-208) (Communications by Edward Robertson, p. 208; E. B. W. Chappelow, pp. 208-210; H. S. Curr, pp. 210-211; J. B. Anderson, p. 210)]

R. Gordis, "Some Relationships of Biblical and Rabbinic Hebrew," *JBL* 64 (1945) viii-ix.

Joseph L. Mihelic, "The Study of Hebrew in England," *JAAR* 14 (1946) 94-100.

*G. R. Driver, "Theological and Philological Problems in the Old Testament," *JTS* 47 (1946) 156-166. [I. Theological Problems (i) *The god* Ym *in proper names;* (ii) *Cain's warning;* II. Philological Problems (i) *Words misread;* (ii) *Roots confused; Dr. Guillaume's Comments*]

Alexander Sperber, "Biblical Hebrew," *PAAJR* 18 (1948-49) 301-382.

*David Diringer, "The Early Hebrew Hand-Book," *PEQ* 82 (1950) 16-24.

*Harry M. Orlinsky, "Studies in Talmudic Philology," *HUCA* 23 (1950-51) Part 1, 499-514.

W. Chomsky, "What was the Jewish Vernacular During the Second Commonwealth?" *JQR, N.S.,* 42 (1951-52) 193-212.

James Lewis, "On the Value of Hebrew," *LQHR* 178 (1953) 11-13.

Ludwig Koehler, "Problems in the Study of the Language of the Old Testament," *JSS* 1 (1956) 3-24.

Albert Carver, "The Value of Hebrew to the Ministerial Student," *SR* 4 (1957-58) 75-80.

*William H. Rossell, "Preaching Values in Hebrew Words," *SWJT, N.S.,* 2 (1959-60) #1, 19-25.

Paul Kahle, "Pre-Masoretic Hebrew," *ALUOS* 2 (1959-61) 6-10.

Jehoshua M. Grintz, "Hebrew as the Spoken and Written Language in the Last Days of the Second Temple," *JBL* 79 (1960) 32-47.

James Barr, "The Position of Hebrew Language in Theological Education," *IRM* 50 (1961) 435-444.

George Howard, "Hebrew in First Century Palestine," *RestQ* 5 (1961) 57-61.

James Barr, "The Position of Hebrew Language in Theological Education," *PSB* 55 (1962) #3, 16-24.

A. S. Halkin, "The Medieval Jewish Attitude toward Hebrew," *LIST* 1 (1963) 233-248.

John C. L. Gibson, "Hebrew Writing as a Subject of Linguistic Investigation," *GUOST* 20 (1963-64) 49-62.

Ernst E. Ettisch, "The Monumental Pictorial Script of the Hebrews," *JQR, N.S.,* 54 (1963-64) 28-57.

*E. Y. Kutscher, "Aramaic Calque in Hebrew,"*Tarbiz* 33 (1963-64) #2, II-III.

Hugh R. Harcourt, "The Hebraic Void in the University," *TT* 20 (1963-64) 347-361.

*U. Ornan, "The Tiberian Vocalisation System and the Principles of Linguistics," *JJS* 15 (1964) 109-123.

*Jean-Georges Kahn, "Did Philo Know Hebrew?" *Tarbiz* 34 (1964-65) #4 IV-V.

*Marvin H. Pope, "Marginalia to M. Dahood's *Ugaritic-Hebrew* Philology," *JBL* 85 (1966) 455-466.

William Chomsky, "The Growth of Hebrew During the Middle Ages," *JQR, 75th* (1967) 121-136.

P. P. Saydon, "Hebraico-Maltese Notes," *RDSO* 41 (1967) 115-154.

*Sh. Yeivin, "Philological Notes 10," *Lĕš* 32 (1967-68) #1/2, I-II. [1. Joshua's defeat of the Jerusalemite Confederation, 2. I Sam. 15:22-23; 3. Technical Terms describing Solomon's Temple]

M. Z. Kaddari, "On Semantic Parallelism in Biblical Hebrew," *Lĕš* 32 (1967-68) #1/2, III.

Henoch Yalon, "Gleanings on Mishnaic Hebrew,"*Tarbiz* 37 (1967-68) #2, II.

Joseph Naveh, "A Palaeographic Note on the Distribution of the Hebrew Script," *HTR* 61 (1968) 68-74.

*E. Brønno, "Samaritan Hebrew and Origin's Secunda," *JSS* 13 (1968) 192-201.

*Otto W. Heick, "Biblical Inerrancy and the Hebrew Mode of Speech," *LQ, N.S.,* 20 (1968) 7-19.

M. Sokoloff, "The Hebrew of *Bĕrēšit Rabba* According to Ms. Vat. Ebr. 30," *Lĕš* 33 (1968-69) #1, n.p.n., #2/3, n.p.n., #4, 2.

J. H. Eaton, "The Teaching of Hebrew for Degrees in Theology," *Theo* 72 (1969) 352-355.

*J. Yahalom, "The Palestinian Vocalization in Hedwata's Qĕduštot, and the Language Tradition it Reflects," *Lĕš* 34 (1969-70) #1/2, 3-4 *[English Supplement]*

N. Berggrün, "The Language Spoken by the Jews in the Diaspora as a Source for the Study of Hebrew," *Lĕš* 34 (1969-70) #3, n.p.n.

Y. Yitzhaki, "The Hebrew Authors of the Haskalah: Their Views on the Hebrew Language and Their Ways and Means of Perfecting it," *Lĕš* 34 (1969-70) #4, n.p.n.

§504 *3.3.3.2.1.4.1 Hebrew Lexicography*

*†Anonymous, "Dr. Geedes on the Hebrew Scriptures," *BCQTR* 19 (1802) 1-15, 134-154, 283-293, 348-355, 524-530, 623-631; 20 (1802) 53-61, 165-171. *(Review)*

*[Wilhelm] Gesenius, "Sources of Hebrew Philology and Lexicography," *BRCR* 3 (1833) 1-44. *(Trans. by Edward Robinson)*

M. Stuart, "Hebrew Lexicography," *BRCR* 8 (1836) 448-494. *(Review)*

I. Nordheimer, "Hebrew Lexicography," *BRCR* 11 (1838) 482-503. *(Review)*

(   ) Benisch, "On the Conjectural Affinity of Certain Hebrew and English words," *TPS* (1848-50) 122-124.

T. A., "Hebrew Synonyms," *JSL, 4th Ser.,* 5 (1864) 429.

Edward Biley, "On the Confusion of Certain Hebrew Forms," *JSL, 4th Ser.,* 10 (1866-67) 172-177. [(A) קָדְשִׁים קֹדֶשׁ (B) הַקֳּדָשִׁים (C) קָדְשֵׁי (D) הַקֳּדָשִׁים (E) הַקֹּדֶשׁ קָדְשׁ מָקוֹם (F) הַקֹּדֶשׁ מְקוֹם]

*George H. Whittemore, "Hebrew Grammar and Lexicography," *BS* 29 (1872) 547-553.

Charles J. Elliott, "The Sacrificial Terms of the Old Testament," *CM* 7 (1878) 65-83.

*A. B. Rich, "Do the Scriptures Prohibit the Use of Alcoholic Beverages?" *BS* 37 (1880) 99-133, 305-327, 401-418. *[Word Studies of Old Testament Terms]*

A Lowy, "On Technological Terms in Ancient Semitic Culture and Fokelore[sic]*," *SBAP* 6 (1883-84) 138-144.

Francis Brown, "The Needs of Hebrew Lexicography," *PR* 6 (1885) 114-118.

*R[obert] D[ick] Wilson, "Hebrew Lexicography and Assyriology," *PR* 6 (1885) 319-328.

Stanley Leathes, "Foreign Words in the Hebrew Text of the Old Testament," *JRAS* (1886) 527-542.

Cyrus Adler, "Hebrew Words in the Latin Glossary Codex Sangellensis 912," *PAPA* 18 (1886) iv-vii.

*P. A. Nordell, "Old Testament Word Studies: 'Man and Woman'," *ONTS* 8 (1888-89) 6-10. ['Îsh—'Îshshah; 'Ādhām; 'ᵉnôsh; Gĕbhĕr; Mᵉthîm; Nă'ăr; Bachûr; Zēqēn]

*P. A. Nordell, "Old Testament Word-Studies: 2. Constituent Parts of Man," *ONTS* 8 (1888-89) 49-54. [Rû(ă)ḥ *spirit;* Nĕphĕsh *soul;* Nᵉshāmā(h) *breath;* Bāsār *flesh;* Lēbh or Lēbhābh *heart;* Kᵉlāyôth *kidneys, reins]*

*P. A. Nordell, "Old Testament Word-Studies: 3. Moral Good," *ONTS* 8 (1888-89) 101-105. [Qādhăsh *to be holy;* Qōdhĕsh *holiness;* Qādhôsh *holy;* Ḥĕsĕdh *love, grace;* Tsĕdhĕqāh *righteousness;* Yāshār *upright;* 'ᵉmeth *truth;* Tôbh *good]*

*P. A. Nordell, "Old Testament Word-Studies: 4. Moral Evil," *ONTS* 8 (1888-89) 143-147. ['āvĕn *vanity;* 'āshām *guilt;* Bᵉlīyyă'ăl *worthlessness;* Hăvvāh *destructive wickedness;* Hăttā'th *sin;* 'āvĕl, 'ăvᵉlāh *unfairness;* 'āvōn *iniquity;* 'āmāl *toil, misery;* Pĕshă' *transgression, felony;* Ră' *wicked, evil;* Rāshă' *wicked]*

*P. A. Nordell, "Old Testament Word Studies: 5. Divine Law," *ONTS* 8 (1888-89) 176-180. [Dîn *cause, judgment;* Dāth *edit, law;* Ḥōq, Ḥŭqqāh *statute, ordinance;* Mĭtsvāh *commandment;* Mĭsmĕrĕth *charge;* Mĭshpāt *judgment;* 'ēdhûth *testimony;* Pĭqqûdhîm *precepts;* Tôrāh *law]*

*P. A. Nordell, "Old Testament Word Studies: 6. Theocratic Functionaries," *ONTS* 8 (1888-89) 220-224. [Rŏ'ĕh *seer;* Ḥōzĕh *seer, gazer;* Nābhî' *prophet;* Kōhēn *priest;* Lēvî *Levite;* Mĕlĕk *king*]

*P. A. Nordell, "Old Testament Word Studies: 7. Sacrifice and Worship," *ONTS* 8 (1888-89) 257-261. [Mĭnḥāh *present, offering;* Qŏrbān *offering;* Zēbhăḥ *sacrifice;* 'ōlāh *burnt offering;* Ḥăṭṭā'th *sin offering;* 'āshām *guilt offering;* Kĭppĕr *to make atonement*]

*P. A. Nordell, "Old Testament Word Studies: 8. Idols and Images," *ONTS* 8 (1888-89) 296-301. [Mĭnḥāh *present, offering;* Qŏrbān *offering;* Zēbhăḥ *sacrifice;* 'ōlāh *burnt offering;* Ḥăṭṭā'th *sin offering*]

*P. A. Nordell, "Old Testament Word Studies: 9. Angels, Demons, etc.," *ONTS* 8 (1888-89) 341-345. [Rû(ă)ḥ rā'āh *evil spirit;* Măl'ākh *messenger, angel;* Măl'ākh Jehōvāh *angel of Jehovah;* Măhănăyîm tᵉsbhā'ôth *hosts;* Kᵉrûbhîm *cherubim;* Sᵉrāphîm *seraphim;* Ṣātān*[sic]* *adversary, Satan;* Sā'îr *satyr;* lîlîth *night monster*]

*C[laude] R. Conder, "Jews and Gentiles in Palestine," *PEFQS* 22 (1890) 310-326. [*Comparative Word Study - Hebrew/Greek*]

D. S. Margoliouth, "Requests and Replies," *ET* 6 (1894-95) 420-421. [Etymology - "Mistletoe (mazzal-tov); Hogmanay (Chag-meni); Cholera (Choli-ra)]

*Fritz Hommel, "Belial and Other Mythological Terms," *ET* 8 (1896-97) 472-473.

*T. K. Cheyne, "Hebrew Mythological Terms," *ET* 8 (1896-97) 525-526.

A. B. Davidson, "'Studies in Hebrew Synonyms'," *ET* 9 (1897-98) 286. *(Review)*

C. Levias, "Etymological Notes," *AJSL* 16 (1899-1900) 248-251. [1. בַּדְיָא; 2. בַּרְקָא; 3. כַּבָּא; 4. כִּכָּרָא; 5. מִין; 6. מוּקְרָא; 7. שְׁצִנִיתָא; 8. מַמְזֵר; 9. מְנָזֵר; 10. narâbu]

D. S. Margoliouth, "Armenian as Illustrative of Hebrew," *ET* 11 (1899-1900) 235-237. [1. צמק; 2. גִּבּוֹר; 3. נֵאץ; 4. רֶסוּ; 5. הפרשדנה, המסדרונה; 6. כֶּתֶר; 7. צְבָאוֹת]

*Julius A. Bewer, "Lexical Notes," *AJSL* 17 (1900-01) 168-170. [שמר,
Amos 1:11; אתה, Deut. 33:21; אשר, Isa. 1:17; זר, Isa. 1:7 (and often);
רגמה, Psa. 68:28; פחח, Isa. 42:22]

*Julius A. Bewer, "New Lexical and Critical Suggestions," *AJSL* 18 (1901-
02) 120-122. [נביא "Prophet"; קוש, Isa. 29:21; קוץ, 1 Kings 11:25; Isa
7:6; שׂא, Psa. 35:17; זאבי ערב, Zeph. 3:3; Hab. 1:8; מורה, Job 36:22]

N. Herz, "Doubtful Hebrew Words," *ET* 13 (1901-02) 190. [אשׁפר; כן, כנם,
or כנם; סרפד]

C[aspar] Levias, "B. Word Studies," *HUCA* (1904) 147-157. [1.מסקרת; 2.
זע טוט.6; איירי, ארא.5; סבר, גרס, גמר.4; גפן=גנף=גלף.3; אפודה;
7. (בגתפי)טט בכתפי ; 8. גיתאפי.9; מילי מוליאתא.10; מרדו.11; מחם;
12.הלם, המולה.13; הויא, הוא.14; עשיק]

*Henry Preserved Smith, "Old Testament Notes," *JBL* 24 (1905) 27-30. [I.
Nisroch and Nusku; II. Nabi'; III. Naioth; IV. 1 Chronicles 22:2; V.
Genesis 35:11; VI. Judges 9:29; VII. The Emphatic ל or לא]

*Felix Perles, "The Fourteenth Edition of Gesenius-Buhl's Dictionary," *JQR*
18 (1905-06) 383-390. *(Review)* [I. Lexical Remarks. בן; ברית = biritu;
סרן; ספר, סנפיר; המריא; משך=to acquire; מעט; ילפת; חשך; גרע;
שלח; צלפחד; ערכך; עצב=nerve; עז, סתר (as a *musical* expression); תהומות=Tiâmat, pp. 384-388; תימרות עשן]

C[laude] R. Conder, "Notes on Biblical Antiquities. 4.," *PEFQS* 37 (1905)
156-157.[Oboth ('ôbôth); Parah פרתה;The Tapsar תפסר ;(Sumir
סמר)]

*St[ephen] Langdon, "Lexicographical Notes," *ZA* 21 (1908) 283-292. [1.
כתר to be complete, successful, etc.; 2. *pûḫu* = "image"; 3. פחה; 4.
sirdū abālu = sardū abālu:aplu = "replacer"; 5. *ardu* and *ardatu*]

*Max L. Margolis, "Complete Induction for the Identification of the
Vocabulary in the Greek Versions of the Old Testament with its Semitic
Equivalents: Its Necessity and the Means of obtaining it," *JAOS* 30
(1909-10) 301-312.

*Felix Perles, "A Miscellany of Lexical and Textual Notes on the Bible, Chiefly in connection with the Fifteenth Edition of the Lexicon by Gesenius-Buhl," *JQR, N.S.,* 2 (1911-12) 97-132. [אמץ, אפם, בארים, בְּתָה,
= לֹמד, כשיל וכילפות, דְּגָלֹות הֹמר, זמרי as the name of a people, גורל
drive on, מחה, מכרה, מְלֹא, מנהרוה, מַשְׂאֹות, נולי, עֲמֹיהוּד, עמקם?,
[שֹתֹר בוזני, שֹמֹת, שֹמֹאל, שֹמֹא, שֹהֹד, קְלֹקֹל, קֹדֹם, פֹּרֹק, פֹּרֹח, נעתרות]

*James A. Montgomery, "Notes on the Old Testament," *JBL* 31 (1912) 140-146. [1. יגר, Gen. 31:47; 2. עֹל שֹים, 1 Kgs. 20:12; 3. Sukkoth-Benoth, 2 Kgs. 17:30; 4. The barbarous Syllables in Isa. 28:10; 5. חֹזֹה, Isa. 28:15; 6. מֹבֹליג, Am. 5:9; 7. הֹכֹל, Eccles. 11:5, etc.; 8. The Interrogative particle מֹי or מֹה; 9. The Correlative use of כֹי and אֹכֹן]

Felix Perles, "Additions and Corrections to Miscellany of Lexical and Textual Notes on the Bible," *JQR, N.S.,* 3 (1912-13) 313-314.

Emil Lund, "Biblical Hebrew and Common English,"*TTKF* 15 (1913) 39-54.

*E. Ben Yehuda, "Three Notes in Hebrew Lexicography," *JAOS* 37 (1917) 324-327.

H. Geers, "Hebrew Textual Notes," *AJSL* 34 (1917-18) 129-134. [Neh. 12:8, עַל־הַיְדֹות; Ezek. 30:9, בַּצֹּים מֹלְפָנַי מַלְאָכֹים יֵצְאֹוּ; 2 Sam. 20:14, אֶל נֹחֹילֹות, Psa. 5:1; וֹכֹל־הֹבֹרֹים וֹיֹקֹהֹלֹוּ וֹיֹבֹאֹוּ אֹף־אֹחֹרֹיו; Job. 12:21 בֹּאָה הֹצֹפֹרֹה אֹלֹיךֹ יֹוֹשֹׁב; Isa. 11:5; Ezek 7:7 וֹמֹזֹיֹחֹ אֹפֹיֹקֹים רֹפֹה; Isa. 31:8b-9a.]

*Robert Dick Wilson, "Scientific Biblical Criticism," *PTR* 17 (1919) 190-240, 401-456. [E. The Vocabulary, pp. 413-435]

W[illiam] F[oxwell] Albright, "The Hebrew Stems *dlk, grš, škḥ,*" *JBL* 39 (1920) 167-168.

James Robertson Buchanan, "A Study in Hebrew Synonyms. *Verbs signifying 'shut,' 'close,' 'stop up.',*" *SSO* 1 (1920) 1-12.

David Yellin, "Some Fresh Meanings of Hebrew Roots," *JPOS* 1 (1920-21) 10-14. [דֹרֹך, אֹמֹן, אֹבֹד]

G. R. Driver, "Notes on Hebrew Lexicography," *JTS* 23 (1921-22) 405-410.
[Corr. *JTS* 31 (1929-30) p. 284] [אדב;אח ;אמה ;אמץ ;אסף ;באר ;דבה;
;מלתעות ;כתם ;כישור ;חשמן ;חשל ;חרם ;חפה ;חסידה ;חמל ;Iדומה;
;שהין ;רכס ;קיץ ;קבע ;IIIצי ;פתח ;פתיחה ;פורים ;סרים ;נחשת II; מרא
שחיף ;שגיון ;שמר ;שרב ;תמך]

*Israel Efros, "Glosses on the Hebrew Bible," *JAOS* 42 (1922) 390. [Ex.
32:2; Deut. 32:35; Isa. 1:18 (cf. 57:2, Amos 3:10); Isa. 2:12 (cf. Hab.
2:4); Isa. 5:7; 10:13 (cf. 2 Kings 17:6; 18:11 & Ezek. 1:3); Hos. 11:4;
Eccl. 1:5; 1:8; 2:1; 5:5; 9:12; 12:5]

*Herbert H. Gowen, "Hebrew Trade and Trade Terms in O.T. Times," *JSOR*
6 (1922) 1-16. [אהל,אהלות), (once אהלים);כרכם ,נרד ,אל־מגים, ט ל,
אזוב ,ברית ,נתר ,מר ,חלבנם ,כמן ,קנמון ,קנה ,קציעה ,בדלח ,צרי ,בשם,
אגוז ,מֶשִׁי ,שֵׁש ,בוץ ,אטון מורים ,אטין ,מָדין ,כתנת ,קִשָּׁא ,שִׂקְמָה,
גמל ,תכיים ,קפים ,בזל]*[sic] (see Ezek. 27:15);* הבנם ,שֶׁנְהַבִּים

*Israel Eitan, "The Bearing of Ethiopic on Biblical Exegesis and Lexi-
cography," *JPOS* 3 (1923) 136-143.

A. Cohen, "Studies in Hebrew Lexicography," *AJSL* 40 (1923-24) 153-185.
[אבנים, אגם, אוד, אכל, אסון, אפל, בדלח, בקא, בזק, הבן בן ,בצץ,
בקיע, ברה, גב, גב(?), גבן, גדוד, גדל, גלד, גליון, גלש, גרע, דלל,
דק, הדר, חלל, זמרה, חגב, חרק, חיה (?), IIIIחלה, חלש, חתן, ילפת,
כלוב, כמס, לבב, מן, משך , נוף, נזה, נחץ (?), סריס, עב, עב, עבר,
עדר, עדר, (פח), צנצנת, קסס, קרס, רדיד, שחיף, שים, שמיכה, שלח,
שמץ, שפלות, תך, תנה]

*Israel Eitan, "Ethiopic and Hebrew Etymologies," *AJSL* 40 (1923-24) 269-
276.

J. Morgenstern, "Two Compound Technical Terms in Biblical Hebrew,"
JBL 43 (1924) 311-320. [מקרא קדש יובל הוא]

Samuel Feigin, "Word Studies," *AJSL* 41 (1924-25) 274-278. [I. Etymology
of *Madaktu,* "Camp"; II. *Sandanakum,* "A Tree Cultivator"; III.
Sattakka, "Always"; IV. "Fixed Price" ערכך]

Joseph Reider, "Studies in Hebrew Roots and Their Etymology," *HUCA* 2
(1925) 87-97. [גו. ,חלץ ,שמד ,אבחה ,אנן ,נהר ,קדד and קרר]

*Samuel Feigin, "Word Studies," *AJSL* 43 (1926-27) 44-53. [I. שֶׁגֶר, "Womb of Beasts"; II. שׁגל, "Womb," שָׁגֵל, "Rape"; שֵׁגֵל, "Foreign Woman"; III. Sumerian Origin of שֶׁגֶר and שֵׁגֵל, שֵׁגֵל; IV. כַּלָּה, "Bride"; V. פֶּתַח, "Pudenda"; VI. שַׁ, "Heart, Inside"; VII. שׁכל, "Abort"; VIII. Etymology of Sal, "Woman," in Sumerian; IX. פִּילֶגֶשׁ, "Concubine"; X. לְחֵנָה, "Concubine"; XI. Talmudic כרן, "Same"; The Date Formula še-ga dingir "gal-gal"]

G. R. Driver, "Some Hebrew Words," *JTS* 29 (1927-28) 390-396. [אבך; נכר; נמרץ; הַנְּבִיאִים; לְבָה; חלה; אלח]

G. R. Driver, "Some Hebrew Verbs, Nouns, and Pronouns," *JTS* 30 (1928-29) 371-378. [בְּרֻבְּרִים; סאסאה (בשלחה) (סאסא); וְהֶעֱלִיָה; הַשּׁוֹק; שׁוּף; לֵך הִתְרַפֵּס וּרְהַב רֵעֶיךָ] (Corr. *JTS* 31 (1929-30) p. 284)

G. R. Driver, "Studies in the Vocabulary of the Old Testament," *JTS* 31 (1929-30) 275-284.

G. R. Driver, "Studies in the Vocabulary of the Old Testament. II," *JTS* 32 (1930-31) 250-257.

G. R. Driver, "Studies in the Vocabulary of the Old Testament. III," *JTS* 32 (1930-31) 361-366. (with additions and corrections)

G. R. Driver, "Studies in the Vocabulary of the Old Testament. IV," *JTS* 33 (1931-32) 38-47. [Additions and Corrections, pp. 383-385]

G. R. Driver, "Studies in the Vocabulary of the Old Testament. V.," *JTS* 34 (1933) 33-44.

G. R. Driver, "Studies in the Vocabulary of the Old Testament. VI.," *JTS* 34 (1933) 375-385.

H. L. Ginsberg, "Lexicographical Notes," *ZAW* 51 (1933) 308-309. [1. יגע, to torture; 2. *יָרֵה or *יָדִי voice; רֹבַע, dust]

*N. S. Doniach, "Studies in Hebrew Philology," *AJSL* 50 (1933-34) 177-179. [קההו√ עתר√, גוה√]

G. R. Driver, "Studies in the Vocabulary of the Old Testament. VII.," *JTS* 35 (1934) 380-393. (Corrections, p. 393)

*James A. Montgomery, "Some Hebrew Etymologies," *JQR, N.S.,* 25 (1934-35) 261-269. [(2) Roots: רכב; צפצף; נים, pp. 265-266; (3) Varia: יהוה; שֵׁי; עַד, עולם, מַס; יֶחְדָו, pp. 267-269.]

G. R. Driver, "Studies in the Vocabulary of the Old Testament. VIII.," *JTS* 36 (1935) 293-301.

*Joseph Reider, "Contributions to the Hebrew Lexicon," *ZAW* 53 (1935) 270-277. [כְּמוֹכֶן, הַיַּת, כֹּל, יָשַׁר עַל אנשים, מֶלֶךְ]

Robert Gordis, "Studies in Hebrew Roots of Contrasted Meanings," *JQR, N.S.,* 27 (1936-37) 33-58. [1. אפו. 2. חדל. 3. חפה. 4. חפש. 5. כסה 11. אלמן אשכל. 10. אלם. 9. יאב איב אהב. 8. און. 7. שאל. 6. (כסא), 18. סנורים. 17. מלל. 16. חלף. 15. חגר. 14. בקק. 13. בחל. 12. אצל 25. שחר. 24. רפה רפא. 23. רגע. 22. קלס. 21. פסח. 20. עזב. 19. עור, סכל שכל. 26. שתם. 27. שחר. 28. האב]

*Joseph Reider, "The Etymology of Hebrew *mūl, or mōl* and its Bearing on *tmōl* and *'etmōl,*" *HUCA* 12&13 (1937-38) 89-96.

Julius Lewy, "Lexicographical Notes," *HUCA* 12&13 (1937-38) 97-101. [I. גנח "To Groan"; II. אָחֵז "Learned"; III. עָצוּר וְעָזוּב "(The) yet Unborn and (the) Born"]

*Joseph Reider, "Contributions to the Hebrew lexicon," *RDSO* 17 (1937-38) 103-110. [כְּמוֹכֶן, הַיַּת, כֹּל, יָשַׁר עַל אנשים, מֶלֶךְ]

*James A. Montgomery, "Hebraica," *JAOS* 58 (1938) 130-139. [(1) *dârôm,* 'the South' = the circle of the ecliptic? (2) *yām sûp* ('the Red Sea') = *Ultimum Mare*? (3) The land of Cabul *[1 Kings 9:13]*; (4) 'in the land' = Akk. *ina māti*; (5) the Multiplicative expression *[Jer. 16:18]*; (6) A case of arithmetical proportion *[1 Kings 5:27, 30//2 Chron. 2:2, 17]*; (7) The word for the harlot's fee *['eṭnā(h) 'eṭnān]*; (8) Hebrew 'word' = 'reason' (9) Light from Arabic, (a) Daniel 9:4; I Kings 18:42, II Kings 4:34,35, (b) I Kings 10:25 (= II Chron. 9:24), (c) I Kings 2:46a (LXX) (d) 'His delight is in the fear of the LORD,' Isa. 11:3 (e) 'After thee, O Benjamin!', Judg. 5:14; Hos. 5:8, (f) The cartitative name-form 'Solomon', (g) The Rash Shamra locative with *Hē*]

Frank Zimmermann, "Some Studies in Biblical Etymology," *JQR, N.S.,* 29 (1938-39) 241-246. [1. מִסְפָּר = boundary; 2. חלץ = oppress; 3. שׁוה = ripen, to bring to maturity]

T[heophile] J. Meek, "Use of *Lamedh* in *lᵉpī hereḇ,*" *JBL* 59 (1940) xiv.

*Steven T. Byington, "Hebrew Marginalia I," *JBL* 60 (1941) 279-288. [Terms of Hebrew Daily Life Surviving Only in Metaphor and Simile, pp. 279-281]

*Norval Gerhard Hegland, "Sermons in Hebrew Words," *JTALC* 6 (1941) 817-835, 935-944. [Part I. Chief Names for God, 'Elohim, Jhwh, 'El Shaddaj, Jhwh Zeba'oth; Part II. Chief Words for Man, 'Adam, 'Ish, 'Enosh, Gebher]

Alfred Guillaume, "Magical Terms in the Old Testament," *JRAS* (1942) 111-131; (1946) 79-80.

G. R. Driver, "Hebrew Notes," *JRAS* (1944) 165-171. *[Ref. Guillaume's article, above]*

*William Foxwell Albright, "The Old Testament and Canaanite Language and Literature," *CBQ* 7 (1945) 5-31. [VI. Canaanite Light on Hebrew Grammar and Lexicography, pp. 22-26]

*Steven T. Byington, "Hebrew Marginalia III," *JBL* 64 (1945) 339-355. [1.) The Sense of Certain Words: באשים ;נבא ;פנינים + ראמות ;נא ;יד ;דכא (Isa. 5:2, 4) pp. 339-343]

*Steven T. Byington, "Some Bits of Hebrew. I. Topography in Hebrew," *ET* 57 (1945-46) 26-27.

*Steven T. Byington, "Some Bits of Hebrew. II. Medical and Physiological Hebrew," *ET* 52 7 (1945-46) 52.

*Steven T. Byington, "Zoological Hebrew," *ET* 57 (1945-46) 81-82.

A. S. Yahuda, "Hebrew Words of Egyptian Origin," *JBL* 66 (1947) 83-90. הִתְוָה (7 ;אַטֵּים (6 ;הַמָּנִים (5 ;תַּחְרָא (4 ;מֶרְבֶּכֶת (3 ;מֶרְחָשָׁת (2 ;יָעִים (1] פַּקַח־קוֹחַ (8 ;פְּרָוִים (9 ;פָּרְוָר (10

*G. R. Driver, "Mistranslations," *PEQ* 79 (1947) 123-126.[קפוּ ;√wrd ;יֹשֵׁב [רוד ;יום ;ירד

*H. A. Wolfson, "Arabic and Hebrew Terms for Matter and Element with Especial Reference to Saadia," *JQR, N.S.*, 38 (1947-48) 47-61.

G. R. Driver, "Mistranslations in the Old Testament," *WO* 1 (1947-52) 29-31.

*Godfrey Rolles Driver, "Misreadings in the Old Testament," *WO* 1 (1947-52) 234-238.

*Godfrey Rolles Driver, "Hebrew Roots and Words," *WO* 1 (1947-52) 406-415. [I. גָּעַשׁ = חֵׁעַס ; גָּעַר = جَعَر ; אלח = أَلَخ ;(חול) חִיל קָוֶה =

;قَوَى ; פּוּר = فَار (و);ראה = רוה ;רוה ;נָחָה = نَحَا ; שָׁנָה = سَمِحَا ; עֵצָה ;

*עָצְמָה = عَظِيمَة ;*חָמָה*=حَمِى ; הָיָה = שִׁיר נָפַל ;II. יָקַח* חנק =

وقَمح [

*G. R. Driver, "Mistranslations," *PEQ* 80 (1948) 64-65. [Nu. 21:24; Deut. 3:16; √'*dw* ; aḏ; yāraḏ]

*G. J. Thierry, "Notes on Hebrew Grammar and Etymology," *OS* 9 (1951) 1-17. [hōḏ; 'el—; *kn; wâw copulativum and consecutivum; ǰǎ'ǎn; Psalm xxiii; Kaftor; m; ḥaǐ]

*Joseph Reider, "Miscellanea Hebraica," *JJS* 3 (1952) 78-86. 1.) מַאן ממאן, Ex. 7:27; 9:2; 10:4; Jer. 38:21; 2.) Prepositional prefix בּ; 3.) enclitic-*ma*; 4.) Verb לבש; 5.) לקח; 6.) Etymon שלח; 7.) Gen. 4:7; 8.) Gen. 21:16; 9.) Gen. 26:14; Job 1:3; 10.) Gen. 41:56; 11.) Num. 21:17; 12.) Num. 23-קבב;קבה; 13.) Num. 24:3, 15; 14.) Job 2:6; Nah. 2:11; 15.) Jer. 20:14ff., Job 3:3ff.; 16.) I. Cor. 15:55 = Hos. 13:14b; 17.) Ecclus. 33:2; 18.) Ecclus. 33:4; 19.) homen loci בשן; 20.) Phrase ועל האבנים וידבר על העצים]

*Joseph Reider, "Etymological Studies in Biblical Hebrew," *VT* 2 (1952) 113-130. [1 קעקע; 2 תְּרָאוּ; 3 חמת לֹבָא; 4 ונחת; 5 ידק הדה; 6 ערות; 7 והיו; 12 הרבים; 11 רשעים//עשיר; 10 המסכן תרומה; 9 חרוץ; 8 צפא; ואהיה להם כמרימי על על לחיהם 15; רעמו פנים 14; יער השדה 13 ;אלם 18; אני שמרתי ארחות פריץ 17; שבת חמס 16; ואט אליו אוכיל במות אדם רשע תאבד תקוה ותוחלת אונים 19; מרים 20; בהם 21 ;ספר 27; כידור 26; בטחות 25; יעיר 24; מעצמותי 23; עשר 22; אבדה; יחפרו בעמק וישיש 29; אך לא בעי ישלח יד אם בפידו להן שוע 28 בכח 30; יחוש//יאכל]

*Cyrus H. Gordon, "Marginal Notes on the Ancient Middle East," *JKF* 2 (1952-53) 50-61. [I. Hebrew Parallels to Linguistic Features in King Azitawad's Phoenician Inscriptions from Karatepe, p. 51]

*R. B. Y. Scott, "Meteorological Phenomena and Terminology in the Old Testament," *ZAW* 64 (1952-53) 11-25.

*G. R. Driver, "Some Hebrew Medical Expressions," ZAW 65 (1953-54) 255-262.

*A. Guillaume, "A Contribution to Hebrew Lexicography," *BSOAS* 16 (1954) 1-12. {I. Words with no Arabic Equivalent in the Hebrew Lexicon; II. Words with Weak or Doubtful Equivalents; III. Words that may rest on Both ف and ث; Philological and Exegetical Notes: *(a)* ריפח

(g) ; فاق *(f)* שנה *(e)* ; עשק *(d)* ; גרש *(c)* ; געש *(b)* [רפות (2) ,כתש (1)]

;תושיה *(m)* שֵׁי *(l)* ; רשׁע *(k)* ; רגש *(j)* ; עישׁ *(i)* Deut. xxxii, 26; *(h)* ;שׁולל

[קשׁח *(q)* ;לקשׁ *(p)* ;נחשׁלים *(o)* ; שׁקע *(n)*]

*G. R. Driver, "Babylonian and Hebrew Notes," *WO* 2 (1954-59) 19-26. [1. Three Hebrew Words (בדיל, מצהב ,כסף), (i) בְּדִיל 'tin; antimony' and 'dross, slag', pp. 21-24; (ii) נחשׁת מצהב 'orichalc', pp. 24-25; (iii) כֶּסֶף 'silver', pp. 25-26]

*G. R. Driver, "Technical Terms in the Pentateuch," *WO* 2 (1954-59) 254-263. [I. גְּבְלֻות 'welding'; II. חשׁב 'embroiderer'; חֵשֶׁב 'band'; III. כָּלִיל 'woven in one piece'; IV. מָר־דְרֹור; V. קְדָה 'cassia in strips' and קצִי טָה 'powdered cassia'; VI. שָׁבֵץ 'lined, quilted']

*Edw. Ullendorff, "The Contribution of South Semitics to Hebrew Lexicography," *VT* 6 (1956) 190-198.

Jonas C. Greenfield, "Lexicographical Notes I," *HUCA* 29 (1958) 203-228. [געשׁ I; דלף II; טרד III; להק IV; נפל V; פתק VI; קנט VII; שׁתע VIII]

N. Wieder, "Three Terms for 'Tradition'," *JQR, N.S.,* 49 (1958-59) 108-121. [הירושׁה I; העתקה II; הגדה III]

*A. Guillaume, "Hebrew and Arabic Lexicography. A Comparative Study (I)," *Abr-N* 1 (1959-60) 3-35.

C. S. Rodd, "Modern Issues in Biblical Study. Rediscovered Hebrew Meanings," *ET* 71 (1959-60) 131-134.

*Zeev W. Falk, "Hebrew Legal Terms," *JSS* 5 (1960) 350-354.

*A. Guillaume, "Hebrew and Arabic Lexicography. A Comparative Study (II)," *Abr-N* 2 (1960-61) 5-35.

*John C. L. Gibson, "Observations on Some Important Ethnic Terms in the Pentateuch," *JNES* 20 (1961) 217-238.

*Chaim Rabin, "Etymological Miscellanea," *SH* 8 (1961) 384-400. [1. אהל Qal; 2. בֿר־אוני Gen. xxxv, 18; 3. אזנ(י)ך Dt. xxiii.14 ≠ Aram. *zēnā;* 4. אחר(י) Gen. xxii, 13; 5. בוך Niph. Ex. xvi, 3; 6. דון; 7. הבו אהבו Hos. iv. 18; 8. הרן Gen. iii. 16; 9. חרה אפו; 10. מלתחה, 2 Kings. x, 22; 11. *ām* of *kinnām* = "lice"; 12. לחם; 13. מין Gen. i, 21; 14. מסדרון Jud. iii, 23; 15. מהים(מ)משֹה הבית ימעט (ואם Ex. xii, 4; 16. "hollow measure"; 17. סכן; 18. עלוה Hos. x, 9; 19. עלז; 20. התפאר Ex. viii, 5; 21. פחז; 22. כחכה צר Pr. xxiv, 10; 23. Egyptian *q'bt* "nipple" = (?) Hebrew *qēbhāh* "Fourth stomach of a ruminant"; 23.*[sic]* קריא, קרוא, 'invited to a meal, etc."; 24. שֹאת Gen. iv, 7; 25. √שכח; Additional notes]

*Harris H. Hirschberg, "Some Additional Arabic Etymologies in Old Testament Lexicography," *VT* 11 (1961) 373-385.

*A. Guillaume, "Hebrew and Arabic Lexicography. A Comparative Study (III)," *Abr-N* 3 (1961-62) 1-10.

*J. V. Kinnier Wilson, "Hebrew and Akkadian Philological Notes," *JSS* 7 (1962) 173-183. [I המר; II ירד; III ערבה and ṣarbatu; IV šasûII; V שֹממIII(?); VI. *sekrtu;* VII עיר and *âru]*

*M[itchell] Dahood, "Hebrew-Ugaritic Lexicography I," *B* 44 (1963) 289-303.[אבוה-בעל]

*Svi Rin, "Ugaritic-Old Testament Affinities," *BZ, N.S.,* 7 (1963) 22-33.

*C. Rabin, "Hittite Words in Hebrew," *Or, N.S.,* 32 (1963) 113-139. [1. *a-a-pi* "sacrificial pit" — Heb. *ob;* 2. Luwian *arkammana-*, Hitt. *arkamma(n)-* "tribute" — Heb. *argaman* "stuff dyed with purple"; 3. ^DUG*ḫarši* - "large pottery vessel, pithos" — Heb. *ḫaeraeś* "pottery vessel, potsherd", unic *chirs, ers* "potsherd"; 4. *ḫīla-, ḫēla-* "fence, court, halo" — Heb. *ḫēl* (written *ḫl, ḫyl*) "ring of fortifications surrounding a wall"; 5. *ḫuttulli-* "flock of wool" — Heb. nouns *ḫittul, ḫătullah*, verb *ḫuttul* in passive; Ug. noun *ḫtl;* perhaps also Mishnaic Hebrew *ḫotal* "packing for dates"; 6. *kalleś-* "to all, invite" (in cultic contexts) — Heb. *qls* Hitp. "to deride", *qeles, qallasah* "derision", Ugar. *qlṣ* "to deride", *qlṣ, qlṣt* "derision" or "baseness"; 7. *kariulli-* "a female garment covering head and body, hood" — late(?) Heb. *mĕkurbal* "dressed in a *KRBL* (?)"; 8. *kullupi-* "hatchet, mattock" — Heb. *keylappot* (Ps. lxxiv, 6), probably *keylap* parallel to *qardummot* "hatchets or mattocks";*(continued)*

*C. Rabin, "Hittite Words in Hebrew," *Or, N.S.,* 32 (1963) 113-139. *(continued)* 9. *kupaḫi-* "helmet"(?) — Heb. *k/qobaʿ* "helmet"; 10. *gurta-* "fortress" — Heb. *qaeraet (*qartu)* "city", Phoenician *qart-,* Aramaic *qartā;* 11. *kurtal* "container made of wood or basketwork" — Heb. construct pl. *ăgarṭĕley,* name of a bowl-shaped vessel used in the Temple, made of gold and silver; 12. *lappiya-* "glowing thing", "torch"(?), Luw. *lappi(ya)-* — Heb. *lappid* "torch", "lightning"; 13. *maŝŝi(ya)-* "shawl" — Heb. *maeŝi* (Theodotion: μεσσι), Ezek. xvi, 10, 13; 14. Luwian *mitgaimi* "sweet" (particle of an unattested verb *mitgai-)* — Heb. *mtq* in Qal "be sweet", in Hiph'il "make sweet"; 15. Hittite, Luwian, Hieroglyphic Hittite *muwat(t)alli-* "strong", especially of weapons — Heb. construct state *mĕṭil;* 16. *naḫŝariya-* "to fear" or another form of the same root — Heb. *naḫŝir* in (1QM); 17. *ŝalli-* "great, important", nominative *ŝalliŝ* — Heb. *ŝaliŝ,* pl. *ŝaliŝim,* some kind of adjutant or officer; 18. *tarkummāi-, tarkummiya-,* Luwian *tarkummiya-,* "to announce, explain, translate"— Heb. (or Imperial Aramaic) *trgm* "to translate" or "to explain" or "to read out"; 19. *tuekka-,* late *tukka-,* also *tuikamma-* "body, self" — (a) Heb. *tawaek,* construct sate *tok* "centre", "inside", *bĕ-tok* "within, in", Ugaritic *tk, btk* "within", (b) DDS Hebrew *tkmy* (construct plural) meaning probably "body"; 20. Hierogl. Hittite *tuwarsa-* "vine" — Heb. *tiroŝ* "wine", Ug. *trṭ* "wine"; 21. *wiyana-,* Luwian *winiyant-,* Hierogl. Hittite *wa(i)ana-* "wine" — Heb. *yayin* "wine", Ugaritic *yn* "wine"; 22. *zapzagai-, zapzi/aki-* "glass(?) glass vessel" — Heb. *sapsaggim* (?) "glaze"; Ugaritic. *spsg* "glaze"(?)]

*A. Guillaume, "Hebrew and Arabic Lexicography. A Comparative Study (IV)," *Abr-N* 4 (1963-64) 1-18.

C[haim] Rabin, "Etymological Notes," *Tarbiẓ* 33 (1963-64) #2, II. [1. Abēl; 2. Hit'appēq; 3. Ḥăriṭīm; 4.ʾApār; 5. Tĕshūqāh]

*M[itchell] Dahood, "Hebrew-Ugaritic Lexicography II," *B* 45 (1964) 393-412. [גְּבוּל - טָרַח]

*M[itchell] Dahood, "Hebrew-Ugaritic Lexicography III," *B* 46 (1965) 311-332.[*כָּשִׁיר - יָבָם]

*Arnold A. Wieder, "Ugaritic-Hebrew Lexicographical Notes," *JBL* 84 (1965) 160-164. [1. שׁוה—*ṭwy;* 2. More on עמק—*ʾmq;* 3. פרד—*brd;* 4. גשׁם נדבות—*mdlk mṭrtk*]

E. Y. Kutscher, "Marginal Notes to the Biblical Lexicon," *Lĕŝ* 30 (1965-66) #1, n.p.n. [6. דרבן; 7. נשׁא ובל נטל; 8. גלגל; 9. $C_1 \ni C_2 VC_3$-(<$C_1 \ni C_2 CV_3 C_3$-); 10. אָסֹף] *[No English Summaries for Numbers 1-5]*

*M[itchell] Dahood, "Hebrew-Ugaritic Lexicography IV," *B* 47 (1966) 403-419.[מַלְתָּעוֹת - ל]

*E. Y. Kutscher, "Marginal Notes to the Mishnaic Lexicon and a Grammatical Note," *Lěš* 31 (1966-67) #2, n.p.n. [1. אילתית; 2. אפר; 3. הֵיל; 4. קמצוץ; 9. פרקד; 8. עֲדָיִן; 7. סכין; 6. יבל; 5. טפה]

*M[itchell] Dahood, "Hebrew-Ugaritic Lexicography V," *B* 48 (1967) 421-438.[ממך - כָחָה]

*Svi Rin and Shifra Rin, "Ugaritic-Old Testament Affinites II," *BZ, N.S.,* 11 (1967) 174-192.

J. F. A. Sawyer, "Root-meanings in Hebrew," *JSS* 12 (1967) 37-50.

*Z[eev] W. Falk, "Hebrew Legal Terms II," *JSS* 12 (1967) 241-244.

*A. T. Hanson, "Philo's Etymologies," *JTS, N.S.,* 18 (1967) 128-139.

*Daniel Sperber, "Numismatic Hapax-Legomena," *Muséon* 80 (1967) 265-268. [TASHSIGA; QASQAS - Rabbinical Hebrew]

*S. Liberman, "Forgotten Meanings," *Lěš* 32 (1967-68) #1/2, V-VI. פגעים, 42:12 שנה; 42:1 שותף) with (שוֹתָף) דרך; Ben Sira 41:2 אפס המרה [המרה]; ארקחה, רוחא, רוח, הררה; נאץ, נקק; דבוי מיתה; דבקים; בדקים; שמיר ושית (Isa. 7:25)]

N. Berggrün, "Notes on the Talmudic Lexicon," *Lěš* 32 (1967-68) #1/2, VI-VII. [1. עשה; 2. קרחה]

E. E. Urbach, "Words and Content," *Lěš* 32 (1967-68) #1/2, VII. [1. קטריקו; 2. Gen. Rab. 9, 9 פגה אמרה איוב; 3. עומדים במים; 4. ערער]

*E. Y. Kutscher, "Marginal Notes to the Biblical Lexicon," *Lěš* 32 (1967-68) #4, n.p.n. [11. מרר) אל תמֶּר, Ex. 23:21) תַּמֶּר (root מרר); 12. דרך; 13. חֵלֶב = 'hill']

*M[itchell] Dahood, "Hebrew-Ugaritic Lexicography VI," *B* 49 (1968) 355-369.[נָחָה - (cont.) נָצַר]

*J. Pairman Brown, "Literary Contexts of the Common Hebrew-Greek Vocabulary," *JSS* 13 (1968) 163-191.

*R. Weiss, "Textual Notes," *Text* 6 (1968) 127-131. [Isa. 38:12; פקד—ספר; מסעד hap. leg. I Kings 10:12; Psa. 14 and 53]

H. J. van Dijk, "A Neglected Connotation of Three Hebrew Verbs," *VT* 18 (1968) 16-30. [NĀTAN, ŚĪM, ŠÎT]

N. Berggrün, "Note on the Talmudic Lexicon: כלך, או לכה לך, הולכה לך," *Lĕš* 33 (1968-69) #2/3, n.p.n.

*M[itchell] Dahood, "Hebrew-Ugaritic Lexicography VII," *B* 50 (1969) 337-356.[נָשָׂה - עֲרָפֶל]

*Z[eev] W. Falk, "Hebrew Legal Terms III," *JSS* 14 (1969) 39-44.

*Stanislav Segert, "Hebrew Bible and Semitic comparative lexicography," *VTS* 17 (1969) 204-211.

*J. A. Emerton, "Notes on Jeremiah 12:9 and on some suggestions of J. D. Michaelis about the Hebrew Words *naḥā, 'æbrā,* and *jadaʿ,*" *ZAW* 81 (1969) 182-191.

*L. Kopf, "Structure and Arrangement of Medieval Arabic Dictionaries (A Contribution to the Study of the Dependence of Hebrew Lexicography on Arabic Lexicography)," *Lĕš* 34 (1969-70) #1/2, 5-6. [English Supplement]

*M[itchell] Dahood, "Hebrew-Ugaritic Lexicography VIII," *B* 51 (1970) 391-404. [פֶּ - צָרִין]¹

*M[itchell] Dahood, "Hebrew-Ugaritic Lexicography IX," *B* 52 (1971) 337-356. [צוֹרְרִי - לָחַץ בְּ]¹

*M[itchell] Dahood, "Hebrew-Ugaritic Lexicography X," *B* 53 (1972) 286-403. [רחק ב - שדד]¹

*M[itchell] Dahood, "Hebrew-Ugaritic Lexicography XI," *B* 54 (1973) 351-366. [שדף - שתע]¹

*M[itchell] Dahood, "Hebrew-Ugaritic Lexicography XII," *B* 55 (1974) 381-383. [תאב - תשמורים*]¹

---

1. Since the articles by Mitchell Dahood are published in their entirety, the editor has gone beyond the normal cut-off period of 1969-70, in order to complete the series.

§505 *3.3.3.2.1.4.2 Alphabetical Listing of Hebrew Words*
[See also: Exegetical Studies →]

א

*P. A. H. de Boer, "The counsellor," *VTS* 3 (1955) 42-71. [אב, pp. 57-58, 62-67]

R. J. Lau, "Abel (אָבֵל) in the Bible," *JAOS* 27 (1906) 301-302.

*W. E. Crum, "Bricks as Birth-Stool," *JEA* 28 (1942) 69. [Correction, *JEA* 29 (1943) p. 79 [אבנים]

Maurice H. Farbridge, "Notes on Philology, etc. The Word *'Abnēṭ* in Hebrew. I.," *JMUEOS* #2 (1912-13) 73. [אַבְנֵט]

M. A. Canney, "Notes on Philology, etc. The Word *'Abnēṭ* in Hebrew. II.," *JMUEOS* #2 (1912-13) 74. [אַבְנֵט]

*M. E. Weichselfish, "The Plants באשה and אגא, איזמא, איזמא," *Lěš* 34 (1969-70) #4, n.p.n. [אגא]

*Israel Eitan, "Two Unknown Verbs," *JBL* 42 (1923) 22-28. [1. אָד (root איד), pp. 22-24]

Benjamin B. Warfield, "The Meaning of 'Adam' in the Old Testament," *CFL, 3rd Ser.,* 8 (1908) 130-138. [אָדָם]

Paul Haupt, "Heb. *adám,* man, and *ădamâ,* earth," *BAVSS* 10 (1927) Heft 2, 203-206. [אָדָם, אֲדָמָה]

*Steven T. Byington, "יהוה" and "אדני," *JBL* 76 (1957) 58-59.

G. W. Ahlström, "אדר," *VT* 17 (1967) 1-7.

D. Winton Thomas, "The Root אָהֵב 'love' in Hebrew," *ZAW* 57 (1939) 57-64.

D. H. Gordon, "The Mistress of the Bottle: A Query," *Man* 31 (1931) #244. [אוב]

*H. J. Rose, "Ba'alathobh," *Man* 32 (1932) #69. [אוב]

Harry A. Hoffner Jr., "Second Millennium Antecedents to the Hebrew *'oḇ,*" *JBL* 86 (1967) 385-401. [אוֹב]

*Fritz Hommel, "Assyriological Notes," *SBAP* 17 (1895) 199-207. [§8. Etymology of עוֹלָם, אוּלָם, עֵילָם, pp.200-201]

*A. A. Bevan, "Hebrew Words אָוֶן, אוֹן and אֵיד," *JP* 26 (1898-99) 300-302. [אוֹן, אָוֶן]

*Paul Haupt, "Labor and Sorrow," *BAVSS* 10 (1927) Heft 2, 150-164. [אָוֶן]

*Herbert Loewe, "The Name אוֹפִיר," *JQR, N.S.,* 15 (1924-25) 503-506.

W. T. "On the Meaning and Structure of אָז,"*JSL, 1st Ser.,* 6 (1850) 223-227.

*Paul Haupt, "Hebrew *az* = Ethiopic *enza,*" *JSOR* 1 (1917) 41-44. [אָז]

W. Robertson Smith, "Notes on Hebrew Words, I.," *JQR* 4 (1892-93) 289-292. [אֵזוֹר]

*G. R. Driver, "Three Technical Terms in the Pentateuch," *JSS* 2 (1956) 97-105. [II. אזכרה "Token", pp. 99-100]

*Ed[uard] König, "The Name 'Ahab'," *ET* 16 (1904-05) 566-567. [אחב]

W. J. Peter Boyd, "Notes on the Secondary Meanings of אַחַר," *JTS, N.S.,* 12 (1961) 54-56.

R. B. Y. Scott, "Secondary Meanings of אַחַר, *After, Behind,*" *JTS* 50 (1949) 178-179.

*A. A. Bevan, "Hebrew Words אָוֶן, אוֹן and אֵיד," *JP* 26 (1898-99) 300-302. [אֵיד]

*I. Eitan, "Two Unknown Verbs," *JBL* 42 (1923) 22-28. [1. אָד (root אֵיד)]

*J. Dyneley Prince, "Ichabod," *JBL* 32 (1913) 151-154. [איכבוד]

*M. E. Weichselfish, "The Plants באשה and אגא, אִיזְמָא," *Lĕš* 34 (1969-70) #4, n.p.n. [אִיזְמָא]

A. Guillaume, "The Root אין in Hebrew," *JTS* 34 (1933) 62-64.

*John Muir, "The Significance of אַיִן in Genesis V. 24 and Psalm XXXIX. 13," *ET* 50 (1938-39) 476-477.

Y.   Brand,   "איטלין,"   *Lěš*   32   (1967-68)   #3,   n.p.n.

N[orman] H. Snaith, "The Meaning of the Hebrew אָך," *VT* 14 (1964) 221-225.

Hinckley G. Mitchell, "The Preposition אֶל," *JBL* 8 (1888) 43-120.

*John L. McKenzie, "The Appelative use of *El* and *Elohim*," *CBQ* 10 (1948) 170-181. [אֱלֹהִים, אֵל]

Samuel I. Feigin, "The Origin of *'ĕlôh*, 'god,' in Hebrew," *JNES* 3 (1944) 259. [אֱלוֹהַּ]

*Otto Eissfeldt, "'My God' in the Old Testament," *EQ* 19 (1947) 7-20. [אלהי/אלי]

George Balderson Kidd, "Proposal on the Interpretation of the Word (אֱלֹהִים) Elohim," *JSL, 1st Ser.*, 2 (1848) 332-341.

*J. Battersby Harford, "Since Wellhausen," *Exp, 9th Ser.*, 4 (1925) 4-26. [Supplementary Note On the Use of Elohim in the Pentateuch, pp. 20-26 [אֱלֹהִים]]

*Robert H. Pfeiffer, "Three Assyriological Footnotes to the Old Testament," *JBL* 47 (1928) 184-187. [*1. Ilāni = Elohim*, pp. 184-185] [אלהים]

Cyrus H. Gordon, "אלהים in Its Reputed Meaning of *Rulers, Judges*," *JBL* 54 (1935) 134-144.

*John L. McKenzie, "The Appelative use of *El* and *Elohim*," *CBQ* 10 (1948) 170-181. [אֱלֹהִים, אֵל]

*P. A. H. de Boer, "The counsellor," *VTS* 3 (1955) 42-71. [אָם, pp. 58-67]

Edmund Perry, "The Meaning of *'emuna* in the Old Testament," *JAAR* 21 (1953) 252-256. [אֱמוּנָה]

Ḥ.   Yalon,   "אמץ,"   *Lěš*   32   (1967-68)   #1/2,   I.

*Paul Haupt, "Heb. *Ämš*, Yesterday = Assyr. *Ina Mûši*, at Night," *JBL* 36 (1917) 147-148. [אֶמֶשׁ]

Albert Ehrman, "A Note on the Verb אָמַר," *JQR, N.S.,* 55 (1964-65) 166-167.

*C. J. Labuschagne, "Some Remarks on the Translation and Meaning of *'āmartî* in the Psalms," *OTW* 5 (1962) 27-33.

*Henri Blocher, "The Biblical Concept of Truth," *Them* 6 (1969) #1, 47-61. [אֱמֶת, pp. 48-56] *(Trans. by H. O. J. Brown)*

Jonas C. Greenfield, "The Etymology of אַמְתַּחַת," *ZAW* 77 (1965) 90-92.

*J. P. Lesley, "Notes on Hebrew Etymologies from Egyptian ANX. Enoch; Anoki; Enos," *PAPS* 29 (1891) 17-20. [אָנֹכִי]

*Herbert Gordon May, "*Ephod* and *Ariel*," *AJSL* 56 (1939) 44-69. [אֵפוֹד]

*Samuel Daiches, "Etymological Notes. I. Talmudic אפש = Assyrian *epēšu*," *JRAS* (1919) 63-64.

*Paul Haupt, "Heb. *Argamân* and *Tekéleth*," *JBL* 33 (1914) 298-299. [אַרְגָּמָן]

*E. Sapir, " *'argăz,* A Philistine Word," *JAOS* 56 (1936) 272-281. [אַרְגַּז]

Samuel Feigin, "The Meaning of Ariel," *JBL* 39 (1920) 131-137. [אֲר(י)אֵל]

W. D. Morris, "אֲרִיאֵל," *ET* 40 (1928-29) 237.

*Herbert Gordon May, "*Ephod* and *Ariel*," *AJSL* 56 (1939) 44-69. [אֲרִיאֵל]

*Paul Haupt, "Heb. ärz, cedar < Ass. irêšu, balsamic juice," *JAOS* 45 (1925) 322-323. [אֶרֶז]

P. J. Heawood, "ארמין and ארם," *JTS* 13 (1911-12) 66-73.

E[phraim] A. Speiser, "The Etymology of אַרְמוֹן," *JQR, N.S.,* 14 (1923-24) 329.

*G. M. FitzGerald, "Two Inscriptions from Beisān," *PEFQS* 59 (1927) 154. [ארמנות]

*W[illiam] L. Holladay, " *'Ereṣ*—'underworld': two more suggestions," *VT* 19 (1969) 123-124. [אֶרֶץ]

B. Gross, "To the etymology of אשבורן," *Lĕš* 32 (1967-68) #3, n.p.n.

*Luther Link, "What is Asherah?" *USR* 16 (1904-05) 352-357. [אֲשֵׁרָה/אֲשִׁירָה]

*T. K. Cheyne, "On the Hebrew words אשכר and סגור," *SBAP* 21 (1899) 246.

*J. Martin Plumley, "Notes on אֶשֶׁל the Tamarisk Tree," *JMUEOS* #23 (1942) 15-18.

*James Barr, "Seeing the Wood for the Trees? An Enigmatic Ancient Translation," *JSS* 13 (1968) 11-20. [אֶשֶׁל]

Leon Morris, "'Asham," *EQ* 30 (1958) 196-210. [אָשָׁם]

H. C. Thomson, "The Significance of the Term 'Asham in the Old Testament," *GUOST* 14 (1950-52) 20-26. [אָשָׁם]

*S[tephen H.] Langdon, "*Šurru,* Shoulder. A*šāru,* Assemble," *SBAP* 30 (1908) 178-181. [אשר]

*Max L. Margolis, "The Mode of Expressing the Hebrew *'ā'id* in the Greek Hexateuch," *AJSL* 29 (1912-13) 237-260. [אשר]

Carl Gaenssle, "The Hebrew Particle אשׁר," *AJSL* 31 (1914-15) 3-66, 93-159.

*B. Jacob, "A Study in Biblical Exegesis," *JQR* 12 (1899-1900) 434-451. [אֲשֶׁר־חי]

Waldemar Janzen, "*'ašrê* in the Old Testament," *HTR* 58 (1965) 215-226. [אשרי]

Alfred M. Wilson, "The Particle את in Hebrew. I.," *AJSL* 6 (1889-90) 139-150.

Alfred M. Wilson, "The Particle את in Hebrew. II.," *AJSL* 6 (1889-90) 212-224.

P. P. Saydon, "The Meanings and Uses of the Particle את,"*VT* 14 (1964) 192-210.

J. Macdonald, "The Particle את in Classical Hebrew," *VT* 14 (1964) 263-275.

J. Hoftijzer, "Remarks Concerning the Use of the Particle *'t* in Classical Hebrew," *OTS* 14 (1965) 1-99. [את]

*P. J. van Zijl, " 'tb'l in the Phoenician and Biblical literature," *OTW* 9 (1966) 159-162. [אתבעל]

*Raphael Weiss, "A Note on אתָה in Ex 10:11," *ZAW* 76 (1964) 188.

*P. Wernberg- Møller, "The Pronoun אתמה and Jeremiah's Pun," *VT* 6 (1956) 315-316.

*J. P. van der Westhuizen, "The Term *'ětnān* in Micah," *OTW* 11 (1968) 54-61. [אתנן]

ב

F. R. Blake, "The Hebrew Expres. בָּאמָה after Numerals," *JBL* 34 (1915) 180-182.

*P[eter] R. Ackroyd, "A Note on the Hebrew Roots באש and בוש," *JTS* 43 (1942) 160-161.

Peter R. Ackroyd, "The Hebrew Root באש," *JTS, N.S.,* 2 (1951) 31-36.

*M. E. Weichselfish, "The Plants באשה and אגא, איזמא," *Lěš* 34 (1969-70) #4, n.p.n. [באשה]

*Louis H. Gray, "Observations on the Phonology of the *BͰΓΑΔΚͰΦΑΘ*," *AJSL* 52 (1935-36) 171-177. [Transcription of בגדכפת]

*Avi Hurvitz, "The Usage of שש and בוץ in the Bible and Its Implication for the Date of P," *HTR* 60 (1967) 117-121.

*P[eter] R. Ackroyd, "A Note on the Hebrew Roots באש and בוש," *JTS* 43 (1942) 160-161.

A. Guillaume, "A Note on the Meaning of בין," *JTS, N.S.,* 13 (1962) 109-111.

*W. W. Davies, "House, Tabernacle and Temple," *HR* 26 (1893) 80-82. [בית]

(   ) Gimel, "The Meaning of the Word בָּכָה," *QCS, N.S.,* 2 (1828) 345.

T. K. Cheyne, "The Development of the Meanings of 'Belial'," *Exp, 5th Ser.,* 1 (1895) 435-439. [בְּלִיַּעַל]

T. K. Cheyne, "The Origin and Meaning of 'Belial'," *ET* 8 (1896-97) 423-424. [בְּלִיַּעַל]

Anonymous,   "Belial,"   *CFL,   O.S.,*   1   (1897)   240.   [בְּלִיַּעַל]

Wolf Baudissin, "The Original Meaning of 'Belial'," *ET* 9 (1897-98) 40-45. [בְּלִיַּעַל]

T. K. Cheyne, "On 'Belial,' In Reply to Professor v. Baudissin," *ET* 9 (1897-98) 91-92. [בְּלִיַּעַל]

P. Jensen, "On 'Belial,' In Reply to Professor Cheyne," *ET* 9 (1897-98) 283-284. [בְּלִיַּעַל]

T. K. Cheyne, "On 'Belial'," *ET* 9 (1897-98) 332. [בְּלִיַּעַל]

Fritz Hommel, "Supplementary Note on Belîli (Belial)," *ET* 9 (1897-98) 567. [בְּלִיַּעַל]

*John A. Maynard, "Sheol and Belial," *ATR* 1 (1918-19) 92-93. [בְּלִיַּעַל]

James Edward Hogg, "'Belial' in the Old Testament," *AJSL* 44 (1927-28) 56-58. [בְּלִיַּעַל]

A. Guillaume, "A Note on the √בלע," *JTS, N.S.,* 13 (1962) 320-322.

Moses Gaster, "The Grandson," *ET* 28 (1916-17) 518-520. [בֶּן בֵּן]

*I. Yeivin, "Two Terms of the Babylonian Masora to the Bible," *Lěš* 30 (1965-66) #1, n.p.n. [דֹּק, בֹּע]

W. Emery Barnes, "Biḳ'ah—'Valley' or 'Plain'?" *PEFQS* 66 (1934) 45. [בִּקְעָה]

*C. J. Ball, "A Study in Biblical Philology," *SBAP* 33 (1911) 243-253. [בָּעַד, pp. 243-247]

Harold M. Wiener, "A vital new element in Old Testament criticism," *TTL* 52 (1918) 164-169. [בַּעַל]

*Philip A. Nordell, "The Hebrew Synonyms בִּקֵּשׁ and דָּרַשׁ," *AJSL* 2 (1885-86) 162-163.

*Willis J. Beecher, "ברא in Josh. 17:15, 18; and Ezek. 21:24; 23:47," *JBL* 2 (1882) 128-133.

A. A. Bevan, "The Hebrew verb ברא 'to create'," *JP* 29 (1903-04) 263-265.

*William M. McPheeters, "Meaning of Bārā' in Genesis i," *CFL, N.S.,* 8 (1903) 10-16. *(Editorial)* [בָּרָא]

*William M. McPheeters, "The Meaning of Bārā' in Genesis," *CFL, 3rd Ser.,* 7 (1907) 367-372. [בָּרָא]

*R. J. Wilson, "Wilhelm Vischer on 'God Created' בָּרָא," *ET* 65 (1953-54) 94-95.

*John Eliot Howard, "The Early Destinies of Mankind," *JTVI* 15 (1881-82) 159-190. (Discussion, p. 190) [Appendix A. בָּרָא, p. 187]

J. J. Rabinowitz, "An Additional Note on בראש," *VT* 9 (1959) 209-210.

C. Rabin, "Bāriᵃḥ," *JTS* 47 (1946) 38-41. [בָּרְחַ]

Bernard J. Bamberger, "Baruch," *Jud* 5 (1956) 167-168. [בָּרוּךְ]

J. M., "Observations on the Verb בָּרֵךְ *barek,* 'to Bless'," *JSL, 1st Ser.,* 6 (1850) 437-443.

Hugh Rose Rae, "'Bless' and 'Curse' in One Word: A Question," *HR* 46 (1903) 371-375. [בָּרֵךְ]

Rembert D. M'Neer, "Interpretation and Translation of בָּרֵךְ (Barak)," *MQR, 3rd Ser.,* 48 (1922) 532-535.

*Oswald T. Allis, "The Blessing of Abraham," *PTR* 25 (1927) 263-298. [III. The Verb "To Bless" in Hebrew, pp. 287-295] [ברך]

Thomas Plassmann, "The Semitic Root *Brk,*" *CBQ* 11 (1949) 445-446. [ברך]

*M. H. Goshen-Gottstein, "ברך in Ugaritic and Hebrew," *Lěš* 32 (1967-68) #1/2, IV.

Maurice A. Canney, "Berākah," *ET* 39 (1927-28) 381-382. [בְּרָכָה]

A. Murtonen, "The Use and Meaning of the Words l^ebârek and b^eråkå^h in the Old Testament," *VT* 9 (1959) 158-177. [בְּרָכָה]

A. Murtonen, "A Note to *V.T.* IX, No. 2, p. 176 sq.," *VT* 9 (1959) 330. [בְּרָכָה]

W[illiam] F[oxwell] Albright, "The Hebrew Expression for 'Making a Covenant' in Pre-Israelite Documents," *BASOR* #121 (1951) 21-22. [בְּרִית]

P. Peters, "The First Published Extra-Biblical Occurrence of the Old Testament Word for Covenant," *WLQ* 48 (1951) 149. [בְּרִית]

*Ernest D[e Witt] Burton, "Spirit, Soul and Flesh II. נֶפֶשׁ רוּחַ, and בָּשָׂר in the Old Testament," *AJT* 18 (1914) 59-80.

*Cornelius Walker, "Basar and Sarx, (בשר and Σαρξ)—Their Contrasts and Modifications," *HR* 35 (1898) 65-68.

*Morris Jastrow Jr., "The element בשת in Hebrew proper names," *JBL* 13 (1894) 19-30.

J. L. Helberg, "A Communication on the Semasiological Meaning of Basar," *OTW* 2 (1959) 23-28. [בָּשָׂר]

William R. Arnold, "The Meaning of בתרין," *AJSL* 28 (1911-12) 274-283.

ג

A. R. Johnson, "The primary meaning of גאל√," *VTS* 1 (1953) 67-77.

N. H. Snaith, "The Hebrew Root G'L (I)," *ALUOS* 3 (1961-62) 60-67. [גאל]

*H. Torczyner, "*Semel Ha-qin'ah Ha-maqneh,*" *JBL* 65 (1946) 293-302. [6. קנה synonym of גאל, pp. 300-302]

A. B. Davidson, "Requests and Replies," *ET* 10 (1898-99) 444. [גָּאוֹן]

*J. C. Greenfield, "The Root 'GBL' in Mishnaic Hebrew and the Hymnic Literature of Qumran," *RdQ* 2 (1959-60) 155-162. [גבל]

G. J. Thierry, "Gebál, Byblos, Bible:—Paper," *VT* 1 (1951) 130-131. [גבל]

*Hans Kosmala, "The term *geber* in the Old Testament and in the Scrolls," *VTS* 17 (1969) 159-169. [גֶּבֶר]

*P. H. de v. Uys, "The term gᵉbîrâ in the Book of Proverbs," *OTW* 11 (1968) 82-85.[גְּבִרְתָּה]

*E[phraim] A. Speiser, "'People' and 'Nation' of Israel," *JBL* 79 (1960) 157-163. [גּוֹי]

*A. Cody, "When is the Chosen People called a gôy?" *VT* 14 (1964) 1-6. [גּוֹי]

*David Neumark, "Crescas and Spinoza. A Memorial Paper in Honor of the Five Hundredth Anniversary of the 'Or Adonoi'," *YCCAR* 18 (1908) 277-318. [גּוֹרָל]

*W. R. Hutton, "Tumbleweed," *ET* 61 (1949-50) 59-60. [גַּלְגַּל]

*S[tephen] Langdon, "Philological Notes," *RAAO* 28 (1931) 13-22. [1] *Gilinu, gullimu* (?), גלּם, a garment, p. 13]

*Aylward M. Blackman, "Philological Notes," *JEA* 11 (1925) 210-215. [גלשׁ]

*Mitchell Dahood, "The Root GMR in the Psalms," *ThSt* 14 (1953) 595-597. [גמר]

*Henry George Tomkins, "The Name Genubath," *SBAP* 10 (1887-88) 372. (Note by W. Harry Rylands, "The Ḳenbetu and the Semitic South," pp.

373-376 [جذرب] (גנבת] // Γαυηβὰθ]

Samuel Krauss, "A Misunderstood Word," *JQR, N.S.,* 4 (1913-14) 111-114. [גנוניות]

T. K. Cheyne, "Occurrences of גער in the Old Testament," *ZAW* 31 (1911) 315.

A. A. Macintosh, "A consideration of Hebrew גער," *VT* 19 (1969) 471-479.

*Francis M. Seely, "Note on G'RH with Especial Reference to Proverbs 13:8," *BTr* 10 (1959) 20-21. [גְּעָרָה]

P. J. van Zijl, "A Discussion of the root *ga'ar* (rebuke). A Semasiological Study," *OTW* 12 (1969) 56-63. [גָּעַר]

Gershon Tchernowitz, "On the Conception of 'Ger' in the Torah," *JIQ* 2 (1925-26) #1, 20-24. [גֵּר]

*Th[eophile] J. Meek, "The Translation of *Gêr* in the Hexateuch and its Bearing on the Documentary Hypothesis," *JBL* 49 (1930) 172-180. [גֵּר]

Thomas M. Horner, "Changing Concepts of the 'Stranger' in the Old Testament," *ATR* 42 (1960) 49-53. [גֵּר]

*Sidney Smith, "The Threshing Floor at the City Gate," *PEQ* 78 (1946) 5-14. [גֹּרֶן]

Sidney Smith, "On the Meaning of *Goren*," *PEQ* 85 (1953) 42-45. [גֹּרֶן]

*John Gray, "The *Goren* at the City Gate: Justice and the Royal Office in Ugaritic Text 'Aqht," *PEQ* 85 (1953) 118-123. [גֹּרֶן]

*W. G. Lambert, "Two Akkadian Cognates," *JJS* 5 (1954) 40-41. [2. *MAGRANU, MAGRATTU* = גרן, p. 41]

ד

C. Rabin, "Hebrew *D* = '*Hand*'," *JJS* 6 (1955) 111-115. [ד]

*M. Z. Kadari, "The Use of ד־-Clauses in the Language of Targum Onkelos," *Text* 3 (1963) 35-59.

*Frank M. Cross Jr., "Ugaritic *db'at* and Hebrew Cognates," *VT* 2 (1952) 162-164. [דְּבָאָה]

C. Taylor, "Mr. Taylor, on the meaning of the Hebrew Root, דבר," *JP* 1 (1868) #2, 56-65.

Thomas Plassmann, "Notes on the Stem d-b-r. A Semasiological Study," *CBQ* 4 (1942) 119-132. [דבר]

G. Buchanan Gray, "The Meaning of the Hebrew Word דֶּגֶל," *JQR* 11 (1898-99) 92-101.

T. K. Cheyne, "Further Remarks on the Hebrew Word דֶּגֶל," *JQR* 11 (1898-99) 232-236.

*Leroy Waterman, "דוֹדִי in the Song of Songs," *AJSL* 35 (1918-19) 101-110.

P[eter] R. Ackroyd, "The Meaning of Hebrew דּוֹר Considered," *JSS* 13 (1968) 3-10.

James A. Montgomery, "Note on the Etymology of דְּמָאִי," *JQR, N.S.,* 23 (1932-33) 209.

*P. A. Nordell, "Contributions to Hebrew Synonymy," *AJSL* 1 (1884-85) 13-14. [מִשְׁפָּט = דִּין]

*Anonymous, "Questions and Answers. 2.," *AJSL* 1 (1884-85) 20-21. [The prefixed Article in the Infinitive construction of דַּעַת]

*I. Heivin, "Two Terms of the Babylonian Masora to the Bible," *Léš* 30 (1965-66) #1, n.p.n. [דֹּק, בע]

Nathaniel West, "DIQDUQ," *AJSL* 3 (1886-87) 41-43. [דִּקְדּוּק]

*M[itchell] J. Dahood, "Ugaritic *drkt* and Biblical *derek,*" *ThSt* 15 (1954) 627-631. [דֶּרֶךְ]

Frank J. Neuberg, "An Unrecognized Meaning of Hebrew *dôr,*" *JNES* 9 (1950) 215-216. [דּוֹר]

*Philip A. Nordell, "The Hebrew Synonyms בָּקֵשׁ and דָּרַשׁ," *AJSL* 2 (1885-86) 162-163.

*Julius Lewy, "The Biblical Institution of *Derôr* in the Light of Akkadian Documents," *EI* 5 (1958) 21*-31*. [דְּרוֹר]

ה

*J[ames] A. Montgomery, "The *Hemzah-H* in the Semitic," *JBL* 46 (1927) 144-146. [ה]

*George R. Entler, "The Origin of the Hebrew Article ה," *PAPA* 8 (1875-86) 4-5. *[Bound with Transactions, but paged separately]*

William Chomsky, "Note on the Meaning of הדיוט in Mishnaic Hebrew," *JQR, N.S.,* 42 (1951-52) 329-330.

*J[ames] A. Montgomery, "The Hebrew Divine Name and the Personal Pronoun *hū,*" *JBL* 63 (1944) 161-163. [הוּא]

*G. R. Driver, "Witchcraft in the Old Testament," *JRAS* (1943) 6-16. [הֹוָה, הַוָּה]

Richard J. Clifford, "The use of *hôy* in the Prophets," *CBQ* 28 (1966) 458-464. [הֹוי]

*Ed[uard] König, "The Hebrew יָלַד and הֹולִיד, etc.," *ET* 9 (1897-98) 286-288.

*W. Bacher, The Talmudical Particle הֹולכך," *JQR* 17 (1904-05) 583.

*Robert Polzin, "*HWQY'* and Covenantal Institutions in Early Israel," *HTR* 62 (1969) 227-240. [הֹוקִיעַ Hiph. of יָקַע]

*J. Wijngaards, "הֹוצִיא and הֶעֱלה, A Twofold Approach to the Exodus," *VT* 15 (1965) 91-102.

*M. Smith, "Another Criterion for the καίγε Recension," *B* 48 (1967) 443-445. [הֹורָה = φωτιζειν]

*C. Taylor, "An Interpretation of יזה גוים," *JP* 8 (1879) 62-66. [On the root הִזָּה, pp. 64-66]

*Th. C. Vriezen, "The Term *Hizza:* Lustration and Consecration," *OTS* 7 (1950) 201-235. [הִזָּה Hiph. of נזה]

*J. Blau, "הֵחֵל denoting 'to begin and continue' (the 'Stretching' of Ingressive Verbs to Duratives in Biblical and Mishnaic Hebrew, in Classical, Middle and Modern Arabic, and in Syriac),"*Lěš* 32 (1967-68) #1/2, III-IV.

*P. P. Saydon, "The Inceptive Imperfect in Hebrew and the Verb הֵחֵל 'to Begin'," *B* 35 (1954) 43-50.

*William Wright, "Observations on the Assyrian Verb *Basu,* as compared with the Hebrew Verb הָיָה, *Hâyâ,* 'He was'," *SBAT* 3 (1874) 104-109.

*W. W. Davies, "House, Tabernacle and Temple," *HR* 26 (1893) 80-82. [הֵיכָל]

*Franz Praetorias, "הלך and ילך," *ONTS* 2 (1882-83) 24-25.

*J. M. Allegro, "HLK/YLK 'go'," *WO* 2 (1954-59) 264-266. [הלך]

*J. Colver Wightman, "הַמָּשִׁיחַ The Messiah," *BQ* 10 (1876) 302-311.

*Fritz Hommel, "Hena' and 'Awwâ," *ET* 9 (1897-98) 330-331. [הֵנַע]

*Joseph Offord, "Dancing Worship," *SBAP* 21 (1899) 253. [הַסְּעָפִּים]

H. B., "Biblical Query," *PEFQS* 5 (1873) 80. [הָעִיר]

A. B., "*To the Editor of the 'Quarterly Statement' of the Palestine Exploration Fund*," *PEFQS* 5 (1873) 117-118. [הָעִיר]

*J. Wijngaards, "הוציא and העלה, A Twofold Approach to the Exodus," *VT* 15 (1965) 91-102.

Morton A. Cogan, "A Technical Term for Exposure," *JNES* 27 (1968) 133-135. [השליך]

A. D. Singer, "The Derivation of Hebrew התל," *JQR, N.S.*, 36 (1945-46) 255-259.

ו

*E. Adkins, "The Particles *ΔE* and ו in Bible Translation," *BQ* 5 (1871) 99-107.

*Hinckley G. Mitchell, "והיה of the Past," *JBL* 33 (1914) 48-55.

*H. F. B. Compston, "The Accentuation of *Wayyomar* in Job," *JTS* 13 (1911-12) 426-427. [וַיֹּאמֶר]

*Jacob Leveen, "The Meaning of וַיִּכְתֹּב in Judges viii, 14," *JRAS* (1948) 61-62.

C[harles] Cutler Torrey, "Old Testament Notes," *JBL* 16 (1897) 166-170. [1. The Meaning of וּכְעֵנֶת, pp. 166-168]

ז

A. H. W., "The Origin of Z," *JSL, 4th Ser.*, 4 (1863-64) 473. [ז]

*Lloyd Gaston, "Beelzebul," *TZ* 18 (1962) 247-255. [O. T. Refs., pp. 247-250] [זְבוּל]

*Moshe Held, "The Root ZBL/SBL in Akkadian, Ugaritic and Biblical Hebrew," *JAOS* 88 (1968) 90-96. [זבל]

*Paul Haupt, "Heb. *zed,* haughty = Assyr. *sittu,* remnant," *JBL* 34 (1915) 184-185. [זד]

*Frank R. Blake, "The Word זדה in the Siloam Inscription," *JAOS* 22 (1901) 55-60.

*H. Birkeland, "Hebrew *zœ* and Arabic *ḏū,*" *ST* 2 (1949-50) 201-202. [זה]

*A. D. Singer, "Philological Notes," *JPOS* 21 (1948) 104-109. [II. On Two Biblical Verbs: Hiph. תזדו; זוד]

*Harris R. Schenck, "The Old Testament Eldership—Its Origins and Functions," *PQ* 11 (1897) 433-466. [זקני]

L. A. Snijders, "The Meaning of זר in the Old Testament," *OTS* 10 (1954) 1-154.

*A. Lowy, "Notices concerning Glass in Ancient Jewish Records," *SBAP* 4 (1881-82) 84-86. [זכוכית]

*Robert Hutcheson, "On the syntax of זרע with especial reference to its bearing on Gal. iii 16," *SBLP* (June, 1880) 11-13.

*†Robert Hutcheson, "The Syntax of זרע with special reference to its bearing on Gal. 3[16]," *JBL* 49 (1930) xxxiii-xxxiv. *[Reprint of the Proceedings of the first meeting of SBL (may be bound separately)]*

Robert Hutcheson, "The Syntax of זרע," *BS* 38 (1881) 317-322.

ח

J. J. Finkelstein, "Hebrew חבר and Semitic *ḪBR,*" *JBL* 75 (1956) 328-331.

*D. Sperber, "A Note on Hasmonean Coin-Legends. Heber and Rosh Heber," *PEQ* 97 (1965) 85-93. [חבר]

*Sidney B. Hoenig, "I. *Heber Ir* II. City-Square," *JQR, N.S.,* 48 (1957-58) 123-139. [חבר עיר]

*Julian Morgenstern, "The Etymological History of the Three Hebrew Synonyms for 'to Dance,' ḤGG, ḤLL, and KRR, and their Cultural Significance," *JAOS* 36 (1916) 321-332. [חגג]

D. Winton Thomas, "*ḤDL*-II in Hebrew," *CBQ* 24 (1962) 154. [חדל]

R. F., "חִדְקֵל," *AJSL* 1 (1884-85) 129-130.

*Frederick Baepler, "A Study on the Hebrew Name for Eve," *TM* 6 (1926) 363-367. [חַוָּה]

G. R. Driver, "Two Forgotten Words in the Hebrew Language," *JTS* 28 (1926-27) 285-287. [1) חוח 'bramble'; 2.) חוח 'hole', 'hollow place']

Fritz Hommel, "Havilah," *ET* 8 (1896-97) 473. [חוילה]

*Alfred Guillaume, "Is Episcopacy a Jewish Institution?" *BSOAS* 13 (1949-51) 23-26. [(חֲזֹון (*חַזָּן]

*Anonymous, "Who Were the Seers (Chozim)?" *HR* 22 (1891) 266-269. [חֹזֶה]

*M[orris] Jastrow Jr., "Ro'ēh and Ḥozēh in the Old Testament," *JBL* 28 (1909) 42-56. [חֹזֶה]

*F. D. Coggan, "The Meaning of חטא in Job V. 24," *JMUEOS* #17 (1932) 53-56.

*C. Levias, "Šᵉvâ and Ḥâṭēph," *AJSL* 13 (1896-97) 79-80. [חָטֵף]

*Moshe Greenberg, "The Hebrew Oath Particle ḥay/ḥē," *JBL* 76 (1957) 34-39. [חֵי/חַי]

Arnold B. Ehrlich, "חַי and חֵי," *AJSL* 6 (1889-90) 309-311.

*William Cosser, "The Meaning of 'Life' (Ḥayyim) in Proverbs, Job, and Ecclesiastes," *GUOST* 15 (1953-54) 48-53. [חַיִּים]

Grey Hubert Skipwith, "*Pi-Haḫīrōth*, 'The Mouth of the Canals'," *PEFQS* 45 (1913) 94-95. [חירת]

*Shlomo Marenof, "A Forgotten Root," *AJSL* 52 (1935-36) 116-117. [חל or חלל]

A. M. Haberman, "Ancient Hebrew and Aramaic Epistles and the Word 'Hela'," *EI* 4 (1956) IX. [חֵלָה]

*Richard L. Ruble, "The Doctrine of Dreams," *BS* 125 (1968) 360-364. [חֲלוֹם]

*Julian Morgenstern, "The Etymological History of the Three Hebrew Synonyms for 'to Dance,' HGG, HLL, and KRR, and their Cultural Significance," *JAOS* 36 (1916) 321-332. [חלל]

*Shlomo Marenof, "A Forgotten Root," *AJSL* 52 (1935-36) 116-117. [חלל or חלל]

M. Z. Kaddary, "חלל = 'Bore,' 'Pierce'?" *VT* 13 (1963) 486-489.

*Israel Eitan, "Two Unknown Verbs," *JBL* 42 (1923) 22-28. [2. חָלַשׁ, pp. 25-28]

*A. Guillaume, "The Use of חלשׁ in Exod. XVII. 13, Isa. XIV. 12, and Job XIV. 10," *JTS, N.S.,* 14 (1963) 91-92.

Herbert H. Gowen, "Note on חמד," *ATR* 1 (1918-19) 426-428.

G. R. Driver, "On *Hēmāh* 'hot anger, fury' and also 'firey wine'," *TZ* 14 (1958) 133-135. [חֵמָה]

*G. Ernest Wright, "'Sun-Image' or 'Altar of Incense'?" *BA* 1 (1938) 9-10. [חַמָּנִים]

M. A. Canney, "The Hebrew חֹמֶשׁ," *JTS* 24 (1922-23) 175-176.

Frank R. Blake, "Hebrew חֲמִשָּׁה, הֲמִשִּׁים," *JAOS* 26 (1905) 117-119.

*W. H. Lofthouse, "Hen and Hesed in the Old Testament," *ZAW* 51 (1933) 29-35. [חֵן]

*William L. Reed, "Some Implications of *hēn* for Old Testament Religion," *JBL* 69 (1950) ix-x. [חֵן]

*William L. Reed, "Some Implications of *hēn* for Old Testament Religion," *JBL* 73 (1954) 36-41. [חֵן]

*B. D. Eerdmans, "The Chasidim," *OTS* 1 (1942) 176-257. [חָסִיד]

Johannes Pedersen, "Note on Hebrew Hofšī," *JPOS* 6 (1926) 103-105. [חֹפֶשׁ]

*William F[oxwell] Albright, "Canaanite Ḥapši and Hebrew Ḥofsî," *JPOS* 6 (1926) 106-108. [חֹפֶשׁ]

*Duncan Cameron, "Covenant Loyalty," *ET* 27 (1915-16) 26-29. [חֶסֶד]

*W. H. Lofthouse, "Ḥen and Ḥesed in the Old Testament," *ZAW* 51 (1933) 29-35. [חֶסֶד]

*James A. Montgomery, "Hebrew *Hesed* and Greek *Charis,*" *HTR* 32 (1939) 97-102.

Steven T. Byington, "Hebrew Marginalia I," *JBL* 60 (1941) 279-288. [חסד and Hushai, pp. 282-283]

Norman H. Snaith, "The Meaning of חֶסֶד," *ET* 55 (1943-44) 108-110.

P. Peters, "The Old Testament Covenant Term Chesed," *WLQ* 50 (1953) 181-188, 252-262; 51 (1954) 126-136, 167-172, 236-242. [חֶסֶד]

*Aubrey R. Johnson, "Ḥesed and Ḥāsîd," *NTTO* 56 (1955) 100-112. [חֶסֶד, הָסִיד]

Harry M. Orlinsky, "*Ḥasēr* in the Old Testament," *JAOS* 59 (1939) 22-37. [חָסֵר]

P. Victor, "A Note on חֹק in the Old Testament," *VT* 16 (1966) 358-361.

*Eberhard Hommel, "The Forms Σειραχ and 'Ακελδαμαχ as Transcriptions of סירא and חקלדמא," *ET* 25 (1913-14) 285.

Samuel Daiches, "The Meaning of חָרְבוֹת," *JQR* 20 (1907-08) 637-639.

*A. Leo Oppenheim, "Assyriological Notes to the Old Testament," *JQR, N.S.,* 37 (1946-47) 175-176. [חֲרִי יוֹנִים = ḫalla summati]

Fritz Hommel, "Babylonian Origin of Khartummim," *ET* 11 (1899-1900) 234. [חַרְטֻמִּים]

S. E. Loewenstamm, "The Hebrew root חרשׁ in the light of the Ugarit texts," *JJS* 10 (1959) 63-65.

*M. D. Goldman, "Lexicographical Notes on the Hebrew Text of the Bible (2): 'Thinking' in Hebrew," *ABR* 1 (1951) 135-137.[חשׁב]

S[teven] T. Byington, "חשׁך," *JBL* 39 (1920) 80-81.

*M. Stuart, "Have the Sacred Writers any where asserted that the Sin or Righteousness of one is imputed to another?" *BRCR* 7 (1836) 241-330. [§2. Use of the verb חָשַׁב in the Hebrew Scriptures, pp. 248-257]

Philip J. Calderone, "*ḤDL*-II in Poetic Texts," *CBQ* 23 (1961) 451-460. [חדל]

Philip J. Calderone, "Supplementary Note on *ḤDL*-II," *CBQ* 24 (1962) 412-419. [חדל]

D. Winton Thomas, "Some observations on the Hebrew Root חדל," *VTS* 4 (1957) 8-16.

D. R. Ap-Thomas, "Some Aspects of the Root ḤNN in the Old Testament," *JSS* 2 (1957) 128-148. [חנן]

T. C. Mitchell, "The Meaning of the noun *ḤTN* in the Old Testament," *VT* 19 (1969) 93-112. [חתן]

ט

*C. Taylor, "Notes on the translation of Genesis," *JP* 3 (1871) 291-327. [IV. On טהר, to purify, pp. 310-313]

R[obert] Gordis, "A Note on טוב," *JTS* 35 (1934) 186-188.

E[phraim] A. Speiser, "ṬWṬPT," *JQR, N.S.,* 48 (1957-58) 208-217. [טוטפת]

Paul Haupt, "Heb *ṭum'â*, uncleanness," *BAVSS* 10 (1927) Heft 2, 207-209. [טָמֵא]

Edward P. Rice, "'Little Ones'," *ET* 29 (1917-18) 427. [טַף]

*W. Muss-Arnolt, "Assyrian Etymologies," *AJSL* 7 (1890-91) 183-185, 253-256. [II. A-ṭap-pu = ṭap-pu = Hebrew טֶפַח, *coping*, pp. 253-254]

י

David ben Abraham al-Fāsī, "A Study of the Uses of the Letter 'Yod' by David ben Abraham al-Fāsī," *JAOS* 58 (1938) 167-172. *(Trans. from the Arabic by Solomon L. Skoss)* [י]

Anonymous, "The Word יאר," *AJSL* 1 (1884-85) 16.

M. Delcor, "Two Special Meanings of the Word יד in Biblical Hebrew," *JSS* 12 (1967) 230-240.

Aloysius Fitzgerald, "Hebrew *yd* = 'Love' and 'Beloved'," *CBQ* 29 (1967) 368-374. [יד]

Robert Gordis, "A Note on *Yad*," *JBL* 62 (1943) 341-344. [יד]

Robert North, "*Yâd* in the Shemitta-law," *VT* 4 (1954) 196-199. [יד]

*H. F. Lutz, "The root ידל, *edelu* in Egyptian," *JAOS* 42 (1922) 202-203.

D. W[inton] Thomas, "The Root ידע in Hebrew," *JTS* 35 (1934) 298-306.

D. W[inton] Thomas, "The Root ידע in Hebrew, II," *JTS* 36 (1935) 409-412.

D. W[inton] Thomas, "More Notes on the Root ידע in Hebrew," *JTS* 38 (1937) 404-405.

*D. Winton Thomas, "Some Rabbinic Evidence for a Hebrew Root ידע = ودع," *JQR, N.S.,* 37 (1946-47) 177-178.

*Leon J. Liebreich, "Observations on 'Some Rabbinic Evidence for a Hebrew Root ידע = ودع (*JQR, N.S.,* XXXVII, 177-8)," *JQR, N.S.,* 37 (1946-47) 337-339.

*D. Winton Thomas, "A Note on the Meaning of ידע in Hosea ix. 7 and Isaiah ix. 8," *JTS* 42 (1941) 43-44.

D. W[inton] Thomas, "Julius Furst and the Hebrew Root ידע," *JTS* 42 (1941) 64-65.

*Joseph Reider, "Etymological Studies: ידע or ירע and רעע," *JBL* 66 (1947) 315-317.

M. D. Goldman, "Lexicographical Notes on Exegesis. (4): The Root ידע*[sic]* and the Verb 'To Know' in Hebrew," *ABR* 3 (1953) 46-47 [ידע]

D. Winton Thomas, "Some Remarks on the Hebrew Root ידע," *JJS* 6 (1955) 50-52.

David H. Wallington, "Difficult Words and Phrases," *BTr* 12 (1961) 42-43. (Adapted from an unpublished article by J. L. Swellengrebel) [יָדַע]

D. Winton Thomas, "Additional Notes on the Root ידע in Hebrew," *JTS, N.S.,* 15 (1964) 56-57.

*Herbert B. Huffmon, "The Treaty Background of Hebrew *Yāda'*," *BASOR* #181 (1966) 31-37. [ידע]

*Herbert B. Huffmon and Simon B. Parker, "A Further Note on the Treaty Background of Hebrew *Yāda'*," *BASOR* #184 (1966) 36-37. [ידע]

*H. F. Lutz, "The root ידל, *edelu* in Egyptian," *JAOS* 42 (1922) 202-203.

יהוה *[See also: YHWH (Doctrine of God), and Tetragrammaton ⟶]*

( ) B., "The Septuagint and the New Testament Rendering of 'Jehovah': or, the Reasons why the New Testament seems to Sanction the Septuagint Rendering יהוה by κύριος," *BRCM* 3 (1847) 21-28.

*Fritz Hommel, "The Etymology of יהוה," *ET* 10 (1898-99) 48.

*James A. Montgomery, "Some Hebrew Etymologies," *JQR, N.S.,* 25 (1934-35) 261-269. [(3) Varia: יהוה pp. 268-269]

*Cyrus H. Gordon, "The Pointing of יְהֹוָה," *ZAW* 56 (1938) 174.

G. R. Driver, "Reflections on Recent Articles," *JBL* 73 (1954) 125-136. [I. The Interpretation of YHWH as a Practical Form from a Causative Theme of the Verb, pp. 125-131]

Peter Katz, "יְהֹוָה = JᵉJā, יהיה = JāJā?" *VT* 4 (1954) 428-429.

*Steven T. Byington, "יהוה and אדני," *JBL* 76 (1957) 58-59.

A. Gelston, "A Note on מלך יהוה," *VT* 16 (1966) 507-512.

*W. Taylor Smith, "Joshua and Jesus," *ET* 4 (1892-93) 47-48. [יְהוֹשׁוּעַ]

H. M. Jonson, "The Meaning of יום," *MR* 32 (1850) 257-281.

*Herbert W. Magoun, "The Cosmogony Problem and the Meaning of Hebrew 'Yom'," *CFL, 3rd Ser.,* 34 (1928) 604-611. [יוֹם]

H[erbert] W. Magoun, "The Content of Hebrew *Yôm*," *BS* 86 (1929) 338-342. [יוֹם]

Hebert W. Magoun, "More Light on 'Yom'," *CFL, 3rd Ser.,* 35 (1929) 184-188 [יוֹם]

F. D. Nichol, "Yom-Day," *CFL, 3rd Ser.,* 36 (1930) 541-542 [יוֹם]

*Paul Haupt, "Heb. *jayén,* misery," *BAVSS* 10 (1927) 210-212. [יְוֵן]

*Charles C[utler] Torrey, "The Evolution of the Financier in the Ancient Near East," *JNES* 2 (1943) 295-301. [יוֹצֵר, pp. 298-301]

*John Mauchline, "The Uses of *Yaḥad* and *Yaḥdāu* in the Old Testament," *GUOST* 13 (1947-49) 51-53. [יַחַד, יַחְדָּו]

J. C. De Moor, "Lexical Remarks concerning *Yaḥad* and *Yaḥdaw*," *VT* 7 (1957) 350-355. [יַחַד, יַחְדָּו]

M. D. Goldman, "Lexicographic Notes on Exegesis: Misunderstood Polaric Meaning of a Word," *ABR* 1 (1951) 61-63. [יחד]

S. Talmon, "The Sectarian יחד—a biblical noun," *VT* 3 (1953) 133-140.

*Alvah Hovey, "Bible Wine: The Meaning of Yayin and Oinos in Scripture," *BQR* 9 (1887) 151-180. [יַיִן]

*Anonymous, "Tirosh and Yayin," *ONTS* 13 (1891) 181. [יַיִן]

*Hinckley G. Mitchell, "Tirosh and Yayin," *JBL* 10 (1891) 70-72. [יַיִן]

*Hayyim Rosenrauch, "Critical Notes: II. The Hebrew Equivalent to Accadic lip(p)u," *JQR, N.S.,* 36 (1945-46) 81. [ילבב]

*Ed[uard] König, "The Hebrew יֶלֶד and הוֹלִיד, etc.," *ET* 9 (1897-98) 286-288.

*Folker Willesen, "The Yālīḏ in Hebrew Society," *ST* 12 (1958) 192-210. [יֶלֶד]

*Franz Praetorias, "הלךְ and ילךְ," *ONTS* 2 (1882-83) 24-25.

*J. M. Allegro, "HLK/YLK 'go'," WO 2 (1954-59) 264-266. [וַיֵּלֶךְ or וַיֵּלֶךְ]

*P. A. H. de Boer, "The counsellor," VTS 3 (1955) 42-71. (מועצה, עצה, יעץ) pp. 43-56]

Shaul Esh, "Note on יצא," VT 4 (1954) 305-307.

Frederick L. Moriarty, "A Note on the Root YPʻ," CBQ 14 (1952) 62. [יפע]

*C. Taylor, "Note on the Hebrew root יקש," JP 2 (1869) 130-134.

*Julian Obermann, "In the Wake of the Karatepe Discoveries," Oriens 3 (1950) 20-30. [2. The Synonyms *mērîb̠ and *yārîb̠ in Hebrew, pp. 22-25] [ירב]

*Joseph Reider, "Etymological Studies: ידע or ירע and רעע," JBL 66 (1947) 315-317.

*G. R. Driver, "On עלה 'went up country' and ירד 'went down country'," ZAW 69 (1957) 74-77.

*Wolf Leslau, "An Ethiopian Parallel to Hebrew עלה 'went up country' and ירד 'went down country'," ZAW 74 (1962) 322-323.

*Sakae Shibayama, "Notes on Yārad and ʻĀlāh: Hints on Translating," JAAR 34 (1966) 358-362. [ירד]

*Geo. H. Schodde, "Biblical Research Notes. The Name 'Jordan'," ColTM 18 (1898) 255-256. [יַרְדֵּן]

*J. B. Segal, "'YRḤ' in the Gezer 'Calendar'," JSS 7 (1962) 212-221. [ירח]

*A. Guillaume, "A Note on the Roots ריע, ירע, and רעע in Hebrew," JTS, N.S., 15 (1964) 293-295.

Anonymous, "The Hebrew Word יָשַׁב Yashabh," PRev 39 (1867) 337-365.

*Francis Brown, "The imperfect of ישׁב (yêshēb), and kindred forms, in Hebrew," JAOS 13 (1889) lxxv-lxxvii.

*Ralph Marcus, "The Hebrew Sibilant śin and the Name Yiśraʼel," JBL 60 (1941) 141-150. [יִשְׂרָאֵל]

כ

*Paul Haupt, "Heb. kĕ, like and kî, as," *JAOS* 45 (1925) 316-318. [כְ]

*Samuel Daiches, "The Meaning of כאֲרִי in Psalm 22, v.17," *JRAS* (1933) 401-403.

*F. X. Sheehan, "The Glory of God: Doxa-Kavodh," *BibT* #26 (1966) 1815-1821. [כָּבוֹד]

Lewis B[ayles] Paton, "The use of the word 'kohen' in the Old Testament," *JBL* 12 (1893) 1-14. [כֹּהֵן]

A. H. Sayce, "The Origin of the Hebrew *Cohen*," *ET* 24 (1912-13) 38. [כֹּהֵן]

*Paul Haupt, "Heb. *kôhén* and *qahál*," *JAOS* 42 (1922) 372-375. [כֹּהֵן]

*Theodor Gaster, "A Hittite Word in Hebrew," *JRAS* (1933) 909. [כּוֹבַע "helmet" /קוֹבַע = Hittite *kupaḫi*]

Edward Sapir, "Hebrew 'helmet,' a Loanword, and its Bearing on Indo-European Phonology," *JAOS* 57 (1937) 73-77. [קוֹבַע]

E. Y. Kutscher, "כּוּף and its Cognates," *EI* 8 (1967) 77*.

*J. W. Jack, "Cushan-Rishathaim (כּוּשָׁן רִשְׁעָתַיִם)," *ET* 35 (1923-24) 426-428.

*Paul Haupt, "Heb. kĕ, like and kî, as," *JAOS* 45 (1925) 316-318. [כִּי]

James Muilenburg, "The Linguistic and Rhetorical Usages of the Particle כִּי in the Old Testament," *HUCA* 32 (1961) 135-160.

G. Molin, "What is a *Kidon?*" *JJS* 1 (1956) 334-337. [כִּידוֹן]

*H. F. Lutz, "Etymological Miscellanies," *AJSL* 37 (1920-21) 73-74. [כִּכָּר, pp. 74-75]

C. M. Mead, "The Use of כֹּל with Negative Particles," *BS* 31 (1874) 487-506.

*David de Sola Pool, "The Constructive Use of כֹּל in the Book of Psalms," *PAAJR* 13 (1943) 41-46.

*James A. Montgomery, "Adverbial *Kúlla* in Biblical Aramaic and Hebrew," *JAOS* 43 (1923) 391-395. [כְּלָא]

D. Winton Thomas, "*Kelebh* 'dog': Its Origin and Some Usages of it in the Old Testament," *VT* 10 (1960) 410-427. [כֶּלֶב]

J. G. Lansing, "The Reins," *ONTS* 3 (1883-84) 191-196. [כִּלְיוֹת]

*Paul Haupt, "Assyr. *ramku*, 'Priest' = Heb. *komer*," *AJSL* 32 (1915-16) 64-75. [כֹּמֶר]

Jacob Neusner, "Note on *KMR*," *JAOS* 82 (1962) 372-373. [כמר]

*Edouard Naville, "Hebraeo-Aegyptiaca. III," *SBAP* 37 (1914) 208-214. [כנעני]

*John Thomas, "'Double for All Her Sins'. A Critical Exposition," *Exp, 5th Ser.*, 4 (1896) 370-380. [כִּפְלַיִם]

Anonymous, "The Use of the Verb כִּפֶּר," *BWR* 2 (1878) 460-461.

*Willis J. Beecher, "The idea of atonement, as found in the piel verb כִּפֶּר and the nouns כִּפֻּרִים and כַּפֹּרֶת," *JBL* 4 (1884) 144.

*C. H. Dodd, "*ΙΛΑΣΚΕΣΘΑΙ* in the Septuagint," *JTS* 32 (1930-31) 352-360. [כִּפֶּר]

*Leon Morris, "The Biblical Idea of Atonement," *ABR* 2 (1952) 83-95. [כפר]

R. Laird Harris, "Exegetical Notes—Meaning of *Kipper*, 'Atone.'," *BETS* 4 (1961) 3. [כִּפֶּר]

*Willis J. Beecher, "The idea of atonement, as found in the piel verb כִּפֶּר and the nouns כִּפֻּרִים and כַּפֹּרֶת," *JBL* 4 (1884) 144.

*P. le Page Renouf, "Is the Hebrew Word Cherub of Egyptian Origin?" *SBAP* 6 (1883-84) 189-193. [כְּרוּב]

*S. C. Ylvisaker, "Some Old Testament Difficulties," *WLQ* 54 (1957) 262-264. [*Karmel*, p. 264] [כַּרְמֶל]

*Julian Morgenstern, "The Etymological History of the Three Hebrew Synonyms for 'to Dance.' ḤGG, ḤLL, and KRR, and their Cultural Significance," *JAOS* 36 (1916) 321-332. [כרר]

*J. F. McCurdy, "Assyriological Notes," *AJP* 2 (1881) 461-464. [כשר - Root]

Z.   Kallai,   "Katepu—כתף,"   *IEJ*   15   (1965)   177-179.

*F. Charles Fensham, "A Cappadocian Parallel to the Hebrew *kutōnet*," *VT* 12 (1962) 196-198. [כֻּתֹּנֶת]

ל

I. M. Casanowicz, "The Emphatic Particle ל in the Old Testament," *JAOS* 16 (1894-96) clxvi-clxxi.

*Theophile J[ames] Meek, "Old Testament Notes," *JBL* 67 (1948) 233-239. [3. The Temporal Use of ל, pp. 236-238]

*T[heophile] J. Meek, "The Consecutive Use of *l^e* and *l^ema'an*," *JBL* 56 (1937) xii. [לְ]

*Edmund F. Sutcliffe, "A Note on *'al, l^e*, and *from*," *VT* 5 (1955) 436-439. [לְ]

*D. R. Goodwin, "The use of לב and καρδία in the Old and New Testaments," *JBL* 1 (1881) 67-72.

*Wm. R. Harper, "Notes for Beginners," *AJSL* 2 (1885-86) 178-182. [The Word לֵב or לֵבָב, pp. 179-180.]

*Cornelius Walker, "'The Heart'—לב, καρδία—in Scriptural Usage," *HR* 36 (1898) 446-450.

*Hayyim Rosenrauch, "II. The Hebrew Equivalent to Accadic Lib(lib)u," *JQR, N.S.*, 36 (1945-46) 81. [לבב]

*J. J. Gluck, "'^ari and *lavi' (labi')*—An Etymological Study," *ZAW* 81 (1969) 232-235. [לְבִיא]

A. Guillaume, "The Hebrew Root להט," *JTS* 41 (1940) 251-252.

*Theodor H. Gaster, "The Name לֵוִי," *JTS* 38 (1937) 250-251.

*Paul Haupt, "Heb. *lĕḥî,* cheek, and *lô ᵃᶜ,* jaw," *JBL* 33 (1914) 290-295. [לְחִי]

*M. Zeidel, "Leḥayath—a vulture," *BIES* 6 (1938-39) #3, IV. [לְחַיַת]

*Paul Haupt, "Heb. *lêç,* wanton, and *melîç,* spokesman," *BAVSS* 10 (1927) Heft 2, 175-184. [לִיץ]

H. N. Richardson, "Some notes on לִיץ and its Derivatives," *VT* 5 (1955) 163-179.

H. N. Richardson, "Two addenda to 'Some notes on לִיץ and its Derivatives'," *VT* 5 (1955) 434-436.

Paul Haupt, "The Semitic Root *lak,* to press," *JBL* 34 (1915) 183-184. [לָאַךְ*(?)]

J. M. Casanowicz, "Note on Some Usages of לָכֵן," *JAOS* 30 (1909-10) 343-346.

C. S. Macalpine, "For Mine Own Sake," *ET* 18 (1906-07) 15-18. [I. Passages in which the Preposition is used otherwise than of God; II. Passages in which the Preposition is used of God indirectly; III. Passages in which the Preposition is used of God more Directly; IV. Passages in which the Preposition is used of God directly] [לְמַעַן]

*H. G. Mitchell, "The Construction with לְמַעַן," *ONTS* 2 (1882-83) 171-172.

*Paul Haupt, "Heb. *lĕḥî,* cheek, and *lô ᵃᶜ,* jaw," *JBL* 33 (1914) 290-295. [לֹעַ]

S. Kogut, "Double Meaning of the Biblical Root לקח," *Lĕš* 34 (1969-70) #4, n.p.n.

מ

*Horace D. Hummel, "Enclitic *Mem* in Early North-West Semitic, Especially Hebrew," *JBL* 76 (1957) 85-107. [מ]

*A. Guillaume, "מְאֹד in I Samuel XX, 19," *PEQ* 86 (1954) 83-86.

*Fr. Rosenthal, "Māgēn, Māsāk, Māʿōz," *JBL* 63 (1944) 309-312. [מָגֵן]

*Joseph Reider, "The Etymology of Hebrew *mūl, or mōl* and its Bearing on *tmōl* and *'etmōl*," *HUCA* 12&13 (1937-38) 89-96. [מוֹל, מוּל]

*Solomon Zeitlin, "Mumar and Meshumad," *JQR, N.S.,* 54 (1963-64) 84-86. [מוּמָר]

*John A. Wilson, "The Assembly of a Phoenician City," *JNES* 4 (1945) 245. [מוֹעֵד]

*Duncan B. Macdonald, "Notes Critical and Lexicographical," *JBL* 14 (1895) 57-62. [V. מוֹפֵת pp. 58-62]

B. Eshel, "נוֹסֵךְ/מוֹסֵךְ = 'Caster, Founder',"*Lěš* 30 (1968-69) #1, n.p.n.

*C. Taylor, "Note on the Hebrew root יקשׁ," *JP* 2 (1869) 130-134. [מוֹקֵשׁ]

*H[enry] S. Gehman, "Philological Notes on Two Hebrew Words," *JBL* 58 (1939) vi. [מוֹקֵשׁ]

Henry S. Gehman, "Notes on מוֹקֵשׁ," *JBL* 58 (1939) 277-282.

*G. R. Driver, "Reflections on Recent Articles," *JBL* 73 (1954) 125-136. [II. Hebr. *môqēš,* 'Striker', pp 131-136] [מוֹקֵשׁ]

J. Sawyer, "What was a mošia'," *VT* 15 (1965) 475-486. [מוֹשִׁיעַ]

*Svi Rin, "The מות of Grandeur," *VT* 9 (1959) 324-325.

*G. Lefebvre, "A Note on Brit. Mus. 828 (Stela of Simontu)," *JEA* 25 (1939) 218. (Note by Battiscombe Gunn, p. 218-219) [מֶזַח]

*J. Dyneley Prince, "Old Testament Notes,"*JBL* 16 (1897) 175-177. [The Word מזור in Obadiah 7, pp. 176-177]

*B. Gross, "The Origin of the Words; מזנון and תמחוי," *Lěš* 30 (1965-66) #3, n.p.n.

*Isidore Wartski, "*Mezuqqar* and the *Pi'el Ziqqer* in the Midrashim," *Tarbiz* 29 (1959-60) #4, II-III. [מזיקר not מיוקר]

*Eli Eytan, "More on Maṭrūn and Miṭḥan," *JQR, N.S.,* 53 (1962-63) 66-68. [מטחן]

*Eli Eytan, "Maṭrūn," *JQR, N.S.,* 48 (1957-58) 380. [מָטְרוּן]

*Leon Nemoy, *"Maṭrūn* Once More," *JQR, N.S.,* 49 (1958-59) 155-157. [מָטרוֹן]

*Eli Eytan, "More on Maṭrūn and Miṭḥan," *JQR, N.S.,* 53 (1962-63) 66-68. [מָטרוֹן]

Paul Haupt, "Heb., מֶכֶר, abundance," *JBL* 31 (1912) 210.

D. W[inton] Thomas, "The Root מכר in Hebrew," *JTS* 37 (1936) 388-389.

D. Winton Thomas, "A Further Note on the Root מכר in Hebrew," *JTS, N.S.,* 3 (1952) 214.

*Paulo Boneschi, "Is *Malak* an Arabic Word?" *JAOS* 65 (1945) 107-111. [מלאך]

*Robert North, "Separated Spiritual Substances in the Old Testament," *CBQ* 29 (1967) 419-449. [מלאך]

Benjamin Douglass, "The Use of the Verb Malach, 'To Reign,' in the Old Testament," *ONTS* 10 (1890) 213-219. [מלך]

*Julius Boehmer, "MLKH in Semitic Proper Names," *ET* 16 (1904-05) 473-477. [מלך]

Paul Haupt, "The Hebrew Noun *Melkh,* Counsel," *JBL* 34 (1915) 54-70. [מֶלֶךְ]

Maurice A. Canney, "The Hebrew מֵלִיץ," *AJSL* 40 (1923-24) 135-137.

*Paul Haupt, "Heb. *Lêç,* wanton, and *melîç,* spokesman," *BAVSS* 10 (1927) Heft 2, 175-184. [מֵלִיץ]

*James Oscar Boyd, "'He Brake The Battle'," *CFL, N.S.,* 6 (1902) 298-300. [מלחמה]

*T. K. Cheyne, "On an Assyrian Loan-word in Hebrew, and on מֵמְזֵר," *SBAP* 22 (1900) 165-166.

*Samuel Feigin, "Etymological Notes," *AJSL* 43 (1926-27) 53-60. [II. מֵמְזֵר, pp. 56-60]

Fritz Hommel, "ממשת—Mampsis," *ET* 12 (1900-01) 288.

*H. L. Ginsberg, "MMŠT and MṢH," *BASOR* #109 (1948) 20-22. [ממשת]

*Paul Haupt, "Biblical Studies," *AJP* 43 (1922) 238-249. [8. The Etymology of Manna, pp. 247-249] [מָן]

*J. Simons, "Two Connected Problems Relating to the Israelite Settlement in Transjordan," *PEQ* 79 (1947) 27-39, 87-101. [מִן]

Willis J. Beecher, "Should מנחה be translated 'meal-offering'?" *JBL* 5 (1885) 73.

Robert Dick Wilson, "מנה, 'to Appoint,' in the Old Testament," *PTR* 16 (1917) 645-654.

*Fr. Rosenthal, "Māgēn, Māsāk, Māʿōz," *JBL* 63 (1944) 309-312. [מָסָךְ]

*H. L. Ginsberg, "MMŠT and MṢH," *BASOR* #109 (1948) 20-22. [מסה]

*Paul Haupt, "Masora," *JBL* 37 (1918) 219-228. [*מָסוֹרָה]

*Samuel Daiches, "Psalm XXXV, v. 16. The Meaning of מָעוֹג," *JRAS* (1935) 355-358.

*S. D. Goitein, "Māʿōn—A Reminder of Sin," *JSS* 10 (1965) 52-53. [מָעוֹן]

*Fr. Rosenthal, "Māgēn, Māsāk, Māʿōz," *JBL* 63 (1944) 309-312. [מָעוֹז]

P[aul] Haupt, "Heb. *mô ʾēç*, Counsel," *JBL* 38 (1919) 45-48. [מֵעֵצָה]

*Theodor H. Gaster, "The legend M-z-h," *PEFQS* 64 (1932) 104. [מצה]

*Saul Lieberman, "Two Lexicographical Notes," *JBL* 65 (1946) 67-72. [2. מצוה ἐντολή charity alms, pp. 69-72]

*Nathaniel Reich, "The Geographical Terms *Mizraim* and *Pathros*," *JSOR* 12 (1928) 43-45. [מצרים]

*W. Robertson Smith, "On the Hebrew Root קצע and the word מקצוע," *JP* 16 (1887-88) 71-81.

A. Cowley, "The Meaning of מָקוֹם in Hebrew," *JTS* 17 (1915-16) 174-176.

Paul Haupt, "Heb. *mardûṭ*, chastisement and chastity," *JBL* 39 (1920) 156-158. (Addenda, p. 171) [מַרְדּוּת]

*Julian Obermann, "In the Wake of the Karatepe Discoveries," *Oriens* 3 (1950) 20-30. [2. The Synonyms *mērîḇ *and* *yārîḇ in Hebrew, pp. 22-25] [*מְרוּב]

*Anonymous, "Sekel and Maskil," *CFL, O.S.,* 1 (1897) 192. [מַשְׂכִּיל]

*J. Willis Beecher, "Hebrew Word Studies. The Word Maschil in the Psalm Titles," *HR* 33 (1897) 262. [מַשְׂכִּיל]

*Francis Brown, "Geographical," *PR* 3 (1882) 169. [מַשָּׂא]

*Henry S. Gehman, "The 'Burden' of the Prophets," *JQR, N.S.,* 31 (1940-41) 107-121. [מַשָּׂא]

R. B. Y. Scott, "The Meaning of *massā'* as an Oracle Title," *JBL* 67 (1948) v-vi. [מַשָּׂא]

P. A. H. de Boer, "An Inquiry into the Meaning of the Term מַשָּׂא," *OTS* 5 (1948) 197-214.

J. A. Naude, "*maśśā* in the O.T. with special reference to the prophets," *OTW* 12 (1969) 91-100. [מַשָּׂא]

*D. Winton Thomas, "The Meaning of the Name Mishal," *PEFQS* 68 (1936) 39-40. [מְשָׁאָל]

*Th. Sprey, "ܠ ܚܒܘ ‎- משבה," *VT* 7 (1957) 408-410.

*Solomon Zeitlin, "Mumar and Meshumad," *JQR, N.S.,* 54 (1963-64) 84-86. [משומד]

Paul Haupt, "Hebrew *Mašâl,*" *JBL* 36 (1917) 140-142. [מָשָׁל]

Allen Howard Godbey, "The Hebrew *Mašal,*" *AJSL* 39 (1922-23) 89-108. [מָשָׁל]

A. S. Herbert, "The 'Parable' *(Māšāl)* in the Old Testament," *SJT* 7 (1954) 180-196. [מָשָׁל]

A. R. Johnson, "מָשָׁל," *VTS* 3 (1955) 162-169.

*P. A. Nordell, "Contributions to Hebrew Synonymy," *AJSL* 1 (1884-85) 13-14. [מִשְׁפָּט = דִּין]

L. W. Batten, "The Use of משפט," *JBL* 11 (1892) 206-210.

Osborne Booth, "The Semantic Development of the Term *Mishpat* in the Old Testament," *JBL* 61 (1942) xi. [מִשְׁפָּט]

Osborne Booth, "The Semantic Development of the Term מִשְׁפָּט in the Old Testament," *JBL* 61 (1942) 105-110.

Leon Morris, "Judgment and Custom," *ABR* 7 (1959) 72-74. [מִשְׁפָּט]

*Wallace I. Wolverton, "The King's 'Justice' in Pre-exilic Israel," *ATR* 41 (1959) 276-286. [מִשְׁפָּט]

Eliezer Berkovits, "The Biblical Meaning of Justice," *Jud* 18 (1969) 188-209. [מִשְׁפָּט]

*Joseph Reider, "Studies in Hebrew Roots and Their Etymology," *AJSL* 34 (1917-18) 66-70. [משׁק]

*A. Rubinstein, "The Terms משׁתבשׁין and דחזי in the Babylonian Massorah," *VT* 10 (1960) 198-212.

O. O. F., "The Word מְתִים (מְתָם)," *ONTS* 1 (1882) #2, 12-13.

נ

*Henry Preserved Smith, "Old Testament Notes," *JBL* 24 (1905) 27-30. [II. Nabi', pp. 27-28] [נָבִיא]

*Norman Walker, "What is a Nābhî'?" *ZAW* 73 (1961) 99-100. [נָבִיא]

Wolfgang M. W. Roth, "NBL," *VT* 10 (1960) 394-409. [נבל]

R. M. Spence, "Nĕbhêlah," *ET* 8 (1896-97) 428. [נְבֵלָה]

Fritz Hommel, "Nĕbhêlah," *ET* 8 (1896-97) 473-474. [נְבֵלָה]

R. M. Spence, "Nĕbhêlah," *ET* 8 (1896-97) 526. [נְבֵלָה]

*John R. Mackay, "'Knowledge' and 'Revelation' in Hebrew," *Exp, 9th Ser.,* 1 (1924) 139-140. [נגד]

*J. J. Glück, "Nagid-Shepherd," *VT* 13 (1963) 144-150. [נָגִיד]

Theodore Robinson, "Note on the Use of the Hebrew נגף," *AJSL* 46 (1929-30) 198-200.

S[teven] T. Byington, "נדגלות," *JBL* 39 (1920) 82.

Paul Haupt, "The Hebrew Stem Nahal, to Rest," *AJSL* 22 (1905-06) 195-206. [נחל]

G. R. Berry, "The Hebrew Word נוח," *JBL* 50 (1931) 207-210.

*B. Eshel, "נוסך/מוסך = 'Caster, Founder'," *LeŠ* 30 (1968-69) #1, n.p.n.

*J. J. Glück, "Nagid-Shepherd," *VT* 13 (1963) 144-150. [נוקד]

*C. Taylor, "An interpretation of יזה גוים," *JP* 8 (1879) 62-66. [The Constructions of נזה, pp. 62-63]

*Th. C. Vriezen, "The Term *Hizza:* Lustration and Consecration," *OTS* 7 (1950) 201-235. [הזּה Hiph. of נזה]

*M. D. Goldman, "Lexicographical Notes on Exegesis. (2) Some Hebrew Words Used in Their Original Meaning," *ABR* 1 (1951) 141-142. [נזל]

D. Winton Thomas, "A Note on the Hebrew Root נחם," *ET* 44 (1932-33) 191-192.

Geo. B. Michell, "A Note on the Hebrew Root נחם," *ET* 44 (1932-33) 428.

*D. Winton Thomas, "A Study in Hebrew Synonyms; verbs signifying 'to breathe'," *ZS* 10 (1935) 311-314. [נחם and פוח]

*Paul D. Hanson, "Song of Heshbon and David's *Nîr,*" *HTR* 61 (1968) 297-341. [ניר]

J[ulian] Morgenstern, "נכון," *JBL* 37 (1918) 144-148.

Paul Haupt, "On the Etymology of Nekasim," *AJSL* 3 (1886-87) 107-110. [נכסים]

Michael Guttman, "The Term 'Foreigner' (נכרי) Historically Considered," *HUCA* 3 (1926) 1-20.

*Peter R. Ackroyd, "נצח—ἐις τέλος," *ET* 80 (1968-69) 126.

T. K. Cheyne, "The Use of the Hebrew Word נצח," *JQR* 11 (1898-99) 400-403.

D. Winton Thomas, "The Use of נֵצַח as a superlative in Hebrew," *JSS* 1 (1956) 106-109.

H. L. Ginsberg, "An Obscure Hebrew Word," *JQR, N.S.,* 22 (1931-32) 143-145. [נָפָה]

*David Yellin, "A Hitherto Unnoticed Meaning of נפל," *JPOS* 6 (1926) 164-166.

*James Strong, "Scripture Usage of נפש and רוח, and of the Corresponding Greek Words," *ONTS* 2 (1882-83) 105-106.

*C[harles] A. Briggs, "The Use of נפש in the Old Testament," *JBL* 16 (1897) 17-30.

*Ernest D[e Witt] Burton, "Spirit, Soul and Flesh II. רוּחַ, נֶפֶשׁ, and בָּשָׂר in the Old Testament," *AJT* 18 (1914) 59-80.

Wm. Henry Cobb, "The Meaning of נֶפֶשׁ. A Contribution to Biblical Psychology," *BS* 37 (1880) 134-152.

*A. M. Habermann, "The Tomb of Rachel and the Term נפש," *Tarbiz* 25 (1956-57) #4, I-II.

A. Murtonen, "The Living Soul: A Study of the Meaning of the Word *næfæš* in the Old Testament Hebrew Language," *SO* 28 (1958) #1, 1-105. [וְנֶפֶשׁ]

*M. D. Goldman, "The Root 'NQY'," *ABR* 4 (1954-55) 49-55. [נקי]

George E. Mendenhall, "God of Vengeance, Shine Forth!" *WBHDN* 45 (1948) #12, 37-42. [נְקָמָה]

William Henry Cobb, "The Meaning of נָשָׂא," *BS* 30 (1873) 422-464.

*Samuel E. Loewenstamm, "נשׁך and מ/תרבית," *JBL* 88 (1969) 78-80.

T. C. Mitchell, "The Old Testament usage of N°šāmá," *VT* 11 (1961) 177-187. [נְשָׁמָה]

D. W. Young, "Notes on the root נתן in Biblical Hebrew," *VT* 10 (1960) 457-459.

ס

*S. Daiches, "The Assyrian and Hebrew Words for 'Beard of the Ear of Corn'," *SBAP* 37 (1915) 215-216. [סאסא]

P. Artzi, "Sevel-Sablum," *BIES* 18 (1954) #1/2, VII. [סבל-סבלום]

*John A. Maynard, "Short Notes on Assyrian Religious Texts," *JSOR* 12 (1928) 109. [2. Sagullatu, סגלה]

*H. Wheeler Robinson, "The Council of Yahweh," *JTS* 45 (1944) 151-157. [סוד]

*Moshe Greenberg, "Hebrew s⁽e⁾gullā: Akkadian sikiltu," *JAOS* 71 (1951) 172-174. [סְגֻלָּה]

*T. K. Cheyne, "On the Hebrew words אשכר and סגור," *SBAP* 21 (1899) 246.

*Eberhard Hommel, "The Forms Σειραχ and 'Ακελδαμαχ as Transcriptions of סירא and חקלדמא," *ET* 25 (1913-14) 285.

*E[phraim] A. Speiser, "The Verb ṢHR in Genesis and Early Hebrew Movements," *BASOR* #164 (1961) 23-28. [סחר]

*W[illiam] F[oxwell] Albright, "Some Remarks on the Meaning of the Verb ṢHR in Genesis," *BASOR* #164 (1961) 28. [סחר]

Paul Haupt, "Sîrîm, Thorns, and Sîrôṭ, Pots," *JBL* 36 (1917) 256-258. [סירות, סירים]

Wolfgang M. W. Roth, "A Study of the Classic Hebrew Verb ṢKL," *VT* 18 (1968) 69-78. [סכל]

W[illiam] F[oxwell] Albright, "The Assumed Hebrew Stem skt, Be Silent,"*JBL* 39 (1920) 166-167. [סכת]

*B. B. Edwards, "Studies in Hebrew Poetry," *BS* 5 (1848) 58-79. [Explanation of the Word סֶלָה, Selah, pp. 66-79]

Emilie Grace Briggs, "סלה," *AJSL* 16 (1899-1900) 1-29.

*H. Torczyner, "*Semel Ha-qin'ah Ha-maqneh,*" *JBL* 65 (1946) 293-302. [3. סמל, a loan word, pp. 297-298]

D.　Sperber,　"סניס—סנסן,"　*Lĕš*　33　(1968-69)　#1,　n.p.n.

A. M. Honeyman, "Hebrew סַף 'Basin, Goblet'," *JTS* 37 (1936) 56-59.

*Francis　Brown,　"סְפְרוִים,"　*PR*　3　(1882)　169.

*Samuel Feigin, "Etymological Notes," *AJSL* 43 (1926-27) 53-60. [I. סְרָנִים, pp. 56-60]

ע

H. Hirschfeld, "The Pronunciation of the Letter AYN (ע)," *JQR* 4 (1891-92) 499-502.

*Ḥ Allon, "Biblical *'Anan* and *'Av,*" *Lĕš* 31 (1966-67) #3, n.p.n. [עָב]

*E. C. Bissell, "The Use of עבר and its Compounds in the Hexateuch," *AJSL* 2 (1885-86) 9-12.

Herbert G. Grether, "Rendering *'eber* as a Geographical Term," *BTr* 13 (1962) 177-179. [עבר]

Herbert Parzen, "The Problem of the Ibrim ('Hebrews') in the Bible," *AJSL* 49 (1932-33) 254-261. [עברים]

*George Jeshrun, "Note on עד and עולם," *JBL* 53 (1934) 384-385.

J. A. Thompson, "Expansions of the עד Root," *JSS* 10 (1965) 222-240.

H. L. Ginsberg, "A Preposition of Interest to Historical Geographers," *BASOR* #122 (1951) 12-14. [II עַד]

H. L. Ginsberg, "Postscript to Bulletin No. 122, pp. 12-14," *BASOR* #124 (1951) 29-30. [II עַד]

Solomon Speier, "On Hebrew *'Aḏ* Meaning 'At, By, Near'," *BASOR* #126 (1952) 27. [II עַד]

*Philip A. Nordell, "On the Synonyms עדה and קהל," *AJSL* 3 (1886-87) 129-135.

Z. W. Falk, "Forms of Testimony," *VT* 11 (1961) 81-91. [עֵדוּת]

*Fritz Hommel, "Hena' and 'Awwâ," *ET* 9 (1897-98) 330-331. [עַוָּה]

*M. Stuart, "*Aἰών* and *Aἰώνοις*," *SP* 2 (1829) 405-452. [III. (1) The meaning of the Hebrew עוֹרֵם, pp. 434-438]

*Fritz Hommel, "Assyriological Notes," *SBAP* 17 (1895) 199-207. [§8. Etymology of עוֹלָם, אוּלָם, עֵילָם, pp.200-201]

Ezra S. Goodwin, "Meaning of עוֹלָם. Third Letter from the Rev. Mr. Goodwin," *CE* 13 (1832) 225-253.

Ezra S. Goodwin, "Meaning of עוֹלָם. Fourth Letter from the Rev. Mr. Goodwin," *CE* 14 (1833) 246-267. (Editorial note, pp. 245-246)

*George Jeshurun, "Note on עַד and עוֹלָם," *JBL* 53 (1934) 384-385.

Raphael Loewe, "Jerome's Rendering of עוֹלָם," *HUCA* 22 (1949) 265-306. (Addendum, p. 432)

P[aul] Haupt, "The Etymology of 'ôr, Skin," *JBL* 38 (1919) 50-51. [עוֹר]

*G. R. Driver, "Three Technical Terms in the Pentateuch," *JSS* 2 (1956) 97-105. [I. עזאזל "Jagged Rocks, Precipice", pp. 97-98]

*Mitchell Dahood, "The Root עזב II in Job," *JBL* 78 (1959) 303-309.

*N. N., "Additional Note to עָצוּר וְעָזוּב," *Lèš* 33 (1968-69) #1, n.p.n.

*Fritz Hommel, "עֲזֵקָה ('Azeḳa) in an Assyrian Inscription," *ET* 13 (1901-02) 95-96.

*Fritz Hommel, " 'Azeḳa: a Supplementary Note," *ET* 13 (1901-02) 144. [עֲזֵקָה]

*Fritz Hommel, "Assyriological Notes," *SBAP* 17 (1895) 199-207. [§8. Etymology of עוֹלָם, אוּלָם, עֵילָם, pp.200-201]

M. Z. Kaddary, "The Double Meaning of *'Ayef* ' (עָיֵף) in the Bible," *Tarbiz* 34 (1964-65) #4, VI.

*Frank Zimmerman, "עִיר, קִיר and Related Forms," *JQR, N.S.,* 75th (1967) 582-592.

*Edmund F. Sutcliffe, "A Note on *'al, lᵉ,* and *from*," *VT* 5 (1955) 436-439. [עַל]

*G. R. Driver, "Hebrew *'al* ('High One') as a Divine Title," *ET* 50 (1938-39) 92-93. [I עַל]

Joseph Reider, "Substantival *'al* in Biblical Hebrew," *JBL* 53 (1934) iii. [II עַל]

*G. R. Driver, "On עלה 'went up country' and ירד 'went down country'," *ZAW* 69 (1957) 74-77.

*Wolf Leslau, "An Ethiopian Parallel to Hebrew עלה 'went up country' and ירד 'went down country'," *ZAW* 74 (1962) 322-323.

*Sakae Shibayama, "Notes on *Yārad* and *'Ālāh:* Hints on Translating," *JAAR* 34 (1966) 358-362. [עָלָה]

*C. F. Burney, "Old Testament Notes. I. The 'Sign of Immanuel'," *JTS* 10 (1908-09) 580-584. [עלמה]

John E. Steinmueller, "The Etymology and Biblical Usage of *'Almah*," *CBQ* 2 (1940) 28-43. [עַלְמָה]

*Cyrus H. Gordon, "The Patriarchal Age," *JAAR* 21 (1953) 238-243. [*'almah,* pp. 240-241 (עַלְמָה)]

John Joseph Owens, "The Meaning of *'Almah* in the Old Testament," *R&E* 50 (1953) 56-60. [עַלְמָה]

William A. Irwin, "That Troublesome *'Almah* and Other Matters," *R&E* 50 (1953) 337-360. [עַלְמָה]

Albert E. Myers, "The Use of *Almah* in the Old Testament," *LQ, N.S.,* 7 (1955) 137-140. [עַלְמָה]

*Edmund F. Sutcliffe, "A Note on *'al, lᵉ,* and *from*," *VT* 5 (1955) 436-439. [עַל]

M. D. Goldman, "Lexicographical Notes on Exegesis (4): Concerning the Meaning of עַם," *ABR* 3 (1953) 51. [עַם]

*E[phraim] A. Speiser, "'People' and 'Nation' of Israel," *JBL* 79 (1960) 157-163. [עַם]

*George Jeshurun, "On the Meaning of the Silent Yod in a Certain Group of Passages in the M.T.," *JSOR* 16 (1932) 108-112. [עמיו ,עמיה ,עמיך]

*Paul Haupt, "Labor and Sorrow," *BAVSS* 10 (1927) Heft 2, 150-164. [עָמָל]

*Cyrus H. Gordon, "Marginal Notes on the Ancient Middle East," *JKF* 2 (1952-53) 50-61 [VI. Babyloniaca: a. CH²⁷ 3:68 *a-ši-ir;* b. *'mq* 'be strong', Acc. *ina emûqi* = Ugar. *b'mq* 'violently' - Heb. עמק II כה]

*Ḥ Allon, "Biblical *'Anan* and *'Av*," *Lěš* 31 (1966-67) #3, n.p.n. [עָנָן]

D. Winton Thomas, "Hebrew עֲנִי 'Captivity'," *JTS, N.S.,* 16 (1965) 444-445.

*Louis Finkelstein, "A Talmudic Note on the Word for Cutting Flax in the Gezer Calendar," *BASOR* #94 (1944) 28-29. [עצד]

*N. N., "Additional Note to עָצוּר וְעָזוּב," *Lěš* 33 (1968-69) #1, n.p.n.

*A. D. Singer, "Philological Notes," *JPOS* 21 (1948) 104-109. [II. On Two Biblical Verbs: Hiph. וַיַּעְפִלוּ √עפל, pp. 106-109]

*A. Hurvitz, "Ακκαρων = Amaqar(r)una = עֶקְרוֹן," *Lěš* 33 (1968-69) #1, n.p.n.

Raphael Patai, "'Arisah," *JQR, N.S.,* 35 (1944-45) 165-172. [עריסה]

*Samuel Daiches, "The Meaning of עֶרֶף in Leviticus v. 8," *ET* 39 (1927-28) 426-427.

*M. D. Goldman, "Lexicographical Notes on Exegesis. (2) Some Hebrew Words Used in Their Original Meaning," *ABR* 1 (1951) 141-142. [ערף]

Cyrus Adler, "On the use of the Word *'asah* in the Bible," *JAOS* 11 (1885) ccxxv-ccxxvii. [עָשָׂה]

Alfred Guillaume, "A Note on the Verb עשה," *JTS* 44 (1943) 23-24.

D. Winton Thomas, "Translating Hebrew *'āsāh*," *BTr* 17 (1966) 190-193. [עשה]

*Paul Haupt, "Heb. *qîṭôr* a doublet of *'ašán*," *JAOS* 42 (1922) 375-377. [עשן]

*Paul Haupt, "Biblical Studies," *AJP* 43 (1922) 238-249. [6. Heb. *'aštê* and Sum. *aš-tân*, p. 245 (עַשְׁתֵּי)]

פ

*David Neiman, "PGR: A Canaanite Cult-Object in the Old Testament," *JBL* 67 (1948) 55-60. [פגר]

Thos. Laurie, "Mouth," *AJSL* 5 (1888-89) 196-197. [פה]

*D. Winton Thomas, "A Study in Hebrew Synonyms; verbs signifying 'to breathe'," *ZS* 10 (1935) 311-314. [פום and פוח]

W. Sommer, "The Meaning of פוּך in the Old Testament," *JBL* 62 (1943) 33-35.

*D. Sperber, "פילס, פולסא and Follis," *Lěš* 31 (1966-67) #3, n.p.n.

E. Y. Kutscher, "פחוא and its Cognate Forms," *Tarbiz* 30 (1960-61) #2, I-II.

*Samuel I. Feigin, "The Captives in Cuneiform Inscriptions," *AJSL* 50 (1933-34) 217-245. [The Law concerning the Captive Woman in Deut. 21:10-14, pp. 243-245 (פִּילֶגֶשׁ)]

*D. Sperber, "פילס, פולסא and Follis,"*Lěš* 31 (1966-67) #3, n.p.n.

*Maurice A. Canney, "Notes on Philology, Etc. Purim," *JMUEOS* #5 (1915-16) 103. [פור*]

*Paul Haupt, "Biblical Studies," *AJP* 43 (1922) 238-249. [4. Heb. *pěleţâ* and Ger. *flöten gehn*, pp. 241-243. [פְּלֵיטָה]

*M. D. Goldman, "The Root פלל and Its Connotation with Prayer. (Attempted Explanation of Deuteronomy XXXII, 31), *ABR* 3 (1953) 1-6.

E[phraim] A. Speiser, "The Stem *PLL* in Hebrew," *JBL* 82 (1963) 301-306. [פלל]

*Eric Burrows, "Notes on the Pearl in Biblical Literature," *JTS* 42 (1941) 53-64. [פנינים]

Crawford H. Toy, "Meaning of פסח," *JBL* 16 (1897) 178-179.

Francis T. Glasson, "The 'Passover', a Misnomer: The Meaning of the Verb *Pasach*," *JTS, N.S.*, 10 (1959) 79-84. [פָּסַח]

*P. Middelkoop, "A Word Study. The Sense of PAQAD in the second Commandment and its general background in the O. T. in regard to the translation into the Indonesian and Timorese Languages," *SEAJT* 4 (1962-63) #3, 33-47. [פָּקַד]

*P. Middelkoop, "Paqad—A Word Study," *SEAJT* 4 (1962-63) #4, 56-65. [פָּקַד]

Thomas H. Campbell, "The Theological Significance of God's 'Visitations'," *CS* 9 (1961-62) #1, 1-4. [פְּקֻדָּה]

*A. Leo Oppenheim, "Assyriological Notes to the Old Testament," *JQR, N.S.,* 36 (1945-46) 171-176. [Neo-Babyl. *pirku* = Hebrew פֶּרֶךְ]

Louis Finkelstein, "The Meaning of the Word פרס in the Expressions בפרוס החג and ,בפרוס הפסח, בפרוס עצרת, פורס על שמע," *JQR, N.S.,* 32 (1941-42) 387-406; 33 (1942-43) 29-48.

G. R. Driver, "The Root פרץ in Hebrew," *JTS* 25 (1923-24) 177-178.

A. Guillaume, "Some Hebrew Roots and Their Meanings: פָּרַץ," *JTS* 24 (1922-23) 318.

*J. J. Glück, "The Verb PRṢ in the Bible and in the Qumran Literature," *RdQ* 5 (1964-66) 123-127. [פרץ]

William R. Arnold, "The Word פָּרָשׁ in the Old Testament," *JBL* 24 (1905) 45-53.

A. H. Sayce, "Origin of the Hebrew *Pârâsh,*" *JTS* 24 (1922-23) 175. [פָּרָשׁ]

A. E. Cowley, "The Origin of פתגמא," *JTS* 30 (1928-29) 54-56.

*Nathaniel Reich, "The Geographical Terms *Mizraim* and *Pathros*," *JSOR* 12 (1928) 43-45. [פתרוס]

צ

Henry P[reserved] Smith, "צדק and its Derivatives," *PR* 3 (1882) 165-168.

W. E. Addis, "Notes on the Use of צֶדֶק and cognate Words in the Hebrew Bible," *OSHTP* (1900-01) 50-52.

*Toyozo W. Nakarai, "The Prophetic Concept of Righteousness," *SQ/E* 13 (1952) 51-57. [צדק]

*John A. Bollier, "The Righteousness of God. *A Word Study*," *Interp* 8 (1954) 404-413. [צדק]

Jerome P. Jutstesen, "On the Meaning of Ṣāḏāq," *AUSS* 2 (1964) 53-61. [צדק]

W. E. Read, "Further Observations on Ṣāḏāq," *AUSS* 4 (1966) 29-36. [צדק]

*C. Taylor, "Notes on the translation of Genesis," *JP* 3 (1871) 291-327. [II. On the Hebrew root צהר, pp. 302-307]

H. Louis Ginsberg, "A Punic Note. צועת," *AJSL* 47 (1930-31) Number 1, Part 1, 52-53. (Corr. p. 144)

*Paul Haupt, "Arab. táhamah = çánaxah, Heb. çaḥnâ," *JAOS* 43 (1923) 424-425. [צֶחֱנָה]

*W. L. Moran, "Ugaritic ṣîṣûma and Hebrew ṣîṣ," *B* 39 (1958) 69-71. [צִיץ]

*Solomon Gandz, "The Origin of the Term Gnomon or the Gnomon in Hebrew Literature," *PAAJR* 2 (1930-31) 23-38. [ṣēl, p. 29f. (צֵל)]

Maurice A. Canney, "The Hebrew צָלַח," *JMUEOS* #7 (1917-18) 65-68.

K. Budde, "Professor Nöldeke on צַלְמָוֶת and צֶלֶם," *ET* 8 (1896-97) 384.

T. K. Cheyne, "צַלְמוּת or צַלְמָוֶת?" *AJSL* 1 (1884-85) 251-252.

D. Winton Thomas, "צַלְמָוֶת in the Old Testament," *JSS* 7 (1962) 191-200.

C. R. Conder, "The Tsinnor," *PEFQS* 22 (1890) 39. [צִנּוֹר]

M. H. Gottstein, "A Note on צנח," *VT* 6 (1956) 99-100.

*D. Winton Thomas, "The Root צנע in Hebrew and the Meaning of קדרנית in Malachi III, 14," *JJS* 1 (1948-49) 182-188.

*Samuel E. Loewenstamm, "The Nouns צֶמֶר, צעור (Ketīb), צָעִיר (Qeré)," *Tarbiẕ* 36 (1966-67) #2, I-II.

*A. Benisch, "Correspondence," *JSL, 1st Ser.,* 3 (1849) 168-170. [Zaananim] [(בְּ)צַעֲנַנִּים]

*J. Dyneley Prince, "Note on Leprosy in the Old Testament," *JBL* 38 (1919) 30-34. [צרעת]

*J. L. Swellengrebel, "The Translation of 'tsara'ath' and 'Lepra'," *BTr* 11 (1960) 69-79. [צרעת]

F. J. Stephens, "The Ancient Significance of Ṣîṣîth," *JBL* 50 (1931) 59-70. [ציצת]

ק

*G. R. Driver, "The Meaning of קאת and קפד in Hebrew," *JTS* 22 (1920-21) 382-383.

*Jacob J. Rabinowitz, "The Susa Tablets, the Bible and the Aramaic Papyri," *VT* 11 (1961) 55-76. [a. *Maḫâru* = קבל, pp. 63-69]

C. H. W. Brekelmans, "The Saints of the Most High and Their Kingdom," *OTS* 14 (1965) 305-329. [I. The Holy Ones. A. *The Hebrew Old Testament;* B. *The Deuterocanonical Writings (The Apocrypha);* C. *The Apocrypha (or Pseudepigrapha);* D. *The Literature of Qumran;* E. *Conclusion;* II. The Kingdom of the Saints; III. Conclusion] [קדושים]

H[enry] P[reserved] Smith, "The Root קדש in the Old Testament," *PR* 2 (1881) 588-593.

R. H. Altus, "A Lexicographic Study of Qadash," *AusTR* 16 (1945) 53-56. [קדש]

*Paul Haupt, "Heb. *kôhén* and *qahál*," *JAOS* 42 (1922) 372-375. [קהל]

E. Ullendorff, "The Meaning of קהלת," *VT* 12 (1962) 215.

*Philip A. Nordell, "On the Synonyms עדה and קהל," *AJSL* 3 (1886-87) 129-135.

*Theodor Gaster, "A Hittite Word in Hebrew," *JRAS* (1933) 909. [כובע "helmet" / קובע = Hittite *kupaḫi*]

*S. Kogut, "Does the form *Qĕtol* = *qotel* Exist in the Bible?" *Lĕš* 34 (1969-70) #1/2, 3. [קוטל] *[English Supplement]*

*W. Caspari, "The Voice of One Crying in the Wilderness," *JBL* 46 (1927) 266-278. [קוֹל]

Israel Efros, "קוּלכּוּדִיאָה," *JQR, N.S.,* 36 (1945-46) 79.

Harry Wolfson, "Colcodea קוּלקוּדִיאָ," *JQR, N.S.,* 36 (1945-46) 176-182.

*Jacob J. Rabinowitz, "The Susa Tablets, the Bible and the Aramaic Papyri," *VT* 11 (1961) 55-76. [c. *Nazâza* = קוּם, pp. 59-63]

*R. J. H. Gottheil, "On קוּשִׁיהוּ and קִישׁי," *JBL* 17 (1898) 199-202.

F. Zimmermann, "The Root *Kahal* in Some Scriptural Passages," *JBL* 50 (1931) 311-312. [קְהִלָּה]

P. Wernberg-Møller, "The Noun of the Qtwl Class in the Massoretic Text," *RdQ* 2 (1959-60) 448-450. *[Table of Contents reads: "$Q^{\varepsilon}t\bar{o}l$"]* [קטל]

*Paul Haupt, "Biblical Studies," *AJP* 43 (1922) 238-249. [7. Heb. *qĕṭórt* and Gr. *néktar*, pp. 245-247 (קְטֹרֶת)]

*Paul Haupt, "Heb. *qîṭôr* a doublet of *'ašán*," *JAOS* 42 (1922) 375-377. [קטר]

*Frank Zimmerman, "עִיר, קִיר and Related Forms," *JQR, N.S., 75th,* (1967) 582-592.

*R. J. H. Gottheil, "On קוּשִׁיהוּ and קִישׁי," *JBL* 17 (1898) 199-202.

*B. Salomonsen, "Some Remarks on the Zealots with Special Regard to the Term 'Qannaim' in Rabbinic Literature," *NTS* 12 (1965-66) 164-176. [קנאים]

*H. Torczyner, "*Semel Ha-qin'ah Ha-maqneh*," *JBL* 65 (1946) 293-302. [6. קנה synonym of גאל, pp. 300-302]

Peter Katz, "The Meaning of the Root קנה," *JJS* 5 (1954) 126-131.

David Halivni Weiss, "The Use of קנה in Connection with Marriage," *HTR* 57 (1964) 244-248.

*Cyrus H. Gordon, "Marginal Notes on the Ancient Middle East," *JKF* 2 (1952-53) 50-61 [VI. Babyloniaca: c. קנים, pp. 56-57]

N. H. Tur-Sinai, "קְנִישְׁקִין—Q'nê šāqayin, The Canes of the Butlers," *BIES* 16 (1951) #3/4, VII. [Talmudic Word = 'Drinking Straws']

A. A. Bevan, "The Hebrew Word קִצִין," *ZA* 26 (1912) 37.

*W. Robertson Smith, "On the Hebrew Root קצע and the word מִקְצוֹעַ," *JP* 16 (1887-88) 71-81.

*G. R. Driver, "The Meaning of קָאת and קִפֹּד in Hebrew," *JTS* 22 (1920-21) 382-383.

M. D. Goldman, "Lexicographic Notes on Exegesis: The Original Meaning of the Word 'Qara' 'קְרָא'," *ABR* 1 (1951) 66-67.

*F. M. Heichelheim, "New Evidence on the Ebro Treaty," *HJAH* 3 (1954-55) 211-219. [קְרָב]

Solomon Zeitlin, "Korban," *JQR, N.S.,* 53 (1962-63) 160-163. [קָרְבָּן]

Paul Haupt, "*Qaš,* straw, and *qäšt,* bow," *JBL* 39 (1920) 161-163. (Addenda on p. 171 and 172) [קֶשֶׁת / קַשׁ]

ר

Wolf Leslau, "A Parallel to the Non-Gemination of the Hebrew *R,*" *JBL* 68 (1949) 55-56. [ר]

*M[orris] Jastrow Jr., "Rô'êh and Ḥôzēh in the Old Testament," *JBL* 28 (1909) 42-56. [רֹאֶה]

*Anonymous, "The Unicorn," *CRB* 21 (1856) 34-45. [רְאֵם]

*John Theodore Mueller, "Notes on the Unicorn," *CTM* 32 (1961) 286-287. [רְאֵם]

*Virgil M. Rogers, "The Use of ראש in an Oath," *JBL* 74 (1955) 272.

J. R. Bartlett, "The use of the word ראֹשׁ as a title in the Old Testament," *VT* 19 (1969) 1-10.

Hershel Shanks, "Origins of the Title 'Rabbi'," *JQR, N.S.,* 59 (1968-69) 152-157. [רַבִּי]

M. D. Goldman, "The Meaning of 'רגע'," *ABR* 4 (1954-55) 7-16.

*J. Dyneley Prince, "Old Testament Notes," *JBL* 16 (1897) 175-177. [An Assyrian Cognate of the Word רוזנים, pp. 175-176]

*James Strong, "Scripture Usage of נפש and רוח, and of the Corresponding Greek Words," *ONTS* 2 (1882-83) 105-106.

C[harles] A. Briggs, "The Use of רוח in the Old Testament," *JBL* 19 (1900) 132-145.

W. R. Shoemaker, "The Use of רוח in the Old Testament, and of πνεῦμα in the New Testament (A Lexicographical Study)," *JBL* 23 (1904) 13-67.

*John P. Peters, "The Wind of God," *JBL* 30 (1911) 44-54; 33 (1914) 81-86. [רוח]

*Ernest D[e Witt] Burton, "Spirit, Soul and Flesh II. רוּחַ, נֶפֶשׁ, and בָּשָׂר in the Old Testament," *AJT* 18 (1914) 59-80.

*G. R Driver, "Hebrew Studies," *JRAS* (1948) 164-176. [A Note on רוח 'Wind, Spirit', p. 170]

*Peter May, "The Self and the Spirit," *IJT* 6 (1957) 131-142. [רוּחַ]

*W. G. Lambert, "Two Akkadian Cognates," *JJS* 5 (1954) 40-41. [1. *RÂSU* = רוץ]

*S[tephen] Langdon, "The Assyrian Root Raṣānu, Hebrew רזן," *AJSL* 28 (1911-12) 144-145.

Paul Haupt, "Heb. *ro*ʿ, evil = Arab. *ʿurr*," *JBL* 39 (1920) 152-155. (Addenda, p. 170) [רֹעַ]

*John P. Peters, "The Wind of God," *JBL* 30 (1911) 44-54; 33 (1914) 81-86. [רחף]

*B. Gemser, "The *rîb-* or controversy-pattern in Hebrew mentality," *VTS* 3 (1955) 120-137. [1. The Frequency of Disputes in Israelite Life; 2. Semantics; 3. The Rîb in Traditional Phraseology; 4. In the Preaching of the Prophets; 5. Man's Controversy with God; 6. Conclusions]

*James Limburg, "The Root ריב and the Prophetic Lawsuit Speeches," *JBL* 88 (1969) 291-304. [I. The Primary Sense of the Root ריב in the OT; II. The Root רב in the Sphere of International Relationships; III. The Root ריב and the Prophetic Lawsuit Speeches]

M[itchell] Dahood, "Denominative *riḥḥam,* 'to conceive, enwomb'," *B* 44 (1963) 204-205. [רחם]

*A. Guillaume, "A Note on the Roots ידע, ירע, and רעע in Hebrew," *JTS, N.S.,* 15 (1964) 293-295.

Israel Eitan, "An Unknown Meaning of Raḥamīm," *JBL* 53 (1934) 269-271. [רַחֲמִים]

Joseph Reider, "On Raḥamīm," *JBL* 53 (1934) 385. [רַחֲמִים]

*Kevin J. Cathcart, "*TRKB QMḤ* in the Arad Ostracon and Biblical Hebrew *REKEB,* 'Upper Millstone'," *VT* 19 (1969) 121-123. [רֶכֶב]

*N. E. Wagner, "רִנָּה in the Psalter," *VT* 10 (1960) 435-442.

Arch. Henderson, "The Verb 'to Shepherd'," *ET* 28 (1916-17) 234-236. [רָעָה]

Israel W. Slotki, "A Study of רעם," *AJSL* 37 (1920-21) 149-155.

*Joseph Reider, "Etymological Studies: ידע or ירע and רעע," *JBL* 66 (1947) 315-317.

*A. Guillaume, "A Note on the Roots ריע, ירע, and רעע in Hebrew," *JTS, N.S.,* 15 (1964) 293-295.

*Brevard S. Childs, "The Enemy from the North and the Chaos Tradition," *JBL* 78 (1959) 187-198. [II. רעש and the Chaos Tradition, pp. 188-190]

*Paul Haupt, "Critical Notes. II. Assyr. *rabû,* 'To Sink' = Heb. *raphâ,*" *AJSL* 33 (1916-17) 48. [רָפָה]

Norman Walker, "The Renderings of Rāṣôn," *JBL* 81 (1962) 182-184. [רָצָה]

*H. Torczyner, "The Firmament and the Clouds, Rāqîᵃ' and Sheḥāqîm," *ST* 1 (1947-48) 188-196. [Additional Note, *ST* 2 (1949-50) p. 98] [רָקִיעַ]

*S[tephen] Langdon, "Assyrian Lexicographical Notes," *JRAS* (1921) 573-582. [I. *ŠARĀPU,* to burn, Hebrew *RĀŚAPH,* p. 573] (רשׁף)

Geo. Bousfield, "Resheph," *JTS* 31 (1929-30) 397-399. [רֶשֶׁף]

שׁ

*Ralph Marcus, "The Hebrew Sibilant *śin* and the name *Yiśrā'ēl*," *JBL* 60 (1941) x.

A. Guillaume, "A Root שׁאה in Hebrew," *JTS, N.S.,* 17 (1966) 53-54.

John P. Peters, "Miscellaneous Notes," *AJSL* 3 (1886-87) 111-116. [The Meaning of שׁדרה, pp. 115-116]

Cyrus Adler, "Professor Peters' Notes," *AJSL* 3 (1886-87) 269. [שָׂדֶה]

Robert Gordis, "The Root SHDY-SHD in Biblical Hebrew," *JBL* 58 (1939) xii. [שְׂדִי]

*Robert Gordis, "The Biblical Root *ŠDY-ŠD:* Notes on 2 Sam. i. 21; Jer. xviii. 14; Ps. xci. 6; Job v. 21," *JTS* 41 (1940) 34-43. [שְׂדִי]

Maurice A. Canney, "The Hebrew שֶׁהֲרֹנִים," *JMUEOS* #8 (1918-19) 91-92.

Sigmund Mowinckel, "The verb *śi^aḥ* and the nouns *śi^aḥ, śiḥā*," *ST* 15 (1961) 1-10. [שִׂיחַ]

*Anonymous, "Sekel and Maskil," *CFL, O.S.,* 1 (1897) 192. [שׂכל]

Willis J. Beecher, "Hebrew Word Studies. The Word Sekel in the Sense of Trained Skill," *HR* 33 (1897) 261-262. [(שֶׂכֶל) שֵׂכֶל]

*Felix Perles, "A Misunderstood Hebrew Word," *JQR, N.S.,* 17 (1926-27) 233. [שׂכל]

Jonas C. Greenfield, "Lexicographical Notes II," *HUCA* 30 (1959) 141-151. [IX. The Root שׂמח]

*Maurice A. Canney, "The Goat-song," *ZAW* 42 (1924) 145-148. [שׂער]

*D. Winton Thomas, "The Text of Jesaia II 6 and the Word שָׂפַק," *ZAW* 75 (1963) 88-90.

שׁ

שְׁאוֹל - *[See also: Doctrinal Studies, Sheol→]*

Gust. Fred. Oehler, "What is the Meaning of שְׁאוֹל?" *MR* 31 (1849) 75-86.

S. Wieting, "שְׁאוֹל, Sheol," *MR* 38 (1856) 281-287.

[S. Wieting], "שְׁאוֹל, Sheol," *JSL, 3rd Ser.,* 4 (1856-57) 116-122.

R. A. H., "On the Use of 'Sheol'," *JSL, 3rd Ser.,* 5 (1857) 178. [שְׁאוֹל]

*Robert Young, "Sheol, Hades; Gehenna, Tartarus," *HR* 6 (1881-82) 48-49. [שְׁאוֹל]

*(   ) D., "Sheol Passages in the Old Testament," *TQ* 10 (1906) 22-33. [שְׁאוֹל]

*W[illiam] F[oxwell] Albright, "The Etymology of *Še'ol*," *AJSL* 34 (1917-18) 209-210. [שְׁאוֹל]

R. Laird Harris, "The Meaning of the Word Sheol as Shown by Parallels in Poetic Texts," *BETS* 4 (1961) 129-135. [שְׁאוֹל]

*Paul Haupt, "The Original Meaning of Sheol," *JBL* 36 (1917) 258. [שְׁאוֹל]

*John A. Maynard, "Sheol and Belial," *ATR* 1 (1918-19) 92-93. [שְׁאוֹל]

Alvah Hovey, "The Meaning of Sheol in the Old Testament," *ONTS* 5 (1885-86) 49-52. [שְׁאוֹל]

*W. E. M., "Sheol and Hades," *UQGR* 1 (1844) 363-380. [שְׁאוֹל]

*Morris Jastrow Jr., "The Name of Samuel and the Stem שׁאל," *JBL* 19 (1900) 82-105.

*E. W. Heaton, "The Root שׁאר and the Doctrine of the Remnant," *JTS, N.S.,* 3 (1952) 27-41.

*Z. W. Falk, "Ruler and Judge," *Lěš* 30 (1965-66) #4, n.pn. [שׁוֹפֵט = שֵׁבֶט]

*S. E. Loewenstamm, "Ruler and Judge reconsidered," *Lěš* 32 (1967-68) n.p.n. (marginal note by E. Y. Kutscher and S. Eidelberg) [שׁוֹפֵט = שֵׁבֶט]

J. H. Hertz, "An Explanation of Bathsheba, Beersheba, Elisheba," *ET* 45 (1933-34) 142. [שֶׁבַע]

Theodor Herzl Gaster, "שֶׁבַע = 'Fortune': A Correction," *ET* 45 (1933-34) 524.

J. H. Hertz, "שבע = 'Fortune': A Reply," *ET* 46 (1934-35) 285-286.

M. G. Slonim, "The Gender of *Sbt* (Sabbath) in the Hebrew Bible," *JBL* 70 (1951) iv-v. [שַׁבָּת]

*Jacob Milgrom, "The Cultic שגגה and Its Influence in Psalms and Job," *JQR, N.S.,* 58 (1967-68) 115-125.

*Paul Haupt, "Šegál, Queen = Arab. Tajlâ'," *JBL* 35 (1916) 320-322. [שֵׁגַל]

Manfred R. Lehmann, "A new interpretation of the term שדמות," *VT* 3 (1953) 361-371.

*John P. Peters, "Miscellaneous Notes. The Meaning of שדה," *AJSL* 3 (1886-87) 115-116.

*G. T. Manley, "'Officers' in the Old Testament," *EQ* 29 (1957) 149-156. [שֹׁטְרִים, שטר]

*F. J. Coffin, "Third Commandment," *JBL* 19 (1900) 166-188. [II. An inductive study of the word שָׁוְא, pp. 168-171]

R[obert] Gordis, "Some Hitherto Unrecognized Meanings of the Verb *Shub*," *JBL* 52 (1933) 153-162. [שוב]

H. S. Gehman, "Notes on *Shûbh, sh^ebhûth (sh^ebhîth),*" *JBL* 60 (1941) x. [שוב]

G. Gerald Harrop, "Returning unto the Lord," *CJT* 7 (1961) 239-244. [שוב]

*Aloys Dirksen, "Metanoeite!" *BibT* #19 (1965) 1261-1269. [שוב]

*Joseph Reider, "Studies in Hebrew Roots and Their Etymology," *AJSL* 34 (1917-18) 66-70. [שוק]

Paul Haupt, "*Šôr,* Bull, and *Šôrér,* Foe," *JBL* 36 (1917) 255-256. [שׁוֹר, שׁוֹרֵר]

*Joshua Finkel, "Hebrew Shīr and Sūra," *ZAW* 50 (1932) 310-312. [שׁוּר]

*Emil Lund, "הִשְׁתַּחֲוֹת, προσκυνεῖν," *TTKF* 17 (1915) 29-33. [שָׁחָה]

*H. Torczyner, "The Firmament and the Clouds, Rāqîᵃ‘ and Sheḥāqîm," *ST* 1 (1947-48) 188-196. [Additional Note, *ST* 2 (1949-50) p. 98] [שְׁחָקִים]

Felix Perles, "שׂטף = Hair," *JQR, N.S.,* 3 (1912-13) 547.

*N. Wieder, "Notes on the New Documents from the Fourth Cave of Qumran," *JJS* 7 (1956) 71-76. [The Meaning of the Word שׁילה, p. 74]

*Joshua Finkel, "Hebrew Shīr and Sūra," *ZAW* 50 (1932) 310-312. [שִׁיר =

شعر]

*H[arry] M. Orlinsky, "The Hebrew Root *ŠKB*," *JBL* 63 (1944) 19-44. [שׁכב]

*Harry M. Orlinsky, "*Rāḇáṣ* for *Šāḵáḇ* in Numbers 24.9," *JQR, N.S.,* 35 (1944-45) 173-177. [II. On שְׁכַבְ? in Num. 23.24, pp. 176-177]

*Paul Haupt, "Sum. *azalak,* fuller, and Heb. *ašlāḡ,* fullers' earth," *BAVSS* 10 (1927) Heft 2, 268-270. [שָׁלַג]

*Frank Gavin, "*Shaliach* and *Apostolos*," *ATR* 9 (1926-27) 250-259. [שָׁלִיחַ]

J. W. Truron, "The Hebrew Word 'Shaliach'," *Theo* 51 (1948) 166-170. [שָׁלִיחַ]

Gregory Dix, "The Christian Shaliach and the Jewish Apostle—A Reply," *Theo* 51 (1948) 249-256. [שָׁלִיחַ]

J. W. Truron, "'Shaliach'," *Theo* 51 (1948) 341-342. (Note by H. St. J. Hart, pp. 342-343) [שָׁלִיחַ]

*Norman W. Porteous, "Shalem—Shalom," *GUOST* 10 (1940-41) 1-7. [שָׁלוֹם]

W. E[mery] Barnes, "On the Meaning of שְׁלָטִים (Constr. שִׁלְטֵי)," *ET* 10 (1898-99) 43-44.

J. H. Burn, "The Meaning of שְׁלָטִים," *ET* 10 (1898-99) 188.

Paul Haupt, "The Hebrew Term שׁלִיש," *BAVSS* 4 (1902) 583-587.

*A. A. Cowley, "A Hittite Word in Hebrew," *JTS* 21 (1919-20) 326-327. [שָׁלִישׁ]

*David Gill, *"Thysia* and *šᵉlāmīm:* Questions to R. Schmid's *Das Bundesopfer in Israel,"* B 47 (1966) 255-262. [שְׁלָמִים]

*L. H. Gray, "Iranian Miscellanies. c) The Iranian Name בגדאנא," *JAOS* 33 (1913) 285. [שמחיצא = בגדאנא]

*J. G. Baldwin, *"Semaḥ* as a Technical Term in the Prophets," *VT* 14 (1964) 93-97. [שֶׁמַע]

M. G. Slonim, "The Double Gender of *Shamash,"* *JBL* 68 (1949) xii. [שֶׁמֶשׁ]

Cyrus   Adler,   "Shanah,"   *JQR*   1   (1888-89)   288.   [שָׁנָה]

*James A. Kelso, "The Septuagint Rendering of שִׁנְיוֹן," *JBL* 27 (1908) 157-159.

*D. Winton Thomas, "The Root שנה = سنى in Hebrew," *ZAW* 52 (1934) 236-238.

J.   A.   Montgomery,   "שנה = سنى,"   *ZAW*   53   (1935)   207-208.

*D. Winton Thomas, "The Root שנה = سنى in Hebrew II.," *ZAW* 55 (1937) 174-176.

W. H. Griffith Thomas, "'Sheeny'," *ET* 28 (1916-17) 327-328. [שְׁנִינָה]

Henry   Ferguson,   "The   verb   שפט,"   *JBL*   8   (1888)   130-136.

*F. C. Fensham, "The Judges and Ancient Israelite Jurisprudence," *OTW* 2 (1959) 15-22. [šōphēṭ/*stem*- šphṭ] [שפט]

*I. H. Eybers, "The Stem Š-P-Ṭ in The Psalms," *OTW* 6 (1963) 58-63. [שפט]

*Z. W. Falk, "Ruler and Judge," *Lᵉš* 30 (1965-66) #4, n.p.n. [שׁוֹפֵט = שֶׁבֶט]

*Wallace I. Wolverton, "The King's 'Justice' in Pre-exilic Israel," *ATR* 41 (1959) 276-286. [שָׁפַט]

*S. E. Loewenstamm, "Ruler and Judge reconsidered," *Lěš* 32 (1967-68) #3, n.p.n. (marginal note by E. Y. Kutscher and S. Eidelberg) [שבט and שפט]

Sh. Yeivin, "Some Additional Notes on the Problem of שׁוֹפֵט־מֶלֶךְ," *Lěš* 33 (1968-69) #1, n.p.n. [שפט]

A. F. L. Beeston, "The Hebrew Verb špt," *VT* 8 (1958) 216-217. [שפת]

*Joseph Reider, "Studies in Hebrew Roots and Their Etymology," *AJSL* 34 (1917-18) 66-70. [שׁקק]

*Avi Hurvitz, "The Usage of שׁשׁ and בּוּץ in the Bible and Its Implications for the Date of P," *HTR* 60 (1967) 117-121.

Meïr Bravmann, "Hebrew *Štayim* in the Light of Syriac and Turcic," *PAAJR* 21 (1952) 1-2. [שְׁתַּיִם]

*Israel Eitan, "An Egyptian Loan Word in Is. 19," *JQR, N.S.* 15 (1924-25) 419-420. [שָׁתֶיהָ]

ת

*C. J. Ball, "Note on the Wood called *Ukarina*," *SBAP* 11 (1888-89) 143-144. [תְּאַשּׁוּר]

Paul Haupt, "Heb. *tě'ô*, Aurochs," *JBL* 36 (1917) 254. [תְּאוֹ]

*A. L. Frothingham Jr., "Early Bronzes Discovered in the Cave of Zeus on Mount Ida in Krete," *AJA, O.S.*, 5 (1889) 48. [Ref. תֵּבָה]

*George A. Barton, "Tiamat," *JAOS* 15 (1893) 1-27. (corrigendia, p. v) [תְּהוֹם]

Jonathan P. Siegel, "Grammar or *Gematria*?" *JQR, N.S.*, 59 (1968-69) 161-162. [תהילה]

Sidney B. Hoenig, "The *Plene* Writing of תהילים. A Rejoinder," *JQR, N.S.*, 59 (1968-69) 163. (Surrejoinder by S[olomon] Zeitlin, pp. 163-164)

*Paul Haupt, "Tôrâ = Tahrirtu," *JBL* 36 (1917) 258-259. [תּוֹרָה]

*W[illiam] F[oxwell] Albright, "The Names 'Israel' and 'Judah' with an Excursus on the Etymology of Tôdâh and Tôrâh," *JBL* 46 (1927) 151-185. [C. The Etymology of Tôdâh and Tôrâh, pp. 178-185] [תּוֹרָה]

E. C. Broome Jr., "Torah and the Flight of Arrows," *JBL* 61 (1942) iv. [תּוֹרָה]

G. B. Gray, "A Questionable Plural in Hebrew," *JTS* 4 (1902-03) 124-125. [תּוֹצָאוֹת]

Karl J. Grimm, "The Meaning and Etymology of the Word תּוּשִׁיָּה in the Old Testament," *JAOS* 22 (1901) 35-44.

John Franklin Genung, "Meaning and Usage of the Term תּוּשִׁיה," *JBL* 30 (1911) 114-122.

*Samuel Krauss, "Notes on Sirach," *JQR* 11 (1898-99) 150-158. [4. The word תחליף, pp. 157-158]

*Anonymous, "Tirosh and Yayin," *ONTS* 13 (1891) 181. [תִּירוֹשׁ]

*Hinckley G. Mitchell, "Tirosh and Yayin," *JBL* 10 (1891) 70-72. [תִּירוֹשׁ]

*Paul Haupt, "Heb. *argamân* and *tekéleth*," *JBL* 33 (1914) 298-299. [תְּכֵלֶת]

*Paul Haupt, "Heb. Talpî'ôṭ, Siege-Towers," *JBL* 38 (1919) 186-187. [תַּלְפִּאוֹת]

*N. Wieder, "Notes on the New Documents from the Fourth Cave of Qumran," *JJS* 7 (1956) 71-76. [The Term תלה חי, pp. 71-72]

*B. Gross, "The Origin of the Words; מזנון and תמחוי," *Lěš* 30 (1965-66) #3, n.p.n.

B. Halper, "The Root חנן," *AJSL* 24 (1907-08) 366-369.

*G. R. Driver, "Three Technical Terms in the Pentateuch," *JSS* 2 (1956) 97-105. [III. תנופה "Special Contribution", pp. 100-105]

*Georges Vajda, "'unṣur and te'âlâh," *JQR, N.S.*, 38 (1947-48) 481. (Rejoinder by H. A. Wolfson, pp. 481-482) [תְּעָלָה]

*W. Houghton, "The Tree and Fruit represented by the *Tappūakh* (תַּפּוּחַ) of the Hebrew Scriptures," *SBAP* 12 (1889-90) 42-48.

H. F. Lutz, "The Hebrew word for 'to sew'," *JAOS* 40 (1920) 71-72. [תפר]

*Samuel E. Loewenstamm, "נשך and מ/תרבית," *JBL* 88 (1969) 78-80.

*Paul Haupt, "Assyr. *tamêrtu* and Heb. *tĕrûmâ,*" *JSOR* 2 (1918) 87. [תְּרוּמָה]

*H. H. Rowley, "Review of Foreign Theology. The cultic cry in the Old Testament," *ET* 58 (1946-47) 220-221. *(Review)* [תְּרוּעָה]

C. J. Labuschagne, "*Teraphim*—A new proposal for its etymology," *VT* 16 (1966) 115-117. [תְּרָפִים]

*Harry A. Hoffner Jr., "Hittite *Tarpiš* and Hebrew *Terāphîm,*" *JNES* 27 (1968) 61-68. [תְּרָפִים]

M. Mishor, "תרשיש 'sea', in Talmudic Sources," *Lěš* 34 (1969-70) #4, n.pn.

§506 3.3.3.2.1.4.3 Hebrew Phrases (includes Idioms, Figures of Speech and Alphabetical Listing of Phrases)

*M. A. Canney, "'Heart and Reins.' Further Notes on Hebrew Idioms," *JMUEOS* #1 (1911) 93-94.

*J. Oscar Boyd, "The Science of Semantics and the Words of the Old Testament," *BM* 1 (1913) 336-345. *[Use of Idioms]*

*Charles Eugene Edwards, "A Hebrew Idiom," *BS* 90 (1933) 232-235. *[Combining a finite tense and an infinitive of the same verb to express intensity, etc.]*

*Joseph Reider, "*Itba'* in Hebrew and Aramaic," *JQR, N.S.,* 24 (1933-34) 321-330.

A. M. Honeyman, "*Merismus* in Biblical Hebrew," *JBL* 71 (1952) 11-18.

*G. R. Driver, "Forgotten Hebrew Idioms," *ZAW* 78 (1966) 1-7.

*E[phraim] A. Speiser, "The Biblical Idiom *Pānîm Hōlᵉkîm,*" *JQR, 75th* (1967) 515-517. [פָּנֶיךָ הֹלְכִים]

א-ת

*Yehoshua Blau, "On Two Biblical Expresssions," *EI* 3 (1954) v. [II. אחזת שמרות עיני in שמורות (Ps. 77:5)]

*Joseph Rauch, "Apocalypse in the Bible," *JJLP* 1 (1919) 163-195. [V. אחרית הימים (End of Days) pp. 176-178]

*H. Kosmala, "'At the End of the Days'," *ASTI* 2 (1963) 27-37. [אחרית הימים]

Raphael Hallevy, "Man of God," *JNES* 17 (1958) 237-244. [איש אלהים]

Wm. Henry Cobb, "Al-Tashheth," *ONTS* 3 (1883-84) 49-52. [אַל־תַּשְׁחֵת]

*Hyman Klein, "The Significance of the Technical Expression 'אלא אי איתמר הכי איתמר' in the Babylonian Talmud," *Tarbiz* 31 (1961-62) #1, v-vi.

*N. A. van Uchelen, "אנשי דמים in the Psalms," *OTS* 15 (1969) 205-212.

*B. Jacob, "A Study in Biblical Exegesis. אֲשֶׁר־חַי," *JQR* 12 (1899-1900) 434-451.

*David Halivni Weiss, "A Note on אשר לא ארשה," *JBL* 81 (1962) 67-69.

*Joshua Brand, "The Title 'אשר על הבית'," *Tarbiz* 36 (1966-67) #3, I-II.

*Moshe Held, "A Difficult Biblical Expression and its Parallel in Ugaritic," *EI* 3 (1954) iv. [בִּגְדֵי שְׂרָד]

*Samuel Daiches, "Ezekiel and the Babylonian Account of the Deluge. Notes on Ezek. XIV. 12-20," *JQR* 17 (1904-05) 441-455. [Appendix: Note on the term בן אדם, pp. 447-448]

*F. Charles Fensham, "The Son of a Handmaid in Northwest-Semitic," *VT* 19 (1969) 312-321. [בן אמה]

*Cornelius Walker, "Divine Sonship, Sons of God, Bene Elohim," *HR* 39 (1900) 447-449. [בְּנֵי־הָאֱלֹהִים]

G. Brin, "On the Title בן המלך," *Léš* 31 (1966-67) #1, n.p.n.

G. Brin, "On the Title בן המלך *(concl.),*" *Lĕš* 31 (1966-67) #2, n.p.n.

*T. Grahame Bailey, "Contributions and Comments. Note on Two Passages in Dr. Moffatt's 'Old Testament'," *ET* 36 (1924-25) 380-381. [בֶּן־נַעֲוַת הַמַּרְדּוּת]

*James G. Williams, "The Prophetic 'Father': A Brief Explanation of the Term 'Sons of the Prophets'," *JBL* 85 (1966) 344-348. [בְּנֵי הַנְּבִיאִים]

W. Scott Watson, "בעבר הירדן," *AJSL* 13 (1896-97) 214-216.

*H. J. Rose, "Ba'alathobh," *Man* 32 (1932) #69. [בַּעֲלַת־אוֹב]

*S. E. Lowenstamm, "The Formula בעת ההיא in Deuteronomy," *Tarbiẓ* 38 (1968-69) #2, I.

*Nathaniel Schmidt, "Was בר נשא a Messianic Title?" *JBL* 15 (1896) 36-53.

W. Sibley Towner, "'Blessed be YHWH' and 'Blessed art Thou, YHWH': The Modulation of a Biblical Formula," *CBQ* 30 (1968) 386-399. [בָּרוּךְ יהוה;בָּרוּךְ אַתָּה יהוה]

R. F., "גַּן־בְּעֵדֶן," *AJSL* 1 (1884-85) 129.

*Hosua Podro, "חותמו של הקב"ה אמת—'God's Seal is Truth'," *JJS* 5 (1954) 107-109.

*S. A. Hirsch, "Isaiah 14:12. הילל בן שחר," *JQR, N.S.,* 11 (1920-21) 197-199.

*M. Haran, "Zebaḥ Hayyamîm," *VT* 19 (1969) 11-22. [זֶבַח הַיָּמִים]

*M. Haran, "*ZBḤ YMM* in the Karatepe Inscriptions," *VT* 19 (1969) 372-373. [זֶבַח הַיָּמִים]

T. C. Foote, "The Old Testament Expresssion zanáh ahrê," *JAOS* 22 (1901) 64-69. [זָנָה אַחֲרֵי]

*Paul Chertoff, "עשרה בטלנים and חבר עיר," *JQR, N.S.,* 34 (1943-44) 878-98.

Ralph Marcus, "The Phrase Ḥokmat Yᵉwanit," *JNES* 12 (1954) 86.

*Maurice A. Canney, "The Primordial Mound," *JMUEOS* #20 (1936) 25-40. [Judges 9:37; Ezek. 38:12; ṭabbur hā'āreṣ]

*Daniel Leibel, "'צדקנו יהוה'," *Tarbiz* 34 (1964-65) #3, v. *[23:5-6]*

Eb. Nestle, "'God Save the King.' A Query," *ET* 16 (1904-05) 43. [יחי המלך]

H. F. Moule, "'God Save the King'," *ET* 16 (1904-05) 186-187. [יחי המלך]

S[olomon] Zeitlin, "The Phrase יתלח אנשים חיים," *JJS* 8 (1957) 117-118.

N. Wieder, "Rejoinder," *JJS* 8 (1957) 119-121. [יתלח אנשים חיים]

*T. Grahame Bailey, "Contributions and Comments. Note on Two Passages in Dr. Moffatt's 'Old Testament'," *ET* 36 (1924-25) 380-381. [כֹּה יַעֲשֶׂה יהוה לִי וְכֹה יֹסִיף]

*N. Wieder, "A Controversial Mishnaic and Liturgical Expression, *JJS* 18 (1967) 1-8. [וכל באי (ה) עולם עוברים לפניו כבני מרון]

R. Yaron, "*Ka'eth Ḥayyah* and *Koh Leḥay*," *VT* 12 (1962) 500-501. [כֹּוֹה לֹחָ and כָּעֵת הַיָּה]

*Theophile J. Meek, "Archaeology and a Point in Hebrew Syntax," *BASOR* #122 (1951) 31-33. [לְפִי־חָרֶב]

*Samuel Belkin, "Some Obscure Tradition Mutually Clarified in Philo and Rabbinic Literature," *JQR, 75th,* (1967) 80-103. [6. Eternal Death (Gen. 2:17) pp.93-96.] [מות תמות]

*H[erbert] G. May, "Cosmic Connotations of Mayim Rabbim," *JBL* 72 (1953) v. [מַיִם רַבִּים]

*H[erbert] G. May, "Cosmic Connotations of *Mayim Rabbîm,* 'Many Waters'," *JBL* 74 (1955) 9-21. [מַיִם רַבִּים]

G. Ernest Loosley, "מַלֵּא אֶת־יָד," *ET* 15 (1903-04) 382.

*J. G. Weiss, "On the formula melekh ha-'olam as anti-Gnostic protest," *JJS* 10 (1959) 169-171. [מֶלֶךְ הָעוֹלָם]

*E. J. Wiesenberg, "The Liturgical Term melek ha-'olam," *JJS* 15 (1964) 1-56. [מֶלֶךְ הָעוֹלָם]

*E. Wiesenberg, "Gleanings of the Liturgical Term *Melekh Ha-'olam*," *JJS* 17 (1966) 47-72. [מֶלֶךְ הָעוֹלָם]

Morris Jastrow Jr., "On מִמָּחֳרַת הַשַּׁבָּת ('The Day After the Sabbath')," *AJSL* 30 (1913-14) 94-110.

Hinckley G. Mitchell, "מקרא קדש," *JBL* 8 (1888) 159-161.

*Leon J. Liebreich, "The Term Miqra' qodesh in the Synagogue Liturgy," *JQR, 75th* (1967) 381-397. [מִקְרָאֵי קֹדֶשׁ]

Miriam Seligson, "The Meaning of נפש מת in the Old Testament," *SO* 16 (1951) #2, 7-100.

*Samuel Daiches, "Exodus 5.4-5, The Meaning of עַם־הָאָרֶץ," *JQR, N.S.*, 12 (1921-22) 33-34.

S[amuel] Daiches, "The Meaning of עם הארץ in the Old Testament," *JTS* 30 (1928-29) 245-249.

E. W. Nicholson, "The Meaning of the Expresssion עם הארץ in the Old Testament," *JSS* 10 (1965) 59-66.

*Fritz Hommel, "The Babylonian Ammi-Satana and the Hebrew Ammi-Shaddai," *ET* 9 (1897-98) 235. [עַמִּי שַׁדַּי]

*Israel Efros, "Brief Notes. *Textual Notes on the Hebrew Bible*," *JAOS* 45 (1925) 152-154. [2. proverbial expression—עצור ועזוב, pp. 152-153]

P. P. Saydon, "The Meaning of the Expression עָצוּר וְעָזוּב," *VT* 2 (1952) 371-374.

*A Ăhuvya, "עצור ועזוב בישראל," *Lĕš* 30 (1965-66) #3, n.p.n.

*Paul Chertoff, "חבר עיר and עשרה בטלנים," *JQR, N.S.*, 34 (1943-44) 87-98.

*E. E. Hallevy, "The Correct Interpretation of 'פוטריו אותו' (Sanhedrin 17a)," *Tarbiz* 36 (1966-67) #1, IV-V.

*A. L. Oppenheim, "A Note on *ṣôn barzel*," *IEJ* 5 (1955) 89-92. [צֹאן בַּרְזֶל]

*E[phraim] A. Speiser, "The Biblical Idiom *Pānīm Hōlᵉkīm*," *JQR, 75th* (1967) 515-517. [פָּנֶיךָ הֹלְכִים]

*Leon Morris, "Καὶ ἅπαξ καὶ δίς," *NT* 1 (1956) 205-208. [פַּעַם וּשְׁתָּיִם]

*Saul Lieberman, "Two Lexicographical Notes," *JBL* 65 (1946) 67-72. [1. קְמִץ צלח ἅλλομαι, pp. 67-69]

W[illiam] A. Irwin, *"qrî'ê ha-'edhah," AJSL* 57 (1940) 95-97. [קְרִיאֵי הָעֵדָה]

Howard Crosby, "Light on Important Texts. NO. X," *HR* 5 (1880-81) 586-587. [רֹאשׁ פִּנָּה]

*E. Power, "A Study of the Hebrew Expresssion 'Wide of Heart'," *B* 1 (1920) 59-75. [וְרֹחַב לֵב; רְחַב לֵבָב]

Julian Morgenstern, "The Rest of the Nations," *JSS* 2 (1957) 225-231. [הַגּוֹיִם שְׁאֵרִית]

*J. M. Allegro, "The Meaning of the Phrase *šeṭūm hā'ayin* in Num. XXIV 3, 15," *VT* 3 (1953) 78-79. [שְׁתֻם הָעָיִן]

B. De-Vries[sic]*, "The Talmudic Formula רתו לא מידי," *Tarbiẓ* 37 (1967-68) #1, IV.

*Cyrus H. Gordon, "Marginal Notes on the Ancient Middle East," *JKF* 2 (1952-53) 50-61 [V. Hebraica: c. Construct + Adjective: The Formation עגלת שלשיה (Jer. 48:34), pp. 54-55]

Solomon Zeitlin, "The Phrase תולים אותו חי," *JQR, N.S.,* 48 (1957-58) 398-399.

Harry M. Orlinsky, "On Biblical Tôp̄eś-Tôp̄śê," *JQR, N.S.,* 34 (1943-44) 281-297. [תֹּפֵשׂ-תֹּפְשֵׂי]

Hyman Klein, "On Biblical Topes-Topse," *JQR, N.S.,* 35 (1944-45) 351-353. [תֹּפֵשׂ-תֹּפְשֵׂי]

Harry M. Orlinsky, "On Biblical Topes-Topse," *JQR, N.S.,* 35 (1944-45) 354. [תֹּפֵשׂ-תֹּפְשֵׂי]

§507 *3.3.3.2.1.4.4 Hebrew Concordances and Lexicons*

†Anonymous, "Parkhurst's Hebrew and English Lexicon," *BCQTR* 2 (1793) 43-51. *(Review)*

Anonymous, "Joa. Simonis Lexicon Manuale Hebraicum et Chaldaicum, post Joa. Godf. Eichhorn Curas, denuo castigavit, emendavit, multisque modis auxit Dr. Georg. Benedict. Winer, in Academiâ Erlangensi Prof. P. O., Seminarii Exeget. Director," *CE* 6 (1829) 347-352. *(Review)*

Anonymous, "Roy's Hebrew Lexicon," *CRB* 3 (1838) 124-129 *(Review)*

Anonymous, "Nordheimer's Hebrew Concordance," *LTR* 6 (1839) 571-579. *(Review)*

Tayler Lewis, "Review of Nordheimer's Hebrew Concordance," *BRCR, N.S.,* 7 (1842) 467-478. *(Review)*

Anonymous, "Omissions in the Hebrew and Chaldean Lexicon," *JSL, 3rd Ser.,* 14 (1861-62) 191.

*D. G. Lyon, "Assyrian Research and the Hebrew Lexicon," *BS* 41 (1884) 376-385.

B. Felsenthal, "Finn's New Hebrew Dictionary," *AJSL* 3 (1886-87) 255-260. *(Review)*

*K. Kohler, "Jastrow's Talmudic Dictionary," *AJSL* 5 (1888-89) 1-6. *(Review)*

A. Lukyn Williams, "The New Hebrew Concordance," *ET* 7 (1895-96) 361. *[Veteris Testamenti Concordantiae Hebraicae atque Chaldaicae]*

S. R. Driver, "Hebrew Concordance," *ET* 7 (1895-96) 431-432. *[Veteris Testamenti Concordantiae Hebraicae atque Chaldaicae]*

A. Lukyn Williams, "Hebrew Concordances," *ET* 7 (1895-96) 477-478.

*Felix Perles, "The Fourteenth Edition of Gesenius-Buhl's Dictionary," *JQR* 18 (1905-06) 383-390. *(Review)*

Irwin Hoch De Long, "The Brown-Driver-Briggs Hebrew-English Lexicon," *RChR, 4th Ser.,* 11 (1907) 307-329.

*Felix Perles, "A Miscellany of Lexical and Textual Notes on the Bible, Chiefly in connection with the Fifteenth Edition of the Lexicon by Gesenius-Buhl," *JQR, N.S.,* 2 (1911-12) 97-132.

H. F. B. Compston, "Corrigenda and Addenda in 'B.D.B.'," *ET* 26 (1914-15) 376-377.

James Donald, "Corrigenda and Addenda to the Oxford Hebrew Lexicon," *ET* 26 (1914-15) 477.

W. B. Stevenson, "Linguistic Errors in Brown-Driver-Briggs's Lexicon," *GUOST* 9 (1938-39) 21-22.

*Donald G. Miller, "Implements of Interpretation. I. Concordances," *Interp* 1 (1947) 52-62.

*Blamer H. Kelly, "Implements of Interpretation. VI. Hebrew Grammars and Lexicons," *Interp* 2 (1948) 186-198.

Solomon Skoss, "Corrections to Mandelkern's Concordance, היכל הקדש' Second Edition by Margolin (1925)," *JQR, N.S.,* 40 (1949-50) 173-188.

§508 *3.3.3.2.1.4.5 Hebrew Grammar - General Studies (includes Studies on Grammarians)*

Anonymous, "Concerning two Dialects of the Aramic[sic]* Language," *MMBR* 5 (1798) 245-246. *[Hebrew]*

†Anonymous, "Dowling's Elements of Hebrew," *BCQTR* 14 (1799) 250-253. *(Review)*

Anonymous, "A Manual of Hebrew Grammar for the use of Beginners. By J. Seixas," *CE* 15 (1833) 65-69. *(Review)*

Anonymous, "A Manual of Hebrew Grammar for the use of Beginners. By J. Seixas. Second Edition," *CE* 18 (1835) 160-166. *(Review)*

Anonymous, "Bush's Hebrew Grammar," *PRev* 7 (1835) 341-367. *(Review)*

Anonymous, "Gesenius' Hebrew Grammar," *CRB* 4 (1839) 419-426. *(Review)*

Tayler Lewis, "Review of Nordheimer's Hebrew Grammar," *BRCR, N.S.,* 5 (1841) 438-463. *(Review)*

F. B., "History of the Study of Hebrew in England until the Accession of James I," *CRB* 11 (1846) 485-499.

F. B., "Hebrew Study in England During the Seventeenth Century," *CRB* 12 (1847) 109-127.

John Nicholson, "Hebrew Criticism," *JSL, 1st Ser.,* 1 (1848) 160-167. *(Review)*

F. Bosworth, "Hebrew in the Time of Jerome," *JSL, 1st Ser.,* 3 (1849) 283-308.

John Nicholson, "Professor Von Ewald on Dr. Samuel Lee's Accusations," *JSL, 1st Ser.,* 3 (1849) 374-375.

H. Von Ewald, "Letter by Professor Von Ewald," *JSL, 1st Ser.,* 3 (1849) 375-376. [*Ref.* Samuel Lee, *Churchman's Monthly Review,* May, 1847]

Samuel Lee, "Dr. Samuel Lee in Answer to Professor Von Ewald," *JSL, 1st Ser.,* 4 (1849) 159-160.

John Nicholson, "Professor Von Ewald's Reply to Professor Lee's Last Letter," *JSL, 1st Ser.,* 4 (1849) 383-386.

C. M., "Mr. Keightley's Hebrew Criticism," *JSL, 3rd Ser.,* 7 (1858) 160-167.

*Tayler Lewis, "The Emotional Element in Hebrew Translation [First Article]," *MR* 44 (1862) 85-108.

*Tayler Lewis, "The Emotional Element in Hebrew Translation [Second Article]," *MR* 45 (1863) 55-74.

*Tayler Lewis, "The Emotional Element in Hebrew Translation [Third Article]," *MR* 45 (1863) 382-406.

*Tayler Lewis, "The Emotional Element in Hebrew Translation [Fourth Article]," *MR* 46 (1864) 57-77.

George E. Day, "Critical Note on Dr. Friedrich Böttcher's Hebrew Grammar," *JAOS* 9 (1871) xxxiii-xxxiv.

*George H. Whittemore, "Hebrew Grammar and Lexicography," *BS* 29 (1872) 547-553.

*Charles Warren, "Arabic and Hebrew," *PEFQS* 7 (1875) 227-228.

Alfred Jones, "Davidson's Hebrew Grammar," *SPR* 30 (1879) 738-753. *(Review)*

B. Maimon, "The Hebrew Language—its Spirit and Characteristics," *UQGR, N.S.,* 17 (1880) 36-51.

(   ) Craik, "Biblical Hebrew," *ONTS* 2 (1882-83) 87-88.

George H. Schodde, "Methods in Hebrew Grammars," *AJSL* 1 (1884-85) 75-79.

Wilhelm Bacher, "משרתים־מלכים. A Contribution to the History of the Terminology of Hebrew Grammar," *AJSL* 1 (1884-85) 96-97.

Frederic Gardiner, "Advantages of a Slight Knowledge of Hebrew," *AJSL* 2 (1885-86) 90-92.

Cyrus Adler, "Qamḫi*[sic]*," *AJSL* 2 (1885-86) 116. *[Hebrew Grammarian - Kimchi]*

Geo[rge] H. Schodde, "The Study of Hebrew and the Dialects," *AJSL* 2 (1885-86) 223-227.

Cyrus Adler, "'Professor Peters' Notes'," *AJSL* 3 (1886-87) 269.

Morris Jastrow Jr., "Jewish Grammarians of the Middle Ages," *AJSL* 3 (1886-87) 103-106, 171-174. *[Parts I-III]*

Morris Jastrow Jr., "Jewish Grammarians of the Middle Ages," *AJSL* 4 (1887-88) 26-33, 118-122. *[Parts IV-V]*

W[illiam] R. Harper, "The Hebrew Movement; Its Past and Future," *PQ* 1 (1887-88) 338-343.

Morris Jastrow Jr., "Jewish Grammarians of the Middle Ages. VI," *AJSL* 5 (1888-89) 115-120.

*M[orris] Jastrow, "On transposed stems in Talmudic, Hebrew, Chaldaic," *JAOS* 14 (1890) xl-xlii.

*Duncan B. Macdonald, "Notes critical and lexicographical," *JBL* 14 (1895) 57-62.

Samuel David Luzzatto, "Prolegomena to a Grammar of the Hebrew Language," *PJTSA* 5 (1896) [paged separately] i-viii, 1-71. *(Trans. by Sabato Morais)*

C. Levias, "A Trace of Syriac Influence on Hebrew Grammar," *AJSL* 14 (1897-98) 129-130.

Max L. Margolis, "The Twenty-Seventh Edition of Gesenius's Hebrew Grammar," *AJSL* 19 (1902-03) 159-170. *(Review)*

*Moses H. Segal, "Mišnaic Hebrew and Its Relation to Biblical Hebrew and to Aramaic," *JQR* 20 (1907-08) 647-737.

*J. Oscar Boyd, "The Science of Semantics and the Words of the Old Testament," *BM* 1 (1913) 336-345. *[Use of Idioms]*

‡*T. Witton Davies, "Survey of Recent Work on Semitic Philology and Hebrew Grammar," *RTP* 9 (1913-14) 685-713.

*Robert Dick Wilson, "Scientific Biblical Criticism," *PTR* 17 (1919) 190-240, 401-456. [D. The Grammar, pp. 401-413]

*A. S. Tritton, "Hebrew and Arabic: Similarities in Thought and Grammar," *GUOST* 5 (1923-28) 24.

*‡John A. Maynard, "Hebrew Studies since 1918 (including Biblical Aramaic)," *JSOR* 9 (1925) 32-40.

*W. E. Staples, "The Hebrew of the Septuagint," *AJSL* 44 (1927-28) 6-30.

A. L. Williams, "A Grammar of Mishnaic Hebrew," *JTS* 29 (1927-28) 69-71. *(Review)*

*H. Louis Ginsberg, "The So-called Šĕụȧ Medium in the Light of the Christian Palestinian Idiom," *JAOS* 53 (1933) 352-356.

*George B. Michell, "The Linguistic Criticism of the Old Testament," *BS* 92 (1935) 178-186.

Henry Englander, "Grammatical Elements and Terminology in Rashi's Biblical Commentaries," *HUCA* 11 (1936) 367-389.

*S. Yeivin, "Studies in comparative Egypto-Semitics, IV," *Kêmi* 6 (1936) 63-80. [Parts I & II published in *Lĕš;* Part III under separate title]

Henry Englander, "Grammatical Elements and Terminology in Rashi," *HUCA* 14 (1939) 387-429.

W[illiam] F[oxwell] Albright, "What is Biblical Hebrew?" *JBL* 58 (1939) vii.

Helmuth Galliner, "Agathius Guidacerius 1477-1540, An Early Hebrew Grammarian," *HJud* 2 (1940) 85-101.

Henry Englander, "Rabbenu Jacob ben Meir Tam as Grammarian," *HUCA* 15 (1940) 485-495.

*Henry Englander, "Rashi as Bible Exegete and Grammarian," *YCCAR* 50 (1940) 342-359.

W. E. Staples, "The Reading of Hebrew," *AJSL* 58 (1941) 139-145.

*Henry Englander, "A Commentary on Rashi's Grammatical Comments," *HUCA* 17 (1942-43) 427-498.

Alexander Sperber, "Hebrew Grammar: A New Approach," *JBL* 62 (1943) 137-262. [I. Introduction; II. Vocalization Through Vowel Letters; III. The Verb; IV. The Noun; V. Prepositions and Particles. Index of Biblical Passages p. 243; Table of Contents, p. 261]

Frank R. Blake, *"Hebrew Grammar: A New Approach,* by Alexander Sperber (Journal of Biblical Literature, Vol. LXII, Part III, pp. 137-262)," *JBL* 63 (1944) 195-199. *(Review)*

Amos Edelheit, "Blake's Review of 'Hebrew Grammar: A New Approach', by A. Sperber," *JBL* 63 (1944) 438-439.

William Chomsky, "How the Study of Hebrew Grammar Began and Developed," *JQR, N.S.,* 35 (1944-45) 281-301.

*William Foxwell Albright, "The Old Testament and Canaanite Language and Literature," *CBQ* 7 (1945) 5-31. [IV. The Ugaritic Dialect and Biblical Hebrew, pp. 14-19]

*Alexander Sperber, "Biblical Exegesis: Prolegomena to a Commentary and Dictionary to the Bible," *JBL* 64 (1945) 39-140. [I. Introduction; II. Hebrew Dictionaries Lack Method; III. Grammatical Terms Misleading; IV. Accentuation and Exegesis; V. The Composite Character of the Bible; VI. Hebrew Syntax; VII. My Grammar Put to the Test]

*H. H. Rowley, "Recent Foreign Theology. Pre-massoretic Hebrew Grammar," *ET* 58 (1946-47) 220. *(Review)*

*Blamer H. Kelly, "Implements of Interpretation. VI. Hebrew Grammars and Lexicons," *Interp* 2 (1948) 186-198.

*G. R. Driver, "Hebrew Studies," *JRAS* (1948) 164-176.

*Alexander Sperber, "Biblical Hebrew," *PAAJR* 18 (1948-49) 301-382.

*G. R. Driver, "Ugaritic and Hebrew Problems," *ArOr* 17 (1949) Part 1, 153-157.

D[avid] N[oel] Freedman and F[rank] M. Cross Jr., "Notes on Pre-exilic Hebrew," *JBL* 69 (1950) ix.

*G. J. Thierry, "Notes on Hebrew Grammar and Etymology," *OTS* 9 (1951) 1-17.

Solomon L. Skoss, "Saadia Gaon, the Earliest Hebrew Grammarian," *PAAJR* 21 (1952) 75-100; 22 (1953) 65-90; 23 (1954) 59-73.

Cyrus H. Gordon, "North Israelite Influence on Postexilic Hebrew," *EI* 3 (1954) v.

C[yrus] H. Gordon, "North Israelite Influence on Postexilic Hebrew," *IEJ* 5 (1955) 85-88.

*Z[e'ev] Ben-Hayyim, "Traditions in the Hebrew Language, with Special Reference to the Dead Sea Scrolls," *SH* 4 (1957) 200-214.

*A. Murtonen and G. J. Ormann, "Materials for a Non-Masoretic Grammar I. Liturgical Texts and Psalm Fragments Provided with the So-Called Palestinian Punctuation," *SO* 24 (1958) 1-126, ס-א.

William Chomsky, "Toward Broadening the Scope of Hebrew Grammar," *JQR, N.S.,* 49 (1958-59) 179-190.

*Allan R. McAllaster, "Hebrew Language and Israelite Faith. *Insights Provided by Language Structure,*" *Interp* 14 (1960) 421-432.

*J. Blau, "The Dual in Judaeo-Arabic and its Linguistic Background," *Tarbiz* 30 (1960-61) #2, III.

E. Y. Kutscher, "Yemenite Hebrew and Ancient Pronunciation," *JSS* 11 (1966) 217-225.

M. Rottenberg, "The Implicit Construct Phrase in the Bible," *Lĕš* 32 (1967-68) #4, n.p.n.

*E. Y. Kutscher, "Canaanite (=*C*)—Hebrew (=*H*)—Phoenician (=*Ph*)—Aramaic (=*A*)—Mishnaic Hebrew (=*MH*)—Punic (=*P*)," *Lĕš* 33 (1968-69) #2/3, n.p.n.

*Ze'ev Ben-Hayyim, "The Contribution of the Samaritan Inheritance to Research into the History of Hebrew," *PIASH* 3 (1969) 162-174.

§509 **3.3.3.2.1.4.5.1** *Etymology - General Studies*

Charles A. Hay, "Meier's Lexicon of Hebrew Roots," *BS* 4 (1847) 369-386. *(Review)*

*James Strong, "Affinity of the Hebrew and Greek Languages," *MR* 47 (1865) 430-444.

C[rawford] H. Toy, "Hebrew Etymology," *PAPA* 8 (1875-76) 41-42. *[Bound with Transactions, but paged separately]*

Crawford H. Toy, "On Hebrew Verb-Etymology," *TAPA* 7 (1876) 50-72.

Henry S. Morais, "Neubauer's Etymologies," *AJSL* 3 (1886-87) 186-187.

J. P. MacLean, "Gaelic Elements in the Hebrew Language," *UQGR, N.S.*, 25 (1888) 173-183.

A. J. Maas, "Pronominal Roots," *AJSL* 5 (1888-89) 192-195.

*M[orris] Jastrow [Jr.], "On transposed stems in the Talmudic, Hebrew, and Chaldaic," *JAOS* 14 (1890) xl-xlii.

J. Cheston Morris, "Notes on Hebrew Phonetics," *PAPS* 39 (1891) 7-11.

*J. P. Lesley, "Notes on Hebrew Etymologies from the Egyptian ANX. Enoch; Anok; Enos," *PAPS* 29 (1891) 17-20.

Max L. Margolis, "Dogmatic Influences in Our Vocalization," *AJSL* 14 (1896-97) 208.

Wm. Rollo, "Euphony in Hebrew," *GUOST* 2 (1901-07) 38.

George V. Schick, "The Stems **dûm** and **damám** in Hebrew," *JBL* 32 (1913) 219-243. [דום, דמם] *[Index of passages referred to, p. 243]*

*G. R. Driver, "Some Hebrew Roots and Their Meanings," *JTS* 23 (1921-22) 69-73. [Postscript by C. F. Burney, p. 73]

Israel Eitan, "Studies in Hebrew Roots," *JQR, N.S.*, 14 (1923-24) 31-52.

Ephraim A[vigdor] Speiser, "The Pronunciation of Hebrew According to the Transliterations in the Hexapla, Chapters I-II," *JQR, N.S.*, 16 (1925-26) 343-382.

H. C. R. Eltoft, "Rashi's Knowledge of the Triliteral Root in Hebrew," *JMUEOS* #14 (1929) 53-60.

Ephraim Avigdor Speiser, "The Pronunciation of Hebrew Based Chiefly on the Transliterations in the Hexapla (Chapter II—cont.)," *JQR, N.S.*, 23 (1932-33) 233-265.

Ephraim Avigdor Speiser, "The Pronunciation of Hebrew Based Chiefly on the Transliterations in the Hexapla (Chapter III)," *JQR, N.S.*, 24 (1933-34) 9-46.

Alexander Sperber, "Hebrew Based Upon Greek and Latin Transliterations," *HUCA* 12&13 (1937-38) 103-274.

Alexander Sperber, "Hebrew Phonology," *HUCA* 16 (1941) 415-482.

Solomon L. Skoss, "A Study of Inflection in Hebrew from Saadia Gaon's Grammatical Work 'Kutub al-Lughah'," *JQR, N.S.,* 33 (1942-43) 171-212.

E[dmund] F. Sutcliffe, "St. Jerome's Pronunciation of Hebrew," *B* 29 (1948) 112-125.

O. R. Sellers, "Hebrew Roots and Stems," *JBL* 67 (1948) vi.

*G. J. Thierry, "Notes on Hebrew Grammar and Etymology," *OTS* 9 (1951) 1-17.

Joseph Reider, "Etymological Studies in Biblical Hebrew," *VT* 2 (1952) 113-130.

Raphael Patai, "The Phonology of 'Sabra'-Hebrew," *JQR, N.S.,* 44 (1953-54) 51-54.

J[oseph] Reider, "Etymology Studies in Biblical Hebrew," *VT* 4 (1954) 276-295.

Alan D. Corre, "The Anglo-Sephardic Pronunciation of Hebrew," *JJS* 7 (1956) 85-90.

*P. Kahle, "The Massoretic Text of the Bible and the Pronunciation of Hebrew," *JJS* 7 (1956) 133-154.

J. Mansour, "The Arabic Dialect of the Jews of Bagdad and the Pronunciation of Hebrew," *JJS* 8 (1957) 187-198.

S. Morag, "Mēša'. A Study of Certain Features of Old Hebrew Dialects," *EI* 5 (1958) 92*.

Cynthia M. Crews, "The Vulgar Pronunciation of Hebrew in the Judaeo-Spanish of Salonica," *JJS* 13 (1962) 83-95.

*A[nson] F. Rainey, "Private Seal-Impressions: A Note on Semantics," *IEJ* 16 (1966) 187-190.

David Téné, "Is the Hebrew Root content structured?" *Lěš* 32 (1967-68) #1/2, IX-X.

*A. T. Hanson, "Philo's Etymologies," *JTS, N.S.,* 18 (1967) 128-139.

*A. Hurvitz, "The Chronological Signifiance of 'Aramaisms' in Biblical," *IEJ* 18 (1968) 234-240.

David Robertson, "The Morphemes -y(-ī) and -w(-ō) in Biblical Hebrew," *VT* 19 (1969) 211-223.

§510 *3.3.3.2.1.4.5.2 Accents, Vowels, Vowel Points, and Punctuation*

P., "On the Hebrew Vowel Points," *QCS* 3 (1821) 236-238.

Jacob I. M. Falkenau, "Criticism on Gesenius's Doctrine of the Accents and Makkeph," *BS* 7 (1850) 650-655.

*C. Graham, "Note on the Hebrew Alphabet and Vowel Points," *JTVI* 6 (1872-73) 404.

B. Pick, "The Vowel-Points Controversy in the XVI, XVII, and XVIII Centuries," *PQPR* 6 (1877) 163-168.

[Samuel] Davidson, "Antiquity and Authority of the Hebrew Accents," *ONTS* 2 (1882-83) 164-169. *[Adapted from 'Outlines of Hebrew Accentuation']*

Anonymous, "The Study of the Hebrew Vowel-System," *AJSL* 2 (1885-86) 119-120.

*Wm. R. Harper, "Notes for Beginners," *AJSL* 2 (1885-86) 178-182. [Origin of Various Vowel-Sounds, p. 178; Relative Occurrence of Vowel Sounds, pp. 178-179]

*Wm. R. Harper, "Notes for Beginners. II," *AJSL* 2 (1885-86) 244-247. [The Origin of Long Vowels in Hebrew]

D. Chwolson, "The Quiescents (or Vowel-Letters) הוי in Ancient Hebrew Orthography," *AJSL* 6 (1889-90) 89-108. *(Trans. by T. K. Abbott)*

G. F. Moore, "Note on the origin of the supralinear system of vowel points in Hebrew," *JAOS* 14 (1890) xxxvii-xxxviii.

*Hinckley G. Mitchell, "Prose Accents," *JBL* 9 (1890) 132-135.

*Hinckley G. Mitchell, "Poetical Accents," *JBL* 10 (1891) 144-146.

B. Pick, "The Vowel-Points Controversy," *AJSL* 8 (1891-92) 150-173.

G. Margoliouth, "The Superlinear Punctuation, its origin, the different stages of its development, and its relation to other Semitic systems of Punctuation," *SBAP* 15 (1892-93) 164-205.

M. Friedlander, "A Third System of Symbols for the Hebrew Vowels and Accents," *JQR* 7 (1894-95) 564-568.

C. Levias, "On the Etymology of the Term Šᵉvâ," *AJP* 16 (1895) 28-37.

Grey Hubert Skipwith, "Suggestions for a Simpler Mode of Pointing," *JQR* 8 (1895-96) 707-709.

C. Levias, "Šᵉvâ and Ḥâṭēph," *AJSL* 13 (1896-97) 79-80. [שְׁוָא]

C. Levias, "The Palestinian Vocalization," *AJSL* 20 (1898-99) 157-164.

Arthur Davis, and Miss Nina Davis, "Ben Asher's Rhymes on the Hebrew Accents," *JQR* 12 (1899-1900) 452-455.

Paul Haupt, "The Names of the Hebrew Vowels," *JAOS* 22 (1901) 13-17.

R. B. Pattie, "Notes on Exceptional Pointing," *GUOST* 2 (1901-07) 27.

J. A. Selbie, "The 'Note-Line' in Hebrew," *ET* 15 (1903-04) 500-501. *[Pāsēḳ]*

C[aspar] Levias, "A. The Names of the Hebrew Vowels," *HUCA* (1904) 138-146.

A. M. Macdonald, "Sermons in Accents," *ET* 18 (1906-07) 238-239. *[Hebrew Accents]*

Fred T. Kelly, "Some Notes on the Shewa," *JSOR* 4 (1910) 82-86.

Max L. Margolis, "The Place of the Word-Accent in Hebrew," *JBL* 30 (1911) 29-43.

Frank R. Blake, "The Hebrew Metheg," *JAOS* 32 (1912) 78-102.

Frank R. Blake, "The Hebrew Vowel Seghol," *OOR* 1 (1926) #2, 10-13.

Phineas Mordell, "The Discovery of a Vowel Point System Based on the Sephardic Pronunciation," *JQR, N.S.,* 19 (1928-29) 479-488. *(Review)*

H. Biddulph, "The Paseḳ in the Scriptures. A Suggestion," *JQR, N.S.*, 20 (1929-30) 249-253.

*George Jeshurun, "On the Meaning of the Silent Yod in a Certain Group of Passages in the M.T.," *JSOR* 16 (1932) 108-112.

*C. Levias, "Enallage in the Bible," *AJSL* 50 (1933-34) 104-108. [Vowel-Obscuration in Hebrew and Aramaic, pp. 106-107; The Connecting Nun, p. 108]

Phineas Mordell, "The Beginning and Development of Hebrew Punctuation," *JQR, N.S.*, 24 (1933-34) 137-149. (corr. p. 280)

Phineas Mordell, "The Sephardic Vocalization," *JQR, N.S.* 24 (1933-34) 277-280. *(Review)*

Henry Englander, "Grammatical Elements and Terminology in Rashi's Commentaries, Part II—Rashi's Vowel Terminology," *HUCA* 12&13 (1937-38) 505-521.

*Arno Poebel, "The Antepenult Stressing of Old Hebrew and Its Influence on the Shaping of Vowels," *AJSL* 56 (1939) 225-230.

Arno Poebel, "Penult Stressing Replacing Ultimate Stressing in Pre-Exilic Hebrew," *AJSL* 56 (1939) 384-387.

Albrecht Goetze, "Accent and Vocalism in Hebrew," *JAOS* 59 (1939) 431-459.

J. Finkel, "The *Paseq* and the *Puncta Extraodinaria*," *JBL* 58 (1939) xii.

William Chomsky, "The History of Our Vowel-System," *JQR, N.S.*, 32 (1941-42) 27-49.

R[alph] Marcus, "Stress and Vowel Quality in Hebrew," *JBL* 61 (1942) xii.

*A. M. Honeyman, "Traces of an Early Diacritic Sign in Isaiah 8:6b," *JBL* 63 (1944) 45-50.

John Bowman, "A Forgotten Controversy," *EQ* 20 (1948) 46-68. *[Hebrew Vowel Points]*

Frank R. Blake, "Pretonic Vowels in Hebrew," *JNES* 10 (1951) 243-255.

Solomon L. Skoss, "A Study of Hebrew Vowels from Saadia Gaon's Grammatical Work 'Kutub al-Lughah'," *JQR, N.S.*, 42 (1951-52) 283-317.

*I. Yeivin, "Notes and Communications. 1. A Unique Combination of Accents," *Text* 1 (1960) 209-210.

*C. Rabin, "The Hebrew Development of the Proto-Semitic ā," *Tarbiz* 30 (1960-61) #2, I.

H. B. Rosen, "A Marginal Note on Biblical Hebrew Phonology," *JNES* 20 (1961) 124-126.

A. Dothan, "The Minor *Ga'ya*," *Text* 4 (1964) 55-75.

Henoch Yalon, "The Pronunciation of Vowels," *Tarbiz* 34 (1964-65) #2, II.

David Weisberg, "The Rare Accents of the Twenty-one Books," *JQR, N.S.*, 56 (1965-66) 315-336; 57 (1966-67) 57-70, 227-238.

§511 *3.3.3.2.1.4.5.3 Consonants, Syllables, and Orthography*

*Richard Cull, "On the Existence and Expression in Assyrian of the hard guttural sound of the Hebrew ע," *SBAP* 2 (1879-80) 43-45.

*Richard Cull, "On the Expression in Assyrian of the soft sound of the Hebrew ע," *SBAP* 2 (1879-80) 62-66.

*C[rawford] H. Toy, "Semitic Notes," *AJP* 5 (1884) 493-500. [II. The Syllable in Hebrew, pp. 494-500]

T. J. Dodd, "The Intermediate Syllable," *AJSL* 1 (1884-85) 10-13. (Editorial note, p. 19)

B. Felsenthal, "On 'Intermediate Syllables'," *AJSL* 1 (1884-85) 60-65. (Editorial note, pp. 67-68)

Hermann L. Strack, "The Syllables in the Hebrew Language," *AJSL* 1 (1884-85) 73-75.

Anonymous, "Unaccented Open Syllables with a Short Vowel," *AJSL* 1 (1884-85) 132.

Hartwig Hirschfeld, "The Dot in Semitic Palaeography," *JQR, N.S.,* 10 (1919-20) 159-183. [I. The Dot Disjunctive; II. The Dot Diacritical; III. The Dot Vocalic; IV. The Dot Grammatical]

*W. E. Staples, "The Hebrew of the Septuagint," *AJSL* 44 (1927-28) 6-30.

H. Louis Ginsberg, "The So-called Šĕyá Medium in the Light of the Christian Palestinian Idiom,"*JAOS* 53 (1933) 352-356.

*Arno Poebel, "The Antepenult Stressing of Old Hebrew and Its Influence on the Shaping of Vowels," *AJSL* 56 (1939) 225-230.

R[obert] Gordis, "The Asseverative Kaph," *JBL* 61 (1942) xii.

*Robert Gordis, "The Asseverative Kaph in Ugaritic and Hebrew," *JAOS* 63 (1943) 176-178.

Frank R. Blake, "The Origin and Development of the Hebrew Daghesh," *JBL* 62 (1943) 89-107.

G. Slonim, "The Substitution of the *raphē* for the *mappîq* in the Hebrew Bible," *JBL* 67 (1948) vii.

D[avid] N[oel] Freedman, "The Evolution of Early Hebrew Orthography," *JBL* 68 (1949) xii.

Frank R. Blake, "The Apparent Interchange Between a and i in Hebrew," *JNES* 9 (1950) 76-83.

Carl Cohen, "The Pronunciation of Hebrew," *CJ* 7 (1950-51) #3, 1-6.

W[illiam] S[anford] LaSor, "Secondary Opening of Syllables Originally Closed with Gutturals," *JBL* 70 (1951) xv.

William Sanford LaSor, "Secondary Opening of Syllables Originally Closed with Gutturals (in Hebrew)," *JNES* 15 (1956) 246-250.

I[srael] Yeivin, "Some Manifestations of *Milra'* Tendency in Hebrew," *EI* 5 (1958) 92*.

M. Z. Segal, "*Pisqa* in the Middle of a Verse," *Tarbiz* 29 (1959-60) #3, I-II.

Daniel Leibel, "A Note regarding the Development of Biblical Orthography," *Tarbiz* 32 (1962-63) #2, I-II.

Raphael Weiss, "On Ligatures in the Hebrew Bible (מכ=בן)," *JBL* 82 (1963) 188-194.

*U. Ornan, "The Tiberian Vocalisation System and the Principles of Linguistics," *JJS* 15 (1964) 109-123.

J[ames] Barr, "St. Jerome and the Sounds of Hebrew," *JSS* 12 (1967) 1-36.

§512 *3.3.3.2.1.4.5.4 Particles, Prepositions, Adverbs, and Prefixes*

Thomas Keightley, "Critical Examination of Some Passages of Scripture," *JSL, 3rd Ser.,* 6 (1857-58) 427-433. *[Preposition ב]*

Francis Crawford, "On the existence of biconsonantal prefixes of composition in Hebrew, as evidenced by a comparision with the Indo-European class," *TPS* (1858) 63-93.

Francis Crawford, "On constant affixes and afformatives in the Hebrew language, as illustrated by reference to Indo-European analogies. Part II," *TPS* (1858) 179-192.

Robert Young, "The Hebrew Particles and Young's Concordance," *HR* 6 (1881-82) 353.

*Henry Preserved Smith, "Old Testament Notes," *JBL* 24 (1905) 27-30. [VII. The Emphatic ל or לא, p. 30]

*Max L. Margolis, "The Greek Preverb and Its Hebrew-Aramaic Equivalent," *AJSL* 26 (1909-10) 33-61. *[Prepositional element in a compound verb]*

*C. J. Ball, "A Study in Biblical Philology," *SBAP* 33 (1911) 243-253. [Preformative ב in the Transliteration of Semitic Roots, pp. 247-253]

*James A. Montgomery, "Notes on the Old Testament," *JBL* 31 (1912) 140-146. [8. The interrogrative particle מי or מה, p. 144; 9. The correlative use of כי and אכן, pp. 144-146]

Frank R. Blake, "The Interrogative Particle א in Hebrew," *AJSL* 33 (1916-17) 146-148.

*Israel Eitan, "Hebrew and Semitic Particles. Comparative Studies in Semitic Philology," *AJSL* 44 (1927-28) 177-205, 254-260.

*Israel Eitan, "Hebrew and Semitic Particles—*Continued.* Comparative Studies in Semitic Philology," *AJSL* 45 (1928-29) 48-63, 130-145, 197-211; 46 (1929-30) 22-51.

Israel Eitan, "Three 'im Particles in Hebrew," *JAOS* 54 (1934) 295-297.

Charles E. Edwards, "Suggestive Hebrew Particles," *EQ* 9 (1937) 34-37.

H. H. Rowley, "Some Hebrew prepositional forms," *ZDMG* 92 (1938) 53-59.

Joseph Reider, "Substantival 'al in Biblical Hebrew," *JQR, N.S.,* 30 (1939-40) 263-270.

*H[arry] M. Orlinsky, "Some Biblical Prepositions and Pronouns," *JBL* 59 (1940) x.

*Steven T. Byington, "Hebrew Marginalia I," *JBL* 60 (1941) 279-288. [Constructions with אֶל, pp. 281-282]

Harry M. Orlinsky, "The Biblical Prepositions *Táḥaṭ, Bēn, Báʿaḏ,* and Pro-

nouns *ʾᵃnû* (or *ʾanū*), *zōʾṭāh Q*" *HUCA* 17 (1942-43) 267-292. [I. Introduction, II. תַּחַת; III. בֵּין; IV. בַּעַד; V. אָנוּ (or אָנוּ); VI. זֹאתָה; Appendix. On the origin of the *yōḏ* in forms like אֵלָיו, עָלָיו, and אַחֲרָיו]

A. M. Honeyman, "The So-Called *Nota Accusativi* in Biblical Hebrew," *GUOST* 12 (1944-46) 48. [אֵת]

*Steven T. Byington, "Hebrew Marginalia III," *JBL* 64 (1945) 339-355. [2. אִם Before Noun or Pronoun, p. 344]

G. D. Young, "Nominalized Prepositions," *JBL* 72 (1953) xv.

*Edmund F. Sutcliffe, "A Note on 'al, lᵉ, and *from,*" *VT* 5 (1955) 436-439. [לְ; עַל]

*Moshe Greenberg, "The Hebrew Oath Particle *Ḥay/Ḥē,*" *JBL* 76 (1957) 34-39.

Naum M. Sarna, "The Interchange of the Prepositions *Beth* and *Min* in Biblical Hebrew," *JBL* 78 (1959) 310-316.

P. Wernberg-Møller, "Observations on the Hebrew Particle," *ZAW* 71 (1959) 54-67.

Frederic J. Goldbaum, "Two Hebrew Quasi-Adverbs: לכן and אכן," *JNES* 23 (1964) 132-135.

Esra Shereshevsky, "The Use of Prepositions and Conjunctions in Rashi's Commentary," *JQR, N.S.,* 57 (1966-67) 200-211.

*H. J. Van Dijk, "A neglected connotation of three Hebrew verbs," *VT* 18 (1968) 16-30. [Ballast Prepositions, pp. 17-18]

§513   *3.3.3.2.1.4.5.5 Pronouns and Pronominal Suffixes*

F. B. Denio, "Prepositions of the Verbs Meaning to Believe or Trust," *ONTS* 2 (1882-83) 277-279. [בָּטַח, הָסָה, הֶאֱמִין, נִשְׁעַן]

C[harles] R. Brown, "The Relatives שֶׁ· and אֲשֶׁר, *AJSL* 1 (1884-85) 249-250.

A. H. Sayce, "A Note on the Relative (אֲשֶׁר)," *AJSL* 2 (1885-86) 51.

Charles R. Brown, "A Note on the Relative (אֲשֶׁר)," *AJSL* 2 (1885-86) 117-118.

Richard Kraetzschmar, "The Origin of the Notae Relationis in Hebrew," *AJSL* 6 (1889-90) 296-302. [אשר and שׁ]

*[Grey] H[ubert] Skipwith, "The Relative שׁ in Genesis," *JQR* 8 (1895-96) 706-707.

*W. B. Stevenson, "The Second Person Singular and Second Person Plural of Address in Isaiah 40-55. *Preface,"* *GUOST* 3 (1907-12) 31-32.

*S. F. Hunter, "The Second Person Singular and Second Person Plural of Address in Isaiah 40-55," *GUOST* 3 (1907-12) 32-36.

*Max L. Margolis, "The Mode of Expressing the Hebrew *'ā'id* in the Greek Hexateuch," *AJSL* 29 (1912-13) 237-260. [אֲשֶׁר/أَلْعَائِذ]

Frank R. Blake, "The Expression of Indefinite Pronominal Ideas in Hebrew," *JAOS* 34 (1914) 115-228.

Charles E. Edwards, "Emphatic Hebrew Pronouns," *EQ* 5 (1933) 420-430.

Mayer G. Slonim, "The Substitution of the Masculine for the Feminine Hebrew Pronominal Suffixes to Express Reverence," *JQR, N.S.,* 29 (1938-39) 397-403.

*H[arry] M. Orlinsky, "Some Biblical Prepositions and Pronouns," *JBL* 59 (1940) x.

Mayer G. Slonim, "The Deliberate Substitution of the Masculine for the Feminine Pronominal Suffixes in the Hebrew Bible," *JQR, N.S.,* 32 (1941-42) 139-158.

Harry M. Orlinsky, "The Biblical Prepositions *Táḥaṭ, Bēn, Bá'aḏ,* and Pronouns *'ᵃnū̃* (or *'anū*), *zō'ṭāḥ,*" *HUCA* 17 (1942-43) 267-292. [I. Introduction, II. תַּחַת; III. בֵּין; IV. בַּעַד; V. אֲנוּ (or אָנוּ); VI. זֹאתָה; Appendix. On the origin of the *yōḏ* in forms like אַחֲרָיו, עָלָיו, אֵלָיו, and]

M[ayer] G. Slonim, "Masculine Predicates with Feminine Subjects in the Hebrew Bible," *JBL* 63 (1944) 297-302.

*G. R. Driver, "Hebrew Studies," *JRAS* (1948) 164-176. [I. The Pronominal Suffix attached to one noun with the force being carried through to the parallel noun; Exceptions to the rule of agreement between subject and attribute or predicate in Hebrew; a Note on רוּחַ 'Wind, Spirit'; A masculine pronominal suffix may occasionally resume as a feminine noun after an interval; a plural participle with a pronominal suffix can take a predicate in a singular number.]

M[ayer] G. Slonim, "Masculine Suffixes versus Feminine Antecedents," *JBL* 71 (1952) xii.

*Frank R. Blake, "Studies in Semitic Grammar V," *JAOS* 73 (1953) 7-16. [3. The Hebrew Possessive Suffixes *-ām, -ān,* pp. 8-9]

M[ayer] G. Slonim, "Feminine Nouns in Plural with Predicates in Masculine Singular and Feminine Singular," *JBL* 72 (1953) xvi.

J. M. Allegro, "Uses of the Semitic Demonstrative element *z* in Hebrew," *VT* 5 (1955) 309-312.

*P. Wernberg-Møller, "Pronouns and Suffixes in the Scrolls and the Masoretic Text," *JBL* 76 (1957) 44-49.

*Chr. Brekelmans, "Pronominal suffixes in the Hebrew Book of Psalms," *JEOL* #17 (1963) 202-206.

§514 *3.3.3.2.1.4.5.6 The Article*

M. Stuart, "Correspondence between Prof. M. Stuart and Dr. I. Nordheimer, on the Use and Omission of the Hebrew Article in some important passages of Scripture," *BRCR, N.S.,* 6 (1841) 404-411. (Reply by Isaac Nordheimer, pp. 412-418)

*Anonymous, "Questions and Answers. 2.," *AJSL* 1 (1884-85) 20-21. [The prefixed Article in the Infinitive construction of דַּעַת]

Anonymous, "Questions and Answers. 3.," *AJSL* 1 (1884-85) 21. [The use of אֵת as a sign of the definite object]

Duncan B. Macdonald, "The Massoretic Use of the Article as a Relative," *AJSL* 13 (1896-97) 213-214.

§515 *3.3.3.2.1.4.5.7 The Verb - General Studies*

Anonymous, "Illustration of Some Passages of Sacred Scripture, from the Manner in which the Hebrews used their Active Verb," *MR* 4 (1821) 97-99.

[Heinrich] Ewald, "The Hebrew Tenses," *BRCR* 11 (1838) 131-174. *(Trans. with remarks by M. Stuart)*

N. B., "Gesenius' Hebrew Grammar, Fourteenth Edition, as Revised by Dr. E. Rödiger," *MQR* 1 (1847) 202-210. *(Review) [Hebrew Tenses]*

D[un.] H. Weir, "Observations on the Tenses of the Hebrew Verb, *JSL, 1st Ser.,* 4 (1849) 308-334.

James G. Murphy, "On Hebrew Tenses," *JSL, 1st Ser.,* 5 (1850) 194-202.

Samuel Lee, "Dr. Samuel Lee on the Tenses of the Hebrew Verbs," *JSL, 1st Ser.,* 6 (1850) 193-207.

Dun. H. Weir, "Professor Weir's Answer to Dr. Samuel Lee," *JSL, 1st Ser.,* 6 (1850) 484-497. *[Hebrew Tenses]*

J[ames] G. Murphy, "Tenses of Hebrew Verbs," *JSL, 1st Ser.,* 7 (1851) 216-223.

Samuel Lee, "Tenses of Hebrew Verbs," *JSL, 1st Ser.,* 7 (1851) 469-484.

Κεραία, "Tenses of Hebrew Verbs," *JSL, 1st Ser.,* 7 (1851) 484-488.

G. T., "The Hebrew Tenses. Mason and Bernard versus Lee," *JSL, 2nd Ser.,* 6 (1854) 111-120.

Σ., "On the Absence of the Substantive Verb in Hebrew," *JSL, 2nd Ser.,* 6 (1854) 237-238.

E. L. Rockwell, "Analogy between the Formation of the Pihel[sic]* Conjugation in Hebrew and the Perfect Tense in Latin," *SPR* 14 (1861-62) 444-449.

Francis Barham, "The Moods and Tenses of the Hebrew Verb," *JSL, 4th Ser.,* 4 (1863-64) 468-469.

*Richard Cull, "The Assyrian Verbs *Basu,* 'To Be,' *Qabah,* 'To Say,' and *Isu,* 'To Have,' identified as Variant Forms of Verbs having the same signification in Hebrew Language," *SBAT* 1 (1872) 281-293.

*Richard Cull, "A ת Conjugation, such as exists in Assyrian, shown to be a character of early Shemitic speech, by its vestiges found in the Hebrew, Phoenician, Aramaic, and Arabic Languages," *SBAT* 2 (1873) 83-109.

A. B. Rich, "The Hebrew Tense," *BS* 31 (1874) 115-135.

C[rawford] H. Toy, "The Nominal Basis of the Hebrew Verb," *PAPA* 9 (1876-77) 29-30. *[Bound with Transactions, but paged separately]*

Crawford H. Toy, "On the Nominal Basis of the Hebrew Verb," *TAPA* 8 (1877) 18-38.

C[rawford] H. Toy, "The Termination of *un* as a Means of Determining Date," *PAPA* 12 (1879-80) 28-30. *[Bound with Transactions, but paged separately]*

Crawford H. Toy, "The Hebrew Verb-termination *un,*" *TAPA* 11 (1880) 18-34.

*( ) R., "'Time' in the Old Testament," *ONTS* 3 (1883-84) 205-207. *[Use of the Past Tense in Hebrew]*

*Anonymous, "Questions and Answers. 2.," *AJSL* 1 (1884-85) 20-21. [The prefixed Article in the Infinitive construction of דַּעַת]

F. B. Denio, "Grammatical Questions. The Repetition of the Construct State Before a Second Genitive," *AJSL* 1 (1884-85) 244-246.

Wm. G. Ballantine, "Suggestions Toward a More Exact Nomenclature and Definition of the Hebrew Tenses," *AJSL* 2 (1885-86) 53-55.

James Strong, "Driver on the Hebrew Tenses," *AJSL* 2 (1885-86) 107-108.

Wm. Henry Bennett, "Notes on the Use of the Hebrew Tenses," *AJSL* 2 (1885-86) 193-208.

L. N. Dembitz, "The Passive of Qal," *AJSL* 3 (1886-87) 39-40.

Henry S. Morais, "Mr. Bennett's Articles on the Hebrew Tenses," *AJSL* 3 (1886-87) 45-46.

*John P. Peters, "Miscellaneous Notes," *AJSL* 3 (1886-87) 111-112. [Feminine Plural of Verbs, pp. 111-112]

John P. Peters, "Notes on the Hebrew Verb—Plural in Â," *AJSL* 5 (1888-89) 190-191.

W[illiam] H[enry] Bennett, "The Use of the Tenses in Hebrew Narrative," *AJSL* 5 (1888-89) 202-204.

*Francis Brown, "The imperfect of יֵשֵׁב *(yêshēb),* and kindred forms, in Hebrew," *JAOS* 13 (1889) lxxv-lxxvii.

William Henry Green, "On the Hebrew Tenses," *JAOS* 14 (1890) xxxiv-xxxv.

F. P. Ramsey, "New Names for the Forms of the Hebrew Finite Verb," *AJSL* 8 (1890-91) 101-102.

A. R. R. Hutton, "Hebrew Tenses," *AJSL* 14 (1897-98) 57-80.

J. D. Wijnkoop, "Hebrew Verbs with a Biliteral Stem," *JQR* 10 (1897-98) 503-512.

Louis B. Wolfenson, "The Pi'lēl in Hebrew," *JAOS* 27 (1906) 303-316.

B. Halper, "The Principal Formations of Geminate Verbs," *ZAW* 30 (1910) 42-57, 99-126, 201-228.

*Hinckley G. Mitchell, "וְהָיָה of the Past," *JBL* 33 (1914) 48-55.

T. Witton Davies, "The Infinitive, Especially the Infinitive Absolute in Hebrew and its Cognates: A Study in Comparative Philology and Translation," *JMUEOS* #8 (1918-19) 55-69. [Comparative Philology; Two Types of the Infinitive in Hebrew; The Intensifying (or Continuing) Infinitive in the Languages Cognate to Hebrew; The Intensive Infinitive in the Versions; Bibliography]

C. F. Burney, "A Fresh Examination of the Current Theory of the Hebrew Tenses," *JTS* 20 (1918-19) 200-214.

Israel Eitan, "Light on the History of the Hebrew Verb (נִפְעַל or intensive נִפְעַל)," *JQR, N.S.,* 12 (1921-22) 25-32.

H. Distenfeld, "Was There a Form נִפְעַל in Early Hebrew?" *JQR, N.S.,* 13 (1922-23) 337-342.

W[illiam] F[oxwell] Albright, "The Hebrew Nippa'el in the Light of Comparative Philology," *JQR, N.S.,* 13 (1922-23) 503-505.

*David Yellin, "The Hippa'el-Nif'al Conjugation in Hebrew and Aramaic; and the Assimilation of ת in the Hitpa'el Conjugation," *JPOS* 4 (1924) 85-106.

*Oswald T. Allis, "The Blessing of Abraham," *PTR* 25 (1927) 263-298. [II. The Passives and Reflexives in Hebrew, pp. 279-287]

H. Louis Ginsberg, "Studies on the Biblical Hebrew Verb," *AJSL* 46 (1929-30) 53-58, 127-138. [I. Masoretically Misconstrued Internal Passives; II. Heterogeneous Infinitive-Finite Combinations; III. Phonetic Problems]

R. B. Pattie, "Notes on the Syntax of the Hebrew Construct," *GUOST* 6 (1929-33) 63-64.

R. M., "Observations on Verbs עי״א*[sic]* with Virtual Doubling of the א in the Intensives," *TF* 2 (1930) 58-62.

*Charles Eugene Edwards, "A Hebrew Idiom," *BS* 90 (1933) 232-235. *[Combining a finite tense and an infinitive of the same verb to express intensity, etc.]*

Harry M. Orlinsky, "On the Cohortative and Jussive after an Imperative or Interjection in Biblical Hebrew," *JQR, N.S.,* 31 (1940-41) 371-382; 32 (1941-42) 191-205, 273-277.

H[arry] M. Orlinsky, "On Suffixed Forms of Qal Infinitive Construct in *i* and *a*," *JBL* 61 (1942) xi-xii.

Harry M. Orlinsky, "Notes on the Qal Infinitive Construct and the Verbal Noun in Biblical Hebrew," *JAOS* 67 (1947) 107-126.

William Chomsky, "Some Irregular Formations in Hebrew," *JQR, N.S.,* 38 (1947-48) 409-418.

*Theophile James Meek, "Old Testament Notes," *JBL* 67 (1948) 233-239. [4. The Infinitive Construct of אהב, p. 238]

*G. J. Thierry, "Miscellanea Hebraica," *OTS* 7 (1950) 143-148. [1. A Hypothesis on the Origin of the Hifîl, pp. 143-145; 2. Baur-Leander's Terminology on the Hebrew tempora, pp. 145-146]

*M. M. Bravmann, "Notes on the Forms of the Imperative in Hebrew and Aramaic," *JQR, N.S.,* 42 (1951-52) 51-56.

A. Rubinstein, "A Finite Verb Continued by an Infinitive Absolute in Biblical Hebrew," *VT* 2 (1952) 362-367.

*Cyrus H. Gordon, "Marginal Notes on the Ancient Middle East," *JKF* 2 (1952-53) 50-61. [V. a. *t*-causatives; c. Construct + Adjective: שלשיה עגלת The formation (Jer. 48:34), pp. 54-56]

C. J. Mullo Weir, "Hebrew 3rd Singular Feminine Perfects in -āth and -ath," *GUOST* 15 (1953-54) 10-15.

*Frank R. Blake, "Studies in Semitic Grammar V," *JAOS* 73 (1953) 7-16. [4. The ending *ēh* in Hebrew verbs tertiae *h*, p. 9; 5. The Construct Ending *ē(h)* in Hebrew, pp. 9-11; 12. Addendum to Study 4, p. 16]

*P. P. Saydon, "The Inceptive Imperfect in Hebrew and the Verb הֵחֵל 'to Begin'," *B* 35 (1954) 43-50.

Lawrence N. Manross, "Bêth Essentiae," *JBL* 73 (1954) 238-239.

*E[phraim] A. Speiser, "The Durative Hithpaʻel: A *tan*- Form," *JAOS* 75 (1955) 118-121.

*J. Huesman, "Finite Uses of the Infinitive Absolute," *B* 37 (1956) 271-295.

S. Morag, "The Pāʻēl and Hitpāʻēl Verbal Stems," *Tarbiz* 26 (1956-57) #4, I-II.

F. C. Fensham, "The Stem *HTL* in Biblical Hebrew," *VT* 9 (1959) 310-311.

*Jerzy Kuryłowicz, "Accentuation of the Verb in Indo-European and in Hebrew," *Word* 15 (1959) 123-129.

*Bruno W. W. Dombrowski, "Some Remarks on the Hebrew Hithpaʻel and Inversative -t- in the Semitic Languages," *JNES* 21 (1962) 220-223.

P. P. Saydon, "The Conative Imperfect in Hebrew," *VT* 12 (1962) 124-126.

*John D. W. Watts, "Infinitive Absolute as Imperative and Interpretation of Exodus 20:8," *ZAW* 74 (1962) 141-145.

W. L. Moran, "**taqtul*—Third Masculine Singular?" *B* 45 (1964) 80-82.

*Moshe Held, "The Action-Result (Factitive-Passive) Sequence of Identical Verbs in Biblical Hebrew and Ugaritic," *JBL* 84 (1965) 272-282.

S. E. Loewenstamm, "The Plusquamperfect in Talmudic Hebrew," *Lĕš* 31 (1966-67) #1, n.p.n.

Delbert R. Hillers, "Delocutive Verbs in Biblical Hebrew," *JBL* 86 (1967) 320-324.

C. Rabin, "The Vocalization of the Third Singular Perfect of *Piʻēl* in Tiberian Hebrew," *Lĕš* 32 (1967-68) #1/2, II.

R. Mirkin, "*Mĕfuʻal* Forms; Material on the Passive and Perfective Participle," *Lĕš* 32 (1967-68) #1/2, VIII-IX.

*Moshe Held, "The Root *ZBL/SBL* in Akkadian, Ugaritic and Biblical Hebrew," *JAOS* 88 (1968) 90-96.

Werner Weinberg, "The *Qamāṣ Qāṭān* Structures," *JBL* 87 (1968) 151-165.

*C. Rabin, "*L-* with Imperative (Gen. XXIII)," *JSS* 13 (1968) 113-124.

*H. J. Van Dijk, "A neglected connotation of three Hebrew verbs," *VT* 18 (1968) 16-30.

A. Kohén, "The Infinitive plus *Hé*," *Lĕš* 33 (1968-69) #2/3, n.p.n.

Francis I. Andersen, "A Short Note on Construct *k* in Hebrew," *B* 50 (1969) 68-69.

*C. Rabin, "The Nature and Origin of the Šaf'el in Hebrew and Aramaic," *EI* 9 (1969) 138. [English Summary]

*J. C. Greenfield, "The 'Periphrastic Imperative' in Aramaic and Hebrew," *IEJ* 19 (1969) 199-210.

*R. Hetzron, "The Evidence for Perfect **y'aqtul* and Jussive **yaqt'ul* in Proto-Semitic," *JSS* 14 (1969) 1-21. [3. Hebrew, pp. 8-18]

H. B. Rosén, "The Comparative Assignment of Certain Hebrew Tense Forms," *PICSS* (1969) 212-234.

H. J. van Dijk, "Does third masculine singular **taqtul* exist in Hebrew?" *VT* 19 (1969) 440-447.

*David Marcus, "The Stative and *Waw* Consecutive," *JANES* 2 (1969-70) 37-40.

S. Kogut, "Does the form *Qětol* = *qotel* Exist in the Bible?" *Lěš* 34 (1969-70) #1/2, 3. *[English Supplement]*

§516 *3.3.3.2.1.4.5.7.1 The Strong Verb*

Frank R. Blake, "The So-called Intransitive Verbal Forms in Hebrew," *JAOS* 24 (1903) 145-204.

§517 *3.3.3.2.1.4.5.7.2 The Weak Verb*

Anonymous, "Questions and Answers. 1.," *AJSL* 1 (1884-85) 20. [The vowel û in the Hoph'al of ע"ע verbs]

Morris Jastrow Jr., "On a fragment of Ḥayyuǵ's treatise on weak verbs," *JAOS* 14 (1890) xxxviii-xl.

George Ricker Berry, "Original Waw in ל"ה Verbs," *AJSL* 20 (1903-04) 256-257.

Henry Englander, "Rashi's View of the Weak ע"ע, and פ"ן roots," *HUCA* 7 (1930) 399-437.

§518 *3.3.3.2.1.4.5.8 Studies on the Use of "Waw"*

†Anonymous, "Sharp on the Hebrew Tongue," *BCQTR* 27 (1806) 53-57. *(Review)* [ו]

*John P. Peters, "Miscellaneous Notes," *AJSL* 3 (1886-87) 112-113. [Waw Consecutive with the Imperfect, pp. 112-113]

George Ricker Berry, "Waw Consecutive with the Perfect in Hebrew," *JBL* 22 (1903) 60-69.

*C. F. Burney, "The Book of Isaiah: A New Theory," *CQR* 74 (1912) 99-123. *[Note on the use of the Imperfect with Waw Consecutive in continuation of a Prophetic Perfect, pp. 123-126]*

J. Courtenay James, "One-Tense Semitic," *ET* 29 (1917-18) 376-377. *[waw conversive]*

F. T. Kelly, "The Imperfect with Simple Waw in Hebrew," *JBL* 39 (1920) 1-23.

Cyrus H. Gordon, "The Accentual Shift in the Perfect with *Waw* Consecutive," *JBL* 57 (1938) 319-326.

F. R. Blake, "The Hebrew Waw Conversive," *JBL* 63 (1944) 271-295.

Frank R. Blake, "The Form of Verbs After *Waw* in Hebrew," *JBL* 65 (1946) 51-57.

*Cyrus H. Gordon, "Marginal Notes on the Ancient Middle East," *JKF* 2 (1952-53) 50-61. [IV. The Semitic Conjunction *wa,* pp. 53-54]

G. Douglas Young, "The Origin of the Waw Conversive," *JNES* 12 (1953) 248-252.

J. Huesman, "The Infinitive Absolute and Waw + Perfect Problems," *B* 37 (1956) 410-434.

P. Wernberg-Møller, "'Pleonastic' *Waw* in Classical Hebrew," *JSS* 3 (1958) 321-326.

A. Rubinstein, "The Anomalous Perfect with *Waw*-Conjunctive in Biblical Hebrew," *B* 44 (1963) 62-66.

*David Marcus, "The Stative and the *Waw* Consecutive," *JANES* 2 (1969-70) 37-40.

§519 *3.3.3.2.1.4.5.9 Syntax - General Studies*

Jas. Strong, "Hebrew Syntax," *AJSL* 2 (1885-86) 228-233.

*John P. Peters, "Miscellaneous Notes," *AJSL* 3 (1886-87) 111-116. [Masculine Plural in ÔTH, p. 114]

*Alois Barta, "Syntax of the Sentences in Isaiah 40-66," *AJSL* 17 (1900-01) 22-46.

*Ed. König, "Is There a Rhetorical Use of 'Not' in Hebrew?" *ET* 12 (1900-01) 44-45.

W. H. Carslaw, "Peculiarities of Gender," *ICMM* 1 (1905) 254-257.

W. H. Carslaw, "Additional Facts Regarding the Sun and Moon," *ICMM* 1 (1905) 442-445. *[Gender]*

J. P. Wilson, "Hebrew Syntax in the Septuagint," *GUOST* 4 (1913-22) 71-72.

*Israel W. Slotki, "'Breaks in the Midst of Verses' or פָּסוּק בְּאֶמְצַע פִּסְקָא," *JTS* 22 (1920-21) 263-265.

Frank R. Blake, "A new method of syntactical arrangement," *JAOS* 41 (1921) 467-471.

*Israel Eitan, "Talmudic Syntax," *JQR, N.S.*, 24 (1933-34) 161-164. *(Review)*

*Theophile James Meek, "The Syntax of the Sentence in Hebrew," *JBL* 64 (1945) 1-13.

Zellig S. Harris, "Componential Analysis of a Hebrew Paradigm," *Lang* 24 (1948) 87-91.

*Theophile J. Meek, "Archaeology and a Point in Hebrew Syntax," *BASOR* #122 (1951) 31-33. [*lᵉfî ḥereḇ*]

J. Wash Watts, "A Survey of Syntax in the Hebrew Old Testament," *R&E* 48 (1951) 442-452.

*A. M. Honeyman, "The Syntax of the Gezer Calendar," *JRAS* (1953) 53-58.

*M. Z. Kadari, "Studies in the Syntax of Targum Onqelos," *Tarbiz* 32 (1962-63) #3, III-IV.

*Mitchell Dahood, "Ugaritic—Hebrew Syntax and Style," *UF* 1 (1969) 15-36.

M. Z. Kaddari, "Problems in Biblical Hebrew Syntax (On the So-Called 'Double Object')," *Lĕš* 34 (1969-70) #4, n.p.n.

§520 *3.3.3.2.1.4.5.9.1 The Noun (includes Syntax of the Noun)*

G. Bosworth, "The Idiomatic Use of Certain Hebrew Nouns in Construction," *BRCR, 3rd Ser.,* 2 (1846) 756-763.

William Lindsay Alexander, "On Certain Idiomatic Uses of the Plural in Hebrew," *JSL, 1st Ser.,* 1 (1848) 279-289.

*Robert Hutcheson, "On the Syntax of זֶרַע with especial reference to its bearing on Gal. iii. 16," *SBLP* (June, 1880) 11-13.

Robert Hutcheson, "The Syntax of זֶרַע," *BS* 38 (1881) 317-322.

Anonymous, "The Ethical Dative," *AJSL* 1 (1884-85) 15-16.

*Wm. R. Harper, "Notes for Beginners," *AJSL* 2 (1885-86) 178-182. [The Nominative Absolute, p. 179]

F. B. Denio, "Relations expressed by the genitive in Hebrew," *JBL* 19 (1900) 107-113.

*James A. Kelso, "Is the Divine Name in Hebrew Ever Equivalent to the Superlative?" *AJSL* 19 (1902-03) 152-158.

R. B. Pattie, "The Double Genitive, and Allied Constructions," *GUOST* (1907-12) 6-7.

M. Seidel, "*Û* as an Old Plural Ending in the Hebrew Noun," *JAOS* 37 (1917) 165-167. [ו]

M. Seidel, "*Â* as an Old Plural Ending of the Hebrew Feminine Noun," *AJSL* 37 (1920-21) 311-313.

Fred T. Kelly, "Stray Notes on the 'A' Class Segholate," *JSOR* 5 (1921) 96-99.

G. R. Driver, "The Origin of 'Ḥireq Compaginis' in Hebrew," *JTS* 26 (1924-25) 76-77.

*J. M. Powis Smith, "The Use of Divine Names as Superlatives," *AJSL* 45 (1928-29) 212-213.

*†Robert Hutcheson, "The Syntax of זֶרַע with special reference to its bearing on Gal. 3^{16}," *JBL* 49 (1930) xxxiii-xxxiv. *[Reprint of the Proceedings of the first meeting of SBL (may be bound separately)]*

William Chomsky, "The Plural of Nouns in the (קְ)טֶלֶת Formations," *JAOS* 54 (1934) 425-428.

T[heophile] J[ames] Meek, "The Hebrew Accusative of Time and Place," *JBL* 58 (1939) vii.

Theophile James Meek, "The Hebrew Accusative of Time and Place," *JAOS* 60 (1940) 224-233.

M. G. Slonim, "Hebrew Nouns Used in Both Genders," *JBL* 66 (1947) vii.

D. Winton Thomas, "A Consideration of Some Unusual Ways of Expressing the Superlative in Hebrew," *VT* 3 (1953) 209-224.

J. Weingreen, "The Construct-Genitive Relation in Hebrew Syntax," *VT* 4 (1954) 50-59.

*P. P. Saydon, "Some Unusual Ways of Expressing the Superlative in Hebrew and Maltese," *VT* 4 (1954) 432-433.

Norman Walker, "Concerning the Function of *'ēth,*" *VT* 5 (1955) 314-315.

*N[orman] Walker, "Do Plural Nouns of Majesty Exist in Hebrew?" *VT* 7 (1957) 208.

*P. Wernberg-Møller, "The Noun of the Qṭwl Class in the Massoretic Text," *RdQ* 2 (1959-60) 448-450. *[Table of Contents reads: "Q^{e}ṭōl"]*

Svi Rin, "ʾ. . as an absolute Plural Ending," *BZ, N.S.,* 5 (1961) 255-258.

W. F. Stinespring, "No Daughter of Zion. *A Study of the Appositional Genitive in Hebrew Grammar,*" *SQ/E* 26 (1965) 133-141.

M. Z. Kaddari, "Dvandva-Type 'Composite' Substantives in Biblical Hebrew," *Lĕš* 30 (1965-66) #2, n.p.n.

*A. van Selms, "*Pa'yal* Formations in Ugaritic and Hebrew Nouns," *JNES* 26 (1967) 189-295.

D. Winton Thomas, "Some Further Remarks on Unusual Ways of Expressing the Superlative in Hebrew," *VT* 18 (1968) 120-124.

§521 *3.3.3.2.1.4.5.9.2 Hebrew Numerals [See also: §122 Mathematics and Numbering Systems ←]*

*John P. Peters, "Miscellaneous Notes. Hebrew Use of Numbers," *AJSL* 1 (1885-86) 174.

*John P. Peters, "Miscellaneous Notes," *AJSL* 3 (1886-87) 111-116. [The Use of Numbers in Hebrew, pp. 113-115]

Hinckley G. Mitchell, "Two Papers. Partitives after numerals in Hebrew," *JBL* 7 (1887), Part 1, 61-64.

Frank R. Blake, "The Dual Ending *-aim* in the Hebrew Multiplicative Numerals," *AJSL* 33 (1916-17) 148-149.

*Frank R. Blake, "Studies in Semitic Grammar," *JAOS* 35 (1917) 375-385. [III. The Multiplicative Numerals in Aramaic and Hebrew, pp. 381-382]

*Solomon Gandz, "Hebrew Numerals," *PAAJR* 4 (1932-33) 53-112.

*G. R. Driver, "Gender in Hebrew Numbers," *JJS* 1 (1948-49) 90-104.

*G. Sarfatti, "Arithmetical Fractions in Biblical and Mishnaic Hebrew," *Tarbiz* 28 (1958-59) #1, I-II.

§522 *3.3.3.2.1.4.5.10 The Sentence - General Studies*

Henry Ferguson, "An Examination of the use of tenses in conditional sentences in Hebrew," *JBL* 2 (1882) 40-94.

*H. G. Mitchell, "The Construction with לְמַעַן‎," *ONTS* 2 (1882-83) 171-172.

H. G. Mitchell, "Purpose without a Connective," *AJSL* 1 (1884-85) 253-255.

*Wm. R. Harper, "Notes for Beginners," *AJSL* 2 (1885-86) 178-182. [The Nominative Absolute, p. 179; Circumstantial Clauses, pp. 180-182]

*Wm. R. Harper, "Notes for Beginners. II," *AJSL* 2 (1885-86) 244-247. [A Noun in the Construct Relation with a Clause, p. 247]

C. Albrecht, "The Arrangement of the Words in the Hebrew Nominal Sentence," *AJSL* 4 (1887-88) 95-98. *(Trans. unknown)*

*Dean A. Walker, "The Semitic Negative with Special Reference to the Negative in Hebrew," *AJSL* 12 (1895-96) 230-267.

H. G. Mitchell, "Final Constructions of Biblical Hebrew," *JBL* 34 (1915) 83-161.

Theophile James Meek, "The Co-ordinate Adverbial Clause in Hebrew," *JAOS* 49 (1929) 156-159.

R[obert] Gordis, "Note on General Conditional Sentences in Hebrew," *JBL* 49 (1930) 200-203.

Theophile J[ames] Meek, "The Co-ordinate Adverbial Clause in Hebrew," *AJSL* 47 (1930-31) Number 1, Part 1, 51-52.

Robert Gordis, "A Rhetorical Use of Interrogative Sentences in Biblical Hebrew," *AJSL* 49 (1932-33) 212-217.

J. A. Thompson, "The Relative Negative in the Old Testament," *JBL* 64 (1945) viii.

M. H. Gottstein, "Afterthought and the Syntax of Relative Clauses in Biblical Hebrew," *JBL* 68 (1949) 35-47.

*Marvin Pope, "'Pleonastic' *Wāw* before Nouns in Ugaritic and Hebrew," *JAOS* 73 (1953) 95-98.

P. P. Saydon, "Assonance in Hebrew as a Means of Expressing Emphasis," *B* 36 (1955) 36-50, 287-304.

Theophile J[ames] Meek, "Result and Purpose Clauses in Hebrew," *JQR, N.S.,* 46 (1955-56) 40-43.

Aaron Mirsky, "The Origin of the *Anadiplosis* in Hebrew Literature," *Tarbiz* 28 (1958-59) #2, IV.

*C. Rabin, "The Ancient Versions and the Indefinite Subject," *Text* 2 (1962) 60-76.

*A. D. Crown, "Aposiopesis in the O.T. and the Hebrew Conditional Oath," *Abr-N* 4 (1963-64) 96-111.

M. Morešet, "The Predicate Preceding a Compound Subject in the Biblical Language," *Lĕš* 31 (1966-67) #4, n.p.n.

M. Rottenberg, "The Implicit Construct Phrase in the Bible," *Lĕš* 32 (1967-68) #4, n.p.n.

E. A. Levenston, "The Structure of the Hebrew Clause," *Lĕš* 32 (1967-68) #4, n.p.n.

M. Rottenberg, "The Implicit Construct Phrase in the Bible (*concl.*)," *Lĕš* 33 (1968-69) #1, n.p.n.

Francis I. Andersen, "A Short Note on Construct *k* in Hebrew," *B* 50 (1969) 68-69.

*S. E. Lowenstamm, "The Expanded Colon in Ugaritic and Biblical Verse," *JSS* 14 (1969) 176-196.

§523 *3.3.3.2.1.4.6 Related Studies in Modern Hebrew*

W. Willner, "Modern Ideas in Hebrew," *AJSL* 2 (1885-86) 52. *[Means employed to express modern ideas]*

William O. Sproull, "Hebrew and Rabbinical Words in Present Use," *AJSL* 7 (1890-91) 72-74.

A. Ben-Oliel, "Hebrew in Palestine," *EN* 3 (1891) 20-23.

Aaron Ember, "Pronunciation of Hebrew Among the Russian Jews," *AJSL* 19 (1902-03) 223-234.

J. Garrow Duncan, "Modern Hebrew. How the Language of the Old Testament is adapting itself to Modern Needs," *PEFQS* 56 (1924) 78-84.

R. Thornhill, "The Rise in Modern Hebrew," *DUJ, N.S.,* 12 (1950-51) 103-114.

Matitiahu Tsevat, "Learned Intentions and Free Development in Modern Hebrew," *SQ/E* 14 (1953) 135-138.

Haiim B. Rosén, "Book-Review: A Grammar of Israeli Hebrew," *Tarbiz* 24 (1954-55) #2, VI-VII.

Z. Ben-Hayyim, "About the Nature of Spoken Hebrew," *Tarbiz* 24 (1954-55) #3, V.

Ezekiel G. Kutscher, "Modern Hebrew and 'Israeli' Hebrew," *CJ* 10 (1955-56) #3, 28-45.

R. Bachi, "A Statistical Analysis of the Revival of Hebrew in Israel," *SH* 3 (1956) 179-247.

S. Morag, "Studies in the Living Traditions of Post-Biblical Hebrew as Preserved by Jewish Communities," *Tarbiz* 26 (1956-57) #1, I-II.

Yehudah Ratzhabi, "Concerning the Status of the Hebrew Language in the Synagogues of Yemen," *Tarbiz* 26 (1956-57) #3, IX.

E. Ullendorff, "Modern Hebrew as a Subject of Linguistic Investigation," *JSS* 2 (1957) 251-262.

Haiim B. Rosén, "Syntactical Notes on Israeli Hebrew, Determination, Indetermination, and the Article," *JAOS* 81 (1961) 21-26.

*Zvi Keren, "The Influence of the Hebrew Language on Contemporary Israeli Art Music," *BSOAS* 25 (1962) 209-224.

Ḥanokh Yallon, "The *Kamaz* in Babylonian Phonetics and in Yemen," *Tarbiẓ* 33 (1963-64) #2, I-II.

Gerd Fraenkel, "A Structural Approach to Israeli Hebrew," *JAOS* 86 (1966) 32-38. *(Review)*

Aaron Bar-Adon, "New Imperative and Jussive Formations in Contemporary Hebrew," *JAOS* 86 (1966) 410-413.

W. Weinberg, "Spoken Israeli Hebrew: Trends in the Departures from Classical Phonology," *JSS* 11 (1966) 40-68.

*E. Y. Kutscher, "Yemenite Hebrew and Ancient Pronunciation," *JSS* 11 (1966) 217-225.

Š Aškĕnazi, "Hebrew Lexicography," *Lĕš* 31 (1966-67) #2, n.p.n. *[Modern Hebrew]*

R. Pine, "Remarks on the Improvement of ḥireq and ḥolem Notation in Hebrew Spelling," *Lĕš* 31 (1966-67) #2, n.p.n.

Y. Carmiel, "On Haskala Vocabulary," *Lĕš* 31 (1966-67) #4, n.p.n.

S. Morag and R. Sappan, "Notes on the Hebrew Idiom of Fishermen and Sailors in Israel," *Lĕš* 31 (1966-67), #4, n.p.n.; 32 (1967-68) #3, n.p.n.

P. Enoch and G. Kaplan, "The Physical Nature of Syllabic Stress in Israeli Hebrew," *Lĕš* 33 (1968-69) #2/3, n.p.n.

S[amuel] E. Loewenstamm, "A Remark on the Question of אוֹ שֶׁ־," *Lĕš* 33 (1968-69) #4, 4.

§524 *3.3.3.2.1.5 Word Studies Keyed to English*
- Alphabetical Listing

J. B. Bittinger, "A Bible Glossary," *ER* 13 (1861-62) 248-264. [Addicted; Allow; Artillery; By-and-by; Cabin; Carriage; Charity; Cheer; Coast; College; Comfortable; Commune; Conceit; Consider; Curious; Cunning; Damnation; Dealings; Debate; Decently; Deliciously; Desire; Disciples; Doctor; Duke; Equal; Estimation; Estate; Exactor; Fairs; Faithful; Fame; Fashion; Fault; Fearful; Folly; Forwardness; Ghost; Grief] *(Never Completed)*

A

Henry Goodwin Smith, "'Adam' in the Revised Version," *AJT* 6 (1902) 758-761.

*Norman Walker, "'Adam' and 'Eve' and 'Adon'," *ZAW* 74 (1962) 66-68.

Trude Weiss Rosemarin, "The Terms for 'Air' in the Bible," *JBL* 51 (1932) 71-72.

Douglas Brice, "Alleluia," *ClR* 42 (1957) 257-264.

*Σ., "'Table' or 'Altar'?" *BFER* 16 (1867) 625-630.

H. W. Hogg, "'Amen.' Notes on Its Significance and Use in Biblical and Post-Biblical Times," *JQR* 9 (1896-97) 1-23.

Charles H. Richards, "Amen," *HR* 55 (1908) 378-380.

*Jos[eph] A. Seiss, "Some Sacred Words. The Triasgion, The Hallelujah, and The Amen," *LCR* 16 (1897) 190-202.

*S. Talmon, "*Amen* as an Introductory Oath Formula," *Text* 7 (1969) 124-129.

†H. A., "On the Word Angel," *MMBR* 7 (1799) 213-214.

James Hope Moulton, "'It is His Angel'," *JTS* 3 (1901-02) 514-527. *[Study of the term as applied to human sent messengers]*

*Robert North, "Separated Spiritual Substances in the Old Testament," *CBQ* 29 (1967) 419-449. *[Angel]*

Ed[uard] König, "The Hebrew Word for 'Atone'," *ET* 22 (1910-11) 232-234, 378-380.

Stephen H. Langdon, "The Hebrew Word for 'Atone'," *ET* 22 (1910-11) 320-325.

C. F. Burney, "The Hebrew Word for 'Atone',"*ET* 22 (1910-11) 325-327.

S[tephen] H. Langdon, "Supplementary Note on the Hebrew Word for 'Atone',"*ET* 22 (1910-11) 380-381.

C. J. Ball, "The Hebrew Term for 'Atone',"*ET* 22 (1910-11) 478-479.

A. B. Davidson, "The Word 'Atone' in Extra-Ritual Literature," *Exp, 5th Ser.,* 10 (1899) 92-103.

B

*T. Stenhouse, "Baal and Belial," *ZAW* 33 (1913) 295-305.

J. Marshall, "The Name Baal-zebub," *SBAP* 8 (1885-86) 76-77.

†Anonymous, "A New Etymology of the Word Babel," *MMBR* 13 (1802) 24-26.

†M. W., "Derivation of Babel," *MMBR* 15 (1803) 298.

*Anonymous, "On the Bdellium of the Bible," *SPR* 2 (1848-49) 94-99.

*Anonymous, "In the Study. Behind and Before," *ET* 20 (1908-09) 408-410.

*T. Stenhouse, "Baal and Belial," *ZAW* 33 (1913) 295-305.

Eb. Nestle, "The Aramaic Equivalent of 'Blessed'," *ET* 20 (1908-09) 564-565.

Harry Mowvley, "The Concept and Content of 'Blessing' in the Old Testament," *BTr* 16 (1965) 74-79.

Toyozo W. Nakarai, "The Blood is the Life," *SQ/E* 1 (1940) 124-132.

L[eon] Morris, "The Biblical Use of the Term 'Blood'," *JTS, N.S.,* 3 (1952) 216-227; 6 (1955) 77-82.

L. Dewar, "The Biblical Use of the Term 'Blood'," *JTS, N.S.,* 4 (1953) 204-208.

*Edward F. Siegman, "The Blood of the Covenant," *AER* 136 (1957) 167-174. *[Blood]*

David Mack, "The Meaning of Blood in the Old Testament," *RefR* 11 (1957-58) #3, 37-42.

*H. B. Hackett, "Scripture Facts and Illustrations, Collected During a Journey in Palestine," *CRB* 18 (1853) 405-424, 517-537. [Use of the word "Brother", pp. 419-420]

C

*Michael C. Astour, "The Origin of the Terms 'Canaan,' 'Phoenician,' and 'Purple'," *JNES* 24 (1965) 346-350.

*Samuel I. Feigin, "The Captives in Cuneiform Inscriptions," *AJSL* 50 (1933-34) 217-245. *[Word Studies of 'Captive' in Several Ancient Foreign Languages]*

*Samuel I. Feigin, "The Captives in Cuneiform Inscriptions—Continued," *AJSL* 51 (1934-35) 22-29. *[Word Studies of 'Captive' in Several Ancient Foreign Languages]*

*P. le Page Renouf, "Is the Hebrew Word Cherub of Egyptian Origin?" *SBAP* 6 (1883-84) 189-193.

Jack P. Lewis, "The Jewish Background of the Church," *RestQ* 2 (1958) 154-163.

*E[phraim] A. Speiser, "'Coming' and 'Going' at the 'City' Gate," *BASOR* #144 (1956) 20-23.

*Sidney B. Hoenig, "I. *Heber Ir.* II. City-Square," *JQR, N.S.,* 48 (1957-58) 123-139.

*Herbert H. Gowen, "The Color Terms of the Old Testament," *ATR* 3 (1920-21) 141-151.

*Eb. Nestle, "Rest and Comfort," *ET* 10 (1898-99) 48.

*E[phraim] A. Speiser, "'Coming' and 'Going' at the 'City' Gate," *BASOR* #144 (1956) 20-23.

*Geoffrey Evans, "'Coming' and 'Going' at the City Gate—A Discussion of Professor Speiser's Paper," *BASOR* #150 (1958) 28-33.

Maurice G. Hansen, "The Word 'Conscience' in the Bible," *ONTS* 3 (1883-84) 387-388.

Jacob W. Heikkinen, "A Biblical Study," *MidS* 8 (1968-69) #3, 92-114. *[Conversion]*

*T. A. Rickard, "The Nomenclature of Copper and its Alloys," *JRAI* 62 (1932) 281-290.

*J. C. Hindley, "The Translation of the Words for 'Covenant'," *IJT* 10 (1961) 13-24.

*J. C. Hindley, "The Meaning and Translation of Covenant," *BTr* 13 (1962) 90-101.

*Geerhardus Vos, "'Covenant' or 'Testament'?" *BM* 2 (1914) 205-225.

*†Anonymous, "On the Meaning of the Word 'Created,' in Genesis," *MMBR* 21 (1806) 221-224.

*A. G. Hebert and N[orman] H. Snaith, "A Study of the Words 'Curse' and 'Righteousness'," *BTr* 3 (1952) 111-116.

D

*Julian Morgenstern, "The Etymological History of the Three Hebrew Synonyms for 'to Dance.' ḤGG, ḤLL, and KRR, and their Cultural Significance," *JAOS* 36 (1916) 321-332.

James Robertson, "The 'Dawn' in Hebrew," *Exp, 8th Ser.,* 3 (1912) 86-96.

*J. P. J. Olivier, "The concept *day* in Nahum and Habakkuk," *OTW* 12 (1969) 71-74.

*L. H. Muirhead, "The Terms 'Life' and 'Death' in the Old Testament and the New," *OSHTP* (1904-05) 34-44.

*S[igmund] Mowinckel, "Drive and/or Ride in the O.T.," *VT* 12 (1962) 278-299.

M. D. Goldman, "Lexicographic Notes on Exegesis: Euphemism for Dying and Its Implications," *ABR* 1 (1951) 64-65.

E

Anonymous, "Ear. As an obsolete word in the Bible," *ET* 20 (1908-09) 410.

Richard   Roberts,   "Ear,"   *ET*   20   (1908-09)   475.

*J[ulian] Morgenstern, "The King-God among the Western Semites and the Meaning of Epiphanes," *VT* 10 (1960) 138-197.

F. Rendall, "History of the Word 'Eternal'," *Exp, 3rd Ser.,* 7 (1888) 266-278.

Joseph Angus, "Of Scripture Terms Used to expresss 'eternity,' with Special Reference to the Future Punishment," *Exp, 3rd Ser.,* 6 (1887) 274-286.

*Norman Walker, "'Adam' and 'Eve' and 'Adon'," *ZAW* 74 (1962) 66-68.

Stanislas Lyonnet, "Scriptural meaning of 'expiation'," *TD* 10 (1962) 227-232.

F

*Edward A. Lawrence, "Faith and Trust," *PQPR* 6 (1877) 695-702.

Anonymous, "The Meaning of 'Faith'," *HR* 50 (1905) 42.

George G. Findlay, "Faith: a Bible Study," *LQHR* 107 (1907) 193-208.

Frank R. Neff Jr., "An Exegetical Theology of Faith," *TUSR* 3 (1952-54) 1-13.

L[eande]r S. K[eyser], "Notes on the Word 'Firmament'," *CFL, 3rd Ser.,* 33 (1927) 494-496.

Samuel E. Loewenstamm, "The Development of the Term 'First' in the Semitic Languages," *Tarbiz* 24 (1954-55) #3, I.

*Ernest D[eWitt] Burton, "Spirit, Soul, and Flesh. I. ΠΝΕῖΜΑ, ΨΥΧΗ', and ΣΆΡΞ in Greek Writers from Homer to Aristotle," *AJT* 17 (1913) 563-598.

*Ernest D[e Witt] Burton, "Spirit, Soul and Flesh II. רוּחַ, נֶפֶשׁ, and בָּשָׂר in the Old Testament," *AJT* 18 (1914) 59-80.

*Ernest D[eWitt] Burton, "Spirit, Soul, and Flesh. III. ΠΝΕῖΜΑ, ΨΥΧΗ', and ΣΆΡΞ in Greek Writers from Epicurus to Arius Didymus," *AJT* 18 (1914) 395-414, 571-599.

*Ernest D[eWitt] Burton, "Spirit, Soul, and Flesh. IV. ΠΝΕῖΜΑ, ΨΥΧΗ', and ΣΆΡΞ in Greek Writers of the Early Christian Period and in Jewish-Greek Literature," *AJT* 20 (1916) 390-413.

*Leonard Johnston, "Scripture Words—II: World and Flesh," *LofS* 16 (1961-62) 237-244.

W. P. Paterson, "The Fools of the Bible," *ET* 11 (1899-1900) 13-16.

G

Calvin Thomas, "The Derivation of the Word 'God'," *OC* 4 (1890-91) 2306-2307.

*E[phraim] A. Speiser, "'Coming' and 'Going' at the 'City' Gate," *BASOR* #144 (1956) 20-23.

*Geoffrey Evans, "'Coming' and 'Going' at the City Gate—A Discussion of Professor Speiser's Paper," *BASOR* #150 (1958) 28-33.

*Paul Haupt, "The Hebrew Terms for Gold and Silver," *JAOS* 43 (1923) 116-127.

*Leonard Johnston, "Scripture Words—III: Holiness, Justice, Truth and Grace," *LofS* 16 (1961-62) 381-387. [Grace, pp. 386-387]

H

Eb. Nestle, "Hallelujah," *ET* 22 (1910-11) 564-565.

*Jos[eph] A. Seiss, "Some Sacred Words. The Triasgion, The Hallelujah, and The Amen," *LCR* 16 (1897) 190-202.

Thomas J. Packard, "The Meaning of Heart in the Old Testament," *PER* 2 (1888-89) 82-85.

Edward Mack, "The Heart in the Bible," *USR* 28 (1916-17) 40-49.

*E. C. Blackman, "A Study of the Words 'Thought', 'Mind', and 'Heart'," *BTr* 4 (1953) 36-40.

*Norman [H.] Snaith, "Heart and Soul and Spirit," *PQL* 3 (1957) 19-24.

*E. R. Lacheman, "The Meaning of the Words *Hebrew-Israel* in the Light of Biblical Archaeology," *JBL* 65 (1946) iv.

Julius Lewy, "Origin and Signification of the Biblical Term 'Hebrew'," *HUCA* 28 (1957) 1-13.

J. P. McLean, "The Word 'Hell' in Various Languages," *UQGR, N.S.,* 25 (1888) 450-465.

Hans Gustav Güterbock, "Toward a Definition of the Term 'Hittite'," *Oriens* 10 (1957) 233-239.

Agar J. Beet, "Holiness, Symbolic and Real," *LQHR* 112 (1909) 268-287.

*Leonard Johnston, "Scripture Words—III: Holiness, Justice, Truth and Grace," *LofS* 16 (1961-62) 381-387. [Holiness, pp. 381-383]

*Jos[eph] A. Seiss, "Some Sacred Words. The Trisagion, The Hallelujah, and The Amen," *LCR* 16 (1897) 190-202. *[Holy, Holy, Holy]*

William Scott, "Hosanna," *ET* 54 (1942-43) 167.

Ch. Callow, "'House'," *ET* 26 (1914-15) 378.

G. Herbert King, "'House'," *ET* 26 (1914-15) 378.

I

*[W. B.] Stevenson, "The Use of the Name 'Israel' in Old Testament Times. *In Isaiah and Micah*," *GUOST* 3 (1907-12) 51-52.

*D. F. Roberts, "The Usage in Samuel, Kings, Amos, and Hosea," *GUOST* 3 (1907-12) 52-53. *[Use of the Name 'Israel']*

*W[illiam] F[oxwell] Albright, "The Names 'Israel' and 'Judah' with an Excursus on the Etymology of Tôdâh and Tôrâh," *JBL* 46 (1927) 151-185. [A. The Name 'Israel', pp. 154-168]

*E. R. Lacheman, "The Meaning of the Words *Hebrew-Israel* in the Light of Biblical Archaeology," *JBL* 65 (1946) iv.

Norman   Walker,   "Israel,"   *VT*   4   (1954)   434.

J

*Anonymous,   "The   Name   Jerusalem,"   *ONTS*   13   (1891)   120.

A[lbert] T. Clay, "The Amorite Name Jerusalem," *JPOS* 1 (1920-21) 28-32.

*J[ames] A. Montgomery, "Paronomasias on the Name Jerusalem," *JBL* 49 (1930) 277-282.

*D. W. Amram, "A Further Example of Paronomasia on Jerusalem," *JBL* 49 (1930) 429.

*Samuel Krauss, "Zion and Jerusalem. A Linguistic and Historical Study," *PEQ* 77 (1945) 15-33.

Eb. Nestle, "'Jew,' 'Jewess,' 'Jewish,' 'Jewry'," *ET* 13 (1901-02) 432.

J.   A.   Cross,   "'Jew,'   'Jewry'," *ET*   13   (1901-02)   477.

J. H. Adeney, "Sheeny," *ET* 28 (1916-17) 426-427. *[Origin of the name 'Jew']*

*Geo. H. Schodde, "Biblical Research Notes. The Name 'Jordan'," *ColTM* 18 (1898) 255-256.

*W[illiam] F[oxwell] Albright, "The Names 'Israel' and 'Judah' with an Excursus on the Etymology of Tôdâh and Tôrâh," *JBL* 46 (1927) 151-185. [B. The Name 'Judah', pp. 168-178]

*Donald A. McKenzie, "The Judge in Israel," *VT* 17 (1967) 118-121.

A.   van   Selms,   "The   Title   'Judge'," *OTW*   2   (1959)   41-50.

*John L. McKenzie, "The Judge of All the Earth," *Way* 2 (1926) 209-218. *[Justice]*

*Wallace I. Wolverton, "The King's 'Justice' in Pre-Exilic Israel," *ATR* 41 (1959) 276-286. [The *Shafaṭ* Function of Rule; The Early Period; The King's *Mishhpaṭ;* The Eighth Century Prophets and *Mishpaṭ* and Messiah; Conclusions]

*Zeev W. Falk, "Two Symbols of Justice," *VT* 10 (1960) 72-74.

*Leonard Johnston, "Scripture Words—III: Holiness, Justice, Truth and Grace," *LofS* 16 (1961-62) 381-387. [Justice, pp. 383-385]

K

Thos. Laurie, "The Word 'Kidron'," *AJSL* 2 (1885-86) 176-177.

*Crawford H. Toy, "The King in Jewish Post-exilian Writings," *JBL* 18 (1899) 156-166.

R[obert] D[ick] Wilson, "The Words for 'Kingdom' in the Old Testament," *PTR* 23 (1925) 133-137.

Paul Haupt, "To Know = To have Sexual Commerce," *JBL* 34 (1915) 71-76.

*John R. Mackay, "'Knowledge' and 'Revelation' in Hebrew," *Exp, 9th Ser.,* 1 (1924) 139-140.

L

G. Buchanan Gray, "The Misuse of the Term 'Lamb' in the E.V.," *Exp, 8th Ser.,* 22 (1921) 241-262.

*Sheldon H. Blank, "The Septuagint Renderings of Old Testament Terms for Law," *HUCA* 7 (1930) 259-283.

*Eugene A. Nida, "The Translation of 'Leprosy', a brief contribution to the discussion," *BTr* 11 (1960) 80-81.

*Charles F. Pfeiffer, "Lotan and Leviathan," *EQ* 32 (1960) 208-211.

*L. H. Muirhead, "The Terms 'Life' and 'Death' in the Old Testament and the New," *OSHTP* (1904-05) 34-44.

*William Cosser, "The Meaning of 'Life' *(Ḥayyim)* in Proverbs, Job, and Ecclesiastes," *GUOST* 15 (1953-54) 48-53.

*James Wood, "The Idea of Life in the Book of Job," *GUOST* 18 (1959-60) 29-37.

*James D. Roche, "Light as a Figure and Symbol in St. John and in the Old Testament," *MH* 15 (1960) #2, 18-29.

Anonymous, "Longsuffering," *ET* 12 (1900-01) 330-332.

Philip Johnson, "A Biblical Word Study of the Concept of Love," *GR* 1 (1955) 23-29.

Douglas N. Morgan, "Love in the Hebrew Bible," *Jud* 5 (1956) 31-45.

*Maurice G. Hansen, "The Name Lucifer," *ONTS* 4 (1884-85) 71-73.

M

[Robert Baker] Girdlestone, "Hebrew Words for Man," *ONTS* 1 (1882) 72.

*P. A. Nordell, "Old Testament Word Studies: 'Man and Woman'," *ONTS* 8 (1888-89) 6-10. ['Îsh—'Îshshah; 'Ādhām; 'ᵉnôsh; Gĕbhĕr; Mᵉthîm; Nă'ăr; Bachûr; Zēqēn]

*Paul Haupt, "Biblical Studies," *AJP* 43 (1922) 238-249. [8. The Etymology of Manna, Ex. 16:15, pp. 247-249]

James Wells, "Mercy. An Exegetical Study," *ET* 11 (1899-1900) 409-411, 452-454, 559-562.

*Archibald Duff, "The Rise of the Title 'Messiah'," *Exp, 8th Ser.,* 25 (1923) 205-215.

Edward J. Hamilton, "Historical Development of the Word Messiah," *HR* 48 (1904) 39-41.

W. F. Stinespring, "The Term *Messianic* in the Old Testament," *JBL* 57 (1938) vii.

*E. C. Blackman, "A Study of the Words 'Thought', 'Mind', and 'Heart'," *BTr* 4 (1953) 36-40.

*James Moffatt, "Twisted Sayings—Mizpah," *HR* 78 (1919) 27.

Raymond E. Brown, "The Pre-Christian Semitic Concept of 'Mystery'," *CBQ* 20 (1958) 417-443.

N

*E[phraim] A. Speiser, "'People' and 'Nation' of Israel," *JBL* 79 (1960) 157-163.

Anonymous, "Newness," *ET* 12 (1900-01) 233-234.

*Eduard König, "Is There a Rhetorical Use of 'Not' in Hebrew?" *ET* 12 (1900-01) 44-45.

O

*A. M. Walmsley, "'Worship' and 'Obeisance' in the Bible," *ET* 24 (1912-13) 478.

*G. T. Manley, "'Officers' in the Old Testament," *EQ* 29 (1957) 149-156.

J. Murphy, "'Oriental'," *JMUEOS* #23 (1942) 9-11.

*Paul Haupt, "Critical Notes. II. The Hebrew Names for 'Ostrich'," *AJSL* 32 (1915-16) 142-143.

P

*Leonard Prestige, "Paradise," *Theo* 10 (1925) 141-149.

H. G. G. Hertklots, "The Pastor in the Bible," *LQHR* 181 (1956) 4-7.

W. Meikle, "The Vocabulary of 'Patience,' in the Old Testament," *Exp, 8th Ser.,* 19 (1920) 219-225.

*Eric Burrows, "Notes on the Pearl in Biblical Literature," *JTS* 42 (1941) 53-64.

*E[phraim] A. Speiser, "'People' and 'Nation' of Israel," *JBL* 79 (1960) 157-163.

F. Mason, "Scriptural View of Perfection," *CRB* 9 (1844) 232-255.

P. le Page Renouf, "The Name of Pharaoh," *SBAP* 15 (1892-93) 421-422.

*Michael C. Astour, "The Origin of the Terms 'Canaan,' 'Phoenician,' and 'Purple'," *JNES* 24 (1965) 346-350.

*Kathryn Sullivan, "The God of All Power," *Way* 3 (1963) 247-256. *[Power]*

Anonymous, "The Word 'Prophet'," *ONTS* 11 (1890) 246.

V. H. Hegstrom, "The Term 'Prophet'," *AQ* 4 (1925) 228-231.

*Michael C. Astour, "The Origin of the Terms 'Canaan,' 'Phoenician,' and 'Purple'," *JNES* 24 (1965) 346-350.

Lysander Dickerman, "On the etymology and synonyms of the word *Pyramid*," *JAOS* 15 (1893) xxv-xxxi.

R

Anonymous, "Refreshing. A Study in the Religious Language of the Bible," *ET* 13 (1901-02) 463-464.

*W. I. Distant, "On the Term 'Religion' as used in Anthropology," *JRAI* 6 (1876-77) 60-68. (Discussion, pp. 68-70)

Shinya Nomoto, "Renewal in the Old Testament," *NEAJT* 2 (1969) #1, 97-109.

Benjamin B. Warfield, "On the Biblical Notion of 'Renewal'," *PTR* 9 (1911) 242-267.

*Eb. Nestle, "Rest and Comfort," *ET* 10 (1898-99) 48.

Anonymous, "A Note on 'Rest'," *ET* 24 (1912-13) 110-111.

*John R. Mackay, "'Knowledge' and 'Revelation' in Hebrew," *Exp, 9th Ser.,* 1 (1924) 139-140.

*S[igmund] Mowinckel, "Drive and/or Ride in the O.T.," *VT* 12 (1962) 278-299.

*A. G. Hebert and N[orman] H. Snaith, "A Study of the Words 'Curse' and 'Righteousness'," *BTr* 3 (1952) 111-116.

*Larry R. Thornton, "God's Standards for the Kings of Judah," *CCBQ* 11 (1968) #3, 16-30. [Righteousness in the Old Testament, pp. 18-21]

*Toyozo W. Nakarai, "The Prophetic Concept of Righteousness," *SQ/E* 13 (1952) 51-57.

S

H. F. Talbot, "On the Origin of the Word Sabbath," *JSL, 3rd Ser.,* 5 (1857) 175.

W. W., "On the Origin of the Word 'Sabbath'," *JSL, 3rd Ser.,* 5 (1857) 440-442.

H. Hirschfeld, "Remarks on the Etymology of 'Sabbath'," *JRAS* (1896) 353-359.

*T. Witton Davies, "Some Notes on Hebrew Matters, Literary and Otherwise," *R&E* 9 (1912) 551-556. [Anent Some Technical Terms for Old Testament Sacrifice, pp. 553-555]

T. Paul Verghese, "Salvation. Meanings of a Biblical Word," *IRM* 57 (1968) 399-416. [I. The Old Testament, pp. 400-407; II. The Inter-Testament Period, pp. 407-411; III. The New Testament Concept of Salvation, pp. 411-416]

Howard Crosby, "Light on Important Texts. No. IX," *HR* 5 (1880-81) 465-466. *[Sanctuary]*

*Joseph Offord, "Archaeological Notes on Jewish Antiquities. LVII. *The Word for Satrap*," *PEFQS* 51 (1919) 138-139.

J. Donovan, "The Word 'Scripture' and Its Synonyms," *IER, 5th Ser.,* 29 (1927) 462-480.

*[James S.] Blackwell, "Shemitic or Semitic?" *PAPA* 13 (1881) 27-29. *[Bound with Transactions but paged separately]*

*T. T. Titus, "The Shekinah," *ER* 11 (1859-60) 344-369.

*Herbert H. Gowen, "'Sound' Terms and 'Shine' Terms (As illustrated in the Hebrew Vocabulary)," *JSOR* 5 (1921) 70-80.

*Edgar J. Goodspeed, "The Shulammite," *AJSL* 50 (1933-34) 102-104.

*H. H. Rowley, "The Meaning of 'The Shulammite'," *AJSL* 56 (1939) 84-91.

Edward Malatesta, "The Silent Word," *Way* 7 (1967) 217-223. [Silence in the O.T., pp. 218-221]

*Paul Haupt, "The Hebrew Terms for Gold and Silver," *JAOS* 43 (1923) 116-127.

James Stalker, "Names for Sin," *Exp, 4th Ser.,* 10 (1894) 214-219.

Byron H. DeMent, "Bible Terms for Sin," *SWJT* 1 (1917) #4, 25-33.

*Samuel A. B. Mercer, "Words for Sin in the Old Testament," *ATR* 2 (1919-20) 234-236.

B. A. Copass, "Hebrew Terminology for Sin," *SWJT* 8 (1924) #1, 65-68.

Kenneth Grayston, "A Study of the Word 'Sin' With its correlatives *Sinner, Err, Fault, Guilt, Iniquity, Offence, Malefactor, Mischief, Perverse, Transgress, Trespass, Wicked, Wrong,* Part I - Old Testament," *BTr* 4 (1953) 138-140.

*Gnana Robinson, "A Terminological Study of the Idea of Sin in the Old Testament," *IJT* 18 (1969) 112-123.

*David Noel Freedman, "The Slave of Yahweh," *WW* 10 (1959) #1, 1-19. *[Slave]*

*Edwin [M.] Yamauchi, "Slaves of God," *BETS* 9 (1966) 31-50. [The Word 'Slave' and the Translators of the King James Version, pp. 40-43]

*Robert E. Bailey, "Is 'Sleep' the Proper Biblical Term for the Intermediate State?" *ZNW* 55 (1964) 161-167.

Tayler Lewis, "Names for Soul," *BRCR, 3rd Ser.,* 6 (1850) 674-703.

*William H. Hodge, "Biblical Usage of 'Soul' and 'Spirit'," *PRR* 8 (1897) 251-266.

*Ernest D[eWitt] Burton, "Spirit, Soul, and Flesh. I. ΠΝΕῦΜΑ, ΨΥΧΗ΄, and Σ΄ΑΡΞ in Greek Writers from Homer to Aristotle," *AJT* 17 (1913) 563-598.

*Ernest D[e Witt] Burton, "Spirit, Soul and Flesh II. רוּחַ נֶפֶשׁ, and בָּשָׂר in the Old Testament," *AJT* 18 (1914) 59-80.

*Ernest D[eWitt] Burton, "Spirit, Soul, and Flesh. III. *ΠΝΕῖΜΑ, ΨΥΧΗ΄,* and *Σ΄ΑΡΞ* in Greek Writers from Epicurus to Arius Didymus," *AJT* 18 (1914) 395-414, 571-599.

*Ernest D[eWitt] Burton, "Spirit, Soul, and Flesh. IV. *ΠΝΕῖΜΑ, ΨΥΧΗ΄,* and *Σ΄ΑΡΞ* in Greek Writers of the Early Christian Period and in Jewish-Greek Literature," *AJT* 20 (1916) 390-413.

W. E. Staples, "The 'Soul' in the Old Testament," *AJSL* 44 (1926-27) 145-176.

*Norman [H.] Snaith, "Heart and Soul and Spirit," *PQL* 3 (1957) 19-24.

Edmund Hill, "'Soul' in the Bible," *LofS* 13 (1958-59) 530-537.

*Willⁱ ım H. Hodge, "Biblical Usage of 'Soul' and 'Spirit'," *PRR* 8 (1897) 251-266.

J. B. Burkhart, "The Spirit and the Spirits," *HR* 94 (1927) 220-222.

*Ernest D[eWitt] Burton, "Spirit, Soul, and Flesh. I. *ΠΝΕῖΜΑ, ΨΥΧΗ΄,* and *Σ΄ΑΡΞ* in Greek Writers from Homer to Aristotle," *AJT* 17 (1913) 563-598.

*Ernest D[e Witt] Burton, "Spirit, Soul and Flesh II. רוּחַ נֶפֶשׁ, and בָּשָׂר in the Old Testament," *AJT* 18 (1914) 59-80.

*Ernest D[eWitt] Burton, "Spirit, Soul, and Flesh. III. *ΠΝΕῖΜΑ, ΨΥΧΗ΄,* and *Σ΄ΑΡΞ* in Greek Writers from Epicurus to Arius Didymus," *AJT* 18 (1914) 395-414, 571-599.

*Ernest D[eWitt] Burton, "Spirit, Soul, and Flesh. IV. *ΠΝΕῖΜΑ, ΨΥΧΗ΄,* and *Σ΄ΑΡΞ* in Greek Writers of the Early Christian Period and in Jewish-Greek Literature," *AJT* 20 (1916) 390-413.

*Peter May, "The Self and the Spirit," *IJT* 6 (1957) 131-142. *[Spirit]*

*Norman [H.] Snaith, "Heart and Soul and Spirit," *PQL* 3 (1957) 19-24.

*Herbert H. Gowen, "'Sound' Terms and 'Shine' Terms (As illustrated in the Hebrew Vocabulary)," *JSOR* 5 (1921) 70-80.

T

*Σ., "'Table' or 'Altar'?" *BFER* 16 (1867) 625-630.

Roy B. Zuck, "Hebrew Words for 'Teach'," *BS* 121 (1964) 228-235.

Jesse W. Ball, "The Biblical Use of the Word Temptation," *LCR* 24 (1905) 551-556.

*Harry A. Hoffner, "The Linguistic Origins of Teraphim," *BS* 124 (1967) 230-238.

Leonard Johnston, "Scripture Terms—I: Testament," *LofS* 16 (1961-62) 17-22.

*Geerhardus Vos, "'Covenant' or 'Testament'?" *BM* 2 (1914) 205-225.

*M. D. Goldman, "Lexicographical Notes on Exegesis. (2) 'Thinking' in Hebrew," *ABR* 1 (1951) 135-137.

*E. C. Blackman, "A Study of the Words 'Thought', 'Mind' and 'Heart'," *BTr* 4 (1953) 36-40.

Willis J. Beecher, "Notes on Hebrew Words in the Old Testament," *HR* 33 (1897) 541-544. [I. The Word 'Torah' in the Book of Job; II. The Word 'Torah' in the Book of Proverbs]

Anonymous, "The Word 'Torah' in Job and Proverbs," *CFL, O.S.,* 1 (1897) 191-192.

Willis J. Beecher, *"Torah:* A Word-Study in the Old Testament," *JBL* 24 (1905) 1-16.

A. H. Sayce, "What is Meant by the Torah?" *CFL, 3rd Ser.,* 12 (1910) 40-44.

*W[illiam] F[oxwell] Albright, "The Names 'Israel' and 'Judah' with an Excursus on the Etymology of Tôdâh and Tôrâh," *JBL* 46 (1927) 151-185.

Robert Eisler, "Loan-Words in Semitic Languages Meaning 'Town'," *Antiq* 13 (1939) 449-455.

*Leonard Johnston, "Scripture Words—III: Holiness, Justice, Truth and Grace," *LofS* 16 (1961-62) 381-387. [Truth, pp. 385-386]

*Henri Blocker, "The Biblical Concept of Truth," *Them* 6 (1969) #1, 47-61. *(Trans. by H. O. J. Brown)*

*Edward A. Lawrence, "Faith and Trust," *PQPR* 6 (1877) 695-702.

*David Künstlinger, "The Numeral 'Two' in the Semitic Language," *JQR* 10 (1897-98) 462-469.

U

*D. Kaufmann, "What was the Word for 'Unhappy' in Later Hebrew?" *JQR* 1 (1888-89) 442-444.

V

Raymond H. Swartzbak, "A Biblical Study of the Word 'Vengeance'," *Interp* 6 (1952) 451-457.

L[eander] S. K[eyser], "The Hebrew Words for Virgin," *CFL, 3rd Ser.,* 32 (1926) 409-410.

W

Edmund   Steimle,   "Wait,"   *USQR*   22   (1966-67)   139-145.

Norman Kerr, "Wines: Scriptural and Ecclesiastical," *CM* 13 (1881) 321-335; 4 (1882) 46-56. [The Old Testament, pp. 329-332] *[Words Translated 'Wine' in the Bible]*

R. Butim, "Scriptural Use of the Word 'Wine'," *AER* 52 (1915) 149-162.

Francis Cosgrove, "'Wisdom, Not Weapons...'," *MH* 2 (1945-46) #4, 5-9.

*John Warwick Montgomery, "Wisdom as Gift. *The Wisdom Concept in Relation to Biblical Messianism,"* *Interp* 16 (1962) 43-57. [The Religious Meanings of Wisdom, pp. 43-46]

T. Witton Davies, "The Words 'Witch' and 'Witchcraft'," *Exp, 8th Ser.,* 7 (1914) 19-29.

*P. A. Nordell, "Old Testament Word Studies: 'Man and Woman'," *ONTS* 8 (1888-89) 6-10. ['Îsh—'Îshshah; 'Ādhām; 'enôsh; Gĕbhĕr; Methîm; Nă'ăr; Bachûr; Zĕqēn]

Gregory Manly, "'Work' in the Bible," *BibT* #44 (1969) 3062-3067.

William H. Bates, "The World: An Inductive Exegesis and an Exposition," *BS* 68 (1911) 105-131.

*Leonard Johnston, "Scripture Words—II: World and Flesh," *LofS* 16 (1961-62) 237-244.

*A. M. Walmsley, "'Worship' and 'Obeisance' in the Bible," *ET* 24 (1912-13) 478.

Y

*Paul E. Kretzmann, "The word 'year' in the Book of Genesis," *CTM* 4 (1933) 216.

§525 *3.3.3.2.1.6 Phrases Keyed to English*

*H. C. Ackerman, "The Principle of Differentiation Between 'The Word of the Lord' and 'The Angel of the Lord'," *AJSL* 37 (1920-21) 145-149.

*E. Robertson, "The Apple of the Eye in the Masoretic Text," *JTS* 38 (1937) 56-59.

Lewis Bayles Paton, "The Meaning of the Expression 'Between Two Walls'," *JBL* 25 (1906) 1-13.

G. Buchanan Gray, "'Breach for Breach,' and 'The Breach of His People'," *ET* 26 (1914-15) 347-351.

*H[ope] W. Hogg, "Dan to Beersheba: The Origin and Significance of the Phrase," *OSHTP* (1897-98) 31-34.

*H[ope] W. Hogg, "'Dan to Beersheba': The Literary History of the Phrase and the Historical Problems it Raises," *Exp, 5th Ser.,* 8 (1898) 411-421.

*W. W. Crump, "A Day's Journey," *Exp, 6th Ser.,* 2 (1900) 211-215.

Thos. Laurie, "Devise Evil," *AJSL* 5 (1888-89) 196.

H. O. A. Keinath, "The Term 'Fear of God' in the Old Testament. (A Linguistic Study)," *CTM* 19 (1948) 93-97.

*Samuel E. Loewenstamm, "'From this Time forth and for evermore'," *Tarbiz* 32 (1962-63) #4, I.

Leon Liebreich, "The Expression 'God Drew Us Near (Unto)' in Various Liturgical Contexts," *JQR, N.S.,* 33 (1942-43) 461-469.

*G. Elliot Smith, "'Heart and Reins' in Mummification," *JMUEOS* #1 (1911) 41-44. [Supplementary note, pp. 45-48]

*H. Wheeler Robinson, "'Heart and Reins' in the Ancient Literatures of the Nearer East. Notes on Biblical Usage from a letter of H. Wheeler Robinson," *JMUEOS* #1 (1911) 55-56.

*M. A. Canney, "'Heart and Reins.' Further Notes on Hebrew Idioms," *JMUEOS* #1 (1911) 93-94.

Thos. Laurie, "House of Their Fathers," *AJSL* 5 (1888-89) 196.

*James Barr, "The Image of God in the Book of Genesis—A Study of Terminology," *BJRL* 51 (1968-69) 11-26. *[Image of God]*

*H. L. Ginsberg, "'King of Kings' and 'Lord of Lords'," *AJSL* 57 (1940) 71-74.

*Joseph Offord, "Archaeological Notes on Jewish Antiquities. XXV. *The Title 'King of Kings'*," *PEFQS* 48 (1916) 194-196.

*Joseph Offord, "Archaeological Notes on Jewish Antiquities. XXVII. *The Title 'King of Persia'*," *PEFQS* 49 (1917) 181-183.

*Robert Dick Wilson, "The Title 'King of Persia' in the Scriptures," *PTR* 15 (1917) 90-145. [(I) The Forms and Use of the Titles of the Persian Kings in Dates; II. Use of the Title 'King of Persia' in Decrees, Commands and Grants, A. Evidence of Royal Inscriptions, B. Evidence of Titles Used by Subjects, C. Evidence of Titles Used by Foreigners, D. Indirect Evidence for the Title 'King of Persia'; Conclusions]

*A. van Selms, "The Origin of the Title 'The King's Friend'," *JNES* 16 (1957) 188-122.

*A[nson] F. Rainey, "'The King's Son' at Ugarit and among the Hittites," *Lěš* 33 (1968-69) #4, 3.

*C. L. E. Hoopmann, "The Meaning of the Term, 'The Last Times'," *AusTR* 7 (1936) 7-12.

*James Edward Hogg, "'Living Water'—'Water of Life'," *AJSL* 42 (1925-26) 131-133.

*H. L. Ginsberg, "'King of Kings' and 'Lord of Lords'," *AJSL* 57 (1940) 71-74.

*Raphael Hallevy, "Man of God," *JNES* 17 (1958) 237-244.

*Otto Eissfeldt, "'My God' in the Old Testament," *EQ* 19 (1947) 7-20.

*William L. Holladay, "On Every High Hill and Under Every Green Tree," *VT* 11 (1961) 170-176.

*Jacob J. Rabinowitz, "Demotic Papyri of the Ptolemaic Period and Jewish Sources," *VT* 7 (1957) 398-400. [a."On the Head of", pp. 398-399]

F. F. North, "The Expression the Oracle of Yahweh as an Aid to Critical Analysis," *JBL* 71 (1952) x.

P[aul] Haupt, "The Biblical Phrase *To Ordain a Lamp,*" *JBL* 25 (1916) 319.

A. [James] Orr, "The Seventy Years of Babylon," *VT* 6 (1956) 304-306.

C. F. Whitley, "The Term Seventy Years Captivity," *VT* 4 (1954) 60-72.

C. F. Whitley, "The Seventy Years Desolation—A Rejoinder," *VT* 7 (1957) 416-418.

Richard de Bary, "The Titles 'Son of God' and 'The Son of God'," *HR* 48 (1904) 437-438.

*Stephen H. Stackpole, "Sons of God. A Study of the Scriptural Uses of the Title," *BQR* 2 (1880) 315-333.

Tryon Edwards, "'The Sons of God'," *HR* 25 (1893) 547-548.

*Cornelius Walker, "Divine Sonship, Sons of God, Bene Elohim," *HR* 39 (1900) 447-449.

*Gerald Cooke, "The Sons of (the) God(s)," *ZAW* 76 (1964) 22-47.

*James G. Williams, "The Prophetic 'Father': A Brief Explanation of the term 'Sons of the Prophets'," *JBL* 85 (1966) 344-348.

*Anonymous, "What is the Scriptural Meaning of the Phrase *'The Spirit of God'*," *CD* 1 (1813) 178-180, 206-210.

*Alexander M'Nair, "'Thus Saith Jahweh'," *ET* 32 (1920-21) 508-509.

H. Wheeler Robinson, "The Psychology and Metaphysic of 'Thus saith Yahweh'. (A paper read before the Society for Old Testament Study, meeting in London, January 3rd, 1923.)," *ZAW* 41 (1923) 1-15.

G. Vermes, "The Torah is Light," *VT* 8 (1958) 436-438.

Brevard S. Childs, "A Study of the Formula, 'Until This Day'," *JBL* 82 (1963) 279-292.

J. G. Thomson, "Wait on the Lord," *ET* 65 (1953-54) 196-198.

*James Edward Hogg, "'Living Water'—'Water of Life'," *AJSL* 42 (1925-26) 131-133.

*Edward J. Kissane, "'Who Maketh Lightnings for the Rain'," *JTS, N.S.*, 3 (1952) 214-216.

*E. Power, "A Study of the Hebrew Expresssion 'Wide of Heart'," *B* 1 (1920) 59-75.

N. L. F., "On the Phrase, 'The Word of God'," *CE* 54 (1853) 277-284.

*R. H. Fuller, "The Word of God," *Theo* 47 (1944) 267-271.

*Richard C. Caemmerer, "A Concordance Study of the Concept 'Word of God'," *CTM* 22 (1951) 170-186. [II. Word: Old Testament, pp. 172-179]

*H. C. Ackerman, "The Principle of Differentiation Between 'The Word of the Lord' and 'The Angel of the Lord'," *AJSL* 37 (1920-21) 145-149.

Frank North, "The Origin and Signification of the Phrase 'The Word of the Lord'," *JBL* 70 (1951) v.

*C. R. Milley, "The Word of Yahweh—Its Implications in OT Prophecy," *JBL* 71 (1952) x.

§526 *3.3.3.2.1.7 Moabite*

F. I. Andersen, "Moabite Syntax," *Or, N.S.,* 35 (1966) 81-120. [Table of Contents, pp. 119-120; Index of Words discussed, p. 120]

§527 *3.3.3.2.1.8 Phoenician, including Carthaginian*

*Richard Cull, "A ח Conjugation, such as exists in Assyrian, shown to be a character of early Shemitic Speech, by its vestiges found in the Hebrew, Phoenician, Aramaic, and Arabic Languages," *SBAT* 2 (1873) 83-109.

*Anonymous, "Hieroglyphics and Pre-Phœnician Script," *AAOJ* 16 (1894) 310-311.

Julius L. Siegel, "Epigraphical Notes," *AJSL* 46 (1929-30) 58-59. [אֱזְרֹם, Eshmunazar Inscription; אֶדְלָן, Tabnith Inscription]

*S[tephen] Langdon, "Adonis in Assyrian?" *RAAO* 27 (1930) 23-25.

Charles C[utler] Torrey, "A New Phoenican Grammar," *JAOS* 57 (1937) 397-410. *(Review)*

Julian Obermann, "Phoenician *yqtl 'nk,*" *JNES* 9 (1950) 94-100.

*Julian Obermann, "In the Wake of the Karatepe Discoveries," *Oriens* 3 (1950) 20-30. [1. Participles of the Yqtl Pattern Outside Phoenican, pp. 20-22]

John Wm. Wevers, "The Infinitive Absolute in the Phoenician Inscription of Azitawadd," *ZAW* 62 (1950) 316-317.

Frank M. Cross Jr. and David Noel Freedman, "The Pronominal Suffixes of the Third Person Singular in Phoenician," *JNES* 10 (1951) 228-230.

*Cyrus H. Gordon, "Marginal Notes on the Ancient Middle East," *JKF* 2 (1952-53) 50-61. [III. Phoenicana: a. The ancient vocalization of *gbl* 'Byblos', p. 53]

*J. Huesman, "Finite Uses of the Infinitive Absolute," *B* 37 (1956) 271-295. [1. Phoenician, pp. 271-280]

Stanley Gevirtz, "On the Etymology of the Phoenican Particle אשׁ,"*JNES* 16 (1957) 124-127.

*M[itchell] Dahood, "Punic *hkkbm 'l* and Isaiah 14,13," *Or, N.S.,* 34 (1965) 170-172.

*S. Segert, "Some Phoenician Etymologies of North African Toponyms," *OA* 5 (1966) 19-25.

*P. J. van Zijl, "'tb 'l in the Phoenician and Biblical literature," *OTW* 9 (1966) 159-162.

M[itchell] Dahood, "G. R. Driver and the Enclitic *mem* in Phoenican," *B* 49 (1968) 89-90.

*E. Y. Kutscher, "Canaanite (=*C*)—Hebrew (=*H*)—Phoenician (=*Ph*)—Aramaic (=*A*)—Mishnaic Hebrew (=*MH*)—Punic (=*P*)," *Lěš* 33 (1968-69) #2/3, n.p.n.

William R. Lane, "The Phoenician Dialect of Larnax Tes Lapethou," *BASOR* #194 (1969) 39-45.

C. Krahmalkov, "Observations on the Affixing of Possesive Pronouns in Punic," *RDSO* 44 (1969) 181-186.

§528 *3.3.3.2.1.9 Aramaic - General Studies*

*W. C. D., "The Syro-Arabian Languages and Literature," *CRB* 17 (1852) 393-424. [I.—The Aramean Languages. §1. *The Old Aramean,* pp. 397-402; §3. *The Aramaic Dialect of Northern Palestine,* pp.410-418]

*Richard Cull, "A ה Conjugation, such as exists in Assyrian, shown to be a character of early Shemitic Speech, by its vestiges found in the Hebrew, Phoenician, Aramaic, and Arabic Languages," *SBAT* 2 (1873) 83-109.

*†Edward Sachau, "The Cappadocian Cuneiform Inscription," *SBAP* 4 (1881-82) 117. [*Kutin* = *mule* // Aramaic כּוּדָנְיָא or כּוּדְנָא]

E. Kautzsch, "The Aramaic Language," *AJSL* 1 (1884-85) 98-115. *(Trans. by Charles R. Brown)* [Correction p. 132]

*W. O. Sproull, "The Native Language of Abraham," *AJSL* 4 (1887-88) 186.

*M[orris] Jastrow, "On transposed stems in the Talmudic, Hebrew, and Chaldaic," *JAOS* 14 (1890) xl-xlii.

*Fritz Hommel, "Assyriological Notes," *SBAP* 16 (1893-94) 209-212. [§2. 'Ass. *mindema* = Aram. *minda'am, meddem*, pp. 210-211]

Richard J. H. Gottheil, "The Judæo-Aramæ Dialect of Salamās," *JAOS* 15 (1893) 297-310.

*C. Levias, "A Grammar of the Aramaic Idiom Contained in the Babylonian Talmud," *AJSL* 13 (1896-97) 21-78, 118-139, 177-208; 14 (1897-98) 17-37, 106-128, 195-206, 252-266; 15 (1898-99) 242-243; 16 (1899-1900) 83-109.

*Fritz Hommel, "The Earliest Language of the Israelites," *ET* 12 (1900-01) 96.

Ed. König, "The Emphatic State in Aramaic," *AJSL* 17 (1900-01) 209-221.

*C. H. W. Johns, "The Divine Name Auršt in Assyrian," *ET* 16 (1904-05) 144.

Herbert Harry Powell, "The Supposed Hebraisms in the Grammar of the Biblical Aramaic," *UCPSP* 1 (1907-23) 1-55.

*Moses H. Segal, "Mišnaic Hebrew and Its Relation to Biblical Hebrew and to Aramaic," *JQR* 20 (1907-08) 647-737.

*Claude R. Conder, "Notes on New Discoveries," *PEFQS* 41 (1909) 266-275. [bar, p. 273]

*James A. Montgomery, "Brief Communications," *JBL* 33 (1914) 78-80. [3. TARWAH, Sachau's Elephantine Papyrus 7, p.80]

J. N. Epstein, "Notes on Post-Talmudic-Aramaic Lexicography I," *JQR, N.S.*, 5 (1914-15) 233-251.

P[aul] Haupt, "Aramaic *lĕhenâ*, Concubine,"*JBL* 35 (1916) 322-324.

*Moïse Schwab, "Amulets and Bowls with Magic Inscriptions," *JQR, N.S.*, 7 (1916-17) 619-628. [Aramaic Word List, pp. 624-627]

*Frank R. Blake, "Studies in Semitic Grammar," *JAOS* 35 (1917) 375-385. [II. The Etymology of the Aramaic particle אִיתַ, אִיתִי, pp. 377-381; III. The Multiplicative Numerals in Aramaic and Hebrew, pp. 381-382; IV. Mixed Constructions in Hebrew and Aramaic, pp. 382-385]

*Paul Haupt, "Aramaic *Bárrâ*, wilderness = Sumerian *Bar*," *JBL* 36 (1917) 254-255.

J. N. Epstein, "Notes on Post-Talmudic-Aramaic Lexicography II," *JQR, N.S.*, 12 (1921-22) 299-390. [Index of Words, pp. 289-390]

*James A. Montgomery, "Adverbial *Kulla* in Biblical Aramaic and Hebrew," *JAOS* 43 (1923) 391-395 [כְּלָא]

*David Yellin, "The Hippa'el-Nif-'al Conjunction in Hebrew and Aramaic; and the Assimilation of ח in the Hitpa'el Conjunction," *JPOS* 4 (1924) 85-106.

R[obert] Dick Wilson, "Aramaisms in the Old Testament,"*PTR* 23 (1925) 234-266.

‡*John A. Maynard, "Hebrew Studies since 1918 (including Biblical Aramaic)," *JSOR* 9 (1925) 32-40.

*G. R. Driver, "The Aramaic Language," *JBL* 45 (1926) 323-325.

*George A. Barton, "On the Anticipatory Pronominal Suffix Before the Genitive in Aramaic and Akkadian," *JAOS* 47 (1927) 260-262.

R[obert] D[ick] Wilson, "Foreign Words in the Old Testament as an Evidence of Historicity," *PTR* 26 (1928) 177-247. [Foreign Words in Biblical Aramaic; Foreign Words in Biblical Hebrew; Excursus on the Name "Cyrus"]

Maurice A. Canney, "'Eating the Pieces'," *JMUEOS* #14 (1929) 62-72. [Aramaic compound expression found in Daniel 3:8; 6:25 and the Targums, eg. Prov. 11:13; 20:19]

*Joseph Reider, "*Itba'* in Hebrew and Aramaic," *JQR, N.S.*, 24 (1933-34) 321-330.

H. Louis Ginsberg, "Aramaic Dialect Problems," *AJSL* 50 (1933-34) 1-9.

*C. Levias, "Enallage in the Bible," *AJSL* 50 (1933-34) 104-108. [Vowel-Obscuration in Hebrew and Aramaic; The Connecting Nûn]

*Charles C. Torrey, "Hebrew and Aramaic from Beth Shemesh," *JAOS* 55 (1935) 307-310.

H. L. Ginsberg, "Aramaic Dialect Problems. II," *AJSL* 52 (1935-36) 95-103.

*Cyrus H. Gordon, "Aramaic Incantation Bowls," *Or, N.S.,* 10 (1941) 116-141, 272-284, 339-360.

H. L. Ginsberg, "Aramaic Studies Today," *JAOS* 62 (1942) 229-238.

E. Rosenthal, "An Aramaic Root נְרַע?" *JMUEOS* #23 (1942) 20.

*Frank R. Blake, "Studies in Semitic Grammar IV," *JAOS* 66 (1946) 212-218. [3. Aramaic *z* for Semitic z_1 and *d*, pp. 217-218]

D. K. Andrews, "The Translations of the Aramaic *dî* in the Greek Bibles," *JBL* 66 (1947) 15-51.

*Raymond A. Bowman, "Arameans, Aramaic, and the Bible," *JNES* 7 (1948) 65-90.

*M. M. Bravmann, "Notes on the Forms of the Imperative in Hebrew and Aramaic," *JQR, N.S.,* 42 (1951-52) 51-56.

*Cyrus H. Gordon, "Marginal Notes on the Ancient Middle East," *JKF* 2 (1952-53) 50-61. [VII. Egypto-Semitica: Eg. *y* = Aram. הֹא, p. 57]

*Frank R. Blake, "Studies in Semitic Grammar V," *JAOS* 73 (1953) 7-16. [2. Additional note on Etymology of Aramaic *'ît*, pp. 7-8; 6. The Aramaic plural endings *-ôn* and *-ên*, pp. 11-12; 7. The mixing of forms of verbs tert.*j* and tert. ' in verbs tertiae infirmae in Aramaic, pp. 12-14; 8. The confusion in the forms of Aramaic nouns derived from monosyllabic and dissyllabic bases with short vowels, pp. 14-15; 9. Apparent exceptions in the treatment of the diphthong *aj* in Biblical Aramaic, p. 15; 10. Peculiar Hephel forms in Biblical Aramaic, p. 15; 11. Peculiar passive forms in Biblical Aramaic, pp. 15-16]

C[yrus] H. Gordon, "'Holy Wâw'? A Case of Contrasting Methodologies," *Or, N.S.,* 22 (1953) 415-416.

Jacob J. Rabinowitz, "The Meaning of the Phrase מחר או יום אחרן in the Aramaic Papyri," *JNES* 14 (1955) 59-60.

*P. Grelot, "On the Root עבק/עבץ in Ancient Aramaic and in Ugaritic," *JSS* 1 (1956) 202-205.

J[acob]. J. Rabinowitz, "The Meaning of תתב על מוזנא in Aramaic Papyri," *VT* 6 (1956) 104.

J[oseph] A. Fitzmyer, "The Syntax of *kl, kl'* in the Aramaic Texts from Egypt and in Biblical Aramaic," *B* 38 (1957) 170-184.

*S. C. Ylvisaker, "Some Old Testament Difficulties," *WLQ* 54 (1957) 262-264. [*Bar* in the expression *nashsh'qu bar,* Ps. 2:12, pp. 263-264]

*J[acob] J. Rabinowitz, "Grecisms and Greek Terms in the Aramaic Papyri," *B* 39 (1958) 77-82.

W. F. Stinespring, "History and Present Status of Aramaic Studies," *JAAR* 26 (1958) 298-303.

*H. L. Ginsberg, "Notes on Some Old Aramaic Texts," *JNES* 18 (1959) 143-149. [I. Biblical Texts, A. The Feminine Third Person Plural of the Finite Verb, pp. 143-145]

*J[acob] J. Rabinowitz, "More Grecisms in Aramaic Documents," *B* 41 (1960) 72-74.

Shelomo Morag, "On the Yeminite Tradition of Babylonian Aramaic," *Tarbiz* 30 (1960-61) #2, II.

Stanislav Segert, "Concerning the Methods of Aramaic Lexicography (Notes on the Dictionaries by I. N. Vinnikov)," *ArOr* 30 (1962) 505-506.

*Jonas C. Greenfield, "Studies in Aramaic Lexicography I," *JAOS* 82 (1962) 290-299. [1. ghk; 2. ṣbt; 3. 'bṭ; 4. kwṣ; Addendum]

*F. Charles Fensham, "The Wild Ass in the Aramean Treaty Between Barga'ayah and Mati'el,"*JNES* 22 (1963) 185-186 [Aramaic סרם]

*E. Y. Kutscher, "Aramaic Calque in Hebrew," *Tarbiz* 33 (1963-64) #2, II-III.

*H. J. Polotsky, "Aramaic, Syriac, and Ge'ez," *CNI* 15 (1964) #4, 19-26.

James G. Williams, "A Critical Note on the Aramaic Indefinite Plural of the Verb," *JBL* 83 (1964) 180-182.

*H. J. Polotsky, "Aramaic, Syriac, and Ge'ez," *JSS* 9 (1964) 1-10.

*B. Uffenheimer, "The 'Awakeners'—A Cultic Term from the Ancient Near East," *Lĕš* 30 (1965-66) #3. n.p.n. [עדרן]

T. Muraoka, "Notes on the Syntax of Biblical Aramaic," *JSS* 11 (1966) 151-167.

Stanislav Segert, "Contribution of Professor I. N. Vinnikov to Old Aramaic Lexicography," *ArOr* 35 (1967) 463-466.

R.   Degen,   "עבבן,"   *Lěš*   32   (1967-68)   #4,   n.p.n.

Jonas C. Greenfield, "Dialect Traits in Early Aramaic," *Lěš* 32 (1967-68) #4, n.p.n.

*A. Hurvitz, "The Chronological Significance of 'Aramaisms' in Biblical Hebrew," *IEJ* 18 (1968) 234-240.

*R[euven] Yaron, "Minutiae Aramaicae," *JSS* 13 (1968) 202-211. [I. "Silver *zuz* to the Ten"; II. An Allegation of Theft; III. Once More Pap. Kraeling 2; IV. Observations Minimae]

*E. Y. Kutscher, "Canaanite (=*C*)—Hebrew (=*H*)—Phoenician (=*Ph*)—Aramaic (=*A*)—Mishnaic Hebrew (=*MH*)—Punic (=*P*)," *Lěš* 33 (1968-69) #2/3, n.p.n.

*C. Rabin, "The Nature and Origin of the Šaf'el in Hebrew and Aramaic," *EI* 9 (1969) 138 *[English Summary]*

*J[onas] C. Greenfield, "The 'Periphrastic Imperative' in Aramaic and Hebrew," *IEJ* 19 (1969) 199-210.

M. Z. Kaddari, "Construct State and *dī*-Phrases in Imperial Aramaic," *PICSS* (1969) 102-115.

E. Y. Kutscher, "Two 'Passive' Constructions in Aramaic in the Light of Persian," *PICSS* (1969) 132-151.

*Samuel [E.] Loewenstamm, "Remarks upon the Infinitive Absolute in Ugaritic and Phoenician," *JANES* 2 (1969-70) 53.

M. Ben-Asher, "The Conjugation of the Aramaic Verb in 'Hălakot Pěsuqot'," *Lěš* 34 (1969-70) #4, n.p.n.

§529 *3.3.3.2.1.9.1 Samarian (Samaritan)*

*[Morris] Jastrow [Jr.], "On Assyrian and Samaritan," *JAOS* 13 (1889) cxlvii-cl.

Zĕ'ēv Ben-Ḥayyīm, "The Samaritan vowel-system and graphic representation," *ArOr* 22 (1954) 515-530.

A. Murtonen, "Materials for a Non-Masoretic Hebrew Grammar. II. An Etymological Vocabulary to the Samaritan Pentateuch," *SO* 24 (1960) 1-228. *[Part I published in Paul Kahle's* The Cairo Geniza*]*

*Ivan Tracy Kaufman, "A Note on the Place Name *Spr* and the Letter *Samek* in the Samaria Ostraca," *BASOR* #172 (1963) 60-61.

A. Murtonen, "Materials for a Non-Masoretic Hebrew Grammar. III. A Grammar of the Samaritan Dialect of Hebrew," *SO* 29 (1964) 3-368; part II follows p. 368 and numbered 1-113]

*E. Brønno, "Samaritan Hebrew and Origen's Secunda," *JSS* 13 (1968) 192-201.

Zĕ'ēv Ben-Ḥayyīm, "The Contribution of the Samaritan Inheritance to Research into the History of Hebrew," *PIASH* 3 (1969) 162-174.

§530 *3.3.3.2.1.9.2 Syriac*

James Murdock, "The Syriac Words for Baptism," *BS* 7 (1850) 733-743.

Benjamin Davies, "An Investigation in Syriac Philology," *BS* 8 (1851) 554-563.

*W. C. D., "The Syro-Arabian Languages and Literature," *CRB* 17 (1852) 393-424. [§4. *Neo-Aramaic Dialect*—the Syriac, pp. 418-424]

D. T. Stoddard, "Grammar of the Modern Syriac Language, as spoken in Oroomiah, Persia, and in Koordistan," *JAOS* 5 (1855-56) 1-180h.

W. W., "On the Syriac Word ܥܡܕ *'Emadh*, 'To be Baptized'," *JSL, 3rd Ser.,* 8 (1858-59) 405-407.

Anonymous, "The Syriac Language and Literature," *JSL, 4th Ser.,* 2 (1862-63) 75-87.

Jules Ferrette, "On a Neo-Syriac Language still spoken in the Anti-Lebanon," *JRAS* (1863) 431-436.

C[rawford] H. T[oy], "Exegetical Notes. The Syriac Stem *'amad,*" *BQ* 6 (1872) 106-110.

James A. Corcoran, "Syriac Grammars," *ACQR* 2 (1877) 722-745.

Geo. Phillips, "Syriac accents," *JP* 9 (1880) 221-229.

Anonymous, "The Study of Syriac," *AJSL* 3 (1886-87) 51-52.

*Richard J. H. Gottheil, "Syriac and Assyrian," *AJSL* 3 (1886-87) 187.

Richard J. H. Gottheil, "A Tract on the Syriac Conjunctions," *AJSL* 4 (1887-88) 167-173.

Richard [J. H.] Gottheil, "Ḳalilag W^edamnag in Syriac Literature," *AJSL* 4 (1887-88) 251.

Frederick James Bliss, "Ma'lula and its Dialect," *PEFQS* 22 (1890) 74-98. *[Syriac]*

C[laude] R. Conder, "The Malula Dialect," *PEFQS* 22 (1890) 186. *[Syriac]*

J. Van den Gheyn, "On the Syriac word ܢܚܘܬܐ," *BOR* 5 (1891) 17.

Richard J. H. Gottheil, "Dawidh bar Paulos, a Syriac grammarian," *JAOS* 15 (1891) cxi-cxviii.

*Fritz Hommel, "Assyriological Notes," *SBAP* 17 (1895) 199-207. [§11a. Babylonian *šutapú* = Syr. שׁוּתָפָא *šautâphâ,* pp. 205-206]

C[laude] R. Conder, "The Syrian Language," *PEFQS* 28 (1896) 60-78.

Benjamin Labaree, "Maclean's Grammar of the Dialects of Vernacular Syriac," *AJSL* 15 (1898-99) 87-99.

Gabriel Oussani, "The Modern Chaldeans and Nestorians, and the Study of Syriac among them," *JAOS* 22 (1901) 79-96

Abraham Yohannan, "Some Remarks regarding the Pronunciation of Modern Syriac," *JAOS* 25 (1904) 76-78.

*Paul Haupt, "Well and Field = Wife," *JAOS* 36 (1916) 418-420.

Paul Haupt, "Syriac *sífṯâ,* lip, and *sáy̆pâ,* end," *JSOR* 1 (1917) 92.

Giuseppe Furlani, "A Short Physiognomic Treatise in the Syriac Language," *JAOS* 39 (1919) 289-294.

*Frank R. Blake, "Studies in Semitic Grammar II," *JAOS* 62 (1942) 109-118. [6. Syriac Connecting Vowel *â* before Verbal Suffixes; 7. The Orthography of the Syriac Ittafal; 8. New Syriac *k,* pp. 114-115]

*Th. Sprey, "ܐܠܡܣܐ - מֹשֶׁבָה," *VT* 7 (1957) 408-410.

*J. A. Emerton, "Notes on Three Passages in Psalm Book III," *JTS, N.S.,* 14 (1963) 374-381. [III. Psalm 74:41 and the Syriac verb ܚܒ , 'to be angry', p. 381]

*H. J. Polotsky, "Aramaic, Syriac, and Ge'ez," *CNI* 15 (1964) #4, 19-26.

*H. J. Polotsky, "Aramaic, Syriac, and Ge'ez," *JSS* 9 (1964) 1-10.

*P. Wernberg-Møller, "Some Scribal and Linguistic Features of the Genesis Part of the Oldest Peshiṭta Manuscript (B.M. Add 14425)," *JSS* 13 (1968) 136-161.

J. Blau, "The Origins of the Open and Closed *e* in Proto-Syriac," *BSOAS* 32 (1969) 1-9.

§531 *3.3.3.2.2 Ugaritic*

Anonymous, "Notes and Comments. A New Language Reported from Syria," *A&A* 28 (1929) 145.

Anonymous, "New Language Discovered in Syria," *Antiq* 3 (1929) 350.

Theodor Herzl Gaster, "An Egyptian Loan-Word at Ras Shamra," *AEE* 19 (1934) 21. [ḫptš]

Zellig S. Harris, "The Structure of Ras Shamra C," *JAOS* 54 (1934) 79-83.

*Eric Burrows, "Origins of the Ras Shamra Alphabet," *JRAS* (1936) 271-277.

Zellig S. Harris, "A Conditioned Sound Change in Ras Shamra," *JAOS* 57 (1937) 151-157.

*Zellig S. Harris, "Ras Shamra: Canaanite civilization and language," *SIR* (1937) 479-502.

Zellig S. Harris, "Expression of the Causative in Ugaritic," *JAOS* 58 (1938) 103-111.

Albrecht Goetze, "The Tenses of Ugaritic," *JAOS* 58 (1938) 266-309.

*Cyrus H. Gordon, "*TRḤ, ṬN* and *NKR* in Ras Shamra Tablets," *JBL* 57 (1938) 407-410.

Albrecht Goetze, "Is Ugaritic a Canaanite Dialect?" *Lang* 17 (1941) 127-138.

A. D. Singer, "The 'Final' -m' (=mă?) in the Ugarit Tablets," *BIES* 10 (1942-44) #2/3, II-III.

*Robert Gordis, "The Asseverative Kaph in Ugaritic and Hebrew," *JAOS* 63 (1943) 176-178.

*William Foxwell Albright, "The Old Testament and Canaanite Language and Literature," *CBQ* 7 (1945) 5-31. [III. Decipherment and Interpretation of the Tablets, pp. 9-14; IV. The Ugaritic Dialect and Biblical Hebrew, pp. 14-19; VI. Canaanite Light on Hebrew Grammar and Lexicography, pp. 22-26]

Julian Obermann, "Sentence Negation in Ugaritic," *JBL* 65 (1946) 233-248.

Albrecht Goetze, "Ugaritic *mẓrḡl*," *JCS* 1 (1947) 72.

Marvin H. Pope, "A Note on Ugaritic *ndd - ydd*," *JCS* 1 (1947) 337-341.

A. D. Singer, "The Vocative in Ugaritic," *JCS* 2 (1948) 1-10.

Y. Sukenik, "Note on *tlt swsm* in the Legend of Keret," *JCS* 2 (1948) 11-12.

*G. R. Driver, "Hebrew Studies," *JRAS* (1948) 164-176. *[Pronominal Suffix in Ugaritic Poetry, pp. 164-165]*

*G. R. Driver, "Ugaritic and Hebrew Problems," *ArOr* 17 (1949) Part 1, 153-157.

Theodor H. Gaster, "Ugaritic Philology," *JAOS* 70 (1950) 8-18.

H. L. Ginsberg, "Interpreting Ugaritic Texts," *JAOS* 70 (1950) 156-160.

*G. D. Young, "Ugaritic Poetic Style and the Old Testament," *JBL* 69 (1950) viii.

Cyrus H. Gordon, "Ugaritica," *JNES* 9 (1950) 178-181.

J. M. Paul Bauchet, "Philological Note," *ITQ* 18 (1951) 71. *[GPNM in Ugaritic]*

M. Pope, "Ugaritic enclitic *-m*," *JCS* 5 (1951) 123-128.

Edward Ullendorff, "Ugaritic Marginalia," *Or, N.S.*, 20 (1951) 270-274. [1. *tḥm*; 2. *yprq lṣb wyṣḥq*; 3. *wypḥ bhm aqht yb llqh* (1AQHT 145/46); 4. *širh ltikl 'ṣrm mnth ltkly npr* "so that the birds eat his flesh the...finish of his portion" (49:II:36, 37)]

Bruce Vawter, "The Ugaritic Use of GLMT," *CBQ* 14 (1952) 319-322.

*R. T. O'Callaghan, "The Word *ktp* in Ugarit and Egypto-Canaanite Mythology," *Or, N.S.*, 21 (1952) 37-46.

John Gray, "*Dtn* and *Rp'um* in Ancient Ugarit," *PEQ* 84 (1952) 39-41.

*Frank M. Cross Jr., "Ugaritic *db'at* and Hebrew Cognates," *VT* 2 (1952) 162-164.

*Cyrus H. Gordon, "Marginal Notes on the Ancient Middle East," *JKF* 2 (1952-53) 50-61 [VI. Babyloniaca: a. CH^{27} 3:68 *a-ši-ir;* b. *'mq* 'be strong', Acc. *ina emûqi* = Ugar. *b'mq* 'violently' - Heb. עמק ‖ כה]

G. Douglas Young, "The Present Status of Ugaritic Studies," *JKF* 2 (1952-53) 225-245.

*Cyrus H. Gordon, "The Patriarchal Age," *JAAR* 21 (1953) 238-243. [*betulah,* pp. 240-241]

*Marvin Pope, "Pleonastic *Wāw* before Nouns in Ugaritic and Hebrew," *JAOS* 73 (1953) 95-98.

*M[eir] M. Bravmann, "An Arabic Cognate of Ugaritic *ǧmrm,*" *JCS* 7 (1953) 27.

*Moshe Held, "A Difficult Biblical Expression and its Parallel in Ugaritic," *EI* 3 (1954) IV. [בִּגְרֵי שָׂרָד]

*E[phraim] A. Speiser, "The Terminative-Adverbial in Canaanite- Ugaritic and Akkadian," *IEJ* 4 (1954) 108-115.

*M[itchell] M. Dahood, "Ugartic *drkt* and Biblical *derek,*" *ThSt* 15 (1954) 627-631.

E[dward] Ullendorff, "The Position of Ugaritic within the Framework of the Semitic Languages," *Tarbiz* 24 (1954-55) #2, I.

*A. M. Honeyman, "Ugarit and Semitic Usage," *JAOS* 75 (1955) 121-122.

C. J. Labuschagne, "The Root *MḤH* attested in Ugaritic," *VT* 5 (1955) 312-313.

*J. Huesman, "Finite Uses of the Infinitive Absolute," *B* 37 (1956) 271-295.

*P. Grelot, "On the Root עבק/עבץ in Ancient Aramaic and in Ugaritic," *JSS* 1 (1956) 202-205.

M[itchell] Dahood, "Some Aphel Causatives in Ugaritic," *B* 38 (1957) 62-73.

*W. L. Moran, "Ugaritic *şîşûma* and Hebrew *şîş,*" *B* 39 (1958) 69-71.

*William W. Hallow, "Isaiah 28:9-13 and the Ugaritic Abecedaries," *JBL* 77 (1958) 324-338.

M[itchell] Dahood, "The Value of Ugaritic for Textual Criticism," *B* 40 (1959) 160-170.

*Moshe Held, "*mḫṣ/*mḫš* in Ugaritic and Other Semitic Languages (A Study in Comparative Lexicography)," *JAOS* 79 (1959) 169-176.

Joseph A. Reif, "The Loss of Consonantal Aleph in Ugaritic," *JSS* 4 (1959) 16-20.

*M[itchell] Dahood, "The value of Ugaritic for textual criticism," *SBO* 1 (1959) 26-36.

*M. H. Goshen-Gottstein, "'Ephriam is a well-trained heifer' and Ugaritic *mdl*," *B* 41 (1960) 64-66.

*Dennis Dickman, "The Ugaritic Language and the Old Testament," *Amb* 10 (1960-61) #5, 15, 18-27.

*William A. Ward, "Comparative Studies in Egyptian and Ugaritic," *JNES* 20 (1961) 31-40.

Edward Ullendorff, "Ugaritic Marginalia II," *JSS* 7 (1962) 339-351. [I. *thbr;*

II. *ngš;* III. *ḥtk;* IV. *bmdgt br nrt;* V. *'db úḫry mt ydh;* VI. *'nṭ;* VII. 𝒱

or ⌐𝜸]

*M[itchell] Dahood, "Hebrew-Ugaritic Lexicography I," *B* 44 (1963) 289-303.[אָבוֹת - בָּעַל]

*Svi Rin, "Ugaritic-Old Testament Affinities," *BZ, N.S.,* 7 (1963) 22-33. [Meanings and Forms: *ḥzt; tġly/tġl; wyp'r; yrḥm; yṭkḥ; bṭbrn qnh; ḏmr; rbtm; rḥtm; 'šdk; lnḥt; wtpq; td; dll; w'an; sprnhn; bšlḥ; ṣḥ; msrr; tqtnṣn; t'td; 'tdb; gh; m'id; 'aṭt; bht; yhbr; mġrm; tmġyn; btrbš; ht; sp'; 'ib; ṭrml;* Idiomatic Usages: *'al; dbḥ dnt; 'm'il; ṭlṭ r'b ym; šrd b'l bdbḥk; ṣ'it npšh; šm' -- bn; 'ahbt ṭr t'rrk; w'ṣr 'udnh; b'dn ksl ṭṭbr; bmm'; lyrz 'm b'l;* lymm -- lyrḥm; *byrdm 'arṣ; šlmm šlmm; b'lṣ 'lṣm; lm 'ank; ṣrrt ṣpn; 'lk bd 'iṭt*]

*A[nson] F. Rainey, "A Canaanite at Ugarit," *IEJ* 13 (1963) 43-45.

*Harry A. Hoffner Jr., "An Anatolian Cult Term in Ugaritic," *JNES* 22 (1963) 66-68.[*dġt*]

*C. J. Labuschagne, "Ugaritic *blt* and *blt̂* in Is. X 4," *VT* 14 (1964) 97-99.

Edward Ullendorff, "Ugaritic Studies Within Their Semitic and Eastern Mediterranean Setting," *BJRL* 46 (1963-64) 236-249.

*M[itchell] Dahood, "Hebrew-Ugaritic Lexicography II," *B* 45 (1964) 393-412. [גְּבוּל - טָרַח]

J. C. Greenfield, "Ugaritic *mdl* and Its Cognates," *B* 45 (1964) 527-534.

*E[phraim] A. Speiser, "The Syllabic Transcription of Ugaritic [h] and [ḥ]," *BASOR* #175 (1964) 42-47.

*A. Haldar, "The Position of Ugaritic among the Semitic Languages," *BO* 21 (1964) 267-277.

*J[ohannes] C. de Moor, "Ugaritic *ṯkḥ* and South Arabian *mṯkḥ*," *VT* 14 (1964) 371-372.

*M[itchell] Dahood, "Hebrew-Ugaritic Lexicography III," *B* 46 (1965) 311-332.[*יָבַם - כָּשִׁיר]

*Arnold A. Weider, "Ugaritic-Hebrew Lexicographical Notes," *JBL* 84 (1965) 160-164. [1. שׁוה—*ṯwy;* 2. More on עמק—*'mq;* 3. פרד—*brd;* 4. גשׁם נדבות—*mdlk mṯrtk*]

*Moshe Held, "The Action-Result (Factitive Passive) Sequence of Identical Verbs in Biblical Hebrew and Ugaritic," *JBL* 84 (1965) 272-282.

*Johannes C. de Moor, "Frustula Ugaritica," *JNES* 24 (1965) 355-364. [1. *dġt;* 2. *phy;* 3. *UM* Text 77:40-45; 4. Some Instances of *'an,* Read *n;* 5. Inflected Forms of *iṯ;* 6. The Pronominal Suffix 3 Sg. Masc. *-n;* 7. A Malicious Informer; 8. *yḥ,* "May He Live"; 9. Some Garments; 10. III Aqht: 14-15; 11. Arboriculture; 12. *ġr;* 13. *'iṯl,* "Spittle"? 14. A Case of *'ank* = "This"]

*John Pairman Brown, "Kothar, Kinyras, and Kythereia," *JSS* 10 (1965) 197-219. *[KTR]*

J. A. Emerton, "Notes and Studies. Ugaritic Notes," *JTS, N.S.,* 16 (1965) 438-443.

S[amuel] E. Loewenstamm, "Ugaritic Gleanings,"*Lěš* 30 (1965-66) #2, n.p.n.

A[nson] F. Rainey, "New Tools for Ugaritic Study," *Lěš* 30 (1965-66) #4, n.p.n. *(Review)*

*M[itchell] Dahood, "Ugaritic *ušn,* Job 12, 10 and 11 Ps[a]Plea 3-4," *B* 47 (1966) 207-208.

*M[itchell] Dahood, "Hebrew-Ugaritic Lexicography IV," *B* 47 (1966) 403-419.[לְ - מַלְתָּעוֹת]

*Martin H. Pope, "Marginalia to M. Dahood's *Ugaritic-Hebrew* Philology," *JBL* 85 (1966) 455-466.

*M[itchell] Dahood, "Hebrew-Ugaritic Lexicography V," *B* 48 (1967) 421-438.[מִמֶּךָ - כָּחָה]

*Svi Rin and Shifra Rin, "Ugaritic-Old Testament Affinities II," *BZ, N.S.,* 11 (1967) 174-192. [Personal Names: *ṯpṯ nhr; 'Al'iyn - 'Al'iyn b'l; šmb'l; yqy; gmr hd; ybnt; 'mr; 'mmym; ṯ'y;'aṯr b'l; yš'u gh wyṣḥ bl mt my l'im bndgn my hmlt 'aṯr b'l; ypt; 'atn; nqmd; yrgb; rḥmy; krtn; yṯpn; 'ablm. Qrt 'ablm;* Miscellanea: *rgmm; ph; 'amr; kḫt;mlḫt - ḫrb mlḫt; y'šr; mm' - brkm. tġll bdm ḏmr ḥlqm bmm' mhrm; 'išdk: 'my p'nk tlsmn 'my twtḥ 'išdk; mdl: b'l mdlh yb'r; kmn; 'aḫth; gm sḫ; mk; akrt; ḫlq; bmt; db'atk - qrn db'atk; gl; hll b'l gml; mṯdṯt ġlm ym; mġd; ṯrrṯ - wtmġy l'udm ṯrrṯ; qr; mswnh; ṯlṯ: 'dt 'ilm ṯlṯh; mr; 'aḫt 'rš mdw; ḥbš; 'qbm; bntb pš'; mz' - tmz' kst Dn'il; yr - yr 'rpt* More on the Construct with Final *m;* On The Superlative]

*Harry A. Hoffner Jr., "Ugaritic *pwt:* A Term from the Early Canaanite Dyeing Industry," *JAOS* 87 (1967) 300-303.

*A. van Selms, "*Pa'yal* Formations in Ugaritic and Hebrew Nouns," *JNES* 26 (1967) 289-295.

J. C. Greenfield, "Ugaritic Lexicographical Notes,"*JCS* 21 (1967) 89-93. [1. *'mq;* 2. *ḥmdrt;* 3. *ṣml;* 4. *ġprt;* 5. *abn ṣrp;* 6. *mqb;* 7. *krk;* 8. *niṯ*]

A[nson] F. Rainey, "*Āširu* and *Asīru* in Ugarit and the Land of Canaan," *JNES* 26 (1967) 296-301.

*S[amuel] E. Loewenstamm, "Remarks on Stylistic Patterns in Biblical and Ugaritic Literatures," *Lěš* 32 (1967-68) #1/2, II-III.

*M. H. Goshen-Gottstein, "ברך in Ugaritic and Hebrew," *Lěš* 32 (1967-68) #1/2, IV.

Y. Blau, "'ęśrę <*'išrayh (followed by a short vowel)," *Lěš* 32 (1967-68) #3, n.p.n. [Reply by E. Y. Kutscher]

S[amuel] E. Loewenstamm, "*Matres Lectionis* in Ugaritic," *Lěš* 32 (1967-68) #4, n.p.n. [Reply by E. Y. Kutscher]

Stanislav Segert, "Recent Progress in Ugaritology," *ArOr* 36 (1968) 443-467.

*M[itchell] Dahood, "Hebrew-Ugaritic Lexicography VI," *B* 49 (1968) 355-369.[נָצַר - (cont.) נָחָה]

*Moshe Held, "The Root *ZBL/SBL* in Akkadian, Ugaritic and Biblical Hebrew," *JAOS* 88 (1968) 90-96.

Joshua Blau, "On Problems of Polyphony and Archaism in Ugaritic Spelling," *JAOS* 88 (1968) 523-526.

W[olf] Leslau, "Observations on Semitic Cognates in Ugaritic," *Or, N.S.,* 37 (1968) 347-366.

*S. P. Brock, "Νεφεληγερέτα = rkb 'rpt," *VT* 18 (1968) 395-397. [רכב ערפת]

*Arvid S. Kapelrud, "The number seven in Ugaritic texts," *VT* 18 (1968) 494-499.

David Marcus, "The Three Alephs in Ugaritic," *JANES* 1 (1968-69) #1, 50-60.

David Marcus, "Studies in Ugaritic Grammar 1," *JANES* 1 (1968-69) #2, 55-61.

S[amuel] E. Loewenstamm, "*Yod* as *Mater Lections* in Ugaritic," *Lěš* 33 (1968-69) #2/3, n.p.n.

*M[itchell] Dahood, "Hebrew-Ugaritic Lexicography VII," *B* 50 (1969) 337-356.[נָשָׂה - עֲרָפֶל]

Samuel E. Loewenstamm, "Ugaritic Formulas of Greeting," *BASOR* #194 (1969) 52-54.

A[nson] F. Rainey, "Notes on the Syllabic Ugaritic Vocabularies," *IEJ* 19 (1969) 107-109.

*William A. Ward, "The Semitic Root *HWY* in Ugaritic and Derived Stems in Egyptian," *JNES* 28 (1969) 265-267.

J. A. Emerton, "The Meaning of the Root *mzl* in Ugaritic," *JSS* 14 (1969) 22-33.

T. L. Fenton, "Command and Fulfilment in Ugaritic—TQTL:YQTL and QTL:QTL," *JSS* 14 (1969) 34-38.

*S[amuel] E. Loewenstamm, "The Expanded Colon in Ugaritic and Biblical Verse," *JSS* 14 (1969) 176-196.

*J. C. Greenfield, "Amurrite, Ugaritic and Canaanite," *PICSS* (1969) 92-101.

*S. E. Loewenstamm, "The Numerals in Ugaritic," *PICSS* (1969) 172-179.

*A[nson] Rainey, "Some Prepositional Nuances in Ugaritic Administrative Texts," *PICSS* (1969) 205-211.

*Mitchell Dahood, "Ugaritic—Hebrew Syntax and Style," *UF* 1 (1969) 15-36.

Johannes C. de Moor, "Ugaritic *hm* - never 'behold'," *UF* 1 (1969) 201-202.

*F. Charles Fensham, "The Son of a Handmaid in Northwest-Semitic," *VT* 19 (1969) 312-321. [*ben-'āmāh*]

*Samuel [E.] Loewenstamm, "Remarks upon the Infinitive Absolute in Ugaritic and Phoenician," *JANES* 2 (1969-70) 53. *[Ugaritic]*

E. Y. Kutscher, "Ugaritica Marginalia," *Lěš* 34 (1969-70) #1/2, 1-3. *[English Supplement]* [I. (א)מחוז Karum = Harbour, Market(place); II. Some entries from the Vocabulary, *Adanu* 'father'; III. חלב Hill, Mountain]

A[nson] F. Rainey, "Notes on the Syllabic Vocabularies from Ugarit," *Lěš* 34 (1969-70) #3, n.p.n.

*M[itchell] Dahood, "Hebrew-Ugaritic Lexicography VIII," *B* 51 (1970) 391-404. [פָ - צֶרִי][1]

*M[itchell] Dahood, "Hebrew-Ugaritic Lexicography IX," *B* 52 (1971) 337-356. [צוֹרְרִי - לָחַץ בְּ][1]

*M[itchell] Dahood, "Hebrew-Ugaritic Lexicography X," *B* 53 (1972) 286-403. [רחק ב - שׁדד][1]

*M[itchell] Dahood, "Hebrew-Ugaritic Lexicography XI," *B* 54 (1973) 351-366. [שׁרף - שׁתע]¹

*M[itchell] Dahood, "Hebrew-Ugaritic Lexicography XII," *B* 55 (1974) 381-383. [תאב - תשמורים*]¹

1. Since the articles by Mitchell Dahood are published in their entirety, the editor has gone beyond the normal cut-off period of 1969-70, in order to complete the series.

§532 *3.3.3.2.3 East Semitic/Akkadian - General Studies*

*[C.] Lottner, "Remarks on the nation by which the cuneiform mode of writing was invented.—On the most ancient ethnographical state of Western Asia historically known," *TPS* (1858) 124-136, 137-142.

*A. [H.] Sayce, "The Casdim and the Chaldees," *JSL, 4th Ser.,* 4 (1863-64) 165-171.

W. T., "The Decipherment of Cuneiform Inscriptions Described and Tested," *JSL, 4th Ser.,* 5 (1864) 114-125; 6 (1864-65) 91-106.

A. [H.] Sayce, "The Ethnography of Early Chaldea—No. II," *JSL, 4th Ser.,* 5 (1864) 187-194.

Edw. Hincks, "Chaldean Interpretations," *JSL, 4th Ser.,* 5 (1864) 421-425.

*A. [H.] Sayce, "Ethnography of Early Chaldea—No. III.," *JSL, 4th Ser.,* 6 (1864-65) 171-176.

*A. H. Sayce, "The Accadian numerals," *ZDMG* 27 (1873) 696-702.

Otis T. Mason, "Progress and Results of Cuneiform Decipherment," *BQ* 8 (1874) 191-208.

A. H. Sayce, "Accadian Phonology," *TPS* (1877-79) 123-142.

Hyde Clarke, "Preliminary Notes on the Characters, Phonetics, and Language of the Akkadians and pre-Akkadians," *SBAP* 2 (1879-80) 51-52.

*†Geo. Bertin, "Notes on Akkadian Poetry," *SBAP* 3 (1880-81) 121-122.

S. J. Barrows, "Chinese and Akkadian. M. Terrien de Lacouperie's Discoveries," *URRM* 15 (1881) 310-322.

*Theo[philus] G. Pinches, "The Akkadian Numerals," *SBAP* 4 (1881-82) 111-116.

*George Bertin, "On the Character and Influence of the Accent in the Akkadian and Assyrian Words," *SBAP* 5 (1882-83) 19-21.

*†John P. Peters, "The Akkadian Numerals," *SBAP* 5 (1882-83) 120-121.

*G[eorge] Bertin, "Notes on the Assyrian and Akkadian Pronouns," *JRAS* (1885) 65-88.

*A. H. Sayce, "Miscellaneous Notes," *ZK* 2 (1885) 399-405. [1. Assyrian *R* for *S;* 2. *Tisâ* "nine"; 3. Accadian *das-bi* "in one"; 4. Interchange of *b* and *m* in Accadian; 5. Accadian *dan-ga* "powerful"; 6. Accadian values of ⟨𒀹⟩ and ⟨; 7. *Teretu* "written knowledge"; 8. NA-BI "that man"; 9. Gudibir; 10. *Irad* and *Enoch* in Genesis; 11. The Sagartians of the Behistun Inscription; 12. *Eramu* "bare skin"; 13. *Khamtu* and *maru*]

*A. H. Sayce, "Miscellaneous Notes," *ZA* 2 (1887) 331-340. [14. *Kuru* "a scourge", p. 331]

*A. H. Sayce, "Miscellaneous Notes," *ZA* 3 (1888) 231-232. [20. 𒇷𒀹𒅆𒋼𒍦 "barbers"; 21. *Nu-bat-ti,* "day of morning"; 22. *arad kitti,* "trustworthy servant"; 23. *Birit,* "in the sight of"]

*A. H. Sayce, "Miscellaneous Notes," *ZA* 4 (1889) 382-393. [29. *Khandal* or *Khindil* "a trunk"; 30. The Accadian *sebi* "clothing"; 31. *Ursânu,* "a hero"; 33. The name of Eve in Assyrian]

*Terrien de Lacouperie, "Akkadian and Sumerian in Comparative Philology," *BOR* 1 (1886-87) 1-7.

*Robert Brown Jr., "Ugro-Altaic Numerals: One — Five," *SBAP* 10 (1887-88) 207-214.

*A. H. Sayce, "The Woman's Language of Chaldea," *Exp, 3rd Ser.,* 8 (1888) 319. [Assy. NAQBU = (?) Accadian EME-SAL]

*Claude R. Conder, "On Comparisons of Hieroglyphics," *PEFQS* 20 (1888) 252-259. *[Akkadian]*

*C[laude] R. Conder, "The Three Hieroglyphic Systems," *ARL* 3 (1889) 99-117. *[Cuneiform]*

A. H. Sayce, "The Accadian Word for King," *PEFQS* 21 (1889) 210.

C. J. Ball, "The New Accadian," *SBAP* 12 (1889-90) 4-41, 53-80, 207-222, 269-287, 394-418.

C[laude] R. Conder, "Ku for King," *PEFQS* 22 (1890) 40.

C. J. Ball, "Ideograms common to Accadian and Chinese. Part I," *SBAP* 13 (1890-91) 83-105.

C. J. Ball, "Ideograms common to Accadian and Chinese. Part II," *SBAP* 13 (1890-91) 368-382.

C. J. Ball, "Ideograms common to Accadian and Chinese. Part III," *SBAP* 13 (1890-91) 484-495.

C[laude] R. Conder, "The Hebrews on the Tell Amarna Tablets," *PEFQS* 23 (1891) 251.

C. J. Ball, "The Ideogram ⊨⫯⫯⫷⫷⫴⊟," *SBAP* 15 (1892-93) 48-50.

Robert F. Harper, "The Decipherment of the Assyro-Babylonian Inscriptions," *BW* 1 (1893) 294-297, 371-373.

George A. Barton, "A peculiar use of *ilani* in the tablets from El-Amarna," *JAOS* 15 (1893) cxcvi-cxcix.

Christopher Johnston, "The Sumero-Akkadian Question," *JAOS* 18 (1893) 317-322.

C[laude] R. Conder, "Notes on Akkadian," *JRAS* (1893) 855-867.

*Fritz Hommel, "Assyriological Notes," *SBAP* 16 (1893-94) 209-212. [§1. Origin of the Expression *Sumir and Akkad* ⊨⫯⫷⫷⫷ ⟨⫻⊟ ⊢⫯⫯ ⊢⫯⫯⟐ ⟨⫻⊟ ⧖⫶⧗ ⊨⫯⫯⫯⫯ ; §2. Etymology of ידע/מדע‎ compares with Babylonian *mindi;* §3. The name ⧖⫶ ⫯⫻ ⧖⧖ ⫺ ⊢⫻⫯⫯ ⊢⫻⫯⫯ ; §4. *a-na* ⊢⫯⫯ ⊨⫯⫯ ⫯⫯⫯ ⊢⫻⫯ *ras-shi-bat Ninua at-ta-shi ka-ti;* §5. *Sha* ⊢⫯ *Maru, mâr A-bi-í-ra-mu*]

*Fritz Hommel, "Assyriological Notes," *SBAP* 17 (1895) 199-207. [§6. לעלנסחמלשי‎; §7. *Sha-ma-num ghar-sag Me-nu-a-ta,* ⊢⫻⊞⊟ *šal-la ghar-sag Mar-tu-ta tag na-gal im-ta-dul-du, na-rù-a-ku mu-gim;* §8. Etymology of עֵילָם, אוּלָם, עוֹלָם‎; §9 4R. 34, No. 2; §10. Inscription of *Agu-kak-rimi* (5 R. 33); §11a. Babylonian *šutapú* = Syr. שַׁוְתָּפָא‎, 11b. Arabic لُرْن‎ = Babylonian *lânu;* §12a. A town ⫯⫻ ⫯⫴⫯⫴⫯-*ki;* §12b. Gen. iv. 17]

*Fritz Hommel, "Assyriological Notes," *SBAP* 18 (1896) 17-24. [§13. Geographical term *mât A-* ◁𝍦*-ri-í;* §14. K. 257, Lines 29 and 30 ⊨𝍦𝍦𝍦 *anna* ⊨𝍦𝍦𝍦 *ki-a šú-mu-ta ni . . . . ;* §15. S^b 287-8 ⊨𝍦𝍦𝍦 𝍦𝍦, Sumerian *sur-ru* = Semitic *kalû* "priest, sorcerer"; §16. Babylonian Poetry; §17. K. 2455; §18. K. 9852 ⤙𝍦 ; §19. Expression ⤙𝍦𝍦𝍦𝍦𝍦 ; §20. Elamitic proper name *Ma-uk-ti-ti*]

*Fritz Hommel, "Assyriological Notes," *SBAP* 19 (1897) 78-90, 312-315. [§21. فُعَال = *nupâru;* §22. *nabâsu, napâsu* = נפש "to pick wool"; §23. Babylonian *p* = Hebrew, Aramaic, and Arabic *b;* §24. Sumerian *ǧilib,* "god"; §25. Hethitic gods *Maura* and *Ḫattu;* §26. Place name *Khâna;* §27. *Tuktû,* "blood, vengeance" = תּנּת (*tektô*) "blood (of the woman)"; §28. *Amat-*⤙𝍦 *Su-'u-la;* §29. *Collection de Clereq,* Vol II, Pl. X, No. 6. ▱ ⫸▷ = ⊨𝍦𝍦 ⤬ ⤬; §30. Sc. 289, *i-mi,* ◁𝍦, *a-ḫu* and *ṭu-ṭu;* §31. Babylonian gods, ⤙𝍦 ⤬𝍦𝍦 ⊨𝍦𝍦 and ⤙𝍦 ◁-𝍦𝍦; §32. Name of the god ⤙𝍦 ⤬𝍦𝍦 ⊨𝍦𝍦 to be read *Nin-dar* or *Nin-ib;* §33. *surdú* = falcon; §34. *madâdu* = "to love", *namaddu* = "the beloved", *shudadu* = *râimu* "loving"; §35. *akhulâpi* = *matî;* §36. Babylonian *umâm* "beast" = *ubhâmu, buhâmu;* §37. *pishannu;* §38. Babylonian *ashlaku* = Arab. *silk*]

Anonymous, "How the Cuneiform Characters were Deciphered," *CFL, O.S.,* 3 (1899) 28-30, 108-111.

*C. P. Tiele, "Akkadian and Sumerian," *JRAS* (1900) 343-344.

*Theophilus G. Pinches, "Akkadian and Sumerian," *JRAS* (1900) 551-552.

*Joseph Offord, "Notes and Queries. 4. *The Origin of the Cuneiform Syllabary,*" *PEFQS* 36 (1904) 181-182.

*Andrew Craig Robinson, "The Bearing of Recent Oriental Discoveries on Old Testament History," *JTVI* 38 (1906) 154-176. [(Discussion, pp. 176-181) (The Cuneiform System of Writing, pp. 155-156)]

*Stephen [H.] Langdon, "The Derivation of *šabattu* and other notes," *ZDMG* 62 (1908) 29-32. [*šabattu,* 29-30; *buganu šutuk,* 31-32; *tam* distributive, 32]

Hope W. Hogg, "Two Cuneiform Heart Symbols. ⌂𝍦𝍦𝍦 and ⫷𝍦," *JMUEOS* #1 (1911) 109-121.

*C. J. Ball, "On the Compound Heart Ideogram (LID + ŠAG, Br. 8890)," *JMUEOS* #1 (1911) 123-127.

D. D. Luckenbill, "Notes on the Brussels Vocabulary," *RAAO* 11 (1914) 197.

W[illiam] F[oxwell] Albright, "Some Unexplained Cuneiform Words," *JAOS* 35 (1915) 394-398. [kamir; utte'izzi; çarçar]

William Wallace Martin, "Certain Cuneiform Groups for Babylon," *MQR, 3rd Ser.,* 48 (1922) 712-715.

*Sidney Smith, "Miscellanea," *RAAO* 21 (1924) 75-92. (Addendum to p. 79, *p.155.*) [(2) Lexicographical (i) *šallaru* (ii) (iii) *uppu* (iv) *dalbu, dalbanu* (v) *šibbu, šippu, sippu* (vi) *bur simatim* (vii) *azu = izzu,* strong (viii) *šadahu* (ix) *šalahu,* "to extend" (x) *tallu* (xi) *uṭṭatu, kibatu* (xii) *immeru zalamu* (xiii) *ḫaramu* (xiv) *ṣabatu niati* (xv) *garum* (xvi) *ganinu* and *ganunu* (xii)[sic] *ummanu*]

*Sidney Smith and C. J. Gadd, "A Cuneiform Vocabulary of Egyptian Words," *JEA* 11 (1925) 230-239. [Additional Note by T. Eric Peet, pp. 239-240]

Sidney Smith, "Miscellanea," *RAAO* 22 (1925) 57-70. [(2) Lexicographical (continued) (xviii) *namkaru,* sump-hold; xix. *šadadu;* xx. *šitu, šittu;* xxi. *šahatu;* xxii. *mala* "a first time, once"; (4) Grammatical Notes: I. *lama;* II. *makasu;* III. *šanat* in Dates; IV. C.T.C.T., I. 48, 7-8]

*S[tephen H.] Langdon, "Assyriological Comments on Some Difficult Passages," *SO* 1 (1925) 97-101. [I. The Sumerian Original of the Aramaic Transcription of the name *NIN-IB;* II. *Šitim-íd-da = sīki (sākiru),* Canal-repairer; III. *ki-g'ur,* to bend the earth, to crush]

*W[illiam] F[oxwell] Albright, "The New Cuneiform Vocabulary of Egyptian Words," *JEA* 12 (1926) 186-190.

*Paul Haupt, "The Cuneiform Terms for Sport," *BAVSS* 10 (1927) 127-132.

*George A. Barton, "On the Anticipatory Pronominal Suffix Before the Genitive in Aramaic and Akkadian," *JAOS* 47 (1927) 260-262

John A. Maynard, "Lexicographical Notes on Akkadian Religious Texts," *JSOR* 13 (1929) 101-102. [*Malâlu,* to mix; *Nagbu,* deep; *EZEN, uzun; Turdu,* posthumous son; *Nurmu,* nut; *The land of no death*]

*W[illiam] F[oxwell] Albright, "Mitannian maryannu, 'chariot-warrior', and the Canaanite and Egyptian Equivalents," *AfO* 6 (1930-31) 217-221.

*S[tephen H.] Langdon, "Philological Notes," *RAAO* 28 (1931) 13-22. [1) *Gilinu, gullimu(?)*, גלֹם, a garment; 2) The Accadian word for Anus 𒂖; 3) BA-RA-ZAL; 4) *Piltum, pistum,* fleece, hair 𒂖𒐊▶ ; 5) A Grammatical Text from Kish (W. 1928-2); 6) NIRDA, sin, transgression, treachery]

S[tephen H.] Langdon, "Philological note on the Verb 'šarû'," *RAAO* 28 (1931) 103-104.

*S[tephen H.] Langdon, "Note on the Legal Commentary *Ana itti-šu*," *AJSL* 48 (1931-32) 51-53.

S[tephen H.] Langdon, "The Transcription of Cuneiform Signs," *AfO* 8 (1932-33) 223-224.

Sidney Smith, "*b/pukk/qqu* and *mekku,*" *RAAO* 30 (1933) 153-168.

S[tephen H.] Langdon, "ṬULIMU: TULIMĀTU," *AJSL* 50 (1933-34) 179-180.

*Samuel I. Feigin, "The Captives in Cuneiform Inscriptions," *AJSL* 50 (1933-34) 217-245. [1. *asirtu,* "Captive Women," in the Omen Text K. 3, pp. 217-220; 3. *asīru* and *ašīru* in Palestinian Letters of the Amarna Time, pp. 226-227; 8. *esrêti-* Women in Nuzi Documents, pp. 234-237]

*Theodor Herzl Gaster, "An Egyptian Loan-Word in a Tel-Amarna Letter," *AEE* 19 (1934) 21. *[ḫa-ab-ši]*

*Cyrus H. Gordon, "Numerals in the Nuzi Tablets," *RAAO* 31 (1934) 53-60.

*E[phraim] A. Speiser, "A Figurative Equivalent for Totality in Akkadian and West-Semitic," *JAOS* 54 (1934) 200-203.

Cyrus H. Gordon, "The Pronoun in the Nuzi Tablets," *AJSL* 51 (1934-35) 1-21.

*Samuel I. Feigin, "The Captives in Cuneiform Inscriptions—*Continued,*" *AJSL* 51 (1934-35) 22-29. [Appendix III: The Meaning of *ziianatum,* pp. 26-29]

Cyrus H. Gordon, "Nouns in the Nuzi Tablets," *Baby* 16 (1936) 1-154.

*S[tephen] Langdon, "Philological Notes," *RAAO* 33 (1936) 191-196. [I. *Uārsu, Urāšu,* chamberlain, king's attendant; II. Ideograms for *assinnu,* eunuch; III. *amirānu,* totality, assembly, confinement; IV. *erû, urrû,* to enclose, collect; V. *ikuku,* fish-oil; VI. The length of daylight in each month]

I[gnace] J. Gelb, "Additional Akkadian Values," *AJSL* 53 (1936-37) 34-44, 180-187.

A. Sachs, "Two Notes on the Taanach and Amarna Letters," *AfO* 12 (1937-39) 371-373. [I. idu (Amarna 16,30), "wages"; II. KAK.Ú.TAG.GA, "arrow"]

Moshe Bar-Am, "The Subjunctive in the Cappadocian Texts," *Or, N.S.,* 7 (1938) 12-31.

Cyrus H. Gordon, "The Dialect of the Nuzu Tablets," *Or, N.S.,* 7 (1938) 32-63, 215-232.

A. Poebel, "Etymology of qâtum, 'Hand'," *JAOS* 60 (1940) 95-97.

A. Leo Oppenheim, "Idiomatic Accadian (Lexicographical Researches)," *JAOS* 61 (1941) 251-271.

A. L[eo] Oppenheim, "Studies in Accadian Lexicography I," *Or, N.S.,* 11 (1942) 119-133.

A. L[eo] Oppenheim, "Akkadian *pul(u)ḫ(t)u* and *melammu,*" *JAOS* 63 (1943) 31-34.

*Frank R. Blake, "Studies in Semitic Grammar III," *JAOS* 65 (1945) 111-116. [1. *E* for *a* Adjacent to Gutturals in Akkadian; 2. Supposed Influence of Preceding and Following *i* in Akkadian]

Frederick W. Geers, "The Treatment of Emphatics in Akkadian," *JNES* 4 (1945) 65-67.

A. L [eo] Oppenheim, "Studies in Akkadian Lexicography. II," *Or, N.S.,* 14 (1945) 235-241.

*Hayyim Rosenrauch, "Critical Notes: II. The Hebrew Equivalent to Accadic lib(lib)u," *JQR, N.S.,* 36 (1945-46) 81.

*H. Torczyner, *"Semel Ha-qin'ah Ha-maqneh,"* *JBL* 65 (1946) 293-302. [2. Akkadian *šamallū(m),* pp. 299-300]

Albrecht Goetze, "The Akkadian Masculine Plural -ānū/ī and its Semitic Background," *Lang* 22 (1946) 121-130.

A[lbrecht] Goetze, "Sequence of Two Short Syllables in Akkadian," *Or, N.S.,* 15 (1946) 233-238.

*J. Lewy, "Studies in Akkadian Grammar and Onomatology," *Or, N.S.,* 15 (1946) 361-415.

G. R. Driver, "Additions to the Cuneiform Syllabary," *JCS* 1 (1947) 47-49. [I. Thureau-Dangin, Syllabaire Accadien (1926); II Thureau-Dangin, Homophones Sumériens (1929)]

Albrecht Goetze, "The Akkadian Passive," *JCS* 1 (1947) 50-59.

Albrecht Goetze, "Akk. *antalū* and *namtallūm* 'eclipse'," *JCS* 1 (1947) 251-252.

E[phraim] A. Speiser, "A Note on the Derivations of *šumma," JCS* 1 (1947) 321-328.

M. M. Bravmann, "The Plural Ending -*ut*- of Masculine Attributive Adjectives in Akkadian," *JCS* 1 (1947) 343.

*A[lbrecht] Goetze, "Short or Long *a*? (Notes on some Akkadian words)," *Or, N.S.,* 16 (1947) 239-250. [(1) terḫatu(m); (2) kallatu(m); (3) āwatu(m); (4) piḫatu(m)/pāḫatu(m); (5) ḫatanu(m); (6) kŭdanu(m); (7) rāmanu(m)]

R. Marcus, "On the Genitive after *umma* in the Amarna Tablets," *JCS* 2 (1948) 223-224.

*E[phraim] A. Speiser, "A Note on Certain Akkadian Terms for Door-Equipment," *JCS* 2 (1948) 225-227.

Albrecht Goetze, "The Etymology of Akk. *qātum* 'hand'," *JCS* 2 (1948) 268-270.

Alexander Heidel, "The Meaning of 'Mummu' in Akkadian Literature," *JNES* 7 (1948) 98-105.

*Julius Lewy, "Apropos of the Akkadian Numerals *iš-ti-a-na* and *iš-ti-na," ArOr* 17 (1949) Part 2, 110-123.

*A. Leo Oppenheim, "Akk. *arad ekalli* = 'Builder'," *ArOr* 17 (1949) Part 2, 227-235.

Armas Salonen, "Notes on the Stem R-K-B in Akkadian," *ArOr* 17 (1949) Part 2, 313-322.

Alexander Heidel, "A Special Usage of the Akkadian Term *šadû*," *JNES* 8 (1949) 233-235.

I. J. Gelb, "Reorganisation of the Akkadian Dictionary," *Or, N.S.,* 18 (1949) 376-377.

*Roger T. O'Callaghan, "Notes on Mesopotamian History," *CBQ* 12 (1950) 132-135. [3. Ḥammu, pp. 134-135]

†Anonymous, "B. Landsberger's Lexicographical Contributions," *JCS* 4 (1950) 1-62. [Bibliography, pp. 3-7; Index of Akkadian Words, pp. 8-56; Index of Sumerian Words, pp 57-62]

Alfred Haldar, "On the Problem of Akkadian *šumma*," *JCS* 4 (1950) 63-64.

*W. L. Moran, "The Use of the Canaanite Infinitive as a Finite Verb in the Amarana Letters from Byblos," *JCS* 4 (1950) 169-172.

A[rmas] Salonen, "Akkadian Lexicography," *Or, N.S.,* 19 (1950) 404-407.

*Moshe Greenberg, "Hebrew *sᵉgullā:* Akkadian *sikiltu*," *JAOS* 71 (1951) 172-174.

Armas Salonen, "Some Akkadian Etymologies," *JNES* 9 (1950) 108-110.

*Julian Oberman, "Does Amarna Bear on Karatepe?" *JCS* 5 (1951) 58-61.

E[phraim] A. Speiser, "The Semantic Range of *dalāpu*," *JCS* 5 (1951) 64-66.

W. L. Moran, "'Does Amarna Bear on Karatepe?'—An Answer," *JCS* 6 (1952) 76-80.

*E[phraim] A. Speiser, "The 'Elative' in West-Semitic and Akkadian," *JCS* 6 (1952) 81-92.

I. J. Gelb, "Present State of the Akkadian Dictionary," *Or, N.S.,* 21 (1952) 358-359.

*Cyrus H. Gordon, "Marginal Notes on the Ancient Middle East," *JKF* 2 (1952-53) 50-61 [VI. Babyloniaca: a. CH^{27} 3:68 *a-ši-ir;* b. *'mq* 'be strong', Acc. *ina emûqi* = Ugar. *b'mq* 'violently' - Heb. עמק II כה]

E[phraim] A. Speiser, "Comments on Recent Studies in Akkadian Grammar," *JAOS* 73 (1953) 129-138.

W. L. Moran, "Amarna *summa* in Main Clauses," *JCS* 7 (1953) 78-80.

*Thomas O. Lambdin, "Another Cuneiform Transcription of Egyptian *msḥ,* 'crocodile'," *JNES* 12 (1953) 284-285. [NUM.ŠA.ḪU]

*E[phraim] A. Speiser, "The Terminative-Adverbial and Canaanite-Ugaritic and Akkadian," *IEJ* 4 (1954) 108-115.

*W. G. Lambert, "Two Akkadian Cognates," *JJS* 5 (1954) 40-41. [1. *RÂṢU* = רקץ; 2. *MAGRANU, MAGRATTU* = גרן]

Julius Lewy, "On Some Akkadian Expressions for 'Afterwards' and Related Notions," *WO* 2 (1954-59) 432-437.

Jussi Aro, "Remarks on the Language of the Alalakh Texts," *AfO* 17 (1954-56) 361-365.

I. J. Gelb, "Notes on von Soden's Grammar of Akkadian," *BO* 12 (1955) 93-111. *(Review)*

*E[phraim] A. Speiser, "Nuzi or Nuzu?" *JAOS* 75 (1955) 52-55.

J. Huesman, "Finite Uses of the Infinitive Absolute," *B* 37 (1956) 271-295.

*E[phraim] A. Speiser, "Nuzi Marginalia," *Or, N.S.,* 25 (1956) 1-23. [1. The Hurrian equivalent of *sikiltu(m);* 2. OB *k/ḫiššātum:* Nuzi *ḫi/eššumaku;* 3. The Hurrian element *maku;* 4. Ceremonial Payment; 5. The terminology of the oath by the gods]

G. Castellino, "Observations on the Akkadian Personal Pronouns in the Light of Semitic and Hamitic," *MIO* 5 (1957) 185-218.

G. R. Driver, "Acc *šimê/ītān* 'two evenings'," *ZA* 52 (1957) 307-308.

B. Landsberger and O. R. Gurney, "igi-duḫ-a = *támartu,* short version," *AfO* 18 (1957-58) 81-86.

R. F. G. Sweet, "Logogram PA.PA = Akk *ša ḫaṭṭātim?*" *AfO* 18 (1957-58) 360.

*M[itchell] Dahood, "Hebrew and Ugaritic Equivalents of Accadian *pitū pūridā*," *B* 39 (1958) 67-69.

Hayim Tadmor, "Historical Implications of the Correct Rendering of Akkadian *dâku*," *JNES* 17 (1958) 129-141.

Loren R. Fisher, "An Amarna Age Prodigal," *JSS* 3 (1958) 113-122.

*E[phraim] A. Speiser, "The *muškênum*," *Or, N.S.*, 27 (1958) 19-28.

H. Lewy, "The Meaning of NÍG·DU in the Mari Texts," *Or, N.S.*, 27 (1958) 55-58.

*Jørgen Læssøe, "Akkadian Annakum: 'Tin' or 'Lead'?" *AO* 24 (1959) 83-94. *[SH 868]*

Matitiahu Tsevat, "Additions to the Akkadian Syllabary," *JCS* 13 (1959) 15-18.

H[ildegard] Lewy, "Miscellania Nuziana I.," *Or, N.S.*, 28 (1959) 1-25.

Hildegard Lewy, "Miscellania Nuziana II," *Or, N.S.*, 28 (1959) 113-129. [*Ḫurizati; Mušni; Taluḫlu; Artamašši*]

Erica Reiner, "ME.UGU = *mēlu*," *AfO* 19 (1959-60) 150-151.

Mesrob K. Krikorian, "A further Argument about 'Annakum'," *AO* 25 (1960) 171-172.

*Robert Gordis, "A West-Semitic Cognate to Akkadian 'Suhatu'," *JSS* 5 (1960) 151-152.

*A[lbrecht] Goetze, "Suffixes in 'Kanishite' Proper Names," *RHA* 18 (1960) 45-55.

E. E. Knudsen, "Cases of Free Variants in the Akkadian *q* Phoneme," *JCS* 15 (1961) 84-90.

*Jacob J. Rabinowitz, "An Egyptian Parallel to the *Šalmukēnu* Clause of Accadian Documents," *JNES* 20 (1961) 50-51.

I. J. Gelb, "WA = *aw, iw, uw* in Cuneiform Writing," *JNES* 20 (1961) 194-196.

*Wolf Leslau, "Southeast Semitic Cognates to the Akkadian Vocabulary. I," *JAOS* 82 (1962) 1-4.

*J. V. Kinnier Wilson, "Hebrew and Akkadian Philological Notes," *JSS* 7 (1962) 173-183. [I. הֹמֶר; II. יָרַד; III. עֶלְבָּה and ṣarbatu; IV. šasû II; V. שָׁמֵם III(?); VI. sekrītu; VII. עִיר and âru]

*F. Charles Fensham, "A Cappadocian Parallel to the Hebrew *Kutōnet*," *VT* 12 (1962) 196-198. [ku-ta-nu/ku-ta-ni]

*Rivkah Harris, "The organization and administration of the cloister in Ancient Babylonia," *JESHO* 6 (1963) 121-157. [Akk *gagûm*]

Thorkild Jacobsen, "The Akkadian Ablative Accusative," *JNES* 22 (1963) 18-29.

*F. Charles Fensham, "The Wild Ass in the Aramean Treaty Between Barga'ayah and Mati'el," *JNES* 22 (1963) 185-186. [Akk. sirrimu]

A. Haldar, "The Akkadian Verb System. 1. *paris* Form," *Or, N.S.,* 32 (1963) 246-279.

A. L. Oppenheim, "Mesopotamian Conchology," *Or, N.S.,* 32 (1963) 407-412.

*Wolf Leslau, "Southeast Semitic Cognates to the Akkadian Vocabulary. II," *JAOS* 84 (1964) 115-118.

A. Haldar, "The Akkadian Verb System. 2. *iprus:iparras* Forms," *Or, N.S.,* 33 (1964) 15-48.

H. Lewy, M. Mayrhofer, "Apropos of the Texts HSS XV 32," *Or, N.S.,* 34 (1965) 30-31. [*ta-mar-ti-a[n-n]i; sa mar-ti-a[n-n]i*]

*Harry A. Hoffner Jr., "A Native Akkadian Cognate to West Semitic *GBN* 'Cheese'?" *JAOS* 86 (1966) 27-31.

W. L. Moran, "Some Akkadian Names of the Stomachs of Ruminants," *JCS* 21 (1967) 178-182.

*Moshe Held, "The Root *ZBL/SBL* in Akkadian, Ugaritic and Biblical Hebrew," *JAOS* 88 (1968) 90-96.

Giorgio Buccellati, "An Interpretation of the Akkadian Stative as a Nominal Sentence," *JNES* 27 (1968) 1-12.

J. V. Kinnier Wilson, "'Desonance' in Accadian," *JSS* 13 (1968) 93-103.

*David Sperling, "The Akkadian Legal Term *dīnu u dabābu*," *JANES* 1 (1968-69) #1, 35-40.

*M. M. Bravmann, "Akk. *kipru(m)*, pl. *kipratu(m)* and Ethiopic *kanfar*," *JCS* 22 (1968-69) 85-87.

*Wolf Leslau, "Southeast Semitic Cognates to the Akkadian Vocabulary. III," *JAOS* 89 (1969) 18-22.

Nahum M. Waldman, "Akkadian *kaṣāru* and Semantic Equivalents," *JNES* 28 (1969) 250-254.

P. B. Adamson, "*Bubu'tu* and *Birdu* Lesions in Akkadian Texts," *JRAS* (1969) 10-12.

*R. Hetzron, "The Evidence for Perfect *y'aqtul* and Jussive *yaqt'ul* in Proto-Semitic," *JSS* 14 (1969) 1-21. [1. Akkadian, pp 1-5]

*A[nson] Rainey, "Some Prepositional Nuances in Ugaritic Administrative Texts," *PICSS* (1969) 205-211.

*R. Kutscher, "The Sumerian Equivalents of Akkadian *māḫāzu*," *Lěš* 34 (1969-70) #4, n.p.n.

§533 *3.3.3.2.3.1 Assyrian - General Studies*

*†Anonymous, "The Monuments of Nineveh and the Cuneiform Characters," *DR* 24 (1848) 329-349. *(Review)*

*H[enry] C. Rawlinson, "On the Orthography of some of the later Royal Names of Assyrian and Babylonian History," *JRAS* (1855) 398-402. (Reply by Ed. Hincks, pp. 402-403)

E. Hincks, "On Assyrian Verbs," *JSL, 3rd Ser.,* 1 (1855) 381-393; 2 (1855-56) 141-162; 3 (1856) 152-171, 392-403.

George E. Day, "Brandis on the Assyrian Inscriptions and the Mode of Interpreting Them," *BS* 14 (1857) 413-425.

George E. Day, "Brandis on the Assyrian Inscriptions and the Mode of Interpreting Them," *JSL, 3rd Ser.,* 5 (1857) 343-352.

*A[lexander] McW[horter], "Yav in Assyrian; or 'Jehovah' on the Bricks and Inscribed Cylinders of 'Ur of the Chaldees'," *JSL, 3rd Ser.,* 9 (1859) 174-175.

Edwin Norris, "Specimen of an Assyrian Dictionary," *JRAS* 2 (1866) 225-256. *[A-ADR]*

E[dward] Hincks, "Specimen Chapters of an Assyrian Grammar," *JRAS* (1866) 480-519.

H. F. Talbot, "Contributions towards a Glossary of the Assyrian Language," *JRAS* (1867-68) 1-64; (1869-71) 1-80.

William Hayes Ward, "Assyrian Studies—Text-Books," *BS* 27 (1870) 184-191. *(Review)*

*Richard Cull, "The Assyrian Verbs *Basu,* 'To Be,' *Qabah,* 'To Say,' and *Isu,* 'To Have,' identified as Variant Forms of Verbs having the same signification in Hebrew Language," *SBAT* 1 (1872) 281-293.

*Richard Cull, "A ה Conjugation, such as exists in Assyrian, shown to be a character of early Shemitic Speech, by its vestiges found in the Hebrew, Phoenician, Aramaic, and Arabic Languages," *SBAT* 2 (1873) 83-109.

*William Wright, "Observations on the Assyrian Verb *Basu,* as compared with the Hebrew Verb הָיָה, *Hâyâ,* ' He was'," *SBAT* 3 (1874) 104-109.

*A. H. Sayce, "On the Study of Assyrian and Egyptian: An Opening Address," *BFER* 24 (1875) 294-301.

A. H. Sayce, "The Dual of the Assyrian Perfect," *ZDMG* 30 (1876) 310-312.

A. H. Sayce, "The Tenses of the Assyrian Verb," *JRAS* (1876-77) 22-58.

W. Houghton, W. R. Cooper, A. H. Sayce, and G[eorge] Bertin, "On some further Desired Aids to the Study of Assyrian," *SBAT* 6 (1878-79) 249-256.

William Houghton, "On the Hieroglyphic or Picture Origin of the characters of the Assyrian Syllabary," *SBAT* 6 (1878-79) 454-483.

*George Bertin, "Notes on the Assyrian Numerals," *SBAP* 2 (1879-80) 37-38.

*Richard Cull, "On the Existence and Expression in Assyrian of the hard guttural sound of the Hebrew ע," *SBAP* 2 (1879-80) 43-45.

Robert Brown Jr., "An Examination of the Ideograph 𒀯," *SBAP* 2 (1879-80) 61-62. (Remarks by Theo[philus] G. Pinches, p. 62)

*Richard Cull, "On the Expression in Assyrian of the soft sound of the Hebrew ע," *SBAP* 2 (1879-80) 62-66.

†Theo[philus] G. Pinches, "The consonants Š, R, and L, in Assyrian," *SBAP* 3 (1880-81) 82-85. (Corr. p. 104)

*George Bertin, "The Assyrian Numerals," *SBAT* 7 (1880-82) 370-389.

F. W. Eastlake, "Uruku *versus* Šišku," *SBAP* 4 (1881-82) 36-40.

*A. H. Sayce, "Notes on the Assyrian Numerals," *SBAP* 4 (1881-82) 105-107.

*†Edward Sachau, "The Cappadocian Cuneiform Inscription," *SBAP* 4 (1881-82) 117. [*Kutin = mule //* Aramaic כּוּדְנָא ר כּוּדְנְיָא]

Theo[philus] J. Pinches, "Introductory Paper upon Assyrian Grammar," *ONTS* 2 (1882-83) 214-216.

*George Bertin, "On the Character and Influence of the Accent in the Akkadian and Assyrian Words," *SBAP* 5 (1882-83) 19-21.

Theo[philus] G. Pinches, "Papers on Assyrian Grammar. Introductory," *SBAP* 5 (1882-83) 21-31.

D. G. Lyon, "On the Study of Assyrian," *ONTS* 3 (1883-84) 249-252. (Corr. p. 263)

Theo[philus] G. Pinches, "Papers on Assyrian Grammar, II," *SBAP* 6 (1883-84) 62-67. [The Permansive of the other Forms; Remarks; Further Remarks upon the Permansive Kal]

†Geo[rge] Bertin, Theo[philus] G. Pinches, and E. A. Budge, "The Transcription of Assyrian," *SBAP* 6 (1883-84) 125-126.

*C[rawford] H. Toy, "Semitic Notes," *AJP* 5 (1884) 493-500. [I. Assyrian Case-endings, pp. 493-494]

Anonymous, "The Study of Assyrian," *AJSL* 1 (1884-85) 130-132.

Paul Haupt, "On the Etymology of Mutninu," *AJSL* 2 (1885-86) 4-6.

Anonymous, "An Important Help for the Study of Assyrian," *AJSL* 2 (1885-86) 56-58.

*†Theo[philus] G. Pinches, "Assyriological Notes," *SBAP* 8 (1885-86) 240-245. [An Interesting Numeral-form; Âgarrûtu, 'workmen'; 𒅴 šaṭāru, 'a written document'; Nadānu, and natānu, 'to give'; The Name of Sargon of Agade; Assyrian Bird-Names]

*Morris Jastrow Jr., "Assyrian, in its Relation to Hebrew and Arabic," *PAPA* 18 (1886) xviii-xix.

*Richard J. H. Gottheil, "Syriac and Assyrian," *AJSL* 3 (1886-87) 187.

Bêl-ibnî, "An Assyrian Lexicon," *BOR* 1 (1886-87) 124-126. *(Review)*

G. A. Simcox, "Note on the name Bit-hilani," *SBAP* 9 (1886-87) 193-194. (Reply by C. J. Ball, pp. 194-195)

Paul Haupt, "The Assyrian *E-* Vowel," *AJP* 8 (1887) 265-291.

( ) E., "Dr. Delitzsch's Assyrian Dictionary," *Exp, 3rd Ser.,* 6 (1887) 228-232. *(Review)*

Habib Anthony Salmoné, "Zumru and Zamaru," *BOR* 2 (1887-88) 64.

.Morris Jastrow Jr., "Delitzsch's Assyrian Dictionary, Part I.," *PAPA* 19 (1887) xii-xiv. *(Review)*

( ) E., "Brevia. Assyrisches Worterbuch, von F. Delitzsch, 2. Lieferung, Hinrichs, Leipzig, 1888," *Exp, 3rd Ser.,* 8 (1888) 233-240, 320.

*A. H. Sayce, "The Woman's Language of Chaldea," *Exp, 3rd Ser.,* 8 (1888) 319. [Assy. NAQBU =(?) Accadian EME-SAL]

S. Alden Smith, "Assyriological notes," *ZA* 3 (1888) 100-102. [𒀸𒁺 𒀭𒈨𒌋; 𒄑 𒁲𒄑 𒀸 ; 𒊹 𒌋 𒈨; 𒂊𒊩 𒀭𒋼 𒈨]

*A. H. Sayce, "Pronominal Forms in Egyptian," *SBAP* 11 (1888-89) 80-82.
[Ref. ᵗ𒁹 𒁹, pp. 81-82]

*[Morris] Jastrow [Jr.], "On Assyrian and Samaritan," *JAOS* 13 (1889) cxlvii-cl.

David G. Lyon, "Notice of Delitzsch's *Assyrisches Wörterbuch, Erste Lieferung*," *JAOS* 13 (1889) clxi-clxviii.

Morris Jastrow Jr., "On Ikonomatic writing in Assyrian," *JAOS* 13 (1889) clxviii-clxxii.

Edgar P. Allen, "Announcement of a new Assyrian-English Glossary," *JAOS* 13 (1889) ccxliv-ccxlix.

Paul Haupt, "Prolegomena to a Comparative Assyrian Grammar," *JAOS* 13 (1889) ccxlix-cclxvii.

Paul Haupt, "Explanation concerning a remark in the notes of the Prolegomena to a Comparative Assyrian Grammar," *JAOS* 13 (1889) cccii.

*A. H. Sayce, "Miscellaneous Notes," *ZA* 4 (1889) 382-393. [33. The name of Eve in Assyrian, p. 393]

Morris Jastrow Jr., "Êpêšu," *ZA* 4 (1889) 406.

V. Scheil, "Assyriological Notes," *BOR* 4 (1889-90) 44-48. [šallaru; kalakku; alluḫappu]

Morris Jastrow Jr., "On the Assyrian *kudûru* and the ring of the Sun-god in the Abu-Habba tablet," *JAOS* 14 (1890) xcv-xcviii.

Cyrus Adler, "Assyrian verbs ל״ו and ל״י," *JAOS* 14 (1890) xcviii-c.

M[orris] Jastrow Jr., "Azûru," *ZA* 5 (1890) 295-296.

*W. Muss-Arnolt, "Assyrian Etymologies," *AJSL* 7 (1890-91) 183-185, 253-256. [I. Tup-šikku = *a badge of servitude;* II. A-ṭap-pu = ṭap-pu = Hebrew שֶׂפַח, *coping;* III. antalû *eclipse;* IV. Tamkaru and Timkallu; V. ŠE-BAR and ŠE-ZIR]

Charles F. Kent, "Annexion in Assyrian," *AJSL* 7 (1890-91) 289-301.

Lester Bradner Jr., "The Order of the Sentence in the Assyrian Historical Inscriptions," *AJSL* 8 (1891-92) 1-14.

Robert Francis Harper, "A-bi-e-shu-' = Ebishum," *AJSL* 8 (1891-92) 103-104.

*George A. Barton, "Tiamat," *JAOS* 15 (1893) 1-27.

William R. Harper, "Some notes on historical Assyrian syntax," *JAOS* 15 (1893) lxxiv-lxxvi.

Lester Bradner Jr., "The order of the sentence in the Assyrian historical inscriptions," *JAOS* 15 (1893) cxxviii.

Robert F[rancis] Harper, "On Kraetzschar's views as to the *a*-vowel in an overhanging syllable," *JAOS* 15 (1893) cxix-cxx.

George A. Reisner, "The construct case in Assyrian," *JAOS* 15 (1893) cxxi-cxxvi.

Charles Foster Kent, "Annexion in Assyrian," *JAOS* 15 (1893) cxxvi-cxxvii.

Carl J. Elofson, "Position of the adjective in Assyrian historical inscriptions," *JAOS* 15 (1893) cxxviii-cxxx.

Robert Francis Harper, "Assyriological Notes," *AJSL* 10 (1893-94) 196-201.

*Fritz Hommel, "Assyriological Notes," *SBAP* 16 (1893-94) 209-212. [§1. 𒀭𒀭𒀭𒀭𒀭; §2. 'Ass. *mindema* = Aram. *minda am, meddem;* §3. 𒀭𒀭𒀭𒀭𒀭; §4. *a-na* 𒀭𒀭𒀭𒀭 *ra-shi-bat Ninua at-ta-shi ka-ti;* §5. Sha 𒀭 *Martu, mâr A-bi-i-ra-mu*]

G[eorge] A. Reisner, "The Berlin Vocabulary V. A. Th. 244," *ZA* 9 (1894-95) 149-164.

*Fritz Hommel, "Assyriological Notes," *SBAP* 17 (1895) 199-207. [§6. לעלנסחממלכי; §7. *Sha-ma-num ghar-sag Me-nu-a-ta,* 𒀭 *-šal-la ghar-sag Mar-tu-ta tag na-gal im-ta-dul-du, na-rù-a-ku mu-gim;* §8. Etymology of עוֹלָם אוּלָם דֶּעִילָם; §9. A Palestinian Letter of the Amarna Period - 4 R. 34, No. 2.; §10. Inscription of *Agu-kak-rimi* (5 R.33)]

*Fritz Hommel, "Assyriological Notes," *SBAP* 18 (1896) 17-24. [§13. *mât A-* 𒀀𒂅 *- ri-î;* §14. . K. 257 lines 29 and 30 𒄀𒐊; §15. S^b 287-8 𒐊 𒂊, Sumerian *sur-ru;* §16. K. 8204; §17. K2455; §18. K. 9852; §19. The expression ᐅ𒅀 𒂊𒊺𒀀 ; §20. Elamite proper name *Ma-uk-ti-tî*]

*Theophilus G. Pinches, "Assyriological Gleanings," *SBAP* 18 (1896) 250-258. [81-11-3, 435; 81-11-3, 478; 81-1-18. 1846; A. H. 83-1-18, 1866; 83-1-18, 1847; 81-11-8,154]

*Fritz Hommel, "Assyriological Notes," *SBAP* 19 (1897) 78-90, 312-315. [§21. *lubâru;* §22. *nabâsu, napâsu;* §23. Hebrew *b* // Babylonian *p;* §24. Sumerian *ĝilib,* "god"; §25. *-sar* or *-sir;* §26. W.A.I. 28. 17 - *Akhânu* and *Arpad;* §27. *Tuktü,* "blood, vengeance = 𒋼𒅗𒌋 *(tektô)* "blood (of the woman)"; §28. *Amat-* ᐅᐟ *Su-'u-la;* §29. Inscription in *Collection de Clereq,* Vol. II, Pl. X, No. 6; §30. *i-mi,* 𒀀𒀹, *a-ḫu* and *ṭi-ṭu;* §31. Babylonian gods, ᐅᐟ 𒍦𒂖 𒅗𒐊 and ᐅᐟ𒀀𒀹; §32. The name of the god ᐅᐟ 𒍦𒂖 𒅗𒐊; §33. falcon, *surdu;* §34. madâdu - ma-da-du, namaddu, shudadu = râimu; §35. akhulâpi = adî matî; §36. umâmu; §37 pishannu; §38 ashlaku]

J. Dyneley Prince, "On the syntax of the Assyrian preposition *ina,*" *JAOS* 16 (1896) ccxviii-ccxxvii.

*Robert Francis Harper, "Assyriological Notes," *AJSL* 13 (1896-97) 209-212. [II]

Charles Foster Kent, "The Origin and Signification of the GUNU-Signs," *AJSL* 13 (1896-97) 299-308.

J. Dyneley Prince, "The Syntax of the Assyrian Preposition *ana,*" *JAOS* 18 (1897) 355-360.

*Robert Francis Harper, "Assyriological Notes," *AJSL* 14 (1897-98) 1-16. [III]

Robert Francis Harper, "Assyriological Notes. IV," *AJSL* 14 (1897-98) 171-182.

Charles Boutflower, "On the Meaning of the Word Asîtu," *AJSL* 15 (1898-99) 49-51.

*Robert Francis Harper, "Assyriological Notes. V," *AJSL* 15 (1898-99) 129-144.

J. Dyneley Prince, "Assyrian Prepositional Usage," *JAOS* 20 (1899) 1-11.

Christopher Johnston, "Two new Assyrian words," *JAOS* 20 (1899) 250-252. [jâmútu; pâgu]

†C. H. W. Johns, "The words *Adar* and *Sartu*," *SBAP* 21 (1899) 79-80.

*Fritz Hommel, "Assyriological Notes *(Continuation)*," *SBAP* 21 (1899) 115-139.[§38a. *ashlaku,* rope-maker, hence Arabic *silk;* §39. The Lulubaean king *Anu-banî-ni*; §40. The list of Assyrian gods, K. 252 (W.A.I., III, 66), and Ahura-mazda; §41. The true reading of 𒌍, UR-, as the first element of proper names; §42. The true reading of 𒀭 Nin 𒌍 as Nin-ib; §43. *shanunkatu,* "queen"; §44. AMIAUD, *ikkaru,* "peasant"; §45. *Ḫu-ḫu-tar-ri, Ḫu-uḫ-tar-ri* not *Ḫu-ḫu-nu-ru* (-ki), var. *Ḫu-uḫ-nu-ri;* §46. Assyrian *kakku,* "weapon"; §47. שׁנגלא = *ushumgallu;* §48. *lardu* = spikenard, Hebrew נֵרְדְּ, νάρδος; §49. *Proper names;* §50. Ahura-mazda and *Varuna* in Assyrian inscriptions]

*C. H. W. J[ohns], "Assyriological Notes," *SBAP* 21 (1899) 140-141, 254-255.

C. H. W. Johns, "The Offical Title LU-SU-PA-MEŠ," *SBAP* 21 (1899) 172-173.

George R. Berry, "The Assyrian Word mašâru or magarru," *AJSL* 16 (1899-1900) 50-51.

*T. K. Cheyne, "On an Assyrian Loan-word in Hebrew, and on מִמְזָר," *SBAP* 22 (1900) 165-166. *[mindidu]*

C[harles] Boutflower, "On a Not Uncommon Rendering of the Word ÍKALLU," *AJSL* 17 (1900-01) 244-249.

Christopher Johnston, "Note on two Assyrian words hitherto unexplained," *JAOS* 22 (1901) 23-26 [(1) da' âlu; (2) ûlâ]

Mary Inda Hussey, "A Supplement to Brunnow's Classified List of Cuneiform Ideographs," *JAOS* 22 (1901) 201-220.

Theophilus G. Pinches, "Assyriological Gleanings. II," *SBAP* 23 (1901) 188-210. [82-5-22, 956 (54626); Rm. IV, 97 (33,541); Rm. IV, 90 (33,534)]

*C. H. W. Johns, "Some Secondary Formations Among Assyrian Proper Names," *AJSL* 18 (1901-02) 149-166, 246-253.

*Francis R. Harper, "Assyriological Notes. VI," *AJSL* 19 (1902-03) 228-232.

W. Muss-Arnolt, " ŠUPAR, (amêl)ŠUPARŠÂḲ(Û), (amêl)ŠAḲŠUPP(BB)AR, and Related Terms," *AJSL* 20 (1903-04) 186-193.

W. Muss-Arnolt, "Lexicographical Notes," *AJSL* 20 (1903-04) 223-234. [1. šêrêti; 2. šêrtu; 3. šêrtu; 4. šêrtu; 5. tam-gi-ti; 6. ti-'-u-tu; 7. têlu; 8. te-el-tum; 9. têl(i)tu; 10. šanû; 11. (amêl)šanû; 12. šina; 13. šinîtum; 14. šanû; 15. ši-pi šaṭiṭi; 16. (ilat)Ereš-ki-gal; 17. ḫabûnu, Šerru; 18. šarûru; 19. ša-ra IBARI ša-a-ru; 20. šâru; 21. Ša-riš; 22. Têbiltu; 23. ti-šit; 24. ta-a-an]

*A. H. Godbey, "SISINNU = 'Horsebird' = Ostrich," *AJSL* 20 (1903-04) 257-258.

H. A. Godbey, "(amêl)KUL - ḫêpû = Woodcutter," *AJSL* 20 (1903-04) 258-259.

*A. H. Godbey, "Political, Religious, and Social Antiquities of the Sargonid Period," *AJSL* 21 (1904-05) 65-82.

*A. H. Godbey, "The Assyro-Babylonian amelTU.BÎTI," *AJSL* 22 (1905-06) 45-62.

*Stephen [H.] Langdon, "Sumerian-Assyrian Vocabularies," *Baby* 2 (1907-08) 199-208, 282-288; 3 (1909-10) 145-196, 259-265; 4 (1910-11) 9-56.

Stephen [H.] Langdon, "Lexicographical note," *Baby* 2 (1907-08) 121-125. [*naṭū; galādu-galātu*]

*A. M. Skelly, "The Resurrection of Ancient Egypt and Assyria," *IER, 4th Ser.,* 23 (1908) 510-522.

S[tephen H.] Langdon, "Lexicographical Studies," *SBAP* 30 (1908) 266-271. [I. The Root *Šakāku* and its Derivatives; II. *Pušḳu,* IV. Rawlinson]

*S[tephen H.] Langdon, "Lexicographical Studies," *ZA* 21 (1908) 283-292. [1. כתר to be complete, successful, etc.; 2. *pûḫu* = "image"; 3. פחה; 4. *sirdū abālu* = *sardū abālu:aplu* = "replacer"; 5. *ardu* and *ardatu*]

S[tephen H.] Langdon, "Lexicographical Studies," *SBAP* 30 (1908) 266-271. [I. The Root *Šakāu* and its Derivatives; II. *Pušku*]

Christopher Johnston, "Assyrian *qanânu* 'to coil'; and *xarâpu* 'to abound'," *JAOS* 29 (1909) 224-226.

*S[tephen H.] Langdon, "Lexicographical Studies," *SBAP* 31 (1909) 74-77. [III. Semitic words for "sorrow," "distress"; Sumerian *šag-dib*, Br. 8072-7; IV. *Niknakku*]

S[tephen H.] Langdon, "Lexicographical Studies," *SBAP* 31 (1909) 110-114. [V. The Assyrian Adverbial Endings *iš, aš, uš, ussu, uššu*]

Paul Haupt, "Some Assyrian Etymologies," *AJSL* 26 (1909-10) 1-26.

*Morris Jastrow Jr., "Signs and Names of the Planet Mars," *AJSL* 27 (1910-11) 64-83.

*Christopher Johnston, "Assyrian Lexicographical Notes," *AJSL* 27 (1910-11) 187-189. [*a)* b a t t u 'side', *b)* k a l a k u 'raft', *c)* b â s i, 'on account of, in order that', *d)* t i k p u 'row, course of stone, or brick']

S[tephen] Langdon, "The Signs ⊬𒁹 (A) and ⊬𒁹 (B)," *SBAP* 33 (1911) 50-52.

L. W. King, "The Meaning and Use of *Ḳutaru* in Assyrian Magic," *SBAP* 33 (1911) 62-67.

*S[tephen H.] Langdon, "The Assyrian Root Raṣānu, Hebrew רזן," *AJSL* 28 (1911-12) 144-145.

Paul Haupt, "The five Assyrian stems la'u," *JAOS* 32 (1912) 17-20.

Christopher Johnston, "Assyrian Karâru 'to wind' and Pilurtu 'tablet'," *AJSL* 29 (1912-13) 122-125.

*S. C. Ylvisaker, "Dialectic Differences between Assyrian and Babylonian, and some Problems they Present," *JAOS* 33 (1913) 397-401.

S[tephen H.] Langdon, "Concerning the use of the word *Ullānu* in Assyrian," *SBAP* 35 (1913) 193-195.

S[tephen H.] Langdon, "Lexicographical Notes," *SBAP* 35 (1913) 277-281. [(1) The Sign 𒀭𒁉 = *arḫu;* (2) The Ideogram 𒀭𒁉 𒀭𒁉; (3) 𒀭𒁉 𒀭𒁉, *galu-kàs = mar šipri,* "messenger"]

S[tephen H.] Langdon, "Lexicographical Note on Uluskinnu, Balsam, Pistacea Wine," *AJSL* 30 (1913-14) 288-289.

*S[tephen H.] Langdon, "Critical Notes," *AJSL* 31 (1914-15) 282-286. [I. The Sign *aragub-minnabi;* II. e p ē š u, "to attach, inclose, bind"; III. k u s a r i k k u, "goat-fish"; IV. K I D - n i - e = s i ḫ - l i - e, "Mustard"(?)]

Paul Haupt, "Assyr. *atmu,* fledgling, in the Old Testament," *JBL* 34 (1915) 77-82.

*S[tephen H.] Langdon, "Philological Comments on K. 45. An Omen Tablet in the British Museum," *SBAP* 37 (1915) 42-43.

*S. Daiches, "The Assyrian and Hebrew Words for 'Bread of the Ear of Corn'," *SBAP* 37 (1915) 215-216. *[sussa]*

*Paul Haupt, "Assyr. *Ramku,* 'Priest' = Heb. *Komer, " AJSL* 32 (1915-16) 64-75.

*Felix von Oefele, "Assyrian 'kalmat,' Arabic 'kaemlet'," *JAOS* 36 (1916) 416.

*Paul Haupt, "Askari, *'soldier,'* and Lascar, *'sailor', " JAOS* 36 (1916) 417-418.

*S[tephen H.] Langdon, "Lexicographical and epigraphical notes," *RAAO* 13 (1916) 1-4. [(1) *Li-ga, ga-li - duḫdu,* "Cream"; (2) 𒀭𒁉; The Sign 𒀭𒁉 *(šita),* "Weapon, Mace"]

*Paul Haupt, "Critical Notes," *AJSL* 33 (1916-17) 45-48. [I. Assyr. *mûrnisqui,* "War-Horse"; II. Assyr. *rabû,* "To Sink" = Heb. *raphâ*]

*Paul Haupt, "Assyrian *lânu,* 'aspect'—Arabic *láyn,* 'color'," *JAOS* 37 (1917) 253-255.

*Paul Haupt, "Heb. *Ämš,* Yesterday = Assyr. *Ina Mûši,* at Night," *JBL* 36 (1917) 147-148.

*Paul Haupt, "Tôrâ = Tahrirtu," *JBL* 36 (1917) 258-259.

*A. H. Sayce, "Assyriological Notes," *SBAP* 39 (1917) 207-212.

S[tephen H.] Langdon, "Lexicographical Notes, Contribution to the Assyrian Dictionary," *AJSL* 34 (1917-18) 206-209. [1. *papaḫu*, "Chamber"; 2. *esigu*, "Overflowing Canal"; *egēru*, "to Surround, Bind, Place a Girdle Around"; 4. *kaṣāṣu*, "Press, Harass, Be Harassed, Be Angry"; 5. *kunnâ*, "Solicitously"/*kunnû*, "Solicitous"; 6. *lakû*, "Growl, Howl"]

A. H. Godbey, "The Rab-Šiṭirtê," *AJSL* 34 (1917-18) 13-20

W[illiam] F[oxwell] Albright, "Ninib-Ninurta," *JAOS* 38 (1918) 197-201.

*Paul Haupt, "Assyr. *dagâlu*, to look for, in the OT," *JBL* 37 (1918) 229-232.

*Paul Haupt, "Assyr. *tamêrtu* and Heb. *tĕrûmâ*," *JSOR* 2 (1918) 87.

*St[ephen] Langdon, "Assyriological notes," *RAAO* 15 (1918) 107-114. [1) The Sign ⟨⟨⟩⟩; 2) The Assyrian Root BAGĀRU; 3) The fourth tablet of GAR-RA = ḪUBULLU; 4) Mathematical Observations on the Scheil-Esagila Tablet; 5) *piḫû* a vessel, a liquid measure; 6) Identification of the sign ⸙⸙]

Michel Sidersky, "The Assyrian Word iḳdu," *AJSL* 35 (1918-19) 222-223.

*S[tephen H.] Langdon, "Four Assyriological Notes," *JRAS* (1919) 37-42. [1. The Identification of the Name [d.]Tagtug; 2. *Apsasû*, a Kind of Wild Cattle; 3. *IR = zu'tu*, Sweat; 4. *ARA = namāru*, Blaze, Shine]

*Samuel Daiches, "Etymological Notes. I. Talmudic אפש = Assyrian *epēšu*," *JRAS* (1919) 63-64.

*Stephen [H.] Langdon, "Contribution to Assyrian Lexicography," *JSOR* 3 (1919) 36-41. [1. *ba' ālu* to shine; 2. *EN E-NU-ŠUB = šipat bit pašāri?* 3. *GIŠ = rigmu*; 4. *DURU*, to flood, immerse, in omen texts; 5. [aban]*PA= ja'ertu, ja'artu, ja'āru*, red coral]

Stephen [H.] Langdon, "Contributions to Assyrian Lexicography," *JSOR* 3 (1919) 81-85. [6. *tartābu*, be covered with dust, be begrimed, dark; 7. *kallatu*, "she that is confined in a house"; 8. *ana la ḫâzim rîga*, Code of Hammurabi, Epilogue, 198-199; 9. *gabraḫ*, Code of Hammurabi, Epilogue, 260]

*W[illiam] F[oxwell] Albright, "Notes on assyrian lexicography and etymology," *RAAO* 16 (1919) 173-194. [1. *Abunnatu* = "backbone, back, stature"; 2. *edû,* "tide"; 3. *amûtu,* "intestines, omen"; 4. *ipû,* "womb"; 5. *açîtu* = "tunic, shirt"; 6. *eçîttu* = "burial cairn"; 7. *êru* = "inundate"; 8. *išittu* (pl. *išnâti*), "storehouse"; 9. *ištu,* "from"; 10. *bûbûtu,* "hunger, nourishment"; 11. *bêlu,* "weapon"; 12. *bašû,* "to be, exist"; 13. *batûlu,* "youth"; *batûltu,* "maiden"; 14. *giššu* = "hip, side"; 15. *dallalu* = "water-carrier"; 16. *zâzu,* "divide, distribute"; 17. *ḫamû* = "hold, support, rely, trust"; 18. *ḫamâmu* = "cut, decide"; 19. *ḫamâru* = "cover, veil"; 20. *ḫaçânu,* "hold, carry (in the bosom), protect"; 21. ḫardatu = *"pudendum muliebre";* 22. *lîlâtu,* "evening"; 23. *lamûtânu,* "attendant, minister"; 24. *nablu,* "flame, beam"; 25. *nabâsu,* "(red) wool"; 26.*naḫâšu,* "flood with fertility"; 27. *nalâšu,* (pres. *ináluš*), "to sleet" = Heb. *nāšál,* "drop (shoe, olives, etc.); 28. *nannabu,* "offspring"; 29. *nâpalû,* "interlocutor"; 30. *niqilpû,* "float, pass"; 31. *narâbu* = "swell"; 32. *sûsapînu,* "bridal attendant"; 33. *sarâḫu* —see ḫamâmu; 34. **pêmu,* "leg"; 35. *pisnuqû,* synonym of *enšu,* "weak", *ulâlu* "infant"; 36. *pâru,* "skin"; 37. *çaddu* = "road-sign, mark (of guidance)"; 38. *quluptu,* "slough of serpent"; 39. *qiççu,* "cell, chamber, chapel"; 40. *qarâšu* = "judicial massacre, slaughter of prisoners"; 41. *qattu,* "human form"; 42. *šizbu,* "milk" means properly "cream"; 43. *šêmu* = "grease"; 44. *šapru* = "arse, rump"; 45. *šapâtu,* "complete, decide" (syn. of *gamaru,* "complete", and *dânu,* "decide"; 46. *tû'amu,* "twin"]

*H. F. Lutz, "A Loanword in Egyptian," *JAOS* 40 (1920) 71. [*ṭakapu* = Assy. *zaqapu*]

*S[tephen H.] Langdon, "Assyrian Lexicographical Notes," *JRAS* (1920) 325-331. [1. Bararitu, evening, first watch; 2. Guannakku = καννάκης, frilled mantle; 3. The Babylonian Name of the Milky Way]

Paul Haupt, "Assyr. *birku,* knee, and *karâbu,* to bless," *JBL* 39 (1920) 163-165. (Addenda on p. 172)

Stephen [H.] Langdon, "Contribution to Assyrian Lexicography," *JSOR* 4 (1920) 33-34. [10. The compound preposition and adverb *murgu-ta*]

*Morris Jastrow Jr., *"Ḫuruppati,* 'betrothal gifts'," *JAOS* 41 (1921) 314-316.

G. R. Driver, "Three Assyrian Roots," *JRAS* (1921) 389-393. [1. The Root and meaning of *Kamtum;* 2. Note on the Root *Šimêtan;* 3. The Meaning of *Simkurru*]

*S[tephen] Langdon, "Assyrian Lexicographical Notes," *JRAS* (1921) 573-582. [I. *ŠARĀPU*, to burn, Hebrew *RĀŠAPH*, p. 573; IV. ⟨ᛉ⟨ (SIKUR), to sacrifice, pp. 574-575]

A. H. Sayce, "The Name by Which the Assyrian Language was Known in the Ancient World," *JRAS* (1921) 583.

*D. D. Luckenbill, "Assyriological Notes," *AJSL* 39 (1922-23) 56-65. [I. *daurdu-taurtu,* "minor, orphan (fatherless)"; II. *Ašmanu,* "bachelor or widower(?)"; III. *ubtaeru, uktainu,* not preterites of II 2; IV. *naṭû* and *baḳânu;* V. Was there a God Zababa? VI. Urta, one of the many gods identified with Ninib; VII. On some "Hittite" Proper Names]

Robert H. Pfeiffer, "On the Babylonian-Assyrian Feudalism (*ilku*)," *AJSL* 39 (1922-23) 66-68.

*S[tephen H.] Langdon, "Contributions to the Assyrian Lexicon," *AJSL* 39 (1922-23) 136-142. [1) *eṭirritu,* treaty, alliance; 2) *ṣîta rašû,* to run away; 3) *ilam rašû;* 4) *dullulu;* 5. *giparu;* 6) *šaman ḫalṣa,* filtered oil; 7) A Letter of Hammurabi; 8) *ibizzû,* loss, injury; 9) *imirtu,* field, meadow]

Robert H. Pfeiffer, "Assyrian Epistolary Formulae," *JAOS* 43 (1923) 26-40.

Stephen [H.] Langdon, "Assyriological Notes," *JSOR* 7 (1923) 53-55. [1) The Semitic Word for 'hermaphrodite'; 2) *Zaḫannu,* a vessel; 3) KA-KA-SI-GA, 'The meaning is the same']

George A. Barton, "Lexicographical notes," *JAOS* 44 (1924) 271-272. [1. *i-ga-ad-di-mj-uš;* 2. (phrase) *šum-ma amelu ta-ḫu-ú-ma raba-a ša-a tap-pa-i-šu us-sa-am-mi-iḫ;* 3. *it-tam-ra-a-ak*]

R. Campbell Thompson, "*ᵘKur.Kur.* = Hellebore," *JRAS* (1924) 669-671.

Leroy Waterman, "Abbreviated Ideograms in the Assyrian Letter-Literature," *AJSL* 41 (1924-25) 17-23.

D. D. Luckenbill, "Assyrian *be-dak,* 'to spend the night'," *AJSL* 41 (1924-25) 136-138.

*Paul Haupt, "Heb. ärz, cedar ‹ Ass. irêšu, balsamic juice," *JAOS* 45 (1925) 322-323.

*Sidney Smith, "Assyriological Notes," *JRAS* (1925) 508-513. [Adumu, Adummatu, Abubu, Anu and Adapa, Ea and Mummu]

*S[tephen H.] Langdon, "Philological Note on *Nalbaš Šamê* = *Ishtar,*" *JRAS* (1925) 717.

Ephraim Avigdor Speiser, "Vocalic N in Assyrian," *Lang* 1 (1925) 107-108.

*S[tephen H.] Langdon, "Assyriological Notes," *RAAO* 22 (1925) 31-38. [I. *ŠUTUR* = *šuturu,* cloth in the roll, "hank"; II. *UTTUKU,* weaver, fuller, (male and female); III. *ILLURI: ILLULU,* javelin, boomerang, bow (?); Corrigenda; Note: *utukku, uttukku, utuku* = *Ôdakôn(?)*]

*A. H. Sayce, "Notes," *RAAO* 22 (1925) 93. [LAL-KI, a bee hive - 𒆷𒆠]

*Paul Haupt, "Arab. *tâjir* and Ass. *tamkaru,*" *BAVSS* 10 (1927) Heft 2, 31-68.

Paul Haupt, "Ass. *ablu,* mourner, heir," *BAVSS* 10 (1927) Heft 2, 69-83.

*Paul Haupt, "Ass. *talîmu,* full brother," *BAVSS* 10 (1927) Heft 2, 114-120.

Paul Haupt, "Ass. *pâtu,* blowy, and *pâṭu,* brim," *BAVSS* 10 (1927) Heft 2, 137-140.

*Paul Haupt, "Ass. *miṭpânu,* longbow," *BAVSS* 10 (1927) Heft 2, 144-145.

*Paul Haupt, "Ass. *napšu,* lust," *BAVSS* 10 (1927) 148-149.

Paul Haupt, "The Personal Prefixes of the Imperfect," *BAVSS* 10 (1927) Heft 2, 198-202.

Paul Haupt, "Ass. *kamâsu, kanâšu,* and *qamâçu,*" *BAVSS* 10 (1927) Heft 2, 253-257.

*Paul Haupt, "Ass. *budulxu,* bdellium, and Arab. *taḥállub,* secretion," *BAVSS* 10 (1927) Heft 2, 258-263.

*Paul Haupt, "Ass. *zâzu,* halve, and Eth. *azzáza,* command," *BAVSS* 10 (1927) Heft 2, 264-267.

*Paul Haupt, "Ass. *marçu,* sick, and *marçu,* arduous," *BAVSS* 10 (1927) Heft 2, 271-273.

*Paul Haupt, "Ass. *xamâdu,* to help = Arab. *mádaxa,*" *BAVSS* 10 (1927) Heft 2, 274-275.

*R. Campbell Thompson, "Assyrian *Garidu* = 'Beaver'," *JRAS* (1927) 723.

*S[tephen H.] Langdon, "Assyriological Note," *JRAS* (1927) 323-326. [The Assyrian Root, *Katātu,* Sumerian, *Tuku*]

*Robert H. Pfeiffer, "Three Assyriological Footnotes to the Old Testament," *JBL* 47 (1928) 184-187. [*1. Ilāni* = *Elohim,* pp. 184-185]

S[tephen H.] Langdon, "Assyriological Notes," *JRAS* (1928) 143-148. [(1) *GIR-PAD-DU* = *ḳursinnu* "leg bone, leg," *eṣimtu* "bone"; (2) parû ẏarû "to empty," *vomere*]

*Leroy Waterman, "Some Proposed Assyrian-Hebrew Parallels," *AJSL* 45 (1928-29) 281-285.

*R. Campbell Thompson, "(1) On *KUR.GI.ḪU, kurkû* = the Crane; (2) šikkû = 'cat'; (3) *kamunu* = 'red worms'," *JRAS* (1929) 339-343.

*S[tephen] Langdon, "Adonis in Assyrian?" *RAAO* 27 (1930) 23-25.

*S[tephen H.] Langdon, "Assyriological Notes," *JRAS* (1932) 327-332. [I. Agalla = *mu'iru;* II. The Sign 𒀹𒀹 (eri, era) = *mu'irru,* Director; III. Note on the Year Date 2 of Samsuiluna; IV. The sign TAG, value *paḫ, baḫ;* V. Sumerian *bad-bad* = *babbad* = *tapdû, padanû, taḫtû;* VI. *birîš* = In Hunger, Hungrily]

*A. Poebel, "Sumerian Mu-an-na 'year' and Egyptian *Rnpt* 'year'," *AJSL* 49 (1932-33) 1-8.

*S[tephen H.] Langdon, "Assyriological Notes," *RAAO* 30 (1933) 105-110. [I. *Anduḫallatu, imduḫallatu,* gecko, salamander; II. A) ZARAḪ, wailing, misery. B) ZARAḪ, stork. C) ZARAḪ, some part of the body; III. K. 8827; IV. *ḫamû, ḫammu,* slime, marsh grass, not *ḫamû, ḫammu;* V. *Gurgurru,* a plant, a love potion, rocket]

*R. Campbell Thompson, "On Some Assyrian Minerals," *JRAS* (1933) 885-895.

*Samuel I. Feigin, "The Captives in Cuneiform Inscriptions," *AJSL* 50 (1933-34) 217-245. [5. *esirtu* in the Assyrian Laws, pp. 228-230]

*R. Campbell Thompson, "On the Assyrian words for 'whetstone' and 'corundum'," *JRAS* (1934) 343-346.

S[tephen H.] Langdon, "Assyriological Notes," *RAAO* 31 (1934) 109-113. [I. Upšāšû not aršāšû; II. Nalbānu, nalbantu, nalbattu, Brick mould; CT., 19, 10, K. 5425B, 6-9 (Restoration); *(No part IV)* V. CT., 12, 42, A 28, (Restoration)]

*Samuel I. Feigin, "The Captives in Cuneiform Inscriptions—*Continued*," *AJSL* 51 (1934-35) 22-29. [Appendix II: The Word *batiqânu* in the Assyrian Laws, pp. 24-26]

Julius Lewy, "Old Assyrian *puru'um* and *pūrum*," *RHA* 5 (1938-40) 117-124.

*R. Campbell Thompson, "*ú*Kurangu* and *ú*Lal(l)angu* as Possibly 'Rice' and 'Indigo' in Cuneiform," *Iraq* 6 (1939) 180-183.

*A. Leo Oppenheim, "Assyriological Notes to the Old Testament," *JQR, N.S.,* 36 (1945-46) 171-176. [Neo-Babyl. *pirku* = Heb. פֶּרֶךְ]

*H. Torczyner, "*Semel Ha-qin'ah Ha-maqneh*," *JBL* 65 (1946) 293-302. [5. Šamala napṭur, pp. 299-300]

*A. Leo Oppenheim, "Assyriological Notes to the Old Testament," *JQR, N.S.,* 37 (1946-47) 175-176. [הֲרֵי יוֹנִים = ḫalla summati]

Julius Lewy, "Ḫatta, Ḫattu, Ḫatti, Ḫattuša, and 'Old Assyrian' Ḫattum," *ArOr* 18 (1950) Part 3, 366-441.

Theophile J. Meek, "The Explicative Pronoun *šu/ša* in the Code of Hammurabi," *ArOr* 18 (1950) Part 4, 78-81.

J[ulius] Lewy, "Studies in Old Assyrian Grammar and Lexicography," *Or, N.S.,* 19 (1950) 1-36.

*M. B. Rowton, "*Ṭuppu* and the Date of Hammurabi," *JNES* 10 (1951) 184-204.

*J[ulius] Lewy, "Old Assyrian *ḫusârum* and Sanchunyâtôn's Story about Chusor," *IEJ* 5 (1955) 154-162.

Ralph Marcus, "Logogram or Lexigram?" *JAOS* 76 (1956) 200.

*Hildegard Lewy, "On Some Old Assyrian Cereal Names," *JAOS* 76 (1956) 201-204.

M. B. Rowton, "*Ṭuppū* in the Assyrian King-Lists," *JNES* 18 (1959) 213-221.

J[ulius] Lewy, "Old Assyrian *izêzum* and its Implications," *Or, N.S.,* 28 (1959) 351-360.

*J[ulius] Lewy, "The Old Assyrian Surface Measure *Šubtum*," *SBO* 3 (1959) 216-226.

J[ulius] Lewy, "Lexical and Grammatical Studies," *Or, N.S.,* 29 (1960) 20-45. [1. À propos of the Stative in Prohibitive Clauses; 2. Old Assyrian *abâtum;* 3. Signification and Etymology of *assurri* and Related Terms; 4. Old Assyrian *šušalšum*]

H[ayim] Tadmor, "Que and Muṣri," *IEJ* 11 (1961) 143-150.

J. A. Brinkman, "New Evidence on Old Assyrian *ḫamuštum*," *Or, N.S.,* 32 (1963) 387-394.

J. A. Brinkman, "Note on Old Assyrian *ḫamuštum,* " *JNES* 24 (1965) 118-120.

Kemal Balkan, "Contributions to the Understanding of the Idiom of the Old Assyrian Merchants of Kanish," *Or, N.S.,* 36 (1967) 393-415. [kabāsum]

Julius Lewy and Hildegard Lewy, "Old Assyrian *subrum,* " *HUCA* 39 (1968) 1-15.

*Michael Ford, "The Contradictory Records of Sargon II of Assyria and the Meaning of *palûi*," *JCS* 22 (1968-69) 83-84.

*A. Hurvitz, "Ακκαρων = *Amaqar(r)una* = עקרון," *Lěš* 33 (1968-69) #1, n.p.n.

*W. G. Lambert, "The Reading of the God Name ᵈKA.DI," *ZA* 59 (1969) 100-103.

David Sperling, "The Informer and the Conniver," *JANES* 2 (1969-70) 101-104. *[lišānu]*

*David Neiman, "*URBI* 'Irregulars' or 'Arabs'," *JQR, N.S.,* 60 (1969-70) 237-258.

§534 *3.3.3.2.3.2 Babylonian - General Studies*

Edward Hincks, "Chaldean Interpretations," *JSL, 4th Ser.,* 5 (1864) 421-425.

Paul Haupt, "The Babylonian 'Woman's Language'," *AJP* 5 (1884) 68-84.

A. H. Sayce, "Kikkisu-GAB.RI," *ZK* 1 (1884) 257-258. [1. *Kikkisu:* Deluge-table I. 18, 19 (Haupt); 2. GAB-RI]

Carl F. Lehmann, "On the dialectic Equivalence of *sh* and *n* in Proto-Babylonian," *JAOS* 11 (1885) cxciii-cxciv.

Theo[philus] G. Pinches, "Archaic Forms of Babylonian Characters," *ZK* 2 (1885) 149-156.

*†Theo[philus] G. Pinches, "Assyriological Notes," *SBAP* 8 (1885-86) 240-245. [𒀭𒁾 šaṭāru, 'a written document', p. 241-242]

Eberhard Schrader, "Note on a Legal Term in the *Babylonian Contract Tablets,*" *BOR* 1 (1886-87) 147. [𒁹𒁹𒁹𒁹𒁹]

Theo[philus] G. Pinches, "Babylonian Etymologies: The Pronunciation of the Divine Name 𒀭𒀭𒁹," *BOR* 1 (1886-87) 207-208.

G. Bertin, "Origin and Development of the Cuneiform Syllabary," *JRAS* (1887) 625-654.

Theo[philus] G. Pinches, "Babylonian Etymologies, &c.," *BOR* 2 (1887-88) 39. [The Letter *M* in Semitic Babylonian]

T[errien] de Lacouperie, "The old Babylonian Characters and their Chinese Derivates," *BOR* 2 (1887-88) 73-99.

A. H. Sayce, "The Old Babylonian Characters and their Chinese Derivates," *BOR* 2 (1887-88) 218-220.

*W. St. Chad Boscawen, "Babylonian Canals," *BOR* 2 (1887-88) 226-233. (Explanatory Note, p. 263) [𒁹]

Terrien de Lacouperie, "Chips of Babylonian and Chinese Palæography," *BOR* 2 (1887-88) 257-263.

Terrien de Lacouperie, "The Origin of the Babylonian Characters from the Persian Gulf," *JRAS* (1888) 316-319.

C. Bezold, "The 'Woman's Language' of Ancient Chaldea," *SBAP* 11 (1888-89) 16-17. [⊬⛉ ⛨ instead of ⊬⛫ ⛨⊢]

Theo[philus] G. Pinches, "Ammatu^m," *BOR* 4 (1889-90) 69-71. (With letter by O. C. Whitehouse, p. 70)

Richard Kraetzschmar, "The Sign of the Breath at the End of Words in the New-Babylonian and Achaemenian Inscriptions," *AJSL* 7 (1890-91) 149-151.

*Robert Brown Jr., "Remarks on the Euphratean Astonomical Names of the Signs of the Zodiac," *SBAP* 13 (1890-91) 246-271.

Fritz Hommel, "The Ideogram ⊨⫯⫯," *SBAP* 15 (1892-93) 111-112.

Morris Jastrow Jr., "Mušannîtu(m)," *AJSL* 10 (1893-94) 193-195.

*Fritz Hommel, "Assyriological Notes," *SBAP* 16 (1893-94) 209-212. [§2. Etymology of ידע/מדע compares with Babylonian *mindi*, pp. 210-211]

*Fritz Hommel, "Assyriological Notes," *SBAP* 17 (1895) 199-207. [§11a. Babylonian *šutapú* = Syr. שׁוּרְתָּפָא, 11b. Arabic لُرن = Babylonian *lânu*; pp. 205-206]

*Fritz Hommel, "Assyriological Notes," *SBAP* 19 (1897) 78-90, 312-315. [§23. Babylonian *p* = Hebrew, Aramaic, and Arabic *b*; §31. Babylonian gods, ⊢⟨ ⛨⊟ ⊨⫯⫯ and ⊢⟨ ⛛⊢⫯⫯; §32. Name of the god ⊢⟨ ⛨⊟ ⊨⫯⫯ to be read *Nin-dar* or *Nin-ib*; §36. Babylonian *umâm* "beast" = *ubhâmu, buhâmu*; §37. *pishannu*; §38. Babylonian *ashlaku* = Arab. *silk*]

Morris Jastrow Jr., "The Babylonian Term Šu'âlu," *AJSL* 14 (1897-98) 165-170.

C. J. Ball, "Babylonian Hieroglyphics," *SBAP* 20 (1898) 9-23, 296-298. [(1) ⊨⫯⫯,(2) ⟨⊟⫯,(3) ⊢⟨⫯⛛,(4) ⊢⟨⫯⛛,(5) ⊢⟨⫯⟨,(6) ⊢⟨⫯⛨,(7) ⛨⫯⫯,(8) ⊨⫯⫯,(9) ⊨⫯⫯,(10) ⛨⊨⫯⫯,(11) ⛨,(12) ⊨⛛⫯ ⛨⊟⫯; ⛛⛨ ⟨⛨⊨]

Fritz Hommel, "The Babylonian Ideogram for 'Image' and the Slate Palette from Hieraconopolis," *SBAP* 20 (1898) 291-295. [𒄲 𒐋𒂷]

*A. H. Godbey, "Political, Religious, and Social Antiquities of the Sargonid Period," *AJSL* 21 (1904-05) 65-82.

*Theophilus G. Pinches, "The Element *îlu* in Babylonian Divine Names," *JRAS* (1905) 143-150.

*A. H. Godbey, "The Assyro-Babylonian ^amelTU.BÎTI," *AJSL* 22 (1905-06) 45-62.

R. J. Lau, "Supplement to the Old-Babylonian Vocabularies," *JAOS* 27 (1906) 297-300.

Morris Jastrow Jr., "The Signs and Names for the Liver in Babylonian," *ZA* 20 (1907) 105-129.

*Morris Jastrow Jr., "The Sign and Name for Planet in Babylonian," *PAPS* 47 (1908) 141-156.

*S[tephen H.] Langdon, "*Šurru,* Shoulder. *Ašāru,* Assemble," *SBAP* 30 (1908) 178-181.

George A. Barton, "The Development of Babylonian Picture Writing," *AJA* 13 (1909) 53.

*S[tephen H.] Langdon, "Lexicographical Studies. III.," *SBAP* 31 (1909) 74-77. [IV. Niknalthu, pp. 75-77]

*C. H. W. Johnes, "The Sissiktu," *SBAP* 31 (1909) 78-80.

*Morris Jastrow Jr., "Signs and Names of the Planet Mars," *AJSL* 27 (1910-11) 64-83.

Stephen [H.] Langdon, "The Sign A + HA," *Baby* 4 (1910-11) 192.

*George A. Barton, "On the Etymology of Ishtar," *JAOS* 31 (1910-11) 355-358.

S[tephen H.] Langdon, "The Babylonian *Zuḫaru*," *SBAP* 33 (1911) 121-127.

*T[heophilus] G. Pinches, "Babylonian Inscriptions," *SBAP* 33 (1911) 155-161. [Note on the title 'King of Eridu', p. 161]

L. W. King, "A Neo-Babylonian Syllabary of the class S^c," *ZA* 25 (1911) 298-301.

S[tephen H.] Langdon, "Concerning two unidentified signs," *RAAO* 9 (1912) 161-162. [A = ; B =]

S[tephen H.] Langdon, "The Babylonian Interrogative Adverbs," *AJSL* 29 (1912-13) 205-206.

Geo[rge] A. Barton, "The Origin and Development of Babylonian Writing," *BAVSS* 9 (1913) Part I, I-XXIV, 1-296; Part II, 1-300.

*S. C. Ylvisaker, "Dialectic Differences between Assyrian and Babylonian, and some Problems they Present," *JAOS* 33 (1913) 397-401.

*Theophilus G. Pinches, "Êridu = Babylon, Unuk and Uruk, Kibêgi = Kingi," *SBAP* 35 (1913) 154-155.

*J. Dyneley Prince, "The Babylonian Equations for Syria," *AJSL* 30 (1913-14) 212-218.

Stephen [H.] Langdon, "The Grammatical Term *KA-KA-SI-GA*," *Baby* 7 (1913-23) 87-92.

Stephen [H.] Langdon, "The Etymology of the Babylonian Relative Pronoun," *AJSL* 31 (1914-15) 271-281.

*William J. Hinke, "The Significance of the Symbols on Babylonian Boundary Stones," *AJA* 20 (1916) 76-77.

*Joseph Offord, "Archaeological Notes on Jewish Antiquities. XII. *Abel and Cuneiform* Ibila," *PEFQS* 48 (1916) 138-139.

*S[tephen H.] Langdon, "Lexigraphical Notes," *SBAP* 38 (1916) 37-40, 55-59. [III. *Şamāru*, "To Heap up, Store up", pp. 39-40]

James B. Nies, "The Reading of GIŠ-ÚḪ^{ki}," *JAOS* 37 (1917) 255-256.

*James A. Montgomery, "Babylonian *niš* 'oath' in West-Semitic," *JAOS* 37 (1917) 329-330.

*A. H. Sayce, "Assyriological Notes," *SBAP* 39 (1917) 207-212. [The Babylonian Name of NIN-IP, p. 212]

James B. Nies, "The Origin of *MAŠ* or *BAR* and the Development of its Meanings," *JAOS* 39 (1919) 91-99. [*MAŠ* = ▷╪]

George A. Barton, "The Origin of the Sign Urašŝu," *AJSL* 36 (1919-20) 315-316. [𒀭]

A. H. Pruessner, "Abi Ummâni," *AJSL* 39 (1922-23) 52-55.

H. F. Lutz, "The meaning of Babylonian *bittu,*" *JAOS* 42 (1922) 206-207.

*Theophile J. Meek, "Babyloniaca," *JAOS* 34 (1923) 353-357. [Names of Parts of the Doorway, pp. 354-357]

E[phraim] A. Speiser, "The Translation and Etymology of Uṣurtu," *AJSL* 40 (1923-24) 137-139.

William F. Edgerton, "*Amêlu* and *muškênu* in the Code of Hammurabi," *AJSL* 41 (1924-25) 58-63.

George A. Barton, "On the Vocalization of the Ideogram ŠES-AB^ki-MA," *JAOS* 46 (1926) 310-311.

George A. Barton, "Identification of Sign No. 572 of Barton's Babylonian Writing," *JAOS* 46 (1926) 311-312. [𒈨]

Samuel Feigin, "*Liqûm,* 'Portion'," *AJSL* 43 (1926-27) 301-304.

*S[tephen H.] Langdon, "Minîtu, 'Fate.' A Correction," *JRAS* (1930) 402-403. [*lum-ni*]

S[tephen] Langdon, "Philological Note," *RAAO* 28 (1931) 165-166. [*ûmu mašil,* mid-day; *mûšu mašil,* mid-night, *mišil ûmi,* half-day, after-noon, evening]

*G. R. Driver, "A Problem of River-traffic," *ZA* 40 (1931) 228-233.

*S[tephen H.] Langdon, "Note on the Legal Commentary *Ana itti-šu,*" *AJSL* 48 (1931-32) 51-53.

S[tephen H.] Langdon, "Philological Note: Muḫḫû, not Magus," *JRAS* (1932) 391-392.

*S[tephen] Langdon, "Philological Note," *RAAO* 29 (1932) 121-122. [*adudîlu* = Mantis religiosa; *The Bird* URINNU (not SISINNU)]

*Samuel I. Feigin, "The Captives in Cuneiform Inscriptions," *AJSL* 50 (1933-34) 217-245. [9. The ŠU.GE₄-Women in the Code fo Hammurabi and in the Contracts of that Period, pp. 237-243]

*Theodor Herzl Gaster, "An Egyptian Loan-Word in a Tell-Amarna Letter," *AEE* 18 (1934) 21. [*ḫptr*]

George A. Barton, "Some Observations as to the Origin of the Babylonian Syllabary," *JAOS* 54 (1934) 75-79.

Albrecht Goetze, "The *t*- Form of the Old Babylonian Verb," *JAOS* 56 (1936) 297-334.

E. R. Lacheman, "SU = Šiqlu," *JAOS* 57 (1937) 181-184.

A[lbrecht] Goetze, "The Sibilant in Old Babylonian *naẓārum*," *Or, N.S.,* 6 (1937) 12-18.

D. P. T. Winckworth, "Neo-Babylonian *ba-ga-ni-(-')*. I," *BSOAS* 9 (1937-39) 333-343.

O. E. Ravn, "The Substitution of -ss- for -šš- in Babylonian," *AO* 17 (1938-39) 318-328.

A. L[eo] Oppenheim, "The Neo-Babylonian Preposition *la,*" *JNES* 1 (1942) 369-372.

*A. Leo Oppenheim, "Assyriological Gleanings I," *BASOR* #91 (1943) 36-38. [II. Styled maledictions, pp. 37-38]

*Albrecht Goetze, "Number Idioms in Old Babylonian," *JNES* 5 (1946) 185-202.

A. Leo Oppenheim, "Deictic -*ka, -kunu* in Neo-Babylonian," *JCS* 1 (1947) 120-121.

T. Fish, "Giš. Gar.Ra, iškārum," *MCS* 1 (1951) 9-11. [H.S.M. 6795]

*Cyrus H. Gordon, "Marginal Notes on the Ancient Middle East," *JKF* 2 (1952-53) 60-61. [VI. Babyloniaca: a. CH²⁷ 3:68 *a-i-šir;* b. *'mq* 'be strong']

T. Fish, "Gemé at Umma," *MCS* 3 (1953) 47-55.

T. Fish, "É-dub-ba in UR III," *MCS* 3 (1953) 70-71.

*Barbara E. Morgan, "Index of Words and Phrases in the Year-Formulae of the First Babylonian Dynasty," *MCS* 4 (1954) 62-77.

*G. R. Driver, "Babylonian and Hebrew Notes," *WO* 2 (1954-59) 19-26. [I 5 12: *ina šubtêburia;* 23 R. 28 *Sa-mi-da-ḫu-um;* 31 O. 30: *itti atta ù šût-rêši*^MEŠ*-ka rêqu;* II 10 R. 4: *ûm tanaššû;* 26 O. 9: *sinništam na-wa-ri-tam;* 30 R. 9: *annîtam (awīl)baddam uwa'er;* 31 R. 3: *eriššišunnu;* 39 O. 27: *lâma ṣābum ... ikašadam mãssu šallat u ṣû ḫaš;* 42 R. 23: atalli = *"je monterai";* 46 17-18: *akkîma ṣābašu itarrû;* 50 R. 8-9. *ṣābum šû itbê-ma issakip enūssu sâ ... u (qãn) ṣinnassu uštaddi;* 50 O. 8-9 *ištu warḫim mãdam-mã [mu]-ú waššuru;* 78 O. 9: *ûm biblim;* III. 24 O. 20-1: *aḫšušam-ma assakpam* = *»je me suis hâté de mettre (à l'eau)";* 79 R. 8-10: *mala naklim u (awīl)muškênim labīrêm šipram šâ kênãtim ušeppeš*]

T. Fish, *"Gala* on Ur III tablets," *MCS* 7 (1957) 25-27.

A. Leo Oppenheim, "An 'etymology' for *andinãnu," AfO* 18 (1957-58) 278.

B. Landsberger and O. R. Gurney, "Practical Vocabulary of Assur," *AfO* 18 (1957-58) 328-341. [Selected Philological Remarks by B. Landsberger, pp. 336-340; Appendix: Practical Vocabulary of Nineveh, pp. 340-341]

*Albrecht Goetze, "Remarks on Some Names Occurring in the Execration Texts," *BASOR* #151 (1958) 28-33.

Albrecht Goetze, "The Sibilants of Old Babylonian," *RAAO* 52 (1958) 137-149.

*J[acob] J. Rabinowitz, "The puzzle of the 'Tirhatum bound in the bride's girdle'," *BO* 16 (1959) 188-190.

Thorkild Jacobsen, *"Ittallak niãti," JNES* 19 (1960) 101-116.

M. B. Rowton, "The Use of the Permansive in Classical Babylonian," *JNES* 21 (1962) 233-303.

Ebbe E. Knudsen, "Notes on Two Grammars of Susa Old Babylonian. A Review Article," *AO* 28 (1964-65) 347-353. *(Review)*

A. Shaffer, "TA *ša kīma* A *ītenerrubu:* A Study in Native Babylonian Philology," *Or, N.S.,* 38 (1969) 433-446.

§535　*3.3.3.2.3.3 Sumerian - General Studies* *

Fritz Hommel, "The Sumerian Language and its Affinities," *JRAS* (1886) 351-363.

*Terrien de Lacouperie, "Akkadian and Sumerian in Comparative Philology," *BOR* 1 (1886-87) 1-7.

*A. H. Sayce, "Miscellaneous Notes," *ZA* 4 (1889) 382-393. [24. The language of the *Šu*, pp. 382-384]

Fritz Hommel, "Sumerological Notes III.," *BOR* 6 (1892-93) 157-159.

Christopher Johnston, "The Sumero-Akkadian Question," *JAOS* 15 (1893) 317-322.

*Fritz Hommel, "Assyriological Notes," *SBAP* 18 (1896) 17-24. [§15. S^b 287-8 ⊭⫯⫯ 𒂖, Sumerian *sur-ru* = Semitic *kalû* "priest, sorcerer", pp. 19-21]

*Fritz Hommel, "Assyriological Notes," *SBAP* 19 (1897) 78-90, 312-315. [§24. Sumerian *ǵilib,* "god", pp. 79-80]

*C. P. Tiele, "Akkadian and Sumerian," *JRAS* (1900) 343-344.

*Theophilus G. Pinches, "Akkadian and Sumerian," *JRAS* (1900) 551-552.

J. Dyneley Prince, "The First and Second Persons in Sumerian," *AJSL* 19 (1902-03) 203-227.

J. Dyneley Prince, "The Vocabulary of Sumerian," *JAOS* 25 (1904) 49-67.

A. H. Sayce, "Recent Biblical and Oriental Archaeology. The Study of Sumerian," *ET* 17 (1905-06) 414-416.

J. Dyneley Prince, "Sumerian as a Language," *AJSL* 23 (1906-07) 202-219.

Stephen [H.] Langdon, "Prolegomenon to Sumerian Lexicography," *Baby* 1 (1906-07) 287-290.

Stephen [H.] Langdon, "The Particle *ma,* " *Baby* 1 (1906-07) 291-292.

---

* Listed here as a matter of convenience due to geographical distribution. Actual linguistic family has not been determined.

J. Dyneley Prince, "The Verbal Prefixes and Infixes in Sumerian," *AJSL* 24 (1907-08) 354-365.

Stephen [H.] Langdon, "Syntax of compound verbs in Sumerian," *Baby* 2 (1907-08) 65-101.

*Stephen [H.] Langdon, "Sumerian loan-words in Babylonian," *Baby* 2 (1907-08) 102-120.

*Stephen [H.] Langdon, "Sumerian-Assyrian Vocabularies," *Baby* 2 (1907-08) 199-208, 282-288; 3 (1909-10) 145-196, 259-265; 4 (1910-11) 9-56.

C. J. Ball, "Sidelights on Sumerian. I," *SBAP* 31 (1909) 70-73. [𒀭 ; 𒀭 ; 𒀭 ĒL (US + SIG); ĒL SURRU; 𒀭 ; ĒL MA + SIG + GAM]

*Stephen [H.] Langdon, "Lexicographical Studies," *SBAP* 31 (1909) 74-77. [III. Semitic Words for "sorrow," "distress;" Sumerian *šag-dib*, Br., 8072-7; IV. *Niknakku*]

C. J. Ball, "Sidelights on Sumerian. II," *SBAP* 31 (1909) 239-246. [1. 𒀭 MA-NA; 2. 𒀭 AK-KIL; 3. 𒋗 ŠU-SI; 4. 𒀭 DUB-BIN]

*Alan S. Hawkesworth, "Semitic and Sumerian; A Study in Origins," *OC* 24 (1910) 574-575.

J. Dyneley Prince, "Certain Grammatical Phenomena in Sumerian," *AJSL* 27 (1910-11) 328-330.

Stephen [H.] Langdon, "Sumerian noun formation," *Baby* 4 (1910-11) 1-8.

George A. Barton, "The Expression SÁ-DÚG in Early Sumerian Texts," *AJSL* 28 (1911-12) 63-65. [𒀭 𒀭]

*Stephen [H.] Langdon, "The Sumerian expresssion *si-ni-tum.* capital, balance carried forward," *Baby* 6 (1912) 41-53.

*J. Dyneley Prince, "The God Name 𒀭 𒀭 ," *AJSL* 29 (1912-13) 248-287.

J. Dyneley Prince, "𒀭 𒀭 𒀭 ," *ZA* 27 (1912-13) 258-261.

M. Tseretheli, "Sumerian and Georgian: a study in Comparative Philology,"
JRAS (1913) 783-821; (1914) 1-36.

*Theophilus G. Pinches, "Êridu = Babylon, Unuk and Uruk, Kibêgi =
Kingi," *SBAP* 35 (1913) 154-155.

*A. Boissier, "A Sumerian Word in the Bible," *SBAP* 35 (1913) 159-160.
[kisurru (kišurru)]

Stephen [H.] Langdon, "Intensive Compound Verbs. A critique of the
Précis d'Allographie of M. Halévy," *Baby* 7 (1913-23) 81-86.

J. Dyneley Prince, "Has ⚹⚹ the value of *tik* in Sumerian?" *ZA* 28 (1913-
14) 362-364.

J. Dyneley Prince, "Striking Phenomena of Sumerian," *JAOS* 34 (1914) 321-
328. [A. Multiplicity of Meanings; B. Abbreviated Roots]

Theophilus G. Pinches, "Further Light on the Sumerian Language," *JRAS*
(1914) 436-440.

L. C. Hopkins, "Chinese and Sumerian," *SBAP* 36 (1914) 269-273; 37
(1915) 24-33, 50-59, 75-86.

J. Dyneley Prince, "Delitzsch's Sumerian Grammar," *AJSL* 31 (1914-15) 67-
78. *(Review)*

J. Dyneley Prince, "Delitzsch's 'Sumerisches Glossar'," *AJSL* 31 (1914-15)
160-167. *(Review)*

*Theophile James Meek, "Critical Notes," *AJSL* 31 (1914-15) 286-287. [VI.

The Sign ⚹⚹ , ⚹⚹ ; VII. Glosses in H. 1396 and H. 1449.]

J. Dyneley Prince, "The Pronouns and Verbs of Sumerian," *PAPS* 54 (1915)
27-46.

M. Tseretheli, "Sumerian and Georgian: a study in Comparative Philology.
Part II," *JRAS* (1915) 255-288; (1916) 1-58.

*S[tephen H.] Langdon, "Lexicographical and epigraphical notes," *RAAO* 13

(1916) 1-4. [The Sign ⚹⚹ *(šita)*, "Weapon, Mace", pp. 3-4]

*Stephen [H.] Langdon, "Lexigraphical Notes," *SBAP* 38 (1916) 37-40, 55-59. [I. The (Conditional Particle *Mā;* II. *Našbaṭu,* "Branch of the Male Date-Palm"; III. *Ṣamāru,* "To Heap up, Store up"; IV. The Sumerian Original of the Descent of Ishtar]

Stephen [H.] Langdon, "Critical Notes. III. The Sign 𒍞 in the Name of the Fourth Month at Umma," *AJSL* 33 (1916-17) 48-49.

Paul Haupt, "Tones in Sumerian," *JAOS* 37 (1917) 309-323.

*H. F. Lutz, "On the Reading of the Date-formula of the Fourth Year of Gimil-Sin," *JAOS* 37 (1917) 330-331.

*Paul Haupt, "Aramaic *Bárrâ,* wilderness = Sumerian *Bar,* " *JBL* 36 (1917) 254-255.

*Paul Haupt, "Sumerian *tu,* dove, and *nam,* swallow," *JSOR* 1 (1917) 3-9.

*Stephen [H.] Langdon, "Lexigraphical Notes," *SBAP* 38 (1916) 37-40, 55-59. [II. *Našbaṭu,* "Branch of the Male Date-Palm", pp.38-39]

H. F. Lutz, "Two Sumerian Lexicographical Notes," *AJSL* 34 (1917-18) 284. [ur-tur-ri; en(n)a]

Paul Haupt, "Sumerian *ḡul-gik,* 'obstinate refusal'," *JAOS* 38 (1918) 66-68.

C. J. Ball, "The Relation of Tibetan to Sumerian," *SBAP* 40 (1918) 95-100.

W[illiam] F[oxwell] Albright, "Some Cruces in the Langdon Epic," *JAOS* 39 (1919) 65-90.

J. Dyneley Prince, "Phonetic Relations in Sumerian," *JAOS* 39 (1919) 265-279.

*Stephen [H.] Langdon, "Contribution to Assyrian Lexicography," *JSOR* 3 (1919) 36-41. [2. EN E-NU-ŠUB = *šipat bit pašāri?* pp. 36-37]

Morris Jastrow Jr., "Ê-nu-šub = bît šipti," *AJSL* 87 (1920-21) 51-61.

*Paul Haupt, "Biblical Studies," *AJP* 43 (1922) 238-249. [6. Heb. *'aštê* and Sum. *aš-tân,* p. 245]

Paul Haupt, "The Sumerian Affixes *Tam* and *Kam,* " *JAOS* 42 (1922) 301-304.

George A. Barton, "The Expression of the Comparative Degree in Sumerian," *JAOS* 43 (1923) 243-244.

George A. Barton, "On the Significance of Compound Postpositives in Early Sumerian," *JAOS* 43 (1923) 317-322.

*W[illiam] F[oxwell] Albright, "The Sumerian Conception of *Giš-Xar*—A Correction," *JSOR* 7 (1923) 79.

J. Dyneley Prince, "Phonetic Possiblities in Sumerian," *AO* 2 (1923-24) 63-76.

J. Dyneley Prince, "Personal Pronominal Elements in Sumerian," *AO* 3 (1924) 153-160.

*A. H. Sayce, "Hittite katral, Sumerian balag," *AfO* 2 (1924-25) 106.

J. Dyneley Prince, "The Elements of the Plural in Sumerian," *AO* 4 (1925) 306-310.

*Paul Haupt, "Arab. *samm,* poison = Sum. *šem, ἄρωμα,*" *BAVSS* 10 (1927) Heft 2, 84-95.

Paul Haupt, "Fr. *cire* and *glu* = Sum. *gir,* " *BAVSS* 10 (1927) Heft 2, 146-147.

Paul Haupt, "Sum. *nimur,* salt, smoke, salt-swamp," *BAVSS* 10 (1927) Heft 2, 242-252.

*Paul Haupt, "Sum. *azalak,* fuller, and Heb. *ašlāḡ,* fullers' earth," *BAVSS* 10 (1927) Heft 2, 268-270.

Ira M. Price, "The Partical *Nam* in Sumerian," *JAOS* 47 (1927) 258-259.

*S[tephen H.] Langdon, "Assyriological Note," *JRAS* (1927) 323-326. [The Assyrian Root, *Katātu,* Sumerian *Tuku*]

*H[enry Ludwig] Fr. Lutz, "A Sumerian loanword in Egyptian," *AfO* 5 (1928-29) 185-186 [Sumerian *unu* written: *(áb-ku)* = Egyptian *mniw*]

Anonymous, "Archaeological Notes," *HR* 98 (1929) 48-50. *[Sumerian Language]*

*S[tephen] Langdon, "Philological Notes," *RAAO* 28 (1931) 13-22. [4) *Piltum, pistum,* fleece, Hair, 𒀭𒈨, pp. 16-17; 6) NIRDA, sin, transgression, treachery, pp. 20-22]

S[tephen] Langdon, "Epigraphical Note," *RAAO* 28 (1931) 115-116. [𒀭 = 𒂍𒅗, 𒂍𒅗𒌋, 𒂍𒅗𒌋, and 𒅗, 𒅗𒌋]

Henry [Ludwig] Frederick Lutz, "The Unidentified Sign 𒀭," *UCPSP* 10 (1931-40) 185.

*S[tephen] Langdon, "Assyriological Notes," *JRAS* (1932) 327-332. [V. Sumerian *bad-bad* = *babbad* = *tapol*u, *padanû, taḫtû*, pp. 330-331]

Samuel N[oah] Kramer, "A Matter of Method in Sumerology," *AJSL* 49 (1932-33) 229-247.

*S[tephen H.] Langdon, "Notes on Sumerian Etymology and Syntax," *JRAS* (1933) 857-866. [I. ŠANDANAKU "Gardener"; II. É-SAL (*áma, ame, âm*) = *maštaku;* III. The Sign BU-doubled Criss-cross; IV. [sìg-úz = *šarti enzi* "fleece of a she goat" also *šartu* "hair of humans"]; V. ARÛTU "relatives, relations"; VI. UKKIN-ŠUB "a title"; VII. Postfixed GE, KA = KIMA]

A. Poebel, "The Tenses of the Intransitive Verb in Sumerian," *AJSL* 50 (1933-34) 143-170.

*Ferris J. Stephens, "Concerning Sumerian *mu-an-na,* 'Year'," *AJSL* 51 (1934-35) 48-49.

*W[illiam] F[oxwell] Albright, "The Words for 'Year' in Egyptian and Sumerian," *AJSL* 51 (1934-35) 126-127.

A. Poebel, "The Sumerian Genitive Element," *AJSL* 51 (1934-35) 145-176.

*S[tephen H.] Langdon, "The Sumerian Word for 'Year' and Origin of the Custom of Dating by Events," *RAAO* 32 (1935) 131-149.

G. R. Driver, "Sumerian ITU ŠE.GU(R).KUD," *AfO* 10 (1935-36) 362.

*Albrecht Goetze, "The Meaning of the Sumerian ki slaḫ and Its Akkadian Equivalents," *AJSL* 52 (1935-36) 143-159.

*S[tephen] Langdon, "Philological Notes," *RAAO* 33 (1936) 191-196. [VII. Sumerian ⟨𒀹𒈪𒌋⟩ (šanešu) = *unnīnu*, pp. 195-196]

A. Poebel, "The Root Forms sì(m) and su$_{11}$ (m), 'to give,' in Sumerian," *JAOS* 57 (1937) 35-72.

S[tephen H.] Langdon, "Sumerian Philological Notes," *JRAS* (1937) 91-96. [I. ZAGSAL, ZAGMIN = ZAMEN; II. The Velar Nasal *ng(ṅ)*, Palatal *ń (ñ)*]

Arno Poebel, "Another Case of the Predicative Use of the Genitive in Sumerian," *JAOS* 58 (1938) 148-150.

*T. Fish, "KI.SU$_7$ on Umma Texts," *MCS* 2 (1952) 54-58, 63-68.

T. Fish, "Notes on NIN-DINGIR and UGULA," *MCS* 3 (1953) 80-83.

*Edmund I. Gordon, "Of Princes and Foxes: The Neck-Stock in the Newly-Discovered Agade Period Stele," *AJA* 60(1956)183. [Sumerian: *giš$_{az-gú}$*]

*Edmund I. Gordon, "Of Princes and Foxes: The Neck-Stock in the Newly-Discovered Agade Period Stele," *Sumer* 12 (1956) 80-84. [Sumerian: *gish $_{az-gú}$*]

Ferris J. Stephens, "Sumerian KA.TAB," *JCS* 13 (1959) 12-14.

*W[illiam] W. Hallo, "Lexical Notes on the neo-Sumerian Metal Industry" *BO* 20 (1963) 136-142.

H. Kizilyay and M. Çiğ, "Two Sumerian Verbs meaning 'take delivery'," *AAI* 2 (1965) 287-289.

M. Civil, "Notes on Sumerian Lexicography, I," *JCS* 20 (1966) 119-124. [1. dum-dam-za; 2. The Reading of ANŠE.KUR.RA; 3. ^{ú}KI.^{d}NANNA = *^{ú}munzur]

*Å. W. Sjöberg, "Contributions to the Sumerian Lexicon," *JCS* 21 (1967) 275-278. [1. á-sì g-g e (á-sì g) "sling stone" Akk. *assukku;* 2. b a r - a$_5$ (= A[rie] K[lindler]) = *bêru* "to select, to examine"; 3. d i - i r - g a (k i - i r - g a) = *riksu;* 4. g i š - e r i n, Akk. *gišrinnu,* "bolt"; 5. k u š $_x$ (=IŠ), k u š $_x$ -s u = *naspantu.;* 6. l u - ḫ u - u m - m a, Akk. *luḫmmû,* "mud"; 7. m u r u $_x$ = (IM.DUGUD), a n - m u r u $_x$ = *akāmu* "cloud of dust, mist"; 8. s í g - b a r - r a (s i g $_7$ - b a r - r a) = *sigbarrû*]

Mamoru Yoshikawa, "On the Grammatical Function of *-e-* of the Sumerian Verbal Suffix *-e-de/-e-da(m),* " *JNES* 27 (1968) 251-261.

M[amoru] Yoshikawa, "The Marû and Ḫamṭu Aspects in the Sumerian Verbal System," *Or, N.S.,* 37 (1968) 401-416.

*R. Kutscher, "The Sumerian Equivalents of Akkadian *māḫāzu,* " *Lěš* 34 (1969-70) #4, n.p.n.

§536 *3.3.3.2.4 South Semitic - General Studies*

*Edw. Ullendorff, "The Contribution of South Semitics to Hebrew Lexicography," *VT* 6 (1956) 190-198.

*Wolf Leslau, "Southeast Semitic Cognates to the Akkadian Vocabulary. I," *JAOS* 82 (1962) 1-4.

*Wolf Leslau, "Southeast Semitic Cognates to the Akkadian Vocabulary. II," *JAOS* 84 (1964) 115-118.

§537 *3.3.3.2.4.1 Arabic*

(   ) Carlyle, "On the Dialects of the Arabic Language," *TRAS* 1 (1827) 580-582. *(Communicated by William Marsden)*

Joseph Packard, "Claims of the Arabic Language and Literature," *BRCR* 8 (1836) 429-448.

T. M. Dickinson, "Remarks on the Arabic Language," *JRAS* (1839) 316-327.

*W. Wright, "The Arabic Term for *Hare,*" *JSL, 4th Ser.,* 10 (1866-67) 180-182.

*C. Taylor, "Notes on translation of Genesis," *JP* 3 (1871) 291-327. [III. The Arabic root ظهر, pp. 307-310]

*Richard Cull, "A ח Conjugation, such as exists in Assyrian, shown to be a character of early Shemitic speech, by its vestiges found in the Hebrew, Phoenician, Aramaic, and Arabic Languages," *SBAT* 2 (1873) 83-109.

Charles Warren, "Arabic and Hebrew," *PEFQS* 7 (1875) 227-228.

Claude R. Conder, "Notes on the Language of the Native Peasantry in Palestine," *PEFQS* 8 (1876) 132-140. [I. Horographic Terms; II. Hydrographic Terms; III. Forests; IV. Topographical Terms; Table of conversion of Hebrew sounds into Arabic]

E. T. Rogers, "Dialects of Colloquial Arabic," *JRAS* (1879) 365-379.

(Miss) E. M. Clerke, "Arabic Analogies in Western Speech," *IAQR, 1st Ser.*, 2 (1886) 324-357.

*Morris Jastrow Jr., "Assyrian, in its Relation to Hebrew and Arabic," *PAPA* 18 (1886) xviii-xix.

Lawrence M. Simmons, "On the Separation which may take place between the so-called Defined and Defining Noun in Arabic," *AJSL* 4 (1887-88) 87-91, 250-251.

*Henry George Tomkins, "The Name Genubath," *SBAP* 10 (1887-88) 372. (Note by W. Harry Rylands, "The Ḳenbetu and the Semitic South," pp. 373-376 [جذرب]

L. C. Casartelli, "The Order of the Characters in the Arabic Alphabet," *BOR* 3 (1888-89) 141-142.

C[laude] R. Conder, "Notes by Major Conder, D.C.L., R.E. I. Palestine Peasant Language," *PEFQS* 21 (1889) 133-142.

C[rawford] H. Toy, "On some phonetic peculiarities of Cairo Arabic," *JAOS* 14 (1890) cxii-cxiv.

Frederick J. Bliss, "Ma'lula and Its Dialect," *PEFQS* 22 (1890) 74-98.

R. F. Hutchinson, "'Ma'lula and Its Dialect', by F. J. B.," *PEFQS* 22 (1890) 332. [Note by C. R. Conder, *PEFQS* 23 (1891) pp. 73-74]

George N. Newman, "On contraction in Arabic," *JAOS* 15 (1893) cxix.

C[onrad] Schick, "Letters from Herr Baurath Schick. II. Arabic Building Terms," *PEFQS* 25 (1893) 194-201.

Joseph K. Arnold, "The Present Order of the Alphabet in Arabic," *AJSL* 11 (1894-95) 203-208.

*Fritz Hommel, "Assyriological Notes," *SBAP* 17 (1895) 199-207. [11b. Arabic لُرْن = Babylonian *lânu*, p. 206]

*Fritz Hommel, "Assyriological Notes," *SBAP* 19 (1897) 78-90, 312-315. [§21. فُعَال = *nupâru*, p. 78]

Talcott Williams, "The spoken Arabic of North Morocco," *BAVSS* 3 (1898) 561-587.

Budgett Meakin, "The spoken Arabic of Morocco," *BAVSS* 4 (1899) 575-582.

*Fritz Hommel, "The Earliest Language of the Israelites," *ET* 12 (1900-01) 96.

Gabriel Oussani, "The Arabic dialect of Baghdad," *JAOS* 22 (1901) 97-114.

W. M. Christie, "Notes on the Arabic Dialect of Aleppo," *GUOST* 2 (1901-07) 39. *[Abstract prepared by T. H. Weir]*

P. Molesworth Sykes, "Anthropological Notes on Southern Persia," *JRAI* 32 (1902) 339-352. *[Arabic Vocabulary]*

A. H. Kisbany, "Arabic Verbs," *IAQR, 3rd Ser.,* 21 (1906) 318-322.

P. Molesworth Sykes, "The Gypsies of Persia. A Second Vocabulary," *JRAI* 36 (1906) 302-311.

William Hoyt Worrell, "The Interrogative Particle دَفَل in Arabic according to Native Sources and the Ḳur'ān," *ZA* 21 (1908) 116-150.

Duncan B. Macdonald, "Arabic for the Wayfarer," *AJSL* 27 (1910-11) 92-94.

"Arif", "The Arabic Language Question in Egypt," *IAQR* 34 (1912) 351-362.

William H. Worrell, "The Consonants Z and Ẓ in Egyptian Colloquial Arabic," *JAOS* 34 (1914) 278-281.

*Paul Popenoe, "The Propagation of the Date Palm: Materials for a Lexicographical Study in Arabic," *JAOS* 35 (1915) 207-212.

*Felix von Oefele, "Assyrian 'kalmat,' Arabic 'kaemlet'," *JAOS* 36 (1916) 416.

*Paul Haupt, "*Seḡál*, Queen = Arab. *Tajlāʿ*," *JBL* 35 (1916) 320-322.

*Paul Haupt, "Assyrian *lânu*, 'aspect'—Arabic *láyn*, 'color'," *JAOS* 37 (1917) 253-255.

*A. H. Sayce, "Assyriological Notes," *SBAP* 39 (1917) 207-212. [The Nunnation in Arabic, pp. 209-210]

T. W. Arnold, "The Study of Arabic," *BSOAS* 1 (1917-20) #1, 112-121.

*Anonymous, "Transliteration of Arabic and Persian," *PBA* 8 (1917-18) 505-521.

G. R. Driver, "Linguistic Affinities of Syrian Arabic," *JRAS* (1920) 305-318.

*H. F. Lutz, "A note regarding the garment called بَدْن and its etymology," *JAOS* 42 (1922) 207.

D. B. Macdonald, "Wahm in Arabic and its Cognates," *JRAS* (1922) 505-521.

Paul Haupt, "Arabic Doublets," *JAOS* 43 (1923) 422-423.

Paul Haupt, "Arabic ɥ = r," *JAOS* 43 (1923) 423-424.

*Paul Haupt, "Arab. táhamah = çánaxah, Heb. çaḥnâ," *JAOS* 43 (1923) 424-425.

*A. S. Tritton, "Hebrew and Arabic: Similarities in Thought and Grammar," *GUOST* 5 (1923-28) 24.

William H. Worrell, "The Formation of Arabic Broken Plurals," *AJSL* 41 (1924-25) 179-182.

*Samuel Poznanski, "New Material on the History of Hebrew and Hebrew-Arabic Philology during the X-XII Centuries," *JQR, N.S.*, 16 (1925-26) 237-266.

*A[aron] Ember, "Several Egypto-Semitic Etymologies," *OOR* 1 (1926) #1, 5-8.[1. - Eg. mʿbꜣ. *harpoon, spear* = Eth. mâʿbal, *sharp instrument, arrow;* 2. - Eg. mʿbꜣ. *thirty* = *Post-Biblical* מְעֻבָּר *intercalated;* 3. Eg.

Fnḫ-ụ =(Φοῖνιξ, Phoenician) = Arab فَلّاح *fellah* < Aram. פלח *split, plough, cultivate the ground;* 4. Eg. ʿr, *enter* = Aram. עלל *enter;* 5. Eg.

gm-ụ, *grief, mourning* = Arab. غَمّ ḡamm, *grief, sadness;* 6. Eg. pzḫ,

be dishevelled, disarray, dismayed = Arab. فزع, *be frightened, terrified, dismayed;* 7. Eg. ḫꜣm, *catching of fish and birds* = חים *net for catching fish;* 8. ḫꜣp, erroneously חפה لِحَف *cover;* 9. Eg. ḫnḡ, *thigh, hip-bone (Pyr. Texts* 124, 133, 1547) = Assyr. ḫinçu, Arab. خُضَر, Heb.

חֲלָצַיִם, *lion, hip;* 10. Eg. ʾinʿ, *chin (Pyr. Texts* 1308) = Heb. לַע *jaw-bone* (probably = Arab. نيع *jaw, mandible*)]

*Paul Haupt, "Arab. *tâjir* and Ass. *tamkaru*, " *BAVSS* 10 (1927) Heft 2, 31-68.

*Paul Haupt, "Arab. *samm*, poison = Sum. *šem*, ἄρωμα," *BAVSS* 10 (1927) Heft 2, 84-95.

*Paul Haupt, "Ass. *budulxu*, bdellium and Arab. *taḥállub*, secretion," *BAVSS* 10 (1927) Heft 2, 258-263.

*Paul Haupt, "Ass. *xamâdu*, to help = Arab. *mádaxa*," *BAVSS* 10 (1927) Heft 2, 274-275.

Adolph August Brux, "Arabic-English Transliteration for Library Pruposes," *AJSL* 47 (1930-31) Number 1, Part 2, 1-30.

Mahmoud Teymour, "The Battle Between the Arab Languages in Modern Egyptian Literature," *IAQR* 28 (1932) 635-639.

*Joshua Finkel, "Hebrew Shīr and Sūra," *ZAW* 50 (1932) 310-312. [שִׁיר =

[سنى

*De Lacy O'Leary, "Notes on the Coptic Language. II. How far can Coptic influence be traced in the Egyptian dialect of Arabic?" *Or, N.S.,* 3 (1934) 249-258.

*D. Winton Thomas, "The Root שׁנה = سنی in Hebrew," *ZAW* 52 (1934) 236-238.

J. A. Montgomery, "שׁנה = سنی," *ZAW* 53 (1935) 207-208.

St. H. Stephan, "Some Personifications in Colloquial Arabic Speech," *JPOS* 17 (1937) 93-99.

*D. Winton Thomas, "The Root שׁנה = سنی in Hebrew II.," *ZAW* 55 (1937) 174-176.

Harold W. Glidden, "A Comparative Study of the Arabic Nautical Vocabulary from Al-'Aqabah Transjordan," *JAOS* 62 (1942) 68-72.

Sidney Glazer, "A Noteworthy Passage from an Arab Grammatical Text," *JAOS* 62 (1942) 106-108.

*Paulo Boneschi, "Is *Malak* an Arabic Word?" *JAOS* 65 (1945) 107-111.

*D. Winton Thomas, "Some Rabbinic Evidence for a Hebrew Root ידע = ودع ," *JQR, N.S.,* 37 (1946-47) 177-178.

*Leo J. Liebreich, "Observations on 'Some Rabbinic Evidence for a Hebrew Root ידע = ودع (*JQR, N.S.,* XXXVII, 177-8)," *JQR, N.S.,* 37 (1946-47) 337-339.

Wolf Leslau, "Four Modern South Arabic Languages," *Word* 3 (1947) 180-203.

*H[arry] A[ustryn] Wolfson, "Arabic and Hebrew Terms for Matter and Element with especial reference to Saadia," *JQR, N.S.,* 38 (1947-48) 47-61.

*Georges Vajda, " 'unṣur and te'ālāh," *JQR, N.S.,* 38 (1947-48) 481. [Rejoinder by H. A. Wolfson, p. 481-482]

*Godfrey Rolles Driver, "Hebrew Roots and Words," *WO* 1 (1947-52) 406-415. [I. גָּעַשׁ = חָעֵס ; גָּעַר = جَعَر ; אלח = أَلَغ (חוּל) חִיל קָוֶה = قَوِى;

= פוּר = فَار (و); ראה = רוח; רוה = נָחָה = حَا ; שָׁנָה = سَحبا ; עֵצָה; עָצְמָה*

عَظِيمَة ;חָמָה*=Arab. حَمِىَ; הָיָה = שִׁיר נָפַל; II. חנק יָקַח* = وَقِم]

*H. Birkeland, "Hebrew *zœ* and Arabic *ḏū*," *ST* 2 (1949-50) 201-202.

*M. M. Bravmann, "An Arabic Cognate of Ugaritic *ǧmrm*," *JCS* 7 (1953) 27. [*ǧumur* or *ǧumr*]

*A. Guillaume, "A Contribution to Hebrew Lexicography," *BSOAS* 16 (1954) 1-12. {I. Words with no Arabic Equivalent in the Hebrew Lexicon; II. Words with Weak or Doubtful Equivalents; III. Words that may rest on Both ف and ث; Philological and Exegetical Notes: *(f)* فاق, p. 9]

*Morris Sigel Seale, "Arabic and Old Testament Interpretation," *ET* 66 (1954-55) 92-93.

Charles A. Ferguson, "The emphatic *l* in Arabic," *Lang* 32 (1956) 446-452.

*Wolf Leslau, "Arabic Loanwords in Argobba (South Ethiopic)," *JAOS* 77 (1957) 36-39.

*Soheil Afnan, "Some Arabic and Persian Terms of Philosophy," *Oriens* 10 (1957) 71-76.

John A. Haywood, "Arabic Lexicography in Perspective," *DUJ, N.S.,* 19 (1957-58) 5-13.

*W[olf] Leslau, "Arabic Loan-Words in Geez," *JSS* 3 (1958) 146-168.

Irene Garbell, "Remarks on the Historical Phonology of an East Mediterranean Arabic Dialect," *Word* 14 (1958) 303-337.

Charles A. Ferguson, "The Arabic Koine," *Lang* 35 (1959) 616-630.

*A. Guillaume, "Hebrew and Arabic Lexicography. A Comparative Study (I)," *Abr-N* 1 (1959-60) 3-35.

*Wilson B. Bishai, "Notes on the Coptic Substratum in Egyptian Arabic," *JAOS* 80 (1960) 225-229.

*William C. Cowan, "Arabic evidence for Proto Semitic */awa/ and */ǒ/," *Lang* 36 (1960) 60-62.

*A. Guillaume, "Hebrew and Arabic Lexicography. A Comparative Study (II)," *Abr-N* 2 (1960-61) 5-35.

*J[oshua] Blau, "The Dual in Judaeo-Arabic and its Linguistic Background," *Tarbiẓ* 30 (1960-61) #2, III.

*Wilson B. Bishai, "Nature and Extent of Coptic Phonological Influence on Egyptian Arabic," *JSS* 6 (1961) 175-182.

*Harris H. Hirschberg, "Some Additional Arabic Etymologies in Old Testament Lexicography," *VT* 11 (1961) 373-385.

*A. Guillaume, "Hebrew and Arabic Lexicography. A Comparative Study (III)," *Abr-N* 3 (1961-62) 1-10.

*Nicholas Rescher, "Some Arabic Technical Terms of Syllogistic Logic and Their Greek Originals," *JAOS* 82 (1962) 203-204.

A. F. L. Beeston, "Arabian Sibilants," *JSS* 7 (1962) 222-233.

Gene M. Schramm, "An outline of Classical Arabic verb structure," *Lang* 38 (1962) 360-375.

E. S. Kennedy, "Transcription of Arabic Letters in Geometrical Figures," *JAOS* 82 (1962) 204.

*Wilson B. Bishai, "Coptic Grammatical Influence on Egyptian Arabic," *JAOS* 82 (1962) 285-289.

*A. Guillaume, "Hebrew and Arabic Lexicography. A Comparative Study (IV)," *Abr-N* 4 (1963-64) 1-18.

Joshua Blau, "On Some Convergent and Divergent Features in Judaeo-Arabic and Christian-Arabic," *Tarbiẓ* 33 (1963-64) #2, III-IV.

Jaroslav Oliverius, "Contribution to the Arabic Historical Dialectology," *ArOr* 31 (1963) 625-629.

Ray L. Cleveland, "A Classification for the Arabic Dialects of Jordan," *BASOR* #171 (1963) 56-63.

Walter Lehn, "Emphasis in Cairo Arabic," *Lang* 39 (1963) 29-39.

A. Guillaume, "Stroking an Idol," *BSOAS* 27 (1964) 430. [*waṯḥan*]

Wojciech Skalmowski, "A Note on the Distribution of Arabic Verbal Roots," *FO* 6 (1964) 97-100.

Maria Tsiapera, "Greek Borrowings in the Arabic Dialect of Cyprus," *JAOS* 84 (1964) 124-126.

George Krotkoff, "Arabic 'lm 'to know'," *JAOS* 84 (1964) 170-171.

Edwin E. Calverley, "The Arabic Generic Negative," *JAOS* 84 (1964) 171-172.

George Krotkoff, "Some Philological Remarks on a Linguistic Publication," *JAOS* 84 (1964) 263. *(Review)*

A[ndrzej] Czapkiewicz, "The Hypothetical Standard-Length of Words in Arabic and Its Realization in the Vocabulary," *FO* 7 (1965) 309-313.

Heikki Palva, "Lower Galilean Arabic: An Analysis of its Anaptyctic and Prothetic Vowels with Sample Texts," *SO* 32 (1965) 1-171.

Wilson B. Bishai, "Modern Inter-Arabic," *JAOS* 86 (1966) 319-323.

William Cowan, "Two notes on Arabic dialectology," *JAOS* 86 (1966) 416-418.

Ray L. Cleveland, "Notes on an Arabic Dialect of Southern Palestine," *BASOR* #185 (1967) 43-57.

T. M. Johnstone, "Aspects of Syllabication in the Spoken Arabic of "Anaiza," *BSOAS* 30 (1967) 1-16.

Andrzej Czapkiewicz, "The d-Form of the Verb in the Spoken Arabic of Baghdad," *FO* 9 (1967) 5-10.

Ladislav Drozdík, "Towards Defining the Structural Level of the Stem in Arabic," *OrS* 16 (1967) 85-95.

Khalil I. H. Semaan, "A Linguistic View of the Development of the Arabic Writing System," *WZKM* 61 (1967) 22-40.

Joshua Blau, "To Which Dialect Group Did Sicilian Arabic Belong?" *JAOS* 88 (1968) 522-523.

H[eikki] Palva, "On the Diphthongs *aw* and *ay* in Syrian Arabic," *SO* 37 (1968) #2, 1-17.

R. C. Delk, "Arabic Verb Forms XI-XV," *Arb-N* 8 (1968-69) 85-91.

Miroslav Krek, "E. W. Lane's working copy of his *Lexicon,*" *JAOS* 89 (1969) 419-420.

*R. Hetzron, "The Evidence for Perfect **y'aqtul* and Jussive **yaqt'ul* in Proto-Semitic," *JSS* 14 (1969) 1-21. [4. Arabic, pp. 18-20]

Meïr M. Bravmann, "'Satisfying' and 'Restraining': Arabic *KAFĀ (KFY)* › *KAFFA,*" *Muséon* 82 (1969) 197-205.

*Heikki Palva, "Notes on the Alleged Coptic Morphological Influence on Egyptian Arabic," *OrS* 18 (1969) 128-136.

*H. Blanc, "The Fronting of Semitic *g* and the *qāl-gāl* Dialect Split in Arabic," *PICSS* (1969) 7-37.

Charles A. Ferguson, "The /g/ in Syrian Arabic: Filling a Gap in a Phonological Pattern," *Word* 25 (1969) 114-119.

*Federico C. Corriente, "A Survey of Spirantization in Semitic and Arabic Phonetics," *JQR, N.S.,* 60 (1969-70) 147-171.

*L. Kopf, "Structure and Arrangement of Medieval Arabic Dictionaries (A Contribution to the Study of the Dependence of Hebrew Lexicography on Arabic Lexicography)," *Lěš* 34 (1969-70) #1/2, 5-6. [English Supplement]

Haim Blanc, "The Arabic Dialect of the Negev Bedouins," *PIASH* 4 (1969-70) 112-150.

A. A. Nadwi, "Notes on the Arabic Dialects of the Bilad Ghāmid and Zahrān Region of Saudi Arabia," *ALOUS* 7 (1969-73) 75-88.

T. M. Johnstone, "The Spoken Arabic of Tikrīt," *ALOUS* 7 (1969-73) 89-109.

A. A. Dohaish and M. J. L. Young, "Modes of Address and Epistolary Forms in Saudi Arabia," *ALOUS* 7 (1969-73) 110-117.

§538 **3.3.3.2.4.1.1 *South Arabian (includes Safaitic)***

*E. L. Pilcher, "The Himyaritic Script derived from the Greek," *SBAP* 29 (1907) 123-132.

James A. Montgomery, "The Words 'law' and 'witness' in the South Arabic," *JAOS* 37 (1917) 164-165.

Bertram Thomas, "Four Strange Tongues from Central South Arabia—The Hadara Group," *PBA* 23 (1937) 231-331. [Shahari; Mahri; Harsusi; Botahari]

Dorothy Stehle, "Sibilants and Emphatics in South Arabic," *JAOS* 60 (1940) 507-543.

*Wolf Leslau, "South-East Semitic (Ethiopic and South-Arabic)," *JAOS* 63 (1943) 4-14.

Wolf Leslau, "The Parts of the Body in the Modern South Arabic Languages," *Lang* 21 (1945) 230-249.

A. F. L. Beeston, "Notes on Old South Arabian Lexicography I," *Muséon* 63 (1950) 53-57.

A. F. L. Beeston, "Notes on Old South Arabian Lexicography II," *Muséon* 63 (1950) 261-268.

A. F. L. Beeston, "Notes on Old South Arabian Lexicography III," *Muséon* 64 (1951) 127-132.

A. F. L. Beeston, "Phonology of the Epigraphic South Arabian Unvoiced Sibilants," *TPS* (1951) 1-26.

A. F. L. Beeston, "Notes on Old South Arabian Lexicography IV," *Muséon* 65 (1952) 139-147.

A. F. L. Beeston, "Notes on Old South Arabian Lexicography V," *Muséon* 66 (1953) 109-122.

A. F. L. Beeston, "Notes on Old South Arabian Lexicography VI," *Muséon* 67 (1954) 311-322.

A[lbert] Jamme, "Syntax of the Adjective in South Arabian," *JSS* 2 (1957) 176-181.

William Sanford LaSor, "The Sibilants in Old South Arabic," *JQR, N.S.,* 48 (1957-58) 161-173.

A. F. L. Beeston, "The Syntax of the Adjective in Old South Arabian: Remarks on Jamme's Theory," *JSS* 3 (1958) 142-145.

G. Rychmans, "Heaven and Earth in the South Arabian Inscriptions," *JSS* 3 (1958) 225-236. *[Safaitic]*

A[lbert] Jamme, "The Syntax of South-Arabian Adjectives Again," *JSS* 4 (1959) 264-267.

A. K. Irvine, "Some Notes on Old South Arabian Monetary Terminology," *JRAS* (1964) 18-36.

*J. C. deMoor, "Ugaritic *ṯkḥ* and South Arabian *mṯkḥ,*" *VT* 14 (1964) 371-372.

Albert Jamme, "The Safaitic Noun *nq't* and its Synonyms," *CBQ* 29 (1967) 386-392.

A[lbert] Jamme, "The Safaitic Verb *wgm,*" *Or, N.S.,* 36 (1967) 159-172.

A[lbert] Jamme, "The Safaitic Expression *rġm mny* and Its Variants," *Or, N.S.,* 36 (1967) 345-348.

Charles D. Matthews, "Modern South Arabian Determination—A Clue Thereto from Shaḥri," *JAOS* 89 (1969) 22-27.

§539 *3.3.3.2.4.1.2 Sabaean*

W. F. Prideaux, "A Sketch of Sabaean Grammar, with Examples of Translation," *SBAT* 5 (1876-77) 177-224, 384-425.

C[rawford] H. Toy, "On Noun-Inflection in the Sabean," *JAOS* 11 (1885) xxix-xxxi.

A. G. Lundin, "The List of Sabaean Eponyms Again," *JAOS* 89 (1969) 533-541.

§540 *3.3.3.2.4.2 Ethiopian*

W[illiam] H[enry] Green, "An Account of Dillmann's Ethiopic Grammar, with some Remarks respecting the Ancient Ethiopic Language," *JAOS* 7 (1862) lvii-lviii.

Francis Barham, "Ethiopic Language and Literature," *JSL, 4th Ser.*, 4 (1863-64) 172-73.

*Paul Haupt, "Hebrew *az* = Ethiopic *enza*," *JSOR* 1 (1917) 41-44.

Hartwig Hirschfield *(editor and translator)*, "An Ethiopic-Falasi Glossary," *JRAS* (1919) 209-230; (1920) 573-582; (1921) 211-237.

*Israel Eitan, "The Bearing of Ethiopic on Biblical Exegesis and Lexicography," *JPOS* 3 (1923) 136-143.

*Israel Eitan, "Ethiopic and Hebrew Etymologies," *AJSL* 40 (1923-24) 269-276.

*Paul Haupt, "Etymological and Critical Notes," *AJP* 47 (1926) 305-318. [4. The pronunciation of Ethiopic, pp. 311-312]

*Paul Haupt, "Ass. *zâzu*, halve, and Eth. *azzáza*, command," *BAVSS* 10 (1927) Heft 2, 264-267.

James A. Montgomery, "Origin of the Ethiopic gerund," *JAOS* 48 (1928) 283-284.

*Frank R. Blake, "Studies in Semitic Grammar II," *JAOS* 62 (1942) 109-118. [5. Distributive Expressions in Ethiopic, pp. 113-114]

*Wolf Leslau, "South-East Semitic (Ethiopic and South-Arabic)," *JAOS* 63 (1943) 4-14.

*Wolf Leslau, "Vocabulary Common to Akkadian and South-East Semitic (Ethiopic and South-Arabic)," *JAOS* 64 (1944) 53-58.

Wolf Leslau, "The Position of Gafat in Ethiopic," *Lang* 20 (1944) 56-65.

*Wolf Leslau, "The Verb in Tigré (North-Ethiopic)," *JAOS* 65 (1945) 1-26.

*Wolf Leslau, "Grammatical Sketches in Tigré (North Ethiopic)," *JAOS* 65 (1945) 164-203.

Wolf Leslau, "The Influence of Cushitic on the Semitic Languages of Ethiopia. A Problem of Substratum," *Word* 1 (1945) 59-82.

Wolf Leslau, "Supplementary Observations on Tigré Grammar," *JAOS* 68 (1948) 127-139.

Wolf Leslau, "Archaic Features in South Ethiopic," *JAOS* 71 (1951) 212-230.

Wolf Leslau, "The Imperfect in South-East Semitic," *JAOS* 73 (1953) 164-166. (Reply by Joseph Greenberg, pp. 167-168)

*Frithiof Rundgren, "The Root *šft* in the Modern Ethiopic Language (Tigrē, Tigrina, and Amharic) and Old Egyptian *ḫfty,* Coptic *šft,*" *OrS* 2 (1953) 19-25.

‡W[olf] Leslau, "Ten years of Ethiopic Linguistics," *AE* 2 (1957) 277-313.

*Wolf Leslau, "Arabic Loanwords in Argobba (South Ethiopic)," *JAOS* 77 (1957) 36-39.

Wolf Leslau, "The Phonetic Treatment of the Arabic Loan Words in Ethiopic," *Word* 13 (1957) 100-123.

*W[olf] Leslau, "Arabic Loan-Words in Geez," *JSS* 3 (1958) 146-168.

F. R. Palmer, "Comparative Statement and Ethiopic Semitic," *TPS* (1958) 119-143.

Wolf Leslau, "The Verb in Harari (South Ethiopic)," *UCPSP* 21 (1958) 1-86.

Wolf Leslau, "Sidamo Features in the South Ethiopic Phonology," *JAOS* 79 (1959) 1-7.

Wolf Leslau, "A Preliminary Description of Argobba," *AE* 3 (1959) 251-273.

Wolf Leslau, "An Analysis of the Harari Vocabulary," *AE* 3 (1959) 275-298.

*W[olf] Leslau, "Traces of the Laryngeals in the Ethiopic Dialect of Ennemor. A Contribution to Semitic Laryngeals," *Or, N.S.,* 28 (1959) 257-270.

Wolf Leslau, "Homonyms in Gurage," *JAOS* 80 (1960) 200-217.

Wolf Leslau, "Echo-Words in Ethiopic," *AE* 4 (1961) 205-238.

W[olf] Leslau, "Remarks on the Gemination of the Gurage Dialect of Azarnat-Mugo," *BO* 18 (1961) 19-20.

*Wolf Leslau, "The Names of the Weekdays in Ethiopic," *JSS* 6 (1961) 62-70.

Wolf Leslau, "'Yes' and 'No' in the Ethiopian Language," *Lang* 38 (1962) 147-148.

Wolf Leslau, "Ethiopic Denominatives with Nominal Morphemes," *Muséon* 75 (1962) 139-175.

*Wolf Leslau, "An Ethiopian Parallel to Hebrew עלה 'went up country' and ירד 'went down country'," *ZAW* 74 (1962) 322-323.

*H. J. Plotsky, "Aramaic, Syriac, and Ge'ez," *CNI* 15 (1964) #4, 19-26.

*H. J. Plotsky, "Aramaic, Syriac, and Ge'ez," *JSS* 9 (1964) 1-10.

Wolf Leslau, "Gleanings in Harari Grammar I," *JAOS* 85 (1965) 153-159.

Marvin L. Bender, "Notes on Some Lexical Correlations in Some Ethiopian Languages," *JES* 4 (1966) #1, 5-30.

Bruce G. Trigger, "Spoken and written Meroïtic: a note on the terminal formulae in the Meroïtic funerary inscriptions from Armenna West," *JEA* 53 (1967) 166-169.

Wolf Leslau, "An Archaic Vowel of the Jussive in Gurage, Gafat, and Harari," *Or, N.S.,* 37 (1968) 90-93.

*M. M. Bravmann, "Akk *kipru(m),* pl. *kipratu(m)* and Ethiopic *kanfar,*" *JCS* 22 (1968-69) 85-87.

*R. Hetzron, "The Evidence for Perfect **y'aqtul* and Jussive **yaqt'ul* in Proto-Semitic," *JSS* 14 (1969) 1-21. [2. Gə'əz, pp. 5-8]

W[olf] Leslau, "Is There a Proto-Gurage?" *PICSS* (1969) 152-171.

§541 *3.3.4 Caucasian (Aryan) Family - General Studies*

*[William D.] Whitney, "On Pictets' Work: Indo-European Origins, or the Primitive Aryans," *JAOS* 8 (1866) lxxxv-lxxxvi.

*W[illiam] D. Whitney, "The Question of Indo-European and Semitic Relationship," *PAPA* 8 (1875-76) 26-28. *[Bound with Transactions, but paged separately]*

*James F. McCurdy, "Relations of the Aryan and Semitic Languages. I.—History and Present State of Inquiry," *BS* 33 (1876) 78-101.

*James F. McCurdy, "Relations of the Aryan and Semitic Languages. II.—Criteria of Relationship," *BS* 33 (1876) 352-381.

Thomas A. Becker, "The Aryan Language and Literature," *ACQR* 3 (1878) 73-103.

*James F. McCurdy, "Relations of the Aryan and Semitic Languages. III.—Comparative Phonology," *BS* 36 (1879) 674-706.

*James F. McCurdy, "Relations of the Aryan and Semitic Languages. IV.—Morphology of Roots," *BS* 37 (1880) 528-565.

*James F. McCurdy, "Relations of the Aryan and Semitic Languages. V.—Comparison of Roots," *BS* 37 (1880) 752-776.

*James F. McCurdy, "Relations of the Aryan and Semitic Languages. V.—Comparison of Roots (Continued)," *BS* 38 (1881) 116-146.

H. Collitz, "On the existence of primitive Aryan $\check{s}$," *JAOS* 15 (1893) lxv-lxvi.

R. A. Stewart Macalister, "A Sketch of the Grammatical Structure of the Nuri Language," *PEFQS* 40 (1908) 64-70.

*Allison Emery Drake, "Some Evidences of Aryo-Semitic Kinship," *BS* 70 (1913) 607-621.

D. A. Hester, "Recent Developments in the Mediterranean 'Substrate' Studies," *Minos* 9 (1968) 219-235.

*G. A. Melikishvili, "Names of Metals in Ancient Oriental and Caucasian Languages," *VDI* (1968) #4, 127.

§542 *3.3.4.1 Elamite (Kassite)*

A. H. Sayce, "The Languages of the Cuneiform Inscriptions of Elam and Media," *SBAT* 3 (1874) 465-485.

Paul Haupt, "The Language of Nimrod, the Kashite," *AR* 2 (1884) 88-98.

*Fritz Hommel, "Assyriological Notes," *SBAP* 18 (1896) 17-24. [§20. Elamite proper name *Ma-uk-ti-ti,* pp. 23-24]

Theophile G. Pinches, "The Question of the Kassite Language," *JRAS* (1907) 685.

Theophile G. Pinches, "The Language of the Kassites," *JRAS* (1917) 101-114.

E. Reiner, "Elamite *ḫawir sukkir,*" *JCS* 7 (1953) 33-35.

Herbert H. Paper, "An Elamite etymology," *Lang* 29 (1953) 66-68.

*J. Harmatta, "An Old Persian Loan-Word in Elamite," *AOASH* 5 (1955) 195-203. [ak-ka$_4$-ia-še]

Richard T. Hallock, "Notes on Achaemenid Elamite," *JNES* 17 (1958) 256-262.

Richard T. Hallock, "The Finite Verb in Achaemenid Elamite," *JNES* 18 (1959) 1-19.

Richard T. Hallock, "The Pronominal Suffixes in Achaemenid Elamite," *JNES* 21 (1962) 53-56.

*William C. Brice and Ernst Grumach, "Studies in the Structures of Some Ancient Scripts," *BJRL* 45 (1962-63) 15-57. [I. The Writing System of the Proto-Elamite Account Tablets of Susa, pp. 15-39]

Richard T. Hallock, "The Verb *šara-* in Achaemenid Elamite," *JNES* 24 (1965) 271-273.

*Ilya Gershevitch, "Iranian Nouns and Names in Elamite Garb," *TPS* (1969) 165-200.

§543 *3.3.4.2 Indo-European Family*

*W[illiam] Henry Green, "On the Relation of Hebrew to the Indo-European Tongues," *PAOS* (November, 1858) 7-8.

[James] Halley, "On the Indo-European Verb, by Dr. Leonard Tafel and Prof. Rudolph L. Tafel, of St. Louis, Mo.," *JAOS* 8 (1866) xxiii-xxiv.

W[illiam] D. Whitney, "On the Beginnings of Indo-European Speech," *JAOS* 9 (1871) vi.

James Gow, "Notes on Gender, Especially in Indo-European Languages," *JP* 10 (1881-82) 39-66.

Maurice Bloomfield, "On some alleged Indo-European Languages in Cunei-form Character," *AJP* 25 (1904) 1-14.

*Edgar H. Sturtevant, "Hittite *h* Initial = Indo-European *bh*," *Lang* 3 (1927) 109-122.

*E[dgar] H. Sturtevant, "Notes on Hittite and Indo-European Pronouns and Morphology," *JAOS* 47 (1927) 174-184. [I Hittite *ta* = Indo-European **to-*; II. Hittite *ašta* = Sanskrit *tatas;* III. The Ablative]

*Edgar Howard Sturtevant, "The Relationship of Hittite to Indo-European," *TAPA* 60 (1929) 25-37.

*Walter Petersen, "Hittite and Indo-European Nominal Plural Declension," *AJP* 51 (1930) 251-272.

*Edgar H. Sturtevant, "Indo-European *bh* Corresponds to Hittite *p*," *JAOS* 50 (1930) 125-128.

Edgar Howard Sturtevant, "The Indo-European Dative and Locative," *TAPA* 62 (1931) 18-25.

A. Campbell, "The Indo-European Accent," *TPS* (1936) 1-42.

*Edgar H. Sturtevant, "*o*-Stem Adjectives from Declined Genitives," *TAPA* 71 (1940) 573-578.

Alf Sommerfelt, "Some New Ideas on the Structure of the Indo-European Parent Language," *TPS* (1945) 206-212.

*R. A. Crossland, "A Reconsideration of the Hittite Evidence for the existance of 'Laryngeals' in Primitive Indo-European," *TPS* (1951) 88-130.

*E. P. Hamp, "Hittite Evidence for 'Laryngeals'—An Addendum," *TPS* (1952) 110-113.

I. J. Gelb, "A contribution to the Proto-Indo-European question," *JKF* 2 (1952-53) 23-36.

*R. A. Crossland, "Indo-European Origins: The Linguistic Evidence," *P&P* #12 (1957) 16-46.

*Jerzy Kuryłowicz, "Accentuation of the Verb in Indo-European and in Hebrew," *Word* 15 (1959) 123-129.

G. B. Jahukyan, "The Hayaša Language and its Relation to the Indo-European Languages," *ArOr* 29 (1961) 353-405.

E. Adelaide Hahn, "Was There a Nominative Gerund? (Interum de gerundio et gerundivo)," *TAPA* 96 (1965) 181-207.

Roland F. Willetts, "The Birmingham Symposium of Aegean Writing," *KZFE* 7 (1968) 176-178.

§544 **3.3.4.2.1** *Hittite (including Hieroglyphic Hittite)*

†J. Dunbar Heath, "Method of Deciphering the Hittite Inscriptions," *SBAP* 3 (1880-81) 23-24 [Remarks by Hyde Clarke, 23; by W. F. Birch, pp. 23-24]

T[errien] de Lacouperie, "Deciphering the Hittite Inscriptions: A Retrospect," *BOR* 1 (1886-87) 85-90.

Claude R. Conder, "The Hittite Language," *PEFQS* 19 (1887) 231-233.

C[laude] R. Conder, "The Hittite Language," *PEFQS* 20 (1888) 77-103.

Claude R. Conder, "Chinese and Hittite," *PEFQS* 20 (1888) 246-249.

*Claude R. Conder, "On Comparisons of Hieroglyphics," *PEFQS* 20 (1888) 252-259. *[Hittite]*

*C[laude] R. Conder, "The Three Hieroglyphic Systems," *ARL* 3 (1889) 99-117. *[Hittite]*

C[laude] R. Conder, "Tarku," *PEFQS* 21 (1889) 25. [𐤉 ⋈⋈ ⟨]

Claude R. Conder, "Essebu," *PEFQS* 21 (1889) 27.

C[laude] R. Conder, "Notes by Major Conder, D.C.L., R.E. VII. Was there a Word *Ko* 'King'?" *PEFQS* 21 (1889) 149.

*A. H. Sayce, "Miscellaneous Notes," *ZA* 4 (1889) 382-393. [26. A Hittite(?) word for Fortress, pp. 386-387]

C[laude] R. Conder, "Note on the Hittite Writing," *JRAS* (1893) 823-853.

A. H. Sayce, "The decipherment of the Hittite Inscriptions," *RTR* 15 (1893) 21-32.

*A. H. Sayce, "The Hittite inscriptions of Cappodicia and their decipherment," *RTR* 14 (1893) 43-53.

Anonymous, "The Language of the Hittites," *MR* 79 (1897) 307-309.

W. M. Ramsay, "Hittite Decipherment, I," *ET* 10 (1898-99) 384.

A. H. Sayce, "Hittite Decipherment, II," *ET* 10 (1898-99) 384.

Fritz Hommel, "Notes on 'Hittite' Inscriptions," *SBAP* 21 (1899) 224-238.

*A. H. Sayce, "Notes," *SBAP* 22 (1900) 77-79. *[Hittite Language]*

A. H. Sayce, "The Decipherment of the Hittite Inscriptions," *ET* 13 (1901-02) 490-492.

A. H. Sayce, "Hittite Decipherment," *ET* 14 (1902-03) 480.

A. H. Sayce, "The Decipherment of the Hittite Inscriptions," *SBAP* 25 (1903) 141-156, 173-194, 277-287, 305-310, 347-362.

W. F. Badè, "The Decipherment of the Hittite Inscriptions and the Determination of the Language," *PAPA* 37 (1905) lxvi.

*D. D. Luckenbill, "Some Hittite and Mitannian Personal Names," *AJSL* 26 (1909-10) 96-104.

A. H. Sayce, "Hittite Notes," *SBAP* 33 (1911) 43-45. [I. The name of Gurgum in the Hittite Texts; Bit-Adin and Bit Agusi; II. The name of Gurgum on the Mer ash Lion; III. King Mita or Midas; IV. The King of the Aleppo Inscriptions]

A. H. Sayce, "Notes on the Hittite Language of Boghaz Keui," *JRAS* (1913) 1043-1047.

*A. H. Sayce, "The Solution of the Hittite Problem," *SBAP* 35 (1913) 6-12.

A. H. Sayce, "Hittite Vocabularies from Boghaz Keui," *JRAS* (1914) 965-972.

J. Dyneley Prince, "The Hittite Material in the Cuneiform Inscriptions," *AJSL* 32 (1915-16) 38-63.

L. W. King, "Note on the Hittite Problem," *JEA* 4 (1916) 190-193.

Anonymous, "The Hittite Language," *MR* 98 (1916) 798-802.

S. J. Crawford, "The Decipherment of the Hittite Language," *JRAS* (1919) 1-13.

*A. Cowley, "A Hittite Word in Hebrew," *JTS* 21 (1919-20) 326-327. [*šalliš*]

A. H. Sayce, "The Hittite Language of Boghaz Keui," *JRAS* (1920) 49-83.

Maurice Broomfield, "The Hittite Language," *JAOS* 41 (1921) 195-209.

J. Dyneley Prince, "Possible Non-Indo-European Elements in 'Hittite'," *JAOS* 41 (1921) 210-224.

*H. R. Hall, "The Egyptian Transliteration of Hittite Names," *JEA* 8 (1922) 219-222.

A. H. Sayce, "The Decipherment of the Hittite Texts,"*JRAS* (1922) 537-572.

*D. D. Luckenbill, "Assyriological Notes," *AJSL* 39 (1922-23) 56-65. [VII. On some "Hittite" Proper Names, pp.. 63-65]

*A. H. Sayce, "Hittite katral, Sumerian balag," *AfO* 2 (1924-25) 106.

George A. Barton, "Unlocking the Secrets of the Hittite Language," *BASOR* #17 (1925) 13-15.

A. H. Sayce, "The Decipherment of the Hittite Hieroglyphic Inscriptions Verified," *JRAS* (1925) 707-715.

A. H. Sayce, "Animal cries in Hittite," *AfO* 3 (1926) 64-65.

Anonymous, "Unlocking the Hittite Language," *HR* 91 (1926) 303-304.

E[dgar] H. Sturtevant, "On the Position of the Hittite among the Indo-European Languages," *Lang* 2 (1926) 25-34.

*W[illiam] M. Ramsay, "Specimens of Anatolian Words," *OOR* 1 (1926) #2, 1-7. [I. Sbida; Pomegranate; II. The Peacock: Name imported into Anatolia; III. Korud: The Lark; IV. Lustra-Sultra; V. The Wagon (Benna); V.*[sic]* Trogla: A Hole in the Ground; VI. Oa, Owa, *Οὐά,* Turkish Ova; VII. Kume and Rume, Village and Street: Ros Head; VIII. Paga and Kranna: Fountain, Water-source; IX. Skanna, Tents or Booths used by Traders ακηνή ὡς Ἀσιαγνῆ τὴν λέξιν (Photius from Meander)]

E[dgar] H. Sturtevant, "Hittite *Katta(n)* and Related Words," *AJP* 48 (1927) 247-257.

*E[dgar] H. Sturtevant, "Notes on Hittite and Indo-European Pronouns and Morphology," *JAOS* 47 (1927) 174-184. [I. Hittite *ta* = Indo-European **to-* ; II. Hittite *ašta* = Sanskrit *tatas* ; III. The Ablative]

*Edgar H. Sturtevant, "Hittite *h* Initial = Indo-European *bh,*" *Lang* 3 (1927) 109-122.

E[dgar] H. Sturtevant, "The *e-* Perfect in Hittite," *Lang* 3 (1927) 161-168.

Edgar H. Sturtevant, "Stems of the Hittite *hi-* Conjugation," *Lang* 3 (1927) 215-225.

A. H. Sayce, "The Names of the Parts of the Body in Hittite," *RAAO* 24 (1927) 45-53.

E[dgar] H. Sturtevant, "Initial *sp* and *st* in Hittite," *Lang* 4 (1928) 1-6.

Edgar H. Sturtevant, "The Parts of the Body in Hittite," *Lang* 4 (1928) 120-127.

E[dgar] H. Sturtevant, "Original *h* in Hittite and the Medio-Passive in *r,*" *Lang* 4 (1928) 159-170.

Edgar H. Sturtevant, "The Sources of Hittite *z,*" *Lang* 4 (1928) 227-231.

*Edgar Howard Sturtevant, "Some Nouns of Relationship in Lycian and Hittite," *TAPA* 59 (1928) 48-56.

*E[dgar] H. Sturtevant, "Hittite Denominatives in *a(i)* and one Source of Indo-European Nouns in Long *ā,*" *Lang* 5 (1929) 8-14.

E[dgar] H. Sturtevant, "Place Whither in Hittite and the Use of Proper Nouns in the Stem Form," *Lang* 5 (1929) 139-146.

E[dgar] H. Sturtevant, "Some Hittite Words," *Lang* 5 (1929) 228-231. [*waggašnuanzi; uppeššaran; hukanzi; memal; meranda*]

*Edgar Howard Sturtevant, "The Relationship of Hittite to Indo-European," *TAPA* 60 (1929) 25-37.

*Walter Petersen, "Hittite and Indo-European Nominal Plural Declension," *AJP* 51 (1930) 251-272.

*Edgar H. Sturtevant, "Indo-European *bh* Corresponds to Hittite *p*," *JAOS* 50 (1930) 125-128.

A. H. Sayce, "The Decipherment of the Moscho-Hittite Inscriptions," *JRAS* (1930) 739-759.

E[dgar] H. Sturtevant, "The Original Diphthongs in Hittite," *Lang* 6 (1930) 25-35.

E[dgar] H. Sturtevant, "Can Hittite *h* be Derived from Indo-Hittite ə," *Lang* 6 (1930) 149-158.

*Clive H. Carruthers, "Some Hittite Etymologies," *Lang* 6 (1930) 159-163. [1. *duddu-* 'rage, be furious'(?), *duddumiya(h)-* 'make furious, cause to show rage', *duddumili* 'blindly, furiously'; 2. *akuwakuwaš* 'frog, toad'; 3. *išhaš* 'master', *ishatar* 'lordship'; 4. *šumanza* 'cord, string', *šuel* 'cord'; 5. *šenah(h)aš* 'battle-line, army in the field (?)'; 6. *tepuš* 'small', *tepnu-* 'make small, revile', *tepawaš-* 'make light of (?)', *tepaweš-* 'be, become small']

*E[dgar] H. Sturtevant, "The Gutturals in Hittite and Indo-European," *Lang* 6 (1930) 213-228.

A. H. Sayce, "Additions to the List of Names of Parts of the Body in Hittite," *RAAO* 27 (1930) 165-167.

E[dgar] H. Sturtevant, "Reduced vowels and syllabic liquids and nasals in Hittite," *RHA* 1 (1930-32) 76-88.

E[dgar] H. Sturtevant, "Hittite Etymologies," *Lang* 7 (1931) 1-13. [1. The prefixes *u-, we-, wa-,* and the adverb *awan;* 2. *har(k)-* 'have', *pe-har(k)-* 'have with one, carry'; 3. *pai-* 'go', *we-, wa-* 'come']

E[dgar] H. Sturtevant, "Changes of Quantity Caused by Indo-Hittite *h,*" *Lang* 7 (1931) 115-124.

E[dgar] H. Sturtevant, "Hittite Verbs with Suffix *na, sa,* or *a,*" *Lang* 7 (1931) 167-172.

E[dgar] H. Sturtevant, "The Origin of the Medio-Passive," *Lang* 7 (1931) 242-251.

Charles L. Mudge, "Ten Hittite Etymologies," *Lang* 7 (1931) 252-253. [1. *alpaš* 'cloud'; 2. *maniyah-* 'govern, assign, appoint'; 3. *kuttar* 'neck, strength'; 4. *lappaš* 'glowing, hot'; 5. *malta-* 'recite'; 6. *parsiya-* 'break, share'; 7. *haraš, haranaš* 'eagle(?)'; 8. *huwantiš* 'wind, storm'; 9. *mugai* 'lament, implore'; 10. *tukka-* 'fall to one's lot(?)']

Walter Petersen, "The Personal Endings of the Hittite Verb," *AJP* 53 (1932) 193-212.

Edgar H. Sturtevant, "The Development of the Stops in Hittite," *JAOS* 52 (1932) 1-12.

*E[dgar] H. Sturtevant, "The Ablative in Indo-European and Hittite," *Lang* 8 (1932) 1-10.

E[dgar] H. Sturtevant, "The *s-* aorist in Hittite," *Lang* 8 (1932) 119-132.

Stefán Einarsson, "Parallels to the Stops in Hittite," *Lang* 8 (1932) 177-182.

*Theodor [H.] Gaster, "A Hittite Word in Hebrew," *JRAS* (1933) 909. [כּוֹבַע "helmet/קוֹבַע = Hittite *kupaḫi*]

E[dgar] H. Sturtevant, "Archaism in Hittite," *Lang* 9 (1933) 1-11.

Walter Petersen, "Hittite and Tocharian," *Lang* 9 (1933) 12-34.

*Clive H. Carruthers, "More Hittite Words," *Lang* 9 (1933) 151-161. [1. *kutrus* 'witness'; *akugallit* (inst. sg) 'wash-basin, water vessel' *kunkunuzzi* 'diorite'; 4. *pupus* 'paramour, lover, adulterer'; 5. *suppalas;* 6. *wantai-* 'be warm, glow, be angry'; 7. *irmas, irmalas, irmalanza* 'ill', 'illness' *irmal(l)iya-* 'be ill'; 8. *ipulli-* 'vagina'; 9. *palwas* 'mud, mire']

Walter Petersen, "The Relation to Hittite Verbs in *-a(i)-* to the Thematic Vowel Class," *Lang* 9 (1933) 291-297.

*E. Adelaide Hahn, "Light from Hittite on Latin Indefinites," *TAPA* 64 (1933) 28-40.

*Samuel I. Feigin, "The Captives in Cuneiform Inscriptions," *AJSL* 50 (1933-34) 217-245. [4. A.SI.RUM in the Hittite Code, pp. 227-228; 6. *és-re-tum* in Hittite Texts, pp. 230-232; *i-sar-ti-* and *napṭarti-* Women in Hittite Texts, pp. 232-234]

W[illiam] F[oxwell] Albright, "The Decipherment of the Hittite Hieroglyphs," *BASOR* #54 (1934) 34-35.

Walter Petersen, "Vowel Assimilation in Hittite," *JAOS* 54 (1934) 161-168.

*E[dgar] H. Sturtevant, "Adjectival *i-* Stems in Hittite and Indo- European," *Lang* 10 (1934) 266-273.

*E. Sapir, "Hittite *hapatis* 'Vassal' and Greek ὀπᾱδός," *Lang* 10 (1934) 274-279.
Walter Petersen, "The Origin of Hittite ḫ," *Lang* 10 (1934) 307-322.

*Albrecht Göetze, "Hittite *šanna-* 'One'," *Lang* 11 (1935) 185-190.

E[dgar] H. Sturtevant, "Two Hittite Words," *JAOS* 56 (1936) 282-287. [1. suppariya-; 2. uwatar]

E. Adelaide Hahn, "Some Hittite Words in *ta-*," *Lang* 12 (1936) 108-120. [1. ta; 2. takku; 3. tamais; 4. takiya]

*Edward Sapir, "Greek ἀτύζομαι, a Hittite Loanword, and Its Relatives," *Lang* 12 (1936) 175-180. [Hittite: adj. *ḫatuki-s* 'terrible, frightful'; adv. *ḫatukā* 'terribly, frightfully']

E[dgar] H. Sturtevant, "Some Hittite Etymologies," *Lang* 12 (1936) 181-189.

E[dgar] H. Sturtevant, "The Meaning and Etymology of Hittite *salik-*," *Lang* 12 (1936) 189-190.

O. R. Gurney, "Note on Hittite Philology: *wappu*," *JRAS* (1937) 113-115.

William M. Austin and Henry Lee Smith Jr., "The Etymology of Hittite *yukas*," *Lang* 13 (1937) 104-106.

E[dgar] H. Sturtevant, "The Values of the *be-* Sign in Hittite," *Lang* 13 (1937) 285-291.

*O. R. Gurney, "Hittite *Paras* = Horse??" *PEQ* 69 (1937) 194-195.

E. Adelaide Hahn, "Hittite *kwis kwis,*" *TAPA* 68 (1937) 388-402.

I[gnace] J. Gelb, "The Dogs of Nikarawas," *AJSL* 55 (1938) 200-203.

Benjamin Schwartz, "On the 'Glossenkeil' in Hittite," *ArOr* 10 (1938) 65-78.

E[dgar] H. Sturtevant, "The Source of the Hittite *hi-* Conjugation," *Lang* 14 (1938) 10-19.

E[dgar] H. Sturtevant, "Hittite Evidence Against Full-Grade *o,*" *Lang* 14 (1938) 104-111.

*E. Adelaide Hahn, "Hittite *kinun* = Latin *nunc* and *num,*" *PAPA* 69 (1938) lii.

Walter Petersen, "Hittite *ḫ* and Saussure's Doctrine of Long Vowels," *JAOS* 59 (1939) 175-199.

E[dgar] H. Sturtevant, "The Pronoun **so, *sā, *tod* and the Indo-Hittite Hypothesis," *Lang* 15 (1939) 11-19.

A. L. Kroeber and C. D. Chrétien, "The Statistical Technique and Hittite," *Lang* 15 (1939) 69-71.

Albrecht Goetze, "Hittite tarkuwa(i)-," *Lang* 15 (1939) 116-119.

Fritz Metzer, "Hittite *ḫa-aš-ša ḫa-an-za-aš-ša,*" *Lang* 15 (1939) 188-189.

E[dgar] H. Sturtevant, "Evidence for Voicing in Indo-Hittite γ," *Lang* 16 (1940) 81-87.

*E[dgar] H. Sturtevant, "The Indo-Hittite and Hittite Correspondences of Indo-European ə," *Lang* 17 (1941) 181-188.

Edgar H. Sturtevant, "Did Hittite Have Pronemes *e* and *o* ?" *Lang* 18 (1942) 181-192.

E[dgar] H. Sturtevant and George L. Trager, "Hittite *u* Before Vowels," *Lang* 18 (1942) 259-270.

Edgar H. Sturtevant, "Hittite *ia-* 'Make, Do, Preform'," *JAOS* 63 (1943) 1-3.

E[dgar] H. Sturtevant and George L. Trager, "Hittite *i* Before Vowels," *Lang* 19 (1943) 209-220.

G[iuliano] Bonfante and I[gnace] J. Gelb, "The Position of 'Hieroglyphic Hittite' among the Indo-European Languages," *JAOS* 64 (1944) 169-190.

Edward H. Sehrt, "Notes on Sturtevant's Indo-Hittite Laryngeals," *Lang* 20 (1944) 88-89.

E. Adelaide Hahn, "The Shift of a Hittite Conjunction from the Temporal to the Conditional Sphere," *Lang* 20 (1944) 91-107.

*Edgar H. Sturtevant, "Hittite Verbal Nouns in *-tar* and the Latin Gerund," *Lang* 20 (1944) 206-211.

*Albrecht Goetze, "Hittite and the Indo-European Languages," *JAOS* 65 (1945) 51-53.

H[ans] G. Güterbock, "The Vocative in Hittite," *JAOS* 65 (1945) 248-257.

G[iuliano] Bonfante, "Hieroglyphic Hittite, 'Indo-Hittite' and Linguistic Method," *JAOS* 65 (1945) 261-264.

Giuliano Bonfante, "'Indo-Hittite' and Areal Linguistics," *AJP* 67 (1946) 289-310.

Albrecht Goetze, "An Answer to Professor Bonfante," *JAOS* 66 (1946) 88.

G[iuliano] Bonfante, "An Answer to Prof. Goetze," *JAOS* 66 (1946) 264-265.

J. Alexander Kerns and Benjamin Schwartz, "Multiple Stem Conjugation: an Indo-Hittite Isogloss?" *Lang* 22 (1946) 57-67.

E. Adelaide Hahn, "The Origin of the Relative *kwi- kwo-*," *Lang* 22 (1946) 68-85.

Holger Pedersen, "Hittite *dalugnula* and *barganula*," *JCS* 1 (1947) 60-64.

*Albrecht Goetze, "Contributions to Hittite Lexicography," *JCS* 1 (1947) 307-320. [(1) *kuwanna(n)-* "copper, azurite, (azurite) bead"; (2) *zapzakai-* "(fine) bowl"; (3) *ḫašuwai-* "soda plant"; (4) *šuppi-wašhar* "onion"]

Edgar H. Sturtevant, "Hittite and Areal Linguistics," *Lang* 23 (1947) 376-382.

Edgar H. Sturtevant, "Indo-Hittite Collective Nouns with a Laryngeal Suffix," *Lang* 24 (1948) 259-261.

Franz Steinherr, "Hittite hieroglyphic 'all, every, whole'," *Oriens* 1 (1948) 198-207.

*Sedat Alp, "GISkalmuş 'Lituus' and HUB.BI 'Earring' in the Hittite Texts," *TTKB* 12 (1948) 320-324.

*Franz Steinherr, "Karatepe, the Key to the Hittite Hieroglyphics," *Arch* 2 (1949) 177-180.

Albrecht Goetze, "Hittite *šani/a-, šannapili,*" *ArOr* 17 (1949) Part1, 288-297.

E. Adelaide Hahn, "The Non-Restrictive Relative in Hittite," *Lang* 25 (1949) 346-374.

I[gnace] J. Gelb, "The Word for seal in Hieroglyphic Hittite," *Or, N.S.,* 18 (1949) 68-72.

Franz Steinherr, "Proposal for a New Reading of the Hittite Hieroglyphic 'TAR'," *Oriens* 2 (1949) 129-142.

*F. J. Tritsch, "Lycian, Luwian and Hittite," *ArOr* 18 (1950) Parts 1&2, 494-518.

*I[gnace] J. Gelb, "The Contribution of the New Cilician Bilinguals to the Decipherment of Hieroglyphic Hittite," *BO* 7 (1950) 129-141.

Benjamin Schwartz, "The Particle *-kan* in Hittite," *JAOS* 70 (1950) 18-24.

Benjamin Schwartz, "Hittite *-kan,*" *JAOS* 70 (1950) 179.

E. Adelaide Hahn, "More About the Vocative in Hittite," *JAOS* 70 (1950) 236-238.

Albrecht Goetze, "Contributions to Hittite Lexicography," *JCS* 4 (1950) 223-225. [(5) *witti meyani-* "New Year's Day"]

Edgar H. Sturtevant, "The Pronunciation of Written *a-i* and *a-u* in Hittite," *Lang* 26 (1950) 1-5.

*Julian Obermann, "In the Wake of the Karatepe Discoveries," *Oriens* 3 (1950) 20-30. [1. Participles of the Yqtl Pattern Outside Phoenician; 2. the Synonyms *mērîḫ and *yārîḫ in Hebrew; 3. On the Correspondence of nominal y- and m- in General]

*E. Adelaide Hahn, "Genesis of the Infinitive with Subject- Accusative," *TAPA* 81 (1950) 117-129.

Albrecht Goetze, "The Hittite Particle *-kan*," *JAOS* 70 (1950) 173-178.

*Julian Obermann, "Does Amarna Bear on Karatepe?" *JCS* 5 (1951) 58-61.

Earnest R. Oney, "The Alleged Occurrence of the Numeral pa^nta, $pa^ntă$ in Hieroglyphic Hittite," *JCS* 5 (1951) 62-63.

Albrecht Goetze, "Contributions to Hittite Lexicography," *JCS* 5 (1951) 67-70. [(6) *mitgaimi-* "sweet, sweetened"]

*Albrecht Goetze, "On the Hittite Words for 'Year' and the Seasons and for 'Night' and 'Day'," *Lang* 27 (1951) 467-476.

*R. A. Crossland, "A Reconsideration of the Hittite Evidence for the Existence of 'Laryngeals' in Primitive Indo-European," *TPS* (1951) 88-130.

W. L. Moran, "'Does Amarna Bear on Karatepe?'—An Answer," *JCS* 6 (1952) 76-80.

Edgar G. C. Polomé, "On the source of Hittite ḫ," *Lang* 28 (1952) 444-456.

*E. P. Hamp, "Hittite Evidence for the 'Laryngeals'—An Addendum," *TPS* (1952) 110-113.

R. D. Barnett, "Karatepe, the Key to the Hittite Hieroglyphs," *AS* 3 (1953) 53-95.

A. S. C. Ross and R. A. Crossland, "Supposed Use of the 2nd Singular for the 3rd Singular in 'Tocharian', Anglo-Saxon, Norse and Hittite," *AL* 6 (1954) 112-121.

*Jaan Puhvel, "Semitic affinities of Hittite ḫar-aš-zi," *JAOS* 74 (1954) 86-88.

Sedat Alp, "the *-N(N)-* Formations in the Hittite Language," *TTKB* 18 (1954) 449-467.

H[ans] G. Güterbock and E. P. Hamp, "Hittite *šuwaya-*," *RHA* 58 (1956) 22-25.

Jaan Puhvel, "'Servant' in Hieroglyphic Hittite," *JAOS* 77 (1957) 137-139.

Paul W. Brosman Jr., "Proto-Indo-Hittite *b* and the allophones of laryngeals," *Lang* 33 (1957) 1-18.

Hans Gustav Güterbock, "Toward a Definition of the Term Hittite," *Oriens* 10 (1957) 233-239.

*H[ans] G. Güterbock, "Lexicographical Notes," *RHA* 15 (1957) 1-8. [1. "Four" in Hittite and Luwian; 2. Hittite palša- = KASKAL?; 3. Hittite šak(u)ruwai- "to water (horses)"]

Paul W. Brosman Jr., "Pre-Indo-Hittite *uw > um:* A suggested restatement," *Lang* 34 (1958) 345-352

L. R. Palmer, "Problems of Hieroglyphic Hittite," *TPS* (1958) 36-74.

*L. R. Palmer, "Luvian and Linear A," *TPS* (1958) 75-100.

Ph. H. J. Houwink ten Cate, "A Luwian connecting Vowel *a* in comparision and derivation," *JEOL* #16 (1959-62) 78-87.

Th. V. Gamkrelidze, "The Akkado-Hittite Syllabary and the Problem of the Origin of the Hittite Script," *ArOr* 29 (1961) 406-418.

Paul W. Brosman Jr., "Neuters Plural in *-i* among Hittite Consonant Stems," *JAOS* 82 (1962) 63-65.

E[dgar] H. Sturtevant, "The Indo-Hittite hypothesis," *Lang* 38 (1962) 105-110.

I. McNeill, "The Metre of the Hittite Epic," *AS* 13 (1963) 237-242.

Albrecht Goetze, "Postposition and Preverb in Hittite," *JCS* 17 (1963) 98-101.

Paul W. Brosman Jr., "Secondary *ns* in Hittite," *Lang* 39 (1963) 617-619.

*C. Rabin, "Hittite Words in Hebrew," *Or, N.S.*, 32 (1963) 113-139. [1. *a-a-pi* "sacrificial pit" — Heb. *ob;* 2. Luwian *arkammana-*, Hitt. *arkamma(n)-* "tribute" — Heb. *argaman* "stuff dyed with purple"; 3. ^{DUG}*ḫarši* - "large pottery vessel, pithos" — Heb. *ḫaeraeś* "pottery vessel, potsherd", unic *chirs, ers* "potsherd"; 4. *ḫīla-, ḫēla-* "fence, court, halo" — Heb. *ḫēl* (written *ḫl, ḫyl*) "ring of fortifications surrounding a wall"; 5. *ḫuttulli-* "flock of wool" — Heb. nouns *ḫittul, ḫătullah*, verb *ḫuttul* in passive; Ug. noun *ḫtl;* perhaps also Mishnaic Hebrew *ḫotal* "packing for dates"; 6. *kalleś-* "to all, invite" (in cultic contexts) — Heb. *qls* Hitp. "to deride", *qeles, qallasah* "derision", Ugar. *qlṣ* "to deride", *qlṣ, qlṣt* "derision" or "baseness"; 7. *kariulli-* "a female garment covering head and body, hood" — late(?) Heb. *měkurbal* "dressed in a *KRBL* (?)"; 8. *kullupi-* "hatchet, mattock" — Heb. *keylappot* (Ps. lxxiv, 6), probably *keylap* parallel to *qardummot* "hatchets or mattocks"; 9. *kupaḫi-* "helmet"(?) — Heb. *k/qobaʿ* "helmet"; 10. *gurta-* "fortress" — Heb. *qaeraet* (**qartu*) "city", Phoenician *qart-*, Aramaic *qartā;* 11. *kurtal* "container made of wood or basketwork" — Heb. construct pl. *ăgarṭěley*, name of a bowl-shaped vessel used in the Temple, made of gold and silver; 12. *lappiya-* "glowing thing", "torch"(?), Luw. *lappi(ya)-* — Heb. *lappid* "torch", "lightning"; 13. *maśśi(ya)-* "shawl" — Heb. *maeši* (Theodotion: μεσσι), Ezek. xvi, 10, 13; 14. Luwian *mitgaimi* "sweet" (particle of an unattested verb *mitgai-*) — Heb. *mtq* in Qal "be sweet", in Hiph'il "make sweet"; 15. Hittite, Luwian, Hieroglyphic Hittite *muwat(t)alli-* "strong", especially of weapons — Heb. construct state *měṭil;* 16. *naḫšariya-* "to fear" or another form of the same root — Heb. *naḫšir* in (1QM); 17. *šalli-* "great, important", nominative *šalliš* — Heb. *šališ*, pl. *šališim*, some kind of adjutant or officer; 18. *tarkummāi-, tarkummiya-*, Luwian *tarkummiya-*, "to announce, explain, translate"— Heb. (or Imperial Aramaic) *trgm* "to translate" or "to explain" or "to read out"; 19. *tuekka-*, late *tukka-*, also *tuikamma-* "body, self" — (*a*) Heb. *tawaek*, construct state *tok* "centre", "inside", *bě-tok* "within, in", Ugaritic *tk*, *btk* "within", (*b*) DDS Hebrew *tkmy* (construct plural) meaning probably "body"; 20. Hierogl. Hittite *tuwarsa-* "vine" — Heb. *tiroš* "wine", Ug. *trt* "wine"; 21. *wiyana-*, Luwian *winiyant-*, Hierogl. Hittite *wa(i)ana-* "wine" — Heb. *yayin* "wine", Ugaritic *yn* "wine"; 22. *zapzagai-, zapzi/aki-* "glass(?) glass vessel" — Heb. *sapsaggim* (?) "glaze"; Ugaritic. *spsg* "glaze"(?)]

H. A. Hoffner Jr., "Some suggested Hittite Etymologies," *RHA* 21 (1963) 34-38.

Paul W. Brosman Jr., "The Neuter Plural of Hittite *i-* and *u-* Stems," *JAOS* 84 (1964) 344-348.

H[ans] G. Güterbock, "Lexicographical Notes II," *RHA* 22 (1964) 95-113. [4. ^{lú}ALAN.KAxUD = ^{lú}ALAN.ZÚ = *aluzinnu;* 5.^{giš}*ḫarau;* 6. ^(dug)GAL = *kāsu* = *zeri;* 7. *alpu-* and *dampu-;* 8. *alwanzena-;* 9. *nekuz;* 10. *pankur;* 11. *dammeli-;* 12. *dannareššar;* 13. *tuḫḫueššar, tuḫš-;* 14 - *ašta;* Addendum (to 7)]

*H. Wittmann, "A Note on the Linguistic Form of Hittite 'sheep'," *RHA* 22 (1964) 117-118.

E. Adelaide Hahn, "Hittite *genuš(š)uš, genus(š)i,* and *pankuš(š)i,*" *JAOS* 85 (1965) 295-307.

Dionys J. N. Lee, "The Hittite Particle *-kan* and Others," *ArOr* 34 (1966) 1-26.

H. A. Hoffner Jr., "Composite Nouns, Verbs and Adjectives in Hittite," *Or, N.S.,* 35 (1966) 377-402.

Ph. H. J. Houwink ten Cate, "The Ending *-d* of the Hittite Possessive Pronoun," *RHA* 24 (1966) 123-132.

Folke Josephson, "Pronominal Adverbs or Anatolian: Formation and Function," *RHA* 24 (1966) 133-154.

Harry A. Hoffner Jr., "An English-Hittite Glossary," *RHA* 25 (1967) 7-99.

H[ans] G. Güterbock, "Lexicographical Notes III," *RHA* 25 (1967) 141-150. [15. *šap-;* 16. *wetti meyani;* 17. *zinnuk;* 18. ŠID; 19. Numerals with *"iš"*]

*Paul W. Brosman Jr., "An Aspect of Hittite Use of the Hurrian Suffix *-ta,*" *JAOS* 88 (1968) 526-528.

*Harry A. Hoffner Jr., "Hittite *tarpiš* and Hebrew *Terāphîm,*" *JNES* 27 (1968) 61-68.

*Albrecht Goetze, "Hittite *šek-/šak-* '(legally) recognize' in Treaties," *JCS* 22 (1968-69) 7-8.

Harry A. Hoffner Jr., "On the Use of Hittite *-za* in Nominal Sentences," *JNES* 28 (1969) 225-230.

*Calvert Watkins, "A Latin-Hittite etymology," *Lang* 45 (1969) 235-242. [Lat. *uespillo* 'undertaker for the poorest classes' cognate with Hitt. *wašpaš* 'clothes']

§545 *3.3.4.2.2 Hurrian*

A. H. Sayce, "The Language of Mitanni," *ZA* 5 (1890) 260-274.

Eric Burrows, "Notes on Harrian*[sic]*," *JRAS* (1925) 277-284. *[Ḫurrian]*

*Zellig S. Harris, "A Hurrian Affricate or Sibilant in Ras Shamra," *JAOS* 55 (1935) 95-100.

E[phraim] A. Speiser, "Notes on Hurrian Phonology," *JAOS* 58 (1938) 173-201.

Albrecht Goetze, "An unrecognized Ḫurrian verbal form," *RHA* 5 (1938-40) 103-108.

Albrecht Goetze, "The Genitive of the Ḫurrian Noun," *RHA* 5 (1938-40) 193-204.

E[phraim] A. Speiser, "Progress in the Study of the Hurrian Language," *BASOR* #74 (1939) 4-7.

E[phraim] A. Speiser, "Studies in Hurrian Grammar," *JAOS* 59 (1939) 289-324.

Albrecht Goetze, "'To Come' and 'To Go' in Ḫurrian," *Lang* 15 (1939) 215-220.

Albrecht Goetze, "The *N*- Form of the Ḫurrian Noun," *JAOS* 60 (1940) 217-223.

E[phraim] A. Speiser, "A New Hurrian Pronominal Form," *JAOS* 60 (1940) 264-267.

Albrecht Goetze, "The Ḫurrian Verbal System," *Lang* 16 (1940) 125-140.

E[phraim] A. Speiser, "Phonetic Method in Hurrian Orthography," *Lang* 16 (1940) 319-340.

Pierre M. Purves, "Hurrian Consonantal Pattern," *AJSL* 58 (1941) 378-404.

*F. R. Steele, "The Points of the Compass in Hurrian," *JAOS* 61 (1941) 286-287.

Sidney Smith, "The 'Hurrian' Language: a review," *Antiq* 16 (1942) 320-329. *(Review)*

E. R. Lacheman, "Note on the Word Ḫupšu at Nuzi," *BASOR* #86 (1942) 36-37.

Albrecht Goetze, "Ḫurrian *muš-* 'twin'," *JCS* 2 (1948) 137-138.

*E[phraim] A. Speiser, "Nuzi Marginalia," *Or, N.S.,* 25 (1956) 1-23. [1. The Hurrian equivalent of *sikiltu(m);* 2. Oscar Broneer *k/ḫiššātum:* Nuzi *ḫi/eššumaku;* 3.The Hurrian element *maku;* 4. Ceremonial Payment; 5. The terminology of the oath by the gods]

*A. Shaffer, "Hurrian **kirezzi,* West-Semitic *krz,* " *Or, N.S.,* 34 (1965) 32-34.

*Paul W. Brosman Jr., "An Aspect of Hittite Use of the Hurrian Suffix *-ta,* " *JAOS* 88 (1968) 526-528.

§546 *3.3.4.2.3 Cypriote, Minoan and Mycenaean (includes Linear A and B)*

D. Pierides, "Notes on Cypriote Palaeography," *SBAT* 5 (1876-77) 88-96.

Isaac H. Hall, "The Declension of the Definite Article in the Cypriote Inscriptions," *PAPA* 12 (1879-80) 19-21. *[Bound with Transactions, but paged separately]*

Isaac H. Hall, "The Declension of the Definite Article in the Cypriote Inscriptions," *TAPA* 11 (1880) 51-66.

Alexander Enmann, "On the Origin of the Cypriote Syllabary," *SBAP* 5 (1882-83) 113-119. (Remarks by W. Boscawen, p. 118; by Samuel Birch, p. 119)

Herbert Weir Smyth, "Arcado-Cyprian Dialect," *PAPA* 19 (1887) xxvii-xxx.

Herbert Weir Smyth, "The Arcado-Cyprian Dialect," *TAPA* 18 (1887) 59-133. [Addenda, pp. 158-159]

*C[laude] R. Conder, "The Three Hieroglyphic Systems," *ARL* 3 (1889) 99-117. *[Cypriote]*

Daniel Quinn, "Pre-Hellenic Writing in the Aegean," *ACQR* 27 (1902) 667-682.

*Arthur J. Evans, "Pre-Phœnician Writing in Crete, and its Bearings on the History of the Alphabet," *Man* 3 (1903) #28.

George Hempl, "Early Cyprian Greek," *TAPA* 46 (1915) 229-248.

*George E. Mylonas, "Prehistoric Epigraphy and Greek Ethnology," *AJA* 41 (1937) 114.

M. G. F. Ventris, "Introducing the Minoan Language," *AJA* 44 (1940) 494-520.

John Franklin Daniel, "Prolegomena to the Cypro-Minoan Script," *AJA* 45 (1941) 249-282.

Alice E. Kober, "Evidence of Inflection in the 'Chariot' Tablets from Knossos," *AJA* 49 (1945) 143-151.

Alice E. Kober, "Inflection in Linear Class B: 1—Declension," *AJA* 50 (1946) 268-276.

Tom B. Jones, "The Minoan Syllabary," *TAPA* 78 (1947) 430, 431.

Johannes Sundwall, "An Attempt at Assigning Phonetic Values to Certain Signs of Minoan, Linear Class B," *AJA* 52 (1948) 311-320.

Alice E. Kober, "'Total' in Minoan (Linear Class B)," *ArOr* 17 (1949) Part 1, 386-398.

Spyriodon Marinatos, "Some General Notes on the Minoan Written Documents," *Minos* 1 (1951) 39-42.

Emmett L. Bennett Jr., "Statistical Notes on the Sign-groups for Pylos," *Minos* 1 (1951) 100-137.

*Henry M. Hoenigswald, "South Etruscan and Cypriote Writing," *AJA* 56 (1952) 174.

T. B. Mitford, "The Status of Cypriot Epigraphy—Cypriot Writing, Minoan to Byzantine," *Arch* 5 (1952) 151-156.

*Bedřich Hronzý, "A$_2$-Lu Jaluka = The Capital of the Empire of Pylos = Ancient Name of Pylos?" *JJP* 6 (1952) 15.

Sterling Dow, "Minoan Writing," *AJA* 58 (1954) 77-129.

Michael Ventris, "King Nestor's Four-Handled Cups: *Greek Inventories in the Minoan Script,* " *Arch* 7 (1954) 21.

Const. D. Ktistopoulos, "Statistical Data on Minoan Words," *Minos* 3 (1954) 100-106.

J. Chadwick, "Mycenaean: A Newly Discovered Greek Dialect," *TPS* (1954) 1-17.

Jane E. Henle, "Have We Criteria for Judging a Decipherment of Minoan?" *AJA* 59 (1955) 171.

Emmett L. Bennett [Jr.], "Miscellanea. Textual Note: KN Sdo450 + 0483," *Minos* 5 (1957) 207.

*Thalia Phillies Howe, "Linear B and Hesiod's Breadwinner's," *TAPA* 89 (1958) 44-65.

*L. R. Palmer, "Luvian and Linear A," *TPS* (1958) 75-100.

Maurice Pope, "On the Language of Linear A.," *Minos* 6 (1958-60) 16-23. [Corrigendum, pp. 164-165]

D. A. Hester, "The i/e Alternation in Mycenaean Greek," *Minos* 6 (1958-60) 24-36.

Saul Levin, "The Problem of Verifying the Linear B Decipherment," *AJA* 63 (1959) 189-190.

*Emmett L. Bennett Jr., "Palaeographical Evidences and Mycenaean Chronology," *AJA* 64 (1960) 182-183.

*Vladimir Georgiev, "Creto-Mycenaean and Homeric," *Klio* 38 (1960) 69-74. [1. Hom. δῶ; 2. Hom. ἰχώρ, ἰχῶ; 3. Hom. κυκε(ι)ῶ; 4. Hesiod ἄλειφα; 5. Cyr. ὁ χακεὐϝ ὁ; 6. Absence of final ν; Conclusion]

S. E. Mann, "The Decipherment of Cypro-Mycenæan," *Man* 60 (1960) #53.

S. E. Mann, "Cypro-Mycenæan," *Man* 60 (1960) #197.

Emmett L. Bennett Jr., "Textual Notes: PY An607," *Minos* 7 (1961-63) 1-13.

Henry D. Ephron, "Mycenaean Greek: A Lesson in Crypt analysis," *Minos* 7 (1961-63) 63-100.

P. H. Ilievski, "Two Notes on the *Fr-* Tablets," *Minos* 7 (1961-63) 143-149.

William C. Brice and Ernst Grumach, "Studies in the Structure of Some Ancient Scripts," *BJRL* 45 (1962-63) 15-57. [II. The Question of Ligatured Signs in the Creatan Linear Scripts, pp. 39-57]

Emmett L. Bennett Jr., "Names for Linear B writing and for its signs," *KZFE* 2 (1963) 98-123.

John Chadwick "The Linear B Ideogram for 'Woman' (No. 102)," *KZFE* 2 (1963) 124-126.

John J. Reich, "The Horse-head Ideogram in the Proto-Elamite Script and Minoan Linear B," *KZFE* 2 (1963) 151-152.

C[yrus] H. Gordon, "Toward a Grammar of Minoan," *Or, N.S.,* 32 (1963) 292-297.

Ernst Grumach, "Studies in the Structure of Some Ancient Scripts," *BJRL* 46 (1963-64) 346-384. [III. The Structure of the Cretan Hieroglyphic Script]

Antonín Bartonêk, "Monophonemic Diphthongs in Mycenaean," *Minos* 8 (1963-67) 51-61.

Emmett L. Bennett Jr., "Linear B-abel. Notes on the transcription of the Mycenaean ideograms," *Minos* 8 (1963-67) 63-99.

John Chadwick, "Mycenaean *pa-wo-ke,*" *Minos* 8 (1963-67) 115-117.

L. R. Palmer, "Some comments on the preceding paper," *Minos* 8 (1963-67) 123-124. [Ref. "Le *damokoro:* un fonctionnaire mycenien," by Jean-Pierre Olivier, *Minos* 8 (1963-67) pp. 118-122]

Machteld J. Millink, "Lycian Wooden Huts and Sign 24 on the Phaistos Disk," *KZFE* 3 (1964) 1-7.

*Warren Cowgill, "The Supposed Cypriote Optatives *duwánoi* and *dókoi* with notes on the Greek infinitive formations," *Lang* 40 (1964) 344-365.

*Carl Blegen and Mabel Lang, "The Palace of Nestor Excavations of 1964," *AJA* 69 (1965) 95-101.

Gregory Nagy, "Observations on the Sign-Grouping and Vocabulary of Linear A," *AJA* 69 (1965) 295-330.

Keith Branigan, "The Origin of the Hieroglyphic sign 18," *KZFE* 4 (1965) 81-83.

William C. Brice and Jane E. Henle, "Studies in the Structure of Some Ancient Scripts," *BJRL* 48 (1965-66) 56-80. [IV. The Minoan "Libation Formula"; V. A Sketch Plan of the Linear B Syllabary]

Dionys J. N. Lee, "Mycenaean *ifo(s),*" *KZFE* 5 (1966) 25-43.

Keith Branigan, "The Prehistory of Hieroglyphic signs 12 and 36," *KZFE* 5 (1966) 115-117.

Thomas B. L. Webster, "Signs on the Base of Mycenaean Vases," *KZFE* 5 (1966) 147.

R. Whitney Tucker, "A Note on the Interpretation of Mycenaean Sibilants," *AJA* 71 (1967) 179-180.

John Chadwick "Greekless Archaeology," *Antiq* 41 (1967) 271-275. [Linear A and B]

W[illiam] C. Brice, "Scriptless Linguistics," *Antiq* 42 (1968) 134-135. (Rejoinder by John Chadwick, pp. 135-136) *[Creatan Script]*

William F. Wyatt Jr., "The Mycenaean ideogram 120 GRANUM," *KZFE* 7 (1968) 100.

Roland F. Willetts, "The Birmingham Symposium on Aegean Writing," *KZFE* 7 (1968) 176-178.

John Chadwick, "The Group *sw* in Mycenaean," *Minos* 9 (1968) 62-65.

Martín Ruipérez, "Some Remarks on the Mycenaean Verbal Ending -TOL," *Minos* 9 (1968) 156-160.

D. A. Hester, "Recent Developments in Mediterranean 'Substrate' Studies," *Minos* 9 (1968) 219-235.

Cyrus H. Gordon, "*KI-DE-MA-WI-NA* (HT 31:4)," *KZFE* 8 (1969) 131-133.

Jon C. Billigmeier, "An Inquiry into the non-Greek Names on the Linear B Tablets from Knossos and their Relationship to Languages of Asia Minor," *Minos* 10 (1969) 177-183.

*J. J. Glück, "' ᵃrî and *lavî* ' (*labî*')— An Etymological Study," *ZAW* 81 (1969) 232-235. [Mycenaean *re-wo*]

N. E. Colligne, "Voice in the Mycenaean Verb," *DUJ, N.S.*, 31 (1969-70) 91-95.

*John Chadwick, "Greek and Pre-Greek," *TPS* (1969) 80-98.

§547 *3.3.4.2.4 Greek - General and Grammatical Studies*

†Meirion, "The Greek and Welsh Languages compared," *MMBR* 3 (1797) 10-12.

†Clericus, "Greek Accents," *MMBR* 4 (1797) 98.

†Anonymous, "Marsh's '*Horæ Pelasgicæ*'," *QRL* 13 (1815) 340-351. *(Review)*

†Anonymous, "Thesaurus Græcæ Linguæ ab H. Stephano constructus," *QRL* 22 (1819-20) 302-348. *(Review)*

*†Anonymous, "An Inquiry into the Structure and Affinity of the Greek and Latin Languages," *BCQTR, 4th Ser.*, 4 (1828) 312-341. *(Review)*

†Anonymous, "Sir D. Sandford's *Translation of Thiersch's Greek Grammar,* " *ERCJ* 52 (1830-31) 472-477. *(Review)*

†Anonymous, "Greek-and-English Lexicography," *QRL* 51 (1834) 144-177; 75 (1845) 293-324. *(Review)*

O. Cockayne, "On the construction of ἵνα, ὅπως, ὡς, with the Past Indicative," *TPS* (1842-44) 227-232.

Robert G. Latham, "On Reciprocal Pronouns and on the Reciprocal Power of the Reflective Verb," *TPS* (1842-44) 232-242.

Richard Garnett, "On the Origin and Import of the Augment in Sanscrit[sic]* and Greek,"*TPS* (1842-44) 265-272.

[Henry] Malden, "On Mistakes in the Use of obsolete Greek Words by Attic Writers," *TPS* (1844-46) 57-67.

[Henry] Malden, "On Mistakes in the Use of Obsolete Greek Words by Attic Writers. Part II," *TPS* (1844-46) 265-274.

G[eorge] C. Renouard, "On the Construction of ὅπως μή with the Past Indicative," *TPS* (1846-48) 17-18.

*[John(?)] Davies, "Attempts to suggest the Derivations and Affinities of some Greek and Latin Words," *TPS* (1846-48) 89-94.

*Anonymous, "Comparative Grammar," *BRCM* 4 (1847-48) 1-22. *(Review)*

*T. H[ewitt] Key, "On the Pronouns of the First and Second Persons,"*TPS* (1848-50) 25-37.

*W. D. Whitney, "A Comparison of the Greek and Latin Verbs," *BS* 7 (1850) 654-568.

*Anonymous, "A Critical History of the Language and Literature of Ancient Greece," *CTPR, 3rd Ser.,* 6 (1850) 332-358. *(Review)*

*†Anonymous, "Mure's *Ancient Greek Language and Literature,*" *ERCJ* 92 (1850) 398-435. *(Review)*

T. O. Cockayne, "On the Greek Middle Verb," *TPS* (1850-52) 159-163.

R[obert] G. Latham, "On the Aorists in -κα, " *TPS* (1852-53) 37-39.

T. Hewitt Key, "Philological Scraps. Απλοος, διπλοος, &c., on the Etymology of," *TPS* (1852-53) 127-128.

[T. Hewitt Key], "Philological Scraps. Στοα, στοια, and Dor. στωα, " *TPS* (1852-53) 138.

*H. L. Aherns, "On Feminines in ω and ως, and on the word γυνή; A Contribution to Greek Grammar and Etymology," *TPS* (1852-53) 155-178. *(Trans. from German by T. H. Key)*

John Stuart Blacke, "A Plea for Greek Accents," *JCSP* 2 (1855) 20-37.

T. Oswald, "On certain instances of Synkope," *TPS* (1854) 201-206.

J. W. Donaldson, "On the Vocalization or Evanescence of the Nasal Liquid in Greek," *TPS* (1854) 282-295.

T. Hewitt Key, "On Greek Accentuation," *TPS* (1855) 119-145.

Henry Malden, "On the Uncontracted Form of the Genitive Case Singular of Greek Nouns of the Second Declension," *TPS* (1855) 146-154.

J. A. Broadus, "Harrison on Greek Prepositions," *CRB* 24 (1859) 78-101. *(Review)*

Leonard Tafel, "A Review of Some Points in Bopp's Comparative Grammar," *BS* 18 (1861) 771-809.

*†T. Hewitt Key, "Miscellaneous Papers. C. On επ' of ειπειν (inquit) and έπ of έπομαι (sequor)," *TPS* (1862-63) 20-26.

*†T. Hewitt Key, "Miscellaneous Papers. D. On *alaceri-* and some related Greek words," *TPS* (1862-63) 26-30.

Henry Malden, "On connecting vowels in Greek," *TPS* (1862-63) 283-316.

*James Strong, "Affinity of the Hebrew and Greek Languages," *MR* 47 (1865) 430-444.

Henry Malden, "On Perfect Tenses in Greek and especially the First Perfect Active," *TPS* (1865) 168-179.

E. H. Knowles, "On Διά as Used in the Final Clause," *TPS* (1865) 181-187.

C. B. Cayley, "On the Verification of Homeric Accentuation," *TPS* (1866) 63-79.

T. Hewitt Key, "On the Formation of Greek Futures and First Aorists," *TPS* (1867) 1-18.

W. G. Clark, "On English pronunciation of Greek," *JP* 1 (1868) #2, 98-108.

*T. Hewitt Key, "On some of the Suffixes of Greek and Latin Prepositions," *TPS* (1868-69) 295-311.

A. H. Wratislaw, "The pronunciation of ancient Greek illustrated by that of modern Bohemian," *JP* 2 (1869) 42-47.

E. M. Geldart, "Remarks on Mr W. G. Clark's Article, Entitled 'English Pronunciation of Greek'," *JP* 2 (1869) 157-160.

E. M. Geldart, "On the Origin and Development of the Modern Greek Language," *JP* 2 (1869) 161-196.

*Evelyn Abbott, "The Cases," *JP* 2 (1869) 206-213.

James Hadley, "On the Nature and Theory of the Greek Accent," *TAPA* 1 (1869-70) 1-19.

William W. Goodwin, "On the Aorist Subjunctive and Future Indicative with Ὅπως and Οὐ μή," *TAPA* 1 (1869-70) 46-55.

James Hadley, "The Theory of the Greek Accent," *PAPA* 2 (1870) 7-8. *[Bound with Transactions, but paged separately]*

W[illiam] W. Goodwin, "The Constructions allowed in Greek, after Ὅπως, Ὅπως μή, and the double negative Οὐ μή," *PAPA* 2 (1870) 9-10. *[Bound with Transactions, but paged separately]*

A. C. Kendrick, "Translation into English of the Greek Aorist Particle," *PAPA* 2 (1870) 17. *[Bound with Transactions, but paged separately]*

James Hadley, "On the Theory of the Greek Accent," *JAOS* 9 (1871) lxii-lxiii.

Charles Short, "On the Order of Words in Attic Greek Prose," *JAOS* 9 (1871) lxiii-lxiv.

Lewis R. Packard, "On Greek Pronunciation," *JAOS* 9 (1871) lxxxvii-lxxxviii.

J[ames] Hadley, "On Westphal's new Greek Grammar," *JAOS* 9 (1871) xc-xci.

*J. B. Mayor, "An Introduction to Greek and Latin Etymology. By John Piele, M. A.," *JP* 3 (1871) 328-347. *(Review)*

F. D. Allen, "The so-called Attic Second Declension," *PAPA* 3 (1871) 12-13. *[Bound with Transactions, but paged separately]*

A. C. Kendrick, "Pronunciation of the Greek Aspirates," *PAPA* 3 (1871) 27-28. *[Bound with Transactions, but paged separately]*

Frederic D. Allen, "On the so-called Attic Second Declension," *TAPA* 2 (1871) 18-34.

*James B. Greenough, "On Some Forms of Conditional Sentences in Latin, Greek, and Sanskrit," *TAPA* 2 (1871) 159-165.

W. A. Stevens, "On the Substantive Use of the Greek Participle," *TAPA* 3 (1872) 45-55.

W[illiam] W. Goodwin, "The Classification of Conditional Sentences in Greek Syntax," *PAPA* 5 (1873) 14-16. *[Bound with Transactions, but paged separately]*

Frederic D. Allen, "The Epic Forms of Verbs in άω, " *PAPA* 5 (1873) 16-17. *[Bound with Transactions, but paged separately]*

William W. Goodwin, "On the Classification of Conditional Sentences in Greek Syntax," *TAPA* 4 (1873) 60-79.

Frederic D. Allen, "The Epic Forms of Verbs in άω, " *TAPA* 4 (1873) 119.

W[illiam] W. Goodwin, "The classification of conditional sentences in Greek syntax," *JP* 5 (1873-74) 186-205.

*W. D. Whitney, "On Peile's Greek and Latin Etymology," *TPS* (1873-74) 299-327.

J. B. Sewall, "The Distinction between the Subjunctive and Optative Modes in Greek Conditional Sentences," *PAPA* 6 (1874) 10-11. *[Bound with Transactions, but paged separately]*

J. B. Sewall, "On the Distinction between the Subjunctive and Optative Modes in Greek Conditional Sentences," *TAPA* 5 (1874) 77-82.

Charles D. Morris, "Some Forms of Greek Conditional Sentences," *PAPA* 7 (1875) 27-28. *[Bound with Transactions, but paged separately]*

Charles D. Morris, "Some Forms of Greek Conditional Sentences," *TAPA* 6 (1875) 44-53.

B[asil] L. Gildersleeve, "The Use of εἰ with the Future Indicative, and that of ἐάν with the Subjunctive, in the Tragic Poets," *PAPA* 8 (1875-76) 17-18. *[Bound with Transactions, but paged separately]*

Milton W. Humphreys, "Negative Commands in Greek," *PAPA* 8 (1875-76) 19. *[Bound with Transactions, but paged separately]*

Augustus C. Merriam, "Temporal Coincidence of the Aorist Participle with the Primary Verb," *TAPA* 9 (1876-77) 4-6. *[Bound with Transactions, but paged separately]*

Basil L. Gildersleeve, "On εἰ with the Future Indicative, and ἐάν with the Subjunctive in the Tragic Poets," *TAPA* 7 (1876) 5-23.

L. A. Sherman, "The Greek Article as a Pronoun," *PAPA* 10 (1877-78) 18-19. *[Bound with Transactions, but paged separately]*

J. B. Sewall, "The Greek Indicative, Subjunctive, and Optative Moods: what is the distinction between them?" *PAPA* 10 (1877-78) 19-21. *[Bound with Transactions, but paged separately]*

M. W. Humphreys, "Elision, especially in Greek," *PAPA* 10 (1877-78) 26-27. *[Bound with Transactions, but paged separately]*

M. W. Humphreys, "On Negative Commands in Greek," *TAPA* 7 (1876) 46-49.

R. Shilleto, "On Greek deponent verbs with Aor. in θνη," *JP* 7 (1876-77) 148-151.

R. Shilleto, "Investigation of some Greek verbs which form or seem to form a parenthetic compound with the negative prefix ἀ-(ἀν), also of similar Anomalies Real or supposed in combination with the Prefixes δυσ- and ευ-," *JP* 7 (1876-77) 157-162.

W[illiam] W. Goodwin, "Greek Expressions of Future-perfect Time," *PAPA* 9 (1876-77) 22-23. *[Bound with Transactions, but paged separately]*

W[illiam] W. Goodwin, "'Shall' and 'Should' in Protasis, and their Greek Equivalents," *TAPA* 7 (1876) 87-107. (Supplementary remark in *PAPA* 9 (1876-77), p. 23 *[Bound with Transactions, but paged separately]*)

B[asil] L. Gildersleeve, "Contributions to the History of the Articular Infinitive in Greek," *PAPA* 10 (1877-78) 24-26. *[Bound with Transactions, but paged separately]*

Basil L. Gildersleeve, "Contributions to the History of the Articular Infinitive," *TAPA* 9 (1878) 5-19.

M. W. Humphreys, "Elision, especially in Greek," *TAPA* 9 (1879) 84-97.

Anton Sander, "On Greek Negatives," *PAPA* 11 (1878-79) 18-19. *[Bound with Transactions, but paged separately]*

W[illiam] W. Goodwin, "'Shall' and 'should' in protasis, and their Greek equivalents," *JP* 8 (1879) 18-38.

F. A. Paley, "On peculiarities in the use of future participles of Greek verbs," *JP* 8 (1879) 79-86.

Maurice Bloomfield, "The 'Ablaut' of Greek Roots which show Variation between E and O," *AJP* 1 (1880) 281-326.

J. B. Greenough, "On Delbrück's recent work, entitled 'the Use of the Subjunctive and Optative in Sanskrit and Greek'," *JAOS* 10 (1880) xiii-xiv. *(Review)*

D. B. Monro, "Traces of Different Dialects in the Language of Homer," *JP* 9 (1880) 252-265.

*J. P. Postgate, "Some Latin and Greek Etymologies, and the Change of *L* to *D* in Latin," *TPS* (1880-81) 335-346.

Fisk P. Brewer, "On the Origin of ν Movable in Greek," *PAPA* 13 (1881) 22-23. *[Bound with Transactions, but paged separately]*

T. D. Seymour, "On the use of the Aorist Participle in Greek," *PAPA* 13 (1881) 24. *[Bound with Transactions, but paged separately]*

T. D. Seymour, "On the Use of the Aorist Participle in Greek," *TAPA* 12 (1881) 88-96.

A. H. Sayce, "Traces of different dialects in the language of Homer," *JP* 10 (1881-82) 110-119.

B[asil] L. Gildersleeve, "Notes from the Greek Seminary," *AJP* 3 (1882) 193-205. [I. The Articular Infinitive in Xenephon and Plato, p. 193-202; II. Οὐ μή, pp. 202-205]

D. B. Monro, "Notes. (2) On the origin of the construction of the Infinitive with πρίν and πάρος, " *JP* 11 (1882) 61-62.

A[ugustus] C. Merriam, "Alien Intrusion between Article and Noun in Greek," *PAPA* 14 (1882) xxv-xxvii.

C. D. Morris, "On οὐ μή with the Future in Prohibitions," *PAPA* 14 (1882) xxxv-xxxviii.

Augustus C. Merriam, "Alien Intrusion between Article and Noun in Greek," *TAPA* 13 (1882) 34-49.

Maurice Bloomfield, "Historical and Critical Remarks, Introductory to a Comparative Study of Greek Accent," *AJP* 4 (1883) 21-63.

B[asil] L. Gildersleeve, "On the Final Sentence in Greek," *AJP* 4 (1883) 416-444.

*Maurice Bloomfield, "Four Etymological Notes," *AJP* 6 (1885) 41-52. [3. On a Probable Equivalent in Sanskrit of the Greek Particle ἄρ, ῥά, pp. 44-45.

B[asil] L. Gildersleeve, "On the Final Sentence in Greek. II," *AJP* 6 (1885) 53-73.

B[asil] L. Gildersleeve, "The Consecutive Sentence in Greek," *AJP* 7 (1886) 161-175.

Herbert Weir Smyth, "The Dialects of North Greece," *AJP* 7 (1886) 421-445.

J. H. Moulton, "On the Greek Treatment of Original Hard Aspirates," *AJP* 8 (1887) 207-213.

B[asil] L. Gildersleeve, "The Articular Infinitive Again," *AJP* 8 (1887) 329-337.

Maurice Bloomfield, "The Origin of the Recessive Accent in Greek," *AJP* 9 (1888) 1-41. [Additional Note and Corrections, p. 220]

B[asil] L. Gildersleeve, "On the Stylistic Effect of the Greek Participle," *AJP* 9 (1888) 137-157.

*Charles S. Halsey, "Peculiarities of Affix in Latin and Greek," *PAPA* 20 (1888) xxiii-xxv.

B[asil] L. Gildersleeve, "On the Article with Proper Nouns," *AJP* 11 (1890) 482-487.

T. D. Goodell, "The Order of Words in Greek," *PAPA* 22 (1890) xxiv-xxv.

B. I. Wheeler, "The origin of Greek nouns in ευς, " *PAPA* 22 (1890) xxxvii-xxxviii.

Thomas Dwight Goodell, "The Order of Words in Greek," *TAPA* 21 (1890) 5-47.

F. B. Tarbell, "Notes. On the Infinitive after Expressions of Fearing in Greek," *AJP* 12 (1891) 70-72.

E. R. Wharton, "The Greek Indirect Negative," *TPS* (1891-94) 221-216.

E. R. Wharton, "Some Greek Etymologies," *TPS* (1891-94) 329-358.

Edwin W. Fay, "Etymological Notes," *PAPA* 24 (1892) xxiii-xxvi.

*William Gardner Hale, "The Origin and Later History of the Clause of Purpose in Latin, Greek and Sanskrit," *PAPA* 24 (1892) xxvi-xxviii.

M. W. Humphreys, "Notes on Greek Grammar," *PAPA* 24 (1892) lxi-lxii. [a. A peculiar use of ὅτι: 2. The dative of measure or difference with μετά, "after"; 3. Negatives in a negative sentence; 4. Ingressive second aorist]

Basil L. Gildersleeve, "Some Problems in Greek Syntax," *PAPA* 25 (1893) xxiv-xxvii.

C. W. E. Miller, "The Imperfect and the Aorist in Greek," *AJP* 16 (1895) 139-185.

Daniel Quinn, "On the Hellenic Pronunciation of Greek," *CUB* 2 (1896) 310-323.

Francis G. Allinson, "On the Accent of Certain Enclitic Combinations in Greek," *TAPA* 27 (1896) 73-78.

[F. J. A. Hort], "A Criticism of Dr. Hatch's 'Essays in Biblical Greek,' by Dr. Hort (A Fragment.)," *Exp, 5th Ser.*, 5 (1897) 81-96, 178-184.

J. E. Harry, "The Omission of the Article with Substantives after οὗτος, ὅδε, ἐκεῖνος in Prose," *TAPA* 29 (1898) 48-64.

Frank Cole Babbitt, "Questions with μή," *PAPA* 33 (1901) xliii-xlv.

Basil L. Gildersleeve, "Problems in Greek Syntax. I," *AJP* 23 (1902) 1-27.

Basil L. Gildersleeve, "Problems in Greek Syntax. II," *AJP* 23 (1902) 121-141.

Basil L. Gildersleeve, "Problems in Greek Syntax. III," *AJP* 23 (1902) 241-260.

James Turney Allen, "On the So-called Iterative Optative in Greek," *TAPA* 33 (1902) 101-126.

F. W. Mozley, "Notes on the Biblical Use of the Present and Aorist Imperative," *JTS* 4 (1902-03) 279-282.

M. L. Earle, "The Supplementary Signs of the Greek Alphabet," *AJA* 7 (1903) 429-444.

Basil L. Gildersleeve, "Temporal Sentences of Limit in Greek," *AJP* 24 (1903) 388-407.

H. W. Magoun, "Is the Present Theory of Greek Elision sound?" *PAPA* 35 (1903) xxiv-xxv.

Cecil Bendall, "Notes on the pronunciation of Greek, as deduced from Greco-Indian bilingual coins B.C. 180-20," *JP* 29 (1903-04) 199-201.

J. E. Harry, "A Misinterpreted Greek Optative," *PAPA* 36 (1904) iv-v.

J. E. Harry, "Some Grammatical Myths," *PAPA* 36 (1904) xxiv-xxvi.

Alfred W. Milden, "The Possessive in the Predicate in Greek," *PAPA* 38 (1906) xxiv-xxv.

J. E. Harry, "The Perfect Forms in Later Greek from Aristotle to Justinian," *TAPA* 37 (1906) 53-72.

H. St. J. Thackeray, "Renderings of the Infinitive Absolute in the Septuagint," *JTS* 9 (1907-08) 597-601.

Basil L. Gildersleeve, "Stahl's Syntax of the Greek Verb. First Article," *AJP* 29 (1908) 257-279.

Basil L. Gildersleeve, "Stahl's Syntax of the Greek Verb. Second Article," *AJP* 29 (1908) 389-409.

Basil L. Gildersleeve, "Stahl's Syntax of the Greek Verb. Third Article," *AJP* 30 (1909) 1-21.

*Hamilton Ford Allen, "The Use of ὥστε in Biblical Greek compared with Hebrew," *PAPA* 41 (1909) xvi-xvii.

Alfred W. Milden, "The Article in the Predicate in Greek," *PAPA* 41 (1909) lxiii-lxiv.

Charles B. Randloph, "On the Use of the Sign of Interrogation in Certain Greek MSS," *PAPA* 41 (1909) lxxiii-lxxiv.

E. B. Clapp, "Notes on Elision in Greek," *PAPA* 41 (1909) xcvii-xcviii.

*Max L. Margolis, "The Greek Preverb and Its Hebrew-Aramaic Equivalent," *AJSL* 26 (1909-10) 33-61. *[Prepositional element in a compound verb]*

Richard Wellington Husband, "Zeta," *PAPA* 43 (1911) xxvi-xxx.

*Edgar Howard Sturtevant, "Notes on the Character of Greek and Latin Accent," *TAPA* 42 (1911) 45-52.

Walter Peterson, "Greek Diminutive Suffix -ΙΣΚΟ- -ΙΣΚΗ-," *CAAST* 18 (1913-15) 139-207.

*Anonymous, "The Value of Hebrew and Greek to the Minister," *MR* 96 (1914) 307-311.

Eugene Watson Burlingame, "The Compound Negative Prefix *an-a-* in Greek and Indic," *AJP* 39 (1918) 299-305.

*Eugene S. McCartney, "Canting Puns on Ancient Monuments," *AJA* 23 (1919) 59-64.

Clara M. Knight, "The change from the ancient to the modern Greek accent," *JP* 35 (1920) 51-71.

Clara M. Knight, "Contamination in morphology," *JP* 35 (1920) 152-160.

*A. Kampmeier, "Roman Tolerance Toward the Greek Language," *OC* 35 (1921) 243-248.

*H. I. Bell and W. E. Crum, "A Greek-Coptic Glossary," *Aeg* 6 (1925) 177-226.

*E[dgar] H. Sturtevant, "Concerning the Influence of Greek on Vulgar Latin," *TAPA* 56 (1925) 5-25.

*D'Arcy Wentworth Thompson, "On Egyptian Fish-names used by Greek Writers," *JEA* 14 (1928) 22-33.

*John C. Grandbery, "Languages of Bible Lands," *MQR, 3rd Ser.,* 55 (1929) 114-119. [Greek, pp. 114-117]

*Francis A. Wood, "Prothetic Vowels in Sanskrit, Greek, Latin and Germanic," *AJP* 52 (1931) 105-144.

Jerzy Kurylowicz, "On the Development of the Greek Intonation," *Lang* 8 (1932) 200-210.

Ashton Waugh McWhorter, "Is Future Subjunctive or is Subjunctive Future?" *PAPA* 64 (1933) l-li.

John Francis Chatterton Richards, "Final νῦ— Ancient Tradition and Modern Practice," *PAPA* 65 (1934) xlvii-xlviii.

*Frank Ringgold Blake, "Necessity for a Combinatory Syntax of Greek and Latin," *PAPA* 65 (1934) l. *[Roman Numeral L not number 1]*

*George E. Mylonas, "Prehistoric Epigraphy and Greek Ethnology," *AJA* 41 (1937) 114.

*William A. Oldfather, "Suggestions for Guidance in the Preparation of a Critical *Index Verborum* for Latin and Greek Authors," *TAPA* 68 (1937) 1-10.

E[dgar] H. Sturtevant, "The Smooth Breathing," *TAPA* 68 (1937) 112-119.

Chauncey E. Finch, "Initial Indo-European y in Greek," *TAPA* 68 (1937) 120-122.

L. A. Post, "Dramatic Uses of the Greek Imperative," *AJP* 59 (1938) 31-59.

F. Stuart Crawford, "Eta as a Syllabic Sign in Greek Inscriptions,"*PAPA* 69 (1938) xxxiii-xxxiv.

Edward Sapir, "Indo-European Prevocalic *S* in Macedonian," *AJP* 60 (1939) 463-465.

T. B. L. Webster, "A Study of Greek Sentence Construction," *AJP* 62 (1941) 385-415.

Martin J. Higgins, "The Renaissance of the First Century and the Origin of Standard Late Greek," *Tr* 3 (1945) 49-100.

L. J. D. Richardson, "Double Gamma as True 'Double-G' in Greek," *TPS* (1946) 156-176.

A. C. Moorhouse, "The Morphology of the Greek Comparative System: Its Rhythmical and Repetitive Features," *AJP* 70 (1949) 159-170.

Kurt von Fritz, "The So-Called Historical Present in Early Greek," *Word* 5 (1949) 186-201.

*G. Bonfante, "The Preposition of Latin and Greek," *Word* 6 (1950) 106-116.

H[enry] S. Gehman, "The Hebraic Cast of Septuagint Greek," *JBL* 70 (1951) xv.

*G. Bonfante, "Addenda to the article 'The Prepositions of Latin and Greek'," *Word* 7 (1951) 250-252.

A. C. Moorhouse, "Derivation in -τερος from Greek ι- Stems," *AJP* 73 (1952) 298-301.

E. Adelaide Hahn, "Partitive Apposition in Homer and the Greek Accusative," *TAPA* 85 (1954) 197-289.

W. Kendrick Pritchett, "Dotted Letters in Greek Epigraphy," *AJA* 59 (1955) 55-61.

W. A. McDonald, "A Linguistic Examination of an Epigraphical Formula," *AJA* 59 (1955) 151-155.

W. Kendrick Pritchett, "The Conditional Sentence in Attic Greek," *AJP* 76 (1955) 1-17.

A. C. Moorhouse, "The Origin of the Infinitive in Greek Indirect Statement," *AJP* 76 (1955) 176-183.

*J. Gwyn Griffiths, "Three notes on Herodotus, Book II," *ASAE* 53 (1955) 139-152. [1. Greek and Egyptian Writing, pp. 139-144]

N. Turner, "The Unique Character of Biblical Greek," *VT* 5 (1955) 208-213.

Alice F. Braunlich, "Goodwin or Gildersleeve?" *AJP* 77 (1956) 181-184. *[Ref. - "The Conditional Sentence in Attic Greek" by W. K. Pritchett]*

A. W. Argyle, "The Genitive Absolute in Biblical Greek," *ET* 69 (1957-58) 285.

William Diver, "On the Prehistory of Greek Consonantism," *Word* 14 (1958) 1-25.

W. S. Allen, "Some Remarks on the Structure of Greek Vowel Systems," *Word* 15 (1959) 240-251.

*E. Adelaide Hahn, "The Origin of the Greek Accusative in Latin," *TAPA* 91 (1960) 221-238.

*R. A. Martin, "Some Syntactical Criteria of Translation Greek," *VT* 10 (1960) 295-310.

*Nicholas Rescher, "Some Arabic Technical Terms of Syllogistic Logic and Their Greek Originals," *JAOS* 82 (1962) 203-204.

George Sotiroff, "A tentative glossary of Thracian words," *CJL* 8 (1962-63) #2, 97-110.

Saul Lieberman, "How Much Greek in Jewish Palestine," *LIST* 1 (1963) 123-141.

Robert Coleman, "The Dialect Geography of Ancient Greece," *TPS* (1963) 58-126.

*Warren Cowgill, "The Supposed Cypriote Optatives *duwánoi* and *dókoi* with notes on the Greek infinitive formations," *Lang* 40 (1964) 344-365.

*C. G. Higgins and W. Kendrick Pritchett, "Engraving Techniques in Attic Epigraphy," *AJA* 69 (1965) 367-371.

G. P. Shipp, "Unusual Sound Combinations in Greek Vocabulary," *AASCS* 1 (1967) 1-11.

Henry R. Immerwahr, "Attic Script and the Young Democracy (510-500 B.C.)," *AJA* 71 (1967) 190.

J. B. Hainsworth, "Greek Views of Greek Dialectology," *TPS* (1967) 62-76.

G. P. Shipp, "Nouns in -σις and -τύς in Homer," *AASCS* 2 (1968) 15-31.

Henry M. Hoenigswald, "A Note on Overlength in Greek," *Word* 24 (1968) 252-254.

T. Whitney Tucker, "Chronology of Greek Sound Changes," *AJP* 90 (1969) 36-47.

*James Drescher, "Graeco-Coptica," *Muséon* 82 (1969) 85-100.

*John Chadwick, "Greek and Pre-Greek," *TPS* (1969) 80-98.

§548 *3.3.4.2.4.1 Greek - Lexicographical Studies*

T. D. Woolsey, "Greek Lexicography," *BS* 1 (1844) 613-632. *(Review)*

Samuel H. Taylor, "Pickering's Greek Lexicon," *BS* 4 (1847) 196-201. *(Review)*

*W. Muss-Arnolt, "On Semitic Words in Greek and Latin," *TAPA* 23 (1892) 35-156. [Index of words, pp. 151-156]

H[enry] A. Redpath, "Concordances to the Old Testament in Greek," *Exp, 5th Ser.,* 3 (1896) 69-77.

*Henry A. Redpath, "Mythological Terms in the LXX," *AJT* 9 (1905) 34-45.

*Adolph Deissmann, "The Philology of the Greek Bible: Its Present and Future. III. Septuagint Philology," *Exp, 7th Ser.,* 4 (1907) 506-520.

*Willis Brewer, "Ethonology of Greek Mythological Terms," *OC* 22 (1908) 480-484.

*C. A. Browne, "Etymology of Greek Mythological Terms According to Plato," *OC* 22 (1908) 680-685.

*Max L. Margolis, "Complete Induction for the Identification of the Vocabulary in the Greek Versions of the Old Testament with its Semitic Equivalents: Its Necessity and the Means of obtaining it," *JAOS* 30 (1909-10) 301-312.

*Max L. Margolis, "Transliterations in the Greek Old Testament," *JQR, N.S.,* 16 (1925-26) 117-125.

*F[rancis] A. Wood, "Greek Fish-Names," *AJP* 48 (1927) 297-325.

*W. E. Staples, "The Hebrew of the Septuagint," *AJSL* 44 (1927-28) 6-30.

*F [rancis] A. Wood, "Greek Fish-Names. Part II," *AJP* 49 (1928) 36-56.

*Francis A. Wood, "Greek Fish-Names. Part III," *AJP* 49 (1928) 167-187.

*Sheldon H. Blank, "The Septuagint Renderings of Old Testament Terms for Law," *HUCA* 7 (1930) 259-283.

Walter Petersen, "Some Greek Examples of Word-contamination," *AJP* 56 (1935) 54-60.

Henry S. Gehman, "The Hebraic Character of Septuagint Greek," *VT* 1 (1951) 81-90.

*R. A. Martin, "Some Syntactical Criteria of Translation Greek," *VT* 10 (1960) 295-310.

*Nicholas Rescher, "Some Arabic Technical Terms of Syllogistic Logic and Their Greek Originals," *JAOS* 82 (1962) 203-204.

*J. Pairman Brown, "Literary Contexts of the Common Hebrew-Greek Vocabulary," *JSS* 13 (1968) 163-191.

G. B. Caird, "Towards a Lexicon of the Septuagint. I," *JTS, N.S.*, 19 (1968) 453-475.

G. B. Caird, "Towards a Lexicon of the Septuagint. II," *JTS, N.S.*, 20 (1969) 21-40.

§549 *3.3.4.2.4.2 Greek Word Studies - General*

*James Yates, "On the Irregularities of the Versification of Homer," *TPS* (1856) 119-142.

*Th[eodore] Aufrecht, "On Some Latin and Greek etymologies," *TPS* (1859) 14-17. [On the derivation of *dulcis* and γλυκυς, γλαυκος, πολυδευκης; On the Original form of μα; On the derivation of *pollex*]

Theodore Aufrecht, "Some Greek Etymologies," *TPS* (1867) 18-22. [1. ξηρός; 2. λήγω; 3. νηδύς; 4. νέννος; 5. ξύω, ξέω, ξύλον]

John E. B. Mayor, "Greek Lexicography," *JP* 6 (1875-76) 288-301.

John E. B. Mayor, "Greek Lexicography. II," *JP* 7 (1876-77) 21-45.

J. E. Sandys, "Suggestions for addenda and corrigenda to Liddell and Scott's Lexicon," *JP* 7 (1876-77) 46-50.

John E. B. Mayor, "Greek Lexicography. III," *JP* 7 (1876-77) 177-199.

R. A. Neil, "Notes on 'Liddell and Scott'," *JP* 7 (1876-77) 200-205.

J. K. Ingram, "Etymological Notes on Liddell and Scott's Lexicon," *Herm* 4 (1881-83) 105-120. [1. αἴξ; 2. ἄλκη; 3. ἀμαλγός; 4. ἀνήρ; 5. ἄχνη; 6. ἀοσσητήρ; 7. ἀπολαύω; 8. ἀρύω; 9. αὐγή; 10. ἄχνη; 11. βατέω; 12. βένθος; 13. γελάω; 14. γηρύω; 15. γλαυκός; 16. Letter δ; 17. δάπεδον; 18. δασύς; 19. δειλός; 20. δειμός; 21. δεύω; 22. εἰλαπίνη; 23. εἴλω; 24. εἰμί; 25. ἔλαφος; 26. ἔλη, εἴλη; 27. ἔνεροι; 28. ἔννυμι; 29. ἔρις; 30. ἔρρω; 31. Letter ζ; 32. ζάω; 33. ἡμί; 34. θέρω; 35. κεῖμαι; 36. κῆρυξ; 37. κηρύσσω; 38. ἡμί; 39. κισσός; 40. κίω; 41. κοίρανος; 42. κραίνω; 43. κραιπνός; 44. κρήνη; 45. κτείς; 46. λαμπήνη; 47. λάσκω; 48. λεῖος; 49. λίπος; 50. Letter μ; 51. μάλη; 52. μορτός, βροτός; 53. νέκταρ; 54. οἰωνός; 55. Πάν; 56. πείρω; 57. πῆμα; 58. πόλχος; 59. πόντος; 60. πούς; 61. πύργος; 62. ῥήγνυμι; 63. ῥίψ; 64. σάλος; 65. σῆμα; 66. σεμνός; 67. σίμβλος; 68. σμῆνος; 69. σῆμα; 70. σοβέω; 71. σπανίς; 72. σπεῖρα; 73. στρέφω; 74. τέρας; 75. τέρην; 76. τηρός; 77. τίκτω; 78. τραχύς; 79. τρίζω; 80. τριήρης; 81. τύρσις; 82. ὑμήν; 83. ὕπνος; 84. φάρω; 85. φαῦλος; 86. φάω; 87. φεύγω; 88. φοξός; 89. φόρμιγξ; 90. φρήν; 91. φώρ; 92. φώς; 93. χάζομαι; 94. χείρ; 95. χεύω; 96. χορός; 97. χρόμαδος; 98. ὥρα; - 1. φέρτατος; 2. κατάβα]

M. W. Humphreys, "Notes. II. Some Errors in Liddell and Scott," *AJP* 8 (1887) 344-345.

*J. Freudenthal, "Are There Any Traces of Greek Philosophy in the Septuagint?" *JQR* 2 (1889-90) 205-222. [1. Ψυχή; 2. Πνοή; 3. Νοῦς; 4. Φρόνησις; 5, 6. Δόξα and λόγος; 7. Αἰσθάνομαι, αἴσθησις; 8. Ἀρετή; 9. Ἀνδρεία, ἀνδρεῖος; 10. Μεγαλοπρεπής, μεγαλοπρέπεια; 11. Πρόνοια; 12. Κόσμος]

*C[laude] R. Conder, "Jews and Gentiles in Palestine," *PEFQS* 22 (1890) 310-326. *[Comparative Word Study - Hebrew/Greek]*

*J. S. Banks, "The Greek of the Septuagint," *ET* 9 (1897-98) 500-503. [Ἀναστρέφομαι; Ἀντίλημψις; Ἀρετή; Γραμματεύς; Γράφω; Ἐντυγχάνω, ἔντευξις; Ἴδιος; Λειτουργέω; Ὄνομα; Πρεσβύτερος; Φίλος; υἱός and τέκνον; Ὁ υἱὸς τοῦ θεοῦ]

A. T. Murray, "Corrections to Liddell and Scott's Greek Lexicon, eighth edition," *PAPA* 33 (1901) lvii-lx. [αβρόπλουτος; ἁβρότης; ἀγκάλη; ἀναπαύω; ἀναπτυχή; ἀπαυθημερίζω; ἀπολαγχάνω; ἄσκη; βλίτον; βοή; γόμφος; γοργόνωτος; δαιμονάω; διάημι; ἔνερσις; ἐξικνέομαι; ἐξομόργνυμι; ἐπιτροπεύω; ἐργάζομαι; Εὐριπιδαριστοφανίζω; ζώστρα; ἠρισάλπιγξ; θῆλυς; θρέμμα; κακορροθέω; καλυπτός; κατόπτης; κνῦμα; κομψεία; λάσκω; μάστιξ; μολύνω; ναυστολέω; ξανθός; οἶτος; ὁμαλός; ὄμβρος; ὀχληρός; παλαμάομαι; πειράω; πεμπταῖος; πινάω; πλίξ; πρᾶγος; προσουρεῖν; προὔργου; πυροπίπης; ῥινός; σπλήν; στάμνος; στομφάζω; στρόβος; στρουθός; σῦριγξ; συρίζω; φίλτερος; χίμαρος; χοροποιός; ψήκτρα]

E.G. Sihler, "Notes on the Greek of the Septuagint and the New Testament," *TQ* 24 (1920) 196-207.

*H. C. Tolman, "Persian Words in the Glosses of Hesychius," *JAOS* 41 (1921) 236-237. [1. ἄρξιφος; 2. βίσταξ; 3. ὀπαστόν; 4. ἀμαζακάραν]

*Ralph Marcus, "Divine Names and Attributes in Hellenistic Jewish Literature," *PAAJR* 3 (1931-32) 43-120. [Concordance, pp. 50-120]

B. E. Perry, "Some Addenda to Liddell and Scott," *AJP* 60 (1939) 29-40.

Gordon M. Messing, "The Etymology of Greek ὁ ἡ τὸ δεῖνα ," *Lang* 23 (1947) 207-211.

Saul Lieberman, "Rays from the East," *AIPHOS* 9 (1949) 409-420. *[Comparative Greek Lexicon from Rabbinic Sources]*

*J[acob] J. Rabinowitz, "Grecisms and Greek Terms in the Aramaic Papyri," *B* 39 (1958) 77-82.

*Vladimir Georgiev, "Creto-Mycenaean and Homeric," *Klio* 38 (1960) 69-74. [1. Hom. δῶ; 2. Hom. ἰχώρ, ἰχῶ; 3. Hom. κυκε(ι)ῶ; 4. Hesiod ἄλειφα; 5. Cyr. ὁ χακεὺϜ ὁ; 6. Absence of final ν; Conclusion]

H[enry] S. Gehman, "Rambles in Septuagint Lexicography," *IJT* 14 (1965) 90-101. [ἀνήρ; ἀπό; ἀποκαλύπτω τὸ ὠτίον (οὖς); δίδωμι; εἰ; ἐν; ἐξαίρω; ἐχθὲς καὶ τρίτην (ἡμέραν); προστίθημι; τρισσός; χείρ; ἀγχιστεύω; ἀναβολή; ἀνάστημα ἀνάστεμα; ἀνατολή; ἀποκλείω; ἀποστολή; ἄρουρα; εἰρήνη; ἐντρέπω; ἐξόδιον; ἐπιτίθημι; ἑτοιμάζω; πιστός]

H[enry] S. Gehman, "Adventures in Septuagint Lexicography," *Text* 5 (1966) 125-132. [ἀνήρ; ἀπό; ἀποκαλύπτω τὸ ὠτίον (οὖς); δίδωμι; εἰ; ἐν; ἐξαίρω; ἐχθὲς καὶ τρίτην (ἡμέραν); προστίθημι; τρισσός; χείρ— ἀγχιστεύω; ἀναβολή; ἀνάστημα /ἀνάστεμα; ἀνατολή; ἀποκλείω; ἀποστολή; ἄρουρα; εἰρήνη; ἐντρέπω; ἐξόδιον; ἐπιτίθημι; ἑτοιμάξω; πιστός]

R. J. Ledogar, "Verbs of Praise in the LXX Translation of the Hebrew Canon," *B* 48 (1967) 29-56.

§550   *3.3.4.2.4.3 Alphabetical Listing of Greek Words*

A

E. M. Cope, "*στοργή, ἔρως, φιλεῖν, ἀγαπᾶν,*" *JP* 1 (1868) #1, 88-93.

*C. F. Hogg, "Note on *ἀγαπάω* and *φιλέω,*" *ET* 38 (1926-27) 379-380.

*H. Highfield, "*ἀγαπάω* and *φιλέω*: A Rejoinder," *ET* 38 (1926-27) 525.

James Hope Moulton, "*Ἀγάπη,*" *ET* 26 (1914-15) 139. (Correction p. 178)

C. C. Tarelli, "*ΑΓΑΠΗ,*" *JTS, N.S.,* 1 (1950) 64-67.

H. A. Wolfson, "On the Septuagint use of *TO HAGION* for the Temple," *JQR, N.S.,* 38 (1947-48) 109-110.

H. S. Gehman, "*Ἅγιος* in the Septuagint, and its Relation to the Hebrew Original," *VT* 4 (1954) 337-348.

F. A. Paley, "On the Word *ἀδάμας,* 'Adamant'," *JP* 2 (1869) 150-151.

Russell Jennings, "*ΑΙΔΗΣ,* Hades," *BQR* 2 (1880) 334-356.

W. E. M., "Sheol and Hades," *UQGR* 1 (1844) 363-380. [*ᾅδης*]

*Herbert Cushing Tolman, "The Etruscan *aisar, ais, aisoi,*" *PAPA* 41 (1909) lxxxviii-lxxxix.

*M. Stuart, "*Αἰών* and *Αἰώνοις,*" *SP* 2 (1829) 405-452. [III. (2) The use of *αἰών* and *αἰώνιος* in the Septuagint, pp. 438-439]

*M. Stuart, "Αἰών and Αἰώνοις," *SP* 2 (1829) 405-452. [III. (2) The use of αἰών and αἰώνιος in the Septuagint, pp. 438-439]

E[zra] S. G[oodwin], "Professor Stuart's *Appendix* to his Exegetical Essay on several Words relating to Future Punishment," *CE* 10 (1831) 34-63, 166-192. [αἰών]

E[zra] S. G[oodwin], "A Second Letter, in which the Investigation of the Meanings of Αἰών[sic] in Ancient Greek is continued," *CE* 12 (1832) 97-105.

*Anonymous, "'Everlasting' and 'Eternity'," *CM* 6 (1878) 321-335. [αἰών]

*C. B. Gohdes, "Æon and Æonios in the Classics," *ColTM* 15 (1895) 65-75. [αἰών]

*C. B. Gohdes, "Æon and Æonios in the Old Testament," *ColTM* 15 (1895) 175-192. [αἰών]

*Anonymous, "'Everlasting' and 'Eternity'," *CM* 6 (1878) 321-335. [αἰώνιος]

*H[osea] B[allou] 2nd, "Αἰώνιος, as used by Philo Judæus," *UQGR* 2 (1845) 133-136.

*C. B. Gohdes, "Æon and Æonios in the Classics," *ColTM* 15 (1895) 65-75. [αἰώνιος]

*C. B. Gohdes, "Æon and Æonios in the Old Testament," *ColTM* 15 (1895) 175-192. [αἰώνιος]

J. H. Wilkinson, "Note on the Meaning of the Word ΑΙΩΝΙΟΣ," *Exp, 5th Ser.,* 5 (1897) 78-80.

*Sp. Marinatos, "Αἰώρα," *AASCS* 2 (1968) 1-14.

*Eberhard Hommel, "The Forms Σειραχ and Ἀκελδαμαχ as Transcriptions of סירא and חקלדמא," *ET* 25 (1913-14) 285.

*A. Hurvitz, "Ακκαρων = Amqar(r)una = עקרון," *Lěš* 33 (1968-69) #1, n.p.n.

*A. J. Festugière, "A Note on ακριμακραγετα," *AJP* 76 (1955) 308-309.

G. H. Whitaker, "The Chief Corner-Stone," *Exp, 8th Ser.,* 22 (1921) 470-472. [ἀκρογωνιαῖος]

*Henri Blocker, "The Biblical Concept of Truth," *Them* 6 (1969) #1, 47-61. *(Trans. by H. O. J. Brown)* [ἀλήθεια, pp. 53-54, 56-60]

*Saul Lieberman, "Two Lexicographical Notes," *JBL* 65 (1946) 67-72. [1. קפ ץפ צלח ἄλλομαι, pp. 67-69]

*Jacob J. Rabinowitz, "Miscellanea Papyrologica," *JJP* 11&12 (1957-58) 167-183. [III. The Meaning of *ΑΛΛΟΣΣΩ* in Some Papyri from Karanis, pp. 182-183]

Philip Whaley Harsh, " 'Ἁμαρτία, Again," *TAPA* 76 (1945) 47-58.

Arthur Patch McKinlay, "On the Meaning of 'Ἁμαυρός," *PAPA* 73 (1942) xxxi.

*Maurice Bloomfield, "Four Etymological Notes," *AJP* 6 (1885) 41-52. [4. ἀμβλακεῖν: Sanskrit mlecchati, pp. 46-52]

A. N. Jannaris, "Does ἀμήν Mean 'Verify'?" *ET* 13 (1901-02) 563-565.

*Stephen Langdon, "History of the Use of ἐάν for ἄν in Relative Clauses," *AJP* 24 (1903) 447-451.

*D. J. N. Lee, "The Modal Particles ἄν, κε(ν), κα," *AJP* 88 (1967) 45-56.

*F. A. Paley, "On ἀναιρεῖν and ἐναίρειν, 'To slay'," *JP* 2 (1869) 147-150.

*Douglas Jones, "ἀνάμνησις in the LXX and the Interpretation of 1 Cor. XI. 25," *JTS, N.S.,* 6 (1955) 183-191.

†W. E., "Word ἀνάστασις," *MMBR* 18 (1804) 193-194.

*Jacob J. Rabinowitz, "Miscellanea Papyrologica," *JJP* 11 &12 (1957-58) 167-183. [I, 6 'Ἁξιόποστος, pp. 175-178]

*Harry M. Orlinsky, " 'Ἁποβαίνω and ἐπιβαίνω in the Septuagint of Job," *JBL* 56 (1937) 361-367.

John A. Massie, "A Contribution to the History of 'Ἁπόλλυμι," *Exp, 2nd Ser.,* 2 (1881) 64-70.

*Campbell Bonner, "Four Lexicographical Notes," *AJP* 62 (1941) 451-459. [ἀποπαιδαρίοω, pp. 451-453]

*Frank Gavin, "*Shaliach* and *Apostolos*," ATR 9 (1926-27) 250-259. [ἀπόστολος]

John E. B. Mayor, "ἄπρακτος—ἄπρατος," JP 15 (1886) 171-173.

*Leicester B. Holland, "Axones," AJA 45 (1941) 346-362. [Ἄξονες]

(   ) DeMorgan, "On the word ἀριθμός," TPS (1859) 8-14.

*Girgis Mattha, "The ἀρτοκοπεῖον in the demotic texts, BIFAO 45 (1947) 59-60.

Peter [M.] Fraser, "ΑΡΧΙΠΡΟΣΤΑΤΗΣ, ΑΡΧΙΠΡΟΤΑΤΕΩ," CdÉ 26 (1951) 162-163.

P[eter] M. Fraser, "Ἀρχιπροστάτης: a correction," CdÉ 27 (1952) 290.

*Paul Haupt, "Arab. *samm*, poison = Sum. *šem*, ἄρωμα," BAVSS 10 (1927) Heft 2, 84-95.

J. Gwyn Griffiths, "Three notes on Herodotus, Book II," ASAE 53 (1955) 139-152. [2. The Deserters on the Left Hand of the King [Ἀσμάχ], pp. 144-149]

*Campbell Bonner, "Four Lexicographical Notes," AJP 62 (1941) 451-459. [ἀσσάλιος, pp. 455-457]

I. Bywater, "ΑΤΑΚΤΑ," JP 10 (1881-82) 67-79, 31 (1908-10) 197-206.

*Edward Sapir, "Greek ἀτύζομαι, a Hittite Loanword, and Its Relatives," Lang 12 (1936) 175-180.

William Linn Westermann, "Dike Corvee in Roman Egypt. On the Meaning of ΑΦΥΛΙΣΜΟΣ," Aeg 6 (1925) 121-129.

*A. E. R. Boak, "Notes on Canal and Dike Work in Roman Egypt," Aeg 7 (1926) 215-219. [ἀφυλισμός]

P. J. Sijpesteijn, "On the meaning of the word ΑΦΥΛΙΣΜΟΣ," Aeg 42 (1962) 128-132.

B

W. D. van Wijngaarden, "On the Origin of the Word βαία," *BBC* 3 (1926) 16-17. (Note by Daniel Plooij, p. 17; by D. C. Hesseling, p. 17]

*Rendel J. Harris, "Symposium on the Pith of Palm Trees (continued)," *BBC* 4 (1927) 16-17. [βαία]

"Laicus", "The Stem ΒΑΠ- and Its Kindred in the Septuagint," *MQR, 3rd Ser.*, 7 (1889-90) 230-254.

"Laicus", "The Stem ΒΑΠ- in Greek Literature to the Fourth Century B.C.," *MQR, 3rd Ser.*, 10 (1891) 285-304.

K. G. Manz, "ΒΑΠΤΙΖΩ. A Lexicographical Study," *CTM* 11 (1940) 667-688. *[O.T. Refs.: 671; 678]*

John Scott, "The Use of *Bapto* in the Old Testament," *RestQ* 1 (1957) 147-151.

*Glanville Downey, "The Words *Stoa* and *Basilike* in Classical Literature," *AJA* 41 (1937) 194-211. [βασίλειος/βασιλική]

George L. Huxley, "Two Notes on Herodotos: II ΒΑΚΟΣ and ΒΕΚΚΟΣ," *GRBS* 4 (1963) 7-8.

*Isidore Wartski, "The Useage of the Greek Words βία—βίος in Midrashic Literature," *Tarbiz* 36 (1966-67) #3, IV.

H. Nettleship, "On the word βουγάιος," *JP* 5 (1873) 18-20.

J. P. Postgate, "On the word βουγάιος and the prefix βου—," *JP* 8 (1879) 116-121.

R. F. Weymouth, "On the Homeric epithet βραιρός," *TPS* (1860-61) 276-278.

Haiim B. Rosén, "Note on βύβλος," *VT* 1 (1951) 306.

*Paul Haupt, "Etymological and Critical Notes," *AJP* 47 (1926) 305-318. [3. Lat. *bucina* and Gr. βυκάνη, pp 309-311]

Γ

E. M. Cope, "γίγνεσθαι, γιγνώσκειν," JP 1 (1868) #1, 79-88.

Joseph Edkins, "Officers," Exp, 5th Ser., 3 (1896) 148-151. [γραμματεῖς]

*John Chadwick, "Mycenaean Wine and the Etymology of γλυκύς," Minos 9 (1968) 192-197.

*Solomon Gandz, "The Origin of the Term Gnomon or the Gnomon in Hebrew Literature," PAAJR 2 (1930-31) 23-28. [γνώμων]

*H. L. Aherns, "On Feminines in ω and ως, and on the word γυνή; A Contribution to Greek Grammar and Etymology," TPS (1852-53) 155-178. (Trans. from the German by T. H. Key)

Δ

Theodore Aufrecht, "On the different Forms of δαίω," TPS (1857) 126-128.

*E. Adkins, "The Particles ΔE and] in Bible Translation," BQ 5 (1871) 99-107.

*William Ridgeway, "δεῖπνον and δόρπον," JP 17 (1888) 159-162.

A. J. Beattie, "The Origin of Greek δεῦρο," TPS (1949) 1-21.

*F. W. Thomas, "ἤδη and δή in Homer," JP 23 (1894-95) 81-115.

[T. Hewitt] Key, "On the derivation of the word δημος," TPS (1859) 143-145.

P. L. Hedley, "ΔΙΑΒΟΥΛΙΑ," JTS 34 (1933) 270.

Paul Peters, "Diatheke in the Old and New Testament," WLQ 39 (1942) 253-282. [διαθήκη]

*J. Swetnam, "Diathēkē in the Septuagint Account of Sinai: A Suggestion," B 47 (1966) 438-444. [διαθήκη]

John Massie, "Righteousness and Justification. Δίκαιος Δικαιοσύνη, and Δικαιοῦν," Exp, 1st Ser., 8 (1878) 257-269.

Martin Scharlemann, "On Etymological Study of Δικαιοσύνη," *CTM* 11 (1940) 899-905.

Nigel M. Watson, "Some Observations on the Use of ΔΙΚΑΙΟΩ in the Septuagint," *JBL* 79 (1960) 255-266.

*C. K. Nelson, "The Force of Δίκη in the Greek Theosophy," *PAPA* 15 (1883) ix.

*Naphtali Lewis, "ΟΚΗΣΙΣ—ΔΙΟΚΗΣΙΣ," *CdÉ* 27 (1952) 413.

Oscar J. E. Seitz, "Antecedents and Signification of the Term δίψυχος," *JBL* 66 (1947) 211-219.

*J. B. Fischer, "The Term ΔΕΣΠΟΤΗΣ in Josephus" *JQR, N.S.,* 49 (1958-59) 132-138.

*William Ridgeway, "δεῖπνον and δόρπον," *JP* 17 (1888) 159-162.

A. Haire Forster, "The Meaning of *doxa* in the Greek Bible," *ATR* 12 (1929-30) 311-316. [δόξα]

*L. H. Brockington, "The Greek Translator of Isaiah and His Interest in ΔΟΞΑ," *VT* 1 (1951) 23-32.

*F. X. Sheehan, "The Glory of God: Doxa-Kavodh," *BibT* #26 (1966) 1815-1821. [δόξα]

*Lawrence Mills, "Philo's δυνάμεις and the Amesha Spenta," *JRAS* (1901) 553-568.

C. B. Cayley, "On the Homeric Word Δύσπαρι[*sic*]," *TPS* (1865) 59-62.

*Reuven Yaron, "Two Greek Words in the Brooklyn Museum Aramaic Papyri," *HUCA* 28 (1957) 49-51. [δώρημα]

E

*Stephen Langdon, "History of the Use of ἐάν for ἄν in Relative Clauses," *AJP* 24 (1903) 447-451.

*†T. Hewitt Key, "Miscellaneous Papers. C. On επ of ειπειν (inquit) and ἐπ of ἔπομαι (sequor)," *TPS* (1962-63) 20-26.

Fordyce H. Argo, "The Essential Meaning of ἐκκλησία," *BW* 25 (1905) 183-195.

John L. Murphy, "'Ekklesia' and the Septuagint," *AER* 139 (1958) 381-390. [ἐκκλησία]

Roy Bowen Ward, "Ekklesia: A Word Study," *RestQ* 2 (1958) 164-179. [ἐκκλησία]

*Leo M. Kaiser, "A Greek Word in 2 Kings 13:6, 9, 10," *CBQ* 10 (1948) 406-407. [ἐκρόφησις; √ροφεῖν]

*Jacob J. Rabinowitz, "Miscellanea Papyrologica," *JJP* 11&12 (1957-58) 167-183. [I, 6. ἐλεύθερος, pp. 175-178]

W. R. Coxwell Rogers, "The Preposition 'ἐν'," *JSL, 4th Ser.*, 6 (1864-65) 183-191.

*F. A. Paley, "On ἀναιρεῖν and ἐναίρειν, 'To slay'," *JP* 2 (1869) 147-150.

John E. B. Mayor, "ἡ ἐνεγκοῦσα in Heliodorus," *JP* 15 (1886) 174-176.

*T. Hewitt Key, "On the Prepositions ἐνι, *in*, and related words," *TPS* (1854) 85-95.

Gerard Gagnon, "The Meaning of the Word *ENTOLĒ* Throughout the Old Testament," *MH* 2 (1945-46) #4, 10-14. [ἐντολή]

*Saul Lieberman, "Two Lexicographical Notes," *JBL* 65 (1946) 67-72. [2. מצוה ἐντολή charity alms, pp. 69-72]

*Walter Leaf, "ἔπειν and ἔπεσθαι," *JP* 14 (1885) 231-251.

*Harry M. Orlinsky, "Ἀποβαίνω and ἐπιβαίνω in the Septuagint of Job," *JBL* 56 (1937) 361-367.

*Allan Chester Johnson, "The ἐπιβολή of land in Roman Egypt," *Aeg* 32 (1952) 61-72.

W. Kay, "On the derivation and the meaning of ἐπιούσιος," *JP* 5 (1873-74) 48-51.

Eb. Nestle, "ἐπιούσιος in Hebrew and Aramaic," *ET* 21 (1909-10) 43.

*Joseph Offord, "Archaeological Notes on Jewish Antiquites. XLVI. Ἐπιπόκων," *PEFQS* 50 (1918) 133.

W. K. Lowther Clarke, "A Note on ἐπισκιάζειν," *Theo* 15 (1927) 102-105.

Livingstone Porter, "The Word ἐπίσκοπος in Pre-Christian Usage," *ATR* 21 (1939) 103-112.

*G. P. Shipp, "*Superstitio* and Ἐπίσταμαι," *AASCS* 3 (1969) 29-31.

Samuel K. Eddy, "Ἐπιφορά in the Tribute Quota Lists," *AJP* 89 (1968) 129-143.

*†T. Hewitt Key, "Miscellaneous Papers. C. on επ of ειπειν (inquit) and ἐπ of ἔπομαι (sequor)," *TPS* (1962-63) 20-26.

E. M. Cope, "στοργή, ἔρως, φιλεῖν, ἀγαπᾶν," *JP* 1 (1868) #1, 88-93.

F. J. A. Hort and J. O. F. Murray, "ΕΥΧΑΡΙΣΤΙΑ, ΕΥΧΑΡΙΣΤΕΙΝ," *JTS* 3 (1901-02) 594-598.

Z

*W. R. French, "Biblical Usage of Ζωή and Ψυχή," *UQGR, N.S.,* 9 (1872) 172-181.

H

Max L. Margolis, "The Particle ἦ in Old Testament Greek," *AJSL* 25 (1908-09) 257-275.

*F. W. Thomas, "ἤδη and δή in Homer," *JP* 23 (1894-95) 81-115.

*Theodore Goldstücker, "On *jecur,* ἧπαρ, यक्कृत् *(yakṛit); stercus,* σκώρ, शकृत् *(śakṛit)* and some words of kindred formation," *TPS* (1854) 157-168.

Theodore Aufrecht, "On the Derivation and Meaning of ἤπιος," *TPS* (1856) 42-47.

Θ

W. Robertson Smith, "Θαλατθ in Berosus," *ZA* 6 (1891) 339. [= θαμτε = Tāmtu]

Roland G. Kent, "The Etymology of Greek *thanatos* and Its Kin," *Lang* 11 (1935) 207-210. [θάνατος]

*C. T. Fritsch, "The Translation of Yahweh by *(ho) Theos* in the Greek Pentateuch," *JBL* 63 (1944) iv-v. [ὁ θεός]

*J. E. Odgers, "Notes on θεὸς Ὕψιστος," *OSHTP* (1905-06) 65-75.

Lionel Casson, "Θυρών: A Note on P. Fuad Univ. *14*," *TAPA* 80 (1949) 425.

*David Gill, "*Thysia* and šelāmīm: Questions to R. Schmid's *Das Bundesopfer in Israel*," *B* 47 (1966) 255-262. [θυσία]

I

*[J. P.] Lesley, "Ἴακχος from [Hor-m] aχu, the Sphinx name of the Solar disc on the Horizon," *PAPS* 19 (1880-81) 110-111.

*Charles H. Weller, "Pausanias's Use of ναός and ἱερόν," *AJA* 13 (1909) 57.

C. M. Mulvany, "ἱερός, ἱερος, ἱρός," *JP* 25 (1896-97) 131-145.

T. W. Manson, "ΊΛαCTHPION," *JTS* 46 (1945) 1-10.

*C. H. Dodd, "ΙΛΑΣΚΕΣΘΑΙ in the Septuagint," *JTS* 32 (1930-31) 352-360.

H. H. Rowley, "The Use of ἱλάσκεσθαι etc. in Biblical Greek," *ET* 62 (1950-51) 227-233.

*K. L. McKay, "Animals in Ward and ἰσονομία," *AJP* 85 (1964) 124-135.

K

*D. J. N. Lee, "The Modal Particles *ἄν, κε(ν), κα*," *AJP* 88 (1967) 45-56.

E. W. Hopkins, "Sanskrit Kabăiras or Kubăiras and Greek Kabeiros," *JAOS* 33 (1933) 55-70. [*κάβειρος*]

*Campbell Bonner, "Four Lexicographical Notes," *AJP* 62 (1941) 451-459. [*καθαπταί*, pp. 453-455]

*T. Hewitt Key, "The Latin *Et, Que, Atque(Ac)*, and the Greek *και, τε*—all of one origin," *TPS* (1866) 49-63.

Edgar R. Smothers, "*Καλός* in Acclamation," *Tr* 5 (1947) 1-57.

*W. F. Lofthouse, "Poneron and Kanon in the Old and New Testaments," *ET* 60 (1948-49) 264-268. [*κανών*]

G. A. Wainwright, "The Septuagint's *Καππαδοκία* for Caphtor," *JJS* 7 (1956) 91-92.

*Cornelius Walker, "'The Heart'—לֵב, *καρδια*—in Scriptural Usage," *HR* 36 (1898) 446-450.

*Herbert Jennings Rose, "Keres and Lemures," *HTR* 41 (1948) 217-228. [*Κᾶρες*]

Peter Katz, "*Καταπαυσαι* as a Corruption of *καταλυσαι* in the LXX," *JBL* 65 (1946) 319-324.

*S[tephen] Langdon, "Assyrian Lexicographical Notes," *JRAS* (1920) 325-331. [2. Guannakku = *καννάκης*, frilled mantle]

*D. J. N. Lee, "The Modal Particles *ἄν, κε(ν), κα*," *AJP* 88 (1967) 45-56.

*Herbert Jennings Rose, "Keres and Lemures," *HTR* 41 (1948) 217-228. [*κῆρες*]

J. Newton Davies, "'Come unto Me, all ye that Labor' (Matthew 11.28). A Study of '*κοπιάω*' in the New Testament and Septuagint," *MR* 107 (1924) 635-639.

George W. Redding, "*ΚΟΣΜΟΣ* From Homer to St. John," *ASW* 4 (1949) 63-65.

Douglas Hilary Corley, "The Coffin," *AJSL* 39 (1922-23) 72. [κόφινος]

Martin P. Nilsson, "Krater," *HTR* 51 (1958) 53-58. [κρατήρ]

Edward Sapir, "*κύβδα,* a Karian Gloss," *JAOS* 56 (1936) 85.

*Marjorie J. Milne, "Kylichnis," *AJA* 43 (1939) 247-254. [κυλιχνίς]

*B., "The Septuagint and New Testament Rendering of 'Jehovah:' or, the Reasons why the New Testament seems to Sanction the Septuagint in Rendering יהוה by κύριος," *BRCM* 3 (1847) 21-28.

J. A. Smith, "The Meaning of *KYPOIΣ*," *JTS* 31 (1929-30) 155-160.

Λ

Max L. Margolis, "*Λαμβάνειν* (including Compounds and Derivatives) and its Hebrew-Aramaic Equivalents in Old Testament Greek," *AJSL* 22 (1905-06) 110-119.

*Victor Tcherikover, "*Syntaxis* and *Laographia,*" *JJP* 4 (1950) 179-207. [λαογραγία]

J. S. Banks, "Requests and Replies," *ET* 10 (1898-99) 14. [λειτουργέω]

*Naphtali Lewis, "*Leitourgia* and Related Terms," *GRBS* 3 (1960) 175-184. [λειτουργία]

*Naphtali Lewis, "*Leitourgia* and Related Terms (II)," *GRBS* 6 (1965) 227-230. [λειτουργία]

*J. L. Swellengrebel, "The Translation of 'Tsara'ath' and 'Lepra'," *BTr* 11 (1960) 69-79. [λέπρα]

M

O. D. Miller, "Use of the Greek Verb *Μέλλω,* by the Sacred Writers," *UQGR, N.S.,* 19 (1882) 192-209.

Arthur Platt, "*Μέλλω,*" *JP* 21 (1892-93) 39-45.

Oswald Szemerenyi, "Greek *μέλλω.* A Historical and Comparative Study," *AJP* 72 (1951) 346-368.

*B[asil] L. G[ildersleeve], "*META* and *ΣΥΝ*," *AJP* 8 (1887) 218-221.

*H. Highfield, "Gleanings from the Septuagint," *ET* 38 (1926-27) 44-45. [2. μεταμελέσθαι and μετανοεῖν]

*B[asil] L. Gildersleeve, "On the Encroachments of μή upon οὐ in Later Greek," *PAPA* 11 (1878-79) 31-33. *[Bound with Transactions, but paged separately]*

*Basil L. Gildersleeve, "Encroachments of μή upon οὐ in Later Greek," *AJP* 1 (1880) 45-47.

W. H., "Critical Miscellanies," *BRCM* 3 (1847) 436-442. [III. (use of μή in Gen. [LXX]), p. 442]

W. Kendrick Pritchett, "*Μή* with the Participle," *AJP* 79 (1958) 392-404.

N

*Charles H. Weller, "Pausanias's Use of ναός and ἱερόν," *AJA* 13 (1909) 57.

*Paul Haupt, "Biblical Studies," *AJP* 43 (1922) 238-249. [7. Hebrew qĕṭorṭ and Gr. *néktar*, pp. 245-247] [νέκταρ]

*S. P. Brock, "*Νεφεληγερέτα* = rkb'rpt," *VT* 18 (1968) 395-397.

D. B. Monro, "Notes. (1) νηγάτεος," *JP* 11 (1882) 61.

Chr[istopher] Wordsworth Jr., "On the etymology of *Νήδυμος*," *JP* 5 (1873) 95-99.

Raphael Taubenschlag, "*Νόμος* in the Papyri," *JJP* 2 (1948) 67-73.

*R. McL. Wilson, "Nomos: The Biblical Significance of the Law," *SJT* 5 (1952) 29-35. [*Νόμος*]

Ξ

Florence M. Bennett, "A Study of the Word *Ξόανον*," *AJA* 21 (1917) 8-21.

O

*James A. Montgomery, "An Aramaic Ostrakon from Nippur and the Greek Obolos," *JAOS* 29 (1909) 204-209. [ὀβολός]

R. F. Weymouth, "On the Homeric epithet ὄβριμος" *TPS* (1860-61) 250-275.

*Naphtali Lewis, "ΟΙΚΗΣΙΣ—ΔΙΟΙΚΗΣΙΣ," *CdÉ* 27 (1952) 413.

*Alvah Hovey, "Bible Wine: The Meaning of Yayin and Oinos in Scripture," *BQR* 9 (1887) 151-180. [οἶνος]

*J. E. Harry, "The Use of οἷος, ποῖος, and ὁποῖος," *PAPA* 39 (1907) xviii-xix.

*T. Hewitt Key, "On the Derivation of *Son, Nurus, Anus, Uxor, Wife,* πας, *omins, solus, every, all,* ὅλος," *TPS* (1868-69) 257-272.

*E. Sapir, "Hittite *hapatis* 'Vassal' and Greek ὀπαδός," *Lang* 10 (1934) 274-279.

*J. E. Harry, "The Use of οἷος, ποῖος, and ὁποῖος," *PAPA* 39 (1907) xviii-xix.

*O. Davies, "ΟΡΕΙΧΑΛΚΟΣ," *Man* 29 (1929) #21.

A. C. Pearson, "On the Use of ὅταν with Causal Implication," *AJP* 33 (1912) 426-435.

*Frank H. Fowler, "Notes. On Greek and Latin Negatives. I. *Latin haud: Greek* οὐ," *AJP* 21 (1900) 443-445.

*B[asil] L. Gildersleeve, "On the Encroachments of μή upon οὐ in Later Greek," *PAPA* 11 (1878-79) 31-33. *[Bound with Transactions, but paged separately]*

*Basil L. Gildersleeve, "Encroachments of μή upon οὐ in Later Greek," *AJP* 1 (1880) 45-47.

*Lionel Horton-Smith, "The Origin of Latin *haud* and Greek οὐ; and the Extentions of the Originally Unextended Form," *AJP* 18 (1897) 43-69.

A. D. Lowe, "The origin of οὐαί," *Herm* #105 (1967) 34-39.

P. T. Stevens, "The Meaning of οὔπω," *AJP* 71 (1950) 290-294.

Karel Janáček, "On the Term 'ὄχλημα'," *ArOr* 18 (1950) 1/2, 307-311.

Π

*Reuven Yaron, "Two Greek Words in the Brooklyn Museum Aramaic Papyri," *HUCA* 28 (1957) 49-51. [παιδευτός/παιδεύω]

*L. J. D. Richardson, "'Winged Words', *Tormentum* and Πάλλω," *TPS* (1936) 101-105.

F. W. Thomas, "Παρεμβολή," *AO* 14 (1936) 109-111.

*Cyrus H. Gordon, "The Patriarchal Age," *JAAR* 21 (1953) 238-243. [*parthenos, pp. 240-241*] (παρθένος)

*Maurice Bloomfield, "Four Etymological Notes," *AJP* 6 (1885) 41-52. [2. πέπων, 'ripe,' and πέπων, 'mild, weak'; pp. 42-44.

*D. B. Monro, "Notes. (3) On πλέες and χέρηες," *JP* 11 (1882) 62-63.

*T. Hewitt Key, "On the Derivation of *Son, Nurus, Anus, Uxor, Wife*, πας, *omins, solus, every, all*, ὅλος," *TPS* (1868-69) 257-272.

R. F. Weymouth, "On πέλωρ, πέλωρος, πελωρίος," *TPS* (1882-84) 389-404.

*Ernest Best, "The Use and Non-Use of Pneuma by Josephus," *NT* 3 (1959) 218-225. [πνεῦμα]

*Ernest D. Burton, "Spirit, Soul, and Flesh. I. ΠΝΕῖΜΑ, ΨΥΧΗ', and ΣΆΡΞ in Greek Writers from Homer to Aristotle," *AJT* 17 (1913) 563-598.

*Ernest D. Burton, "Spirit, Soul, and Flesh. III. ΠΝΕῖΜΑ, ΨΥΧΗ', and ΣΆΡΞ in Greek Writers from Epicurus to Arius Didymus," *AJT* 18 (1914) 395-414, 571-599.

*Ernest D. Burton, "Spirit, Soul, and Flesh. IV. ΠΝΕῖΜΑ, ΨΥΧΗ', and ΣΆΡΞ in Greek Writers of the Early Christian Period and in Jewish-Greek Literature," *AJT* 20 (1916) 390-413.

*D. R. Goodwin, "On the use of ψυχή and πνεῦμα and connected words in the sacred writings," *JBL* 1 (1881) 73-86.

*P. A. Munch, "The Spirits in the Testaments of the Twelve Patriarchs," *AO* 13 (1935) 257-263. [πνεῦμα]

*J. E. Harry, "The Use of οἷος, ποῖος, and ὁποῖος," *PAPA* 39 (1907) xviii-xix.

Walter Petersen, "Greek Pronominal Adjectives of the Type ποῖος," *TAPA* 46 (1915) 59-73.

*W. F. Lofthouse, "Poneron and Kanon in the Old and New Testaments," *ET* 60 (1948-49) 264-268. [πονηρόν]

Campbell Bonner, "Note on the Mosaic of Daphne," *AJA* 38 (1934) 340. [πριβάτον]

Basil L. Gildersleeve, "On πρίν in the Attic Orators," *AJP* 2 (1881) 465-483.

Basil L. Gildersleeve, "On the Use of πρίν in the Attic Orators," *PAPA* 13 (1881) 23-24. *[Bound with Transactions, but paged separately]*

B[asil] L. Gildersleeve, "On ΠΡΙΝ," *AJP* 6 (1885) 482.

*F. Sokolowski, "On *Prothysia* and *Promanteia* in Greek Cults," *HTR* 47 (1954) 165-171. [προθῦσία]

M. L. D'Ooge, "On the Meaning of προμαντεία," *PAPA* 36 (1904) xi-xiii.

*F. Sokolowski, "On *Prothysia* and *Promanteia* in Greek Cults," *HTR* 47 (1954) 165-171.[προμαντεία]

*G. D. Kilpatrick, "προσανοικοδομηθησέται Ecclus. III. 14," *JTS* 44 (1943) 147-148.

W. C. Allen, " On the Meaning of προσήλυτος in the Septuagint," *Exp, 4th Ser.,* 10 (1894) 264-275.

*Emil Lund, "הִשְׁתַּחֲוֹת, προσκυνεῖν," *TTKF* 17 (1915) 29-33.

Józef Modrzejewski, "The πρόσταγμα in the Papyri," *JJP* 5 (1951) 187-206.

*Campbell Bonner, "Four Lexicographical Notes," *AJP* 62 (1941) 451-459. [πρόφασις, pp. 451-453]

*Marjorie J. Milne, "Kylichnis," *AJA* 43 (1939) 247-254. [πυξίς]

*Roland F. Willetts, "ὠνεῖν = πωλεῖν," *KZFE* 4 (1965) 165-168.

P

*Eugene W. Bushala, "ῥόπτρον as a Musical Instrument," *GRBS* 10 (1969) 169-172.

*Leo M. Kaiser, "A Greek Word in 2 Kings 13:6, 9, 10," *CBQ* 10 (1948) 406-407. [ἐκρόφησις; √ῥοφεῖν]

Σ

I. Abrahams, "Σαββαθιον: Note to Page 51 Above," *JQR* 9 (1896-97) 175-176.

D. Ahl, "The Biblical Concept of σάρξ," *ColTM* 18 (1898) 200-209.

*Ernest D. Burton, "Spirit, Soul, and Flesh. I. ΠΝΕῖΜΑ, ΨΥΧΗ', and ΣΆΡΞ n Greek Writers from Homer to Aristotle," *AJT* 17 (1913) 563-598.

*Ernest D. Burton, "Spirit, Soul, and Flesh. III. ΠΝΕῖΜΑ, ΨΥΧΗ', and ΣΆΡΞ in Greek Writers from Epicurus to Arius Didymus," *AJT* 18 (1914) 395-414, 571-599.

*Ernest D. Burton, "Spirit, Soul, and Flesh. IV. ΠΝΕῖΜΑ, ΨΥΧΗ', and ΣΆΡΞ in Greek Writers of the Early Christian Period and in Jewish-Greek Literature," *AJT* 20 (1916) 390-413.

*Cornelius Walker, "Basar and Sarx, (בשר and Σαρξ)—Their Contrasts and Modifications," *HR* 35 (1898) 65-68.

*R[obert] G. Latham, "On the Meaning of the Word σάρος," *TPS* (1844-46) 85-88.

*Eberhard Hommel, "The Forms Σειραχ and Ἀκελδαμαχ as Transcriptions of סירא and חקלדמא," *ET* 25 (1913-14) 285.

*Paul Haupt, "Semachontis = Jungled Region," *JBL* 34 (1915) 185-186. [Σεμαχωνῖτις]

Henry L. F. Lutz, "The Egyptian Derivation of σήραγξ and σηλαγγεύς," *UCPSP* 10 (1931-46) 287-288.

Henry L. F. Lutz, "The Significance and Semasiology of 'Sibinum',"
UCPSP 10 (1931-46) 301-304. [σίβινον]

*Paul Haupt, "Greek *sīrós*, silo, and *sōrós*, stack," *JBL* 40 (1921) 170-173;.
[σιρός (σειρός)]

James Hope Moulton, "Σκάνδαλον," *ET* 26 (1914-15) 331-332.

L. W. Grensted, "Σκάνδαλον," *ET* 27 (1915-16) 139.

B. H. Kennedy, "On σκοποῦμαι as a passive as well as a middle verb," *JP* 5 (1873-74) 84-86.

*Theodore Goldstücker, "On *jecur,* ἧπαρ, यक्रित् *(yakřit); stercus,* σκώρ, शक्रित् *(śakřit)* and some words of kindred formation," *TPS* (1854) 157-168.

*Glanville Downey, "The Words *Stoa* and *Basilike* in Classical Literature," *AJA* 41 (1937) 194-211. [στοά]

F. W. Thomas, "Greek στατήρ in Central Asia," *JRAS* (1926) 507.

*Peter Katz, "Two Kindred Corruptions in the Septuagint," *VT* 1 (1951) 261-266. [III. στερεός; στερεοῦν, pp. 265-266]

E. M. Cope, "στοργή, ἔρως, φιλεῖν, ἀγαπᾶν," *JP* 1 (1868) #1, 88-93.

*B[asil] L. G[ildersleeve], "*META* and *ΣΥΝ*," *AJP* 8 (1887) 218-221.

*Victor Tcherikover, "*Syntaxis* and *Laographia*," *JJP* 4 (1950) 179-207. [σύνταξις]

*Paul Haupt, "Greek *sīrós*, silo, and *sōrós*, stack," *JBL* 40 (1921) 170-173;. [σωρός]

T

*T. Hewitt Key, "The Latin *Et, Que, Atque(Ac),* and the Greek και, τε—all of one origin," *TPS* (1866) 49-63. [τε]

*Herbert Richards, "On the history of the words τετραλογία and τριλογία," *JP* 11 (1882) 64-74.

*Max L. Margolis, "*ΤΕΤΡΟΠΩΜΕΝΟΥΣ* Joshua 11:6," *JBL* 33 (1914) 286-289.

*T. Hewitt Key, "On *titillare* and τικτειν," *TPS* (1862-63) 213-216.

Marjorie J. Milne, "On the Use of τορεύω and Related Words," *AJA* 45 (1941) 390-398.

*Herbert Richards, "On the history of the words τετραλογία and τριλογία," *JP* 11 (1882) 64-74.

Υ

Alfred J. Church, "On a Peculiarity in the Quantity of the Word ὑάδες," *TPS* (1865) 95-96.

Edward B. Pollard, "ΥΠΩΠΙΑΖΕΙΝ, A Word Study," *CQ* 1 (1924) 202-204.

*A. Thomas Kraabel, "Ὕψιστος and the Synagogue at Sardis," *GRBS* 10 (1969) 81-93.

Φ

E. M. Cope, "στοργή, ἔρως, φιλεῖν, ἀγαπᾶν," *JP* 1 (1868) #1, 88-93.

*C. F. Hogg, "Note on ἀγαπάω and φιλέω," *ET* 38 (1926-27) 379-380.

*H. Highfield, "ἀγαπάω and φιλέω: A Rejoinder," *ET* 38 (1926-27) 525.

T. Burrow, "Sanskrit *KSI-:* Greek *ΦΘΙΝΩ*," *JAOS* 79 (1959) 255-262.

E. M. Cope, "On an irregular formation of the Greek passive verb," *JP* 1 (1868) #1, 93-97. [φθονεῖθαι, φθονούμενοι]

*H. R. Hall, "Does *FENKHU* = Φοίνιξ?" *RTR* 34 (1912) 35-36.

[〰️🏺 Ꝑ ı ı ı]

*M. Smith, "Another Criterion for the καίγε Recension," *B* 48 (1967) 443-445. [הוֹרָה = φωτίζειν?]

X

*J[anoslav] Černý, "Philological and Etymological notes (II)," *ASAE* 42 (1943) 341-350 [4. Χάμψαι, pp. 346-348]

*C. M. Mulvany, "Colours in Greek. ΧΑΝΘΟΣ," *JP* 27 (1899-1900) 51-59.

*James A. Montgomery, "Hebrew *Hesed* and Greek *Charis*," *HTR* 32 (1939) 97-102. [χάρις]

*D. B. Monro, "Notes. (3) On πλέες and χέρηες," *JP* 11 (1882) 62-63.

Alexander B. Grosart, "Χριστός and ὁ Χριστός in the Septuagint," *ET* 1 (1889-90) 275-276.

Willis Brewer, "Egyptian Origin of the Word 'Christ'," *OC* 22 (1908) 284-287. [Χριστός]

A. Kampmeier, "The Word 'Christ'," *OC* 22 (1908) 288-290. [Χριστός]

Anonymous, "The Derivation of 'Christ'," *OC* 22 (1908) 376-377. [Χριστός]

ψ

Charles Heber Roberson, "The meaning and use of Psallo (Part II)," *RestQ* 6 (1962) 57-66 [III. Psallō in the Greek Version of the Old Testament] *(Revised and edited by Frank Pack and J. W. Roberts) [ψάλλω]*

*James A. Kelso, "The Septuagint Rendering of שְׁבָיוֹן," *JBL* 27 (1908) 157-159.[ψαλμός]

*Phillips Barry, "Psanterin According to Daniel III. 5," *Monist* 20 (1910) 402-413. [ψαλτήριον]

*Ernest D. Burton, "Spirit, Soul, and Flesh. I. ΠΝΕΥΜΑ, ΨΥΧΗ', and ΣΆΡΞ in Greek Writers from Homer to Aristotle," *AJT* 17 (1913) 563-598.

*Ernest D. Burton, "Spirit, Soul, and Flesh. III. ΠΝΕΥΜΑ, ΨΥΧΗ', and ΣΆΡΞ in Greek Writers from Epicurus to Arius Didymus," *AJT* 18 (1914) 395-414, 571-599.

*Ernest D. Burton, "Spirit, Soul, and Flesh. IV. *ΠΝΕῖΜΑ, ΨΥΧΗ',* and *ΣΆΡΞ* in Greek Writers of the Early Christian Period and in Jewish-Greek Literature," *AJT* 20 (1916) 390-413.

*W. R. French, "Biblical Usage of *Ζωή* and *Ψυχή*," *UQGR, N.S.,* 9 (1872) 172-181.

*D. R. Goodwin, "On the use of *ψυχή* and *πνεῦμα* and connected words in the sacred writings," *JBL* 1 (1881) 73-86.

M. Schwabe, "Varia Epigraphica Judaica," *BIES* 10 (1942-43) #2/3, IV. [*ψυχή* = 'tomb'; cf. *BIES* 10 (1942-43) #1, p. III under "Miscellany"]

Ω

*Roland F. Willetts, "*ὠνεῖν = πωλεῖν,*" *KZFE* 4 (1965) 165-168.

F[rederic] D. Allen, "A certain apparently Pleonastic Use of *ὡς,*" *PAPA* 9 (1876-77) 12. *[Bound with Transactions, but paged separately]*

Frederic D. Allen, "On a Certain Apparently Pleonastic Use of *ὡς,*" *TAPA* 8 (1877) 38-40.

†William Ridgeway, "*ὡς* as a preposition," *JP* 17 (1888) 113-114.

Takamitsu Muraoka, "The Use of *ΩΣ* in the Greek Bible," *NT* 7 (1964) 51-72.

*Hamilton Ford Allen, "The Use of *ὥστε* in Biblical Greek compared with Hebrew," *PAPA* 41 (1909) xvi-xvii.

§551 *3.3.4.2.4.4 Greek Phrases*

W. St. C[had] Boscawen, "Is *Anax andron* a title of Egyptian origin?" *BOR* 7 (1893-94) 92-94.

*Leon Morris, "*ΚΑΙ ΑΠΑΞ ΚΑΙ ΔΙΣ,*" *NT* 1 (1956) 205-208.

*T. C. Skeat, "Two Notes on the Passover 'Haggadah'," *JTS* 50 (1949) 53-57. [*ἐγώ εἰμί*]

*A. F. Knight, "Ego Eimi," *Coll* 1 (1964-66) 219-224.   [*ἐγώ εἰμί*]

*Peter R. Ackroyd, "‏נצח‎—εἰς τέλος," *ET* 80 (1968-69) 126.

Edward Capps, "Ἐπὶ τῆς σκηνῆς and Similar Expressions," *AJA* 5 (1901) 31.

*Jacob J. Rabinowitz, "Miscellanea Papyrologica," *JJP* 11&12 (1957-58) 167-183. [I, 5. ἔργῳ καὶ δυνάμει]

*T. P. Considine, "Two In One Flesh. The Meaning in Sacred Scripture," *ACR* 39 (1962) 111-123. [ἔσονται οἱ δύο εἰς σάρκα μίνα]

B[asil] L. Gildersleeve, "Notes from the Greek Seminary. II. θὐ μή," *AJP* 3 (1882) 202-205.

James D. Rogers, "On the νομίσματα πύργινα of Aeschuylus, Pers. 859," *AJA* 7 (1903) 95-96.

*J. S. Banks, "The Greek of the Septuagint," *ET* 9 (1897-98) 500-503. [Ὁ υἱὸς τοῦ Θεοῦ, p. 503]

W. L. Westermann, "On the meaning of ΠΑΡΟΡΙΑ ΤΗΣ ΠΟΛΕΩΣ," *Aeg* 3 (1922) 80-81.

G. M. A. Grube, "Notes on the περὶ ὕψους," *AJP* 78 (1957) 355-374.

Eunice Burr Couch, "An Interpretation of the Prescript πόλες αὐταὶ φορον ταχσάμεναι in the Athenian Tribute Lists," *AJA* 33 (1929) 502-514.

Naphtali Lewis, "The Meaning of σὺν ἡμιολίᾳ and Kindred Expressions in Loan Contracts," *TAPA* 76 (1945) 126-139.

*Ernest H. Kantorowicz, "ΣΥΝΘΡΟΝΟΣ ΔΙΚΗΙ," *AJA* 57 (1953) 65-70.

*Arthur Darby Nock, "Σύνναος θεός," *PAPA* 60 (1929) xxvii.

C. W. E. Miller, "On τὸ δέ = 'Whereas'," *TAPA* 39 (1908) 121-146.

F. W. Mozley, "The Meaning of ΤΟΥΤΟ ΠΟΙΕΙΤΕ," *Exp, 6th Ser.,* 7 (1903) 370-386.

§552 *3.3.4.2.5 Latin Grammar and Etymology - General Studies*

*†Anonymous, "An Inquiry into the Structure and Affinity of the Greek and Latin Language," *BCQTR, 4th Ser.,* 4 (1828) 312-341. *(Review)*

[T. Hewitt] Key, "On the Origin of certain Latin Words," *TPS* (1844-46) 249-255; (1846-48) 205-212.

*[John(?)] Davies, "Attempts to suggest the Derivations and Affinities of some Greek and Latin Words," *TPS* (1846-48) 89-94.

*Anonymous, "Comparative Grammar," *BRCM* 4 (1847-48) 1-22. *(Review)*

*T. H[ewitt] Key, "On the Pronouns of the First and Second Persons," *TPS* (1848-50) 25-37. [Appendix on the Formation of the Latin Perfect Tenses, *amavi,* &c., pp. 34-37]

*W. D. Whitney, "A Comparison of the Greek and Latin Verbs," *BS* 7 (1850) 654-568.

T. Hewitt Key, "On the Etymology of Certain Latin Words," *TPS* (1850-52) 103-109.

[T. Hewitt] Key, "Miscellaneous Remarks on some Latin Words," *TPS* (1852-53) 93-99.

J. E. B. Mayor, "Latin-English Lexicography," *JCSP* 2 (1855) 271-290.

†Anonymous, "Latin Dictionaries," *QRL* 97 (1855) 451-473. *(Review)*

Theodore Aufrecht, "On the Latin Terminations *tia, tio-,*" *TPS* (1856) 144-146.

Th[eodore] Aufrecht, "Latin Etymologies," *TPS* (1858) 13-21.

T. Hewitt Key, "Miscellaneous remarks suggested by Ritsch's Plautus, especially on the formation of the Latin Perfect," *TPS* (1860-61) 172-197.

E. R. Dickson, "Philological Study of the Latin Language," *MQR* 15 (1861) 231-244.

*E. L. Rockwell, "Analogy between the Formation of the Pihel Conjugation in Hebrew and the Perfect Tense in Latin," *SPR* 14 (1861-62) 444-449.

*Francis W. Newman, "The Text of the Iguvine Inscriptions with Interlinear Latin Translation, and Notes," *TPS* (1864) II, i-xvi, 1-54.

*T. Hewitt Key, "On some of the Suffixes of Greek and Latin Prepositions," *TPS* (1868-69) 295-311.

*Evelyn   Abbott,   "The   Cases,"   *JP*   2   (1869)   206-213.

*James B. Greenough, "On Some Forms of Conditional Sentences in Latin, Greek, and Sanskrit," *TAPA* 2 (1871) 159-165.

*J. B. Mayor, "An Introduction to Greek and Latin Etymology, By John Peile, M.A.," *JP* 3 (1871) 328-347. *(Review)*

Frederick Stengel, "The History of the Pronunciation of Latin," *PAPA* 5 (1873) 19-20. *[Bound with Transactions, but paged separately]*

S. S. Haldeman, "The Pronunciation of Latin as Presented in Several Recent Grammars," *PAPA* 5 (1873) 20-21. *[Bound with Transactions, but paged separately]*

S. S. Haldeman, "On the Pronunciation of Latin as presented in several recent Grammars," *TAPA* 4 (1873) 44-46.

Albert Harkness, "On the Formation of the Tenses for Completed Action in the Latin Finite Verb," *TAPA* 5 (1874) 14-25.

Gustavus Fischer, "The Present Condition of Latin Grammar," *PAPA* 6 (1874) 23-24. *[Bound with Transactions, but paged separately]*

*W. D. Whitney, "On Peile's Greek and Latin Etymology," *TPS* (1873-74) 299-327.

Albert Harkness, "On the Formation of the Tenses for Completed Action in the Latin Finite Verb.—Second Paper," *TAPA* 6 (1875) 5-19.

Tracy Peck, "Certain Differences among the Ancient Romans in the Pronunciation of their Language," *PAPA* 8 (1875-76) 26. *[Bound with Transactions, but paged separately]*

Albert Harkness, "The Development of the Latin Subjunctive in Principal Clauses," *PAPA* 11 (1878-79) 13-14. *[Bound with Transactions, but paged separately]*

Charles Short, "On some points of Latin Syntax, with special reference to Mr. Roby's Grammar," *JAOS* 10 (1880) xcvi-xcviii.

Benjamin Dawson, "The Middle Voice in Virgil's *Aeneid,* Book 6," *TPS* (1880-81) 41-50.

*J. P. Postgate, "Some Latin and Greek Etymologies, and the Change of *L* to *D* in Latin," *TPS* (1880-81) 335-346.

L. L. Bonaparte, "On Neuter Neo-Latin Substantives," *TPS* (1880-81) Appendix III, 45*-64*. [Postscript, pp. 179*-183*]

James S. Blackwell, "The Testimony of the Talmud respecting the Ancient Pronunciation of certain Latin Letters," *PAPA* 13 (1881) 5-6. *[Bound with Transactions, but paged separately]*

J. K. Ingram, "Notes on Latin Lexicography," *Herm* 4 (1881-83) 310-316.

[J. P.] Postgate, "Some Latin Etymologies," *TPS* (1882-84) 149-154.

M. J. O'Brien, "On the Pronunciation of Latin," *IER, 3rd Ser.,* 5 (1884) 445-451, 516-526.

William Gardner Hale, "The Sequences of Tenses in Latin. First Paper. I.," *AJP* 7 (1886) 446-465.

William Gardner Hale, "The Sequences of Tenses in Latin," *PAPA* 18 (1886) xxviii-xxix.

William Gardner Hale, "The Sequences of Tenses in Latin. Second Paper. II.," *AJP* 8 (1887) 46-77.

*Charles S. Halsey, "Peculiarities of Affix in Latin and Greek," *PAPA* 20 (1888) xxiii-xxv.

E. R. Wharton, "On the Vocalic Laws of the Latin Language," *TPS* (1888-90) 43-58.

E. R. Wharton, "Loan-Words in Latin," *TPS* (1888-90) 172-197.

*A. Gudeman, "The Knowledge of the Latin Language and Literature among Greek Writers," *PAPA* 22 (1890) vii-x.

W. G. Hale, "The Syntax of the General Condition of Latin," *PAPA* 23 (1891) xxxviii-xl.

W. G. Hale, "The Tenses in the Subjunctive 'Comparative' Clause in Latin (after *tamquam, tamquam si, velut ac si,* etc.)," *PAPA* 23 (1891) xl-xlii.

*W. Muss-Arnolt, "On Semitic Words in Greek and Latin," *TAPA* 23 (1892) 35-156. [Index of words, pp. 151-156]

*William Gardner Hale, "The Origin and Later History of the Clause of Purpose in Latin, Greek, and Sanskrit," *PAPA* 24 (1892) xxvi-xxviii.

H. C. Elmer, "The Latin Prohibitions," *PAPA* 25 (1893) vi-xiii.

Karl P. Harrington, "A neglected Use of the Latin Imperative," *PAPA* 27 (1895) lxi-lxii.

*Minton Warren, "On the Contributions of the Latin Inscriptions to the Study of the Latin Language and Literature," *TAPA* 26 (1895) 16-27.

Thomas Fitz-Hugh, "A Questionable Tradition in Latin Historical Syntax," *PAPA* 29 (1897) xxxiv-xxxvii.

Karl P. Harrington, "Was there a Letter Z in Early Latin?" *PAPA* 30 (1898) xxxiv-xxxvi.

George Hampl, "The Origin of the Latin Letters *G* and *Z*," *TAPA* 30 (1899) 24-41.

William Gardner Hale, "Is there Still a Latin Potential?" *TAPA* 31 (1900) 138-162.

Charles E. Bennett, "The Stipulative Subjunctive in Latin," *TAPA* 31 (1900) 223-250.

H. C. Nutting, "On the History of the Unreal Condition in Latin," *PAPA* 33 (1901) xlviii-xlix.

H. C. Elmer, "Is there still a Latin Potential?" *PAPA* 33 (1901) cxvii-cxx.

C. L. Meander, "Notes on the Order of Words in Latin," *PAPA* 35 (1903) xxxi-xxxii.

H. C. Elmer, "A Suggestion for a New Latin Dictionary," *PAPA* 36 (1903) xxxiv-xxxvi.

Robert S. Radford, "Studies in Latin Accent and Metric," *TAPA* 35 (1904) 33-64.

Charles W. L. Johnson, "The Accentus of the Ancient Latin Grammarians," *TAPA* 35 (1904) 65-76.

Karl P. Harrington, "The Classification of Latin Conditional Sentences," *PAPA* 37 (1905) xli-xliii.

H. B. Dewing, "The Latin Indirect Object governed by Verbs signifying 'favor, help, injure, please, displease, trust, distrust, command, obey, serve, resist, indulge, spare, pardon, envy, threaten, believe, and persuade'," *PAPA* 37 (1905) lxiii-lxiv.

Clarence Linton Meander, "Types of Sentence Structure in Latin Prose Writers," *TAPA* 36 (1905) 32-51.

Charles E. Bennett, "The Ablative of Association," *TAPA* 36 (1905) 64-81.

Albert Granger Harkness, "The Relation of Accent to Elision in Latin Verse, not including the Drama," *TAPA* 36 (1905) 82-110.

Edwin W. Fay, "Latin-Word Studies," *TAPA* 37 (1906) 5-52.

G. B. Grundy, "The Transliteration and Pronunciation of the Latin letter *v*," *TPS* (1907-10) 1-56.

Thomas Fitz-Hugh, "The Re-acute, Acute, Grave, and Zero Stress in Latin Speech and Rhythm," *PAPA* 40 (1908) xxi-xxvii.

LeRoy C. Barret, "Two Notes on the Latin Present Participle," *PAPA* 41 (1909) xviii-xxi.

F. W. Shipley, "The Effect of Enclitics on Latin Word Accent in the Light of Republican Prose Usage," *PAPA* 41 (1909) lxxxiii-lxxxiv.

Richard Wellington Husband, "The Diphthong -ui in Latin," *TAPA* 41 (1910) 19-23.

*Edgar Howard Sturtevant, "Notes on the Character of Greek and Latin Accent," *TAPA* 42 (1911) 45-52.

Clarence W. Mendell, "The Anticipatory Element in Latin Sentence Connection," *PAPA* 44 (1912) li.

Henry B. Van Hoesen, "The Parentage and Birth Date of the Latin Uncial," *PAPA* 44 (1912) lvii-lix.

R. B. Steele, "The Passive Periphrastic in Latin," *TAPA* 44 (1913) 5-17.

Edgar H. Sturtevant, "The Genitive and Dative Singular of the Latin Pronominal Declension," *TAPA* 44 (1913) 99-105.

Andrew Runni Anderson, "-EIS in the Accusative Plural of the Latin Third Declension," *TAPA* 45 (1914) 129-139.

Albert J. Carnoy, "The Importance of Special Languages in the Study of Vulgar Latin," *TAPA* 46 (1915) 75-85.

Edgar H. Sturtevant and Roland G. Kent, "Elision and Hiatus in Latin Prose and Verse," *TAPA* 46 (1915) 129-155.

Edgar H. Sturtevant, "The Monophthongization of Latin ae," *TAPA* 47 (1916) 107-116.

Albert J. Carnoy, "Some Obscurities in the Assimilation of *ti* and *di* before a Vowel in Vulgar Latin," *TAPA* 47 (1916) 145-152.

Cornelia C. Coulter, "Compound Adjectives in Early Latin Poetry," *TAPA* 47 (1916) 153-172.

*Eugene McCartney, "Canting Puns on Ancient Monuments," *AJA* 23 (1919) 59-64.

John C. Rolfe, "The Use of Devices for Indicating Vowel Length in Latin," *PAPS* 61 (1922) 80-98.

*E[dgar] H. Sturtevant, "Concerning the Influence of Greek on Vulgar Latin," *TAPA* 56 (1925) 5-25.

Edith Francis Claflin, "The Nature of the Latin Passive in the Light of Recent Discoveries," *PAPA* 57 (1926) xxxvi-xxxvii.

*Francis A. Wood, "Prothetic Vowels in Sanskrit, Greek, Latin and Germanic," *AJP* 52 (1931) 105-144.

*A. Cameron, "Latin Words in the Greek Inscriptions of Asia Minor," *AJP* 52 (1931) 232-262.

Hermann Collitz, "A Group of Clipped Words in Latin," *PAPA* 62 (1931) xxii.

*E. Adelaide Hahn, "Light from Hittite on Latin Indefinites," *TAPA* 64 (1933) 28-40.

*Frank Ringgold Blake, "Necessity for a Combinatory Syntax of Greek and Latin," *PAPA* 65 (1934) l. *[Roman numeral 50]*

*William A. Oldfather, "Suggestions for Guidance in the Preparation of a Critical *Index Verborum* for Latin and Greek Authors," *TAPA* 68 (1937) 1-10.

E. Adelaide Hahn, "The Development of Latin Subordinating Conjunctions," *PAPA* 71 (1940) xxxviii.

E. Adelaide Hahn, "Voice of Non-Finite Verb Forms in Latin and English," *TAPA* 74 (1943) 269-306.

*Edgar H. Sturtevant, "Hittite Verbal Nouns in *-tar* and the Latin Gerund," *Lang* 20 (1944) 206-211.

Hans Hendriksen, "The Personal Ending of the 2. Pl. Med.-Pass. in Latin," *ArOr* 17 (1949) Part 1, 310-314.

Demetrius J. Georgacas, "The Latin Fifth Declension," *TAPA* 80 (1949) 426.

*E. Adelaide Hahn, "Genesis of the Infinitive with Subject-Accusative," *TAPA* 81 (1950) 117-129.

O. Szemerényi, "The Latin Gerundive and Other *-nd-* Formations," *TPS* (1950) 169-179.

*G. Bonfante, "The Prepositions of Latin and Greek," *Word* 6 (1950) 106-116.

*G. Bonfante, "Addenda to the article 'The Prepositions of Latin and Greek'," *Word* 7 (1951) 250-252.

E. Adelaide Hahn, "The Moods in Indirect Discourse in Latin," *TAPA* 83 (1952) 242-266.

Philip W. Harsh, "Final *s* after a Short Vowel in Early Latin," *TAPA* 83 (1952) 267-278.

*E. Adelaide Hahn, "The Origin of the Greek Accusative in Latin," *TAPA* 91 (1960) 221-238.

Robert Coleman, "Some Allophonies of Latin /i/," *TPS* (1962) 80-104.

F. A. Mecham, "The Latin Accent," *ACR* 39 (1962) 101-110.

E. Adelaide Hahn, "The Supposed Reflexive Pronoun in Latin," *TAPA* 94 (1963) 86-112.

D. W. Pye, "Latin 3rd Plural Perfect Indicative Active—Its Endings in Verse Usage," *TPS* (1963) 1-27.

E. Adelaide Hahn, "Relative and Antecedent," *TAPA* 95 (1964) 111-141.

§553 *3.3.4.2.5.1 Alphabetical Listing of Latin Words*

A

Theodore Aufrecht, "On the Etymology of the Latin Adverb *Actutum*," *TPS* (1856) 54-56.

*†T. Hewitt Key, "Miscellaneous Papers. D. On *alaceri-* and some related Greek words," *TPS* (1862-63) 26-30.

T. Hewitt Key, "Miscellaneous Papers. A. On *altero-* and its analogies," *TPS* (1862-63) 1-13.

*T. Hewitt Key, "On the Derivation of *Son, Nurus, Anus, Uxor, Wife,* πας, *omnis, solus, every, all,* ὅλος," *TPS* (1868-69) 257-272.

*T. Hewitt Key, "The Latin *Et, Que, Atque(Ac),* and the Greek και, τε—all of one origin," *TPS* (1866) 49-63.

B

*Paul Haupt, "Etymological and Critical Notes," *AJP* 47 (1926) 305-318. [3. Lat. *bucina* and Gr. βυκάνη, pp 309-311]

C

Hensleigh Wedgewood, "On the confusion of meaning between *Corvus* and *Cornix*," *TPS* (1854) 107-108.

D

*Th[eodore] Aufrecht, "On Some Latin and Greek etymologies," *TPS* (1859) 14-17. [On the derivation of *dulcis* and γλυκυς, γλαυκος, πολυλευκης; On the Original form of μα; On the derivation of *pollex*]

Hensleigh Wedgewood, "On the connection of the Latin *dulcis* with *deliciæ, delicatus, delectare*," *TPS* (1860-61) 150-152.

E

*Winnie D. Lowrance, "The Use of *Forem and Essem*," *TAPA* 62 (1931) 169-191.

*T. Hewitt Key, "The Latin *Et, Que, Atque(Ac)*, and the Greek και, τε—all of one origin," *TPS* (1866) 49-63.

F

*D. Sperber, "פילס, פולסא and Follis," *Lĕš* 31 (1966-67) #3, n.p.n.

*Winnie D. Lowrance, "The Use of *Forem and Essem*," *TAPA* 62 (1931) 169-191.

G

*Harold Bennett, "On the Meaning of 'gollere' and 'suscipere' as Applied to Infants," *PAPA* 53 (1922) xvii-xviii.

H

*Frank H. Fowler, "Notes. On Greek and Latin Negatives. *I. Latin haud: Greek οὐ*," *AJP* 21 (1900) 443-445.

*Lionel Horton-Smith, "The Origin of the Latin *haud* and Greek *οὐ*; and the Extensions of the Originally Unextended Form," *AJP* 18 (1897) 43-69.

*J. E. B. Mayor, "On a late use of the particles *hinc, inde*, &c.," *JCSP* 1 (1854) 392-394.

I

*T. Hewitt Key, "On the Prepositions ἐνι, *in*, and related words," *TPS* (1854) 85-95.

*J. E. B. Mayor, "On a late use of the particles *hinc, inde,* &c.," *JCSP* 1 (1854) 392-394.

M

T. Hewitt Key, "On Plural Forms in Latin, with a Singular Meaning, and especially on Virgil's use of *Menta*," *TPS* (1867) 105-114.

T. Hewitt Key, "On the Latin Verb *mittere,* its Origin and Affinities; and generally on Verbs signifiying 'to go' in the Indo-European Family," *TPS* (1855) 1-15.

J. W. Donaldson, "On the Etymology of the Latin particle *modo*," *TPS* (1854) 97-107.

N

*E. Adelaide Hahn, "Hittite *kinun* = Latin *nunc* and *num*," *PAPA* 69 (1938) lii.

*T. Hewitt Key, "On the Derivation of *Son, Nurus, Anus, Uxor, Wife,* πας, *omnis, solus, every, all,* ὁλος," *TPS* (1868-69) 257-272.

O

*T. Hewitt Key, "On the Derivation of *Son, Nurus, Anus, Uxor, Wife,* πας, *omnis, solus, every, all,* ὁλος," *TPS* (1868-69) 257-272.

Theodore Aufrecht, "On the Derivation of the Latin *Otium*," *TPS* (1856) 143-144.

P

Herbert Coleridge, "On the Latin Verb *Ploro,* and some of its Compounds," *TPS* (1857) 129-134.

*Th[eodore] Aufrecht, "On Some Latin and Greek etymologies," *TPS* (1859) 14-17. [On the derivation of *dulcis* and γλυκυς, γλαυκος, πολυδευκης; On the Original form of μα; On the derivation of *pollex*]

*T. Hewitt Key, "On the Latin Prepositions *Re* and *Pro:* their Origin and Primitive Meaning," *TPS* (1866) 30-49.

Q

*T. Hewitt Key, "The Latin *Et, Que, Atque(Ac),* and the Greek καί, τε—all of one origin," *TPS* (1866) 49-63.

*T. Hewitt Key, "On the Latin Prepositions *Re* and *Pro:* their Origin and Primitive Meaning," *TPS* (1866) 30-49.

R

*T. Hewitt Key, "On the Latin Prepositions *Re* and *Pro:* their Origin and Primitive Meaning," *TPS* (1866) 30-49.

S

Joseph Fontenrose, "The Meaning and Use of *Sed Enim,*" *TAPA* 75 (1944) 168-195.

Roland G. Kent, "The Etymology of Latin *sine,*" *TAPA* 73 (1942) 54-57.

*T. Hewitt Key, "On the Derivation of *Son, Nurus, Anus, Uxor, Wife,* πας, *omnis, solus, every, all,* ὅλος," *TPS* (1868-69) 257-272.

Theodore Aufrecht, "On the Derivation of the Latin *Sons,*" *TPS* (1856) 115-118.

*Theodore Goldstücker, "On *jecur,* ἧπαρ, यकृत् *(yakŕit); stercus,* σκώρ, शकृत् *(śakŕit)* and some words of kindred formation," *TPS* (1854) 157-168.

*G. P. Shipp, "*Superstitio* and Ἐπίσταμαι," *AASCS* 3 (1969) 29-31.

*Harold Bennett, "On the Meaning of 'gollere' and 'suscipere' as Applied to Infants," *PAPA* 53 (1922) xvii-xviii.

T

T. Hewitt Key, "On the Latin Words *Temre* and *Temerare*,"*TPS* (1866) 25-30.

*T. Hewitt Key, "On *titillare* and τικτειν," *TPS* (1862-63) 213-216.

*L. J. .D. Richardson, "'Winged Words,' *Tormentum* and Πάλλω," *TPS* (1936) 101-105.

U

*Eric P. Hamp, "Armenian 'gišer', Latin 'uesper'," *AAI* 2 (1965) 257-259.

*Calvert Watkins, "A Latin-Hittite etymology," *Lang* 45 (1969) 235-242. [Lat. *uespillo* 'undertaker for the poorest classes' cognate with Hitt. *wašpaš* 'clothes']

*Maurice Bloomfield, "Four Etymological Studies," *AJP* 6 (1885) 41-52. [1. Latin *usque:* Verdic ácchǎ, pp. 41-42]

*W. M. Gordon, "Interpretation of *Usucapio*," *RIDA, 3rd Ser.*, 9 (1962) 325-333.

T. Hewitt Key, "On the Derivation and Meaning of the Latin Verb *usurpare*," *TPS* (1855) 96-103.

*T. Hewitt Key, "On the Derivation of *Son, Nurus, Anus, Uxor, Wife*, πας, *omnis, solus, every, all*, ὁλος," *TPS* (1868-69) 257-272.

V

Dorothy Paschall, "The Origin and Semantic Development of Latin *Vitium*," *TAPA* 67 (1936) 219-231.

§554 *3.3.4.2.6 Persian Grammar and Lexicography*

Edward E. Salisbury, "On the Identification of the Signs of the Persian Cuneiform Alphabet," *JAOS* 1 (1849) 517-558.

Charles Riev, "Remarks on some Phonetic Laws in Persian," *TPS* (1880-81) 1-22.

William [Aldis] Wright, "On the Persian Word زن گون or گون زنه ," *JP* 15 (1886) 101-102.

W. Bang, "Contributions to the Old Persian Lexicography," *BOR* 3 (1888-89) 239-240.

Herbert C. Tolman, "Points in the syntax of Old-Persian cuneiform inscriptions," *JAOS* 15 (1893) c-ci.

*L. H. Gray, "Iranian Miscellanies," *JAOS* 33 (1913) 281-294. [e. Modern Persian *bi-:* Lithuanian *be-,* pp. 293-294]

Edwin W. Fay, "Indo Iranian Word-Studies (ii)," *JAOS* 34 (1914) 329-343. [(1) Old Persian *mariyam* 'estate', pp. 329-330]

Roland G. Kent, "Studies in the Old Persian Inscriptions," *JAOS* 35 (1915) 321-352. [I. Avahyarādiy; II. Taumā; III. Apariyāya; IV. Hacā darš[a]m[a]; V. Ušabārim; VI. Sim; VII. Ufraštadiy]

*Anonymous, "Transliteration of Arabic and Persian," *PBA* 8 (1917-18) 505-521.

A. V. William Jackson, "The Etymology of Some Words in the Old Persian Inscriptions," *JAOS* 38 (1918) 121-124. [1. Old Persian amuθa 'he fled'; 2-3. OP. aruvastam...niyasaya, NRb. 4-5]

Albert J. Carnoy, "Pre-Aryan Origins of the Persian Perfect," *JAOS* 39 (1919) 117-121.

H. C. Tolman, "An erroneous etymology of New Persian *pādšāh,* in relation to the pr. n. Παταζείθης (Hdt. 3. 61)," *JAOS* 40 (1920) 200-201.

*Georg Morgenstierne, "Iranian Notes," *AO* 1 (1922-23) 245-284. [I. Notes on the Old Persian Inscriptions; II. Modern Iranian Etymologies; III. Miscellaneous Iranian Etymologies; IV. Indian Loan-Words in Baluchi]

Reynold A. Nicholson, "The Subordinate Imperative in Persian," *JRAS* (1923) 264.

James R. Ware, "Old Persian niyaθᵊ̄ārayam, *Bh. 1. 64*," *JAOS* 44 (1924) 285-287.

E. H. Sturtevant, "The Misuse of Case Forms in the Achaemenian Inscriptions," *JAOS* 48 (1928) 66-73.

Louis H. Gray, "Four Old Persian Etymologies," *AJP* 53 (1932) 67-69. [dačaram; θaramiš; yakā; sikaba[+]uda]

Julius J. Price, "Interpretation of Persian Words," *ET* 44 (1932-33) 527.

Jiří Krámský, "A Study in the Phonology of Modern Persian," *ArOr* 11 (1939-40) 66-83.

Roland G. Kent, "Vocalic *r* in Old Persian Before *n*," *Lang* 18 (1942) 79-82.

P. Tedesco, "Slavic *lozā̌* and Persian *rāz*, both 'Vine'," *JAOS* 63 (1943) 149-155.

Roland G. Kent, "The Old Persian Relative and Article," *Lang* 20 (1944) 1-10.

Roland G. Kent, "Old Persian *artācā brazmaniya*," *Lang* 21 (1945) 223-229.

Roland G. Kent, "The Accusative in Old Persian *mām kāma*," *JAOS* 66 (1946) 44-49.

Jiří Krámský, "A Phonological Analysis of Persian Monosyllables," *ArOr* 16 (1947-49) 103-134.

Oswald Szamerenyi, "Contributions to Iranian Lexicography," *JAOS* 70 (1950) 226-236. [1. NPers. *yār*; 2. NPers. *zōr*; 3. NPers. *āšyāne, āšyān* 'nest'; 4. MParth *zxrwb*; 5. Buddh. Sogd. *nyrkčšmy*; 6. OPers. *θrd-*; 7. OPers. *nyāka*]

Manfred Mayrhofer, "Old Persian *kunautiy*: Sanskrit *śṛṇóti*," *JAOS* 72 (1952) 110-111.

Eric P. Hamp, "Final Vowels in Old Persian," *JNES* 13 (1954) 115-117.

*J. Harmatta, "An Old Persian Loan-Word in Elamite," *AOASH* 5 (1955) 193-203. [ak-ka₄-ia-še]

W. B. Henning, "The Middle-Persian Word for 'Beer'," *BSOAS* 17 (1955) 603-604.

Herbert H. Paper, "The Old Persian /L/ Phoneme," *JAOS* 76 (1956) 24-26.

Mansour Shaki, "The Problem of the Vowel Phonemes in the Persian Language," *ArOr* 25 (1957) 45-55.

Ilya Gershevitch, "Sissoo at Susa (Opers. *Yaka- = Dalbergia Sissoo* Roxb.)," *BSOAS* 19 (1957) 317-320.

*Soheil Afnan, "Some Arabic and Persian Terms of Philosophy," *Oriens* 10 (1957) 71-76.

Mansour Shaki, "A Study in the Persian Bound Phraseology and Idioms," *ArOr* 26 (1958) 248-278.

Ilya Gershevitch, "*Ad* 'Sissoo at Susa'," *BSOAS, XIX, 2, 1957, 317, 1. 5," *BSOAS* 21 (1958) 174.

Garland H. Cannon, "Sir William Jones's Persian Linguistics," *JAOS* 78 (1958) 262-273.

J. Duchesne-Guillemin, "Old Persian *Artācā Brazmaniy,*" *BSOAS* 25 (1962) 336-337.

Mansour Shaki, "Nominal Compounds in Neo-Persian," *ArOr* 31 (1963) 138-140.

I[lya] Gershevitch, "Dialect Variation in Early Persian," *TPS* (1964) 1-29.

Bo. Utas, "Old Persian Miscellanea," *OrS* 14&15 (1965-66) 118-140. [1. "Abiš nāviyā āha"; 2. "Mātya" and "drauga"]

J. Harmatta, "The Bisitun[sic]* Inscription and the Introduction of the Old Persian Cuneiform Script," *AAASH* 14 (1966) 255-283.

Jiří Krámský, "Some Remarks on the Problem of Quantity of Vowel Phonemes in Modern Persian," *ArOr* 34 (1966) 215-220.

*Herbert H. Paper, "The Use of *(ha)mē* in Selected Judeo-Persian Texts," *JAOS* 88 (1968) 483-494.

Abdual Azim, "Khan-i Arzu's Observations on the Relationship of Sanskrit and Persian," *ZDMG* 119 (1969-70) 261-269.

§555 *3.3.4.2.7 Other Languages Bearing on Ancient Near Eastern Studies*

Arratoon Isaac Aganoon, "A Dissertation on the Antiquity of the Armenian Language," *JRAS* (1837) 333-344.

*W. C. D., "The Syro-Arabian Languages and Literature," *CRB* 17 (1852) 393-424. [§2. *The Language of Babylon,* pp. 402-410]

*Francis W. Newman, "The Text of the Iguvine Inscriptions with Interlinear Latin Translation, and Notes," *TPS* (1864) II, i-xvi, 1-54.

*Anonymous, "The Etruscans and their Language," *BQRL* 62 (1875) 405-437. *(Review)*

Isaac Taylor, "On the Etruscan Language," *JTVI* 10 (1876-77) 179-202. (Discussion, pp. 202-206)

*A. H. Sayce, "The Karian Language and Inscriptions," *SBAT* 9 (1886-93) 112-154.

J. Imbert, "Notes on the Writings of the Lycian Monuments.—(A.) The Lycian Writing," *BOR* 2 (1887-88) 210-218, 279-288.

J. Imbert, "Notes on the Writings of the Lycian Monuments," *BOR* 3 (1888-89) 252-259; 5 (1891) 105-114.

*Robt. Brown Jr., "The Etruscan Numerals," *ARL* 3 (1889) 376-410.

C[laude] R. Conder, "Asia Minor Words," *PEFQS* 21 (1889) 26.

C[laude] R. Conder, "Notes by Major Conder, D.C.L., R.E. VI. The Speech of Lycaonia," *PEFQS* 21 (1889) 147-148.

C[laude] R. Conder, "The Vannic Language," *PEFQS* 21 (1889) 203-204.

W. Arkwright, "Vocalic Harmony in Lycian," *BOR* 5 (1891) 49-54.

W. Arkwright, "Some Lycian Suffixes," *BOR* 5 (1891) 185-192.

C[laude] R. Conder, "The Lycian Language," *JRAS* (1891) 607-686.

A. H. Sayce, "The Language of Mitanni," *SBAP* 22 (1900) 171-220. (Additional Note, pp. 221-225)

*Herbert Cushing Tolman, "The Etruscan *aisar, ais, αισοί*," *PAPA* 41 (1909) lxxxviii-lxxxix.

W. M. Calder, "The Medial Verbal -*r* Termination in Phrygian," *JMUEOS* #10 (1923) 25-33.

Anonymous, "Notes and Comments. The Etruscan Enigma Again," *A&A* 21 (1926) 145.

*Edgar Howard Sturtevant, "Some Nouns of Relationship in Lycian and Hittite," *TAPA* 59 (1928) 48-56.

*John C. Grandbery, "Languages of Bible Lands," *MQR, 3rd Ser.,* 55 (1929) 114-119. *[Turkish, p. 119]*

Albrecht Goetze, "Indefinites and Negations, Prohibitive and Imperative in the Urarṭean," *RHA* 3 (1934-36) 179-198.

Albrecht Goetze, "On some Urarṭean Verbal Forms," *RHA* 3 (1934-36) 266-282.

Harry Velten, "Some Ancient Eurasian Tool Names and Cultural Terms," *Anthro* 30 (1935) 717-726.

Eva Fiesel, "Χ Represents a Sibilant in Early Etruscan," *AJP* 57 (1936) 261-270.

Cyrus H. Gordon, "Evidence for the Horite Language from Nuzi," *BASOR* #64 (1936) 23-28.

Frank B. Blake, "Urartian *ale* 'says'," *RHA* 5 (1938-40) 109-110.

*Frank R. Blake, "Studies in Semitic Grammar II," *JAOS* 62 (1942) 109-118. [9. Mandaic האנאתה; 10. Lihyanic and Thamudic *b* 'son'; 11. Some Lihyanic and Thamudic Prepositions; 12. The Lihyanic Article; 13. The Personal Pronoun 'I' at the beginning of Inscriptions]

Heinrich M. Hoenigswald, "The Etruscan Language," *AJA* 47 (1943) 101.

Donald C. Swanson, "New Evidence Bearing on a Lydian Sign," *Word* 3 (1947) 204-207. ["↑" "L"]

*F. J. Tritsch, "Lycian Luwian and Hittite," *ArOr* 18 (1950) 1/2, 494-518.

*Henry M. Hoenigswald, "South Etruscan and Cypriote Writing," *AJA* 56 (1952) 174.

Robert Shafer, "Greek transcription of Lukian," *JKF* 2 (1952-53) 1-12.

Massimo Pallottino, "What do we know today about the Etruscan language?" *IALR* 1 (1953) 243-253.

*P. P. Saydon, "Some Unusual Ways of Expressing the Superlative in Hebrew and Maltese," *VT* 4 (1954) 432-433.

*Robert Shafer, "System of Relationship in Lukian," *WO* 2 (1954-59) 484-501.

Richard N. Frye, "Problems in Parthian Epigraphy," *AJA* 59 (1955) 177.

H. W. Bailey, "A Problem of Indo-Iranian Vocabulary," *RO* 21 (1957) 59-69.

J. Aquilina, "Maltese as a Mixed Language," *JSS* 3 (1958) 58-79.

H. W. Bailey, "Iranian *Arya-* and *Daha-*," *TPS* (1959) 71-115. [Supplementary note, *TPS* (1960) 87-88]

*John Wilkins, "Etruscan Numerals," *TPS* (1962) 51-79.

Robert Schafer, "Lycia, Milya, Solymoi: A new Anatolian language," *Minos* 8 (1963-67) 125-129.

V. Sevoroskin, "On Karian," *RHA* 22 (1964) 1-55.

*Eric P. Hamp, "Armenian 'gišer', Latin 'uesper'," *AAI* 2 (1965) 257-259.

P. P. Saydon, "Maltese Etymological Notes," *JSS* 10 (1965) 67-82.

Ph. H. J. Houwink ten Cate, "Short Notes on Lycian Grammar," *RHA* 23 (1965) 17-24.

*Ilya Gershevitch, "Iranian Nouns and Names in Elamite Garb," *TPS* (1969) 165-200.

§556 *3.3.5 The Bible as Literature, including the Old Testament*

T., "Literature of the Bible," *MR* 24 (1842) 485-521.

Anonymous, "The Hebrew Language and Literature," *PQR* 9 (1860-61) 442-475.

Charles A. Briggs, "The Literary Study of the Bible," *ONTS* 2 (1882-83) 65-77.

RIA., "The Bible—Its Position in Literature," *ERG, 9th Ser.,* 2 (1887) 1-7.

J. B. Shearer, "The Universal Book," *PQ* 5 (1891) 517-524.

Anonymous, "The Bible as Literature," *LQHR* 86 (1896) 300-323. *(Review)*

William Henry Green, "The Bible as Literature: A Review of Dr. Lyman Abbott's Lecture," *HR* 33 (1897) 61-67. *(Review)*

Jas. A. Duncan, "Dramatic Literature in the Bible," *MQR, 3rd Ser.,* 23 (1897-98) 260-267.

Alfred Tyler Perry, "The Pre-Eminence of the Bible as a Book" *HSR* 9 (1898-99) 183-209.

J. E. McFadyen, "The Bible as Literature," *BW* 16 (1900) 438-446.

Elkin N. Adler, "Professor Blau on the Bible as a Book," *JQR* 15 (1902-03) 715-728. *(Review)*

A. C. Dixon, "The Bible as Literature and How Much More," *CFL, 3rd Ser.,* 1 (1904) 588-596.

*Matthew Leitch, "Unscientific Criticism of the Bible," *CFL, 3rd Ser.,* 5 (1906) 3-6. [II. Unscientific Criticism of the Bible as a Book of Literature, pp. 3-5]

Fitzgerald Sale Parker, "The Literary Study of the Bible," *MQR, 3rd Ser.,* 34 (1908) 468-484.

Anonymous, "Pagan Books and the Bible Compared," *AAOJ* 31 (1909) 100-103.

W. W. Moore, "The Bible a Literary Necessity," *USR* 21 (1909-10) 87-95.

Anonymous, "The Progress of Thought Contained in the Bible," *AAOJ* 32 (1910) 46-50.

*Willis J. Beecher, "Some Problems Concerning the Bible," *CFL, 3rd Ser.,* 12 (1910) 417-420. [II. Method of Interpreting the Bible as Literature, pp. 418-419]

Huber G. Buehler, "The Bible as Literature," *LQ* 40 (1910) 467-478.

T. E. Rankin, "The Bible the Supreme Product of Literary Art," *HR* 67 (1914) 267-273.

*Thomas E. Barr, "The Bible and Literature," *BS* 75 (1918) 213-236.

William Lyon Phelps, "Literary Aspects of the Bible," *PSB* 13 (1919) #1, 15-17.

Alfred E. Garvie, "The Bible as Literature," *LQHR* 163 (1937) 317-329.

W. Taylor Bowie, "The Bible as Literature," *BQL* 9 (1938-39) 83-90.

R. E. C. Houghton, "The Bible as Literature," *MC* 28 (1938-39) 178-186.

*William Foxwell Albright, " The Old Testament and Canaanite Language and Literature," *CBQ* 7 (1945) 5-31. [VII. Canaanite and Biblical Literature, pp. 27-31]

S. L. Morgan Sr., "The Old Testament as Great Literature," *R&E* 45 (1948) 49-62.

J. Allen Easley, "Appreciation of the Bible as Literature and Religion," *JAAR* 18 (1950) 96-98.

S. D. Goitein, "Form and Spirit in Biblical Literature," *Jud* 3 (1954) 60-67.

T. B. Shepherd, "The Bible as Literature," *LQHR* 180 (1955) 245-249.

R. L. Bruckberger, "The Old Testament as Tragedy," *C&C* 10 (1958) 165-175.

W. R. England, "The Teacher—And the Bible as Literature: 1. The Bible is Literature," *JCE* 2 (1959) 89-96.

W. R. England, "The Teacher—And the Bible as Literature: II. The Bible is Literature," *JCE* 2 (1959) 171-179.

W. R. England, "The Teacher—And the Bible as Literature: III. Bringing the Bible into the Classroom," *JCE* 3 (1960) 95-103.

Francis Seper, "The Bible and Literary Forms," *BibT* #6 (1963) 392-397.

§557 *3.3.5.1 Studies in Hebrew Poetry (includes Ancient Non-Biblical Hebrew Poetry)*

[Johann Gottfried] Herder, "Introductory Dialogue on the Spirit of Hebrew Poetry," *BibR* 2 (1826) 319-345, 505-545; 3 (1827) 429-441. *(Trans. by James Marsh)*

Anonymous, "Biblical Eloquence and Poetry," *PRev* 3 (1831) 447-454.

Anonymous, "The Spirit of Hebrew Poetry, By J. G. Herder. Translated from the German by James Marsh," *CE* 18 (1835) 167-173, n. 174. *(Review)*

Anonymous, "Poetry of the Bible," *ATG* 5 (1838-39) 230-236.

Geo. H. Hastings, "Lyrical Poetry of the Bible," *BRCR, 3rd Ser.,* 3 (1847) 323-347.

*R. B[abcock], "Hebrew Poetry Made Intelligible to Readers of Our Common Bible. Nourse's Edition of the Bible," *CRB* 12 (1847) 387-396.

*B. B. Edwards, "Studies in Hebrew Poetry," *BS* 5 (1848) 58-79. [Age of the Alphabetical Poems; Rhyme in Hebrew Popular Poetry; Explanation of the Word סֶלָה, Selah, General Observations, Jewish Tradition, Hellenistic Interpretations, Recent Explanations of the Word, Masoretic Text, Views of Sommer]

G. H. A. von Ewald, "On Hebrew Poetry," *JSL, 1st Ser.,* 1 (1848) 74-111, 295-325. *(Trans. by John Nicholson)*

W. F., "Parallelistic Poetry," *JSL, 1st Ser.,* 7 (1851) 378-394.

I., "The Bards of the Bible," *JSL, 1st Ser.,* 7 (1851) 419-428.

Anonymous, "Hebrew Poetry," *FBQ* 1 (1853) 75-98.

Anonymous, "The Poetical Element of the Bible," *SPR* 8 (1854-55) 91-112

†P. F., "The Poetical Element in Scripture," *BFER* 11 (1862) 485-511.

[Hermann] Zeller, "Hebrew Poetry.—Translated from Zeller's 'Biblisches Wörterbuch'," *ER* 14 (1862-63) 390-415.

J. A. Brown, "The Poetry of the Bible," *ER* 16 (1864) 283-298.

*Philip Schaff, "Hebrew Poetry," *DTQ* 2 (1876) 422-433.

*W. R. S[mith], "The Poetry of the Old Testament," *BQRL* 65 (1877) 26-70.

*S. M. Drach, "Viceroy Joseph's Offical Despatches. Is Bible Poetry Acrostic?" *SBAT* 6 (1878-79) 244-248.

†J. Chotzner, "Hebrew Poetry," *SBAP* 6 (1883-84) 60-61.

Chas. A. Briggs, "Hebrew Poetry. I.," *AJSL* 2 (1885-86) 164-170.

†C. J. Ball, "Remains of Ancient Hebrew Poetry," *SBAP* 8 (1885-86) 127-129.

Edward L. Curtis, "Some Features of Hebrew Poetry," *ONTS* 6 (1885-86) 1-8.

*Philip L. Jones, "The Poetry of the Bible in its Relation to Exegesis," *BQR* 8 (1886) 365-376.

Charles A. Briggs, "The Strophical Organization of Hebrew Trimeters," *AJSL* 3 (1886-87) 152-165.

*George A. Barton, "The Prayer of Habakkuk," *ONTS* 6 (1886-87) 176-178.

*C. A. Briggs, "The Hebrew Tetrameter," *AJSL* 4 (1887-88) 65-74.

*C. A. Briggs, "The Hebrew Pentameter," *AJSL* 4 (1887-88) 129-139.

*C. A. Briggs, "The Hebrew Hexameter," *AJSL* 4 (1887-88) 201-205.

E. H. Johnson, "The Formal Element in Poetry," *ONTS* 8 (1888-89) 364-366.

Anthony J. Maas, "Scripture Poetry," *ACQR* 14 (1889) 44-59.

Francis Brown, "Measurements of Hebrew poetry as an aid to literary analysis," *JBL* 9 (1890) 71-106.

*Hinckley G. Mitchell, "Poetical Accents," *JBL* 10 (1891) 144-146.

James Neil, "Inspired Hebrew Poetry. Part I," *TML* 6 (1891) 194-206.

James Neil, "Inspired Hebrew Poetry. Part II," *TML* 6 (1891) 257-275.

*W. W. Martin, "A Hebrew Parable and the Poetic Style," *MQR, 3rd Ser.,* 12 (1892) 310-319.

*Karl Budde, "The Folk-Song of Israel in the Mouth of the Prophets," *NW* 2 (1893) 28-51.

*Richard G. Moulton, "Three Biblical Sonnets," *BW* 6 (1895) 328-329. [Prov. 6:6-10; 24:30-34; Ecclescus. 22:11]

*William Hayes Ward, "Light on Scriptural Texts from Recent Discoveries. Hebrew and Babylonian Poetry," *HR* 30 (1895) 408-411.

J. G. Tasker, "Hebrew Poetry," *ET* 9 (1897-98) 445-446.

*C[laude] R. Conder, "Hebrew and Babylonian Poetry," *PEFQS* 30 (1898) 170-176.;

Paul Ruben, "Strophic Forms in the Bible," *JQR* 11 (1898-99) 431-479. [Ezek. 14:12-20; Amos 1:2-2:4; 7:1-11; 8:1-3; Micah 3; Jer. 10:1-16; Isa. 47; 51:9-10, 17-23; 52:1, 2, 7-10; 51:1-5, 6-8, 11; 52:13-53:12; 49:1-7; Ex. 15:1-17, Judges 5; Deut. 32; 2 Sam. 1:19-27; Isa. 1:2-20; Jer. 9:1-21; Hosea. 7; Micah 2:1-11; Hab. 2; 3; Zeph. 2; Zech. 9:9-10:1; Nah. 3; Jer. 46:3-12]

Eneas B. Goodwin, "The Poetry of Israel," *CUB* 6 (1900) 29-49.

H. Y. Arnott, "Hebrew Poetry," *GUOST* 2 (1901-07) 29-30.

*William T. Allison, "The Poetry of the Psalms," *BW* 22 (1903) 42-48.

T. Witton Davies, "The Poetry and Poetical Writings of the Ancient Hebrews," *BW* 22 (1903) 358-362.

Edward Konig, "The Poetizing of the Old Testament," *HR* 45 (1903) 120-126.

*W. T. Allison, "The Nature-Poetry of the Psalms," *BW* 28 (1906) 87-93. [Part I]

*W. T. Allison, "The Nature-Poetry of the Psalms," *BW* 28 (1906) 261-273. [II. The Cosmos]

*W. T. Allison, "The Nature Poetry of the Psalms," *BW* 29 (1907) 208-216. [III The Landscape]

*W. T. Allison, "The Nature-Poetry of the Psalms," *BW* 30 (1907) 111-117. [IV. The Mountains, Sea, Trees and Flowers]

*C. F. Burney, "David as a Poet," *ICMM* 6 (1909-10) 49-65.

A. R. Gordon, "Pioneers in the Study of Old Testament Poetry. I. Lowth," *ET* 22 (1910-11) 444-448.

A. R. Gordon, "Pioneers in the Study of Old Testament Poetry. Herder," *ET* 24 (1912-13) 227-232.

*Anonymous, "Plain Papers on Biblical Literature. Israel's Psalms and Songs," *ICMM* 9 (1912-13) 210-213, 316-318.

G. Buchanan Gray, "The Forms of Hebrew Poetry," *Exp, 8th Ser.,* 5 (1913) 421-441, 552-568; 6 (1913) 45-60, 117-140, 221-244, 306-328, 529-553.

A. R. Gordon, "Pioneers in the Study of Old Testament Poetry. iii. Ewald," *ET* 25 (1913-14) 511-516.

Raymond A. Beardslee, "The Problem of Hebrew Poetry. I.," *BR* 3 (1918) 545-563.

Elcanon Isaacs, "The Origin and Nature of Parallelism," *AJSL* 35 (1918-19) 113-127.

Raymond A. Beardslee, "The Problem of Hebrew Poetry. II.," *BR* 4 (1919) 124-148.

P[aul] Haupt, "The Harmony of the Spheres," *JBL* 38 (1919) 180-183.

R[aymond] A. Beardslee, "Hebrew Poetry: A Criticism," *JBL* 39 (1920) 118-130.

*William F[oxwell] Albright, "The Earliest Form of Hebrew Verse," *JPOS* 2 (1922) 69-86. *[The Song of Deborah]*

T. Berry Smith, "The Poetry of the Bible," *MQR, 3rd Ser.,* 49 (1923) 80-94.

*Herbert H. Gowen, "The Nature Poems of the Psalter," *ATR* 6 (1923-24) 14-28. [Ps. 19:2, 7; Ps. 29; Ps. 28; Ps. 65; Ps. 104]

*Theophile James Meek, "The Poetry of Jeremiah," *JQR, N.S.,* 14 (1923-24) 281-291.

*Israel W. Slotki, "Genesis IV. 7 and a Form of Hebrew Poetry," *ET* 38 (1926-27) 329-330.

Theophile James Meek, "The Structure of Hebrew Poetry," *JR* 9 (1929) 523-550.

O.S. Rankin, "Alliteration in Hebrew Poetry," *JTS* 31 (1929-30) 285-291.

Israel W. Slotki, "Forms and Features of Ancient Hebrew Poetry: A Possible Aid to the Solution of Old Testament Difficulties," *JMUEOS* #16 (1931) 31-49.

I[srael] W. Slotki, "Topographic Arrangement of Ancient Hebrew Poetry. New light on the solution of metrical and textual difficulties," *ZAW* 49 (1931) 211-222.

I[srael] W. Slotki, "The Text and Metre of Some Early Hebrew Poems," *JTS* 34 (1933) 55-61.

Israel W. Slotki, "Long and Shorter Versions of Ancient Hebrew Poems," *AJSL* 50 (1933-34) 15-31.

I[srael] W. Slotki, "Poetry Recitation and Biblical Emendations. Poems of the Bible Retranslated," *ET* 46 (1934-35) 517-522.

Israel W. Slotki, "Antiphony in Ancient Hebrew Poetry," *JQR, N.S.,*26 (1935-36) 199-219.

H. W. Provence, "Lyric Poetry in the Bible," *R&E* 33 (1936) 402-414.

John Mauchline, "The 2:3 Line in Hebrew Poetry," *GUOST* 8 (1936-37) 34-35.

Earle Bennett Cross, "The Appreciation of Hebrew Poetry," *CRDSB* 10 (1937-38) 42-52.

*T[heophile] J. Meek, "Hebrew Poetic Structure as a Translation Guide," *JBL* 57 (1938) viii.

*A. W. Harrison, "The Poetry of the Book of Job," *LQHR* 163 (1938) 327-336.

*Theophile J. Meek, "Hebrew Poetic Structure as a Translation Guide," *JBL* 59 (1940) 1-9.

William McClellan, "The Elements of Old Testament Poetry," *CBQ* 3 (1941) 203-213, 321-336.

*T. H. Robinson, "Hebrew Metre and Old Testament Exegesis," *ET* 54 (1942-43) 246-248.

T. G. Sherman, "Rhyming Poetry in the Biblia Hebraica," *JBL* 62 (1943) vi.

F. E. Hutchinson, "The Poetry of the Bible," *MC* 33 (1943-44) 312-317.

*William Foxwell Albright, "The Old Testament and Canaanite Language and Literature," *CBQ* 7 (1945) 5-31. [V. Ugaritic and Biblical Poetry, pp. 19-22]

James A. Montgomery, "Stanza Formation in Hebrew Poetry," *JBL* 64 (1945) 379-384.

*M. Black, "The Aramaic Liturgical Poetry of the Jews," *JTS* 50 (1949) 179-182.

*G. D. Young, "Ugaritic Poetic Style and the Old Testament," *JBL* 69 (1950) viii.

Merrill F. Unger, "The Nature of Hebrew Poetry," *BS* 108 (1951) 282-285.

W[illiam] F[oxwell] Albright, "On Dating and Interpretation of Early Hebrew Poetry," *JBL* 71 (1952) xvi.

A. M. Honeyman, "*Merisums* in Biblical Hebrew," *JBL* 71 (1952) 11-18.

G. R. Driver, "Hebrew poetic diction," *VTS* 1 (1953) 26-39.

*James Muilenburg, "A study in Hebrew rhetoric: repetition and style," *VTS* 1 (1953) 97-111.

T. H. Robinson, "Hebrew poetic form: the English tradition," *VTS* 1 (1953) 128-149.

Jefrim Schirmann, "Hebrew Liturgical Poetry and Christian Hymnology," *JQR, N.S.*, 44 (1953-54) 123-161.

*Ellis E. Pierce, "The Translation of Biblical Poetry," *BTr* 5 (1954) 62-73.

*Franz Landsburger, "Poetic Units within the Song of Songs," *JBL* 73 (1954) 203-216.

*N. Wieder, "The Term קץ in the Dead Sea Scrolls and in Hebrew Liturgical Poetry," *JJS* 5 (1954) 22-31.

Stanislav Segert, "Problems of Hebrew prosody," *VTS* 7 (1960) 283-291.

David N. Freedman, "Archaic Forms in Early Hebrew Poetry," *ZAW* 72 (1960) 101-107.

E. Z. Melamed, "Break-Up of Stereotype Phrases as an Artistic Device in Biblical Poetry," *SH* 8 (1961) 115-144.

Dominic M. Crossan, "The Biblical Poetry of the Hebrews," *BibT* #13 (1964) 832-837.

H. Kosmala, "Form and Structure in Ancient Hebrew Poetry," *VT* 14 (1964) 423-445.

*Judah Stampfer, "On Translating Biblical Poetry. *Isaiah,* Chapters 1 and 2:1-4," *Jud* 14 (1965) 501-510.

A. Mirski, "The Roots of the Language of the *Piyyuṭ,*" *Lěš* 30 (1965-66) #4, n.p.n.

C. Brandwein, "The Legend of Job According to its Various Stages," *Tarbiz* 35 (1965-66) #1, I-II.

H. Kosmala, "Form and Structure in Ancient Hebrew Poetry (continued)," *VT* 16 (1966) 152-180.

*Dennis J. McCarthy, "'Creation' Motifs in Ancient Hebrew Poetry," *CBQ* 29 (1967) 393-406.

Mitchell Dahood, "A New Metrical Pattern in Biblical Poetry," *CBQ* 29 (1967) 574-579.

A. Mirski, "From *Midraš* to *Piyyuṭ* to Jewish Poetry," *Lěš* 32 (1967-68) #1/2, VII-VIII.

*Elmer B. Smick, "Suggested New Translation of Old Testament Poetry," *BETS* 11 (1968) 85-92.

*Wesley J. Culshaw, "Translating Biblical Poetry," *BTr* 19 (1968) 1-5.

*P. C. Craigie, "The Conquest and Early Hebrew Poetry," *TB* #20 (1969) 76-94.

§558 *3.3.5.2 Studies concerning Rhyme, Metre, Musical Accents and Notations*

Simon Lebl, "An Old Biblical Problem Solved at Last," *ACQR* 8 (1883) 442-462. *[Hebrew Metre]*

C. J. Ball, "The Metres of David," *SBAP* 8 (1885-86) 160-175.

Charles A Briggs, "The Strophical Organization of Hebrew Trimeters," *AJSL* 3 (1886-87) 152-165.

C[harles] A Briggs, "The Hebrew Tetrameter," *AJSL* 4 (1887-88) 65-74.

C[harles] A Briggs, "The Hebrew Pentameter," *AJSL* 4 (1887-88) 129-139.

C[harles] A Briggs, "The Hebrew Hexameter," *AJSL* 4 (1887-88) 201-205.

Morris Jastrow Jr., "Prof. Bickell's System of Hebrew Metre," *AJSL* 5 (1888-89) 197.

Edwin Cone Bissell, "Are There Metres in Old Testament Poetry?" *PRR* 4 (1893) 440-449.

*D. H. Muller, "Strophic Forms in Isaiah XLVII," *JQR* 12 (1899-1900) 377-379.

William Henry Cobb, "Primary Hebrew Rhythm," *JBL* 20 (1901) 158-174.

*C. H. Burney, "Old Testament Notes. II. Rhyme in the Song of Songs," *JTS* 10 (1908-09) 584-587.

*G. Buchanan Gray, "The Forms of Hebrew Poetry. 3. Parallelism and Rhythm in the Book of Lamentations," *Exp, 8th Ser.,* 6 (1913) 117-140.

*Paul Haupt, "Biblical Studies," *AJP* 43 (1922) 238-249. [5. Combined Rhythms, pp. 243-245]

*T[heodore] H. Robinson, "Metre and Textual Criticism," *Exp, 9th Ser.,* 1 (1924) 266-283.

*K. Fullerton, "The Strophe in Hebrew Poetry and Psalm 29," *JBL* 48 (1929) 274-290.

Theodore H. Robinson, "Some Principles of Hebrew Metrics," *ZAW* 54 (1936) 43-48.

Israel Davidson, "Rhymes in Hebrew Poetry," *JQR, N.S.,* 30 (1939-40) 299-398.

Patrick Cummins, "Rhythm, Hebrew and English," *CBQ* 3 (1941) 27-42.

*Theophile J. Meek, "The Metrical Structure of II Kings 19:20-28," *CQ* 18 (1941) 126-131.

Steven T. Byington, "A Mathematical Approach to Hebrew Meters," *JBL* 66 (1947) 63-77.

G. D. Young, "Semitic Metrics and Ugaritic Evidence," *JBL* 68 (1949) xii.

E. Schlesinger, "The Accent Systems of Psalms, Proverbs and Job and of the Other Books of the Bible," *EI* 3 (1954) XII-XIII.

A. Jeschke, "Tropes for Old Testament Scriptures. Part One," *WLQ* 58 (1961) 136-142.

A. Jeschke, "Tropes for Old Testament Scriptures. Part Two," *WLQ* 58 (1961) 196-209.

A. Jeschke, "Tropes for Old Testament Scriptures. Part Three," *WLQ* 58 (1961) 259-278.

*A. Steinsalz, "Rhyming Techniques in the Proems of *Midrash Hagga-dol,*" *Tarbiz* 34 (1964-65) #1, VIII.

*Shelomo Morag, "The Rhyming Techniques in the Proems of *Midrash Haggadol* and the Authorship of the *Midrash,*" *Tarbiz* 34 (1964-65) #3, III-IV.

*S. Bullough, "The Question of Metre in Psalm I," *VT* 17 (1967) 42-49.

E. Kagan, "Notes on the Use of the Spondee in the Hexameter," *Lĕš,* 33 (1968-69) #1, n.p.n.

§559 *3.3.5.3 Studies on Narrative Repetition - "Doublets"*

George C. M. Douglas, "Assumptions of the Radical Critics. *A Narrative Given Twice*," *CFL, N.S.,* 4 (1901) 226-229.

*George C. M. Douglas, "The Higher Criticism. Doublets in the Book of Joshua," *CFL, N.S.,* 5 (1902) 114-119.

Hugh Pope, "Undesigned Coincidences in the Old Testament. The Veracity of the Old Testament Narrative," *DR* 131 (1902) 314-332.

Anonymous, "So-called 'Duplicate Versions of the Same Incident'," *CFL, 3rd Ser.,* 11 (1909) 137-139.

A. F. Schauffler, "Some Illustrations of 'So-Called Duplicate Versions of the Same Incident'," *CFL, 3rd Ser.,* 11 (1909) 203-204.

John Urquhart, "Professor Driver and the Duplicate Records of the Flood and the Origin of Isaac," *CFL, 3rd Ser.,* 12 (1910) 91-94.

John Urquhart, "Driver and Davidson on the 'Duplicate Record' of Hagar," *CFL, 3rd Ser.,* 12 (1910) 259-261.

*Oswald T. Allis, "Old Testament Emphases and Modern Thought. Old Testament Emphases vs. Higher Critical Theories," *PTR* 224 (1926) 252-307. [The Repetitions of Exodus XIV, pp. 259-269]

T. W. Rosmarin, "Motive-Repetition in the Bible," *JBL* 53 (1934) xv.

*Francis Ian Andersen, "Doublets and Contamination," *RTR* 19 (1960) 48-57, 73-81.

*Paul Conners, "Haggadic History," *BC* 3 (1963-64) 162-167.

§560 *3.3.5.4 "Rîb" Patterns/Controversy Studies*

B. Gemser, "The *rîb-* or controversy-pattern in Hebrew mentality," *VTS* 3 (1955) 120-137.

Herbert B. Huffmon, "The Covenant Lawsuit in the Prophets," *JBL* 78 (1959) 285-295.

*Lawrence A. Sinclair, "The Courtroom Motif in the Book of Amos," *JBL* 85 (1966) 351-353.

A. Capbell, "God is the Plaintiff," *Coll* 2 (1966-68) 195-203.

*A. Schoors, "The Rîb-Pattern in Isaiah XL-LX," *BTFT* 30 (1969) 25-38. [1. Is. XLIII, 22-28; 2. The Lawsuit as a Literary Pattern; 3. The Dispute as a Literary Pattern; Conclusion]

*James Limburg, "The Root ריב and the Prophetic Lawsuit Speeches," *JBL* 88 (1969) 291-304.

§561 *3.3.5.5 Sitz im Leben - Specific Studies*

J. F. A. Sawyer, "Context of Situation and Sitz im Leben," *PUNTPS* 1 (1967) #11, 137-147.

§562 *3.3.5.6 Form Criticism of the Old Testament - General Studies*

Frederick C. Grant, "Form Criticism: A New Method of Research," *RL* 3 (1934) 351-366.

Paul Leo, "Form Criticism," *KZ* 67 (1943) 150-160, 311-321. [O.T. Refs., pp. 155-157]

Joseph L. Mihelic, "The Influence of Form Criticism on the Study of the Old Testament," *JAAR* 19 (1951) 120-129.

Reginald Glanville, "Form in Scripture," *PQL* 3 (1957) 11-18.

*Krister Stendahl, "Implications of Form-Criticism and Tradition-Criticism for Biblical Interpretation," *JBL* 77 (1958) 33-38.

James Muilenburg, "Modern Issues in Biblical Studies. The Gains of Form Criticism in Old Testament Studies," *ET* 71 (1959-60) 229-233.

L. Johnston, "Where Do You Stop? or, The Limits of Form Criticism," *CIR* 47 (1962) 385-396. [O.T. Refs., pp. 391-392]

Th. C. Vriezen, "The Credo in the Old Testament," *OTW* 6 (1963) 5-17.

W. M. W. Roth, "Numerical sayings in the Old Testament. a form-critical study," *VTS* 13 (1965) i-x, 1-103.

Ulrich Simon, "The Understanding of Biblical Forms," *Theo* 71 (1968) 54-62.

‡William G. Doty, "The Discipline and Literature of New Testament Form Criticism, I. Bibliography; II. Bibliographic Essay," *ATR* 51 (1969) 257-321. [Form Criticism of the Old Testament, p. 261]

*Roland E. Murphy, "Form Criticism and Wisdom Literature," *CBQ* 31 (1969) 475-483.

James Muilenburg, "Form Criticism and Beyond," *JBL* 88 (1969) 1-18.

Ulrich Simon, "The Problem of Biblical Narrative," *Theo* 72 (1969) 243-253.

*J. L. Crenshaw, "*YHWH Ṣᵉba'ôt Šᵉmô:* A Form-Critical Analysis," *ZAW* 81 (1969) 156-175.

§563 *3.3.5.7 Form-Critical Studies of Individual Books of the Old Testament*

*J. Wm. Wevers, "A Study in the Form Criticism of Individual Complaint Psalms," *VT* 6 (1956) 80-96.

*Paul Watson, "Form Criticism and an Exegesis of Micah 6:1-8," *RestQ* 7 (1963) 61-72.

Martin Kessler, "Form-Critical Suggestions on Jer 36," *CBQ* 28 (1966) 389-401.

*Terence E. Fretheim, "Psalm 132: A Form-Critical Study," *JBL* 86 (1967) 289-300.

*A. Schoors, "The Rîb-Pattern in Isaiah XL-LX," *BTPT* 30 (1969) 25-38. [1. Is. XLIII, 22-28; 2. The Lawsuit as a Literary Pattern; 3. The Dispute as a Literary Pattern; Conclusion]

§564 *3.3.5.8 Literary Style of the Old Testament - General Studies (includes Studies on Genre, Motifs, and Paronomasia)*

Anonymous, "On Scripture Metaphors," *BRCM* 5 (1848-49) 55-69.

Enoch Pond, "The Figurative Character of the Sacred Writings," *TLJ* 4 (1851-52) 686-694.

Edward Robie, "Figurative Language of the Scriptures," *BS* 13 (1856) 314-324.

W. N. B., "The Rhetorical Figures of the Bible," *UQGR* 13 (1856) 175-183.

E. C. Bissell, "The Rhetorical Figures in the Old Testament," *CongR* 10 (1870) 28-40.

W. M. Thomson, "Natural Basis of our Scriptural Language. No. V.—Parables and Similitudes," *BS* 33 (1876) 401-424.

*Charles Morris, "Characteristics of Hebrew Literature," *URRM* 12 (1879) 412-422.

James Robertson, "The Graphic Element in the Old Testament," *Exp, 2nd Ser.,* 6 (1883) 241-258.

Anonymous, "The Vividness of Old Testament Representations," *ONTS* 5 (1884-85) 181-182.

C. G. Montefiore, "A Tentative Catalogue of Biblical Metaphors," *JQR* 3 (1890-91) 623-681.

[J.] Chotzer, "The Humour of the Hebrew Bible and Its English Translations," *IAQR, 2nd Ser.,* 3 (1892) 124-135.

Immanuel M. Casanowicz, "Paronomasia in the Old Testament," *JBL* 12 (1893) 105-167.

Duncan B. Macdonald, "The Drama in Semitic Literature," *BW* 5 (1895) 16-28.

*Samuel Ives Curtiss, "Sytle as an Element in Determining the Authorship of the Old Testament Documents," *AJT* 1 (1897) 312-327.

David Smith, "Biblical Laughter," *ET* 12 (1900-01) 546-549.

J. C. Schacht, "The Beauty of the Bible," *ColTM* 21 (1901) 291-295.

C. V. Anthony, "The Hebrew Hyperbole," *MR* 87 (1905) 742-747.

F. B. Denio, "The Old-Testament Writers and Their Audience," *HR* 52 (1906) 369-371.

John S. Banks, "Literary Aspects of the Old Testament," *LQHR* 105 (1906) 225-241. *(Review)*

*S. A. P. Kermode, "The Influence of Nature on the Literature of the Bible," *ICMM* 4 (1907-08) 315-329.

William Barry, "Literary Aspects of the Old Testament," *DR* 145 (1909) 1-24.

Geo. P. Eckman, "The Humor of the Bible," *MR* 93 (1911) 521-531.

*Robert H. Kennett, "The Development of the Apocalyptic Style in the Old Testament," *ICMM* 8 (1911-12) 386-401.

*J. D. Wynkoop, "A Peculiar Kind of Paronomasia in the Talmud and Midrash," *JQR, N.S.,* 2 (1911-12) 1-23.

John B. Whitford, "The Unique Literary Quality of the Old Testament Writings," *MQR, 3rd Ser.,* 38 (1912) 541-552.

James A. Montgomery, "The Characteristic of Sublimity in the Old Testament," *BW* 46 (1915) 293-300.

*Andrew C. Zenos, "Apocryphal Literature and Bible Study. III. Literary Form," *HR* 70 (1915) 58-59.

*Camden M. Cobern, "Archaeological Discoveries and the Old Testament," *BR* 3 (1918) 9-38. [III. New Light on Some of the Symbolical Language and Literary Forms Used in the Old Testament, pp. 18-36]

R. B. Steele, "The Similes of the Old Testament," *MQR, 3rd Ser.,* 45 (1919) 329-338.

*T. Herbert Bindley, "Some Misunderstood Symbolism," *ICMM* 16 (1919-20) 57-62.

*Francis B. Denio, "Bible Authors and the Imagination," *BS* 77 (1920) 83-101.

Hamilton Schuyler, "Lighter Veins in the Literature of the Bible," *ACM* 8 (1920-21) 409-424.

*W. Ernest Beet, "The Humorous Element in the Old Testament," *Exp, 8th Ser.,* 22 (1921) 59-68.

Harry Torczyner, "The Riddle in the Bible," *HUCA* 1 (1924) 125-150.

William Popper, "Notes on Parallelism," *HUCA* 2 (1925) 63-85.

*Darwin A. Leavitt, "Some Aspects of History-Writing in the Old Testament," *MTSQB* 20 (1925-26) #3, 16-28.

Murdoch MacKinnon, "When the Morning Stars Sang Together," *CJRT* 4 (1927) 469-476.

N. W. Lund, "The Presence of Chiasmus in the Old Testament," *AJSL* 46 (1929-30) 104-126.

*J. A. Montgomery, "Paronomasias on the Name Jerusalem," *JBL* 49 (1930) 277-282.

*D. W. Amram, "A Further Example of Paronomasia on Jerusalem," *JBL* 49 (1930) 429.

Frank James Mallett, "Does the Bible Contain Humor?" *R&E* 27 (1930) 304-310.

J. M. P. Smith, "The Indebtedness of Israel to Its Neighbors," *AJSL* 49 (1932-33) 172-184.

*George B. Michell, "The Linguistic Criticism of the Old Testament," *BS* 92 (1935) 178-186.

A. P. Drucker, "The Dramas of the Bible,"*OC* 50 (1936) 40-54.

*W. E. Staples, "Cultic Motifs in Hebrew Thought," *AJSL* 55 (1938) 44-55.

*Solomon Gandz, "The dawn of literature. Prolegomena to a history of unwritten literature," *Osiris* 7 (1939) 261-522. [Chapter XV, §5. Greek and Hebrew Saga, pp. 409-412]

*H. L. Ginsberg, "Affinities between Semitic Inscriptions and Biblical Literature of Persian and Greek Periods," *JBL* 59 (1940) x.

C. J. Cadoux, "The Use of Hyperbole in Scripture," *ET* 52 (1940-41) 378-381.

T. G. Shearman, "The Thirteen Old Testament Acrostics," *JBL* 61 (1942) ix.

Donald G. Miller, "Art Form and the Genius of the Bible," *USR* 54 (1942-43) 28-46.

*H. L. Ginsberg, "Ugaritic Studies and the Bible," *BA* 8 (1945) 41-58. [IV. The Ugaritic Writings and the Bible, p. 49; 1. Ideas and Ideals, pp. 50-55, 2. Form and Quality of Canaanite Poetry, pp. 55-58]

*Gillis Gerleman, "Synoptic Studies in the Old Testament," *AULLUÅ, N.S.,* 44 (1948) #5, 1-35.

T. H. Gaster, "Dirge and Oracle in the Old Testament," *JBL* 67 (1948) iii.

*Robert Gordis, "Quotations as a Literary Usage in Biblical, Oriental and Rabbinic Literature," *HUCA* 22 (1949) 157-219.

Robert Gordis, "Quotations in Biblical, Rabbinic, and Oriental Literature," *JBL* 68 (1949) xvii-xviii.

Louise P. Smith, "Metrical Lists," *JBL* 69 (1950) xiv.

M. D. Goldman, "Humour in the Hebrew Bible," *ABR* 2 (1952) 1-11. (Errata, p. 129)

M. D. Goldman, "Addenda to 'Humour in the Hebrew Bible'," *ABR* 2 (1952) 128.

M. D. Goldman, "Addenda to 'Humour in the Hebrew Bible'," *ABR* 3 (1953) 72-73.

L. Jacobs, "The Aristotelean Syllogism and the Qal Wa-Ḥomer," *JJS* 4 (1953) 154-157.

*James Muilenburg, "A study in Hebrew rhetoric: repetition and style," *VTS* 1 (1953) 97-111.

J. Weingreen, "Themes in Old Testament Stories," *Herm* #85 (1955) 13-35.

Harold Fisch, "The Analogy of Nature, A Note on the Structure of Old Testament Imagery," *JTS, N.S.,* 6 (1955) 161-173.

Bernard J. LeFrois, "The Semitic Thought-Pattern in Sacred Scripture," *AER* 134 (1956) 374-394.

*Lobes Pierre, "Literary genres in the Bible," *TD* 4 (1956) 67-71.

Bernard J. LeFrois, "The Semitic thought-pattern in Scripture," *TD* 6 (1958) 18. *[Synopsis]*

*Geo Widengren, "Oral Tradition and Written Language among the Hebrews in the Light of Arabic Evidence, with Special Regard to Prose Narratives," *AO* 23 (1958-59) 201-262.

J. Muilenburg, "The Form and Structure of the Conventional Formulations," *VT* 9 (1959) 347-365.

*J. A. Thompson, "Non-Biblical Covenants in the Ancient Near East and their Relevance for Understanding the Covenant Motif in the Old Testament," *ABR* 8 (1960) 39-45.

Dov B. Lang, "On the Biblical Comic," *Jud* 11 (1962) 249-254.

H. McKeating, "But There Do the Angels Resort," *PQL* 8 (1962) 315-319.

Israel Knox, "The Traditional Roots of Jewish Humor," *Jud* 12 (1963) 327-337.

*J. A. Thompson, "The Significance of the Ancient Near Eastern Treaty Pattern," *TB* #13 (1963) 1-6.

*Roy A. Stewart, "The Parable Form in the Old Testament and in Rabbinic Literature," *EQ* 36 (1964) 133-147.

A. Guillaume, "Paronomasia in the Old Testament," *JSS* 9 (1964) 282-290.

*Roy A. Stewart, "The Parable Form in the Old Testament and in Rabbinic Literature," *F&T* 94 (1965-66) 113-127.

D. R. Hillers, "A Convention in Hebrew Literature. The Reaction to Bad News," *ZAW* 77 (1965) 86-89.

*N. Habel, "The Form and Significance of the Call Narratives," *ZAW* 77 (1965) 297-323. [I. The Calls of Gideon and Moses; II. The Call of Jeremiah; III. The Calls of Isaiah and Ezekiel; IV. The Call of II Isaiah; V. Form, Significance and Origin]

*Talmon Shemaryahu, "The 'Desert Motif' in the Bible and in Qumran Literature," *LIST* 3 (1966) 31-63.

A. van Selms, "How do the books of the Bible commence?" *OTW* 9 (1966) 132-141.

Hyacinthe M. Dion, "The Patriarchal Traditions and the Literary Form of the 'Oracle of Salvation'," *CBQ* 29 (1967) 198-206.

*S. E. Loewenstamm, "Remarks on Stylistic Patterns in Biblical and Ugaritic Literature," *Lěš* 32 (1967-68) #1/2, II-III.

*John H. Hayes, "The Usage of Oracles Against Foreign Nations in Israel," *JBL* 87 (1968) 81-92.

*Jay A. Wilcoxen, "Some Anthropocentric Aspects of Israel's Sacred History," *JR* 48 (1968) 333-350.

*J[acob] Weingreen, "The pattern theory in Old Testament studies," *Herm* #108 (1969) 5-13.

*J. N. M. Wijngaards, "The Dramatization of Salvific History in the Deuteronomic Schools," *OTS* 16 (1969) 1-127.

*W. J. Martin, "'Dischronologized' narrative in the Old Testament," *VTS* 17 (1969) 179-186.

§565 *3.3.5.8.1 Literary Style of the Pentateuch*

*O. P. Bestor, "Spirit of the Mosaic Songs," *ONTS* 1 (1882) 67-69. [Ex. 15:1-9; Ex. 17:16; Num. 21:17, 18; 21:27-30; Ex. 32:18; Psa. 19; Deut. 22:1-43; Deut. 33]

Anonymous, "Mr. Gladstone on the Literary Form of the Pentateuch," *EN* 3 (1891) 36-38.

Henry C. Thomson, "An Exercise in Style," *CFL, N.S.,* 8 (1903) 351-354. [Gen. chaps. 6-9]

Harold M. Wiener, "Deuteronomy and the Argument from Style," *PTR* 5 (1907) 605-630.

*Alphonse Mingana, "Remarks on the Hebrew of Genesis," *Exp, 8th Ser.,* 11 (1916) 303-310. [Gen. 1:9; 12:15]

Herbert W. Magoun, "The Literary Form of the First Chapters of Genesis,"
  BS 79 (1922) 153-172.

*Felix Perles, "On the Strophic Form of Exodus 15," *JQR, N.S.,* 17 (1926-
  27) 403-404.

*J[ohn] L. McKenzie, "The Literary Characteristics of Genesis 2-3," *ThSt* 15
  (1954) 541-572.

*John D. W. Watts, "The Song of the Sea—Ex. XV," *VT* 7 (1957) 371-380.

*Meredith G. Kline, "Because It Had Not Rained," *WTJ* 20 (1957-58) 146-
  157. [The Literary Genre of Genesis 1, pp. 155-167]

*John L. McKenzie, "The Literary Characteristics of Genesis 2-3," *TD* 6
  (1958) 19-23.

Martin J. Wyngaarden, "Phenomenal Language According to Dr. Bernard
  Ramm," *BETS* 2 (1959) #4, 10-14. *[The interpretation of Creation in
  Genesis with emphasis on literary style]*

G. Douglas Young, "The Effects of Poetic and Literary Style on Interpretation of the Early Chapters of Genesis," *BETS* 2 (1959) #4, 15-16.

*Robert C. Dentan, "The Literary Affinities of Exodus XXXIV 6f.," *VT* 13
  (1963) 34-51.

Alan R. Cole, "The Patterns in the Book of Exodus," *TTCA* 3 (1966) 12-16.

*Donald B. Redford, "The literary motif of the exposed child (cf. Ex. ii 1-
  10)," *Numen* 14 (1967) 209-228.

(§566) *3.3.5.8.2 Literary Style of the Prophets*

§567   *3.3.5.8.2.1 Literary Style of the
                             Former Prophets*

Willis J. Beecher, "The Literary form of Biblical history of the Judges," *JBL*
  4 (1884) 3-28.

C. Alphonso Smith, "The Literary Aspects of the Book of Judges," *PQ* 6
  (1892) 581-592.

Francis C. Lightbourn, "The 'Story' in the Old Testament," *ATR* 21 (1939)
  94-102. *[1 Kings 17-2 Kings 9]*

*Theophile J. Meek, "The Metrical Structure of II Kings 19:20-28," *CQ* 18 (1941) 126-131.

Gillis Gerleman, "The Song of Deborah in the Light of Stylistics," *VT* 1 (1951) 168-180.

*A. H. van Zyl, "The Message Formula in the Book of Judges," *OTW* 2 (1959) 61-64.

*J. Blenkinsopp, "Ballad Style and Psalm Style in the Song of Deborah: a Discussion," *B* 42 (1961) 61-76.

*J. Blenkinsopp, "Structure and Style in Judges 13-16," *JBL* 82 (1963) 65-76.

*E. J. Smit, "Death and burial formulas in Kings and Chronicles relating to the kings of Judah," *OTW* 9 (1966) 173-177.

*U. Simon, "The Poor Man's Ewe-Lamb. An Example of a Juridical Parable," *B* 48 (1967) 207-242.

J. P. U. Lilley, "A Literary Appreciation of the Book of Judges," *TB* #18 (1967) 94-102.

*Menakhem Perry and Meir Sternberg, "The King Through Ironic Eyes: The Narrator's Devices in the Biblical Story of David and Batsheba. Two Excursuses on the Theory of the Narrative Text," *HS* 1 (1968-69) 452-449.*[sic]* *[English Summary]*

*Menakhem Perry and Meir Sternberg, "Biblical and Literary Criticism. 3. Caution. A Literary Text! Problems in the Poetics and the Interpretation of Biblical Narrative," *HS* 2 (1969-71) 682-679.*[sic]* *[English Summary]*

*Uriel Simon, "Bible and Literary Criticism. 2. An Ironic Approach to a Biblical Story: On the Interpretation of the Story of David and Bathsheba," *HS* 2 (1969-71) 684-683.*[sic]* *[English Summary]*

*Boaz Arpali, "The Bible and Literary Criticism. 1. Caution: A Biblical Story! Comments on the Story of David and Bathsheba and on the Problem of the Biblical Narrative," *HS* 2 (1969-71) 686-684.*[sic]* *[English Summary]*

§568 ***3.3.5.8.2.2   Literary Style of the
Latter Prophets***

Edward B. Pollard, "The Prophet's Use of Contrast," *BW* 18 (1901) 96-100.

Henry Preserved Smith, "Rhetorical Form in the Prophets," *HR* 48 (1904) 37-39.

Henry Thatcher Fowler, "Aeschylus and the Eighth-Century Prophets," *BW* 46 (1915) 134-145.

*A. Bentzen, "Patriarchal 'benediction' and prophetic book," *HTS* 7 (1950-51) 106-109.

*Meir Weiss, "In the Footsteps of one Biblical Metaphor (Methodological Remarks and Exegetical, and Historical Notices)," *Tarbiz* 34 (1964-65) #2, I-II; #3, I-II; #4, I-II. *(Title varies)*

*A. Capell, "God is the Plaintiff," *Coll* 2 (1966-68) 195-203.

M[eir] Wiess, "The Pattern of the 'Execration Texts' in the Prophetic Literature," *IEJ* 19 (1969) 150-157.

§569 ***3.3.5.8.2.2.1 Literary Style of the Major Prophets***

*H. A. Ch. Havernick, "Havernick's Introductory Remarks to His Commentary on Ezekiel," *BS* 5 (1848) 434-447. [Style and Method of Ezekiel, pp. 442-444] *(Trans. by Edward Robie)*

*D. H. Muller, "Strophic Forms in Isaiah XLVII," *JQR* 12 (1899-1900) 377-379.

D. Macrae Tod, "The Poetry and the Wit of Jeremiah," *ET* 15 (1903-04) 461-462.

T. H. Robinson, "The Structure of the Book of Jeremiah," *Exp, 8th Ser.,* 20 (1920) 17-31.

James Muilenburg, "The Literary Character of Isaiah 34," *JBL* 59 (1940) vii, 339-365.

Francis P. Gaines, "Isaiah: Details of Artistry," *USR* 55 (1943-44) 222-233.

*A. van Selms, "Literary Criticism of Ezekiel as a Theological Problem," *OTW* 4 (1961) 24-37.

*William L. Holladay, "Style, Irony, and Authenticity in Jeremiah," *JBL* 81 (1962) 44-54.

*Menaḥem Haran, "The literary structure and chronological framework of the Prophecies of Is. xl-xlviii," *VTS* 9 (1963) 127-155.

§570 *3.3.5.8.2.2.2 Literary Style of the Minor Prophets*

*B. B. Edwards, "Translation of the Prophecy of Nahum with Notes," *BS* 5 (1848) 551-576. [Style and Manner of Nahum, pp. 558-560]

Talbot W. Chambers, "The Literary Character of Amos," *ONTS* 3 (1883-84) 2-6.

*George A. Barton, "The Prayer of Habakkuk," *ONTS* 6 (1886-87) 176-178.

William Rainey Harper, "The Structure of Hosea 1:2-3:5," *AJSL* 17 (1900-01) 1-15.

Fred T. Kelly, "The Strophic Structure of Habakkuk," *AJSL* 18 (1901-02) 94-119.

William Rainey Harper, "The Structure of Hosea 4:1-7:7," *AJSL* 20 (1903-04) 85-94.

William Rainey Harper, "The Structure of Hosea 7:8-14:10," *AJSL* 21 (1904-05) 1-21.

John M[erlin] P[owis] Smith, "The Structure of Obadiah," *AJSL* 22 (1905-06) 131-138.

John Merlin Powis Smith, "The Strophic Structure of the Book of Micah," *AJSL* 24 (1906-07) 187-208.

H. H. Walker and N. W. Lund, "The Literary Structure of the Book of Habakkuk," *JBL* 53 (1934) 355-370.

*J. Reider, "An Acrostic on Ashur in the Bible," *JBL* 56 (1937) x.

C. J. Labuschagne, "The similes in the book of Hosea," *OTW* 7&8 (1964-65) 64-76.

*A. van Selms, "Amos's geographic horizon," *OTW* 7&8 (1964-65) 166-169. *[gattungsgeschtliche]*

*Lawrence A. Sinclair, "The Courtroom Motif in the Book of Amos," *JBL* 65 (1966) 351-353.

M. E. Andrew, "Gattung and Intention in the Book of Jonah," *Orita* 1 (1967) 13-18, 78-85.

*J. J. Glück, *"pārûr—pā'rûr*—A Case of Biblical Paronomasia," *OTW* 12 (1969) 21-26.

(§571) *3.3.5.8.3 Literary Style of the Hagiographa*

§572   **3.3.5.8.3.1 *Literary Style of the Poetical Books***

*O. P. Bestor, "Spirit of the Mosaic Songs," *ONTS* 1 (1882) 67-69. [Psa. 19]

A. W. H. Compton, "The Diligent Husbandman. Proverbs xxvii 23-27," *ET* 3 (1891-92) 233. *(Paraphrase)*

Hugh Cowan, "Israel's Deliverance, A Pledge of Messianic Blessing," *ET* 8 (1896-97) 237-238. *(Psa. 114 - Paraphrase)*

Paul Haupt, "The Poetic Form of the First Psalm," *AJSL* 19 (1902-03) 129-142.

Paul Haupt, "The Poetic Form of Psalm XXIII," *AJSL* 21 (1904-05) 133-152.

F. A. Gast, "The Literary Structure of the Book of Job," *RChR, 4th Ser., 9* (1905) 1-16.

*Anonymous, "Plain Papers on Biblical Literature. Israel's Psalms and Songs," *ICMM* 9 (1912-13) 210-213, 316-318.

Waldo S. Pratt, "Studies in the Diction of the Psalter, First Article," *JBL* 32 (1913) 80-106.

Waldo S. Pratt, "Studies in the Diction of the Psalter, Second Article," *JBL* 32 (1913) 159-183.

Waldo S. Pratt, "Studies in the Diction of the Psalter, Third Article," *JBL* 33 (1914) 1-24.

(1914) 1-24.

Waldo S. Pratt, "Studies in the Diction of the Psalter, Fourth Article," *JBL* 33 (1914) 127-151.

K. Fullerton, "The Feeling for Form in Psalm 104," *JBL* 40 (1921) 43-56.

K. Fullerton, "The Strophe in Hebrew Poetry and Psalm 29," *JBL* 48 (1929) 274-290.

Nils W. Lund, "Chiasmus in the Psalms," *AJSL* 49 (1932-33) 281-312.

William A. Irwin, "Poetic Structure in the Dialogue of Job," *JNES* 5 (1946) 26-39.

H. Kurse, "Two Hidden Comparatives: Observations on Hebrew Style," *JSS* 5 (1960) 333-347. [I. Psalm 42:7-8; II. Psalm 8:3]

J. M. Ward, "The Literary Form and Liturgical Background of Psalm LXXXIX," *VT* 11 (1961) 321-339.

R. N. Whybray, "Some Literary Problems in Proverbs I-IX," *VT* 16 (1966) 482-496.

*D. J. A. Clines, "Psalm Research Since 1955: II. The Literary Genres," *TB* #20 (1969) 105-125.

§573 *3.3.5.8.3.2 Literary Style of the Megilloth*

J. E. Fox, "The Song of Songs," *ET* 7 (1895-96) 105-107, 170-173, 224-225. *[Paraphrase]*

Albert Condamin, "Symmetrical Repetitions in Lamentations I and II," *JTS* 7 (1905-06) 137-140.

*Franz Landsberger, "Poetic Units Within the Song of Songs," *JBL* 73 (1954) 203-216.

*R[obert] Gordis, "Qoheleth and Qumran—A Study of Style," *B* 41 (1960) 395-410.

Stephen Bertman, "Symmetrical Design in the Book of Ruth," *JBL* 84 (1965) 165-168.

§574 ***3.3.5.8.3.3 Literary Style of the Historical Books***

*E. J. Smit, "Death and burial formulas in Kings and Chronicles relating to the kings of Judah," *OTW* 9 (1966) 173-177.

About the Author

William G. Hupper studied at Florida Beacon College and Gordon College. He has continued scholarly pursuits in Ancient Near Eastern studies and biblical languages, as an avocation, studying Hebrew under private tutor. He has spent over twenty-two years compiling, collating and editing the articles included in his multi-volumed index, while continuing his full time profession as a traffic administrator for a leading multi-national corporation. He has developed software for the Macintosh™ computer to produce Egyptian hieroglyphics on screen and in print which is available commercially. He has authored articles in theological journals as well as official government documents related to his vocation. Mr. Hupper has also been a member of the Society of Biblical Literature for over twenty years.